MACROECONOMICS

Sixth Edition

MACRO-ECONOMICS

Volume II of <u>Economics</u>

Richard G. Lipsey
C.D. Howe Institute

Douglas D. Purvis
Queen's University

Peter O. Steiner
The University of Michigan

1817

HARPER & ROW, PUBLISHERS, New York
Cambridge, Philadelphia, San Francisco, Washington,
London, Mexico City, São Paulo, Singapore, Sydney

Sponsoring Editor: John Greenman
Development Editor: Mary Lou Mosher
Project Editor: Lenore Bonnie Biller
Text Design: Leon Bolognese
Cover Design: Lucy Krikorian
Cover Photos: Front—Grain harvest, Alberta, Canada, © 1984,
  Gary Cralle, The Image Bank. Back—Burrard Inlet, Vancouver,
  B.C. Thomas Kitchin, Valan Photos.
Text Art: Vantage Art, Inc.
Production Manager: Kewal Sharma
Compositor: Ruttle, Shaw & Wetherill, Inc.
Printer and Binder: Arcata Graphics/Kingsport Press
Cover Printer: Arcata Graphics/Kingsport Press

Macroeconomics, Volume II of *Economics,* Sixth Edition

Library of Congress Cataloging in Publication Data

Lipsey, Richard G., 1928-
  Macroeconomics. Volume 2 of *Economics.*

  Contains the chapters dealing with macroeconomics
of the author's *Economics,* 6th ed., published in 1988.
    Includes index.
    1. Macroeconomics. I. Purvis, Douglas D. II. Steiner,
Peter Otto, 1922-   . III. Lipsey, Richard G.,
1928-   . Economics. IV. Title.
HB171.5.L73325 1988   339   87-37862

ISBN 0-06-044103-8

89 90 91 9 8 7 6 5 4 3 2

Brief Contents

Detailed Contents

Preface

Economics is a living discipline. Through six editions of *Economics,* our basic motivation has been to provide a text that reflects the tremendous changes in that discipline over the decades.

The first major theme of this book is to reflect the gradual movement of economics today toward becoming a science, exhibiting the key characteristic that marks any science: the systematic confrontation of theory with observation. Today most economists agree that their subject is more than a stage for parading pet theories. Nor is economics just a container for collecting masses of unrelated institutional and statistical material. Economists are expanding the frontiers of knowledge about the economic environment and learning to understand and often to control it. But new problems and new events are always challenging existing knowledge. Economists are therefore continually concerned with how theory, institutions, and facts relate to each other. Every theory is subject to empirical challenge.

A second major theme of this book concerns the relations between economic theory and economic policy. Decades of systematic observations have provided an ever-growing understanding of how things relate to one another quantitatively. This knowledge has increased economists' ability to make sensible and relevant statements about public policy. True, there remain many areas where economists' knowledge is painfully sparse, as current debates about supply-side economics and the nature of an appropriate monetary policy remind us.

The third major feature of the book has to do with the way we view students. We have tried to be as honest with them as possible within the limits of an introductory textbook. No subject worth studying is always easy, and we do not approve of slipping particularly hard bits of analysis past students without letting them see what is happening and what has been assumed, nor do we approve of teaching them things they will have to unlearn if they go on in economics (a practice sometimes justified on the grounds that it is important to get to the big issues quickly). In short, we have tried to follow Albert Einstein's advice: Make things as simple as possible, but not simpler.

Effective criticism of existing ideas is the springboard to progress in science. We believe that introductory economics should introduce students to methods for testing, criticizing, and evaluating the present state of the subject. We do not believe that it is wrong to suggest to students the possibility of criticizing current economic theory. Students will always criticize and evaluate their course content, and their criticisms are more likely to be informed and relevant if they are given practice and instruction in how to challenge what they have been taught in an effective, constructive manner.

Major Revisions in This Edition

Our main theme in this revision has been teachability. Every sentence, the structure of every argument, and every figure has been reviewed. Minor inconsistencies, and passages that our own and other teachers' experiences have told us are unnecessarily difficult, qualifications that belong only in more advanced treatments, unnecessary variations in the labelling of graphs, and a host of other smaller but significant problems have all received our attention. We hope that the result is a smoother and more teachable treatment throughout.

Some dramatic content changes have been made. The most important are listed below.

Changes in Macroeconomics

This is now the third edition in which the material on macroeconomics has relied mainly on the tools of aggregate demand and aggregate supply. Our emphasis in this revision has been on improving the teachability of the material. We have simplified the discussion in several places and restructured the material in a couple of chapters to provide flexibility to the instructor. Perhaps most important, we have introduced and developed the *AD* and *AS* curves only as they are needed; this gives rise to a simpler presentation of the basic theory.

Macroeconomic theory is now developed in three key chapters, Chapters 28, 29, and 30. The first chapter develops the fixed price model, the second allows for variations in the price level but maintains the assumption of fixed wages, while the third introduces the role of wage adjustments.

1. The introduction of the *AD* and *AS* curves that previously occurred in the introductory macro chapter, Chapter 26, has been dropped. This simplifies the introduction to macroeconomics and means that the student no longer meets *AD* and *AS* only to put them aside for several chapters.

2. The detailed treatment of index numbers has been combined with national income accounting in one chapter, Chapter 27. The treatment of both topics is both simpler and more comprehensive than in previous editions. The discussion of the national income accounts has been restructured to reflect the switch from GNP to GDP as the central measure of national income.

3. Chapter 28 develops the fixed-price model in detail. It combines the material from Chapters 28 and 29 in the fifth edition. First the *AE* function is built up and the equilibrium level of income is determined. We then turn to the comparative statics of the fixed-price model, and the development of the simple multiplier.

4. Chapter 29 then develops the model with a variable price level under the assumption of fixed factor prices. In keeping with standard terminology we refer to this as the "short-run" model of the price level and national income. We start by analysing the effects of an exogenous price change in the fixed-price model. This allows us to derive the *AD* curve. We then add the *SRAS* curve in order to allow for an endogenous determination of the price level. The Keynesian flat *AS* curve is mentioned only in passing in the text as a qualification to the general presumption that the *SRAS* has a positive slope. Its historical importance is developed in a box.

5. Chapter 30 allows for factor price adjustments in response to the output gap. (We have moved the box introducing the Phillips curve to this chapter from the inflation chapter.) The implications of wage-price adjustment for the *SRAS* curve are then analysed, and the vertical *LRAS* curve is derived. The treatment of *LRAS* has been thoroughly revised and, where possible, simplified. The distinction, important for most of the remaining chapters, between the *SRAS* and *LRAS* curves is stressed.

We feel that it is worth making the effort required to establish this distinction because, as economists, we are concerned about the many textbooks that carry out the bulk of their analysis with a single, stable *AS* curve. This simplifies teaching, but it risks serious confusion. The alert student faced with a fixed *AS* curve and an *AD* curve that can be shifted by policy, will wonder why anyone would hesitate to pay the price of a once-and-for-all increase in the price level in order to obtain a permanent increase in output and employment. And who would hesitate, faced with such a trade-off? To avoid such serious confusions, we introduce the shifting, short-run *AS* curve and the vertical, long-run *AS* curve at the outset.

6. The structure of Chapter 32, "Fiscal Policy," is mostly unchanged from the last edition, but the material has been rewritten to increase its relevance and teachability. The *AD/AS* apparatus is now fully integrated into the chapter. The historical discussion of fiscal policy in action has been shortened to make room for an extended discussion of the implications of persistent government budget deficits.

7. The chapter on inflation has been reworked and simplified. The emphasis is now more on long-term inflation control and less on the issue—important at the time of writing the previous edition—of how to break an entrenched inflation.

Teaching Aids

Tag lines and captions for figures and tables. The boldface tag line below or next to a figure or table states briefly the central conclusion to be drawn from the illustration; the lightface caption gives information needed to reach that conclusion. Each title, tag line, and caption, along with the figure or table, forms a self-contained unit, useful for reviewing.

Boxes. The "boxes" contain examples or materials that are relevant extensions of the main text but need not be read as part of the text sequence. They are all optional. Some have further theoretical material. Others contain expansions and applications of points already covered in the text. The boxes give flexibility in expanding or contracting the coverage of specific chapters.

End-of-chapter material. Each chapter has a Summary, a list of Topics for Review, and Discussion Questions. The questions are designed for class discussion or for "quiz sections." Answers appear in the Instructor's Manual.

Appendixes. For several editions, the appendixes that give more detailed discussion of certain topics have been gathered in a separate section at the back of the text. In this present edition, for ease of use, we have placed the appendixes directly following the chapters to which they are related.

Mathematical notes. Mathematical notes are collected in a separate section at the end of the book. Since mathematical notation and derivation is not necessary to understand the principles of economics, but is helpful in more advanced work, this segregation seems to be a sensible arrangement. Mathematical notes provide clues to the uses of mathematics for the increasing number of students who have some background in math, without loading the text with notes that are useless and offputting to other readers. Students with a mathematical background have often told us they find the notes helpful.

Glossary. The glossary covers widely used definitions of economic terms. Because some users treat micro- and macroeconomics in that order, and others in the reverse order, words in the glossary are printed in boldface type when they are first mentioned in *either half* of the text.

Endpapers. Inside the front cover on the left is a list of the most commonly used abbreviations in the text; on the right appears a figure representing the relative importance of the national debt. Inside the back cover on the left is an illustration representing the major forms of the federal expenditure. At the right is a table of selected time series, useful data on the Canadian economy since 1929.

Supplements

Our book is accompanied by a workbook, *Study Guide and Problems,* prepared by Professors William Furlong, Kenneth Grant, and Fredric Menz. The workbook is designed to be used either in the classroom or by the students working on their own.

An *Instructor's Manual,* prepared by us, and a *Test Bank,* prepared by Delbert Ogden, are available to instructors adopting the book. The Test Bank is also available in a computerized form; contact the publisher for details.

New to this edition are 50 key theory diagrams reproduced from the text in the form of 2-color acetate transparencies; free to adopters. There are also over 100 transparency masters of important text figures available for classroom use.

Acknowledgments

The starting point for this book was *Economics,* Eighth Edition, by Richard G. Lipsey, Peter O. Steiner, and Douglas D. Purvis. It would be impossible to acknowledge here all the teachers, colleagues, and students who contributed to that book. Hundreds of users have written to us with specific suggested improvements, and much of the credit for the fact that the book does become more and more teachable belongs to them. We can no longer list them individually but we thank them all most sincerely.

David Farnes and Gillian Hamilton provided excellent research assistance. A number of individuals provided reviews of the fifth edition that were most helpful in preparing the present edition. These are Torben Andersen, Red Deer College; Ronald G. Bodkin, University of Ottawa; Chris Clark, British Columbia Institute of Technology; Barry Cozier,

Concordia University; M. H. I. Dore, Brock University; C. M. Fellows, Mount Royal College; S. W. Kardasz, University of Waterloo; George Kondor, Lakehead University; Victor Olshevski, University of Winnipeg; and P. L. Siklos, Wilfred Laurier University. In addition, the key micro chapters of this revision were read by Trudy Ann Cameron, UCLA; Vernon Dow, Cambrian College; and A. Gyasi Nimarko, Vanier College. The core macro chapters were seen by Sohrab Abizadeh, University of Winnipeg; G. C. Church, University of Regina; Geoffrey B. Hainsworth, University of British Columbia; Peter Howitt, University of Western Ontario; and Nicholas Rowe, Carleton University. William Furlong and Kenneth Grant, two of our study guide authors, have contributed to this edition as well.

Special thanks is due to Elaine Fitzpatrick, Patricia Casey-Purvis, Ellen McKay, and Dana Miltchen for careful and efficient handling of the manuscript at all stages.

Finally, this edition is dedicated to Clinton T. Purvis, who celebrates his 90th birthday as we go to press.

Richard G. Lipsey
Douglas D. Purvis
Peter O. Steiner

To the Student

A good course in economics will give you insight into how an economy functions and into some currently debated policy issues. Like all rewarding subjects, economics will not be mastered without effort. A book on economics must be worked at. It cannot be read like a novel.

Each of you must develop an individual technique for studying, but the following suggestions may prove helpful. It is usually a good idea to read a chapter quickly in order to get the general run of the argument. At this first reading you may want to skip the "boxes" of text material and any footnotes. Then, after reading the Topics for Review and the Discussion Questions, reread the chapter more slowly, making sure that you understand each step of the argument. With respect to the figures and tables, be sure you understand how the conclusions stated in the brief tag lines with each table or figure have been reached. You should be prepared to spend time on difficult sections; occasionally, you may spend an hour on only a few pages. Paper and a pencil are indispensable equipment in your reading. It is best to follow a difficult argument by building your own diagram while the argument unfolds rather than by relying on the finished diagram as it appears in the book. It is often helpful to invent numerical examples to illustrate general propositions. The end-of-chapter questions require you to apply what you have studied. We advise you to outline answers to some of the questions. In short, you should seek to understand economics, not merely to memorize it.

After you have read each part in detail, reread it quickly from beginning to end. It is often difficult to understand why certain things are done when they are viewed as isolated points, but when you reread a whole part, much that did not seem relevant or entirely comprehensible will fall into place in the analysis.

We call your attention to the glossary at the end of the book. Any time you run into a concept that seems vaguely familiar but is not clear to you, check the glossary. The chances are that it will be there, and its definition will remind you of what you once understood. If you are still in doubt, check the index entry to find where the concept is discussed more fully. Incidentally, the glossary, along with the captions that accompany figures and tables and the end-of-chapter summaries, may prove very helpful when reviewing for examinations.

The bracketed colored numbers in the text itself refer to a series of 54 mathematical notes that are found starting on page M-1. For those of you who like mathematics or prefer mathematical argument to verbal or geometric exposition, these may prove useful. Others may ignore them.

We hope that you will find the book rewarding and stimulating. Students who used earlier editions made some of the most helpful suggestions for revision, and we hope you will carry on the tradition. If you are moved to write to us, please do.

MACROECONOMICS

PART ONE

The
Nature
of
Economics

1

The Economic Problem

Many of the world's most pressing problems are economic. The dominant problem of the 1930s was the massive unemployment of workers and resources known as the Great Depression. The wartime economy of the 1940s solved that problem but created new ones, especially how to reallocate scarce resources quickly between military and civilian needs. The postwar period from 1945 to 1955 was a time of world-wide economic growth, but with major imbalances as European nations tried to rebuild their war-shattered economies and export to Canada and the United States enough to pay for all that they needed to import. The period from 1955 to 1965 was a time of unparalleled growth and prosperity as the world completed its recovery from the Second World War and entered a period of expanding output and trade. Unemployment was a concern during some years in the decade, as was the inability of most of the world's economies to combine full employment with zero inflation.

From 1965 to 1975 a slowdown in growth and rising inflation became matters for serious concern. The central problems of the period from 1975 to 1985 were the rising cost of energy—oil prices increased tenfold over the decade—and the disturbing combination of rising unemployment and rising inflation, called **stagflation**.[1] By the second half of the 1980s, inflation had fallen to a low level, and the central manufacturing area of Canada was booming. The rest of the country, heavily dependent on resource-based industries whose world markets were shrinking, had severe unemployment problems. Not since the 1930s had Canada seemed so much like two economic nations, the prosperous centre and the stagnant periphery. Thus we see that the world's economic problems change over the decades, yet there are always problems.

Of course, not all the world's problems are primarily economic. Political, biological, social, cultural, and philosophical issues often predominate. But no matter how "noneconomic" a particular problem may seem, it will almost always have a significant economic dimension.

The crises that lead to wars often have economic roots. Nations fight for oil and rice and land to live on, although the rhetoric of their leaders evokes God, Glory, and the Fatherland. The current rate of world population growth is 2.2 persons a second, or about 70 million a year; the economic consequences are steady pressures on the available natural resources, especially arable land. Unless the human race can find ways to increase its food supply as fast as its numbers, increasing millions face starvation.

---

[1] The definitions of the terms in boldface are gathered together in the glossary at the end of the book.

Current Economic Problems

Unemployment and Inflation

Virtually every minister of finance in recent history has included in his budget speeches a statement establishing full employment and low inflation as important goals of economic policy. Reasonable as that may sound, the fact is that we have seldom had both full employment and low inflation at the same time, and in the 10-year period from the mid 1970s to the mid 1980s we had neither. Inflation was reduced to about 4 percent by 1985, but unemployment stayed disturbingly high. By 1987, inflation remained near a 4-percent plateau while the unemployment rate had crept slowly downward to below 9 percent.

If economists are right in saying that zero unemployment is an unattainable goal, what is an "acceptable" level of unemployment? Can we be sure that we will never again experience the trauma of the 1930s, when up to a quarter of all people who sought work were unable to find it? If a completely stable price level is difficult to achieve, what then is an "acceptable" amount of inflation? Why do prices in some countries rise 30 percent or 40 percent a year, while in others they rise at a rate of only 2 percent or 3 percent? Why did inflation accelerate dramatically over most of the world in the 1970s and then fall equally dramatically in the mid 1980s?

Productivity and Growth

Canadians pride themselves on having one of the highest standards of living in the world and a rapid rate of growth in their output of goods and services. During the 1970s the annual rate of growth of total Canadian output averaged 4.2 percent, down from the 5.2 percent average of the 1960s. And although the 1960s witnessed one of the longest periods of *sustained* growth in the nation's history, growth since the 1970s has been sporadic. From 1980 to 1986 the Canadian growth rate averaged 2.5 percent.

Growth in output per person employed, often called **productivity,** slowed dramatically during the seventies. Whereas productivity grew at an average annual rate of 2.7 percent between 1947 and 1973, during the last half of the seventies it averaged less

than 1 percent annually. In the 1980s productivity growth increased slightly, averaging just over 1 percent per year for the first six years of the decade. Since productivity growth accounts for much of the growth in Canadian living standards, this slowdown is a matter of major significance.

What causes such a loss of momentum in the economy? Is it the uncertain state of today's economy? Is it the burden of high taxes on both individuals and business? Is it the heavy drain imposed on the economy by the government's regulation of business to provide cleaner, safer working conditions, bigger unemployment benefits, and more generous pensions and medical care? Or is it the absence of needed government intervention in the form of an industrial policy and other government incentives for growth?

Will the slowdown in our nation's economic growth be reversed? Do we *want* another century of rapid growth and industrialization? Without the automobile, the airplane, and electricity, ours would be a different and less comfortable world. But because of them, air pollution has not only become a major inconvenience but may also be dangerously harming the earth's atmosphere. The coal burned to create the electricity that does so much in homes and factories is a major cause of the acid rain that is polluting lakes and killing trees. Is large-scale pollution the inevitable companion of economic growth? If it is, how can we achieve growth with less pollution?

Two Worlds

By the late 1980s Canada's manufacturing industries were booming—largely as a result of heavy sales to the United States. Unemployment was well below 6 percent in Ontario. But the rest of the country was in difficult straits with unemployment rates of 15 percent in the Atlantic provinces, 13 percent in B.C., 11 percent in Quebec, and 9 percent in the Prairie provinces. The lumber industry was suffering, as were the mining and oil industries. Agriculture's outlook was bleak as a result of world gluts of many products and rising protectionism in many markets. Was Canada splitting into two separate worlds—the two central "have" provinces and the other eight "have nots"?

International Trade and Protectionism

The issue of free trade versus protectionism has been prominent throughout Canada's history because of the crucial role of external trade in the nation's economic development. According to the widely accepted "staples theory," early Canadian economic growth was based on the exploitation of comparative advantages in products with large natural-resource contents. This made Canadian prosperity depend on the strength of export markets for a succession of staples—fish, fur, timber, and wheat—each of which dominated a particular period of Canadian history.

The transcontinental railway was completed in 1855 as a precondition for Confederation. In 1878 Sir John A. MacDonald introduced his National Policy. After Confederation, the protective tariff—a major element in the National Policy—was adopted as a means of fostering domestic manufacturing industries. These two measures, the railway and the tariff, were the key elements in a program of economic nationalism that sought to reduce the country's dependence on unstable export markets for raw materials and to promote an east-west flow of trade that would consolidate the political union of the provinces.

Although a century of industrialization and a series of tariff reductions begun in 1936 have greatly reduced the proportion of the labor force directly engaged in working with raw materials, the issues raised by the National Policy are still at the forefront of public debate. Should Canada continue to reduce the degree of protection that it affords domestic industries from foreign competition? What would be the consequences of another major round of world trade liberalization? If that cannot be achieved, should Canada have free trade with the United States? Would Canadian industries survive and prosper? Would new ones emerge? Or would Canadians resort to being "hewers of wood and drawers of water"?

Government Deficits and the National Debt

Deficits and the national debt were things that governments had talked about for two decades, particularly before elections, but done little about, partic-

ularly after elections. Yet by the mid 1980s economists, bankers, and businesspeople were speaking in alarming terms of the present fiscal position being unsustainable. When the newly elected Conservative government heeded these warnings, it found that major efforts were needed just to stop the deficit from growing. This effort left the deficit still large—it was $32.5 billion in 1986—and the national debt growing rapidly—from 49 percent of national income in 1986 it was projected to grow to 60 percent around 1990. Since the Canadian electorate appeared to reject major cuts in government expenditures, and since most existing taxes were already levied at rates that appeared unproductively high, the only remaining alternative for reducing the debt was finding new tax sources.

How serious was the debt problem? Was there reason to accept the view of the few remaining economists who were willing to argue that the national debt is no problem at all since it is money that we owe to ourselves? Or were the majority of economists right in agreeing that the burden of raising sufficient tax revenues merely to pay the interest on the debt was becoming serious and, if the rise in the debt were not halted, would cause a drastic curtailment in other government expenditures?

Energy

Energy is vital to an industrial economy. Over the past 200 years, North America's output has grown and with it our demand for the earth's limited fossil fuels.

Throughout most of our history, the increase in energy consumption caused no serious problems because new supplies were discovered as rapidly as old ones were exhausted. In the 1970s a dramatic change occurred. The world price of oil rose sharply, and prices of other sources of energy followed suit. By 1976 Canada had become a net importer of oil and natural gas. For a while in the late 1970s and early 1980s talk of an energy crisis was common; many spoke of the need to restore Canada's "energy self-sufficiency." In the last half of the 1980s oil prices plummeted. The end of the oil boom spelled serious economic loss for the oil-producing provinces. Many Canadian workers who had gone west to share in the oil boom joined the reverse trek back to the East, where the jobs were.

Are we cured of our addiction to petroleum, or is the present easing of the energy crisis only apparent, due more to temporarily improved supplies than to our learning to live with less? Are the world's supplies of oil and gas adequate to meet its demands for energy? Can nuclear or solar energy render oil and gas as unnecessary as oil and gas rendered whale oil? What is the appropriate rate at which to deplete our petroleum reserves?

Social Policies

Canadians are both proud and protective of their social policies. These policies help such groups as the poor, the elderly, the sick, the unemployed, and parents with dependent children. Calls for reform have, however, increasingly been heard from those who argue that many existing policies cost too much to deliver too little to those who really need help.

Much of the debate has centred on the so-called principle of universality. Is the universal availability of social policies an essential part of our society that should be maintained whatever the cost? Or is universality a costly frill that should be abandoned if sufficient funds are to remain available to help people in real need?

What Is Economics?

The discussion so far has presented only a handful of the important current issues on which economic analysis is designed to shed light. One way to define the scope of economics is to say that it is the social science that deals with such problems. Another, perhaps better known, is the great English economist Alfred Marshall's: "Economics is a study of mankind in the ordinary business of life." A more penetrating definition is the following:

Economics is the study of the use of scarce resources to satisfy unlimited human wants.

Scarcity is inevitable and is central to economic problems. What are society's resources? Why is scar-

city inevitable? What are the consequences of scarcity?

Resources and Commodities

A society's resources consist of natural gifts such as land, forests, and minerals; human resources, both mental and physical; and manufactured aids to production such as tools, machinery, and buildings. Economists call such resources **factors of production** because they are used to produce things that people desire. The things produced are called **commodities.** Commodities may be divided into goods and services. **Goods** are tangible (e.g., cars or shoes), and **services** are intangible (e.g., haircuts or education). Notice the implication of positive value contained in the terms *goods* and *services.* (Compare the terms *bads* and *disservices.*)

People use goods and services to satisfy many of their wants. The act of making goods and services is called **production,** and the act of using them to satisfy wants is called **consumption.** Goods are valued for the services they provide. An automobile, for example, helps to satisfy its owner's desires for transportation, mobility, and possibly status.

Scarcity

For most of the world's 4 billion human beings, scarcity is real and ever present. In relation to desires (for more and better food, clothing, housing, schooling, entertainment, and so forth), existing resources are woefully inadequate; there are enough to produce only a small fraction of the goods and services that are wanted.

Are not Canada and the United States rich enough that scarcity is nearly banished? After all, they have been characterized as affluent societies. Whatever affluence may mean, it does not mean the end of the problem of scarcity. The small proportion of Canadian households that earn $50,000 a year (a princely amount by world standards) have no trouble spending their after-tax incomes on things that seem useful to them. Yet it would take more than three times the present output of the Canadian economy to produce enough to allow all Canadian households to consume that amount.

Choice

Because resources are scarce, all societies face the problem of deciding what to produce and how to divide the products among their members. Societies differ in who makes the choices and how they are made, but the need to choose is common to all. Just as scarcity implies the need for choice, so choice implies the existence of cost.

Opportunity Cost

A decision to have more of one thing requires a decision to have less of something else. It is this fact that makes the first decision costly. We look first at a trivial example and then at one that vitally affects all of us; both examples involve precisely the same fundamental principles.

Consider the choice that must be made by a small boy who has 10 cents to spend and who is determined to spend it all on candy. For him there are only two kinds of candy in the world: gumdrops, which sell for 1 cent each, and chocolates, which sell for 2 cents. The boy would like to buy 10 gumdrops and 10 chocolates, but he knows (or will soon discover) that this is not possible. (In technical language it is not an *attainable combination* given his scarce resources.) There are, however, several attainable combinations that he might buy: 8 gumdrops and 1 chocolate, 4 gumdrops and 3 chocolates, 2 gumdrops and 1 chocolate, and so on. Some of these combinations leave him with money unspent, and he is not interested in them. Only six combinations (as shown in Figure 1-1) are both attainable and use all his money.

After careful thought, the boy has almost decided to buy 6 gumdrops and 2 chocolates, but at the last moment he decides that he simply must have 3 chocolates. What will it cost him to get this extra chocolate? One answer is 2 gumdrops. As seen in the figure, this is the number of gumdrops he must give up to get the extra chocolate. Economists would describe the 2 gumdrops as the *opportunity cost* of the third chocolate.

Another answer is that the cost of the third chocolate is 2 cents. But given the boy's budget and his intentions, this answer is less revealing than the first one. Where the real choice is between more of this

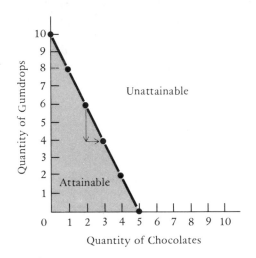

FIGURE 1-1   A Choice Between Gumdrops and Chocolates

A limited amount of money forces a choice among alternatives. Six combinations of gumdrops and chocolates are attainable and use all of the boy's money. The downward-sloping line provides a boundary between attainable and unattainable combinations. The arrows show that the opportunity cost of 1 more chocolate is 2 gumdrops. In this example the opportunity cost is constant and therefore the boundary is a straight line.

and more of that, the cost of "this" is fruitfully looked at as what you cannot have of "that." The idea of opportunity cost is one of the central insights of economics.

The **opportunity cost** is the cost of using resources for a certain purpose, measured in terms of the benefit given up by not using them in an alternative way, that is, measured in terms of other commodities that could have been obtained instead.

Every time scarcity forces one to make a choice, one is incurring opportunity costs. These costs are measured in terms of forgone alternatives.

Production Possibilities

Although the choice between gumdrops and chocolates is a minor consumption decision, the essential nature of the decision is the same whatever the choice being made. Consider, for example, the important social choice between military and civilian goods. Such a choice is similar in form to the one facing the boy deciding what candies to buy with his dime. It is not possible to produce an unlimited quantity of both military and civilian goods. If resources are fully employed and the government wishes to produce more arms, then less civilian goods must be produced. The opportunity cost of increased arms production is forgone production of civilian goods.

The choice is illustrated in Figure 1-2. Because resources are limited, some combinations—those

FIGURE 1-2 A Production Possibility Boundary

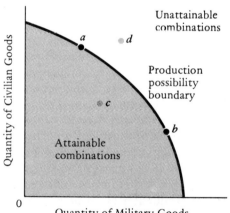

The downward-sloping boundary shows the combinations that are just attainable when all of the society's resources are efficiently employed. The quantity of military goods produced is measured along the horizontal axis, the quantity of civilian goods along the vertical axis. Thus any point on the diagram indicates some amount of each kind of good produced. The production possibility boundary separates the attainable combinations of goods such as *a, b,* and *c* from unattainable combinations such as *d*. It slopes downward because resources are scarce: In a fully employed economy, more of one good can be produced only if resources are freed by producing less of the other goods. Points *a* and *b* represent efficient use of society's resources. Point *c* represents either inefficient use of resources or failure to use all the available resources.

that would require more than the total available supply of resources for their production—cannot be attained. The downward-sloping curve on the graph divides the combinations that can be attained from those that cannot. Points above and to the right of this curve cannot be attained because there are not enough resources; points below and to the left of the curve can be attained without using all of the available resources; and points on the curve can just be attained if all the available resources are used. The curve is called the **production possibility boundary.** It slopes downward because, when all resources are being used, having more of one good requires having less of some other good.

A production possibility boundary illustrates three concepts: scarcity, choice, and opportunity cost. Scarcity is indicated by the unattainable combinations above the boundary, choice by the need to choose among the alternative attainable points along the boundary, and opportunity cost by the downward slope of the boundary.

The shape of the production possibility boundary in Figure 1–2 implies that more and more civilian goods must be given up to achieve equal successive increases in military goods. This shape, referred to as *concave* to the origin, indicates that the opportunity cost of either good grows larger and larger as we increase the amount produced of the other. A slope that forms a straight line, as in Figure 1-1, indicates that the opportunity cost of one good in terms of the other stays constant, no matter how much of it is produced. As we shall see, there are reasons to believe that the case of rising opportunity cost applies to many important choices.[2]

Four Key Economic Questions

While modern economies are complex, many basic decisions that must be made by consumers and pro-

[2] The importance of scarcity, choice, and opportunity cost has led some people to define economics as the problem of allocating scarce resources among alternative and competing ends. The issues emphasized by this definition are important, but, as will be seen in the next section, there are also other important issues.

ducers are not very different from those made in a primitive economy in which people work with few tools and barter with their neighbors. Nor do capitalist, socialist, and communist economies differ in their need to solve the same basic problems, although they do differ, of course, in how they solve them. Most problems studied by economists can be grouped under four main headings.

1. What Is Produced and How?

The allocation of scarce resources among alternative uses, called **resource allocation,** determines the quantities of various goods that are produced. Choosing to produce a particular combination of goods means choosing a particular allocation of resources among the industries or regions producing the goods because, for example, producing a lot of one good requires that a lot of resources be allocated to its production.

Further, because resources are scarce, it is desirable that they be used efficiently. Hence it matters which of the available methods of production is used to produce each of the goods that is to be produced.

2. What Is Consumed and by Whom?

What is the relation between the economy's production of commodities and the consumption enjoyed by its citizens? Economists want to understand what determines the distribution of a nation's total output among its population. Who gets a lot, who gets a little, and why? What role does international trade play in this?

Questions 1 and 2 fall within **microeconomics,** the study of the allocation of resources and the distribution of income as they are affected by the workings of the price system and government policies.

3. How Much Unemployment and Inflation Exist?

When an economy is in a recession, unemployed workers would like to have jobs, the factories in which they could work are available, the managers and owners would like to be able to operate their factories, raw materials are available in abundance,

and the goods that could be produced by these resources are needed by individuals in the community. But for some reason resources remain unemployed. This forces the economy within its production possibility boundary, at a point such as c in Figure 1-2.

The world's economies have often experienced bouts of prolonged and substantial changes in price levels. In recent decades the course of prices has almost always been upward. The 1970s was a period of accelerating inflation not only in North America but in most of the world. Inflation slowed in the early 1980s while unemployment soared. Were these two events related?

Why do governments worry that short-run reductions in either unemployment or inflation will be at the cost of increasing the other?

4. Is Productive Capacity Growing?

The capacity to produce commodities to satisfy human wants grows rapidly in some countries, grows slowly in others, and actually declines in still others. Growth in productive capacity can be represented by a pushing outward of the production possibility boundary, as shown in Figure 1-3. If an economy's capacity to produce goods and services is growing, combinations that are unattainable today will become attainable tomorrow. Growth makes it possible to have more of all goods.

Questions 3 and 4 fall within **macroeconomics,** the study of the determination of economic aggregates such as total output, total employment, the price level, and the rate of economic growth.

Alternative Economic Systems

This book examines the four basic questions just outlined in the context of a market economy in which private firms and households interact in markets with some assistance (and interference) from the government. We study the market economy for several reasons. First, this is the kind of economy we live in. Second, it is the economic environment in which the serious study of economics was born and has grown.

FIGURE 1-3 The Effect of Economic Growth on the Production Possibility Boundary

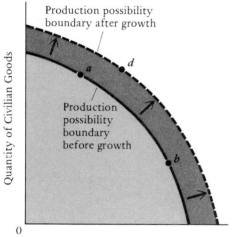

Production possibility boundary after growth

Quantity of Civilian Goods

a   *d*

Production possibility boundary before growth

b

0

Quantity of Military Goods

Economic growth shifts the boundary outward and makes it possible to produce more of all commodities. Before growth in productive capacity, points *a* and *b* were on the production possibility boundary and point *d* was an unattainable combination. After growth, as shown by the dark shaded band, point *d* and many other previously unattainable combinations are attainable.

Today, however, a third of the world's population lives in the Soviet Union and China, countries that reject important elements of our kind of economic system. They rely heavily on centrally planned actions to deal with the four basic questions. At least another third of the world's population lives in countries whose economies have not yet developed to the point where they could accurately be described as either *market* or *planned* economies.

To the extent that economics deals with the ways in which people respond to incentives and mobilize scarce means to given ends, the same economic principles are applicable under a variety of institutional, political, and social arrangements.

All economies face scarcity, and all must decide how to allocate scarce resources and distribute goods and services; all may face problems of inflation, unemployment, and unsatisfactory rates of growth.

Because all economies face many common problems, economic analysis can contribute valuable insights even where familiar institutions are modified or absent.

Differences Among Economies

It is common to speak of only two economic systems, capitalism (or a market-oriented system) and socialism (or a centrally planned system). But this is at best a simplification and at worst a confusion.

There are dozens of economic systems in existence today, not just two. Just as there are many differences among Canada, the United States, the United Kingdom, Germany, Sweden, Japan, and Brazil, so are there differences among the Soviet Union, China, Poland, Cuba, Czechoslovakia, and Yugoslavia. Countries are dissimilar in many respects, including who owns resources, who makes decisions, and the nature of the incentives offered to people. These three aspects are discussed in the next three sections.

Ownership of Resources

Who owns a nation's farms and factories, its coal mines and forests? Who owns its railways, its streams and golf courses? Who owns its houses and hotels?

One characteristic of capitalism is that the basic raw materials, the productive assets of the society, and the goods produced in the economy are predominantly privately owned. By this standard Canada is predominantly a capitalist economy. However, even in Canada public ownership extends beyond the usual basic services such as schools and local transport systems to include other activities such as electric power utilities and housing projects.

In contrast, in a socialist society the productive assets are predominantly publicly owned. Although the Soviets officially designate their economy as socialist, there are three sectors—agriculture, retail trade, and housing—in which some private ownership exists. However, even though the USSR is not a pure socialist economy, public ownership is sufficiently widespread to place the USSR at one end of a spectrum with predominant public ownership, and the United States at the other end. While Canada lies closer to the United States than to the USSR, it is more of a mixed economy than is the United States.

Other countries fall between them on the spectrum. Great Britain has six times in this century elected Labour governments that have been officially committed to socialism to the point of nationalizing key industries, including railroads, steel, coal, electricity, postal services, and telephones. However, the bulk of industries that produce goods and services for household consumption and machinery and equipment for firms remains privately owned. Furthermore, a major thrust for privatization, or the return of publicly owned firms to private ownership, has been under way since 1980.

Ownership patterns are generally mixed and variable rather than exclusive and unchanging. To give some idea of this variability, Figure 1-4 shows the division of investment between public and private sectors in 11 countries.

The Decision Process (Coordinating Principles)

A distinction is sometimes made between two kinds of systems: a *market system*, in which decisions are made impersonally and in a decentralized way by the interaction of individuals in markets, and a *command*

system, in which centralized decision makers decide what is to be done and issue appropriate commands to achieve the desired results.

Again, no country offers an example of either system working alone. But it is true that some economies, such as those of Canada, the United States, France, and Yugoslavia, rely much more heavily on market decisions than do others, such as the economies of East Germany, the Soviet Union, and Cuba. Yet even in Canada the command principle has some sway. Minimum wages, quotas on some agricultural outputs, and quotas on clothing imports are obvious examples. More subtle examples are public expenditures and taxes that in effect transfer command of some resources from private individuals to public officials.

In the planned economies of the Soviet bloc, where targets, quotas, and directives are important aspects of the decision-making system, the command principle dominates. But the market principle also operates. For example, at the retail level people have considerable discretion in how they spend their income on a wide variety of goods.

Much economic behavior depends more on the decision pattern than on the ownership pattern. Thus in the United Kingdom, while many key industries are publicly owned, their control is vested in semi-autonomous boards over which Parliament exerts little control. By and large, the boards try to make their enterprises profitable, and to the extent that

FIGURE 1-4   An Indicator of Differences in Ownership Patterns for Selected Countries

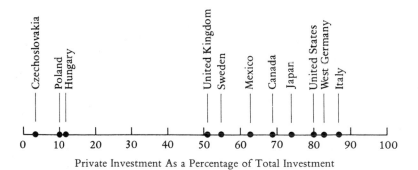

Private Investment As a Percentage of Total Investment

Actual economies never rely solely on private or solely on public investment. These estimates are based on the percentage of gross fixed investment accounted for by the private sector. Such investment provides additions to the stock of productive capital. Private capital investment plays a role even in communist countries; public capital is a significant part of investment in all countries. (*Source*: World Book, *World Tables*.)

TABLE 1-1   Comparative Economic Systems: Ownership and Decision Patterns

| | Ownership pattern | |
Decision pattern	Predominantly private	Predominantly public
Predominantly decentralized with use of market principle	Canada	Yugoslavia
Predominantly centralized with use of command principle	Nazi Germany	USSR

Each of these combinations of private and public ownership and centralized and decentralized control has occurred in practice. This table is a simplification that highlights differences among economic systems. It would be an interesting exercise to use a grid that gives several, rather than just two, gradations for each variable and then attempt to place current and past economies in the appropriate cells.

they succeed, their behavior will be similar to that of profit-seeking, privately owned firms. In contrast, firms in Hitler's Germany were under a high degree of state control, even though they were privately owned. The behavior of these firms was no doubt very different from that of privately owned firms that are managed in order to earn profits for their owners.

Table 1-1, though it makes no subtle distinctions, gives one simple classification of some twentieth century economies according to ownership and decision patterns. Such a classification suggests how communist countries such as the USSR and Yugoslavia differ significantly from one another as well as from Canada.

Incentive Systems

Psychologists know that people (and most other living creatures) respond to incentives. Incentives may be positive or negative—the carrot or the stick—and of almost infinite variety. Among positive incentives, direct monetary rewards, in the form of wages or profits or bribes, are well understood. Indirect monetary rewards, such as special housing, vacations, or subsidized education, are not always as readily identified, but they can be effective. Nonmonetary "carrots" include praise, medals, certificates, and applause. All societies use negative incentives—prison

terms, public ridicule, and other penalties—to discourage aberrant behavior; in some societies indirect negative incentives, such as coercion, fear, and threat of punishment, provide as strong motivation as direct incentives.

Capitalist economies tend to rely heavily on direct monetary rewards. Socialist economies rely more heavily on indirect rewards. Both use negative incentives, but because the command system is relied on in socialist economies, negative nonmonetary incentives are prevalent. In capitalist economies, a major negative monetary incentive that is used is taxation.

Alternative Systems: A Final Word

Perhaps the most important empirical observation about different economies is that a wide variety of economic systems seem able to coexist and to be successful. Three basic points are worth remembering:

1. **All countries have "mixed" economies.**
2. **Among countries, the mixture differs in ways that are appreciable and significant.**
3. **Over time, the mixture changes.**

No economic system seems to do everything better than any major competing system; indeed, each has its strengths and weaknesses. To talk of "better" and "worse" in this context may itself be misleading.

Differences of opinion about which system is best may simply reflect differences in emphasis on particular outcomes. Canadians and Americans may view their economies as being the reason for their high standard of living and see in their well-stocked stores proof of the superiority of free enterprise capitalism. Soviet citizens may look at their economy and see the absence of urban unemployment and the availability of comprehensive welfare services as proof of its superiority to the North American economies. Sweden's slum-free public housing, nationalized medicine, and high productivity in private industry lead many Swedes to regard their "mixed" economy as more desirable than others.

Ends and means.   In many less-developed countries, ordinary people often put more importance on the ends—higher living standards—than on the means of achieving them. They may regard a change of means as unimportant. The choice between a market and a planned economy may seem to be simply a choice of which group will exploit them—government officials or powerful monopoly interests. If a highly planned socialist economy offers them a good chance of a 4 percent growth rate while a market-oriented democratic society offers 2 percent, they may well choose the planned society. To warn them that in so choosing they may throw away their freedom is likely to evoke the reply: What has freedom meant to us in the past but the freedom to be hungry and exploited?

But many people in Western industrialized societies value the means of the free market and democratic processes even more highly than they value the ends of high and rising living standards. Most Canadians distrust the agglomeration of central power and the loss of democratic institutions that accompany a high degree of socialism. Markets are less personal than bureaucrats, and this makes markets more acceptable to many people because they are less arbitrary and less subject to autocratic abuse.

How many Canadians would decide to go over to Russian-style socialism, even if there were *proof* that it would produce higher material living standards than the free-market system? In the 1930s some believed that Fascist dictatorships were more efficient than democracies. Mussolini, it was said, "made the Italian trains run on time." It is debatable that the belief was correct, but many people accepted it. Yet few Canadians advocated that Canada become a Fascist dictatorship.

Of course, many Canadians and citizens of other Western societies believe there is no need to choose. They feel that free markets and democracy produce better results than do alternative systems in terms of both means and ends.

Summary

1. Every generation faces important economic problems. A common feature of such problems is that they concern the use of limited resources to satisfy virtually unlimited human wants.
2. Scarcity is a fundamental problem faced by all economies. Not enough resources are available to produce all the goods and services that people would like to consume. Scarcity makes it necessary to choose. All societies must have a mechanism for choosing what commodities will be produced and in what quantities.
3. The concept of opportunity cost emphasizes the problem of scarcity and choice by measuring the cost of obtaining a unit of one commodity in terms of the number of units of other commodities that could have been obtained instead.
4. Four basic questions must be answered in all economies: What commodities are being produced and how? What commodities are being

consumed and by whom? What are the unemployment and inflation rates? Is productive capacity changing?

5. Not all economies resolve these questions in the same ways or equally satisfactorily. Economists study how these problems are addressed in various societies and the consequences of using one method rather than another to provide solutions.

6. Economies can differ in many ways, and such capsule classifications as "capitalism" and "socialism" represent simplifications of complex matters.

7. Among the important dimensions in which economies can differ are (a) the pattern of ownership of goods and resources, (b) the decision process used, with a particularly important distinction between command and market coordinating principles, and (c) the incentive systems used.

8. All countries have mixed economies in that they exhibit a mixture of public and private ownership, of market and command decision-making systems, and of incentive mechanisms used. The mixtures differ among countries and change over time.

Topics for Review

Scarcity and the need for choice
Choice and opportunity cost
Production possibility boundary
Resource allocation
Unemployed resources
Growth in productive capacity
Alternative economic systems
Public versus private ownership
Market versus command systems

Discussion Questions

1. What does each of the following quotations tell you about the policy conflicts perceived by the person making the statement and about how he or she has resolved them?

   a. "It is an industry worth several hundred jobs to our province; we cannot afford to forgo it." British Columbia Premier William Van der Zam explaining the decision to organize a killing of wolves in northern British Columbia so that more game animals could grow up to be shot by hunters.

   b. "The annual seal hunt must be stopped even if it destroys the livelihood of the seal hunters." An animal rights advocate opposing the seal hunt in the Gulf of St. Lawrence.

   c. "Considering our limited energy resources and the growing demand for electricity, Canada really has no choice but to use all of its possible domestic energy sources, including nuclear energy. Despite possible environmental and safety hazards, nuclear power is a necessity." A representative of the electricity industry replying to criticisms from *Energy Probe*.

2. What is the difference between scarcity and poverty? If everyone in the world had enough to eat, could we say that food was no longer scarce?

3. Consider the right to free speech in political campaigns. Suppose that the Flat Earth Society and the Communist, NDP, Liberal, and Conservative parties all demand equal time on network television in a federal election. What economic questions are involved? Can there be freedom of speech without free access to the scarce resources needed to make one's speech heard?

4. Evidence accumulates that the use of chemical fertilizers, which increases agricultural production greatly, causes damage to water quality. Show the choice involved between more food and cleaner water in using such fertilizers. Use a production possibility curve with agricultural output on the vertical axis and water quality on the horizontal axis. In what ways does this production possibility curve reflect scarcity, choice, and opportunity cost? How would an improved fertilizer that increased agricultural output without further worsening water quality affect the curve? Suppose a pollution-free fertilizer were developed; would this mean there would no longer be any opportunity cost in using it?

5. "What the world of economics needs is an end to ideology and *isms*. If there is a best system of economic organization, it will prove its superiority in its superior ability to solve economic problems." Do you agree with this statement? Would you expect that if the world survives for another hundred years, a single form of economic system would be found superior to all others? Why or why not?

6. Identify the coordinating principle and the incentive system suggested by each of the following:
   a. Taxes on tobacco and alcohol
   b. Production targets assigned to a Russian factory manager by the state planning agency
   c. Legislation establishing minimum wages to be paid
   d. A provincial government directing its agencies to use local suppliers of goods rather than buying from other provinces
   e. Legislation prohibiting the sale and use of cocaine
   f. Rent controls combined with government subsidizing of the building of rental accommodation in Ontario

2

Economics As a Social Science

Economics is generally regarded as a social science. What exactly does it mean to be scientific? Can economics ever hope to be "scientific" in its study of the aspects of human behavior with which it is concerned?

A Scientific Study of Human Behavior

The Distinction Between Positive and Normative

The success of modern science rests partly on the ability of scientists to separate their views on *what does happen* from their views on *what they would like to happen*. For example, until the nineteenth century most people in the Western world believed that the earth was only a few thousand years old. About 200 years ago evidence that some existing rocks were millions or even billions of years old began to accumulate. Most people found this hard to accept: It forced them to rethink their religious beliefs. Many wanted the evidence to be wrong; they wanted rocks to be only a few thousand years old. Nevertheless, the evidence accumulated until today most people accept that the earth is neither thousands, nor millions, but 4 or 5 billion years old.

This advance in our knowledge came because the question "How old are observable rocks?" could be separated from the feelings of scientists (many of them devoutly religious) about the age they would have liked the rocks to be. Distinguishing what *is* true from what we would *like* to be true depends on recognizing the difference between positive and normative statements.

Positive statements concern what is, was, or will be. **Normative statements** concern what one believes ought to be. Positive statements, assertions, or theories may be simple or complex, but they are basically about matters of fact.

Disagreements over positive statements are appropriately handled by an appeal to the facts.

Normative statements, because they concern what ought to be, are inextricably bound up with philosophical, cultural, and religious systems. A normative statement is one that makes, or is based on, a *value judgment*—a judgment about what is good and what is bad.

15

Disagreements over normative statements cannot be handled merely by an appeal to facts.

Some related issues about disagreements among
economists are taken up in Box 2-1.

The Distinction Illustrated

The statement "It is impossible to break up atoms"
is a positive statement that can quite definitely be
(and of course has been) refuted by empirical observations, while the statement "Scientists ought not to
break up atoms" is a normative statement that involves ethical judgments. The questions "What government policies will reduce unemployment?" and
"What policies will prevent inflation?" are positive
ones, while the question "Ought we to be more
concerned about unemployment than about inflation?" is normative.

The Importance of the Distinction

If we think something ought to be done, we can
deduce other things that, if we wish to be consistent,
ought to be done, but we can deduce nothing about
what is done (i.e., is true). Similarly, if we know
that two things are true, we can deduce other things
that must be true, but we can deduce nothing about
what is desirable (i.e., *ought* to be).

It is logically impossible to deduce normative
statements from only positive statements or
positive statements from only normative ones.

As an example of the importance of this distinction in the social sciences, consider the question "Has
the payment of generous unemployment benefits increased the amount of unemployment?" This positive question can be turned into a testable hypothesis
such as "The higher the benefits paid to the unemployed, the higher will be the total amount of unemployment." If we are not careful, however, our
attitudes and value judgments may get in the way of
our study of this hypothesis. Some people are opposed to the welfare state and believe in an individ-
ualist, self-help ethic. They may hope that the hypothesis will be found correct because its truth could

then be used as an argument against welfare measures
in general. Others feel that the welfare state is a good
thing, reducing misery and contributing to human
dignity. They may hope that the hypothesis is wrong
because they do not want any welfare measures to
come under attack. In spite of different value judgments and social attitudes, however, evidence is accumulating on this particular hypothesis. As a result,
we have much more knowledge than we had 10 years
ago of why, where, and by how much unemployment benefits increase unemployment. This evidence
could never have been accumulated or accepted if
investigators had not been able to distinguish their
feelings on how they wanted the answer to turn out
from their assessment of evidence on how people
actually behaved.

Positive statements assert things about the world.
If it is possible for a statement to be proved wrong
by empirical evidence, we call it a *testable statement*.
Many positive statements are testable, and disagreements over them are appropriately handled by an
appeal to the facts.

In contrast to positive statements, which are often
testable, normative statements are never testable.
Disagreements over such normative statements as "It
is wrong to steal" or "It is immoral to have sexual
relations out of wedlock" cannot be settled by an
appeal to empirical observations. Thus, for a rational
consideration of normative questions, different techniques are needed from those used for a rational
consideration of positive questions. Because of this,
it is convenient to separate normative and positive
inquiries. We do this not because we think the former
are less important than the latter but merely because
they must be handled in different ways.

The distinction between positive and normative
allows us to keep our views on how we would like
the world to work separate from our views on how
the world actually does work. We may be interested
in both. It can only obscure the truth, however, if
we let our views on what we would like to be bias
our investigations of what actually is. It is for this
reason that the separation of the positive from the
normative is one of the foundation stones of science
and that scientific inquiry, as it is normally understood, is usually confined to positive questions.
Some important limitations on the distinction be-

BOX 2-1

Why Economists Disagree

If you listen to a discussion among economists on *As It Happens* or *Sunday Morning* or if you read about their debates in the daily press or weekly magazines, you will find economists constantly disagreeing among themselves. Indeed, one widespread reason for rejecting economists' advice is that they seldom completely agree on any issue. Why do economists disagree, and what should we make of this fact?

In a recent column in *Newsweek,* Charles Wolf, Jr., suggests four reasons for the disagreement among economists: (1) Different economists use different benchmarks: Inflation is *down* compared with last year, but *up* compared with the 1950s. (2) Economists fail to make it clear to their listeners whether they are talking about short-term or long-term consequences: Tax cuts will stimulate consumption in the short run and investment in the long run. (3) Economists often fail to acknowledge the full extent of their ignorance. (4) Different economists have different values, and these normative views play a large part in their public discussions.

There is surely some truth in each of these assessments. But there is also a fifth reason: the public's *demand for disagreement.* For example, suppose that all economists were in fact agreed on the proposition that unions are not a major cause of inflation. This view would be unpalatable to some individuals. Those who are hostile to unions, for instance, would like to blame inflation on them and would be looking for an intellectual champion. Fame and fortune would await the economist who espoused their cause, and a champion would soon be found.

Disagreement will always exist. It is also true that by the very nature of reporting this disagreement

tends to get exaggerated in the media. This is not necessarily intentional; indeed, it is hard to see how it might be avoided. When the media cover an issue, they naturally wish to give both sides of it. Normally, the public will hear one or two economists for each side of a debate, regardless of whether the profession is divided right down the middle or is nearly unanimous in its support of one side. Thus the public will not know that in one case a reporter could have chosen from dozens of economists to present each side, while in a second case the reporter had to spend three days trying to locate someone willing to take a particular side because nearly all economists contacted thought it was wrong. On many issues, the profession overwhelmingly supports one side. In their desire to show both sides of the case, however, the media present the public with the appearance of a profession equally split over all matters.

Thus anyone seeking to discredit the economists' advice by showing that they disagree will have no trouble finding evidence to support his or her case. But those who wish to know if there is a majority view or even a strong consensus will find one on a surprisingly large number of issues, such as the housing shortages caused by rent control laws and the unemployment caused by minimum-wage laws. Of course, there are also genuine disagreements among economists on many issues, especially those that involve recent and incompletely understood events, and there will always be controversies at the frontiers of current research. But there is no evidence to suggest that disagreements among economists are more common now than they have been in the past.

---

tween positive and normative are discussed in Box 2-2.

Positive and Normative Statements in Economics

Economics, like other sciences, is concerned with questions, statements, and hypotheses that could

conceivably be shown to be false by actual observations of the world. It is not necessary to show them to be either consistent or inconsistent with the facts tomorrow or the next day; it is only necessary to be able to imagine evidence that could show them to be false. Normative questions cannot be settled by a mere appeal to facts. Of course, this does not mean that they are unimportant. Such questions as "Should

BOX 2-2

Limits on the Positive-Normative Distinction

While the distinction between positive and normative is useful, it has certain specific limitations.

The classification is not exhaustive.   The classifications *positive* and *normative* do not cover all statements that can be made. For example, there is an important class, called *analytic statements,* whose validity depends only on the rules of logic. Thus the sentence "If all humans are immortal and if you are a human, then you are immortal" is a valid analytic statement. It tells us that *if* two things are true, *then* a third thing must be true. The validity of this statement is not dependent on whether or not its individual parts are in fact true. Indeed, the sentence "All humans are immortal" is a positive statement that has been decisively refuted. Yet no amount of empirical evidence on the mortality of humans can upset the truth of the "if-then" sentence quoted above. Analytic statements—which proceed by logical analysis—play an important role in scientific research and form the basis for much of our ability to theorize.

Not all positive statements are testable.   A positive statement asserts something about the universe. It may be empirically true or false in the sense that what it asserts may or may not be true of the universe. If it is true, it adds to our knowledge of what can and cannot happen. Many positive statements are refutable: If they are wrong, this can be ascertained (within a margin for error of observation) by checking them against data. For example, the positive statement that the earth is less than 5,000 years old was tested and

refuted by a mass of evidence accumulated in the nineteenth century.

The statement "Extraterrestrials exist and frequently visit the earth in visible form" is also a positive statement. It asserts something about the universe. But we could never refute this statement with evidence because, no matter how hard we searched, believers could argue that we did not look in the right places or in the right way, or that E.T.s do not reveal themselves to nonbelievers, or any one of a host of other alibis. Thus some positive statements are irrefutable.

The distinction is not unerringly applied.   Because the positive-normative distinction helps the advancement of knowledge, it does not follow that all scientists automatically and unerringly apply it. Scientists are human beings. Many have strongly held values, and they may let their value judgments get in the way of their assessment of evidence. For example, many scientists are not prepared to consider evidence that there may be differences in intelligence among races because as good liberals they feel that all races ought to be equal. Nonetheless, the desire to separate what is from what we would like to be is a guiding light, an ideal, of science. The ability to do so, albeit imperfectly, is attested to by the acceptance, first by scientists and then by the general public, of many ideas that were initially extremely unpalatable—ideas such as the extreme age of the earth and the theory of evolution.

we subsidize higher education?" and "Should we send food to Afghanistan?" must still be decided somehow. In democracies, such questions are often settled by voting.

Economists need not confine their discussions to positive, testable statements. Economists can usefully hold and discuss value judgments as long as they do not confuse such judgments with evaluations of testable statements.

Indeed, the pursuit of what appears to be a nor-

mative statement will often turn up positive hypotheses on which the *ought* conclusion depends. For example, there are probably relatively few people who believe that government control of industry is in itself good or bad. Their advocacy or opposition will be based on beliefs that can be stated as positive rather than normative hypotheses. For example: "Government control reduces efficiency, changes the distribution of income, and leads to an increase of state control in other spheres." A careful study of this subject would reveal enough positive economic questions to keep a research team of economists occupied for many years.

The Scientific Approach

An important aspect of the scientific approach consists of relating questions to evidence. When presented with a controversial issue, scientists will look for all relevant evidence. If they find that the issue is framed in terms that make it impossible to gather evidence for or against it, they will then usually try to recast the question so that it can be answered by an appeal to evidence.

In some fields scientists are able to generate observations that will provide evidence against which to test their hypotheses. Experimental sciences such as chemistry and some branches of psychology have an advantage because it is possible for them to produce relevant evidence through controlled laboratory experiments.

Other sciences such as astronomy and economics cannot do this. They must wait for natural events to produce observations that can be used as evidence in testing their theories. The evidence that then arises does not come from laboratory conditions where everything is held constant except the forces being studied. Instead, it arises from situations where many things are changing at the same time and great care is therefore needed in drawing conclusions from what is observed.

The ease or difficulty with which one can collect evidence does not determine whether a subject is scientific or nonscientific.

Later in this chapter, we shall consider some of the problems that arise when analyzing evidence that is not generated under controlled laboratory conditions. For the moment, however, we shall consider some general problems that are more or less common to all sciences and are particularly important in the social sciences.

Is Human Behavior Predictable?

Social scientists seek to understand and to predict human behavior. A scientific prediction is based on

discovering stable response patterns. But are such patterns possible with anything so complex as human beings? Sometimes this question is answered "no" on the basis of the following argument. While the natural sciences deal with inanimate matter that is subject to natural laws, the social sciences deal with human beings who have free will and therefore cannot be subject to such laws.

This view implies that inanimate matter will show stable response patterns but human beings will not. For example, so goes this argument, if you put a match to a piece of dry paper, the paper will burn, whereas if you subject human beings to torture, some will break down and do what you want them to do and others will not. Even more confusing, the same individual may react differently to torture at different times.

Does human behavior show sufficiently stable responses to factors influencing it to be predictable within an acceptable margin of error? This is a positive question that can be settled only by an appeal to evidence and not by a priori speculation. (**A priori** may be defined as the use of knowledge that is prior to actual experience.) The question itself might concern either the behavior of groups or that of isolated individuals.

Group Behavior Versus Individual Behavior

There are many situations in which group behavior can be predicted accurately without certain knowledge of individual behavior. The warmer the weather, for example, the more people visit the beach and the higher the sales of ice cream. It may be hard to say if or when one individual will buy an ice cream cone, but a stable response pattern from a large group of individuals can be seen. Although social scientists cannot predict what particular individuals will be killed in auto accidents in the next holiday weekend, they can come very close to knowing the total number who will die. The more objectively measurable data they have (for example, the state of the weather on the days in question and the trend in gasoline prices), the more closely they will be able to predict total deaths.

The well-known fact that pollsters usually do a good job of predicting elections on the basis of surveys provides evidence that human attitudes do not change capriciously. If group behavior were truly capricious, there would be no point in trying to predict anything on the basis of such surveys. The fact that 80 percent of the voters who were surveyed said they intended to vote for a certain candidate would give no information about the probable outcome of the election. Today's information would commonly be reversed tomorrow.

The difference between predicting individual and group behavior is illustrated by the fact that economists can predict with fair accuracy what households as a group will do when their take-home pay is increased. Some individuals may do surprising and unpredictable things, but the total response of all households to a permanent change in tax rates that leaves more money in their hands is predictable within quite a narrow margin of error. This stability in the response of households' spending to a change in their available income is the basis of economists' ability to predict successfully the outcome of major revisions in the tax laws.

This does not mean that people never change their minds or that future events can be foretold by a casual study of the past. The stability discussed here is a stable response to causal factors (e.g., next time it gets warm, ice cream sales will rise) and not merely inertia (e.g., ice cream sales will go on rising in the future because they have risen in the past).

The "Law" of Large Numbers

Successfully predicting the behavior of large groups is made possible by the "law" of large numbers. Broadly speaking, this law asserts that random movements of many individual items tend to offset one another. The law is based on one of the most beautiful constants of behavior in the whole of science, and yet it can be derived from the fact that human beings make errors! The law is based on the statistical relation called *normal curve of error*.

What is implied by this law? Ask any one person to measure the length of a room and it will be almost impossible to predict in advance what sort of error of measurement will be made. Dozens of things will affect the accuracy of the measurement, and, furthermore, the person may make one error today

and quite a different one tomorrow. But ask a thousand people to measure the length of the same room, and we can predict within a small margin just how this *group* will make its errors. We can assert with confidence that more people will make small errors than will make large errors, that the larger the error the fewer will be the number making it, that roughly the same number of people will overstate as will understate the distance, and that the larger the number of people that we have making the measurement, the smaller will their *average* error tend to be.

If a common cause should act on each member of the group, the average behavior of the group can be predicted even though any one member may act in a surprising fashion. If, for example, each of the thousand individuals is given a tape measure that understates "actual" distances, it can be predicted that, on the average, the group will understate the length of the room. It is, of course, quite possible that one member who had in the past been consistently undermeasuring distance because of psychological depression will now overmeasure the distance because the state of his health has changed. But some other event may happen to another individual that will turn her from an overmeasurer into an undermeasurer. Individuals may act strangely for inexplicable reasons. But the group's behavior, when the inaccurate tape is substituted for the accurate one, will be predictable precisely because the odd things that one individual does will tend to cancel out the odd things some other individual does.

Irregularities in individual behavior tend to cancel one another out, and the regularities tend to show up in repeated observations.

The Nature of Scientific Theories

When some regularity between two or more things is observed, we may ask why this should be so. A *theory* is an attempt to answer this question, and by providing an explanation for the regularity, it enables us to predict as yet unobserved events. For example, national income theory predicts that a reduction in tax rates will reduce the unemployment rate. The simple theory of market behavior predicts that under specified conditions, a partial failure of the potato crop will cause an increase in the incomes of potato farmers.

Theories are used in explaining observed phenomena. A successful theory enables us to predict behavior.

Any explanation whatsoever of how given observations are linked together is a theoretical construction. Theories are used to impose order on our observations, to explain how what we see is linked together. Without theories there would be only a shapeless mass of meaningless observations.

The choice is not between theory and observation but between better or worse theories to explain observations.

Misunderstanding about the place of theories in scientific explanation gives rise to many misconceptions. One of these is illustrated by the phrase "True in theory, but not in practice." The next time you hear someone say this (or, indeed, the next time you say it yourself) you should immediately reply, "All right, then, tell me what does happen in practice." Usually you will not be told mere facts, but you will be given an alternative theory—a different explanation of the facts. The speaker should have said, "The theory in question provides a poor explanation of the facts (that is, it is contradicted by some factual observations). I have a different theory that does a much better job."

A theory consists of (1) a set of definitions that clearly define the *variables* to be used, (2) a set of *assumptions* that outline the conditions under which the theory is to apply, (3) one or more *hypotheses* about the relationships among the variables, and (4) *predictions* that are deduced from the assumptions of the theory and can be tested against actual empirical observations. We consider these four elements in the following four sections.

Variables

A **variable** is a magnitude that can take on different possible values. Variables are the basic elements of theories, and each one needs to be carefully defined.

Price is an example of an important economic variable. The price of a commodity is the amount of money that must be given up to purchase one unit of that commodity. To define a price we must first define the commodity to which it attaches. Such a commodity might be one dozen grade A large eggs. The price of such eggs sold in, say, supermarkets in Prince Albert, Saskatchewan, defines a variable. The particular values taken on by that variable might be $0.98 on July 1, 1987, $1.02 on July 8, 1988, and $0.99 on July 15, 1989.

There are many distinctions between kinds of variables; two of the most important are discussed below.

Endogenous and exogenous variables.   An **endogenous variable** is a variable that is explained within a theory. An **exogenous variable** influences endogenous variables but is itself determined by factors outside the theory.

For example, consider the theory that the price of apples in Nanaimo, British Columbia, on a particular day is a function of several things, one of which is the weather in the Okanagan Valley during the previous apple-growing season. We can safely assume that the state of the weather is not determined by economic conditions. The price of apples in this case is an endogenous variable—something determined within the framework of the theory. The state of the weather in the Okanagan Valley is an exogenous variable; changes in it influence prices because the changes affect the output of apples, but the state of the weather is not influenced by the prices.

Other words are sometimes used for the same distinction. One frequently used pair is *induced* for endogenous and *autonomous* for exogenous; another is *dependent* and *independent*.

Stock and flow variables.   A flow variable has a time dimension; it is so much per unit of time. The quantity of grade A large eggs purchased in Prince Albert is a flow variable. No useful information is conveyed if we are told that the number purchased was 2,000 dozen eggs unless we are also told the period of time over which these purchases occurred. Two thousand dozen per hour would indicate an active market in eggs, while 2,000 dozen per month would indicate a sluggish market.

A stock variable has no time dimension; it is just so much. Thus if the egg marketing board has 2 million dozen eggs in warehouses around some province that quantity is a stock. All those eggs are there at one time, and they remain there until something happens to change the stock level. The stock variable is just a number, not a rate of flow of so much per day or per month.

Economic theories use both flow variables and stock variables, and it takes a little practice to keep them straight. The amount of income earned is a flow; there is so much per year or per month or per hour. The amount of a household's expenditure is also a flow—so much spent per week or per month. The amount of money in a bank account or a miser's hoard (earned, perhaps, in the past, but unspent) is a stock—just so many thousands of dollars. The key test is always whether a time dimension is required to give the variable meaning.

Assumptions

Assumptions are essential to theorizing. Students are often greatly concerned about the justification of assumptions, particularly if they seem unrealistic.

An example will illustrate some of the issues involved in this question of realism. Much of the theory that we are going to study in this book uses the assumption that the sole motive of all those who run firms is to make as much money as they possibly can, or, as economists put it, firms are assumed to be run so as to *maximize their profits.* The assumption of profit maximization allows economists to make predictions about the behavior of firms. They study the effects that alternatives open to firms would have on profits, and then predict that the alternative selected will be the one that produces the most profits.

But profit maximization may seem like a rather crude assumption. Surely the managers of firms sometimes have philanthropic or political motives. Does this not discredit the assumption of profit maximization by showing it to be unrealistic?

To make successful predictions, however, the theory does not require that managers are solely and always motivated by the desire to maximize profits. All that is required is that profits are a sufficiently

important consideration that a theory based on the assumption of profit maximization will produce predictions that are substantially correct.

This illustration shows that it is not always appropriate to criticize a theory because its assumptions seem unrealistic. All theory is an abstraction from reality. If it were not, it would merely duplicate the world and would add nothing to our understanding of it. A good theory abstracts in a useful way; a poor theory does not. If a theory has ignored some really important factors, then its predictions will be contradicted by the evidence—at least where the factor ignored exerts an important influence on the outcome.

Hypotheses

Relations among variables.   The critical step in theorizing is formulating hypotheses. A hypothesis is a statement about how two or more variables are related to each other. For example, it is a basic hypothesis of economics that the quantity produced of any commodity depends on its own price in such a way that the higher the price, the larger the quantity produced. To illustrate, the higher the price of eggs, the larger the quantity of eggs that the farmers will produce. Stated in more formal terms, the hypothesis is that the two variables, price of eggs and quantity of eggs, are positively related to each other.[1]

Functional relations.   A **function,** or a functional relation, is a formal expression of a relation among variables.[2]

The particular hypothesis that the quantity of eggs produced is related to the price of eggs is an example of a functional relation in economics. In its most general form, it merely says that quantity produced is related to price. The more specific hypothesis is that as the price of eggs rises, the quantity produced also rises.

In the case of many hypotheses of this kind, econ-

[1] When two variables are related in such a way that an increase in one is associated with an increase in the other, they are said to be *positively related.* When two variables are related in such a way that an increase in one is associated with a decrease in the other, they are said to be *negatively related.*

[2] The appendix to this chapter gives a more detailed discussion of functional relations and the use of graphs in economics.

omists can be even more specific about the nature of the functional relation. On the basis of detailed factual studies, economists often have a pretty good idea of how much the quantity produced will change as a result of specified changes in price; that is, they can predict magnitude as well as direction.

Predictions

A theory's predictions are the propositions that can be deduced from that theory. An example of a prediction would be a deduction that *if* firms maximize their profits, and *if* certain other assumptions and hypotheses of the theory hold true, *then* a rise in the rate of corporate tax will cause a reduction in the amount of investment that firms make in new plant and equipment. The prediction is that the rise in the tax rate will be accompanied by a fall in investment. The reasons that lie behind the prediction are contained in the assumptions and hypotheses that constitute the theory in question.

It should be apparent from this discussion that a scientific prediction is not the same thing as a prophecy.

A scientific prediction is a conditional statement that takes the form: *If* **you do this,** *then* **such and such will follow.**

If hydrogen and oxygen are combined under specified conditions, *then* water will be the result. *If* the government cuts taxes, *then* the rate of unemployment will decrease. It is important to realize that this prediction is very different from the statement "I prophesy that in two years' time there will be a large reduction in unemployment because I believe the government will decide to cut tax rates." The government's decision to cut tax rates in two years' time will be the outcome of many influences, both economic and political. If the economist's prophecy about unemployment turns out to be wrong because in two years' time the government does not cut tax rates, then all that has been learned is that the economist is not good at guessing the future behavior of the government. However, *if* the government does cut tax rates (in two years' time or at any other time) and *then* the rate of unemployment does not decrease,

a conditional scientific prediction in economic theory has been contradicted.

Testing Theories

A theory is tested by confronting its predictions with evidence. It is necessary to discover if certain events are followed by the consequences predicted by the theory. For example, is an increase in the corporate tax rate followed by a decline in business investment? (Box 2-3 gives further discussion of what can be learned from testing theories.)

Generally, theories tend to be abandoned when they are no longer useful. And theories cease to be useful when they cannot predict the consequences of actions in which one is interested better than the next best alternative. When a theory consistently fails to predict better than the available alternatives, it is either modified or replaced. Figure 2-1 (p. 25) summarizes the discussion of theories and their testing.

Refutation or confirmation. The scientific approach to any issue consists in setting up a theory that will explain it and then seeing if that theory can be refuted by evidence.

The alternative to this approach is to set up a theory and then look for confirming evidence. Such an approach is hazardous because the world is sufficiently complex that *some* confirming evidence can be found for any theory, no matter how unlikely the theory may be. For example, the advocates of conspiracy theories, such as the theory that U.S. President John Kennedy's assassination was a plot involving many persons and at least two gunmen, can always find some confirming evidence. The scientific way to deal with such questions is to set up the simplest theory—in this case that the president was assassinated by Lee Harvey Oswald acting alone—and then see if the evidence can refute it.

An example of the unfruitful approach of seeking confirmation is frequently seen when a leader, elected or self-appointed, surrounds himself with yes-sayers who feed him only evidence that confirms his existing views. This approach is usually a road to disaster because the leader's decisions become more and more out of touch with reality.

A wise leader adopts a scientific approach instinctively; he constantly checks the realism of his views

BOX 2-3

Can Hypotheses Be Proven or Refuted?

Most hypotheses in economics are universal. They say that whenever certain specified conditions are fulfilled, cause X will always produce effect Y. Such universal hypotheses cannot be proven correct with certainty. No matter how many observations are collected that agree with the hypothesis, there is always some chance that a long series of untypical observations has been made or that there have been systematic errors of observation. After all, the mass of well-documented evidence accumulated several centuries ago on the existence of the power of witches is no longer accepted, even though it fully satisfied most contemporary observers. The existence of observational errors, even on a vast scale, has been shown to be possible, although (one fervently hopes) it is not very frequent. Observations that disagree with the theory may begin to accumulate, and after some time a theory that looked nearly certain may begin to look rather shaky.

By the same token a universal hypothesis can never be proven false with certainty. Even when current observations consistently conflict with the theory, it is still possible that a large number of untypical cases has been selected or systematic errors of ob-

servation have been made. For instance, evidence was once gathered "disproving" the theory that high income taxes tend to discourage work. More recent research suggests that economists may have been wrong to reject this theory. As a result of measurement errors and bad experimental design, the conflicting evidence may not have been as decisive as was once thought.

There is no absolute certainty in any knowledge. No doubt some of the things we now think true will eventually turn out to be false, and some of the things we currently think false will eventually turn out to be true. Yet while we can never be certain, we can assess the balance of evidence. Some hypotheses are so unlikely to be true, given current evidence, that for all practical purposes we may regard them as false. Other hypotheses are so unlikely to be false, given current evidence, that for all practical purposes we may regard them as true. This kind of practical decision must always be regarded as tentative. Every once in a while we will find that we have to change our mind: Something that looked right will begin to look doubtful, or something that looked wrong will begin to look possible.

by encouraging subordinates to criticize them. This tests how far the leader's existing views correspond to all available evidence and encourages amendment in the light of evidence that conflicts with the current views.

Measurement and Testing of Economic Relations

So far we have given an outline of the main elements of theories. Because measurement and testing are so important in evaluating theories, we now present a more detailed discussion of these topics in relation to economic principles.

It is one thing for economists to theorize that two or more variables are related to each other; it is quite

another for them to be able to say how these variables are related. Economists might generalize on the basis of a casual observation that when households receive more income, they are likely to buy more of most commodities. But precisely how much will the consumption of a particular commodity rise as household incomes rise? Are there exceptions to the rule that the purchase of a commodity rises as income rises? For estimating precise magnitudes and for testing general rules or hypotheses, common sense, intuition, and casual observation do not take us very far. More systematic statistical analysis is required.

Statistical analysis is used to test the hypothesis that two things are related and to estimate the numerical values of the function that describes the relation.

**FIGURE 2-1   The Interaction of Deduction and Measurement
in Theorizing**

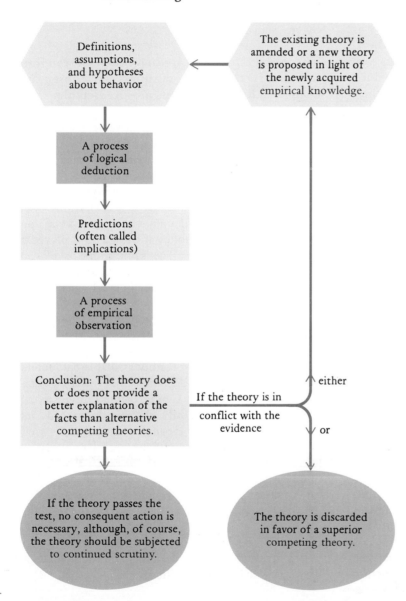

Definitions, assumptions, and hypotheses about behavior

A process of logical deduction

Predictions (often called implications)

A process of empirical observation

Conclusion: The theory does or does not provide a better explanation of the facts than alternative competing theories.

The existing theory is amended or a new theory is proposed in light of the newly acquired empirical knowledge.

If the theory is in conflict with the evidence

either

or

If the theory passes the test, no consequent action is necessary, although, of course, the theory should be subjected to continued scrutiny.

The theory is discarded in favor of a superior competing theory.

Theory and observation are in continuous interaction. Starting (at the top left) with the assumptions of a theory and the definitions of relevant terms, the theorist deduces by logical analysis everything that is implied by the assumptions. These implications are the predictions of the theory. The theory is then tested by confronting its predictions with evidence. If the theory is in conflict with facts, it will usually be amended to make it consistent with those facts (thereby making it a better theory); in extreme cases it will be discarded, to be replaced by a superior alternative. The process then begins again: The new or amended theory is subjected first to logical analysis and then to empirical testing.

In practice, the same data can be used simultaneously to test whether a relationship exists and, when it does exist, to provide a measure of it.

We have seen that economics is a nonlaboratory science. It is rarely possible to conduct controlled experiments with the economy. However, millions of uncontrolled experiments are going on every day. Households are deciding what to purchase given changing prices and incomes; firms are deciding what to produce and how to produce it; and the government is involved in the economy by its various taxes, subsidies, and controls. Because all these activities can be observed and recorded, a mass of data is continually produced by the economy.

The variables that interest economists, such as the volume of unemployment, the price of wheat, and the share of income going to wage earners, are generally influenced by many factors, all of which vary simultaneously. If economists are to test their theories about relations among variables in the economy, they must use statistical techniques designed for situations in which other things cannot be held constant.

An Example of Statistical Testing

To illustrate how data may be used to test theories even while other things are not held constant, we take the very simple and intuitively plausible hypothesis that the federal income taxes paid by households increase as their incomes increase.

A Sample

To begin with, observations must be made of family income and tax payments. It is not practical to do so for all households, so a small number (called a *sample*) are studied on the assumption that these households are typical of the entire group.

It is important that the sample be what is called a random sample. A **random sample** is chosen according to a rigidly defined set of conditions guaranteeing, among other things, that every member of the group from which we are selecting the sample has an equal chance of being selected. Choosing the sample in a random fashion has two important consequences.

First, it reduces the chance that the sample will be unrepresentative of the population from which it is selected. Second, and more important, it allows us to calculate just how likely it is that the sample will be unrepresentative by any specified amount. For example, if the average amount of income tax paid by the households in our sample is $2,000, then it is most likely that the average tax paid by all households in the country is in the vicinity of $2,000. But that is not necessarily so. The sample might be so unrepresentative that the actual figure for average tax

paid by all households is only $1,500, or it might be $2,750. If the sample is random, we are able to calculate the probability that the actual data for the whole population differ from the data in our sample by any stated amount.

The reason for the predictability of random samples is that such samples are chosen by chance, and chance events are predictable.

That chance events are predictable may sound surprising, but consider these questions. If you pick a card from a deck of ordinary playing cards, how likely is it that you will pick a heart? An ace? An ace of hearts? You play a game in which you pick a card and win if it is a heart and lose if it is anything else; a friend offers you $5 if you win against $1 if you lose. Who will make money if the game is played a large number of times? The same game is played again, but now you get $3 if you win and pay $1 if you lose. Who will make money over a large number of draws? If you can answer these questions (we will bet that most of you can), you must believe that chance events are in some sense predictable.

To test the hypothesis about taxes we require relevant data. One set of readily available data refers to a random sample of 212 American families chosen by the Survey Research Center of the University of Michigan. For each family the survey records its income and the federal income tax it pays—as well as some other data that will be useful to us later. Since we are interested in methods rather than in the results at this stage, there is no problem in using data for American rather than Canadian households.

Graphical and Tabular Analysis

There are several ways in which the data may be used to evaluate the hypothesis.

Scatter diagram.   One is the **scatter diagram.**[3] Figure 2-2 is a scatter diagram that relates family income to federal income tax payments. The pattern of the dots suggests that there is a strong tendency

---

[3] The second half of the appendix to this chapter outlines the elements of graphs and the graphical analysis of economic data. If you find graphical analysis baffling, you might read this appendix now.

FIGURE 2-2   A Scatter Diagram Relating Taxes Paid to Family Income in the United States

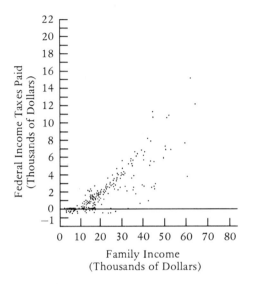

The scatter pattern shows a clear tendency for taxes paid to rise with family income. Family income is measured along the horizontal axis, and federal income taxes paid are measured along the vertical axis. Each dot represents a single family in the sample and is located on the graph according to the family's income and taxes paid. The dots fall mainly within a narrow, rising band, suggesting the existence of a systematic relationship between income and taxes paid. But they do not fall along a single line, which suggests that things other than family income affect taxes paid. The data are for 1979. (Negative amounts of tax liability arise because of such things as capital losses that may be carried forward.)

TABLE 2-1   Federal Tax Payments Cross-Classified by Family Income

Annual family income	Average income tax payment	Number of families
Less than $10,000	$ 70	38
$ 10,000–19,999	893	76
20,000–29,999	2,470	42
30,000–39,999	4,205	28
40,000–99,999	7,755	28
100,000 or more	—	0

Tax payments tend to increase as family income increases. The data on 212 families are grouped into the income classes shown in the first column. The average tax payment for families in each income group is calculated and listed in the second column. When we read down this second column, we find an unbroken rise in tax payments. This cross-classification reduces 212 individual observations to a mere 5. More (or less) detail could have been preserved by varying the size of the income classes used in the first column.

rectly reported its tax payments to the person who collected the data.

Cross-classification table. A cross-classification table provides another way to examine the hypothesis that tax payments vary directly with income. Table 2-1 cross-classifies families by their income and their average tax payments. At the loss of considerable detail, the table makes clear the general tendency for tax payments to rise as income rises.

Regression Analysis

While both the scatter diagram and the cross-classification table reflect the general relationship between federal income tax payments and family income, neither characterizes what the precise relationship is. **Regression analysis,** a widely used technique, provides quantitative measures of the relationship between two variables and how closely it holds.[4] It employs a **regression equation** that represents the best estimate of the *average* relationship between the variables being tested. The equation can be used in

for tax payments to be higher when family income is higher. It thus supports the hypothesis.

There is some scattering of the dots because the relationship is not "perfect"; in other words, there is some variation in tax payments that cannot be associated with variations in family income. These variations in tax payments occur mainly for two reasons. First, factors other than income influence tax payments, and some of these other factors will undoubtedly have varied among the families in the sample. Second, there will inevitably be some errors in measurement. For example, a family might have incor-

[4] Detailed discussion of techniques and conditions that must hold for the technique to be valid is left to courses in statistics and econometrics.

this case to describe the tendency for higher family income to be associated with higher tax payments.[5]

A measure of how closely the relationship holds can be obtained by calculating the percentage of the variance in federal tax payments that can be accounted for by variations in household income.[6] This measure is called the **coefficient of determination** (r^2). For our sample $r^2 = 0.734$. This number tells us that in this case 73.4 percent of the variance in tax payments can be "explained" by associating it with variations in family incomes.

A *significance test* can be applied to determine the odds that the relation discovered in the sample does not exist for the whole population but has arisen by chance because the families selected happen not to be representative of the entire set of American families. It turns out that in this example there is less than one chance in a million that the rising pattern of dots shown in Figure 2-2 would have been observed if there were no positive association between income and tax payments for U.S. families. We conclude with less than one chance in a million of being wrong that the hypothesis that tax payments and family income are positively related is correct. Statistically the relationship is said to be *significant*.

Extending the Analysis to Three Variables

The scatter diagram and the regression equation show that *all* the variation in income tax payments cannot be accounted for by observed variations in family income. If it could, all the dots would lie on a line, and r^2 would equal 1.0. Since these criteria are not met, some other factors must influence tax payments. Why might one family with an income of $12,000 pay 20 percent more in income taxes than another family with the same income?

One reason is difference in family size, for American tax laws provide exemptions based on the number of family members. (There will be other reasons

too, such as differences in itemized deductions for medical expenses or charitable donations.) We anticipate that family size will be an important second reason. The survey also collected data on family size, which we now use.

There are now *three* observations for each of the 212 families: annual income, federal income tax payments, and family size. How should these data be handled? The scatter diagram technique is not available because the relation among three sets of data cannot conveniently be shown on a two-dimensional graph.

The data may, however, be classified into groups once again. This time we are testing two variables that are thought to influence tax payments, and the data have to be cross-classified in a more complicated manner, as shown in Table 2-2.

The table can be used to hold one variable roughly constant while allowing another to vary. Reading across each row, we see that income is held

TABLE 2-2   Federal Tax Payments Cross-Classified by Family Income and Family Size

Annual family income	Number of family members		
	3 or less	4 or 5	6 or more
$ 0–9,999	$ 175	$ 142	$ 26
10,000–19,999	1,028	995	507
20,000–29,999	2,950	2,491	935
30,000–39,999	5,349	3,802	2,372
40,000–99,999	9,459	8,624	4,193
100,000 or more	None in the sample		

Tax payments tend to vary positively with family income and negatively with family size. Each row in the table shows the effect of family size on tax payments for a given level of income. For example, reading across the second row shows that families with incomes between $10,000 and $20,000 paid an average of $1,028 if the family had less than 4 members, $995 if the family had 4 or 5 members, and $507 if the family had 6 or more members. The declining numbers across each row show that for each income group tax payments tend to decline as family size increases. Each column in the table shows the effect of income on tax payments for a given family size. The increase in taxes paid as we move down each column shows that tax payments increase with family income.

---

[5] The equation of a straight line fitted to the data shown in Figure 2-2 is $T = -1,924 + 0.19Y$, where T is taxes paid and Y is income in thousands of dollars per year. The equation shows that for every increase of $1,000 in family income, taxes paid tend to increase by $190.

[6] *Variance* is a precise statistical measure of the amount of variability (dispersion) in a set of data.

constant within a specified range and family size is varied; reading down each column, we see that size of family is held constant within a specified range and income is varied.

To estimate a numerical relation among family income, family size, and tax payments, **multiple regression analysis** is used.[7] This type of analysis allows estimation of both the separate and joint effects on tax payments of variations in family size and variations in income by fitting to the data an equation that "best" describes them. It also permits the measurement of the proportion of the total variation in tax payments that can be explained by associating it with variations in both income and family size. Finally, it permits the use of significance tests to determine how likely it is that the relations found in the sample are the result of chance and thus do not reflect a similar relationship for all U.S. families. Chance plays a role because by bad luck an unrepresentative sample of families might have been chosen.

The Decision to Reject or Accept

In general, a hypothesis can never be proven or refuted with absolute certainty, no matter how many observations are made. Those who are interested in pursuing this matter will find further discussion in Box 2-3.

Although we can never be certain, we do have to make decisions. To do so it is necessary to accept some hypotheses (to act as if they were proven) and reject some hypotheses (to act as if they were refuted). Just as a jury can make two kinds of errors (finding an innocent person guilty or letting a guilty person go free), so can statistical decision makers make two kinds of errors. They can reject hypotheses that are true, and they can accept hypotheses that are false. Luckily, like a jury, they can also make correct decisions—and indeed they expect to do so most of the time.

Although the possibility of error cannot be eliminated in statistics, it can be controlled.

The method of control is to decide in advance how large a risk to take of accepting a hypothesis that is in fact false.[8] Conventionally in statistics this risk is often set at 5 percent or 1 percent. When the 5 percent cutoff point is used, we will accept the hypothesis if the results that appear to establish it could have happened by chance no more than 1 time in 20. Using the 1 percent decision rule gives the hypothesis a sterner test. A hypothesis is accepted only if the results that appear to establish it could have happened by chance no more than 1 time in 100.

Consider the hypothesis that a certain coin is "loaded," favoring heads over tails. The coin is flipped 100 times and comes up heads 53 times. While this result is not inconsistent with the hypothesis, such an unbalanced result could happen by chance more than 22 percent of the time. Thus the hypothesis of a head-biased coin would not be accepted using either a 1 percent or a 5 percent cutoff. Had the experiment produced 65 heads and 35 tails, a result that would occur by chance less than 1 percent of the time, we would (given a 1 percent or a 5 percent cutoff) accept the hypothesis of a loaded coin.[9]

When action must be taken, some rule of thumb is necessary. But it is important to understand, first, that no one can ever be certain about being right in rejecting any hypothesis and, second, that there is nothing magical about arbitrary cutoff points. Some cutoff point must be used whenever decisions have to be made.

Finally, recall that the rejection of a hypothesis is seldom the end of inquiry. Decisions can be reversed should new evidence come to light. Often the result of a statistical test of a theory is to suggest a new hypothesis that "fits the facts" better than the old one. Indeed, in some cases just looking at a scatter

---

[7] Details must be left to a course in statistics. The regression equation for our example is $T = -733 + 0.197Y - 344F$, where F is the number of family members. On average, an additional family member decreases taxes paid by \$344. R^2, the coefficient of determination in multiple regression analysis, is 0.774. Comparison with the previous $r^2 = 0.734$ shows that adding family size to the analysis increased the percentage of variance explained from 73.4 percent to 77.4 percent.

[8] Return to the jury analogy: Our notion of a person's being innocent unless the jury is persuaded of guilt "beyond a reasonable doubt" rests on our wishing to take only a small risk of accepting the hypothesis of guilt if the person being tried is in fact innocent.

[9] The actual statistical testing process is more complex than this example suggests but must be left to a course in statistics.

diagram or making a regression analysis uncovers apparent relations that no one anticipated and leads economists to formulate a new hypothesis.

Economics As a Developing Science

Economics is like other sciences in at least two respects. First, there are many observations of the world for which there are, at the moment, no fully satisfactory theoretical explanations. Second, there are many predictions that no one has yet satisfactorily tested. Serious students of economics must not expect to find a set of answers to all their questions as they progress in their study. Often they must expect to encounter nothing more than a set of problems that provides an agenda for further research. Even when they do find answers to problems, they should accept these answers as tentative and ask even of the most time-honored theory, "What observations would be in conflict with this theory?"

Economics is still a young science. On the one hand, economists know a good deal about the behavior of the economy. On the other hand, many problems are almost untouched. Students who decide to specialize in economics may find themselves, only a few years from now, publishing a theory to account for some of the problems mentioned in this book; or they may end up making a set of observations that will upset some venerable theory described in these pages.

A final word of warning: Having counseled a constructive disrespect for the authority of accepted theory, it is necessary to warn against adopting an approach that is too cavalier. No respect attaches to the person who says, "This theory is for the birds; it is *obviously* wrong." This is too cheap. To criticize a theory effectively on empirical grounds, one must demonstrate, by a careful set of observations, that some aspect of the theory is contradicted by the facts. This is a task worth attempting, but it is seldom easily accomplished.

Summary

1. It is possible, and fruitful, to distinguish between positive and normative statements. Positive statements concern what is, was, or will be, while normative statements concern what ought to be. Disagreements over positive, testable statements are appropriately settled by an appeal to the facts. Disagreements over normative statements can never be settled in this way.

2. The success of scientific inquiry depends on separating positive questions about the way the world works from normative questions about how one would like the world to work, formulating positive questions precisely enough so that they can be settled by an appeal to evidence, and then finding means of gathering the necessary evidence.

3. Some people feel that although natural phenomena can be subject to scientific inquiry and "laws" of behavior, human phenomena cannot. The evidence, however, is otherwise. Social scientists have observed many stable human behavior patterns. These form the basis for successful predictions of how people will behave under certain conditions.

4. The fact that people sometimes act strangely, even capriciously, does not destroy the possibility of scientific study of group behavior. The odd and inexplicable things that one person does will tend to cancel out the odd and inexplicable things that another person does.

5. Theories are designed to give meaning and coherence to observed

sequences of events. A theory consists of a set of definitions of the variables to be employed, a set of assumptions under which the theory is meant to apply, and a set of hypotheses about how things behave. Any theory has certain logical implications that must be true if the theory is true. These are the theory's predictions.

6. A theory provides predictions of the type "*if* one event occurs, *then* another event will also occur." An important method of testing theories is to confront their predictions with evidence. The progress of any science lies in finding better explanations of events than are now available. Thus in any developing science one must expect to discard present theories and replace them with demonstrably superior alternatives.

7. Theories are tested by checking their predictions against evidence. In some sciences these tests can be conducted under laboratory conditions where only one thing changes at a time. In other sciences testing must be done using the data produced by the world of ordinary events. Modern statistical analysis is designed to test hypotheses when many variables are changing at once.

8. Sample data are often used in testing economic theories. If the sample is random, the probability that the measured characteristics of the sample will be misleading (because of the unlucky choice of a nonrepresentative sample) can be calculated.

9. Scatter diagrams or simple cross-classification tables are devices for discovering systematic relationships between two variables. Regression analysis permits more specific measurement of the relationship: what it is, how closely it holds, and whether or not it is "significant."

10. Hypotheses involving several variables require more sophisticated statistical techniques such as the use of complex cross-classification tables and multiple regression analysis. These techniques attempt to identify the separate and joint effects of several variables on one another.

11. Methods of graphing economic observations and the use of functional relations are discussed in more detail in the appendix to this chapter.

Topics for Review

Positive and normative statements
Testable statements
The law of large numbers and the predictability of human behavior
Variables, hypotheses, assumptions, and predictions in theorizing
Endogenous and exogenous variables
Stock and flow variables
Functional relations
Prediction versus prophecy
The scientific approach
Role of statistical analysis: measurement and testing

Scatter diagrams
Cross–classification tables
Rejection and acceptance of hypotheses

Discussion Questions

1. A baby doesn't "know" of the theory of gravity, yet in walking and eating the child soon learns to use its principles. Distinguish between behavior and the explanation of behavior. Does a business executive or a farmer have to understand economic theory to behave in a pattern consistent with economic theory?

2. "If human behavior were completely capricious and unpredictable, life insurance could not be a profitable business." Explain. Can you think of any businesses that do *not* depend on predictable human behavior?

3. Write five statements about unemployment in Canada. (It does not matter whether the statements are correct, but you should confine yourself to those you think might be correct.) Classify each statement as positive or normative. If your list contains only one type of statement, try to add a sixth statement of the other type.

4. Each of the following unrealistic assumptions is sometimes made. See if you can visualize situations in which each of them might be useful.
   a. The earth is a plane.
   b. There are no differences between men and women.
   c. There is no tomorrow.
   d. People are wholly selfish.

5. Polls of voters' intentions are usually based on interviews with a very few thousand voters, yet they are remarkably accurate most of the time. Why can the answers of no more than a thousand or so voters allow us to predict the outcome of elections involving many millions of voters? Why are the predictions based on such data often wrong by a small margin and occasionally wrong by a large margin?

6. What may at first appear to be untestable statements can often be reworded so that they can be tested by an appeal to evidence. How might you do that with respect to each of the following assertions?
   a. The Canadian economic system is the best in the world.
   b. Unemployment insurance is eroding the work ethic and encouraging people to become wards of the state rather than productive workers.
   c. Robotics ought to be outlawed, because it will destroy the future of the working classes.
   d. Laws requiring equal pay for work of equal value will spell disaster for women.

7. "The simplest way to see that capital punishment is a strong deterrent to murder is to ask yourself whether you might be more inclined to commit murder if you knew in advance that you ran no risk of ending in the electric chair, in the gas chamber, or on the gallows." Comment on the methodology of social investigation implied by this statement. What alternative approach would you suggest?

8. Since 1979, when the data used in Figure 2-2 were collected, American tax laws have changed, lowering the tax rates that apply to higher incomes. How would you expect this development to change a scatter diagram of income and tax payments? Would you expect it to change the regression results? Do these changes lead you to reject the conclusions of the analysis of the 1979 data?

9. There are hundreds of eyewitnesses to the existence of flying saucers and other UFOs. There are films and eyewitness accounts of Nessie, the Loch Ness monster. Are you convinced of their existence? If not, what would it take to persuade you? If so, what would it take to make you change your mind?

10. Relate the role of the law of large numbers to the statistical idea that one can test hypotheses by using average relationships based on random samples.

Expressing and Graphing Relations Among Variables

The idea of relationships among variables is one of the basic notions behind all science. Many such relations are found in economics.

Expressing Relations: Correspondences and Functions

When mathematicians want to say that there is a relation between two variables, let us call them X and Y, they say that there is a correspondence between them. When the relation is such that for every value of X there is one and only one value of Y, mathematicians say that Y is a function of X. In what follows we confine ourselves to the subclass of correspondences that are functions.

Consider two examples, one from a natural science and one from economics. The gravitational attraction of two bodies depends on their mass and on the distance separating them, attraction increasing with size and diminishing with distance; the amount of a commodity that people would like to buy depends on (among other things) the price of the commodity, purchases increasing as price falls. Thus gravitational attraction is a function of the mass of the two bodies concerned and the distance between them, and the quantity of a product demanded is a function of the price of the product.

One of the virtues of mathematics is that it permits the concise expression of ideas that would otherwise require long, drawn-out verbal statements. There are two steps in giving compact symbolic expression to functional relations. First, each variable is given a symbol. Second, a symbol is designated to express the idea of one variable's dependence on another. Thus if G equals gravitational attraction, M equals the mass of two bodies, and d equals the distance between the two bodies, we may write

$$G = f(M, d)$$

where f is read "is a function of" and means "is uniquely related to." The whole equation states a hypothesis and is read "gravitational attraction is a function of the mass of the two bodies concerned and the distance between them." The same hypothesis can be written as

$$G = G(M, d)$$

This is read in exactly the same way and means the same thing as the previous expression. Instead of using f to represent "a function of," the left-hand symbol, G, is repeated.[1]

The hypothesis about desired purchases and price can be written

$$q = f(p)$$

or

$$q = q(p)$$

where q stands for the quantity people wish to purchase of some commodity and p is the price of the commodity. The expression says that the quantity of some commodity that people desire to purchase is a function of its price. The alternative way of writing this merely uses a different letter to stand for the same functional relation between p and q.

Functional Forms: Precise Relations Among Variables

The expression $Y = Y(X)$ merely states that the variables Y and X are related; it says nothing about the form that this relation takes. Usually the hypothesis to be expressed says more than that. Does

---

[1] Any convenient symbol may be used on the right-hand side before the parenthesis to mean "a function of." The repetition of the left-hand symbol may be convenient in reminding us of what is a function of what.

Y increase as X increases? Does Y decrease as X increases? Or is the relation more complicated? Take a very simple example, where Y is the length of a board in feet, and X is the length of the same board in yards. Quite clearly, $Y = Y(X)$. Further, in this case the exact form of the function is known, for length in feet (Y) is exactly three times the length in yards (X), so we may write $Y = 3X$.

This relation is a definitional one, for the length of something measured in feet is defined to be three times its length measured in yards. It is nonetheless useful to have a way of writing relationships that are definitionally true. The expression $Y = 3X$ specifies the exact form of the relation between Y and X and provides a rule whereby, if we have the value of one, we can calculate the value of the other.

Now consider a second example. Let C stand for consumption expenditure, the total amount spent on purchasing goods and services by all American households during a year. Let Y_d stand for the total amount of income that these households had available to spend during the year. We might state the hypothesis that

$$C = f(Y_d)$$

and, even more specifically,

$$C = 0.8Y_d$$

The first expression gives the hypothesis that the total consumption expenditure of households depends on their income. The second expression says, more specifically, that total consumption expenditure is 80 percent of the total available for spending. The second equation expresses a specific hypothesis about the relation between two observable magnitudes. There is no reason why it *must* be true; it may be consistent or inconsistent with the facts. This is a matter for testing. However, the equation is a concise statement of a particular hypothesis.

Thus the general view that there is a functional relation between Y and X is denoted by $Y = f(X)$, whereas any precise relation is expressed by a particular equation such as $Y = 2X$, $Y = 4X^2$, or $Y = X + 2.0X^2 + 0.5X^3$.

If Y increases as X increases (e.g., $Y = 10 + 2X$), we say that Y is an *increasing function* of X or that Y and X *vary positively* with each other. If Y decreases as X increases (e.g., $Y = 10 - 2X$), we say that Y is a *decreasing function* of X or that Y and X *vary negatively* with each other. Y varying negatively with X merely means that Y changes in the opposite direction from X.

Error Terms in Economic Hypotheses

Expressing hypotheses in the form of functions is misleading in one respect. When we say that the world behaves so that $Y = f(X)$, we do not expect that knowing X will tell us *exactly* what Y will be, only that it will tell us what Y will be *within some margin of error*.

This error in predicting Y from a knowledge of X arises for two distinct reasons. First, there may be other variables that also affect Y. When, for example, we say that the quantity of butter people wish to purchase is a function of the price of butter, $q_b = f(p_b)$, we know that other factors will also influence this demand. A change in the price of margarine will certainly affect the demand for butter, even though the price of butter does not change. Thus we do not expect to find a perfect relation between q_b and p_b that will allow us to predict q_b exactly from a knowledge of p_b.

Second, variables can never be measured exactly. Even if X is the only cause of Y, measurements will give various Ys corresponding to the same X. In the case of the demand for butter, errors of measurement might not be large. In other cases, errors can be substantial—as, for example, in the case of a relation between the total consumption expenditure of all American households and their total income. The measurements of consumption and income may be subject to quite wide margins of error, and various values of consumption associated with the same measured value of income may be observed, not because consumption is varying independently of income but because the error of measurement is varying from period to period.

When we say Y is a function of X, we appear to say Y is completely determined by X. Instead of the deterministic formulation

$$Y = f(X)$$

it would be more accurate to write

$$Y = f(X, \epsilon)$$

FIGURE 2A-1   A Coordinate Graph

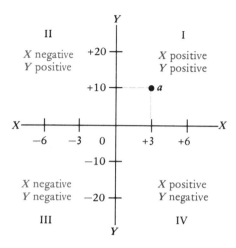

The axes divide the total space into four quadrants according to the signs of the variables. In the upper right-hand quadrant, both X and Y are greater than zero; this is usually called the *positive quadrant*. Point a has *coordinates* $Y = 10$ and $X = 3$ in the coordinate graph. These coordinates *define* point a.

where ϵ, the Greek letter epsilon, represents an **error term.**[2] Such a term indicates that the observed value of Y will differ from the value predicted by the functional relation between Y and X. Divergences will occur both because of observational errors and because of neglected variables. While economists always mean this, they usually do not say so.

The deterministic formulation is a simplification; an error term is really present in all assumed and observed functional relations in economics.

Graphing Relations Among Variables

The popular saying "The facts speak for themselves" is almost always wrong when there are many facts. Theories are needed to explain how facts are linked together, and summary measures are needed to assist

in sorting out what it is that facts show in relation to theories. The simplest means of providing compact summaries of a large number of observations is the use of tables and graphs. Graphs play important roles in economics by representing geometrically both observed data and the correspondence among variables that are the subject of economic theory.

Because the surface of a piece of paper is two-dimensional, a graph may readily be used to represent pictorially any correspondence between two variables. Flip through this book and you will see dozens of examples. Figure 2A-1 shows generally how a coordinate grid can permit the representation of any two measurable variables.[3]

Representing Theories on Graphs

Figure 2A-2 shows a simple two-variable graph, which will be analyzed in detail in Chapter 4. For now it is sufficient to notice that the graph permits us to show the relationship between two variables, the *price* of carrots on the vertical axis and the *quantity* of carrots per month on the horizontal axis.[4] The downward-sloping curve, labeled D for a *demand curve*, shows the relationship between the price of carrots and the quantity of carrots buyers wish to purchase.

Figure 2A-3 is very much like Figure 2A-2, with one difference. It generalizes from the specific example of carrots to an unspecified commodity and focuses on the slope of the demand curve rather than on specific numerical values. Note that the quantity labeled q_0 is associated with the price p_0, while the quantity q_1 is associated with the price p_1.

Straight Lines and Their Slopes

Figure 2A-4 illustrates a variety of straight lines. They differ according to their slopes. **Slope** is defined as the ratio of the vertical change to the corresponding horizontal change as one moves along a curve.

---

[2] The relationship with the error term in it is frequently written $Y = f(X) + \epsilon$.

[3] Economics is often concerned only with the positive values of variables, and the graph is confined to the upper right-hand (or "positive") quadrant. Whenever a variable has a negative value, one or more of the other quadrants must be included.

[4] The choice of which variable to put on which axis is discussed in footnote 2 on page 91 and in math note 8 on page M-2.

FIGURE 2A-2   **The Relationship Between the Price of Carrots and the Quantity of Carrots That Purchasers Wish to Buy: A Numerical Illustration**

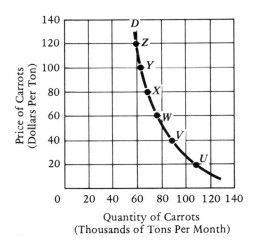

A two-dimensional graph can show how two variables are related. The two variables, the price of carrots and the quantity people wish to purchase, are shown by the downward-sloping curve labeled D. Particular points on the curve are labeled U through Z. For example, Z shows that at a price of $120, the demand to purchase carrots is 60,000 tons per month.

FIGURE 2A-3   **The Relationship Between the Price of a Commodity and the Quantity of the Commodity That Purchasers Wish to Buy**

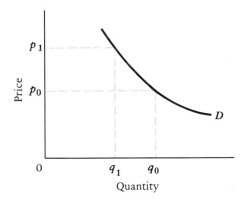

Graphs can illustrate general relationships between variables as well as between specific quantities. Here, in contrast to Figure 2A-2, price and quantity are shown as general variables. The demand curve illustrates a quantitatively unspecified *negative* relationship between price and quantity. For example, at the price p_0 the quantity that purchasers demand is q_0, while at the higher price of p_1 purchasers demand the lower quantity of q_0.

FIGURE 2A-4   **Four Straight Lines with Different Slopes**

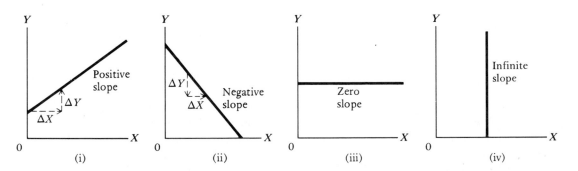

The slope of a straight line is constant but can vary from one line to another. The direction of slope of a straight line is characterized by the signs of the ratio $\Delta Y/\Delta X$. In (i) that ratio is positive because X and Y vary in the same direction; in (ii) the ratio is negative because X and Y vary in opposite directions; in (iii) it is zero because Y does not change as X increases; in (iv) it is infinite.

The symbol Δ is used to indicate a change in any variable. Thus Δ*X* means the change in *X,* and Δ*Y* means the change in *Y.* The ratio Δ*Y*/Δ*X* is the slope of a straight line. Where both increase or decrease together, the ratio is positive and the line slopes upward to the right, as in part (i) of Figure 2A-4. Where Δ*Y* and Δ*X* have the opposite sign, that is, one increases while the other decreases, the ratio is negative and the line slopes downward to the right, as in part (ii). Where Δ*Y* does not change, the line is horizontal, as in part (iii), and the slope is zero. Where Δ*X* is zero, the line is vertical, as in part (iv), and the slope is often said to be infinite, although the ratio Δ*Y*/Δ*X* is indeterminate. **[1]**[5]

Slope is a quantitative measure, not merely a qualitative one. For example, in Figure 2A-5 two upward-sloping straight lines have different slopes. Line *A* has a slope of 2 (Δ*Y*/Δ*X* = 2.0); line *B* has a slope of 1/2 (Δ*Y*/Δ*X* = 0.5).

Curved Lines and Their Slopes

Figure 2A-6 shows four curved lines. The line in part (i) is plainly upward sloping and in part (ii) downward sloping. The other two change from one to the other, as the labels indicate. Unlike straight lines, whose slope is the same at every point on the line, the slope of a curve changes. The slope of a curve must be measured at a particular point and is defined as the slope of a straight line that just touches (is tangent to) the straight line at that point. This is illustrated in Figure 2A-7. The slope at point *A* is measured by the slope of the tangent line *a.* The slope at point *B* is measured by the slope of the tangent line *b.*

Graphing Observations

A coordinate space such as shown in Figure 2A-1 can be used to graph the observed values of two variables as well as the theoretical relationships between them. For example, curve *D* in Figure 2A-2 might have arisen as a freehand line drawn to generalize actual observations of the points labeled *U,*

[5] Notes giving mathematical demonstrations of the concepts presented in the text are designated by colored reference numbers. These notes can be found beginning on page M-1.

FIGURE 2A-5   Two Straight Lines with Different Slopes

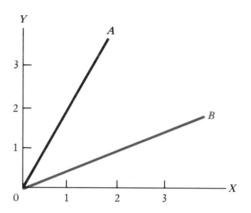

Slope is a quantitative measure. Both lines have positive slopes and thus are similar to Figure 2A-4(i). But curve *A* is steeper (i.e., has a greater slope) than curve *B.* For each 1-unit increase in *X,* the value of *Y* increases by 2 units along curve *A,* but by only 1/2 unit along curve *B.* The ratio Δ*Y*/Δ*X* is 2 for curve *A* and 1/2 for curve *B.*

V, W, X, Y, Z. Although that graph was not constructed from actual observations, many graphs are. Two of the most important kinds are called *scatter diagrams* and *time-series graphs.*

Scatter Diagrams

Scatter diagrams provide a method of graphing any number of *paired* observations made on two variables. In Chapter 2 data for family income and taxes paid for a sample of 212 American families were studied. Figure 2-2 on page 27 shows these data on a scatter diagram. Income is measured on the horizontal axis and taxes paid on the vertical axis. Any point in the diagram represents a particular family's income combined with the tax payment of that family. Thus each family for which there are observations can be represented on the diagram by a dot, the coordinates of which indicate the family's income and the amount of taxes it paid in 1979.

The scatter diagram is useful because if there is a simple relation between the two variables, it will be

FIGURE 2A-6   Four Curved Lines

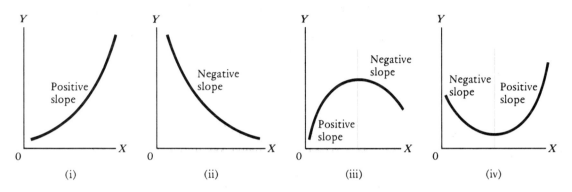

(i)   (ii)   (iii)   (iv)

The slope of a curved line is not constant and may change direction. The slopes of the curves in (i) and (ii) change in size but not direction, whereas those in (iii) and (iv) change in both size and direction. Unlike that of a straight line, the slope of a curved line cannot be defined by a single number because it changes as the value of X changes.

apparent to the eye once the data are plotted. Figure 2-2, for example, makes it apparent that more taxes tend to be paid as income rises. It also made it ap-

FIGURE 2A-7   Defining the Slope of a Curve

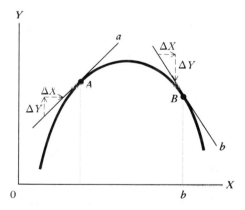

The slope of a curve at any point on the curve is defined by the slope of the straight line that is tangent to the curve at that point. The slope of the curve at point A is defined by the slope of the line a, which is tangent to the curve at point A. The slope of the curve at point B is defined by the slope of the tangent line b.

parent that the relation between taxes and income is approximately linear. A rising straight line fits the data reasonably well between about $10,000 and $40,000 of income. Above $40,000 and below $10,000 the line does not fit the data as well, but since more than two-thirds of the families sampled had incomes in the $10,000 to $40,000 range, the straight line provides a fairly good description of the basic relationship for middle income families.

The diagram also gives some idea of the strength of the relation. If income were the only determinant of taxes paid, all the dots would cluster closely around a line or a smooth curve; as it is, the points are somewhat scattered, and particular incomes are often represented by several households, each with different amounts of taxes paid.

Time-Series Data

The data used in the example of Figure 2–2 are **cross-sectional data.** The incomes and taxes paid of different households are compared over a single period of time—the year 1979. Scatter diagrams may also be drawn for a number of observations taken on two variables at successive periods of time.

For example, if one wanted to know whether there was any simple relation between personal in-

TABLE 2A-1   Income and Consumption in the United States, 1955–1985 (*1982 dollars*)

Year	Disposable personal income per capita	Personal consumption expenditures per capita
1955	$ 5,714	$5,287
1956	5,881	5,349
1957	5,909	5,370
1958	5,908	5,357
1959	6,027	5,531
1960	6,036	5,561
1961	6,113	5,579
1962	6,271	5,729
1963	6,378	5,855
1964	6,727	6,099
1965	7,027	6,362
1966	7,280	6,607
1967	7,513	6,730
1968	7,728	7,003
1969	7,891	7,185
1970	8,134	7,275
1971	8,322	7,409
1972	8,562	7,726
1973	9,042	7,972
1974	8,867	7,826
1975	8,944	7,926
1976	9,175	8,272
1977	9,381	8,551
1978	9,735	8,808
1979	9,829	8,904
1980	9,723	8,784
1981	9,773	8,798
1982	9,732	8,825
1983	9,952	9,148
1984	10,427	9,462
1985	10,504	9,682

Source: Economic Report of the President, 1986.

come and personal consumption in the United States between 1950 and 1985, data would be collected for the levels of personal income and expenditure per capita in each year from 1950 to 1985, as is done in Table 2A-1. This information could be plotted on a scatter diagram, with income on the *X* axis and consumption on the *Y* axis. The data are plotted in Figure 2A-8, and they do indeed suggest a systematic linear relation.

Figure 2A-8 is a scatter diagram of observations taken over successive periods of time. Such data are called **time-series data,** and plotting them on a scat-

ter diagram involves no new technique. When cross-sectional data are plotted, each point gives the values of two variables for a particular unit (say, a family); when time-series data are plotted, each point tells the values of two variables for a particular year.

Instead of studying the relation between income and consumption suggested in the preceding paragraph, a study of the pattern of the changes in either one of these variables over time could be made. Figure 2A-9 shows this information for consumption. Time is one variable, consumption expenditure the other. But time is a special variable; the order in which successive events happen is important. The year 1985 followed 1984; they were not two independent and unrelated years. In contrast, two randomly selected households are independent and unrelated. For this reason it is customary to draw in the line segments connecting the successive points, as has been done in Figure 2A-9.

Such a figure is called a *time-series graph* or a *time series*. This kind of graph makes it easy to see if the variable being considered has varied in a systematic way over the years or if its behavior has been more or less erratic.

Ratio (Logarithmic) Scales

All the foregoing graphs use axes that plot numbers on a natural arithmetic scale, with distances between two values shown by the size of the numerical difference. If *proportionate* rather than *absolute* changes in variables are important, it is more revealing to use a ratio scale rather than a natural scale. On a **natural scale** the distance between numbers is proportionate to the absolute difference between those numbers. Thus 200 is placed halfway between 100 and 300. On a **ratio scale** the distance between numbers is proportionate to the percentage difference between the two numbers (which can also be measured as the absolute difference between their logarithms). Equal distances anywhere on a ratio scale represent equal percentage changes rather than equal absolute changes. On a ratio scale the distance between 100 and 200 is the same as the distance between 200 and 400, between 1,000 and 2,000, and between any two numbers that stand in the ratio 1:2 to each other. For

FIGURE 2A-8   A Scatter Diagram Relating Consumption and Disposable Income

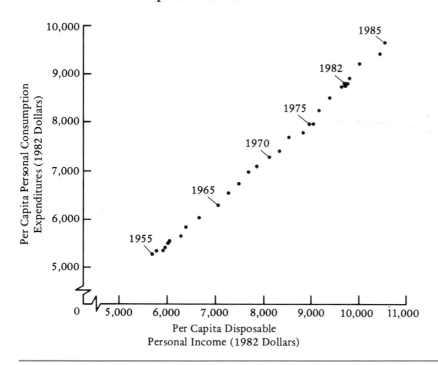

This scatter diagram shows paired values of two variables. The data of Table 2A-1 are plotted here. Each dot shows the values of per capita personal consumption expenditures and per capita disposable personal income for a given year. A close, positive, linear relationship between the two variables is established. Note that in this diagram the axes are shown with a break in them to indicate that not all the values of the variables between $4,000 and zero are given. Since no *observations* occurred in those ranges, it was unnecessary to provide space for them.

FIGURE 2A-9   A Time Series of Consumption Expenditures, 1955–1985

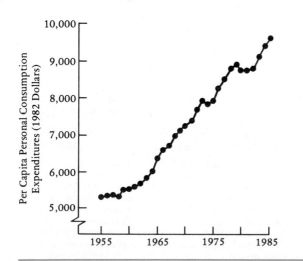

A time series plots values of a single variable in chronological order. The graph shows that, with only minor interruptions, consumption measured in 1982 dollars rose from 1955 to 1985. The data are given in the last column of Table 2A-1.

FIGURE 2A-10   The Difference Between Natural
and Ratio Scales

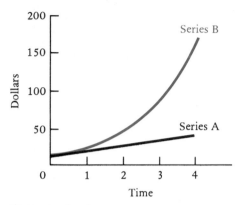

(i) A natural scale

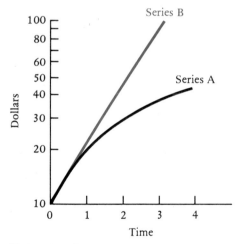

(ii) A ratio scale

**On a natural scale equal distances represent equal
amounts; on a ratio scale equal distances represent
equal percentage changes.** The two series in Table
2A-2 are plotted in each chart. Series A, which grows by
a constant absolute amount, is shown by a straight line
on a natural scale but by a curve of diminishing slope on
a ratio scale because the same absolute growth represents
a decreasing percentage growth. Series B, which grows
at a rising absolute rate but a constant percentage rate, is
shown by a curve of increasing slope on a natural scale
but by a straight line on a ratio scale.

TABLE 2A-2   Two Series

Time period	Series A	Series B
0	$10	$ 10
1	18	20
2	26	40
3	34	80
4	42	160

**Series A shows constant absolute growth ($8 per pe-
riod) but declining percentage growth. Series B
shows constant percentage growth (100 percent per
period) but rising absolute growth.**

obvious reasons a ratio scale is also called a **logarithmic scale.**

Table 2A-2 shows two series, one growing at a
constant absolute amount of 8 units per period and
the other growing at a constant rate of 100 percent
per period. In Figure 2A-10 the series are plotted first
on a natural scale, then on a ratio scale. The natural
scale makes it easy for the eye to judge absolute
variations, and the logarithmic scale makes it easy
for the eye to judge proportionate variations.[6]

Graphing Three Variables in Two Dimensions

Often we want to show graphically more than two
dimensions. For example, a topographic map seeks
to show latitude, longitude, and altitude on a two-
dimensional page. This is done by using contour
lines, as in Figure 2A-11. Now consider the function
$XY = a$, where X, Y, and a are variables. Figure
2A-12 plots this function for three different values
of a. The variables X and Y are represented on the
two axes. The variable a is represented by the labels
on the curves. Several examples of this procedure
occur throughout the book (see, for example, the
discussion of indifference curves in Appendix 7B and
isoquants in the appendix to Chapter 11).

[6] Graphs with a ratio scale on one axis and a natural scale on the
other are frequently encountered in economics. In the cases just
illustrated there is a ratio scale on the vertical axis and a natural
scale on the horizontal (or time) axis. Such graphs are often called
semi-log graphs. In scientific work graphs with ratio scales on both
axes are frequently encountered. Such graphs are often referred to
as *double-log* graphs.

FIGURE 2A-11   **A Contour Map of a Small Mountain**

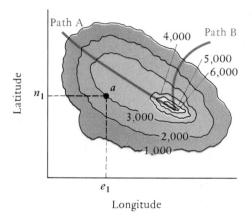

A contour map shows three variables in two-dimensional space. This familiar kind of three-variable graph shows latitude and longitude on the axes and altitude on the contour lines. The contour line labeled 1,000 connects all locations with an altitude of 1,000 feet, that labeled 2,000 connects those with an altitude of 2,000 feet, and so forth. Point a, for example, has a latitude n_1, a longitude e_1, and an altitude of 3,000 feet. Where the lines are closely bunched, they represent a steep ascent; where they are far apart, a gradual one. Clearly, path A is a gentler climb from 3,000 to 4,000 feet on this mountain than path B.

FIGURE 2A-12   **Three Variables Shown in Two Dimensions**

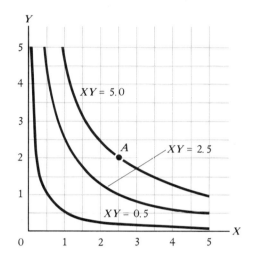

This chart illustrates examples of the three-variable function $XY = a$. The function $XY = a$ is called a *rectangular hyperbola*. The figure shows three members of the family. For example, point A represents $Y = 2.0$, $X = 2.5$, and $a = 5.0$.

3

An Overview of the Economy

The Evolution of Market Economies

The central economic problem of our times—choice under conditions of scarcity—has been with us about 10,000 years. It began with the original agricultural revolution, when human beings first found it possible to stay in one place and survive. Gradually abandoning their nomadic life of hunting and food gathering, people settled down to tend crops that they had learned to plant and animals that they had learned to domesticate. Since that time all societies have faced the problem of choice under conditions of scarcity.

Surplus, Specialization, and Trade

Along with permanent settlement, the agricultural revolution brought surplus production. Farmers could produce substantially more than they needed for survival. The agricultural surplus allowed the creation of new occupations and thus new economic and social classes such as artisans, soldiers, priests, and government officials. Freed from having to grow their own food, these new classes turned their talents to performing specialized services and producing goods other than food. They also produced more than they themselves needed, so they traded the excess to obtain whatever other goods they required.

The allocation of different jobs to different people is called **specialization of labor.** Specialization has proven extraordinarily efficient compared with self-sufficiency for at least two reasons. First, individual talents and abilities differ, and specialization allows each person to do the job he or she can do relatively best, while leaving everything else to be done by others. Second, a person who concentrates on one activity becomes better at it than could a jack-of-all-trades.

The exchange of goods and services in early societies commonly took place by simple mutual agreement among neighbors. In the course of time, however, trading became centered in particular gathering places called markets. Today we use the term **market economy** to refer to a society in which people specialize in productive activities and meet most of their material wants through exchanges voluntarily agreed on by the contracting parties.

Specialization must be accompanied by trade. People who produce only one thing must trade most of it to obtain all the other things they require.

The earliest market economies depended on **barter,** the trading of goods directly for other goods. But barter can be a costly process in terms of time spent searching out satisfactory exchanges. The evolution of money made trade easier. Money eliminates the inconvenience of barter by allowing the two sides of the barter transaction to be separated. If a farmer has wheat and wants a hammer, he does not have to search for an individual who has a hammer and wants wheat. He merely has to find someone who wants wheat. The farmer takes money in exchange, then finds another person who wishes to trade a hammer and swaps the money for the hammer.

By eliminating the need for barter, money greatly facilitates trade and specialization.

The Division of Labor

Market transactions in early economies mainly involved consumption goods. Producers specialized in making a commodity and then traded it for the other products they needed. The labor services required to make the product would usually be provided by the makers themselves, by apprentices learning to be craftsmen, or by slaves. Over the past several hundred years, many technical advances in methods of production have made it efficient to organize agriculture and industry on a large scale. These technical developments have made use of what is called the **division of labor,** which is a further step in the specialization of labor. This term refers to specialization within the production process of a particular commodity. The labor involved is divided into a series of repetitive tasks, and each individual does a single task that may be just one of hundreds of tasks necessary to produce the commodity. Today it is possible for an individual to work on a production line without knowing what commodity emerges at the end of that line!

To gain the advantages of the division of labor, it became necessary to organize production in large factories. With this development urban workers lost their status as craftsmen and became members of the working class, wholly dependent on their ability to sell their labor to factory owners and lacking a plot of land to fall back on for subsistence in times of

need. The day of small craftsmen who made and sold their own goods was over. Today's typical workers do not earn their incomes by selling commodities they personally have produced; rather, they sell their labor services to firms and receive money wages in return. They have increasingly become cogs in a machine they do not fully understand or control. Adam Smith, the eighteenth century Scottish political economist, was the first to develop the idea of the division of labor, as discussed in Box 3-1 (p. 47).

Markets and Resource Allocation

The term **resource allocation** refers to the distribution of the available factors of production among the various uses to which they might be put. There are not enough resources to produce all the goods and services that could be consumed. It is therefore necessary to allocate the available resources among their various possible uses and in so doing to choose what to produce and what not to produce. In a market economy millions of consumers decide what commodities to buy and in what quantities, a vast number of firms produce these commodities and buy the factor services that are needed to make them, and millions of factor owners decide to whom they will sell these services. These individual decisions collectively determine the economy's allocation of resources.

In a market economy the allocation of resources is the outcome of countless independent decisions made by consumers and producers, all acting through the medium of markets.

Our main objective in this chapter is to provide an overview of this market mechanism.

The Decision Makers

Economics is about the behavior of people. Much that we observe in the world and that economists assume in their theories can be traced back to decisions made by individuals. There are millions of individuals in most economies. To make a systematic study of their behavior more manageable, we categorize them into three important groups: households, firms, and the government.[1] These groups are economic theory's cast of characters, and the market is the stage on which their play is enacted.

Households

A **household** is defined as all the people who live under one roof and who make, or are subject to others making for them, joint financial decisions. The members of households are often referred to as consumers. Economic theory gives households a number of attributes.

First, economists assume that each household makes consistent decisions, as though it were composed of a single individual. Thus economists ignore many interesting problems of how the household reaches its decisions. Family conflicts and the moral and legal problems concerning parental control over minors are dealt with by other social sciences.[2] These problems are avoided in economics by the assumption that the household is the basic decision-making atom of consumption behavior.

Second, economists assume that each household is consistently attempting to achieve *maximum satisfaction* or *well-being* or *utility,* as the concept is variously called. The household tries to do this within the limitations of its available resources.

Third, economists assume that households are the principal owners of factors of production. They sell the services of these factors to firms and receive their incomes in return. It is assumed that in making these decisions on how much to sell and to whom to sell it, each household seeks to maximize its utility.

Firms

A **firm** is defined as a unit that employs factors of production to produce commodities that it sells to other firms, to households, or to government. For obvious reasons a firm is often called a *producer.* Economic theory gives firms several attributes.

First, economists assume that each firm makes consistent decisions, as though it were composed of a single individual. Thus economics ignores the internal problems of how particular decisions are reached. In doing this, economists assume that the firm's internal organization is irrelevant to its decisions. This allows them to treat the firm as the atom of behavior on the production or supply side of commodity markets, just as the household is treated as the atom of behavior on the consumption or demand side.

Second, economists assume that most firms make their decisions with a single goal in mind: to make as much profit as possible. This goal of *profit maximization* is analogous to the household's goal of utility maximization.

Third, economists assume that in their role as producers, firms are the principal users of the services of factors of production. In markets where factor services are bought and sold, the roles of firms and households are thus reversed from what they are in commodity markets: In factor markets firms do the buying and households do the selling.

Government

The term **government** is used in economics in a broad sense to include all public officials, agencies, government bodies, and other organizations belonging to or under the direct control of federal, provincial, and municipal governments. For example, in Canada the term *government* includes the prime minister and his cabinet, the Bank of Canada, provincial premiers and legislators, mayors and city councils, commissions and regulatory bodies, income tax inspectors, judges, the military, and the police force. It is not important to draw up a comprehensive list, but one should have in mind a general idea of the organizations that have legal and political power to exert control over individual decision makers and over markets.

---

[1] Although in basic economic theory we can get away with three sets of decision makers, it is worth noting that there are others. Probably the most important are such nonprofit organizations as private universities and hospitals, charities such as the Canadian Cancer Society, and funding organizations such as the Niagara Institute. These bodies are responsible for allocating some of the economy's resources.

[2] In academic work, as elsewhere, a division of labor is useful. However, it is important to remember that when economists speak of "the" consumer or "the" individual, they are in fact referring to the group of individuals composing the household. Thus, for example, the commonly heard phrase *consumer sovereignty* really means *household sovereignty.*

BOX 3-1

The Division of Labor

Adam Smith begins *The Wealth of Nations* (1776) with a long study of the division of labor.

The greatest improvements in the productive powers of labour . . . have been the effects of the division of labour.

To take an example . . . the trade of the pinmaker; a workman not educated to this business (which the division of labour has rendered a distinct trade), nor acquainted with the use of the machinery employed in it could scarce, perhaps, with his utmost industry, make one pin in a day, and certainly could not make twenty. But in the way in which this business is now carried on . . . it is divided into a number of branches. . . . One man draws out the wire, another straightens it, a third cuts it, a fourth points it, a fifth grinds it at the top for receiving the head; to make the head requires two or three distinct operations; to put it on, is a peculiar business, to whiten the pins is another; it is even a trade by itself to put them into the paper; and the important business of making a pin is, in this manner, divided into about eighteen distinct operations, which, in some manufactories, are all performed by distinct hands, though in others the same man will sometimes perform two or three of them.

Smith observes that even in smallish factories, where the division of labor is exploited only in part, output is as high as 4,800 pins per person per day!

Later Smith discusses the general importance of the division of labor and the forces that limit its application.

Each animal is still obliged to support and defend itself, separately and independently, and derives no sort of advantage from that variety of talents with which nature has distinguished its fellows. Among men, on the contrary, the most dissimilar geniuses are of use to one another; the different produces of their respective talents, by the general disposition to truck, barter, and exchange, being brought, as it were, into a common stock, where every man may purchase whatever part of the produce of other men's talents he has occasion for.

As it is the power of exchanging that gives occasion to the division of labour, so the extent of this division must always be limited by the extent of that power, or, in other words, by the extent of the market. When the market is very small, no person can have any encouragement to dedicate himself entirely to one employment for want of the power to exchange all that surplus part of the produce of his own labour, which is over and above his own consumption, for such parts of the produce of other men's labour as he has occasion for.

Smith notes that there is no point in specializing to produce a large quantity of pins, or anything else, unless there are enough persons making other commodities to provide a market for all the pins that are produced. Thus the larger the market, the greater the scope for the division of labor and the higher the resulting opportunities for efficient production.

It is *not* a basic assumption of economics that the government always acts in a consistent fashion. Several important reasons for this may be mentioned here. First, the mayor of Montreal, an Alberta MLA, and the minister of finance in Ottawa represent different constituencies, and therefore they may express different and conflicting views and objectives.

Second, individual public servants, whether elected or appointed, have personal objectives (such as staying in office, achieving higher office, power, prestige, and personal aggrandizement) as well as public service objectives. Although the balance of importance given to the two types of objectives will vary among persons and among types of office, both

will almost always have some importance. It would be a rare MP, for example, who would vote against a measure that slightly reduced the "public good" if this vote almost guaranteed his defeat at the next election. ("After all," he could reason, "if I am defeated, I won't be around to vote against *really* bad measures.")

Decisions on interrelated issues of policy are made by many different bodies. Federal and provincial legislatures pass laws, the courts interpret laws, the governments decide which laws to enforce with vigor and which not to enforce, the Department of Finance and the Bank of Canada influence monetary conditions, and a host of other agencies and semi-autonomous bodies determine actions in respect to different aspects of policy goals. Because of the multiplicity of decision makers, it would be truly amazing if fully consistent behavior resulted.

Another problem arises from the fact that in a democracy legislators and political officials have as important goals their own and their leader's re-election. This means, for example, that any measure that imposes large costs and few benefits obvious to the electorate over the short run is unlikely to find favor, no matter how large the long-term benefits are. There is a strong bias toward shortsightedness in an elective system. Although much of this bias stems from an inability to grasp long-run consequences or a selfish unwillingness to look beyond the present, some of it reflects genuine uncertainty about the future. The further into the future that the economist calculates, the wider the margin of possible error. It is not surprising that politicians, who must worry about the next election, often tend to worry less about the long-term effect of their actions. "After all," they may argue, "who can tell what will happen 20 years hence?"

Markets and Economies

We have seen that households, firms, and the government are the main actors in the economic drama. Their action takes place in individual markets.

Markets

The word *market* originally designated a place where goods were traded. The St. Lawrence Market in Toronto is a modern example of a market in the everyday sense, and most cities have fruit and vegetable markets. Much early economic theory attempted to explain price behavior in just such markets. Why, for example, can you sometimes obtain great bargains at the end of the day and at other times get what you want only at prices that appear exorbitant in relation to prices quoted only a few hours before?

As theories of market behavior were developed, they were extended to cover commodities such as wheat. Wheat produced anywhere in the world can be purchased almost anywhere else in the world, and

the price of a given grade of wheat tends to be nearly uniform the world over. When we talk about the wheat market, the concept of a market has been extended well beyond the idea of a single place to which the producer, the storekeeper, and the homemaker go to sell and buy.

Economists distinguish two broad types of markets: **product markets,** in which outputs of goods and services are sold, and **factor markets,** in which services of factors of production are sold.

Economies

An **economy** is rather loosely defined as a set of interrelated production and consumption activities. It may refer to this activity in a region of one country (for example, the economy of the Maritimes), in a country (the Canadian economy), or in a group of countries (the economy of Western Europe). In any economy the allocation of resources is determined by the production, sales, and purchase decisions made by firms, households, and the government.

A **free-market economy** is an economy in which the decisions of individual households and firms (as distinct from the government) exert the major influence over the allocation of resources.

The opposite of a free-market economy is a **command economy,** in which the major decisions about the allocation of resources are made by the government and in which firms and households produce and consume only as they are ordered.

As we saw in Chapter 1, the terms *free-market* and *command economy* are often used to describe economies. No real economies rely solely on either free markets or commands. In practice all economies are **mixed economies** in the sense that some decisions are made by firms, households, and the government acting through markets and some are made by the government using the command principle.

Sectors of an Economy

Parts of an economy are usually referred to as **sectors** of that economy. For example, the agricultural sector is the part of the economy that produces agricultural commodities.

Market and Nonmarket Sectors

Producers make commodities. Consumers use them. Commodities may pass from one group to the other in two ways: They may be sold by producers and bought by consumers through markets, or they may be given away.

When commodities are bought and sold, producers expect to cover their costs with the revenue they obtain from selling the product. We call this type of production *marketed production,* and we refer to this part of the economy's activity as belonging to the **market sector.**

When the product is given away, the costs of production must be covered from some source other than sales revenue. We call this *nonmarketed production,* and we refer to this part of the economy's activity as belonging to the **nonmarket sector.** In the case of private charities the money required to pay for factor services may be raised from the public by voluntary contributions. In the case of production by the government—which accounts for the bulk of nonmarketed production—the money is provided from government revenue, which in turn comes mainly from taxes.

Whenever a government enterprise *sells* its output, its production is in the market sector. But much state output is in the nonmarket sector by the very nature of the product provided. For example, one could hardly expect the criminal to pay the judge for providing the service of criminal justice. Other products are in the nonmarket sector because governments have decided that there are advantages to removing them from the market sector. This is the case, for example, with much of Canadian education. Public policy places it in the nonmarket sector even though much of it could be provided by the market sector.

Private and Public Sectors

An alternative division of an economy's productive activity is between private and public sectors. The **private sector** refers to all production that is in private hands and the **public sector** to all production that is in public hands. The distinction between the two sectors depends on the legal distinction of ownership. In the private sector the organization that does the producing is owned by households or other firms; in the public sector it is owned by the state. The public sector includes all production of goods and services by the government plus all production by government-operated industries that is sold to consumers through ordinary markets.

The distinction between market and nonmarket sectors is economic; it depends on whether or not the producer earns revenue by selling output to users. The distinction between the private and the public sectors is legal; it depends on whether the producing organizations are privately or publicly owned.

Microeconomics and Macroeconomics

As we saw in Chapter 1, there are two different but complementary ways of viewing the economy. The first, *microeconomics,* studies the detailed workings of individual markets and interrelations between markets. The second, *macroeconomics,* suppresses much of the detail and concentrates on the behavior of broad aggregates.[3]

An Overview of Microeconomics

Early economists observed the market economy with wonder. They saw that most commodities were made by a large number of independent producers and yet in approximately the quantities that people wanted to purchase. Natural disasters aside, there were neither vast surpluses nor severe shortages of products. They also saw that in spite of the ever-changing geographic, industrial, and occupational patterns of demand for labor services, most laborers were able to sell their services to employers most of the time.

How does the market produce this order in the absence of conscious coordination? It is one thing to have the same good produced year in and year out

---

[3] The prefixes *micro-* and *macro-* derive, respectively, from the Greek words *mikros,* "small," and *makro,* "large."

when people's wants and incomes do not change; it is quite another thing to have production adjusting continually to changing wants, incomes, and techniques of production. Yet this adjustment is accomplished relatively smoothly by the market—albeit with occasional, and sometimes serious, interruptions.

A major discovery of eighteenth century economists was that the price system is a social control mechanism.

Adam Smith, in his classic *The Wealth of Nations,* published in 1776, spoke of the price system as "the invisible hand." It allows decision making to be decentralized under the control of millions of individual producers and consumers but nonetheless to be coordinated. Two examples may help to illustrate how this coordination occurs.

A Change in Demand

For the first example, assume that households wish to purchase more of some commodity than previously. To see the market's reaction to such a change, imagine a situation in which farmers find it equally profitable to produce either of two crops, carrots or brussels sprouts, and so are willing to produce some of both commodities, thereby satisfying the demands of households who wish to consume both. Now imagine that consumers develop a greatly increased desire for brussels sprouts and a diminished desire for carrots. This change might have occurred because of the discovery of hitherto unsuspected nutritive or curative powers of brussels sprouts.

When consumers buy more brussels sprouts and fewer carrots, a shortage of brussels sprouts and a glut of carrots develop. To unload their surplus stocks of carrots, merchants reduce the price of carrots—in the belief that it is better to sell them at a reduced price than not to sell them at all. Sellers of brussels sprouts, however, find that they are unable to satisfy all their customers' demands for that product. Sprouts have become scarce, so merchants charge more for them. As the price rises, fewer people are willing and able to purchase sprouts. Thus

making them more expensive limits the quantity demanded to the available supply.

Farmers see a rise in the price of brussels sprouts and a fall in the price of carrots. Brussels sprout production has become more profitable than in the past; the costs of producing sprouts remain unchanged while their market price has risen. Similarly, carrot production is less profitable than in the past because costs are unchanged while the price has fallen. Attracted by high profits in brussels sprouts and deterred by low profits or potential losses in carrots, farmers expand the production of sprouts and curtail carrot production. Thus the change in consumers' tastes, working through the price system, causes a reallocation of resources—land and labor—out of carrot production and into brussels sprout production.

As the production of carrots declines, the glut of carrots on the market diminishes and their price begins to rise. On the other hand, the expansion in brussels sprout production reduces the shortage and the price begins to fall. These price movements will continue until it no longer pays farmers to reduce carrot production and to expand brussels sprout production. When all of the adjustments have occurred, the price of sprouts is higher than it was originally but lower than it was when the shortage sent the price soaring before output could be adjusted, and the price of carrots is lower than it was originally but higher than when the initial glut sent the price tumbling before output could be adjusted.

The reaction of the market to a change in demand leads to a transfer of resources. Carrot producers reduce their production; they will therefore be laying off workers and generally demanding fewer factors of production. Brussels sprout producers expand production; they will therefore be hiring workers and generally increasing their demand for factors of production.

Labor can probably switch from carrot to sprout production without much difficulty. Certain types of land, however, may be better suited for growing one crop than the other. When farmers increase their sprout production, their demands for those factors especially suited to sprout growing also increase—and this creates a shortage of these resources and a consequent rise in their prices. Meanwhile, with carrot production falling, the demand for land and other factors of production especially suited to carrot growing is reduced. A surplus results, and the prices of these factors are forced down.

Thus factors particularly suited to sprout production will earn more and will obtain a higher share of total national income than before. Factors particularly suited to carrot production, however, will earn less and will obtain a smaller share of the total national income than before.

Changes of this kind will be studied more fully later; the important thing to notice now is how a change in demand causes a reallocation of resources in the direction required to cater to the new, higher level of demand.

A Change in Supply

For a second example, consider a change originating with producers. Begin as before with a situation in which farmers find it equally profitable to produce either brussels sprouts or carrots and in which consumers are willing to buy, at prevailing prices, the quantities of these two commodities that are being produced. Now imagine that, at existing prices, farmers become more willing to produce sprouts than in the past and less willing to produce carrots. This shift might be caused, for example, by a change in the costs of producing the two goods—a rise in carrot costs and a fall in sprout costs that would raise the profitability of sprout production and lower that of carrot production.

What will happen now? For a short time, nothing at all; the existing supply of sprouts and carrots on the market is the result of decisions made by farmers at some time in the past. But farmers now begin to plant fewer carrots and more sprouts, and soon the quantities on the market begin to change. The quantity of sprouts available for sale rises, and the quantity of carrots falls. A shortage of carrots and a glut of sprouts result. The price of carrots consequently rises, and the price of sprouts falls. This provides the incentive for two types of adjustments. First, households will buy fewer carrots and more sprouts. Second, farmers will move back into carrot production and out of sprouts.

This example began with a situation in which a

shortage of carrots caused the price of carrots to rise. The rise in the price of carrots removed the shortage in two ways: It reduced the quantity of carrots demanded, and it increased the quantity offered for sale (in response to the rise in the profitability of carrot production). Remember that there was also a surplus of brussels sprouts that caused the price to fall. The fall in price removed the surplus in two ways: It encouraged consumers to buy more of this commodity, and it reduced the quantity of sprouts produced and offered for sale (in response to a fall in the profitability of sprout production).

These examples illustrate a general point:

The price system is a mechanism that coordinates individual, decentralized decisions.

The existence of such a control mechanism is beyond dispute. How well it works in comparison with alternative coordinating systems has been in serious dispute for over a hundred years. It remains today a major unsettled social question.

Microeconomics and Macroeconomics Compared

Microeconomics and macroeconomics differ in the questions each asks and in the level of aggregation each uses. Microeconomics deals with the determination of prices and quantities in individual markets and with the relations among these markets. Thus it looks at the details of the market economy. It asks, for example, how much labor is employed in the fast food industry and why the amount is increasing. It asks about the determinants of the output of brussels sprouts, pocket calculators, automobiles, and Mother's Pizzas. It asks, too, about the prices of these things—why some prices go up and others down. Economists interested in microeconomics analyze how prices and outputs respond to exogenous shocks caused by events in other markets or by government policy. They ask, for example, how a technical innovation, a government subsidy, or a drought will affect the price and output of beet sugar and the employment of farm workers.

In contrast, macroeconomics focuses on much broader aggregates. It looks at such things as the total number of people employed and unemployed, the average level of prices and how it changes over time, national output, and aggregate consumption. Macroeconomics asks what determines these aggregates and how they respond to changing conditions. Whereas microeconomics looks at demand and supply with regard to particular commodities, macroeconomics looks at aggregate demand and aggregate supply.

An Overview of Macroeconomics

We can group together all the buyers of the nation's output and call their total desired purchases **aggregate demand.** We can also group together all the producers of the nation's output and call their total desired sales **aggregate supply.** Determining the magnitude of these and explaining why they change are among the major problems of macroeconomics.

Major changes in aggregate demand are called *demand shocks,* and major changes in aggregate supply are called *supply shocks.* Such shocks will cause important changes in the broad averages and aggregates that are the concern of macroeconomics, including total output, total employment, and average levels of prices and wages. Sometimes government actions are the cause of demand or supply shocks, while at other times they are reactions to such shocks and are used in an attempt to cushion or change the effects of such shocks.

The Circular Flow of Income

One way to gain insight into aggregate demand and aggregate supply is to view the economy as a giant set of flows. A major part of aggregate demand arises from the purchases of consumption commodities by the nation's households. These purchases generate income for the firms that produce and sell commodities for consumption. A major part of aggregate supply arises from the production and sale of consumption goods by the nation's firms. This production generates income for all the factors that are employed in making these goods.

The grey arrows in Figure 3-1 show the interaction between firms and households in two sets of markets—factor markets and product markets—through which their decisions are coordinated. Consider households first. The members of households want commodities to keep themselves fed, clothed, housed, entertained, healthy, and secure. They also want commodities to educate, edify, beautify, stupefy, and otherwise amuse themselves. Households have resources with which to attempt to satisfy these wants. But not all their wants can be satisfied with the resources available. Households are forced, therefore, to make choices as to which goods and services to buy in product markets that offer them myriad ways to spend their incomes.

Now consider firms. They must choose among the products they might produce and sell, among the ways of producing them, and among the various quantities (and qualities) they can supply. Firms must also buy factors of production. Payments by firms to factor owners provide the factor owners with incomes. The recipients of these incomes are households whose members want commodities to keep themselves fed, clothed, housed, and entertained.

We have now come full circle! The action of this drama involves firms and households interacting with one another.

Payments flow from households to firms through product markets and back to households again through factor markets.

If the economy consisted only of households and firms, if households spent all the income they received on buying goods and services produced by firms, and if firms distributed all their receipts to households either by purchasing factor services or by distributing profits to owners, the circular flow would be simple indeed. Everything received by households would be passed on to firms, and everything received by firms would be passed back to households. The circular flow would be a completely closed system, aggregate demand and aggregate supply would consist only of consumption goods, and macroeconomics would involve little more than measuring the flows of production of and expenditure on consumption goods.

The circular flow is not, however, a completely closed system. First, households do not spend all

FIGURE 3-1   The Circular Flow of Expenditures and Income

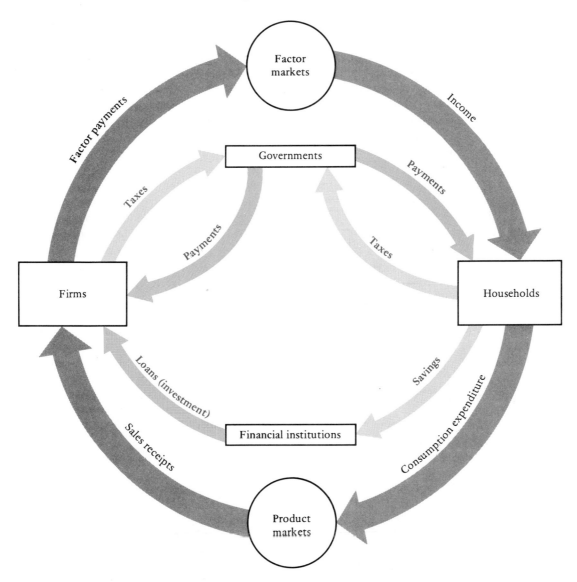

The interaction of firms and households in product and factor markets generates a flow of expenditure and income. These flows are also influenced by other institutions such as governments and the financial system. Factor services are sold by households through factor markets, which leads to a flow of income from firms to households. Commodities are sold by firms through product markets, which leads to a flow of receipts from households to firms. If these primary flows, shown by the grey arrows, were the only flows, the circular flow would be a closed system. But other institutions, such as governments and financial institutions, play roles. For example, governments may inject funds in the form of government payments to households and firms, and banks may inject funds in the form of loans to firms for investment expenditures. Such additions or injections are illustrated by the dark-colored arrows. Similarly, governments may withdraw funds in the form of taxes, and financial institutions may do so by accepting funds that households wish to save. Such leakages or withdrawals are illustrated by the light-colored arrows.

their income. Some of their income is saved, and some goes to governments as taxes. As a result, total household demand for consumption goods and services falls short of total household income. These two *leakages* from the circular flow are shown by the light-colored arrows flowing out of the households in Figure 3-1. As shown in the figure, a third leakage occurs because firms also pay taxes. (Of course, firms may also save, but this leakage is omitted from the figure for simplicity.)[4]

A second reason why the circular flow is not a closed system is that there are elements of aggregate demand that do not arise from household spending. The two main additional elements are investment and government expenditure. A major component of aggregate demand stems from firms that borrow in order to purchase such investment goods as plant and equipment. A further major component of aggregate demand comes from governments—federal, provincial, and municipal. They add to total expenditure on the nation's output by spending on a whole range of goods and services from national defense through the provision of justice to the building of roads and schools. These two major additions to the

[4] Additional elements related to international trade are discussed later in the book.

circular flow of income are shown by the dark-colored arrows flowing into the firms in Figure 3-1. As shown in the figure, a third addition arises because households also receive payments from government. (Of course, households may also borrow from financial institutions to finance current consumption expenditure, but for simplicity this fourth addition is omitted from the figure.)

When any of these elements of aggregate demand changes, aggregate output and total income earned by households are likely to change as a result. Thus studying the determinants of total consumption, investment, and government spending is crucial to understanding the causes of changes both in the nation's total output and in the employment generated by the production of that output.

The Next Step

Soon you will be going on to study micro- or macroeconomics. Whichever branch of the subject you study first, it is important to remember that microeconomics and macroeconomics are complementary, not competing, views of the economy. Both are needed for a full understanding of the functioning of a modern economy.

Summary

1. This chapter provides an overview of the workings of the market economy. Modern economies are based on the specialization and division of labor, which necessitate the exchange of goods and services. Exchange takes place in markets and is facilitated by the use of money. Much of economics is devoted to a study of how markets work to coordinate millions of individual, decentralized decisions.
2. In economic theory three kinds of decision makers—households, firms, and government—interact in markets. Households are assumed to maximize their satisfaction and firms to maximize their profits. Government may have multiple objectives.
3. A free-market economy is one in which the allocation of resources is determined by the production, sales, and purchase decisions made by firms and households acting in response to such market signals as prices and profits.
4. Subdivisions of an economy are called sectors. Economies are commonly divided into market and nonmarket sectors and into public and private sectors. These divisions cut across each other; the first is

based on the economic distinction of how costs are covered, and the second is based on a legal distinction of ownership.

5. A key difference between micro- and macroeconomics is in the level of aggregation to which attention is directed. Microeconomics looks at prices and quantities in individual markets and how they respond to various shocks that impinge on those markets. Macroeconomics looks at broader aggregates such as aggregate consumption, employment and unemployment, and rate of change of the price level.

6. The questions asked in micro- and macroeconomics differ, but they are complementary parts of economic theory. They study different aspects of a single economic system, and both are needed for an understanding of the whole.

7. Microeconomics deals with the determination of prices and quantities in individual markets and the relations among those markets. It shows how the price system provides signals that reflect changes in demand and supply and to which producers and consumers react in an individual but nonetheless coordinated manner.

8. The microeconomic interactions between households and firms through markets may be illustrated in a circular flow diagram that traces money flows between households and firms. These flows are the starting point for studying the circular flows of aggregate income that are key elements of macroeconomics.

9. Household purchases of consumption goods generate income for firms whose payments to factors then flow back to the households as income. This circular flow is not a simple closed system because not all income received by households is spent for the output of firms and some receipts of firms are not paid out to households. Also, some payments to firms do not result from the spending of households and some payments to households do not result from the spending of firms. The flows of expenditure in the economy determine total output, total income, and total employment.

Topics for Review

Specialization and division of labor
Economic decision makers
Markets and market economies
Market and nonmarket sectors
Private and public sectors
The price system as a social control mechanism
Relation between microeconomics and macroeconomics

Discussion Questions

1. Suggest some examples of specialization and division of labor among people you know.
2. There is a greater variety of specialists and specialty stores in large cities than in small towns having populations with the same average income. Explain this in economic terms.

3. Define the household of which you are a member. Consider your household's income last year. What proportion of it came from the sale of factor services? Identify other sources of income. Approximately what proportion of the expenditures by your household became income for firms?

4. "It is not from the benevolence of the butcher, the brewer, or the baker that we expect our dinner, but from their regard to their own self-interest. We address ourselves, not to their humanity, but to their self-love, and never talk to them of our necessities, but of their advantages." Do you agree with this quotation from *The Wealth of Nations*? How are "their self-love" and "our dinner" related to the price system? What are assumed to be the motives of firms and of households?

5. Trace the effect of a sharp change in consumer demand away from cigarettes and toward chewing gum as a result of continuing reports linking smoking with lung cancer and heart disease.

6. List some of the decision makers not mentioned in the text that do not fit into the categories of firm, household, and government. Are you sure that the concept of a firm will not stretch sufficiently to cover some of the items on your list?

7. Trace out some significant microeconomic and macroeconomic effects of the enormous increase in the proportion of women choosing to work rather than to stay at home that has occurred over the past two decades.

8. Which, if any, of the arrows in Figure 3-1 would each of the following events affect first?
   a. Households increase their consumption expenditures by reducing saving.
   b. The government lowers income tax rates.
   c. In view of a recession, firms decide to postpone production of some new products.
   d. Consumers like the new model cars and borrow money from the banking system to buy them in record numbers.

PART TWO

A General View of the Price System

4

Demand, Supply, and Price

Some people believe that economics begins and ends with the "law" of supply and demand. It is, of course, too much to hope for "economics in one lesson." (An unkind critic of a book with that title remarked that the author needed a second lesson.) Still, the so-called laws of supply and demand are an important part of our understanding of the market system.

First we need to understand what determines the demands for commodities and the supplies of them. Then we can see how demand and supply together determine price and how the price system as a whole allows the economy to respond to changes in demand and in supply. Demand and supply help us in understanding the price system's successes and its failures, as well as the consequences of such government interventions as price controls, minimum-wage laws, and sales taxes.

Demand

Canadian consumers spent about $300 billion on goods and services in 1986. Table 4-1 shows the composition of this expenditure and how it has changed over 35 years. Economists ask many questions about the pattern of consumer expenditure: Why is it what it is at any moment? Why does it change in the way it does? Why do consumers spend a higher proportion of their incomes on durable goods and a lower proportion on nondurables than they did 35 years ago? Why has the proportion spent on services risen only slightly (from 40 to 42½ percent) in Canada while in the United States it has increased by nearly 50 percent over the same period? Why do Canadians now heat their homes with electricity, oil, and natural gas when 30 years ago they used coal? How have they reacted to the large changes in fuel prices that occurred in the late 1970s and early 1980s? Why do people who build houses in Norway and the Canadian West rarely use brick, while it is commonly used in England and eastern Canada? Why have the maid and the washerwoman been replaced by the vacuum cleaner and the washing machine?

Quantity Demanded

The total amount of a commodity that all households wish to purchase is called the **quantity demanded** of that commodity.[1] It is important

---

[1] In this chapter we concentrate on the demand of *all* households for commodities. Of course, what all households do is only the sum of what each individual household does, and in Chapters 7 and 8 we shall study the behavior of individual households in greater detail.

TABLE 4-1   Composition of Personal Consumption Expenditures, 1951 and 1986 *(percentages)*

	1951		1986	
Durable goods		9.2		14.6
Automobile and parts	5.4		7.6	
Furniture and household equipment	2.8		2.9	
Other	1.0		4.1	
Semidurable goods		16.0		10.4
Clothing and footwear	9.1		6.1	
Other	6.9		4.3	
Nondurable goods		34.7		28.2
Food	27.1		11.9	
Electricity, gas, and other fuels	3.0		3.2	
Gasoline, oil, and grease	2.0		3.6	
Other	2.6		9.5	
Services		40.1		46.8
Housing and household services	13.6		18.6	
Health services	2.6		4.9	
Other	23.9		23.3	

Source: Statistics Canada, 13–001, 13–20; Department of Finance, *Economic Review.*

Nondurable and semidurables have declined in relative importance, while durables and services have increased.

to notice three things about this concept. First, quantity demanded is a *desired* quantity. It is how much households wish to purchase, given the price of the commodity, other prices, their incomes, tastes, and so on. This may be different from the amount that households actually succeed in purchasing. If sufficient quantities are not available, the amount households wish to purchase may exceed the amount they actually do purchase. To distinguish these two concepts, the term *quantity demanded* is used to refer to desired purchases, and a phrase such as **quantity actually bought** is used to refer to actual purchases.

Second, *desired* does not refer to idle dreams but to effective demands, that is, to the amounts people are willing to buy given the price they must pay for the commodity.

Third, quantity demanded refers to a continuous *flow* of purchases. It must therefore be expressed as so much per period of time: 1 million oranges per day, 7 million per week, or 365 million per year. For

example, being told that the quantity of new television sets demanded (at current prices) in Canada is 10,000 means nothing unless you are also told the period of time involved. Ten thousand television sets demanded per day would be an enormous rate of demand; 10,000 per year would be a very small rate. (The important distinction between stocks and flows was discussed on pages 21–22.)

What Determines Quantity Demanded?

The amount of some commodity that all households are willing to buy in a given time period is influenced by the following important variables. [2][2]

> Commodity's own price
> Average household income
> Prices of related commodities
> Tastes
> Distribution of income among households
> Size of the population

We cannot understand the separate influence of each of these variables if we try to consider what happens when everything changes at once. Instead, we consider the influence of the variables one at a time. To do this, we hold all but one of them constant. Then we let that one selected variable vary and study how it affects quantity demanded. We can do the same for each of the other variables in turn, and in this way we can come to understand the importance of each.[3] Once this is done, we can aggregate the separate influences of the variables to discover what would happen if several things changed at the same time—as they often do in practice.

Holding all other influencing variables constant is often described by the words "other things being equal" or by the equivalent Latin phrase, ***ceteris paribus.*** When economists speak of the influence of the

---

[2] Notes giving mathematical demonstrations of the concepts presented in the text are designated by colored reference numbers. These notes can be found beginning on page M-1.

[3] A relation in which many variables—in this case average income, population, tastes, and many prices—influence a single variable—in this case quantity demanded—is called a *multivariate* relation. The technique of studying the effect of each of the influencing variables one at a time while holding the others constant is common in mathematics, and there is a specific concept, the *partial derivative,* designed to do so.

price of wheat on the quantity of wheat demanded *ceteris paribus,* they refer to what a change in the price of wheat would do to the quantity demanded if all other factors that influence the demand for wheat did not change.

Demand and Price

We are interested in developing a theory of how commodities get priced. To do this we need to study the relation between the quantity demanded of each commodity and that commodity's own price. This requires that we hold all other influences constant and ask: How will the quantity of a commodity demanded vary as its own price varies?

A basic economic hypothesis is that the lower the price of a commodity, the larger the quantity that will be demanded, other things being equal.

Why might this be so? Commodities are used to satisfy desires and needs, and there is almost always more than one commodity that will satisfy any given desire or need. Such commodities compete with one another for the purchasers' attention. Hunger may be satisfied by meat or vegetables, a desire for green vegetables by broccoli or spinach. The need to keep warm at night may be satisfied by several woolen blankets or one electric blanket or a sheet and a lot of oil burned in the furnace. The desire for a vacation may be satisfied by a trip to the seashore or to the mountains, the need to get there by different airlines, a bus, a car, a train. And so it goes. Name any general desire or need, and there will be at least two and often dozens of different commodities that will satisfy it.

Now consider what happens if we hold income, tastes, population, and the prices of all other commodities constant and vary only the price of one commodity. As that price goes up, the commodity becomes an increasingly expensive way to satisfy a want. Some households will stop buying it altogether; others will buy smaller amounts; still others may continue to buy the same quantity. Because many households will switch wholly or partially to other commodities to satisfy the same want, less will

be bought of the commodity whose price has risen. As meat becomes more expensive, for example, households may switch to some extent to meat substitutes; they may also forgo meat at some meals and eat less meat at others.

Alternatively, a fall in a commodity's price makes it a cheaper method of satisfying a want. Households will buy more of it. Consequently, they will buy less of similar commodities whose prices have not fallen and which as a result have become expensive *relative to* the commodity in question. When a bumper tomato harvest drives prices down, shoppers switch to tomatoes and cut their purchases of many other vegetables that now look relatively more expensive.

The Demand Schedule and the Demand Curve

A **demand schedule** is one way of showing the relationship between quantity demanded and price. It is a numerical tabulation showing the quantity that is demanded at selected prices.

Table 4-2 is a hypothetical demand schedule for carrots. It lists the quantity of carrots that would be demanded at various prices on the assumption that all other influences on quantity demanded are held constant. We note in particular that average household income is fixed at $20,000 because later we will wish to see what happens when income changes. The table gives the quantities demanded for six selected prices, but actually a separate quantity would be demanded at each possible price from one cent to several hundreds of dollars.

A second method of showing the relation between quantity demanded and price is to draw a graph. The six price-quantity combinations shown in Table 4-2 are plotted on the graph shown in Figure 4-1. Price is plotted on the vertical axis and quantity on the horizontal axis. The smooth curve drawn through these points is called a **demand curve.** It shows the quantity that purchasers would like to buy at each price. The slope of the curve, downward to the right, indicates that the quantity demanded increases as the price falls.

Each point on the demand curve indicates a single price-quantity combination. The demand curve as a whole shows more.

TABLE 4-2   A Demand Schedule for Carrots

	Price per ton	Quantity demanded when income is $20,000 per year (thousands of tons per months)
U	$ 20	110.0
V	40	90.0
W	60	77.5
X	80	67.5
Y	100	62.5
Z	120	60.0

The table shows the quantity of carrots that would be demanded at various prices, *ceteris paribus.* For example, row *W* indicates that if the price of carrots were $60 per ton, consumers would desire to purchase 77,500 tons of carrots per month, given the values of the other variables that affect quantity demanded, including average household income.

The demand curve shows the relation between quantity demanded and price, other things being equal.

When economists speak of the conditions of demand in a particular market as being given or known, they are referring not just to the particular quantity being demanded at the moment (i.e., not just to one point on the demand curve). Instead, they are referring to the entire demand curve—to the relation between desired purchases and all the possible alternative prices of the commodity.

Thus the term **demand** refers to the entire relation between price and quantity (as shown, for example, by the schedule in Table 4-2 or the curve in Figure 4-1). In contrast, a single point on a demand schedule or curve is the *quantity demanded* at that point (for example, at point *W* in Figure 4-1, 77,500 tons of carrots a month are demanded at a price of $60 a ton).

Shifts in the Demand Curve

The demand schedule is constructed and the demand curve plotted on the assumption of *ceteris paribus.* But what if other things change, as surely they must? What if, for example, households find themselves with more income? If they spend their extra income,

they will buy additional quantities of many commodies *even though their prices are unchanged.*

But if households increase their purchases of any one commodity whose price has not changed, the purchases cannot be represented on the original demand curve. They must be represented on a new demand curve, which is to the right of the old curve. Thus the rise in household income shifts the demand curve to the right as shown in Figure 4-2. This illustrates the operation of an important general rule.

A demand curve is drawn on the assumption that everything except the commodity's own price is held constant. A change in any of the variables previously held constant will shift the demand curve to a new position.

A demand curve can shift in many ways; two of them are particularly important. In the first case more is bought at *each* price, and the demand curve

FIGURE 4-1   A Demand Curve for Carrots

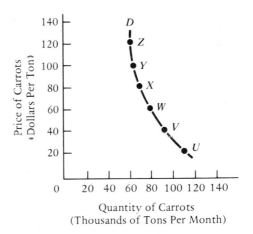

This demand curve relates quantity of carrots demanded to the price of carrots; its downward slope indicates that quantity demanded increases as price falls. The six points correspond to the price-quantity combinations shown in Table 4-2. Each row in the table defines a point on the demand curve. The smooth curve drawn through all of the points and labeled *D* is the demand curve.

TABLE 4-3   Two Alternative Demand Schedules for Carrots

Price per ton p	Quantity demanded when average household income is $20,000 per year (thousands of tons per month) D_0		Quantity demanded when average income is $24,000 per year (thousands of tons per month) D_1	
$ 20	110.0	U	140.0	U'
40	90.0	V	116.0	V'
60	77.5	W	100.8	W'
80	67.5	X	87.5	X'
100	62.5	Y	81.3	Y'
120	60.0	Z	78.0	Z'

An increase in average household income increases the quantity demanded at each price. When average income rises from $20,000 to $24,000 per year, quantity demanded at a price of $60 per ton rises from 77,500 tons per month to 100,800 tons per month. A similar rise occurs at every other price. Thus the demand schedule relating columns p and D_0 is replaced by one relating columns p and D_1. The graphical representations of these two functions are labeled D_0 and D_1 in Figure 4-2.

shifts right so that each price corresponds to a higher quantity than it did before. In the second case less is bought at *each* price, and the demand curve shifts left so that each price corresponds to a lower quantity than it did before.

The influence of changes in variables other than price may be studied by determining how changes in each variable shift the demand curve. Any change will shift the demand curve to the right if it increases the amount people wish to buy, other things remaining equal, and to the left if it decreases the amount households wish to buy, other things remaining equal.

Average household income. If households receive more income on average, they can be expected to purchase more of most commodities even though commodity prices remain the same.[4] Considering all households, we expect that no matter what price we

pick, more of any commodity will be demanded than was previously demanded at the same price. This shift is illustrated in Table 4-3 and Figure 4-2.

A rise in average household income shifts the demand curve for most commodities to the right. This indicates that more will be demanded at each possible price.

Other prices. We saw that the downward slope of a commodity's demand curve occurs because the lower its price, the cheaper the commodity is relative to other commodities that can satisfy the same needs or desires. Those other commodities are called **substitutes.** Another way for the same change to come about is for the price of the substitute commodity to rise. For example, carrots can become cheap relative to cabbage either because the price of carrots falls or because the price of cabbage rises. Either change will increase the amount of carrots households are prepared to buy.

FIGURE 4-2   Two Demand Curves for Carrots

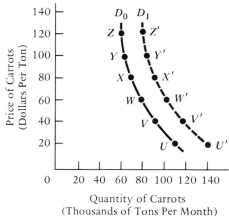

The rightward shift in the demand curve from D_0 to D_1 indicates an increase in the quantity demanded at each price. The lettered points correspond to those in Table 4-3. A rightward shift in the demand curve indicates an increase in demand in the sense that more is demanded at each price and that a higher price would be paid for each quantity.

[4] Such commodities are called *normal goods.* Commodities for which the amount purchased falls as income rises are called *inferior goods.* These concepts are defined and discussed in Chapter 5.

A rise in the price of a substitute for a commodity shifts the demand curve for the commodity to the right. More will be purchased at each price.

For example, a rise in the price of cabbage would shift the demand curve for carrots to the right in Figure 4-2.

Complements are commodities that tend to be used jointly with each other. Cars and gasoline are complements; so are golf clubs and golf balls, electric stoves and electricity, an airplane trip to Calgary and lift tickets at Banff. Since complements tend to be consumed together, a fall in the price of either will increase the demand for both.

A fall in the price of a complementary commodity will shift a commodity's demand curve to the right. More will be purchased at each price.

For example, a fall in the price of airplane trips to Calgary may lead to a rise in the demand for lift tickets at Banff even though their price is unchanged.

Tastes. Tastes have a large effect on people's desired purchases. A change in tastes may be long lasting, such as the shift from fountain pens to ball-point pens or from slide rules to pocket calculators. Or it may be a short-lived fad such as hula hoops. In either case a change in tastes in favor of a commodity shifts the demand curve to the right. More will be bought at each price.

Distribution of income. If a constant total of income is redistributed among the population, demands may change. If, for example, the government increases the deductions that may be taken for children on income tax returns and compensates by raising basic tax rates, income will be transferred from childless persons to households with large families. Demands for commodities more heavily bought by the childless will decline, while demands for commodities more heavily bought by those with large families will increase.

A change in the distribution of income will shift to the right the demand curves for commodities bought most by those gaining income, and it will shift to the left the demand curves for commodities bought most by people losing income.

Population. Population growth does not by itself create new demand. The additional people must have purchasing power before demand is changed. Extra people of working age who are employed, however, will earn new income. When this happens, the demands for all the commodities purchased by the new income earners will rise. Thus it is usually true that:

A rise in population will shift the demand curves for commodities to the right, indicating that more will be bought at each price.

The reasons that demand curves shift are summarized in Figure 4-3.

Movements Along the Demand Curve Versus Shifts of the Whole Curve

Suppose you read in today's newspaper that a soaring price of carrots has been caused by a greatly increased demand for that commodity. Then tomorrow you read that the rising price of carrots is greatly reducing the typical household's purchases of carrots as shoppers switch to potatoes, yams, and peas. The two statements appear to contradict each other. The first associates a rising price with a rising demand; the second associates a rising price with a declining demand. Can both statements be true? The answer is that they can be because they refer to different things. The first describes a shift in the demand curve; the second describes a movement along a demand curve in response to a change in price.

Consider first the statement that the increase in the price of carrots has been caused by an increased demand for carrots. This statement refers to a shift in the demand curve for carrots. In this case the demand curve must have shifted to the right, indicating more carrots demanded *at each price*. This shift will, as we shall see later in this chapter, increase the price of carrots.

Now consider the statement that fewer carrots

FIGURE 4-3   **Shifts in the Demand Curve**

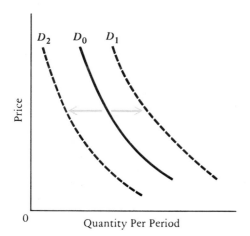

A shift in the demand curve from D_0 to D_1 indicates an increase in demand; a shift from D_0 to D_2 indicates a decrease in demand. An increase in demand means that more is demanded at each price. Such a rightward shift can be caused by a rise in income, a rise in the price of a substitute, a fall in the price of a complement, a change in tastes that favors the commodity, an increase in population, or a redistribution of income toward groups who favor the commodity.

A decrease in demand means that less is demanded at each price. Such a leftward shift can be caused by a fall in income, a fall in the price of a substitute, a rise in the price of a complement, a change in tastes that disfavors the commodity, a decrease in population, or a redistribution of income away from groups who favor the commodity.

---

are being bought because carrots have become more expensive. This refers to a movement along a given demand curve and reflects a change between two specific quantities being bought, one before the price rose and one afterward.

So what lay behind the two stories might have been something like the following.

1. A rise in the population is shifting the demand curve for carrots to the right as more and more are demanded at each price. This in turn is raising the price of carrots (for reasons we will soon

study in detail). This was the first newspaper story.
2. The rising price of carrots is causing each individual household to cut back on its purchase of carrots. This causes a movement upward to the left along any particular demand curve for carrots. This was the second newspaper story.

To prevent the type of confusion caused by our two newspaper stories, economists have developed a specialized vocabulary to distinguish shifts of curves from movements along curves.

We have seen that *demand* refers to the *whole* demand curve. Economists reserve the term **change in demand** to describe a shift in the whole curve, that is, a change in the amount that will be bought at *every* price.

An increase in demand means that the whole demand curve has shifted to the right; a decrease in demand means that the whole demand curve has shifted to the left.

Any one point on a demand curve represents a specific amount being bought at a specified price. It represents, therefore, a particular quantity demanded. A movement along a demand curve is referred to as a **change in the quantity demanded.** [3]

A movement down a demand curve is called an increase (or a rise) in the quantity demanded; a movement up the demand curve is called a decrease (or a fall) in the quantity demanded.

To illustrate this terminology, look again at Table 4-3. When average income is $20,000, an increase in price from $60 to $80 decreases the *quantity demanded* from 77.5 to 67.5 thousand tons a month. An increase in average income from $20,000 to $24,000 increases *demand* from D_0 to D_1.

Figure 4-4 shows the combined effect of a rise in demand, shown by a rightward shift in the whole demand curve, and a fall in the quantity demanded, shown by a movement upward to the left along a given demand curve in response to a change in price.

**FIGURE 4-4   Shifts of and Movements Along
the Demand Curve**

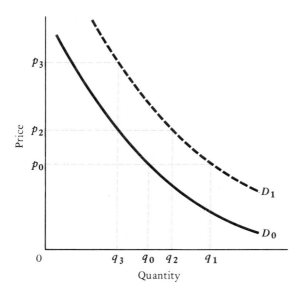

**A rise in demand means that more will be bought
at each price, but it does not mean that more will
be bought under all circumstances.** The demand
curve is originally D_0 and price is p_0 at which q_0 is
bought. Demand then increases to D_1, which implies that
at the old price of p_0, there is a larger quantity demanded, q_1. Now assume the price rises above p_0. This
causes quantity demanded to fall below q_1. *The shift in the
demand curve means that more is bought at each price. A
movement upward along the demand curve causes less to be
bought in response to a rise in price.* The net effect of these
two shifts can be either an increase or a decrease in the
quantity demanded. In the figure a rise in price to p_2
leaves the quantity demanded of q_2 still in excess of the
original quantity q_0, whereas a rise in price to p_3 leaves
the final quantity of q_3 below the original quantity of q_0.

Supply

Canada's private sector produced goods and services
worth nearly $300 billion in 1986. A broad clas-
sification of what was produced is given in Table 4-
4. Economists have as many questions to ask about
production and its changing compositions as they do
about consumption. The percentages shown in Table
4-4 reflect some of the changes in 35 years.

The table shows the growth of services and the
relative decline of primary industries as well as the
relatively stable proportion accounted for by manufacturing. Much more dramatic changes have occurred within each of the categories shown in the
table.

Economists want to know why. Why did the
aluminum industry grow faster than the steel industry? Why, even within a single industry, did some
firms prosper and grow, others hold their own, and
still others decline and fail? Why and how do firms
and industries come into being? All these questions
and many others are aspects of a single question:
*What determines the quantities of commodities that will be
produced and offered for sale?*

Full discussion of these questions of supply will
come later (in Part Four). For now it is enough to
develop the basic relation between the price of a
commodity and the quantity that will be produced

**TABLE 4-4   Domestic Product by Industry
of Origin, 1951 and 1986
(*percentage distribution*)**

Industry group[a]	1951	1986
Agriculture, forestry, fishing, and trapping	15.5	4.9
Mining, quarrying, and oil wells	4.4	6.4
Manufacturing	31.2	22.4
Construction	5.4	8.3
Transportation, storage, and communication	10.0	9.0
Utilities	2.2	3.7
Wholesale and retail trade	11.5	13.9
Finance, insurance, and real estate	9.5	18.1
Other services	10.3	13.3
	100	100

Source: Statistics Canada, 11–003, 13–201.
[a] Excluding government and government enterprises.

Since 1951 agriculture, mining, and manufacturing have
all declined in relative importance, while utilities, finance, and services have gained. Construction, transportation, and trade show considerable fluctuation with no
evident trend.

and offered for sale by firms and to understand what forces lead to shifts in this relationship.

Quantity Supplied

The amount of a commodity that firms wish to sell is called the **quantity supplied** of that commodity. Quantity supplied is a flow; it is so much per unit of time. Note that this is the amount that firms are willing to offer for sale; it is not necessarily the amount they succeed in selling. The term **quantity actually sold** indicates what they succeed in selling.

When we look at desired purchases and sales, it is clear that households may desire to purchase an amount that differs from what sellers desire to sell. Households cannot, however, succeed in buying what someone else does not sell. A purchase and a sale are merely two sides of the same transaction. Looked at from the buyer's side, there is a purchase; looked at from the seller's side, there is a sale.

Since desired purchases do not have to equal desired sales, quantity demanded does not have to equal quantity supplied. But because no one can buy what someone does not sell, the quantity actually purchased must equal the quantity actually sold.

What Determines Quantity Supplied?

The amount of a commodity that firms will be willing to produce and offer for sale is influenced by the following important variables. [4]

> Commodity's own price
> Prices of inputs
> Goals of firms
> State of technology

The situation is the same here as it is on the demand side. The list of influencing variables is long, and we will not get far if we try to discover what happens when they all change at the same time. So again we use the convenient *ceteris paribus* technique to study the influence of the variables one at a time.

Supply and Price

Since we want to develop a theory of how commodities get priced, we study the relation between the quantity supplied of each commodity and that commodity's own price. We start by holding all other influences constant and asking: How do we expect the quantity of a commodity supplied to vary with its own price?

A basic economic hypothesis is that, for many commodities, the higher the price of the commodity, the larger the quantity that will be supplied, other things being equal.

Why might this be so? It is because the profits that can be earned from producing a commodity are almost certain to increase if the price of that commodity rises while the costs of inputs used to produce it remain unchanged. This will make firms, which are in business to earn profits, wish to produce more of the commodity whose price has risen and less of other commodities.[5]

The Supply Schedule and the Supply Curve

The general relationship just discussed can be illustrated by a **supply schedule,** which shows the quantities that producers would wish to sell at alternative prices of the commodity. A supply schedule is analogous to a demand schedule; the former shows what producers would be willing to sell, while the latter shows what households would be willing to buy at alternative prices of the commodity. Table 4–5 presents a hypothetical supply schedule for carrots.

A **supply curve,** the graphical representation of the supply schedule, is illustrated in Figure 4–5. While each point on the supply curve represents a specific price-quantity combination, the whole curve shows more.

The supply curve represents the relation between quantity supplied and price, other things being equal.

---

[5] Notice, however, the qualifying word *many* in the hypothesis. It is used because, as we shall see in Part Four, there are exceptions to this rule. Although the rule states the usual case, a rise in price (*ceteris paribus*) is not always necessary to call forth an increase in quantity in the case of all commodities.

TABLE 4-5   A Supply Schedule for Carrots

	Price per ton	Quantity supplied (thousands of tons per month)
u	$ 20	5.0
v	40	46.0
w	60	77.5
x	80	100.0
y	100	115.0
z	120	122.5

The table shows the quantities that producers wish to sell at various prices, *ceteris paribus*. For example, row *y* indicates that if the price were $100 per ton, producers would wish to sell 115,000 tons of carrots per month.

When economists speak of the conditions of supply as being given or known, they refer not just to the particular quantity being supplied at the moment, that is, not to just one point on the supply curve. Instead, they are referring to the entire supply curve, to the complete relation between desired sales and all possible alternative prices of the commodity.

Supply refers to the entire relation between supply and price. A single point on the supply curve refers to the *quantity supplied* at that price.

Shifts in the Supply Curve

A shift in the supply curve means that at each price a different quantity will be supplied than previously. An increase in the quantity supplied at each price is shown in Table 4-6 and graphed in Figure 4-6. This change appears as a rightward shift in the supply curve. In contrast, a decrease in the quantity supplied at each price would appear as a leftward shift. A shift in the supply curve must be the result of a change in one of the factors that influence the quantity supplied other than the commodity's own price. The major possible causes of such shifts are summarized in the caption of Figure 4-7 (p. 69) and are considered briefly below.

For supply, as for demand, there is an important general rule.

A change in any of the variables (other than the commodity's own price) that affects the amount of a commodity that firms are willing to produce and sell will shift the whole supply curve for that commodity.

Prices of inputs. All things that a firm uses to produce its outputs—such as materials, labor, and machines—are called the firm's inputs. Other things being equal, the higher the price of any input used to make a commodity, the less will be the profit from making that commodity. We expect, therefore, that the higher the price of any input used by a firm, the lower will be the amount that the firm will produce and offer for sale at any given price of the commodity.

A rise in the price of inputs shifts the supply curve to the left, indicating that less will be

FIGURE 4-5   A Supply Curve for Carrots

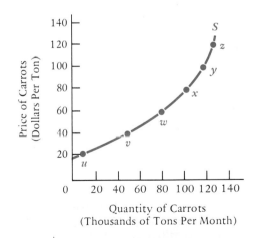

This supply curve relates quantity of carrots supplied to the price of carrots; its upward slope indicates that quantity supplied increases as price increases. The six points correspond to the price-quantity combinations shown in Table 4-5. Each row in the table defines a point on the supply curve. The smooth curve drawn through all of the points and labeled *S* is the supply curve.

TABLE 4-6   **Two Alternative Supply Schedules for Carrots**

Price per ton p	Quantity supplied before cost-saving innovation (thousands of tons per month) S_0		Quantity supplied after innovation (thousands of tons per month) S_1	
$ 20	5.0	u	28.0	u'
40	46.0	v	76.0	v'
60	77.5	w	102.0	w'
80	100.0	x	120.0	x'
100	115.0	y	132.0	y'
120	122.5	z	140.0	z'

A cost-saving innovation increases the quantity supplied at each price. As a result of a cost-saving innovation, the quantity that is supplied at $100 per ton rises from 115,000 to 132,000 tons per month. A similar rise occurs at every price. Thus the supply schedule relating p and S_0 is replaced by one relating p and S_1.

FIGURE 4-6   **Two Supply Curves for Carrots**

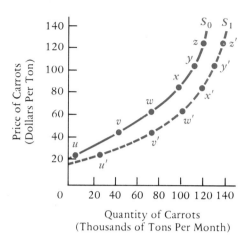

Quantity of Carrots
(Thousands of Tons Per Month)

The rightward shift in the supply curve from S_0 to S_1 indicates an increase in the quantity supplied at each price. The lettered points correspond to those in Table 4-6. A rightward shift in the supply curve indicates an increase in supply in the sense that more carrots are supplied at each price.

supplied at any given price; a fall in the cost of inputs shifts the supply curve to the right.**

Goals of the firm.

In elementary economic theory, the firm is assumed to have the single goal of profit maximization. Firms might, however, have other goals either in addition to or as substitutes for profit maximization. If the firm worries about risk, it will pursue safer lines of activity even though they promise lower probable profits. If the firm values size, it may produce and sell more than the profit-maximizing quantities. If it worries about its image in society, it may forsake highly profitable activities (such as the production of dioxin) when there is major public disapproval. However, as long as the firm prefers more profits to less, it will respond to changes in the profitabilities of alternative lines of action, and supply curves will slope upward.

A change in the importance that firms give to other goals will shift the supply curve one way or the other, indicating a changed willingness to supply the quantity at any given price and hence a changed level of profitability.

Technology.

At any time what is produced and how it is produced depend on what is known. Over time

knowledge changes; so do the quantities of individual commodities supplied. The enormous increase in production per worker that has been going on in industrial societies for about 200 years is largely due to improved methods of production. Yet the Industrial Revolution is more than a historical event; it is a present reality. Discoveries in chemistry have led to lower costs of production of well-established products, such as paints, and to a large variety of new products made of plastics and synthetic fibers. The invention of transistors and silicon chips has radically changed products such as computers, audiovisual equipment, and guidance-control systems, and the consequent development of compact computers is revolutionizing the production of countless other nonelectronic products.

Any technological change that decreases production costs will increase the profits that can be earned at any given price of the commodity. Since increased profitability lead to increased production, this change shifts the supply curve to the right, indicating an

FIGURE 4-7   Shifts in the Supply Curve

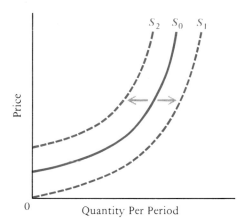

A shift in the supply curve from S_0 to S_1 indicates an increase in supply; a shift from S_0 to S_2 indicates a decrease in supply. An increase in supply means that more is supplied at each price. Such a rightward shift can be caused by certain changes in producers' goals, improvements in technology, or decreases in the costs of inputs that are important in producing the commodity.

A decrease in supply means that less is supplied at each price. Such a leftward shift can be caused by certain changes in producers' goals, or increases in the costs of inputs that are important in producing the commodity.

increased willingness to produce the commodity and offer it for sale at each possible price.

Movements Along the Supply Curve Versus Shifts of the Whole Curve

As with demand, it is important to distinguish movements along supply curves from shifts of the whole curve. The term **change in supply** is reserved for a shift of the whole supply curve. This means a change in the quantity supplied at each price of the commodity. A movement along the supply curve indicates a *change in the quantity supplied* in response to a change in the price of the commodity. Thus an increase in supply means that the whole supply curve has shifted to the right; an increase in the quantity supplied means a movement upward to the right along a given supply curve.

Determination of Price by Demand and Supply

So far demand and supply have been considered separately. The next question is this: How do the two forces interact to determine price in a competitive market? Table 4-7 brings together the demand and supply schedules from Tables 4-2 and 4-5. The quantities of carrots demanded and supplied at each price may now be compared.

There is only one price, $60 a ton, at which the quantity of carrots demanded equals the quantity supplied. At prices of less than $60 a ton there is a shortage of carrots because the quantity demanded exceeds the quantity supplied. This is often called a situation of **excess demand.** At prices greater than $60 a ton there is a surplus of carrots because the quantity supplied exceeds the quantity demanded. This is called a situation of **excess supply.**

To discuss the determination of market price, suppose first that the price is $100 a ton. At this price 115,000 tons would be offered for sale, but only 62,500 tons would be demanded. There would be an excess supply of 52,500 tons a month. We assume that sellers will then cut their prices to get rid of this surplus and that purchasers, observing the stock of unsold carrots, will offer less for what they are prepared to buy.

Excess supply causes a downward pressure on price.

Next consider the price of $20 a ton. At this price there is excess demand. The 5,000 tons produced each month are snapped up quickly, and 105,000 tons of desired purchases cannot be made. Rivalry between would-be purchasers may lead to their offering more than the prevailing price to outbid other purchasers. Also, perceiving that they could have sold their available supplies many times over, sellers may begin to ask a higher price for the quantities that they do have to sell.

Excess demand causes an upward pressure on price.

TABLE 4-7   **Demand and Supply Schedules for Carrots and Equilibrium Price**

(1) Price per ton *p*	(2) Quantity demanded (thousands of tons per month) *D*	(3) Quantity supplied (thousands of tons per month) *S*	(4) Excess demand (+) or excess supply (−) (thousands of tons per month) *D − S*
$ 20	110.0	5.0	+105.0
40	90.0	46.0	+ 44.0
60	77.5	77.5	0.0
80	67.5	100.0	− 32.5
100	62.5	115.0	− 52.5
120	60.0	122.5	− 62.5

Equilibrium occurs where quantity demanded equals quantity supplied—where there is neither excess demand nor excess supply.   These schedules are those of Tables 4-2 and 4-5. The equilibrium price is $60. For lower prices there is excess demand; for higher prices there is excess supply.

Finally, consider a price of $60. At this price producers wish to sell 77,500 tons a month and purchasers wish to buy that quantity. There is neither a shortage nor a surplus of carrots. There are no unsatisfied buyers to bid the price up, nor are there unsatisfied sellers to force the price down. Once the price of $60 has been reached, therefore, there will be no tendency for it to change.

An equilibrium implies a state of rest, or balance, between opposing forces. The **equilibrium price** is the one toward which the actual market price will tend. It will persist once established, unless it is disturbed by some change in market conditions.

The price at which the quantity demanded equals the quantity supplied is called the equilibrium price.

Any other price is called a **disequilibrium price:** the price at which quantity demanded does not equal quantity supplied, and price will be changing. A market that exhibits either excess demand or excess supply is said to be in a state of **disequilibrium.**

Anything that must be true if equilibrium is to be obtained is called an **equilibrium condition.** In the competitive market, the equality of quantity demanded and quantity supplied is an equilibrium condition. [5]

This same story is told in graphical terms in Figure 4-8. The quantities demanded and supplied at any price can be read off the two curves; the magnitude of the shortage or surplus is shown by the horizontal distance between the curves at each price. The figure makes it clear that the equilibrium price occurs where the demand and supply curves intersect. Below that price there will be a shortage and hence an upward pressure on the existing price. Above it there will be a surplus and hence a downward pressure on price. These pressures are represented by the vertical arrows in the figure.

The Laws of Demand and Supply

Changes in any of the variables other than price that influence quantity demanded or supplied will cause a shift in the supply curve or the demand curve or both. There are four possible shifts: (1) a rise in demand (a rightward shift in the demand curve), (2) a fall in demand (a leftward shift in the demand curve), (3) a rise in supply (a rightward shift in the supply curve), and (4) a fall in supply (a leftward shift in the supply curve).

Each of these shifts causes changes that are described by one of the four "laws" of demand and supply. Each of the laws summarizes what happens when an initial position of equilibrium is upset by

**FIGURE 4-8   Determination of the Equilibrium
Price of Carrots**

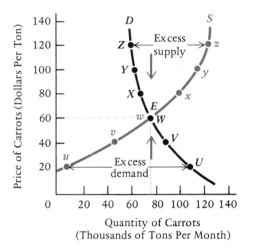

Quantity of Carrots
(Thousands of Tons Per Month)

The equilibrium price corresponds to the intersection of the demand and supply curves. Equilibrium is indicated by *E*, which is point *W* on the demand curve and point *w* on the supply curve. At a price of $60 quantity demanded equals quantity supplied. At prices above equilibrium there is excess supply and downward pressure on price. At prices below equilibrium there is excess demand and upward pressure on price. The pressures on price are represented by the vertical arrows.

some shift in either the demand or the supply curve and a new equilibrium position is then established. The sense in which it is correct to call these propositions "laws" is discussed in Box 4-1.

To discover the effects of each of the curve shifts that we wish to study, we use the method known as **comparative statics.**[6] We start from a position of equilibrium and then introduce the change to be studied. The new equilibrium position is determined and compared with the original one. The differences between the two positions of equilibrium must result

from changes in the data that were introduced, for everything else has been held constant.

The four laws of demand and supply are derived in Figure 4-9 (p. 73), which generalizes our specific discussion about carrots. Previously, we had given the axes specific labels, but from here on we will simplify. Because it is intended to apply to any commodity, the horizontal axis is simply labeled *Quantity*. This should be understood to mean quantity per period in whatever units output is measured. *Price*, the vertical axis, should be understood to mean the price measured as dollars per unit of quantity for the same commodity. The laws of supply and demand are as follows:

1. **A rise in demand causes an increase in both the equilibrium price and the equilibrium quantity exchanged.**
2. **A fall in demand causes a decrease in both the equilibrium price and the equilibrium quantity exchanged.**
3. **A rise in supply causes a decrease in the equilibrium price and an increase in the equilibrium quantity exchanged.**
4. **A fall in supply causes an increase in the equilibrium price and a decrease in the equilibrium quantity exchanged.**

In this chapter we have studied many forces that can cause demand or supply curves to shift. These were summarized in Figures 4-3 and 4-7. By combining this analysis with the four laws, we can link many real-world events that cause demand or supply curves to shift with changes in market prices and quantities.

The theory of the determination of price by demand and supply is beautiful in its simplicity. Yet, as we shall see, it is powerful in its wide range of applications.[7] The usefulness of this theory in interpreting what we see in the world around us is further discussed in Box 4-2 (p. 74), while its application in an open economy in which international trade is important is discussed in the appendix to this chapter.

---

[6] The term *statics* is used because we are not concerned about the actual path by which the market goes from the first equilibrium position to the second. Analysis of that path would be described as dynamic analysis.

[7] The laws of demand and supply apply in competitive markets where a supply curve exists and slopes upward. As we shall see later, not all markets satisfy these conditions.

BOX 4-1

Laws, Predictions, Hypotheses

In what sense can the four propositions developed for supply and demand be called "laws"? They are not like acts passed by Congress, interpreted by courts, and enforced by the police; they cannot be repealed if people do not like their effects. Nor are they like the laws of Moses, revealed to man by the voice of God. Are they natural laws similar to Newton's law of gravity? In labeling them *laws*, classical economists clearly had in mind Newton's laws as analogies.

The term *law* is used in science to describe a theory that has stood up to substantial testing. A law of this kind is not something that has been proven to be true for all times and all circumstances, nor is it regarded as immutable. As observations accumulate, laws may often be modified or the range of phenomena to which they apply may be restricted or redefined. Einstein's theory of relativity, for one example, forced such amendments and restrictions on Newton's laws.

The laws of supply and demand have stood up well to many empirical tests, but no one believes that they explain all market behavior. Indeed, the range of markets over which they seem to meet the test of providing accurate predictions is now much smaller than it was 80 years ago. It is possible—though most economists would think it unlikely—that at some future time they would no longer apply to any real markets. They are thus laws in the sense that they predict certain kinds of behavior in certain situations and the predicted behavior occurs sufficiently often to lead people to continue to have confidence in the predictions of the theory. They are not laws—any more than are the laws of natural science—that are beyond being challenged by present or future observations that may cast their predictions in doubt. Nor is it a heresy to question their applicability to any particular situation.

Laws, then, are hypotheses that have led to predictions that account for observed behavior. They are theories that, in some circumstances at least, have survived attempts to refute them and have proven useful. It is possible, in economics as in the natural sciences, to be impressed both with the "laws" we do have and with their limitations: to be impressed, that is, both with the power of what we know and with the magnitude of what we have yet to understand.

Prices in Inflation

Up to now we have developed the theory of the prices of individual commodities under the assumption that all other prices remained constant. Does this mean that the theory is inapplicable to an inflationary world when almost all prices are rising? Fortunately the answer is no.

The key lies in what are called relative prices. We have mentioned several times that what matters for demand and supply is the price of the commodity in question relative to the prices of other commodities. This is called a **relative price.**

In an inflationary world we are often interested in the price of a given commodity as it relates to the average price of all other commodities. If, during a period when the general price level rose by 40 percent, the price of oranges rose by 60 percent, then the price of oranges rose relative to the price level as a whole. Oranges became *relatively* expensive. However, if oranges had risen in price by only 30 percent when the general price level rose by 40 percent, then the relative price of oranges would have fallen. Although the money price of oranges rose substantially, oranges became *relatively* cheap.

In Lewis Carroll's famous story *Through the Looking-Glass,* Alice finds a country where you have to run in order to stay still. So it is with inflation. A commodity's price must rise as fast as the general level of prices just to keep its relative price constant.

It has been convenient in this chapter to analyze a change in a particular price in the context of a constant price level. The analysis is easily extended to an inflationary period by remembering that any

FIGURE 4-9   The "Laws" of Demand and Supply

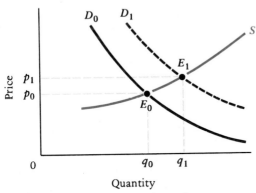

(i) The effect of shifts in the demand curve

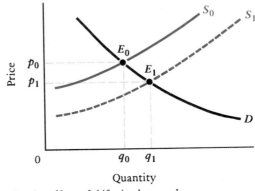

(ii) The effect of shifts in the supply curve

The effects on equilibrium price and quantity of shifts in either demand or supply are called the laws of demand and supply.

A rise in demand. In (i) assume that the original demand and supply curves are D_0 and S, which intersect to produce equilibrium at E_0, with a price of p_0 and a quantity of q_0. An increase in demand shifts the demand curve to D_1, taking the new equilibrium to E_1. Price rises to p_1 and quantity rises to q_1.

A fall in demand. In (i) assume that the original demand and supply curves are D_1 and S, which intersect to produce equilibrium at E_1, with a price of p_1 and a quantity of q_1. A decrease in demand shifts the demand curve to D_0, taking the new equilibrium to E_0. Price falls to p_0 and quantity falls to q_0.

A rise in supply. In (ii) assume that the original demand and supply curves are D and S_0, which intersect to produce an equilibrium at E_0, with a price of p_0 and a quantity of q_0. An increase in supply shifts the supply curve to S_1, taking the new equilibrium to E_1. Price falls to p_1 and quantity rises to q_1.

A fall in supply. In (ii) assume that the original demand and supply curves are D and S_1, which intersect to produce equilibrium at E_1, with a price of p_1 and a quantity of q_1. A decrease in supply shifts the supply curve to S_0, taking the new equilibrium to E_0. Price rises to p_0 and quantity falls to q_0.

---

force that raises the price of one commodity when other prices remain constant will, given general inflation, raise the price of that commodity faster than the price level is rising. For example, a change in tastes in favor of carrots that would raise their price by 20 percent when other prices were constant would raise their price by 32 percent if at the same time the general price level goes up by 10 percent.[8] In each

case the price of carrots rises 20 percent *relative to the average of all prices*.

In price theory, whenever we talk of a change in the price of one commodity, we mean a change relative to other prices.

If the price level is constant, this change requires only that the money price of the commodity in question rise. If the price level is itself rising, this change requires that the money price of the commodity in question rise faster than the price level.

[8] Let the price level be 100 in the first case and 110 in the second. Let the price of carrots be 120 in the first case and x in the second. To preserve the same relative price we need x such that $120/100 = x/110$, which makes $x = 132$.

BOX 4-2

Demand and Supply: What Really Happens

"The theory of supply and demand is neat enough," said the skeptic, "but tell me what really happens."

"What really happens," said the economist, "is that first, demand curves slope downward; second, supply curves slope upward; third, prices rise in response to excess demand; and fourth, prices fall in response to excess supply."

"But that's theory," insisted the skeptic. "What about reality?"

"That is reality as well," said the economist.

"Show me," said the skeptic.

The economist produced the following passages from recent newspaper articles.

As fiber optics substitute for copper wire, Canadian copper mines cut back output in the face of falling world copper prices.

*   *   *

The continuing housing boom in Toronto causes soaring costs of accommodation and attracts construction workers back from Alberta.

*   *   *

Increased demand for macadamia nuts causes price to rise above competing nuts. Major producer now plans to double the size of its orchards during the next five years.

*   *   *

OPEC countries once again fail to agree on output quotas. Output soars and prices plummet. (1985)

OPEC and allied countries agree on quotas, and prices rise gently. (1987)

*   *   *

Last summer, Rhode Island officials reopened the northern third of Narragansett Bay, a 9,500-acre fishing ground that had been closed since 1978 because of pollution. Suddenly clam prices dropped, thanks to an underwater population explosion that had transformed the Narragansett area into a clam harvester's dream.

*   *   *

Increasing third world agricultural production threatens the stability of North American agriculture. In the 1970s North American farm prosperity was built on rising demand due to world prosperity and on falling output in Eastern Europe. Farm experts now worry that the propensity will prove fragile in the face of major increases in world output.

The skeptic's response is not recorded, but you will have no trouble telling which clippings illustrate which of the economist's four statements about "what really happens."

Summary

1. The amount of a commodity that households wish to purchase is called the *quantity demanded*. It is a flow expressed as so much per period of time. It is determined by the commodity's own price, average household income, the prices of related commodities, tastes, the distribution of income among households, and the size of the population.

2. Quantity demanded is assumed to increase as the price of the commodity falls, *ceteris paribus*. The relationship between quantity demanded and price is represented graphically by a demand curve that shows how much will be demanded at each market price. A movement along a demand curve indicates a change in the quantity demanded in response to a change in the price of the commodity.

3. A shift in a demand curve represents a change in the quantity demanded at each price and is referred to as a *change in demand*. The demand curve shifts to the right (an increase in demand) if average income rises, if the price of a substitute rises, if the price of a complement falls, if population rises, or if there is a change in tastes

in favor of the product. The opposite changes shift the demand curve to the left (a decrease in demand).

4. The amount of a commodity that firms wish to sell is called the *quantity supplied*. It is a flow expressed as so much per period of time. It depends on the commodity's own price, the costs of inputs, the goals of the firm, and the state of technology.

5. Quantity supplied is assumed to increase as the price of the commodity increases, *ceteris paribus*. The relationship between quantity supplied and price is represented graphically by a supply curve that shows how much will be supplied at each market price. A movement along a supply curve indicates a change in the quantity supplied in response to a change in price.

6. A shift in the supply curve indicates a change in the quantity supplied at each price and is referred to as a *change in supply*. The supply curve shifts to the right (an increase in supply) if the costs of producing the commodity fall or if, for any reason, producers become more willing to produce the commodity. The opposite changes shift the supply curve to the left (a decrease in supply).

7. The *equilibrium price* is the one at which the quantity demanded equals the quantity supplied. At any price below equilibrium there will be excess demand; at any price above equilibrium there will be excess supply. Graphically, equilibrium occurs where demand and supply curves intersect.

8. Price is assumed to rise when there is a shortage and to fall when there is a surplus. Thus the actual market price will be pushed toward the equilibrium price, and when it is reached, there will be neither shortage nor surplus and price will not change until either the supply curve or the demand curve shifts.

9. Using the method of comparative statics, the effects of a shift in either demand or supply can be determined. A rise in demand raises both equilibrium price and quantity; a fall in demand lowers both. A rise in supply raises equilibrium quantity but lowers equilibrium price; a fall in supply lowers equilibrium quantity but raises equilibrium price. These are the so-called laws of supply and demand.

10. Price theory is most simply developed in the context of a constant price level. Price changes discussed in the theory are changes relative to the average level of all prices. In an inflationary period a rise in the *relative price* of one commodity means that its price rises by more than the rise in the price level; a fall in its relative price means that its price rises by less than the rise in the price level.

Topics for Review

Quantity demanded and quantity exchanged
Demand schedule and demand curve
Quantity supplied and quantity exchanged
Supply schedule and supply curve
Movement along a curve and shift of a whole curve

Change in quantity demanded and change in demand
Change in quantity supplied and change in supply
Equilibrium, equilibrium price, and disequilibrium
Comparative statics
Laws of supply and demand
Relative price

Discussion Questions

1. What shifts in demand or supply curves would produce the following results? (Assume that only one of the two curves has shifted.)
   a. The price of pocket calculators has fallen over the past few years and the quantity exchanged has risen greatly.
   b. As the Canadian standard of living rose over the past three decades, both the prices and the consumption of prime cuts of beef rose steadily.
   c. Summer sublets in Kensington, Ontario, are at rents well below the regular rentals.
   d. Style changes cause the sale of jeans to decline.
   e. Potato blight causes spud prices to soar.
   f. "Gourmet food market grows as affluent shoppers indulge."
   g. Du Pont increased the price of synthetic fibers, although it acknowledged demand was weak.
   h. The Edsel was a lemon when produced in 1958–1960 but is now a best-seller among cars of its vintage.
   i. Some of the first $10 coins minted in Canada to commemorate the Olympics were imperfectly stamped. These flawed pieces are currently worth as much as $1,000.
   j. Do the same for all the examples given in Box 4-2.
2. Recently the U.S. Department of Agriculture predicted that this spring's excellent weather would result in larger crops of corn and wheat than farmers had expected. But its chief economist warned consumers not to expect prices to decrease since the costs of production were rising and foreign demand for American crops was increasing. "The classic pattern of supply and demand won't work this time," the economist said. Discuss his observation.
3. Suppose that compact disk producers find that they are selling more at the same price than they did two years ago. Is this a shift of the demand curve or a movement along the curve? Suggest at least four reasons why this rise in sales at an unchanged price might occur.
4. What would be the effect on the equilibrium price and quantity of marijuana if its sale were legalized?
5. The relative price of personal computers has dropped drastically over time. Would you explain this falling price in terms of demand or supply changes? What factors are likely to have caused the demand or supply shifts that did occur?
6. Classify the effect of each of the following as (i) a decrease in the demand for fish, (ii) a decrease in the quantity of fish demanded, or (iii) other. Illustrate each diagrammatically.
   a. The government of Iceland bars fishermen of other nations from its waters.
   b. People buy less fish because of a rise in fish prices.

   c. The Roman Catholic Church relaxes its ban on eating meat on Fridays.

   d. The price of beef falls and as a result households buy more beef and less fish.

   e. Fears of mercury pollution leads locals to shun fish caught in nearby lakes.

   f. It is discovered that eating fish is better for one's health than eating meat.

7. Predict the effect on the price of at least one commodity of each of the following:

   a. Winter snowfall is at a record high in Quebec, but drought continues in Rocky Mountain ski areas.

   b. A recession decreases employment in Windsor automobile factories.

   c. The French grape harvest is the smallest in 20 years.

   d. The state of New York cancels permission for citizens to cut firewood in state parks.

8. Are the following two observations inconsistent? (a) Rising demand for housing causes prices of new homes to soar. (b) Many families refuse to buy homes as prices become prohibitive for them.

The Laws of Demand and Supply in an Open Economy

So far in this chapter we have discussed the determination of price in a single domestic market. But what about all those goods that are traded internationally? A brief look at these may be a useful exercise at this point.

To start we need to define a few terms. An economy that engages in international trade is called an **open economy.** One that does not is called a **closed economy,** and a situation with no international trade is called **autarky.** In this section we examine the

simple case of a **small open economy (SOE),** which is an economy whose exports and imports are small enough in relation to the total volume of world trade that changes in the quantities it imports or exports do not influence the prices of goods established in world markets. For many countries and commodities, this is an empirically applicable assumption.

We also divide all goods into two types. **Non-tradables** are goods and services that are produced and sold domestically and do not enter into international trade. Their prices are set on domestic markets by domestic supply and demand. **Tradables** are goods and services that enter into international trade. For a small open economy, the prices of tradables, whether the economy imports or exports them, are given, since they are set on international markets.

FIGURE 4A-1 The Domestic Supply and Demand for Wheat (a Typical Exported Good)

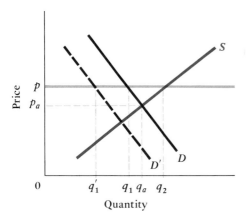

Exports are determined by the domestic excess supply of a tradable good at the world price. D and S are the domestic demand and supply schedules. In autarky, the domestic price would be p_a, and quantity q_a would be produced and consumed domestically. If the world price of wheat, p, exceeds the autarky price, p_a, the country will export wheat. At the world price p, quantity supplied will be q_2, domestic consumption will be q_1, and q_1q_2 will be exported. A fall in domestic demand to D' increases the quantity exported to $q_1'q_2$.

Nontraded Goods

Equilibrium is where the quantity demanded by domestic purchasers is equal to the quantity supplied by domestic producers. In effect, the pricing of nontraded goods is what we discussed in Chapter 4. Price of nontradables is set by the forces of domestic demand and domestic supply.

Traded Goods

Traded goods prices are set on international markets, while domestic demand and supply determine the quantities that are consumed, produced, and traded at that price.

Exports. Domestic demand and supply would establish a domestic price in the absence of world trade. If, however, the given world price exceeds that domestic price, the good will be exported. Since the small open economy's exports are an insignificant fraction of total world production and consumption of the commodity, the world price will dominate, and the excess of domestic quantity supplied over domestic quantity demanded at that price will be exported. This is analyzed in detail in Figure 4A-1.

Notice that trade raises the price of the exported good above its autarky level. Notice also that the equilibrium is no longer where domestic quantity demanded equals domestic quantity supplied; instead, the equilibrium price is the given world price, and the excess of domestic quantity supplied over domestic quantity demanded is exported.

Imports.   If the world price is less than the autarky price, the good will be imported, as shown in Figure 4A-2. Notice that trade lowers the price of the imported good below its autarky level. Notice also that the equilibrium is once again not where domestic quantity demanded equals domestic quantity supplied; price is given by the world price, and the excess of domestic quantity demanded over domestic quantity supplied is met by imports.

For an open economy, equilibrium in markets for traded goods is consistent with domestic demand for those goods being different from domestic supply. If at the world price quantity demanded domestically exceeds quantity supplied domestically, the good will be imported; if quantity supplied domestically exceeds quantity demanded domestically, the good will be exported.

Effects of Changes in Domestic Supply and Demand

Suppose that domestic residents experience a change in tastes. At the same prices, and values of other variables that influence quantity demanded, they decide to consume less of the exported good and more of the imported good. This decision is illustrated in Figure 4A-1, where the demand for the exported good shifts to the left, and in Figure 4A-2, where the demand for imported goods shifts to the right. At the prevailing world prices, these shifts lead to an increase in the quantity of exports and also to an increase in the quantity of imports.

The effects of a change in domestic supply can also be studied. For example, an increase in domestic

FIGURE 4A-2   The Domestic Supply and Demand for Cotton (a Typical Imported Good)

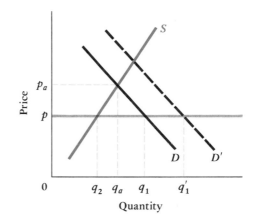

Imports are determined by the excess domestic demand for a tradable good at the world price. D and S are the domestic demand and supply schedules. In autarky, the domestic price would be p_a, and quantity q_a would be produced and consumed domestically. If the world price of cotton, p, is less than the autarky price, p_a, the country will import cotton. At the world price p, quantity supplied will be q_2, domestic consumption will be q_1, and q_2q_1 will be imported. A rise in domestic demand to D' increases the quantity imported to q_2q_1'.

wages would increase the cost of producing both the imported and the exported good. This would reduce the quantity that would be supplied domestically at each price; that is, the supply curves shift upward. The reader can verify that *ceteris paribus* this would lead to an increase in the quantity of imports and a decrease in the quantity of exports.

In a small open economy, other things being equal, shifts in domestic supply and demand lead to changes in quantities imported and exported rather than to changes in prices.

Since the economy we are studying is assumed to be small relative to the whole world, these changes in domestic demand or supply do not have a noticeable effect on world prices. The result of shifts in domestic demand or supply is a change in the *quantities* of imports and exports. The assumption that world prices are constant means that, in effect, the domestic economy can buy or sell any quantities of tradable goods it wants on world markets.

Note in conclusion that the laws of supply and demand derived in Chapter 4 still apply, but they need modification to cover the case of the horizontal demand curve faced by the tradable goods produced by a small open economy. Shifts in demand have the effects given in the text, while shifts in supply have all of their effects concentrated on quantities and none on prices.

PART EIGHT

National Income and Fiscal Policy

26

An Introduction to Macroeconomics

Inflation, unemployment, recession, and economic growth are everyday words. Governments worry about how to prevent recessions and how to increase growth. After having reduced the inflation rate in the early 1980s, governments now worry about how to keep inflation under control while continuing to fight unemployment. Firms are concerned about how inflation affects their costs and how recessions affect their sales. Households are anxious to avoid the unemployment that comes with recessions and to protect themselves against the hazards of inflation.

What Is Macroeconomics?

Each of the concerns mentioned above plays a major role in macroeconomics. As we saw in Chapter 3 (see pages 49–54), economics is customarily divided into two main branches, microeconomics and macroeconomics. Now we look further at the difference between the two approaches to the economy and in more detail at what constitutes macroeconomics.

Macroeconomics studies in broad outline the flow of income in the economy (illustrated in Figure 3-1) without dwelling on much of its interesting but sometimes confusing detail. In contrast, microeconomics deals with the behavior of individual markets, such as the market for wheat, coal, or strawberries.

The following example illustrates the difference between the two branches of economics.

A microeconomic issue. For decades automobile prices fell in relation to the prices of most other commodities. Beginning in the 1970s this trend was reversed, and automobiles became increasingly expensive relative to many other goods and services. In microeconomics we seek to understand the causes and effects of such changes in relative prices.

A macroeconomic issue. Over the decades, as well as changing relative to other prices, automobile prices have tended to follow the general trend of all prices to rise. The average of all prices is called the *price level*. Why does the price level stay relatively stable in some periods and rise rapidly in others? In macroeconomics we seek to understand the causes and effects of changes in the general price level.

Major Macroeconomic Issues

The economy proceeds in fits and starts rather than in a smooth pattern. Why did the 1930s see the greatest economic depression in recorded history, with up to a fifth of the Canadian labor force unemployed and with massive unemployment in all other major industrial countries? Why were the 25 years following World War II a period of sustained boom with only minor interruptions from modest recessions? Why did the early 1980s see the onset of the worst worldwide recession since the 1930s? What fueled the recovery of the mid-1980s?

Why did the pace of inflation during the 1970s and early 1980s reach levels never before seen in peacetime in most advanced Western nations? Has our attitude toward inflation permanently changed? In the early 1970s when inflation crept up to 4 percent, concern was so great that emergency measures were considered. By the mid-1980s the government was claiming credit for having reduced inflation to 4 percent.

Alternating bouts of inflationary boom and deflationary slump have caused many policy headaches in the past. Why were the recessions of the 1970s and early 1980s accompanied not only by their familiar companion, high unemployment, but also by an unexpected fellow traveler, rapid inflation? Will stagflation—simultaneous high unemployment and rapid inflation—return?

Both total output and output per person have risen for several decades in many countries. These long-term trends have meant rising average living standards. Does the slowdown in worldwide growth rates over the 1970s and early 1980s represent a basic change in underlying trends, or is it just a reflection of a prolonged downturn? Can governments do anything to affect growth rates?

Key Macroeconomic Variables

The price level, employment, and total output are key variables in macroeconomics. We hear about them on television; politicians give campaign speeches about them; economists theorize about them. Why are we concerned about them? How have they behaved over the past half century?

Index Numbers

Many key macro variables are expressed as index numbers, so our first task is to understand them.

Macroeconomists frequently ask such questions as "How much have prices risen this year?" or "Has the nation's output increased this year and, if so, by how much?" There is no perfectly satisfactory way to answer these questions because all prices do not move together and because one cannot add tons of steel, pieces of furniture, and gallons of gasoline to get a meaningful total. Yet these are not foolish questions. There *are* trends in prices and production, and thus there are real phenomena to describe. It is of little direct help to someone who wants to know about how prices have changed over some period of time to be given a list of changes in 4,682 individual prices.

Index numbers are statistical measures that are used to give summary answers to the inherently complex questions of the kind just suggested. Note that price indexes provide a measure of the *average* of all prices included, while quantity indexes provide a measure of the *total* of all quantities included. We refer to both the average of prices and the total of quantities as an *aggregate* measure. **Index numbers** measure the percentage change that has occurred in some aggregate over some particular time span. They point to overall tendencies or general drifts, not to detailed facts.

Calculating index numbers.   To calculate any index number, we must have a procedure to add up the individual items that are to be included. Such a procedure involves assigning "weights" to the individual items.

Why do we bother with weights? Why not simply take the average of all prices or the sum of all units of output?

A moment's reflection suggests the answer. Changes in the price of bread, for example, are much more important to the average consumer than changes in the price of, say, caviar. Similarly, producing 1,000 additional automobiles is more important for the economy than producing 1,000 additional can openers. Weights are chosen to reflect the importance of each price. Usually the weights are the quantities from some particular period, called the *base period for weighting purposes*.

Once the weights are chosen, the aggregate can be calculated for each period, usually a year. For example, it might be $600 million in 1982, $720 million in 1985, and $900 million in 1988. Next, some **base period** for comparison purposes (or **base year**) is chosen.[1] The value of the aggregate for each period can then be prorated by dividing it by the value for the base period and multiplying by 100. The resulting series is called an *index number series*; by construction the base period value in this series equals 100. In the example, if 1982 is chosen as the base year for comparison purposes, the index would be 100 in 1982, 120 in 1985, and 150 in 1988.

Index numbers are constructed by assigning weights to reflect the importance of the individual items being combined. The value of the index is set equal to 100 in the base period.

An index number always compares two or more time periods. If a particular index number for 1985 is equal to 130 with 1982 as the base year (i.e., 1982 equals 100), the index shows an increase between 1982 and 1985 of 30 percent in whatever is being measured.

Interpreting index numbers. People often treat these numbers as though they had an accuracy and significance their compilers do not claim for them, but being aware of their limitations should not lead one to neglect index numbers for the useful information they can show: average changes over time. We shall learn more about index numbers in Chapter 27.

The Price Level and Inflation

The **price level** refers to an index number computed from the prices of a broad group of goods and services. It is usually denoted by the symbol *P*. One common index number of prices is the *Consumer Price*

Index, or *CPI,* computed by Statistics Canada. We will learn more about the details of how the CPI and other price indexes are constructed in the next chapter.

The **inflation rate** is the percentage rate of increase in some price index from one period to another. In the rare event of a drop in the price level, we speak of a *deflation*. The formula for measuring the inflation rate is as follows:

$$\text{Inflation rate} = \frac{P_2 - P_1}{P_1} \times 100\%$$

where P_1 is the price level in the first period and P_2 is the price level in the second period.

If the periods being compared are not a year apart, it is common to convert the result to an *annual rate*. For example, if the CPI was 150 last month and rose by 1 percent during the month to 151.5, we might say that over the last month the price level rose at an *annual* rate of approximately 12 percent. This means that *if* the rate of increase persisted for a year, the price level would rise by 12 percent over the year. Box 26-1 (p. 554) identifies a source of confusion that sometimes arises from failing to distinguish other ways of calculating the annual inflation rate.

Inflation: The Historical Experience

Figure 26-1 shows the behavior of the price level and the inflation rate for the period 1930 to 1986. In this figure, the price level is measured by the Consumer Price Index and the inflation rate by the annual rate of change of the CPI. Several facts stand out.

First, the price level is constantly changing, although by a rate that varies considerably from year to year, as reflected by the fluctuations in the inflation rate.

Second, and more important, in only 2 out of the 57 observations did the price level fall; in all 55 other years the inflation rate was positive. The cumulative effect of this sequence of steady price increases is quite dramatic; in 1986 the price level was more than six times higher than that in 1930.

The price level has displayed a distinct upward trend in recent decades.

---

[1] Usually, but not always, the base period *for weighting purposes* and the base period *for comparison purposes* are the same. For simplicity we use the term *base period* to refer to both concepts.

FIGURE 26-1   The Canadian Price Level and Inflation Rate, 1930–1986

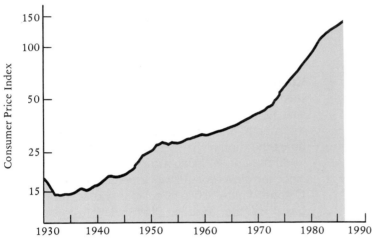

(i) Price level

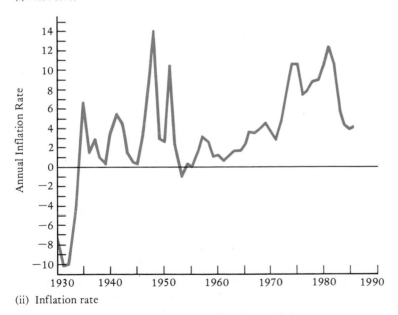

(ii) Inflation rate

(i) The overwhelming trend movement in the price level has been upward over the past 50 years. The data are for the consumer's price index from 1930 to 1986 with 1981 equal to 100. They are plotted on a semi-log scale where equal vertical distances represent equal percentage changes. Any acceleration in the rate of increase in the price level shows up as increasing steepness of the curve.

(ii) The rate of inflation has varied from −10 percent to +14 percent over the period since 1930. Prices fell dramatically during the onset of the Great Depression. They rose sharply during and after World War II and during the Korean War. Although variable, there was no discernible trend in the inflation rate from the end of the Korean War to the mid 1960s. The period starting in the mid 1960s, however, experienced a strong upward trend in the inflation rate, interrupted by short-term fluctuations. In 1983, however, the inflation rate fell to the lowest figure since the early 1970s, and it has remained in the four percent range ever since. (*Source:* M.C. Urquhart, ed., *Historical Statistics of Canada;* Department of Finance, *Economic Review.*)

Third, whereas the long-term trend stands out when one looks at the price level, the short-term fluctuations stand out when one looks at the inflation rate. The general rise in inflation from the mid-1960s through the mid-1980s is quite marked—from 1965 to 1974 inflation averaged 4.7 percent, while from 1975 to 1984 it averaged 9.1 percent! The sharp swings in the inflation rate in the late 1970s and early 1980s are even more dramatic. The increase in the inflation rate to double-digit levels in 1974 and again in 1979 are associated with major shocks to the world price of oil and foodstuffs, while the declines in inflation that followed were delayed responses to major recessions. Note that even when the *inflation rate* falls (as it did in 1982, for example), *as long as inflation remains positive, the price level rises.*

BOX 26-1

Understanding Annual Rates

New values of the index numbers for many key macroeconomic variables are announced each month. But the announcements often lead to a confusing array of interpretations of what the numbers mean for the annual rate of change of the variable in question.

Consider a hypothetical example. The release of the latest monthly figure for a particular price index (PI) for some country, by that country's Bureau of Statistics, elicits the following three responses: "Inflation receding," reads a newspaper headline; "Inflation continues to rise," reports a TV newscaster; "Inflation unchanged," says the official releasing the statistic.

How can this be when all three commentators are talking about the same announcement? The different interpretations arise from different ways of converting monthly statistics into an annual rate of change. (The problem can arise with any index number.)

To understand what is involved, consider the hypothetical values for the PI set out in the table. According to the table, at the end of 1984 the PI (100.0) exceeded its average for the year (95.2). At the end of 1985 it was the same (100.0) as at the start of the year and equal to its average for the year; assume that it was in fact constant and equal to 100 for *each* month of 1985. In 1986 prices started to rise again.

Date	PI	Date	PI
December 1984	100.0	October 1986	106.8
1984 average	95.2	November 1986	108.9
		December 1986	110.0
December 1985	100.0	1986 average	105.0
1985 average	100.0		

Annual averages are the sum of the 12 monthly figures for the calendar year divided by 12.

Comparing annual averages. In stating that the inflation rate was unchanged, the official was comparing annual averages. Comparing the 1984 average PI (95.2) and the 1985 average (100.0) gave a change of approximately 5 percent, as did comparing the 1985 average (100.0) with the 1986 average (105.0). Thus, concludes the official, the annual inflation rate had stayed constant at 5 percent over the two years.

Comparing this month with the same month last year. Using this procedure, the annual inflation rate in December 1986 is 10 percent; in December 1986 the PI is 10 percent higher than it was in December 1985. In November 1986 the annual inflation rate was only 9 percent, since the PI was 9 percent higher than in November 1985. Using this measure the annual inflation rate increased from 9 percent to 10 percent during the month. This procedure could lie behind the television news report that inflation is rising.

Comparing this month with last month. Using this method, the annual inflation rate in December 1986 was 12 percent; the PI had risen by 1 percent over the month, and the annual rate is approximately 12 times the monthly percentage change. In November 1986 the annual inflation rate had been 24 percent, since the November PI was 2 percent higher than the October figure. This calculation would provide the basis for the headline that inflation is receding.

Which Measure Is Best?

Properly understood, all three measures give useful and complementary information.

Comparing annual averages is the least erratic. But because it focuses almost entirely on underlying trends, it is not sensitive to current changes. In our example it misses the stability in prices that prevailed throughout 1985 and the fairly sharp upturn in prices that was apparent in 1986.

Comparing this month with the same month last year is more sensitive to current events. However, it gives a lot of weight to particular events in the most recent month, events that often have little to do with the underlying trend of prices.

Comparing this month with last month is the most erratic measure. The timing of major price changes at or near the end of the month will have a substantial accidental effect on the measure. For some purposes this sensitivity may be desirable, but for understanding the underlying trend in inflation, it is misleading.

The three measures can be used selectively to support almost any position. But people who understand the meaning of each measure need not be fooled by such selective presentation of the data. Figures lie only to those uninformed about what a measure does and does not say.

Why Inflation Is a Matter of Concern

Changes in the price level are associated with changes in the **purchasing power of money** or **value of money**. Both terms refer to the amount of goods and services that can be purchased with a given amount of money. The purchasing power of money is negatively related to the price level. (For example, if the price level doubles, a dollar will buy only half as much.) Thus inflation, which is a rise in the general level of all prices, reduces the purchasing power of money. Conversely, the purchasing power of money rises whenever the price level falls.

Unanticipated inflation.   Any given rate of inflation tends to cause more harm when it is unforeseen than when it is foreseen. Contracts freely entered into when the inflation rate is expected to remain constant will mean hardships for some and windfall gains for others if the inflation rate changes unexpectedly.

For example, consider a wage contract that specifies wage increases of 3 percent. If both employers and workers expect the price level to remain constant, then they expect that the purchasing power of wages paid will rise by 3 percent as a result of the new contract. But if the price level unexpectedly rises by 10 percent over the course of the wage contract, the workers' wages will be able to buy less than they would have before the wage increase was negotiated. A 3 percent increase in money wages combined with a 10 percent increase in prices means a reduction in the purchasing power of wages of about 7 percent.

Inflation also has different effects on borrowers and lenders. Suppose that when the price level is expected to be constant, a bank lends a customer $100 in return for a promise to repay $105 a year hence. If the price level rises during the year, the purchasing power of the $105 repaid will be less than it was expected to be; hence the borrower benefits and the lender suffers relative to their expectations.

One of the most serious effects of inflation is what it does to anyone living on a fixed money income. If a retirement pension specifies an income as so many dollars per year, a rise in the price level lowers the purchasing power of that income. For example, anyone who retired on a fixed money income in 1970 found the purchasing power of that income reduced to about one fourth of its original value by 1985. This means that the retiree could buy in 1985 only one fourth what could be bought in 1970. For such people, rapid inflation causes a great loss of purchasing power.

Some effects of inflation can be avoided by indexing. **Indexing** links the payments made under the terms of a contract to changes in the price level. For example, a retirement pension might specify that it will pay the beneficiary $15,000 per year starting in 1990 and that the amount paid will increase each year in proportion to the increase in some specified index of the price level. Thus if the price index rises by 10 percent between 1990 and 1991, the pension payable in 1991 would rise by 10 percent, to $16,500.

Anticipated inflation.   Indexing provides an automatic correction that does not require anticipating future changes in the price level. However, even without formal indexing, it is possible to allow for the effects of inflation if the rise in the price level is anticipated and contracts take account of the expected rise.

Wage and price contracts are major examples. If, say, inflation of 10 percent is expected over the next year, a money wage that rises by 10 percent over that period will keep the expected purchasing power of wages at a constant level. A money wage that increases by 13 percent will provide a 3 percent increase in the expected purchasing power of wages—10 percent to preserve purchasing power in the face of the expected rise in prices and 3 percent to increase the real purchasing power of the wages.

Labor Force Variables

Employment denotes the number of adult workers (defined in Canada as workers aged 15 and older, including those in the military) who hold jobs. **Unemployment** denotes the number of adult workers who are not employed and are actively searching for a job. The **labor force** is the total number of employed and unemployed. The **unemployment rate**, usually represented by the symbol U, is unemployment expressed as a percentage of the labor force:

$$U = \frac{\text{unemployed}}{\text{labor force}} \times 100\%$$

Unemployment: The Historical Experience

Figure 26-2(i) shows the trends in the labor force, employment, and unemployment since 1930. Despite booms and slumps in the economy, the main trend has clearly been growth in employment that roughly matches growth in the labor force. The growth in both reflects growth in the total population, although the labor force and employment have recently grown faster than the total population. This fact reflects the steadily increasing participation of youths and women in the labor force.

Although the long-term growth trend dominates the employment figures, some unemployment is always present. Figure 26-2(ii) shows that the short-term fluctuations in the unemployment rate have been quite marked. The unemployment rate has been as low as 1.4 percent in 1944 and as high as 19.3 percent in 1933; in the period since 1955 the unemployment rate fell as low as 3.4 percent in 1956 and rose as high as 12.6 percent in 1983.

The high unemployment rate of the Great Depression in the early 1930s tends to dwarf the fluctuations in unemployment that have occurred since then. This is misleading since, as we shall see, the fluctuations in unemployment in recent decades have been neither minor nor unimportant.

Unemployment can rise not only when employment falls but also when the labor force rises. In recent decades the number of people entering the labor force has exceeded the number leaving it. The resulting rise in the labor force has meant that unemployment has sometimes grown even in periods when employment was also growing.

Consideration of employment and unemployment suggests another concept, that of *full employment*. Full employment does not mean zero unemployment. There is a constant turnover of individuals in given jobs and a constant change in job opportunities. New members enter the work force, some people quit their jobs, and others are fired. It may take some time for these people to find jobs. So at any time there is unemployment due to the normal turnover of labor that exists in any economy. Such unemployment is called **frictional unemployment**.

Full employment is said to occur when all existing unemployment is frictional. When the economy is at less than full employment, other types of unemployment, including cyclical (or deficient-de-

mand) unemployment and real-wage unemployment, are present in addition to frictional unemployment. We shall study these in more detail in Chapter 37.[2]

The unemployment rate that occurs when the economy is at full employment is often called the **natural rate of unemployment**. Estimates of the natural rate of unemployment are difficult to obtain and are often a source of disagreement among economists. Nevertheless, such estimates are a useful benchmark against which to gauge the current performance of the economy, as measured by the actual unemployment rate. Estimates indicate that the natural rate rose throughout the 1970s from around 5.5 percent to a high of around 7.5 percent in the late 1970s and has now stabilized or may even be declining. (We shall discuss the reasons for these changes in Chapter 37.)

Why Unemployment Is a Matter of Concern

The social and political significance of the unemployment rate is enormous. The government is blamed when it is high and takes credit when it is low. Few macroeconomic policies are planned without some consideration of how they affect the unemployment rate. No other summary statistic, with the possible exception of the inflation rate, carries as much weight in setting macroeconomic policy as does the unemployment rate.

Unemployment causes economic waste and human suffering. The economic waste is obvious. Human effort is the least durable of economic commodities. If a fully employed economy with a constant labor force has 20 million people willing to work in 1988, their services must either be used in 1988 or wasted. When the services of only 18 million are used because 10 percent of the labor force is unemployed, the potential output of 2 million workers is lost forever. In an economy where there is not enough output to meet everyone's needs, any waste of potential output seems undesirable, and large wastes seem tragic.

The human cost of unemployment is also obvious. Severe hardship and misery can be caused by

---

[2] In that chapter we shall also distinguish a particular type of frictional unemployment called structural unemployment.

FIGURE 26-2   Canadian Labor Force, Employment and Unemployment, 1930–1986

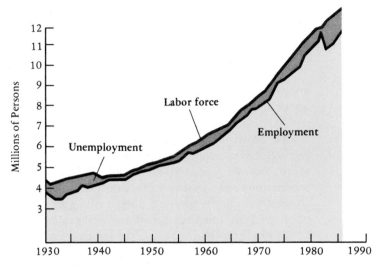

(i) Labor force, employment, and unemployment

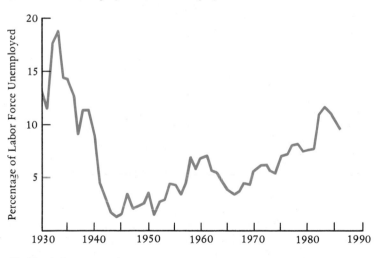

(ii) Unemployment rate

(i) The labor force and employment have grown since the 1930s with only a few interruptions. The size of the Canadian labor force has more than doubled since 1930, and so has the number of the employed. The fall in the labor force in the early 1940s was in the civilian labor force. The missing workers were in the military. Unemployment, the gap between the labor force and employment, has fluctuated. It reached a peak of 800,000 in 1933 and did not reach that level again until 1977. In 1983 it reached 1½ million, although as we see in (ii), as a fraction of the labor force this is smaller than the 1933 figure.

(ii) The unemployment rate responds to the cyclical behavior of the economy. Booms are associated with low unemployment, slumps with high unemployment. The Great Depression of the 1930s produced record unemployment rates for an entire decade. During World War II unemployment rates fell to very low levels. Since 1945, however, the unemployment rate has demonstrated a gradual upward trend. The recession of the early 1980s produced unemployment rates second only to those of the 1930s; these rates were extremely high by the standards of the post-World War II behavior of the Canadian economy. Over the period 1983–1986 the rate fell slowly but steadily, reaching 9.4 percent at the end of 1986. (*Source:* M.C. Urquhart, ed., *Historical Statistics of Canada*; Department of Finance, *Economic Review.*)

prolonged periods of unemployment. A person's spirit can be broken by a long period of wanting work but being unable to find it. Crime, divorce, and general social unrest usually rise with unemployment.

In the not so distant past, only private charity or help from friends and relatives stood between the unemployed and starvation. Today welfare and unemployment insurance have softened those effects. However, when an economic slump is deep and prolonged, as in the mid-1970s and again in the early 1980s, people begin to exhaust their unemployment insurance and must fall back on savings, welfare, or charity. In the early 1980s many people sank below the poverty level for the first time in their lives. They did so because they had used up their unemployment insurance, but were unable to find jobs because of a persistently high unemployment level.

Output and Income Variables

The value of a nation's total production of goods and services is called its *national product*. Since all the value that is produced must ultimately belong to someone in the form of a claim on that value, the national product is equal to the total income claims generated by the production of goods and services. Hence when we study *national product*, we are also studying *national income*.

There are several related measures of the nation's total output and total income. Their various definitions and calculations, and the relationships among them, are discussed in detail in the next chapter. In this chapter we use the generic term **national income** to refer to both the value of total output and the value of the income generated by the production of that output.

Aggregating Total Output

To measure total output, quantities of a variety of goods must somehow be added up, or *aggregated*. Just as there is a problem in obtaining an "average" of the variety of prices in the economy, so is there a problem in obtaining a measure of the total output of the wide variety of goods and services produced in the economy.

Consider this problem in terms of a single firm.

If that firm produces only a single, well-defined commodity, say, loaves of French bread, then to measure its total output all we need do is sum the number of loaves baked during the period under consideration. But if it also produces muffins, fancy pastries, cakes, and doughnuts, we have to find a way of adding its output of these different products.

The same problem arises when we try to add the outputs of literally hundreds of thousands of different goods and services to measure the nation's total output.

We do this by summing *values* of the different products. We cannot add tons of steel to loaves of bread, but we can add the money value of steel production to the money value of bread production. By multiplying the physical output of a good by its price per unit and then summing this value for all goods produced in the nation, we can find the quantity of total output *measured in dollars*.

Real and Nominal Values

The total just described gives the *money value* of national output, often called **nominal national income**. When nominal national income changes, it is important to know to what extent the change is due to a change in prices and to what extent it is due to a change in quantities produced. To answer this question we calculate **real national income**, a measure of total output in which the value of individual outputs is measured not at current prices but at the prices that prevailed in some base period chosen for this purpose.[3] Real national income is denoted by the symbol Y.

Real national income tells us the value of current output measured at base period prices, that is, the sum of the quantities valued at prices prevailing in the base period. Comparing the real national income for different years provides a measure of the change in real output that has occurred during the interval between the years.

Since prices are held constant in calculating it, real national income changes only when output quantities change.

[3] Nominal national income is often referred to as *money* national income or *current dollar* national income. Real national income is often called *constant dollar* national income.

Since our interest is almost exclusively with the real output of goods and services, we shall take the term *national income* (and output) to refer to *real national income* unless otherwise specified. (For an example of this important distinction, see Box 27-3 on page 572.)

National Income: The Historical Experience

In order to look at the actual experience of national income, in this section we look at one of the most commonly used measures, called *gross domestic product*, or GDP.[4] The details of its calculation are discussed in Chapter 27. GDP can be measured in either real or nominal terms; in this section we focus on real GDP.

Part (i) of Figure 26-3 shows real GDP produced by the Canadian economy since 1930; part (ii) shows the annual percentage rate of growth of real GDP for the same period. The series in part (i) shows two kinds of movement. The major one is a trend increase that resulted in a sevenfold increase of real output in the half century from 1932 to 1982. Since the trend has generally been upward in the modern era, it is referred to as *economic growth*.

Long-term growth in real national income is reflected in the trend increase in real GDP.

A second feature of the real GDP series is the short-term fluctuations around the trend, often described as the cyclical behavior of the economy. Overall growth so dominates the real GDP series that this cyclical behavior is hardly visible in part (i) of Figure 26-3. However, as can be seen in part (ii), cyclical fluctuations in real GDP have not been insignificant.

The cyclical behavior of real national income is reflected in the annual fluctuations in the growth rate of real GDP.

Why National Income Is a Matter of Concern

Short-run fluctuations in national income reflect the ebbs and flows of economic activity referred to as the *business cycle*. In periods of high activity, often called *booms* or *expansions*, real GDP and employment are high and unemployment is low. In periods of low activity, called *slumps* or *contractions*, real GDP and employment are low and unemployment is correspondingly high. Policymakers care about short-term fluctuations in national income because slumps bring unwanted unemployment and output foregone, and booms may create strong inflationary pressures.

The long-run trend in real national income is also important. Not only has national income grown, but real income per person (also called real income per capita) has also grown. Indeed, it has more than tripled in the last 60 years. When income per person grows, each generation can expect, on average, to be substantially better off than preceding ones. For example, if real income per capita grows at the relatively modest rate of 1.5 percent per year, the average person's lifetime income expectancy will be *twice* that of his or her grandparents. (Of course, although on average people are better off, it does not follow that every individual will in fact be better off.)

Potential Income and the Output Gap

Actual national income is what the economy does in fact produce. We now introduce the important additional concept of **potential national income**, or just **potential income**, also called *full-employment national income*.[5]

---

[4] Until very recently, national income in Canada was typically discussed in terms of another measure, gross *national* product (GNP). In 1986, in order to follow international convention more closely and thus facilitate international comparisions, Statistics Canada began reporting national income in terms of gross *domestic* product (GDP). As we will see in the next chapter, the two measures are closely related, and for most purposes it does not really matter which measure is used.

[5] The words *real* and *actual* have similar meanings in everyday usage, but they are used quite differently in this context of describing national income. *Real* national income is distinguished from *nominal* national income, while *actual* national income is distinguished from *potential* national income. The latter both refer to real measures, so the full descriptions are actual real national income and potential real national income.

FIGURE 26-3   Canadian Real National Income and Growth Rate, 1930–1986

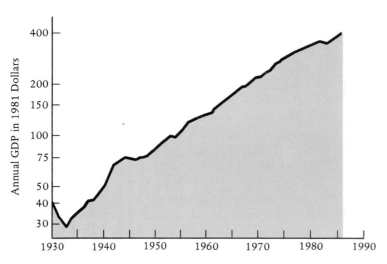

(i) Annual GNP/GDP in constant (1981) dollars

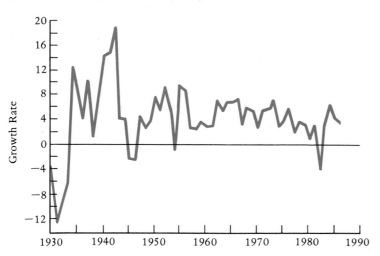

(ii) Annual rate of growth of GNP/GDP in constant (1981) dollars

(i) Real national income, which measures the total production of goods and services produced in the economy over the period of a year, has grown steadily since 1930, with only a few interruptions. In (i) we see the long-term growth of the economy reflected in the upward trend of real national income. Shorter-term fluctuations are obscured by this trend in (i) but are highlighted in (ii).

(ii) Real growth in the economy, as measured by the annual rate of change of real national income, has fluctuated considerably but has been mostly positive. In (ii) the short-term fluctuations are readily apparent, but the long-term upward trend still shows up because the majority of observations are positive.

(Data prior to 1947 are based on GNP; data for 1947–1986 are based on GDP, which is now the standard measure of real national income; see footnote 4 on page 559.) *Source:* M.C. Urquhart, ed., *Historical Statistics of Canada;* Department of Finance, *Economic Review.*

Potential national income is what the economy would produce if its productive resources were fully employed at their normal intensity of use.

This would mean, in terms of labor force variables, that any unemployment of labor is frictional and thus that the unemployment rate is equal to the natural rate of unemployment. It would also mean that the nation's factories and other productive equipment are being used at their normal capacity levels.

Potential national income is represented by the symbol Y^*; it refers to potential *real* income.

The Output Gap

If we subtract actual national income from potential income ($Y^* - Y$), we obtain a measure called the **output gap**.[6] It is the difference between what could have been produced at the potential or full-employment level and what is actually produced, as measured by GDP.

When the gap is positive, that is, when potential income is greater than actual real national income, the output gap is the market value of goods and services that *could have been* produced if the economy's resources had been fully employed but that *actually* went unproduced. This is sometimes referred to as the *deadweight loss of unemployment*.

Slumps in business activity are associated with large positive output gaps, booms with small ones. In a major boom the gap may even become negative, indicating that actual national income exceeds the economy's potential national income. A negative output gap can arise because potential income is defined for a normal rate of utilization of factors of production, and there are many ways in which these normal rates can be exceeded temporarily. Labor may work longer hours than normal; factories may operate an extra shift or not close for routine repairs and maintenance. Although these expedients are only temporary, they are effective in the short run.

Measuring potential national income is not straightforward since it cannot be observed directly. The problem is not only one of observation and measurement but also one of establishing acceptable definitions for such concepts as "normal level of utilization" and "full-employment capacity." Because Y^* is hard to measure, the output gap is correspondingly hard to measure.[7]

Potential Income and the Output Gap: The Historical Experience

Figure 26-4 shows the output gap for the Canadian economy for the years 1954–1986. Growth in the economy's productive capacity means that potential income has risen steadily. Actual real national income has roughly kept pace with potential, but has fluctuated around it. The difference between the two, the output gap, thus reflects fluctuations of real national income around a rising trend.

Fluctuations in economic activity are apparent from fluctuations in the size of the output gap. The deadweight loss from unemployment over any time span is indicated by the overall size of the gap over that span. It is shown in the figure by the shaded area between the curve and the horizontal line, which represents the level at which actual equals potential output.

Why Potential Income and the Output Gap Are Matters of Concern

Potential national income measures the economy's capacity to produce goods and services and hence its capacity to generate income for its people. Because potential income is measured at normal utilization rates of the economy's factors of production, changes in it do not reflect short-term cyclical fluctuations but rather the long-term trend in potential level of output and income. It is this long-term trend that is important for changes in living standards from generation to generation. The low living standards at

---

[6] Unfortunately economics, in common with most living and changing subjects, has no agreed, standard set of terms. In countries where the GNP is the standard measure of output, this gap is often called the GNP gap. Where GDP is the standard measure, it could be called the GDP gap. *Output gap* is more general and is a common international term, so we adopt it here.

[7] Just as the unemployment rate is not zero when the economy is at full employment, measured capacity utilization is not 100 percent. In fact, manufacturing capacity utilization has exceeded 90 percent only once since 1956, and its normal value is in the 80 to 85 percent range.

FIGURE 26-4   The Output Gap, 1954–1986

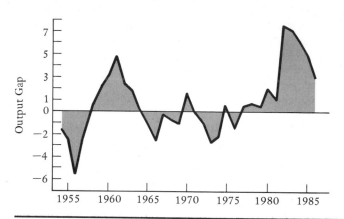

The output gap measures the difference between the economy's potential output and its
actual output; it is expressed here as a percentage of potential output. The cyclical behavior of
the economy is clearly apparent from the behavior
of the output gap from 1954 to 1983. Slumps in
economic activity cause large gaps, booms reduce
the gap. The recession of 1982–1983 and the sustained recovery over the period 1983–1986 are both
evident in the figure. The shaded area above the
zero line represents the deadweight loss from unemployment. (*Source*: Pre 1983, from the Department of Finance, *Economic Review*; post 1983, from
authors' calculations.)

the start of the Industrial Revolution are no longer
with us, primarily because economic growth has resulted in more and more output for less and less
work over the past century.

The output gap is important because it reflects
the actual performance of the economy relative to its
potential. A large output gap means that actual national income falls short of potential, and hence the
unemployment rate will be high. It is therefore in-
dicative of economic waste and human suffering as
540 of failure to use the economy's resources (including its human resources) at their normal intensity
of use.

A negative output gap, indicating that actual national income exceeds potential, also imposes serious
costs. Short-run policies that involve utilizing resources at above normal levels, in order to raise actual output temporarily, create inflationary pressures
in the economy. As we saw earlier, inflation can
impose severe costs on the economy.

The Relation Between Output and Employment

Output and employment (and therefore unemployment) are closely related. If more is to be produced,
either more workers must be used in production or
existing workers must produce more. The first
change means a rise in employment; the second

means a rise in output per person employed, which
is called a rise in **productivity**. Increases in productivity are a major source of economic growth. (Productivity was discussed in Chapter 11 and will be
discussed again in Chapter 38.)

Changes in productivity and in the labor force
dominate the long-term trend of output and employment. But productivity and the labor force usually change slowly. As we study the main elements
of macroeconomic theory over the next few chapters, we will treat both the labor force and productivity as constant. This not only greatly simplifies
our discussion, but it is also a reasonable approximation of reality for purposes of analyzing the short-
term behavior of the Canadian economy. In later
chapters we study productivity changes.

A Preview

Why are the price level, national income, and employment what they are today? What causes them to
change? These are some of the questions that we seek
to answer in macroeconomics.

To answer them, it is useful to make a number
of assumptions that serve to simplify the analysis and
can be dropped later once we have mastered the
simple case. We have just encountered one such assumption: that productivity and the labor force are
constant in the short run, meaning that any increase

in national income will be accompanied by an increase in employment and a decrease in unemployment. Hence we do not need separate theories to explain employment and unemployment—the theory of national income that we develop over the next few chapters will also serve to explain these variables. Hence we focus on explaining national income and the price level.[8]

As we have already seen in this chapter, the time series describing national income and the price level have two important properties. Both series exhibit long-term trends and short-term fluctuations around those trends. The analysis of the next few chapters is to be understood as establishing how the price level, and national income, will behave *relative to trend*. A fluctuation that takes the price level, or national income, above its long-term trend will be indicated by an increase in its value, while a fluctuation that takes the price level, or national income, below its trend will be indicated by a decrease in its value.

For simplicity, in the next few chapters we take these trend values to be constant.[9] When the trend is not constant, the results must be interpreted accordingly. For example, a force that causes national income to fall by 2 percent in the short term when its long-term trend is constant will cause it to increase by 1 percent when its long-term trend is growth at 3 percent per year. Similarly, a force that causes the price level to fall by 3 percent in the short term when the long-term trend is constant will cause the price level to rise by 2 percent when its long-term trend is inflation at 5 percent per year.

---

[8] In fact, we proceed sequentially by first treating the price level as given and only explaining national income, then explaining both.

[9] Later in the book we study long-term trends in inflation and growth in some detail.

Summary

1. Macroeconomics examines the behavior of such broad aggregates and averages as the price level, national income, potential national income, the output gap, employment, and unemployment.

2. Index numbers are summary measures that give the average percentage change in a set of related items between a base year and another given year.

3. The price level has displayed a continual upward trend since 1930. The inflation rate measures the rate of change of the price level. Although it fluctuates considerably, the inflation rate has been consistently positive. Inflation imposes serious costs on the economy.

4. The unemployment rate is the number of adult workers who are not employed and are actively searching for a job, expressed as a percentage of the labor force. The labor force and employment have both grown steadily for the past half century. The unemployment rate fluctuates considerably from year to year. Unemployment imposes serious costs in the form of economic waste and human suffering.

5. The value of total production of goods and services is called national product. Since production of output generates income in the form of claims on that output, it is also common to talk of national income. The most commonly used measure of Canadian national income is gross domestic product (GDP). Nominal national income

evaluates output in current prices. Real national income evaluates output in base period prices. Changes in real national income reflect changes in quantities of output produced.

6. Potential real national income measures the capacity of the economy to produce goods and services when factors of production are employed at their normal intensity of use. The output gap is the difference between potential and actual real national income.

7. The dominant theme of the economy is the growth of real output and employment. A secondary theme involves cyclical factors represented by fluctuations in output and unemployment around their trend values. To study these fluctuations, we focus on the unemployment rate and the output gap.

Topics for Review

The price level and rate of inflation
Employment, unemployment, and labor force
The unemployment rate
Real and nominal national income
Real national income and economic growth
Potential and actual national income and the output gap

Discussion Questions

1. Classify as microeconomic or macroeconomic (or both) the issues raised in the following newspaper headlines.
   a. "Lettuce crop spoils as strike hits B.C. lettuce producers."
   b. "Analysts fear rekindling of inflation as economy recovers toward full employment."
   c. "Index of industrial production falls by 4 points."
   d. "Price of bus rides soars in Centerville as city council withdraws transport subsidy."
   e. "A fall in the unemployment rate signals the beginning of the end of the recession in the Edmonton area."
   f. "Silicon chip technology brings falling prices and growing sales of microcomputers."
   g. "Rising costs of imported raw materials cause most Canadian manufacturers to raise prices."

2. When GDP figures for the fourth quarter of 1986 were released, one headline read "Growth Falls to 0.2%" while another read "Economy Continues to Grow at Steady 3.1%." How could both be right? Which do you think is the most accurate description of what really happened?

3. Between 1979 and 1986, employment in Canada grew by over 10 percent, from 10.4 million to 11.6 million. However, over that same period unemployment grew from 836 thousand to 1.2 million, and the unemployment rate rose from 7.4 percent to 9.6 percent. How do you reconcile these apparently conflicting statistics? Which do you think gives the most accurate description of developments in the economy?

4. During the economic recovery from 1983 through 1986, GDP at current prices grew at an average rate of 8.3 percent per year. To what extent does this imply an improvement in the economic circumstances of the average Canadian? What would we need to know in order to distinguish the effects on (a) a bank president, (b) an autoworker in Oshawa who was unemployed in 1982, (c) a pensioner living in retirement in Victoria, B.C., and (d) an oil-field rigger living in Alberta?

5. Why is unemployment not as serious a matter now as it was at the beginning of this century?

6. If you thought the inflation rate was going to be 10 percent next year, why would most people be unwilling to lend money at 5 percent interest? Say 5 percent was all they could get and they had money they didn't want to spend for a year. Would they do better just to hold the money? What could they do that would be better than lending your money at 5 percent?

27

Measuring Macroeconomic Variables

In Chapter 26 a number of key macroeconomic variables were introduced. Before we delve into the analysis of macroeconomic events, it will be helpful to look in some detail at the measurement and interpretation of these variables. This will give a clearer notion of the concepts. It will also provide some warning about how to avoid misusing or misinterpreting measures that play a prominent role in everyday discussion of the economy.

We focus on two key variables, the price level and real national income.[1] In the first section we study the construction of price indexes and measures of real and nominal national income. In the second section we study the system of National Income Accounts, which provides the framework for gathering and organizing data on the production of output and the generation of income in the economy.

Calculating Price Indexes and Measures of Aggregate Output

We saw in Chapter 26 that in order to measure aggregate variables, we must assign weights to the individual components. We now examine how this is done when calculating price indexes and measures of total output.

The Price Level

The price level refers to an index number computed using some broad group of prices in the economy. A **price index** measures the price level at a *given period* relative to the *base period*. Several issues are involved in the construction of price indexes.

First, what group of prices should be used? This depends on the index. The **Consumer Price Index (CPI)** covers prices of commodities commonly bought by households. Changes in the value of the CPI are meant to measure changes in the typical household's "cost of living." Other price indexes, some of which we will encounter later in this chapter, incorporate prices of different groups of commodities.

[1] The measurement of labor force variables is relatively straightforward, and further details are deferred until our treatment of unemployment in Chapter 37. For present purposes it is sufficient to recall from Chapter 26 that real national income and employment tend to be positively related, while real national income and unemployment tend to be negatively related.

Second, what kind of average should be used? If all prices always changed in the same proportion, this would not matter. A 10 percent rise in each and every price would mean a 10 percent rise in the price level no matter how the index was constructed. But what if, as is always the case, different prices change in different proportions? Now it matters how much importance we give to each price change.

In calculating any price index, statisticians weight each price according to its importance. Let us see how this is done for the CPI. Statistics Canada periodically surveys a group of households to discover how they spend their incomes. The average bundle of goods bought is determined and the quantities of the particular goods in this bundle become the weights attached to the respective prices when calculating the CPI. As a result, the CPI weights rather heavily the prices of commodities on which consumers spend a lot of their income and weights rather lightly the prices of commodities on which consumers spend only a little.

The average *change* in the price level is then calculated by comparing the cost of purchasing the typical bundle of commodities at the prices that prevailed in the base year with the cost of purchasing the same bundle of commodities at the prices pre-vailing in the given year. The procedure is illustrated in Table 27-1.

A price index for a given year gives the ratio of the cost of purchasing a bundle of commodities in that year to the cost of purchasing the *same* bundle in the base year, multiplied by 100. [33]

At the beginning of 1987 the CPI was approximately 136 (1981 = 100). This means that in 1987 it cost 1.36 times as much to buy the representative bundle of goods as it did in the base year of 1981.

A price index is meant to reflect the broad trend in prices rather than the details. This means that although the information it gives may be extremely valuable, it must be interpreted with care. Some of the potential difficulties are discussed in Box 27-1.

Measuring Aggregate Output

We noted in Chapter 26 that there are several related measures of the nation's total output and total income. We now examine a measure obtained by aggregating the contributions to total output made by all producers in the economy. This is called the *output approach,* and the measure arrived at using it, **gross**

TABLE 27-1   The Calculation of a Consumer Price Index Covering Three Commodities

Commodity	Quantity in fixed bundle	Base year 1982		Given year 1987	
		Price in 1982	Value in 1982	Price in 1987	Value in 1987
A	500 units	$1.00	$ 500	$2.00	$1,000
B	200 units	5.00	1,000	7.00	1,400
C	50 units	2.00	100	9.60	480
			1,600		2,880

$$\text{Index value 1982} = \frac{1,600}{1,600} \times 100 = 100$$

$$\text{Index value 1987} = \frac{2,880}{1,600} \times 100 = 180$$

A price index shows the ratio of the costs of purchasing a fixed bundle of goods between two years (multiplied by 100). The cost of purchasing the fixed bundle is calculated at the prices prevailing in each year. The index for year 1987 is the cost of purchasing that bundle in 1987 expressed as a percentage of the cost of purchasing the same bundle in the base year (1982 in this example). The price index is thus always 100 in the base year. The index of 180 means that prices have risen on average by 80 percent between the base year and the year in question. This index weights price changes by their *importance* in the average household's budget in the base year.

BOX 27-1

Problems in Interpreting the Consumer Price Index

First, the weights in the index refer to an average bundle of goods. This average, though typical of what is consumed in the nation, will not be typical of what each household consumes. The rich, the poor, the young, the old, the single, the married, the urban, and the rural household will typically consume different bundles. An increase in air fares, for example, will raise the cost of living of a middle income traveler, while leaving that of a poor stay-at-home unaffected. In the example in Table 27-1, the cost of living would have risen by 100 percent, 40 percent, and 380 percent, respectively, for three different families, one of whom consumed only commodity A, one only commodity B, and one only commodity C. The index in the table shows, however, that the cost of living went up by 80 percent for a family that consumed all three goods in the relative quantities indicated.

The more an individual household's consumption pattern conforms to that of the typical pattern used to weight prices in the price index, the better the price index will reflect the average change in prices relevant to that household.

To assess the importance of this problem, separate indexes are calculated to reflect the different consumption patterns of different groups. For example, separate price indexes are calculated for a number of major Canadian cities.

Second, households usually alter their consumption patterns in response to price changes. A price index that shows changes in the cost of purchasing a *fixed* bundle of goods does not allow for this. For example, a typical cost of living index for middle income families at the turn of the century would have given heavy weight to the cost of maids and laundresses. A doubling of servants' wages in 1900 would have significantly increased the middle-class cost of living. Today it would have little effect, for the rising cost of labor has long since caused middle income families to cease to employ full-time servants. A

household that has dispensed with a commodity altogether finds its cost of living unaffected by any increase in the price of that commodity, no matter how large.

A fixed-weight price index tends to overstate cost of living changes because it does not allow for changes in consumption patterns that shift expenditure away from commodities whose prices rise most and toward those whose prices rise least.

Third, as time passes, new commodities enter the typical consumption bundle and old ones leave. A cost of living index in 1890 would have had a large item for horse-drawn carriages but no allowance at all for automobiles and gasoline.

A fixed-weight index makes no allowance for the increased importance of new products or the declining importance of old in the typical household's consumption bundle.

The longer the period of time that passes, the less some fixed consumption bundle will be typical of current consumption patterns. For this reason Statistics Canada makes a new survey of household expenditure patterns every 15 or 20 years and revises the weights. The base period is then usually changed to be near the year in which the new set of commodity weights was calculated. At the end of 1983, using 1971 weights, the CPI stood at 283.4 (1971 = 100). This meant that the cost of purchasing the bundle of goods bought by a typical household in 1971 had risen 183 percent in the intervening 13 years. (The percentage change in the cost of purchasing the bundle since the base year is the level of the index minus 100.) Thirteen years is a long time for fixed weights to be used, and in 1986 Statistics Canada completed estimating a new set of weights in order to shift the base year for the CPI to 1981.

domestic product (GDP), is the one we used in our historical discussion in Chapter 26.

When we set out to measure GDP, we wish to measure the total output of all producers in the economy. It might appear at first that this could be done simply by adding up the market value of the outputs of every producer. A problem arises, however, because production occurs in stages: One firm may produce output that is used as inputs by other firms, and these other firms in turn may produce output that is used as inputs by yet other firms.

Stages of production, and the consequent inter-firm sales of intermediate products, make it difficult to measure national income from production data. If we merely added up the market values of all outputs of all firms, we would obtain a total greatly in excess of the value of output actually available. Consider as an example the production of bread. If we added the total value of the sales of the wheat farmer, the flour mill, and the baker, we would be counting the value of the wheat three times, the value of the milled flour twice, and the value of the bread once. The error that arises in estimating final output by adding all sales of all firms is called **double counting.** (*Multiple counting* would be a better term, since if we add up the values of all sales, the same output is counted every time it is sold from one firm to another.)

The problem of double counting makes important the distinction between intermediate and final goods. **Intermediate goods** are outputs of some producers that are in turn inputs for other producers in the chain of production. **Final goods** are goods that are not, in the period of time under consideration, used as inputs by other firms. They are goods that are produced for final demand, to be sold—that is, for consumption, for investment (including inventory accumulation), for government, or for export.

Value added.   If the sales of firms could be readily disaggregated into sales for final use and sales for further processing by other firms, measuring GDP would still be straightforward. GDP would equal the value of all *final goods* produced by firms, and all intermediate goods would be excluded. However, when the Steel Company of Canada sells steel to the Ford Motor Company, it does not necessarily know whether the steel is for final use (say, construction of

a new warehouse) or whether it is to be used as an intermediate good in the production of automobiles.[2] The problem of double counting must therefore be resolved in some other manner.

To avoid double counting, statisticians use the important concept of **value added.** Each firm's value added is the value of its output minus the value of the inputs that it purchases from other firms (and which in turn were the outputs of those other firms). Thus a steel mill's value added is the value of its output minus the value of the ore it buys from the mining company, the value of the electricity and fuel oil it uses, and the values of all other inputs that it buys from other firms. A bakery's value added is the value of the baking products it produces minus the value of the flour and other inputs that it buys from other firms.

The concept of value added is further illustrated in Box 27-2, where it is shown that calculating the value of total output of final goods can be achieved by summing all values added.

Gross Domestic Product

Table 27-2 (p. 571) shows the composition of Canadian GDP by industry for 1986. The table also introduces a distinction between GDP valued at factor cost and GDP valued at market prices. The two differ because of indirect taxes—taxes on the production and sale of goods and services—and subsidies.

Suppose that a firm's value added as measured by the market value of its sales less the market value of its purchases of intermediate goods is $10, and that $1 of this represents excise taxes. Then only $9 of the value added is attributable to the costs of factors used producing the output. Thus while the market value of its value added is $10, in terms of factor costs its value added is only $9. The other dollar representing the government's claim on the market value of the firm's value added.

Government subsidies on goods and services also cause the two measures of value added to differ. For example, consider a firm that produces a product

---

[2] Even with our earlier example of bread, a bakery cannot be sure that its sales are for final use since the bread may be further "processed" by a restaurant prior to its final sale to a customer for eating.

BOX 27-2

Value Added Through Stages of Production

Because the output of one firm often becomes the input of other firms, the total value of goods sold by all firms greatly exceeds the value of the output of final products. This general principle is illustrated by a simple example in which firm R starts from scratch and produces goods (raw materials) valued at $100; the firm's value added is $100. Firm I purchases raw materials valued at $100 and produces semi-manufactured goods that it sells for $130. Its value added is $30 because the value of the goods is increased

by $30 as a result of the firm's activities. Firm F purchases the semi-manufactured goods for $130, works them into a finished state, and sells the final products for $180. Firm F's value added is $50. The value of the final goods, $180, is found either by counting only the sales of firm F or by taking the sum of the values added by each firm. This value is much smaller than the $410 that we would obtain if we merely added up the market value of the commodities sold by each firm.

	Firm R	Firm I	Firm F	All firms	
				Transactions at three different stages of production	
A. Purchases from other firms	$ 0	$100	$130	$230	Total interfirm sales
B. Purchases of factors of production (wages, rent, interest, profits)	100	30	50	180	Total value added
A + B = value of product	$100	$130	$180	$410	Total value of all sales

with a market value of $25,000, which, after subtracting $15,000 worth of inputs purchased from other firms, has a value added of $10,000. This is the firm's value added at market prices. But also assume that the firm's wages and other production costs (excluding inputs for other firms) amounted to $14,000, with the extra $4,000 being covered by a government subsidy. The firm's value added measured at factor cost is therefore $14,000.

Real and Nominal National Income

We saw in Chapter 26 that prices of individual outputs are used as weights when constructing an aggregate measure of total output. Although we cannot add tons of steel and loaves of bread, we can add the money value of steel produced to the money value of bread produced. When we add up money values of individual outputs, we end up with a measure of what we have called *nominal national income.*[3] Suppose

[3] To simplify the discussion, in this section we proceed as if all outputs are final products; for the present purpose of distinguishing between real and nominal income, the complications introduced by the presence of intermediate goods are not important.

that we found that our measure of nominal national income had risen by 140 percent between 1980 and 1987. If we wanted to compare *real national income* (i.e., real output) in 1987 to that in 1980, we would need to determine how much of that 140 percent increase in nominal national income was due to increases in prices and how much was due to increases in quantities produced.

There are many possible approaches to distinguishing real from nominal income and many details in the procedures. But the basic principle in calculating real income is to compute the value of output in each period using a common set of (base period) prices. The common set of prices thus provides the weights used in the index of real income. We speak of real income as being measured in *constant (base period) dollars.*

Total output calculated by summing values using current prices is a measure of nominal national income. Total output calculated by summing values using base period prices is a measure of real national income, computed in terms of constant dollars.

TABLE 27-2   Real Gross Domestic Product, 1986

	Billions of 1981 dollars	Percent of GDP
Value added by sector		
Agriculture, fishing, and forestry	$ 14.9	4.2
Mines, quarries, and oil wells	19.0	5.3
Manufacturing	66.2	18.4
Construction	24.6	6.9
Electric power, gas, and water utilities	11.0	3.1
Transportation, storage, and communication	26.5	7.4
Real and wholesale trade	40.9	11.4
Financial, insurance, and real estate	53.2	14.8
Community, business, and personal services	39.1	10.9
Nonbusiness sector	64.1	17.8
GDP (at factor cost)	$358.7	100
Add: Indirect taxes less subsidies	48.3	
GDP (at market prices)	$407.0	

Source: Statistics Canada 11-003E; 15–001.

GDP, a measure of total output produced in Canada, can be decomposed into the contribution to that total by each of a number of sectors. GDP at factor cost equals the sum of values added of each sector. As can be seen, manufacturing is the largest sector, contributing over 18 percent. To convert *GDP at factor cost* to *GDP at market prices,* we have to add indirect taxes net of subsidies to the former.

Any changes in nominal income are due to the combined effects of changes in prices and changes in outputs. But any changes in real income are due solely to changes in output.

The Implicit Deflator

Any differences between nominal and real national income for a given year must be due to changes in prices between that year and the base year used in calculating real income. Such a comparison thus implies a price index relating the two years. This *implicit price index* or *implicit deflator* is defined as follows:

$$\text{Implicit deflator} = \frac{\text{nominal national income}}{\text{real national income}} \times 100\%$$

The implicit deflator is the most comprehensive index of the price level because it covers all the goods and services produced by the entire economy. While the CPI is a fixed-weight index, the implicit deflator is a variable-weight index. It uses the current year's bundle of production to compare the current year's prices with those prevailing in the base period. Thus the 1986 deflator uses 1986 weights and the 1987 deflator will use 1987 weights. Box 27-3 illustrates the calculation of real national income, nominal national income, and the implicit deflator for a simple hypothetical economy that produces only wheat and steel.

Any change in nominal income can be split into a change due to prices and a change due to quantities. For example, in 1986 Canadian nominal income was 147 percent higher than in 1970. This increase was due to a 212 percent increase in prices and an 85 percent increase in real income. Table 27-3 (p. 573) gives nominal and real income and the implicit deflator for selected years since 1935.

National Income Accounting

In Chapter 26 we used the generic term *national income* to describe both the value of output produced and purchased, and the value of income generated

BOX 27-3

Calculation of Nominal and Real National Income

To see what is involved in calculating nominal national income, real national income, and the implicit deflator, an example may be helpful. Consider a simple hypothetical economy that produces only two commodities, wheat and steel.

Table 1 gives the basic data for outputs and prices in the economy for two years.

Table 1   Data for a Hypothetical Economy

	Quantity produced		Prices	
	Wheat (bushels)	Steel (tons)	Wheat (dollars per bushel)	Steel (dollars per ton)
Year 1	110	20	10	50
Year 2	110	16	12	55

Table 2 shows nominal national income, calculated by adding the money values of wheat output and of steel output for each year. In year 1 the value of both wheat and steel production was $1,000, so nominal income was $2,000. In year 2 wheat output rose and steel output fell; the value of wheat output rose to $1,320 and that of steel fell to $880. Since the rise in value of wheat was bigger than the fall in value of steel, nominal income rose by $200.

Table 2   Calculation of Nominal National Income

Year 1 $(100 \times 10) + (20 \times 50) = \$2,000$
Year 2 $(110 \times 12) + (16 \times 55) = \$2,200$

Table 3 shows real national income, calculated by valuing output in each year by year 2 prices; that is, year 2 becomes the base year for weighting purposes. In year 2 wheat output rose but steel output fell. Using year 2 prices, the value of the fall in steel output exceeded the value of the rise in wheat output, and real national income fell.

Table 3   Calculation of Real National Income Using Year 2 Prices

Year 1 $(100 \times 12) + (20 \times 55) = \$2,300$
Year 2 $(110 \times 12) + (16 \times 55) = \$2,200$

In Table 4 the ratio of nominal to real national income is calculated for each year and multiplied by 100. This ratio implicitly measures the change in prices over the period in question and is called the *implicit deflator* or *implicit price index*.

Table 4   Calculation of the Implicit Deflator

Year 1 $(2,000 \div 2,300) \times 100 = 86.96$
Year 2 $(2,200 \div 2,200) \times 100 = 100.00$

The implicit deflator shows that the price level increased by 15 percent between year 1 and year 2.

In Table 4 we used year 2 as the base year for comparison purposes, but we could have used year 1. The implicit deflator would then have been 100 in year 1 and 115 in year 2, and the increase in price level would still have been 15 percent.

by that production. Earlier in this chapter we studied how output could be measured by summing values added; we called this aggregate measure GDP. In this part we examine two other methods of calculating GDP and then relate GDP to other aggregate measures that are sometimes encountered.

It is useful to look again at Figure 3-1, on page 53, which shows the circular flow of expenditure and income. The bottom half of the circular flow focuses on expenditure to purchase the nation's output in product markets, and the top half focuses on factor markets where the receipts of firms are distributed to those factors used in producing the nation's output.

Corresponding to these two halves of the circular flow are two ways of measuring national income: the value of what is produced *and* the value of incomes generated by production. We can add up the total expenditure on each of the main components of final output; this is called *the expenditure approach*.

TABLE 27-3 GDP in Current and Constant Dollars

Year	(1) GDP in billions of current dollars	(2) GDP in billions of 1981 dollars	(3) Implicit national income deflator (1981 = 100)
1935	4,301	34,685	12.4
1945	11,863	66,585	16.8
1955	29,250	109,104	26.8
1965	57,523	175,359	32.8
1975	171,540	283,187	60.5
1980	309,891	343,384	90.2
1985	479,446	393,817	121.7

Source: M. C. Urquhart, ed., *Historical Statistics of Canada;* Department of Finance, *Economic Review.*

Current dollar GDP tells us about the money value of output; constant dollar GDP tells us about changes in physical output. GDP in current dollars gives the total value of all final output in any year, valued in the selling prices of that year. GDP in constant dollars gives the total value of all final output in any year, valued at the prices prevailing in one particular year, in this case, 1981.

The ratio of *GDP in current dollars* to *GDP in constant dollars* times 100 is the implicit GDP deflator. (It is in effect a price index with current year quantity weights.)

We can also measure the incomes generated by the act of production; this is called the *income approach*.

The expenditure approach and the income approach are two different ways of looking at one magnitude: the market value of the nation's output.

The two approaches are conceptually identical, and result in measures of GDP that differ in practice only because of errors of measurement. Each approach is of interest, however, because each gives a different and useful breakdown of national income. Also, having two independent ways of measuring the same thing also gives a useful check on the statistical procedures and unavoidable measurement errors.

National income accounting is the set of rules and techniques for measuring the total flow of output produced and the total flow of incomes generated by this production.

The conventions of double-entry bookkeeping require that all value produced must be accounted for by a claim someone has to that value.

Thus it is merely a matter of accounting convention that the two measures of GDP should be equal.

(Measured values differ only to the extent that measurement errors arise. Any discrepancy arising from such errors is then reconciled so that one common total is given as *the* measure of GDP; that common total is also reconciled with the measure of GDP obtained using the output approach studied earlier in this chapter.)

The Expenditure Approach

The expenditure approach calculates GDP as the market value of final output by adding up the expenditures made to purchase final output. Total expenditure on final output is the sum of four broad categories of expenditure: consumption, investment, government, and net exports.

Consumption Expenditure

Consumption expenditure includes expenditure on all goods and services produced and sold to households during the year (with the exception of residential housing, which is counted as investment). It includes services such as haircuts, medical care, and legal advice; nondurable goods such as fresh meat, cut flowers, and fresh vegetables; and durables such as cars, television sets, and air conditioners. We de-

574 Part Eight National Income and Fiscal Policy

note actual (i.e., measured) consumption expenditure by the symbol C^a.

Investment Expenditure

Investment expenditure is expenditure on the production of goods not for present consumption, including inventories, capital goods such as plant and equipment, and residential housing. Such goods are called **investment goods**.

Inventories. Almost all firms hold stocks of their inputs and their own outputs. These stocks are called **inventories**. Inventories of inputs and unfinished materials allow production to continue at the desired pace in spite of short-term fluctuations in the deliveries of inputs bought from other firms. Inventories of outputs allow firms to meet orders in spite of temporary fluctuations in the rate of outputs or sales.

Inventories are an important part of the production process. They require an investment of the firm's money, since the firm has paid for but not yet sold the goods. An accumulation of inventories counts as current investment because it represents goods produced but not used for current consumption. A drawing down, often called a *decumulation,* counts as disinvestment because it represents a reduction in the stock of finished goods available to be sold.

Additions to inventories are a part of the economy's final production of investment goods. These are valued in the national income accounts at market value, which includes the wages and other costs the firm incurred in producing the goods and the profit the firm will make when the inventories are sold. Thus, in the case of inventories of a firm's own output, the expenditure approach measures what will have to be spent to purchase them when they are sold rather than what has actually been spent to produce them.

Plant and equipment. All production uses capital goods: manufactured aids to production such as tools, machines, and factory buildings. The economy's total quantity of capital goods is called the **capital stock.** Creating new capital goods is an act

of investment and is called fixed business investment, or **fixed investment** for short.

Residential housing. A house is a durable asset that yields its utility over a long life. For this reason housing construction is counted as investment expenditure rather than as consumption expenditure. This is done by assuming that the investment is made by the firm that builds the house and that the sale to a user is a mere transfer of ownership that is not a part of national income.

Gross versus net investment. The total investment that occurs in the economy is called **gross investment.** Gross investment is divided into two parts, replacement investment and net investment. **Replacement investment** is the amount of investment that just maintains the existing capital stock intact; it is called the **capital consumption allowance** or simply **depreciation.** Gross investment minus replacement investment is **net investment.** Positive net investment increases the economy's total stock of capital, while replacement investment keeps the existing stock intact by replacing what has been used up.

All of gross investment is included in the calculation of national income. This is because all investment goods are part of the nation's total output and their production creates income (and employment) whether the goods produced are a part of net investment or are merely replacement investment. Actual (i.e., measured) total investment expenditure is denoted by the symbol I^a.

Government Expenditure on Goods and Services

When governments provide goods and services that households want, such as roads and air traffic control, it is obvious that they are adding to the sum total of valuable output in the same way as do private firms that produce the trucks and airplanes that use the roads and air lanes. With other government activities, the case may not seem so clear. Should expenditures by the federal government to send a scientific probe into space or to pay a civil servant to refile papers from a now defunct department be regarded as contributions to national income? Some people believe that many (or even most) activities "up in Ottawa" or "down at City Hall" are wasteful, if not downright harmful. Others believe that it is governments, not private firms, that produce many of the important things of life, such as education and pollution control.

National income statisticians do not speculate about which government expenditures are or are not worthwhile. Instead, they include all government expenditures on goods and services as part of national income. (Government expenditure on investment goods is included as government rather than investment expenditure.) Just as the national product includes, without distinction, the output of both gin and Bibles, it also includes bombers and the upkeep of parks, along with the services of RCMP officers, members of Parliament, and even Revenue Canada investigators. Actual government expenditure on goods and services is denoted by the symbol G^a.

Government output is typically valued at cost rather than market value. In many cases there is really no choice. What, for example, is the market value of the services of a court of law? No one knows. But we do know what it costs the government to provide these services, so we value them at their cost of production.

Although valuing at cost is the only possible thing to do with many government activities, it does have one curious consequence. If, due to a productivity increase, one civil servant now does what two used to do and the displaced worker shifts to the private sector, the government's contribution to national income will register a decline. In contrast, if two now do what one used to do, the government's contribution will rise. Both changes could occur even though what the government actually does is unchanged. This is an inevitable consequence of measuring the value of the government's output by the cost of the factors, mainly labor, used to produce it.

There is an important exception to the rule that all government expenditure is included in national income. **Transfer payments,** or government payments that are not made in return for factor services, do not lead directly to any increase in output, and they are not included in national income. For example, when a government agency makes welfare payments to a retired person, the government does not receive, nor does it expect to receive, any marketable services from the retiree in return for the welfare payments. The payment itself adds neither to employment of factors nor to total output. The major transfer payments are unemployment insurance, welfare payments, and interest on the national debt (which transfers income from taxpayers to holders of government bonds).

Thus when we refer to government expenditure as part of national income or use the symbol G^a, we include all government expenditure on currently produced goods and services and we *exclude* all government transfer payments. (The term government *outlays* might be used to describe all government spending, including transfer payments.)

Net Exports

The fourth category of aggregate expenditure, and one that is extremely important to the Canadian economy, arises from foreign trade. How do imports and exports influence the national income?

Imports.   One country's national income is the total value of final commodities produced in that country. If your cousin spends $12,000 on a car made in Japan, only a small part of that value will represent expenditure on Canadian production. Some of it goes for the services of the Canadian dealers and transportation; the rest is the output of Japanese firms and expenditure on Japanese products. If you take your next vacation in Italy, much of your expenditure will be on goods and services produced by Italians and thus will contribute to Italian GDP.

Similarly, when a Canadian firm makes an investment expenditure on a Canadian-produced machine tool made partly with imported raw materials, only part of the expenditure is on Canadian production. The rest is expenditure on the production of the countries supplying the raw materials. The same is also true for government expenditure on such things as roads and dams; some of the expenditure is for imported materials and only part of it for domestically produced goods and services.

Consumption, investment, and government expenditures all have an import content. To arrive at total expenditure on Canadian products, we need to subtract from total Canadian expenditure any expenditure on imports. Actual expenditure on imports is given the symbol M^a.

Exports.   If Canadian firms sell goods to German households, the goods are a part of German consumption expenditure but also constitute expenditure on Canadian output. Indeed, all goods and services produced in Canada and sold to foreigners must be counted as part of Canadian production and income; they create incomes for the Canadians who produce them. To arrive at the total value of expenditure on Canadian national product, it is necessary to add in the value of Canadian exports. Actual exports are denoted by the symbol X^a.

It is customary to group actual imports and actual exports together as **net exports.** Net exports are defined as exports minus imports ($X^a - M^a$). The value of net exports is usually small in relation to the total value of either X^a or M^a.

GDP As Measured by the Expenditure Approach

The expenditure approach to measuring national income yields GDP as the sum of consumption, investment, government, and net export expenditures.

Table 27-4(i) shows Canadian GDP for 1986 calculated according to the expenditure approach.

The Income Approach

The income approach calculates the value of GDP as the total of all incomes generated in the process of production.

The production of the nation's output generates income. Labor must be employed, land rented, and capital used. The income approach to measuring GDP involves adding up factor payments and other claims on the value of output until all of it is ac-

counted for. As we have already seen, because all value produced must be owned by someone, the value of production must equal the value of income claims generated by that production.

Factor Payments

National income accountants distinguish four main components of factor incomes: wages, rent, interest, and profits.[4]

Wages.   Wages and salaries (which national income accountants call *compensation to employees* but are usually just called *wages*) are the payment for the services of labor. Wages include take-home pay, taxes withheld, social insurance, and pension fund contributions and other fringe benefits. In total, wages represent the part of the value of production attributable to labor.

Rent.   Rent is the payment for the services of land and other factors that are rented. It includes payments for rented housing and imputed rent for the use of owner-occupied housing. For the purposes of national income accounting, homeowners are viewed as renting accommodation from themselves. This allows national income measures to reflect the value of all housing services used, whether or not the housing is owned by its user.

Interest.   Interest includes interest earned on bank deposits, interest earned on loans to firms, and miscellaneous other investment income. Hence it is one of the payments for the services of capital.

Profits.   Some profits are paid out as **dividends** to owners of firms; the rest are retained for use by firms. The former are called **distributed profits**, the latter **undistributed profits** or **retained earnings.** Both distributed and undistributed profits are included in the calculation of GNP. For accounting purposes, total profits are reported in two separate

---

[4] The concepts of wages, rent, interest, and profits used in macroeconomics do not correspond exactly to the concepts of the same names used in microeconomics, but the details of the differences need not detain us.

TABLE 27-4   Components of GDP, 1986

(i) Expenditure approach

Expenditure category	Billions of dollars	Percentage of GDP
Consumption	299	58.5
Government	101	19.8
Investment	106	21.0
Net exports	6	1.1
Statistical discrepancy	−2	−0.4
GDP at market prices	510	100.0

(ii) Income approach

Income component	Billions of dollars	Percentage of GDP
Compensation to employees	274	53.7
Corporate profits (before taxes)	45	8.8
Net interest	41	8.0
Rental income	36	7.1
Net indirect taxes	54	10.6
Capital consumption allowance	58	11.4
Statistical discrepancy	2	0.4
GDP at market prices	510	100.0

Source: Quarterly Economic Review (Department of Finance, June 1987).

Canada's 1986 nominal gross domestic product (GDP) of $510 billion can be classified according to the expenditure or income approaches. In (i) the expenditure approach shows that consumption is the biggest component of GDP, accounting for almost 60 percent, while net exports account for less than 1 percent. Investment and government expenditure together account for about 40 percent.

In (ii) the income approach shows that compensation to employees accounts for almost 60 percent of GDP. The other 40 percent is accounted for by corporate profits before taxes, capital consumption allowance, indirect taxes less subsidies, interest, and rental income.

---

categories—corporation profits and incomes of unincorporated businesses (mainly small businesses, farms, partnerships, and professionals).

Net domestic income at factor cost.   The sum of the four components of factor incomes—wages, rent, interest, and profits—is called **net domestic income at factor cost.**

Indirect Taxes Net of Subsidies

When using the income approach, we must distinguish between national income valued *at factor cost* and national income valued *at market prices*. The difference between the two results from the effects of indirect taxes and subsidies. An important claim on the market value of output arises out of indirect taxes—taxes on the production and sale of goods and services.

As we saw on page 569, when adding up income claims to determine GDP, it is necessary to add in the part of the total market value of output that is the government's claim arising out of its taxes on goods and services. Recall that we also saw on page 570 that it is also necessary to subtract government subsidies on goods and services, since these allow incomes to *exceed* the market value of output.

Depreciation

Another component in the income approach arises from the distinction between net and gross investment. One claim on the value of final output is depreciation, or capital consumption allowance. This is the value of final output that embodies capital used up in the process of its production. It is part of gross profits, but being the part needed to compensate for capital used up in the process of production, it is not part of net profits. Hence it is not income earned by any factor of production. Instead it is value that must be reinvested just to maintain the existing stock of capital equipment.

GDP As Measured by the Income Approach

Adding depreciation and indirect taxes net of subsidies to net domestic income at factor cost gives gross domestic product at market prices, or GDP.

The income approach measures GDP as the sum of the factor incomes generated in the process of producing final output, plus indirect taxes net of subsidies, plus depreciation.

GDP in the Canadian economy in 1986 as calculated by the income approach is shown in Table 27-4(ii).

Income Produced and Income Received: An Important Distinction

GDP provides a measure of total output *produced in Canada,* and of the total income generated as a result of that production. However, the total income received by Canadians can differ from GDP for two reasons. Some Canadian production creates factor earnings for foreigners who have previously invested in Canada or who sell services to producers in Canada; on this account income received by Canadians will be less than Canadian GDP. Second, many Canadians earn income as a result of foreign investments and of factor services sold abroad; on this account income received by Canadians will be greater than Canadian GDP.

As with total output produced, total income received by Canadians can be measured using either the income or the expenditure approach. The term **Gross National Product (GNP)** is used to describe total income received by Canadians as measured by the income approach. The term **Gross National Expenditure (GNE)** describes the same total measured using the expenditure approach. Hence GNE and GNP give conceptually identical measures of national income.[5]

Total output produced in the economy, measured by GDP, differs from total income received by Canadians, measured by GNP and GNE, due to net foreign factor payments.

Reconciling GDP with GNP and GNE.   Table 27-5 shows the reconciliation of GDP with GNP, and hence with GNE. Recall that GNP and GNE both measure income received by Canadians while GDP measures output produced in Canada. Since Canada has had a long history of importing capital from abroad, factor payments to foreigners exceed factor payments received from foreigners, and hence GDP exceeds GNP. (This does not mean that the net effects of Canada's foreign borrowing has been to reduce incomes of Canadians; most estimates show that foreign investment has contributed more to GDP than

<hr>

[5] In the United States, the term GNP is used to describe *both* measures, and the term GNE is not used in official statistics.

TABLE 27-5   Reconciling GDP with GNP and GNE

	Billions of dollars
GDP at market prices (from Table 27-4)	510
Plus: investment income received from foreigners	7
Less: investment income paid to foreigners	−24
GNP (and GNE) at market prices	493

Source: Quarterly Economic Review (Department of Finance, June 1987).

GNP, income owned or received by Canadians, is equal to GDP, income produced in Canada, plus factor income received from foreigners, less factor income paid to foreigners. Since Canada has traditionally experienced significant net foreign investment, investment income paid to foreigners is large, and hence net international factor payments for Canada are negative. As a result GNP (and GNE, since GNE equals GNP) is less than GDP.

---

it has to the repatriation of factor payments, and hence has increased GNP. We return to this important issue in Chapter 41.)

Other Income Concepts

We have seen how the most comprehensive measures of national income—GDP, GNP, and GNE—are reconciled. We now turn to a discussion of some related but less-comprehensive measures.

Gross national income, however measured, is the most comprehensive income concept. The next most comprehensive measure is net national product (NNP). As we saw in building up the income approach, this is GNP minus the capital consumption allowance. NNP is thus a measure of the net output of the economy after deducting from gross output an amount sufficient to maintain intact the existing stock of capital. It is the maximum amount that could be consumed without actually running down the economy's capital stock.

Personal income is income earned by or paid to individuals before allowance for personal income taxes. Some personal income goes for taxes, some for saving, and the rest for consumption. A number of adjustments to NNP are required to arrive at personal income. The most important are (1) subtracting from NNP indirect taxes (net of subsidies), which are the part of the market value of output that goes directly to governments (this, as we have seen, gives net national income at factor cost), (2) subtracting from NNP business earnings retained by corporations, (3) subtracting from NNP income taxes paid by business, and (4) adding to NNP transfer payments to households. The first three are parts of the value of output not paid to households; the fourth is paid to households and thus is income that households have available to spend or to save, even though the payments are not part of GNP.

Disposable income is the amount of current income that households have to spend and to save; it is personal income minus personal income taxes.

Disposable income is GNP *minus* any part of it that is not actually paid to households *minus* personal income taxes paid by households *plus* transfer payments received by households.

The relations among GNP, NNP, personal income, and disposable income are shown in Table 27-6.

Interpreting National Income Measures

The information provided by measures of national income is useful, but unless carefully interpreted it can also be misleading. Furthermore, each of the specialized measures gives different information. Thus each may be the best statistic for studying a particular range of problems.

Money values and real values. We have seen that national income can be valued in current dollars to yield nominal income or constant dollars to yield real income. When studying the effect of inflation on national income, we need to look at nominal income. When studying changes in the economy's quantity of output, we need to look at real income.

Total values and per capita values. The rise in real GDP during this century has had two main causes:

TABLE 27-6 Various National Income Measures, 1986

	Billions of dollars[a]
A. GDP at market prices	510
Less: net foreign investment income	−17
B. GNP at market prices	493
Less: capital consumption allowance	−58
C. NNP at market prices	435
Less: indirect taxes of net subsidies	−54
D. NDI at factor cost	380
Less: retained earnings and business taxes	−9
Plus: government transfer payments to households	62
E. Personal income	433
Less: personal income taxes	−88
F. Disposable income	343

[a] Figures may not match because of rounding.

Each of the six related national income measures focuses on a different aspect of the national output. GDP measures total output produced in Canada. GNP measures the market value of total income received by Canadians. NNP measures the net value of national income after an allowance for maintaining the capital stock. NNI at factor cost converts market price values to factor costs by adjusting for government indirect taxes net of subsidies. Personal income measures income earned or received by persons before personal income taxes. Disposable income measures after-tax income of persons; it is the amount they have available to spend or to save.

an increase in the amounts of land, labor, and capital used in production and an increase in output per unit of input. In other words, more inputs have been used, and each input has become more productive. For some purposes, such as assessing a country's potential military strength or the total size of its market, we want to measure total output. For other purposes, such as studying changes in living standards, we require per capita measures, which are obtained by dividing a total measure such as GDP by the population.

There are many useful per capita measures. GDP divided by the total population gives a measure of how much GDP there is on average for each person in the country; this is called **per capita GDP**. GDP

FIGURE 27-1   Disposable Income Per Capita in Canada, in Constant (1981) Dollars

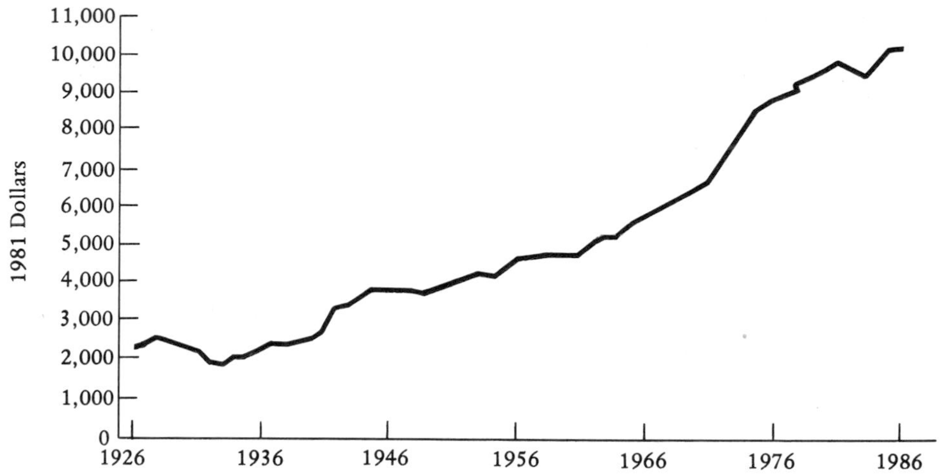

Disposable income per capita in constant dollars provides a measure of the real purchasing power available to the average Canadian household. Disposable income per capita fell during the early 1930s and late 1940s but it has risen in every decade since the thirties, including the 1970s. It underestimates the average living standard because it leaves ou the contribution of government expenditure to such items as police, fire, justice, defense, and recreation. (*Source*: M.C. Urquhart, ed., *Historical Statistics of Canada; Bank of Canada Review.*)

divided by the number of persons employed tells us the average output per employed worker. GDP divided by the total number of hours worked measures output per hour of labor input. A widely used measure of the purchasing power of the average person is disposable income per capita in constant dollars. This measure is shown in Figure 27-1.

Omissions from Measured National Income

Several types of economic activity are not included in GDP and therefore are excluded from other measures based on GDP. The importance of these omissions depends on the purpose for which the data are to be used. Box 27-4 takes up some other aspects of national income accounting.

Illegal activities.   GDP does not measure illegal activities, even though many of them are ordinary

business activities that produce goods and services sold on the market and generate factor incomes. The liquor industry during American Prohibition (1919–1933) is an important example because it accounted for a significant part of total economic activity in the U.S. Today the same is true of many forms of illegal gambling, prostitution, and the drug trade. To gain an accurate measure of the *total* demand for factors of production in the economy or of *total* marketable output, we should include these activities, regardless of whether we as individuals approve of the products.[6]

The omissions of illegal activities is no trivial matter. The drug trade alone is a multibillion dollar business. No one knows the exact value of its output,

[6] Some of them do get included because people sometimes report their earnings from illicit activities as part of their earnings from legal activities in order to avoid the fate of Al Capone, a famous Chicago gangster in the 1930s. Having avoided conviction on many counts, he was finally prosecuted and jailed for tax evasion.

BOX 27-4

The Significance of Arbitrary Decisions

National income accounting uses many arbitrary decisions. Goods that are finished and held in inventories are valued at market value, thereby anticipating their sale even though the actual sales price may not be known. In the case of a Ford in a dealer's showroom, this practice may be justified because the *value* of this Ford is perhaps virtually the same as that of an identical Ford that has just been sold to a customer. But what is the correct market value of a half-finished house or an unfinished novel? Accountants arbitrarily treat goods in process at cost (rather than at market value) if the goods are being made by business firms. They ignore completely the value of the novel in progress. These decisions are arbitrary—but so would any others be. Clearly, practical people must arrive at some compromise between consistent definitions and measurable magnitudes.

The definition of final goods provides further examples. Business investment expenditures are treated as final products, as are all government purchases. Intermediate goods purchased by business for further processing are not treated as final products. Thus when a firm buys a machine or a truck, the purchase is treated as a final good; when it buys a ton of steel, the steel is treated as a raw material that will be used as an input into the firm's production process. But if the steel sits in inventory, it is regarded as a business investment and thus *is* a final good.

Such arbitrary decisions surely affect the size of measured GDP. Does it matter? The surprising answer, for many purposes, is no. In any case, it is wrong to believe that a statistical measure is useless if it falls short of perfection; in fact, all statistical measures do. Crude measures often give estimates to the right order of magnitude, and substantial improvements in sophistication may make only second-order improvements in these estimates.

In the third century B.C. for example, the Alexandrian astronomer Eratosthenes measured the angle of the sun at Alexandria at the moment it was directly overhead 500 miles south at Aswan, and he used this angle to calculate the circumference of the earth to within 15 percent of the distance as measured today by the most advanced measuring devices. For the knowledge he wanted—the approximate size of the earth—his measurement was satisfactory. To launch a modern earth satellite, it would have been disastrously inadequate.

Absolute figures mean something in general terms, although they cannot be taken seriously to the last dollar. In 1985 GDP was measured as $389 billion. It is certain that the market value of all production in Canada in that year was not $100 billion, or $1 trillion, but it might well have been $350 billion or $420 billion had different measures been defined with different arbitrary decisions built in.

International and intertemporal comparisons, though tricky, may be meaningful when they are based on measures all of which contain roughly the same arbitrary decisions. Canadian per capita GDP is a little less than three times the Spanish per capita GDP and is 20 percent higher than the Japanese per capita GDP. Other measures might differ, but it is unlikely that any measure would reveal that either Spanish or the Japanese per capita production was higher than per capita production in Canada. But the statistics also show that per capita GDP was about 2 percent higher in the United States than in Canada, a difference too small to have much meaning. Canadian output grew at a rate of 4.9 percent per year for the 30 years following World War II; it is unlikely that another measure of output would have indicated a 7.5 percent increase. Further, Japanese output grew at about 9 percent per year over the same period. It is inconceivable that another measure would change the conclusion that Japanese national output rose factor than Canadian national output in recent decades.

but even if it were only 1 percent of GDP, that would amount to $5 billion in 1987.

Unreported activities.   An important omission from the measured GDP is the so-called underground economy. The transactions in the underground economy are perfectly legal in themselves. The only illegal thing about them is that they are not reported for tax purposes. For example, a carpenter repairs a leak in your roof and takes payment in cash or in kind in order to avoid tax. Because such transactions go unreported, they are omitted from GDP.

There are many reasons for the growth of the underground economy. Taxes, safety regulations, minimum-wage laws, anti-discrimination regulations, and social insurance payments may all be avoided. Its growth is also facilitated by the rising importance of services in the nation's total output. It is much easier for a carpenter to pass unnoticed by government authorities than it is for a manufacturing establishment.

Estimates of the value of income earned in the Canadian underground economy run from 2 to 15 percent of GDP. In other countries the figures are much higher. The Italian underground economy, for example, was recently estimated at close to 25 percent of that country's total GDP!

Clearly, the omission of unreported activities matters. This causes the actual amount of legal income and employment-creating market transactions to be underestimated. Changes in the proportion of GDP that go unreported can affect measures of growth in output and hence living standards. If, for example, *actual* GDP grows by 2 percent but an additional 1 percent goes unrecorded, *measured* GDP will grow by only 1 percent. (In 1985 and 1986 Italy was one of the fastest-growing countries in Europe, according to official statistics. A number of commentators have argued that this is in part due to a decrease in the proportion of economic activity that was unreported.)

Nonmarketed activities.   If a homeowner hires a firm to do some landscaping, the value of the landscaping enters into GDP; if the homeowner does the landscaping herself, the value of the landscaping is omitted from GDP. Such omissions also include, for example, the services of homemakers, any do-it-yourself activity, and voluntary work such as canvassing for a political party, helping to run a volunteer day-care center, or leading a Boy Scout troop.

In most advanced industrial economies the nonmarket sector is relatively small. The omissions become serious, however, when GDP or disposable income figures are used to compare living standards in very different economies. Generally, the nonmarket sector of the economy is larger in rural than in urban settings and in less developed than in more developed economies. Be a little cautious, then, in interpreting data from a country with a very different climate and culture. When you hear that the per capita GDP of Nigeria is about $900 per year, you should not imagine living in Hamilton Ontario on that income.

Other omitted factors.   Many factors that contribute to human welfare are not included in GDP. Leisure is one. In fact, although a shorter work week may make people happier, it will tend to reduce measured GDP.

Nor does GDP allow for the capacity of different goods to provide different satisfactions. A million dollars spent on a bomber or a missile makes the same addition to GDP as a million dollars spent on a school or on candy bars—expenditures that may produce very different amounts of consumer satisfaction.

Do the Omissions Matter?

If we wish to measure the flow of goods and services through the market sector of the economy or to account for changes in the opportunities for employment for households that sell their labor services in the market, most of these omissions will have negligible effects on our results. If, however, we wish to measure the overall flow of goods and services available to satisfy people's wants, whatever the source of the goods and services, the omissions are undesirable and potentially serious.

Is There a "Best" Measure?

To ask which is *the* best income measure is something like asking which is *the* best carpenter's tool. The answer is that it all depends on the job to be done. Which measure is used will depend on the problem at hand, and solving some problems may require information provided by several different measures or information not provided by any conventional measures. If we wish to predict households' consumption behavior, disposable income may be what we need. If we wish to account for changes in employment, constant dollar GDP is wanted. For an overall measure of economic welfare, we may need to supplement or modify conventional measures of national income, none of which measures the *quality of life*. To the extent that material output is purchased at the expense of overcrowded cities and highways, polluted environments, defaced countrysides, maimed accident victims, longer waits for public services, and a more complex life that entails a frenetic struggle to be happy, conventional

measures of national income include only part of the things that contribute to human well-being.[7]

Even if we do use some new or modified measures for some purposes, we are unlikely to discard GDP (and its relatives) entirely. Economists and politicians who are interested in changes in market activity and in employment opportunities for factors of production will continue to use GDP and GNP as the measures that come closest to telling them what they need to know.

[7] Concepts that come closer to measuring economic welfare have been developed. One was worked out by Professors William Nordhaus and James Tobin. It tries to measure consumption of things that provide utility to households rather than total production; it gives value to such nonmarketed activities as leisure and makes subtractions for such "disutilities" as pollution and congestion.

Summary

1. The Consumer Price Index (CPI) is a price index constructed to reflect changes in the prices of the bundle of goods consumed by a "representative" household. Changes in it are taken as a measure of changes in the "cost of living."

2. Gross Domestic Product (GDP) is the total value of final goods and services produced in the economy during a year. It can be measured by the output approach which sums the values added of all producers in the economy; this avoids the problem of double counting by excluding all intermediate goods produced.

3. Real income is a measure of total output calculated using base period prices as weights; changes in it reflect changes in quantity produced. Nominal income is a measure of total output calculated to reflect changes in both prices and quantities. Any change in nominal income can be split into a change in real income and a change due to prices. Comparing nominal and real income yields the implicit deflator.

4. GDP can also be measured using the expenditure and income approaches. Using the expenditure approach, GDP = $C^a + I^a + G^a + (X^a - M^a)$. C^a is consumption expenditures of households. I^a is investment in plant and equipment, residential construction, and inventory accumulation. Gross investment can be split into replacement investment (necessary to keep the stock of capital intact) and net investment (net additions to the stock of capital). G^a is government expenditures except transfer payments. $(X^a - M^a)$ is the excess of exports over imports; it will be negative if imports exceed exports.

5. The income approach measures GDP according to who has a claim to the value arising from the production and sale of commodities. Wages, interest, rents, profits, depreciation (called capital consumption allowance), and indirect taxes are the major categories. By virtue

of standard accounting conventions, gross domestic product measured by each of the two approaches will be the same.

6. GDP measures total production located in Canada. A distinct concept is total income received by Canadians. The difference is due to income from net foreign investment. Total income received by Canadians can also be measured using either the expenditure or the income approach. When measured by the income approach, it is called gross national product (GNP). When measured by the expenditure approach, it is called gross national expenditure (GNE).

7. Several related but different income measures are used in addition to GDP, GNP, and GNE. Net national product (NNP) measures total income after deducting the capital consumption allowance. Personal income is income actually earned by Canadian households before any allowance for personal taxes. Disposable income gives the amount that is actually available to households to spend or to save.

8. GDP and related measures of national income must be interpreted with care, given their limitations. GDP excludes production resulting from activities that are illegal, take place in the underground economy, or do not pass through markets (such as what is produced by do-it-yourself activities). Moreover, GDP does not measure everything that contributes to human welfare.

9. Notwithstanding their limitations, GDP and GNP remain the best measures available for estimating the total economic activity that passes through the markets of our economy and for accounting for changes in the employment opportunities that face households who sell their labor services on the open market.

Topics for Review

Index numbers and the Consumer Price Index (CPI)
Final goods, intermediate goods, and value added
Gross domestic product (GDP)
Real and nominal national income
Implicit deflator
Output, expenditure, and income approaches to measuring national
    income
Gross national product (GNP) and gross national expenditure (GNE)
National income measured at factor cost and at market prices
Net domestic income (NDI), net national product (NNP), personal
    income, and disposable income
Omissions from measured income

Discussion Questions

1. If Canada and the United States were to join together as a single country, what would be the effect on their total GDP (assuming that output in each country is unaffected)? Would any of the components in their GDPs change significantly?

2. "Every time you rent a U-Haul, brick in a patio, grow a vegetable, fix your own car, photocopy an article, join a food co-op, develop

your own film, sew a dress, avoid purchasing a convenience food, stew fruit, or raise a child, you are committing a productive act, even though these activities are not reflected in the gross domestic product." To what extent are each of these things "productive acts"? Are any of them included in GDP? Where they are excluded, does the exclusion matter?

3. What would be the effect of the following events on the measured value of real GDP? Speculate on the effects of each event on the true well-being of Canadians.
   a. Destruction of a thousand homes by flood water
   b. Passage of a constitutional amendment making abortion illegal
   c. Complete cessation of all imports from South Africa
4. In measuring GNE, which of the following expenditures are included? Why?
   a. Expenditures on automobiles by consumers and by firms
   b. Expenditures on food and lodging by tourists and by business people on expense accounts
   c. Expenditures on new machinery and equipment by Canadian firms
   d. The purchase of one corporation by another corporation
   e. Increases or decreases in business inventories
5. In the United States a Social Security Administration study, using 1972 data, found the "average American housewife's value" to be $4,705 a year. (In 1982 dollars this amount to over 12,000 a year.) It arrived at this total by adding up the hours she spent cooking multiplied by a cook's wage, the hours spent with her children multiplied by a babysitter's wage, and so on. Should the time a parent spends taking children to a concert be included? Are dollar amounts assigned to such activities a satisfactory proxy for market value of production? For what, if any, purposes would such values be excluded from or included in national income?
6. Use the table on the endpaper at the back of this book to calculate the percentage increase over the most recent two decades of each of the following measures. Can you account for the relative size of these changes?
   a. GDP in current dollars
   b. GDP per capita in constant dollars
7. Consider the effect on measured GDP and on economic well-being of each of the following.
   a. Reduction in the standard work week from 40 hours to 30 hours
   b. Hiring of all welfare recipients as government employees
   c. Increase in the salaries of priests and ministers as a result of increased contributions of churchgoers
8. A recent newspaper article reported that Switzerland was considered to be the "best" place in the world to live. In view of the fact that Switzerland does not have the highest per capita income in the world, how can it be ranked the "best"?
9. In 1986 Statistics Canada switched from reporting national income in terms of GNP to reporting it in terms of GDP. How do these two measures differ? Do you think GDP is a better or worse measure of national income than GNP is? Does your answer to the last question depend on the purpose the measure is being used for?

28

National Income and Aggregate Expenditure

In Chapters 26 and 27 we encountered a number of important macro-economic variables. We described how they are measured and how they had behaved over the past half century or so. We now turn to a more detailed study of what *caused* these variables to behave as they did. In particular we wish to study the factors that determine national income, and hence employment and unemployment, and the price level.

Because it is easier to deal with things one at a time, we look first at the forces that determine national income *when the price level is treated as being constant*. In later chapters we will see what happens when the price level also varies. In this chapter, therefore, two questions are key:

1. **Why is national income what it is?**
2. **Why does it change?**

Our answers to these two questions depend on our understanding of why households and firms spend what they do and why they change their spending. Thus our analysis begins with an examination of the expenditure decisions of households and firms. As a first step we distinguish between *desired* expenditure and *actual* expenditure.

Desired Expenditure

In Chapter 27 we discussed how national income statisticians measure gross national expenditure and its components: consumption, C^a; investment, I^a; government, G^a; and net exports, $(X^a - M^a)$.

In this chapter we are concerned with a different concept. It is variously called *desired, planned,* or *intended expenditure*. Of course, all people would like to spend virtually unlimited amounts if only they had the resources. Desired expenditure does not refer, however, to what people would like to do under imaginary circumstances. It refers instead to what people want to spend out of the resources at their command. The *actual* values of the various categories of expenditure are indicated by C^a, I^a, G^a, and $(X^a - M^a)$. We use the same letters without the superscript a to indicate the *desired* expenditure in the same categories: C, I, G, and $(X - M)$.

Everyone with income to spend makes expenditure decisions. Fortunately, it is unnecessary for our purpose to look at each of the millions of such individual decisions. Instead it is sufficient to place decision makers in four main groups: domestic households, firms, governments, and foreign purchasers of domestically produced products. Their actual purchases account for the four main categories of expenditure studied in the preceding chapter: consumption, investment, government, and net exports.

Their desired purchases can also be divided in the same fashion: desired consumption, desired investment, desired government expenditure, and desired exports. Allowing for the fact that some commodities desired by each group will have an import content, we subtract import expenditure to obtain total desired expenditure on domestically produced goods and services, called **aggregate expenditure,** *AE:*

$$AE = C + I + G + (X - M)$$

Desired expenditure need not equal actual expenditure, either in total or in each individual category. For example, firms may not plan to invest in inventory accumulation this year but may do so unintentionally. If they produce goods to meet estimated sales, but demand is unexpectedly low, the unsold goods that pile up on their shelves are undesired, and unintended, inventory accumulation. In this case actual investment expenditure, I^a, will exceed desired investment expenditure, I.

National income accounts measure *actual expenditures* **in each of the four categories: consumption, investment, government, and net exports. National income theory deals with** *desired expenditures* **in each of these four categories.**

To develop a theory of national income determination, we need to know what determines desired aggregate expenditure. First, however, we recall the important distinction between *autonomous* and *induced* expenditure. (The distinction between autonomous and induced variables was first introduced in Chapter 2 on page 21.)

Autonomous and Induced Expenditure

Components of aggregate expenditure that do *not* depend on national income are called autonomous expenditures. Autonomous expenditures can and do change, but such changes do not occur systematically in response to changes in national income. Components of aggregate expenditure that *do* change in response to changes in national income are called induced expenditures. As we will see, the induced response of aggregate expenditure to a change in national income plays a key role in the determination of equilibrium national income.

We need to examine the determinants of each of the components of desired aggregate expenditure. In this chapter we focus on desired consumption expenditures. Consumption is the largest single component of actual aggregate expenditure, and as we will see, desired consumption expenditure provides the single most important link between desired aggregate expenditure and national income.

In an open economy such as Canada's, net exports are also an important link between desired aggregate expenditure and national income. Hence we also examine the factors that influence net exports. The two other components of *AE* are desired investment and government expenditures. We treat each briefly here; we look at both in more detail later in the book.

Desired Consumption Expenditure

Households can do one of two things with their disposable income: spend it on consumption or save it. **Saving** is defined as all disposable income that is not consumed. In effect a household has only one decision to make about disposable income.

Since by definition there are only two possible uses of disposable income, spending or saving, when the household decides how much to put to one use, it has automatically decided how much will go to the other.

What determines the amount that households decide to spend on goods and services for consumption and the amount they decide to save? The factors that influence this decision are summarized in the consumption function and the saving function.

The Consumption Function

The **consumption function** relates the total desired consumption expenditure of all households in the economy to the factors that determine it. It is, as we shall see, one of the central relations in macroeconomics.

While we are ultimately interested in the relationship between consumption and national income, the underlying behavior of households depends on the income they actually have to spend—their disposable income. Therefore, we shall start with the relationship between consumption and disposable income and then go on to relate consumption to national income.

Consumption and Disposable Income

One important influence on desired consumption expenditure is household disposable income, represented by Y_d. As disposable income rises, households have more money to spend on consumption—and the evidence is that they do just that. We therefore treat desired consumption expenditure as varying positively with disposable income.

Other factors such as interest rates and inflation-

ary expectations also exert an influence, but we shall neglect them for the moment. The simple theory of consumption focuses on changes in disposable income to explain changes in consumption.

The term *consumption function* describes the relationship between consumption and disposable income.

In Chapter 27 we examined the calculation of disposable income; for the purposes of this discussion all we need to know is that disposable income tends to be a relatively constant fraction of national income.

Some consumption expenditure is autonomous, but most is induced; that is, most varies with disposable income and hence with national income. A schedule relating disposable income to desired consumption expenditure for a hypothetical economy appears in the first two columns of Table 28-1. In this example autonomous consumption expenditure is $100 billion, whereas induced consumption expen-

Table 28-1 The Calculation of Average Propensity to Consume (*APC*) and Marginal Propensity to Consume (*MPC*) (*billions of dollars*)

Disposable income (Y_d)	Desired consumption (C)	$APC = C/Y_d$	ΔY_d (Change in Y_d)	ΔC (Change in C)	$MPC = \Delta C/\Delta Y_d$
$ 0	$ 100	—			
100	180	1.800	$ 100	$ 80	0.80
400	420	1.050	300	240	0.80
500	500	1.000	100	80	0.80
1,000	900	0.900	500	400	0.80
2,000	1,700	0.850	1,000	800	0.80
3,000	2,500	0.833	1,000	800	0.80
4,000	3,300	0.825	1,000	800	0.80

***APC* measures the proportion of disposable income that households desire to spend on consumption; *MPC* measures the proportion of any *increment* to disposable income that households desire to spend on consumption.** The data are hypothetical. We call the level of income at which desired consumption equals disposable income the break-even level; in this example it is $500 billion. *APC*, calculated in the third column, declines steadily as income rises. APC exceeds unity—that is, consumption exceeds income— below the break-even level of income. Above the break-even level, *APC* is less than unity.

The last three columns are set between the lines of the first three columns to indicate that they refer to changes in the levels of income and consumption. *MPC*, calculated in the last column, is constant at 0.80 at all levels of Y_d. This indicates that in this example $0.80 of *every* additional $1.00 of disposable income is spent on consumption and $0.20 is allocated to saving.

diture is 80 percent of disposable income. In what follows we use this hypothetical example to illustrate the various properties of the consumption function.

Average and marginal propensities to consume. To discuss the consumption function concisely, economists use two technical expressions.

The **average propensity to consume (APC)** is total consumption expenditure divided by total disposable income. The third column of Table 28-1 shows the APCs calculated from the data in the table.

The **marginal propensity to consume (MPC)** relates the *change* in consumption to the *change* in disposable income that brought it about. MPC is the change in disposable income divided into the resulting consumption change, $MPC = \Delta C/\Delta Y_d$ (where the Greek letter Δ, delta, means "a change in"). The last column of Table 28-1 shows the MPCs calculated from the data in the table. [34]

The slope of the consumption function. Part (i) of Figure 28-1 shows a graph of the consumption function plotted from the first two columns of Table 28-1. The consumption function has a slope of $\Delta C/\Delta Y_d$, which is, by definition, the marginal propensity to consume. The upward slope of the consumption function shows that MPC is positive; increases in income lead to increases in expenditure.

Using the concepts of the average and marginal propensities to consume, we can summarize the properties of the short-term consumption function:

1. There is a break-even level of income at which APC equals unity. Below this level APC is greater than unity; above it APC is less than unity.
2. MPC is greater than zero but less than unity for all levels of income.

The 45° line. Figure 28-1(i) contains a line that is constructed by connecting all points where desired consumption (measured on the vertical axis) equals disposable income (measured on the horizontal axis). Since both axes are given in the same units, this line has an upward slope of unity, or (what is the same thing) it forms an angle of 45° with the axes. The line is therefore called the **45° line.**

The 45° line makes a handy reference line. In

Figure 28-1(i) it helps locate the break-even level of income at which consumption expenditure equals disposable income. The consumption function cuts the 45° line at the break-even level of income, in this instance $500. (The 45° line is steeper than the consumption function because MPC is less than unity.)

The saving function. Households decide how much to consume and how much to save. As we have said, this is a single decision: how to divide disposable income between consumption and saving. It follows that once we know the dependence of consumption on disposable income, we also automatically know the dependence of saving on disposable income. (This is illustrated in Table 28-2.)

Two saving concepts are exactly parallel to the consumption concepts of APC and MPC. The **average propensity to save (APS)** is the proportion of disposable income that households want to save, derived by dividing total desired saving by total disposable income, $APS = S/Y_d$. The **marginal propensity to save (MPS)** relates the *change* in total desired saving to the *change* in disposable income that brought it about, $MPS = \Delta S/\Delta Y_d$.

There is a simple relation between the saving and the consumption propensities. APC and APS must sum to unity and so must MPC and MPS. Since

Table 28-2 Consumption and Saving Schedules
(billions of dollars)

Disposable income	Desired consumption	Desired saving
0	100	−100
100	180	− 80
400	420	− 20
500	500	0
1,000	900	+100
2,000	1,700	+300
3,000	2,500	+500
4,000	3,300	+700

Saving and consumption account for all household disposable income. The first two columns repeat the data from Table 28-1. The third column, desired saving, is disposable income minus desired consumption. Consumption and saving both increase steadily as disposable income rises. In this example the break-even level of disposable income is $500 billion.

FIGURE 28-1   The Consumption and Saving Functions

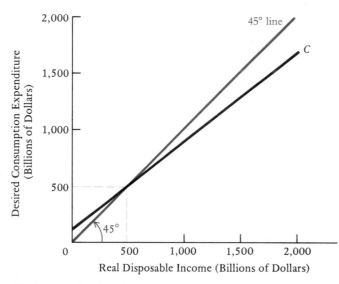

(i) Consumption function

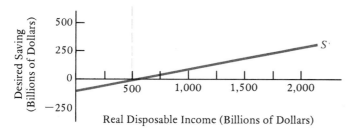

(ii) Saving function

Both consumption and saving rise as disposable income rises. Line *C* in part (i) relates desired consumption expenditure to disposable income using the hypothetical data from Table 28-1. Its slope, $\Delta C/\Delta Y_d$, is the marginal propensity to consume (*MPC*). The consumption line cuts the 45° line at the break-even level of disposable income, $500 in this case.

Saving is all disposable income not spent on consumption ($S = Y_d - C$). The relationship between desired saving and disposable income is derived in Table 28-2, and the resulting relationship is shown in part (ii) by line *S*. Its slope, $\Delta S/\Delta Y_d$, is the marginal propensity to save (*MPS*). The saving line cuts the horizontal axis at the break-even level of income. The vertical distance between *C* and the 45° line in part (i) is by definition the height of *S* in part (ii). That is, any given level of disposable income must be accounted for by the amount consumed plus the amount saved.

income is either spent or saved, it follows that the fractions of incomes consumed and saved must account for all income (*APC* + *APS* = 1). It also follows that the fraction of any increment to income consumed and saved must account for all of that increment (*MPC* + *MPS* = 1). [35]

Calculations from Table 28-2 will allow you to confirm these relations in the case of the example given. *MPC* is 0.80 and *MPS* is 0.20 at all levels of income, while, for example, at income of $2,000 billion *APC* is 0.85 and *APS* is 0.15.

Part (ii) of Figure 28-1 shows the saving schedule given in Table 28-2. At the break-even level of income, where desired consumption equals disposable income, desired saving is zero. The slope of the saving line $\Delta S/\Delta Y_d$ is *MPS*.

Consumption and Wealth

We have seen that disposable income is an important factor in the consumption-saving decision. A second important factor is the real value of each household's wealth. By a household's **wealth** we mean the sum of all the valuable assets it owns. This includes its car, its house and contents, the value of its money in the bank, pension fund, and any stocks, bonds, or other investments that it holds.

Households save in order to add to their wealth. Other things being equal, a rise in wealth tends to reduce the incentive to add further to wealth; that is, it reduces the incentive to save. Obviously, it is the real value of wealth that matters. Should the money value of wealth and the price level change in the same proportion, leaving real wealth unchanged, the household's incentive to save will be unchanged.

A rise in wealth tends to cause a larger fraction of disposable income to be spent on consumption and a smaller fraction to be saved. This shifts the consumption function upward and the saving function downward, as shown in Figure 28-2. A fall in wealth increases the incentive to save in order to restore wealth. This shifts the consumption function downward and the saving function upward.

Individual households experience both expected and unexpected changes in wealth. For example, either planned saving or unplanned bequests will in-

---

FIGURE 28-2   Wealth and the Consumption Function

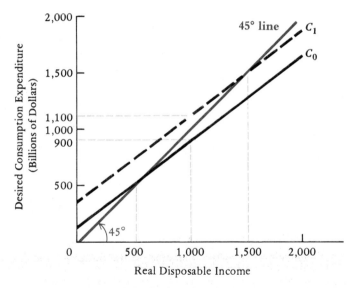

(i) The consumption function shifts up with an increase in wealth

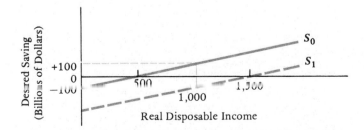

(ii) The saving function shifts down with an increase in wealth

Changes in wealth shift consumption as a function of disposable income. In part (i) line C_0 reproduces the consumption function from Figure 28-1(i). An increase in the level of wealth raises desired consumption at each level of disposable income, thus shifting the consumption line up to C_1. In the figure the consumption function shifts up by $200, so with disposable income of $1,000, for example, desired consumption *rises* from $900 to $1,100. As a result of the rise in wealth, the break-even level of income rises to $1,500.

The saving function in part (ii) shifts down by $200, from S_0 to S_1. Thus, for example, at a disposable income of $1,000, saving *falls* from plus $100 to minus $100.

crease wealth. Similarly, either planned dissaving or unplanned losses reduce wealth.

Many unexpected changes in wealth cancel out across households and so are unimportant for the macroeconomic consumption function. We will see, however, that inflation can be an important source of unexpected changes in wealth in most households.

Planned increases in wealth as a result of past accumulation of wealth can be important for the whole society and can lead to upward shifts in the macro consumption function as wealth accumulates. This effect operates only slowly since wealth accumulates only slowly.

Because for the moment we are focusing on short-term issues, the consumption function used in the text does not include the effects of changes in wealth.

Consumption and National Income

We have related desired consumption to *disposable* income. For a theory of the determination of national income, however, we need to know how consumption is related to national income.

The transition from a relation between consumption and disposable income to one between consumption and national income is readily accomplished since disposable income and national income are themselves related to each other.

The relation between disposable income and national income. On pages 578 and 579 we saw the adjustments required to derive disposable income from national income. Since transfer payments (the major addition) are smaller than total income taxes (the major subtraction), the net effect is for disposable income to be substantially less than national income. (It was about 68 percent of GDP in 1986.)

Relating desired consumption to national income. If we know how consumption relates to disposable income and how disposable income relates to national income, we can derive the relation between consumption and national income.

As an example, assume that disposable income is always 90 percent of national income. Then, whatever the relation between C and Y, we can always

substitute $0.9Y$ for Y_d. Thus if changes in consumption were always 80 percent of changes in Y_d, changes in consumption would always be 72 percent (80 percent of 90 percent) of Y. [36]

Table 28-3 shows that we can write desired consumption as a function of Y as well as of Y_d. We can then derive the marginal response of consumption to changes in Y by determining the proportion of any change in *national income* that goes to a change in desired consumption.

The marginal response of consumption to changes in *national income* ($\Delta C/\Delta Y$) is equal to the marginal propensity to consume out of *disposable income* ($\Delta C/\Delta Y_d$) multiplied by the fraction of national income that becomes disposable income ($\Delta Y_d/\Delta Y$).

Table 28-3   Consumption as a Function of Disposable Income and National Income (*billions of dollars*)

(1) National income (Y)	(2) Disposable income ($Y_d = 0.9Y$)	(3) Desired consumption ($C = 100 + 0.8Y_d$)
100	90	172
1,000	900	820
2,000	1,800	1,540
3,000	2,700	2,260
4,000	3,600	2,980

If desired consumption depends on disposable income, which in turn depends on national income, desired consumption can be written as a function of either income concept. The data are hypothetical. They show deductions of 10 percent of any level of national income to arrive at disposable income. Deductions of 10 percent of Y imply that the remaining 90 percent of Y becomes disposable income. The numbers also show consumption as $100 billion plus 80 percent of disposable income.

By relating columns 2 and 3, one sees consumption as a function of disposable income. By relating columns 1 and 3, one sees the derived relationship between consumption and national income. In this example the change in consumption in response to a change in disposable income (i.e., the *MPC*) is 0.8, while the change in consumption in response to a change in national income is 0.72.

We now have a function showing how desired consumption expenditure varies as national income varies. The relation is defined for real income and real expenditure (i.e., income and expenditure measured in constant dollars). For every given level of real income, measured in terms of purchasing power, households desire to spend some fraction of that purchasing power and to save the rest.

Desired Net Exports

Canada is rich in natural resources and raw materials, which it exports to many other countries that are less favorably endowed. Also, Canada's manufacturing sector is both specialized and export-oriented. As we will see, fluctuations in exports play a key role in explaining fluctuations in the level of economic activity in the Canadian economy.

Similarly, imports play an important role in the Canadian economy; Canadian households typically consume a wide range of imported goods, and Canadian industry uses imported parts and components. A large segment of the Canadian economy is involved in foreign trade—primarily, but not exclusively, with the United States.

The Net Export Function

Exports depend on spending decisions made by foreign households that purchase Canadian goods and services. Therefore, exports will not necessarily change as a result of changes in Canadian national income.

Imports, however, depend on the spending decisions of Canadian households. All categories of expenditure have an import content—even domestic cars, for example, use some imported components in their manufacture. Thus imports rise when the other categories of expenditure rise. Because consumption rises with income, imports of foreign-produced consumption goods and materials that go into the production of domestically produced consumption goods also rise with income.

Desired net exports are negatively related to national income because of the positive relation-

ship between desired expenditure on imports and national income.

This negative relationship between net exports and national income is called the *net export function*. Data for a hypothetical economy with constant exports and with imports that are 10 percent of national income are given in Table 28-4 and illustrated in Figure 28-3. In this example exports form the autonomous component and imports the induced component of the desired net export function.

Shifts in the Net Export Function

We have seen that the net export function relates net exports $(X - M)$ to national income. It is drawn on the assumption that everything that affects net exports except domestic national income remains constant. The major factors that must be held constant are foreign national income, domestic and foreign prices, and the exchange rate. A change in any of these will affect the amount of net exports that will occur at each level of Canadian national income and hence will shift the net export function.

Notice that anything that affects Canadian exports will change the values in the export column in Table 28-4 and so will shift the net export function parallel to itself, upward if exports increase and downward if exports decrease. Also notice that any-

Table 28-4 A Net Export Schedule (*billions of dollars*)

National income (Y)	Exports (X)	Imports (M = 0.1Y)	Net exports
1,000	240	100	140
2,000	240	200	40
2,400	240	240	0
3,000	240	300	−60
4,000	240	400	−160
5,000	240	500	−260

Net exports fall as national income rises. The data are hypothetical. They assume that exports are constant and that imports are 10 percent of national income. Net exports are then positive at low levels of national income and negative at high levels.

FIGURE 28-3   The Net Export Function

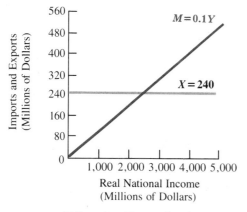

(i) Export and import functions

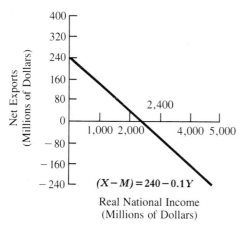

(ii) Net export function

Net exports, defined as the difference between exports and imports, are inversely related to the level of national income. In part (i) exports are constant at $240 million while imports rise with the national income. Therefore net exports, shown in part (ii), decline with national income. The figure is based on the hypothetical data in Table 28-4. With national income equal to $2,400 million, imports are equal to exports at $240 million and net exports are zero. For levels of national income below $2,400 million, imports are less than exports and hence net exports are positive. For levels of national income above $2,400 million, imports are greater than exports and hence net exports are negative.

thing that affects the proportion of income Canadians wish to spend on imports will change the values in the import column in Table 28-4 and thus will change the slope of the net export function by making imports more or less responsive to changes in domestic income.

Foreign income.   An increase in foreign income, other things being equal, will lead to an increase in the quantity of Canadian goods demanded by foreign countries, that is, to an increase in Canadian exports. The increase is in the constant X of the net export function, which shifts upward as a result. A fall in foreign income leads to a downward shift in the net export function.

Foreign prices.   An increase in foreign prices will cause both foreign and domestic agents to substitute cheaper Canadian goods for the now more expensive foreign goods. This will cause changes in both exports and imports. Exports will rise, and the amount of imports associated with any given level of Canadian national income will fall. As a result the net export function will shift upward. A fall in foreign prices has the reverse effect, with substitution away from Canadian goods in favor of foreign goods and a downward shift in the net export curve.

Domestic prices.   An increase in domestic prices leads both foreign and domestic agents to substitute foreign goods for the now more expensive Canadian goods. The export part of net exports falls, and more imports will be associated with each level of domestic income. As a result the net export function shifts downward. A fall in domestic prices leads to substitution in favor of Canadian goods and an upward shift in the net export function.

The exchange rate.   A depreciation of the Canadian dollar has the effect of raising the Canadian price of imports while lowering the prices paid by foreigners for Canadian exports. It thus shifts expenditure away from foreign goods and toward Canadian goods. Canadians will import less at each level of Canadian national income, and foreigners will buy more of our export goods. The net export function thus shifts upward. An appreciation of the Canadian dollar has the opposite effect, causing substitution of foreign for Canadian goods, thus shifting the net export function downward.

Other Expenditure Categories

We have seen that desired consumption expenditure and desired net export expenditure each have an autonomous and an induced component. The induced components mean that desired aggregate expenditure depends on national income.

The relationship between desired aggregate expenditure and national income depends not only on desired consumption and net exports but also on the behavior of the other major expenditure categories, *I* and *G*. As we shall see in later chapters, changes in each of these play an important role in understanding changes in national income. For our present purposes of understanding how the equilibrium level of national income is determined, it is useful to keep things as simple as possible. Where we can, we treat these components as constant and include them in autonomous expenditure.

Desired investment expenditure. For the present it is convenient to study how the level of national income adjusts to a fixed level of planned real investment. So we assume that firms plan to make a constant amount of business fixed investment in plant each year and that they plan to hold their inventories constant. In Chapter 31 we shall drop these assumptions and study the important effects on national income caused by changes in the level of desired investment.

Desired government expenditure. Governments intend to spend, and succeed in spending, many billions of dollars on currently produced goods and services. In this chapter we take desired and actual real government expenditure as a constant. We assume that the real value of government expenditure does not change as the circumstances of the economy change. This assumption allows us to see how national income adjusts to a constant level of real government expenditure. In Chapter 32 we shall drop this assumption and study how national income responds to changes in desired and actual government expenditure.

The Aggregate Expenditure Function

The aggregate expenditure function relates the level of desired real expenditure to the level of real income. Total desired expenditure on the nation's output is the sum of desired consumption, investment, government, and net export expenditures, or

$$AE = C + I + G + (X - M)$$

Table 28-5 illustrates how such a function can be calculated, given the consumption function and the levels of desired investment, government, and net exports expenditures at each level of income. The resulting aggregate expenditure function is illustrated in Figure 28-4 (p. 597).

The Propensity to Spend out of National Income

Earlier we defined propensities to consume and to save that together account for all household disposable income. We now define propensities to spend and not to spend that together account for all national income.

The fraction of any increment to national income that will be spent on domestic production is measured by the change in aggregate expenditure divided by the change in income, symbolized by $\Delta AE/\Delta Y$. It is called the economy's **marginal propensity to spend.** The value of the marginal propensity to spend, which is something greater than zero but less than one, may be indicated by the letter z. The amount $1 - \Delta AE/\Delta Y$ is the fraction of any increment to national income that is not spent. This is the **marginal propensity not to spend.**[1] This makes the value of the marginal propensity not to spend $1 - z$.

---

[1] More fully, these terms would be called the marginal propensity to spend *on national income* and the marginal propensity to not spend *on national income*. Expenditures on imports are included in the latter. The marginal propensity not to spend $(1 - z)$ is often referred to as the *marginal propensity to withdraw.* Not spending a part of one's income amounts to a *withdrawal* from the circular flow of income as described in Figure 3-1.

Table 28-5   The Aggregate Expenditure Function (*billions of dollars*)

National income (Y)	Desired consumption expenditure (C = 100 + 0.72Y)	Desired investment expenditure (I = 250)	Desired government expenditure (G = 170)	Desired net exports expenditure (X − M = 240 − 0.10Y)	Desired aggregate expenditure (AE = C + I + G + [X − M])
100	172	250	170	230	952
400	388	250	170	200	1,008
500	460	250	170	190	1,070
1,000	820	250	170	140	1,380
2,000	1,540	250	170	40	2,000
3,000	2,260	250	170	−60	2,620
4,000	2,980	250	170	−160	3,240
5,000	3,700	250	170	−260	3,860

The aggregate expenditure function is the sum of desired consumption, investment, government, and net export expenditures. The table is based on the hypothetical data given in Tables 28-3 and 28-4. The autonomous components of desired aggregate expenditure are desired investment, desired government, desired export expenditures, and the constant term in desired consumption expenditure. The induced components are the second term in desired consumption expenditure ($0.72Y$) and desired imports ($0.1Y$).

The marginal response of consumption to a change in national income is 0.72, calculated as the product of the marginal propensity to consume (0.8) times the fraction of national income that becomes disposable income (0.9). Because this exceeds the marginal propensity to import out of national income (0.1), desired aggregate expenditure is positively related to national income, as shown in the column at the far right. The marginal response of desired aggregate expenditure to a change in national income, $\Delta AE/\Delta Y$, is 0.62.

To illustrate, suppose that the economy produces $1.00 of extra income and that the response to this is governed by the relationships in Tables 28-3 and 28-4. Since $0.10 is collected by the government as taxes, $0.90 is converted into disposable income, and 80 percent of this amount ($0.72) becomes consumption expenditure. But import expenditure also rises by $0.10, so expenditure on domestic goods, that is, aggregate expenditure, rises by $0.62. Thus *z,* the marginal propensity to spend, is 0.62 (0.62/1.00). What is not spent on domestic output includes the $0.10 in taxes, the $0.18 of disposable income that is saved, and the $0.10 of import expenditure, for a total of $0.38. Hence the marginal propensity not to spend, $1 - z$, is 0.38 = (1 − 0.62).

Determining Equilibrium National Income

Now we can see how equilibrium national income is determined, *given a constant price level.* To do this

we study the *equilibrium conditions,* the conditions that must be fulfilled if national income is to be in equilibrium.

Table 28-6 illustrates the determination of equilibrium national income for our simple hypothetical economy. Suppose that firms are producing a final output of $1,000 and thus national income is $1,000. According to the table, aggregate desired expenditure is $1,380 at this level of income. If firms persist in producing a current output of only $1,000 in the face of an aggregate desired expenditure of $1,380, one of two things must happen.[2]

One possibility is that households, firms, and governments will be unable to spend the extra $380 that they would like to spend, so lines or waiting lists of unsatisfied customers will appear. These queues will send a signal to firms that sales can be increased if production is increased. When the firms increase production, national income rises. Of course, the individual firms are interested only in

[2] A third possibility, that prices would rise, has been excluded by assumption in this chapter.

FIGURE 28-4   An Aggregate Expenditure Function

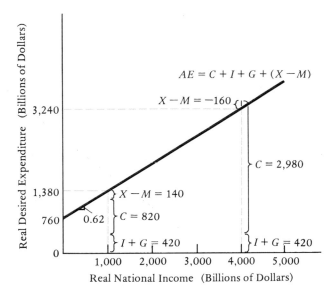

The aggregate expenditure function is derived by adding the four components of expenditure: consumption (*C*), investment (*I*), government (*G*), and net exports (*X* − *M*). The figure is drawn using the hypothetical data from Table 26-5. Substituting in the expressions from the table for each of the four components of *AE* gives

$$AE = (100 + 0.72Y) + 250 + 170 + (240 - 0.1Y)$$

Combining these terms we get

$$AE = 760 + 0.62Y$$

Hence in the figure the *AE* function is drawn as a straight line with an intercept of 760 and a slope of 0.62. The intercept is the sum of the two constant components (*I* + *G* = 420) plus the constant terms from the other two components (100 from *C* and 240 from *X* − *M*). The slope, 0.62, is the marginal propensity to spend. It represents the marginal response of consumption to a change in national income, 0.72, net of the marginal propensity to import, 0.10.

Two examples are illustrated. When income equals $1,000,

$$AE = 760 + (0.62 \times 1,000) = 1,380$$

If income rises by $3,000 to equal $4,000, investment and government expenditures remain at 420, consumption expenditure rises by 2,160 (0.72 × 3,000) to 2,980, and net exports fall by 300 (0.10 × 3,000) to −160. Thus *AE* rises by 1,860 to 3,240.

TABLE 28-6   The Determination of Equilibrium National Income (*billions of dollars*)

National income (Y)	Desired aggregate expenditure (AE = C + I + G + [X − M])	
100	952	Pressure on
400	1,008	income to
500	1,070	rise
1,000	1,380	↓
2,000	2,000	Equilibrium income
3,000	2,620	↑
4,000	3,240	Pressure on
5,000	3,860	income to fall

National income is in equilibrium where aggregate desired expenditure equals national income. The date are taken from Table 28-5. When national income is below its equilibrium level, aggregate desired expenditure exceeds the value of current output. This creates an incentive for firms to increase output and hence for national income to rise. When national income is above its equilibrium level, desired expenditure is less than the value of current output. This creates an incentive for firms to reduce output and hence for national income to fall. Only at the equilibrium level of national income is aggregate desired expenditure exactly equal to the value of the current output.

their own sales and profits, but their individual actions cause an increase in GDP.

The second possibility is that all spenders will spend everything they wanted to spend. But then expenditure will exceed current output, which can happen only when some expenditure plans are fulfilled by purchasing inventories of goods that were produced in the past. In this example the fulfillment of plans to purchase $1,380 worth of commodities in the face of a current output of only $1,000 will reduce inventories by $380. As long as inventories last, more goods can be sold than are currently being produced.

Eventually inventories will run out, but before this happens, firms will increase their output as they see their inventories being drawn down. Extra sales can then be made without a further pulling down of inventories. Once again the consequence of each individual firm's behavior, in search of its own individual profits, is an increase in national income. Thus the final response to an excess of aggregate desired expenditure over current output is a rise in national income toward its equilibrium value.

At any level of national income at which aggregate desired expenditure exceeds total output, there will be pressure for national income to rise.

Next consider national income equal to $4,000 in Table 28-6. At this level desired expenditure on domestically produced goods is only $3,240. If firms persist in producing $4,000 worth of goods, $760 worth must remain unsold. Therefore, inventories must rise. But firms will not allow inventories of unsold goods to rise indefinitely; sooner or later they will reduce the level of output to the level of sales. When they do, national income will fall.

At any level of income for which aggregate desired expenditure falls short of total output, there will be a pressure for national income to fall.

Finally, consider national income equal to $2,000 in the table. At this level, and only at this level, aggregate desired expenditure is exactly equal to national income. Purchasers fulfill their spending plans without causing inventories to change. There is no incentive for firms to alter output. Since total output is the same as national income, national income will remain steady; it is in equilibrium.

The equilibrium level of national income occurs where aggregate desired expenditure equals total output.

This conclusion is quite general and does not depend on the numbers used in the specific example. [37]

Equilibrium Illustrated

Figure 28-5 shows the determination of the equilibrium level of national income. The line labeled *AE* graphs the aggregate expenditure function. Its slope is the marginal propensity to spend. The line labeled *AE = Y* shows the equilibrium condition that de-

FIGURE 28-5   Equilibrium National Income

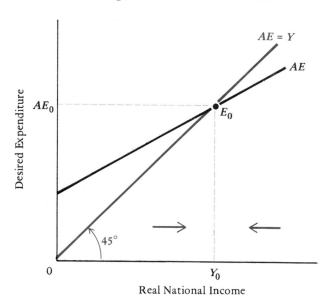

The equilibrium level of national income occurs at E_0, where the desired aggregate expenditure line intersects the 45° line. If real national income is below Y_0, desired aggregate expenditure will exceed national income, and production will rise. This is shown by the arrow to the left of Y_0. If national income is above Y_0, desired aggregate expenditure will be less than national income, and production will fall. This is shown by the arrow to the right of Y_0. Only when real national income is Y_0 will desired aggregate expenditure equal real national income ($AE_0 = Y_0$).

sired aggregate expenditure, *AE,* equals national income, *Y.* Since the *AE = Y* line plots points where the vertical distance equals the horizontal distance, it forms an angle of 45° with the axes. Any point on this line is a possible equilibrium.

Graphically, equilibrium occurs at the level of income at which the aggregate desired expenditure line intersects the 45° line. This is the level of income where desired expenditure is just equal to total national income and therefore is just sufficient to purchase total final output.

We have now explained the equilibrium level of national income that arises at a *given price level.* In the rest of this chapter we study the forces that cause equilibrium income to change; we continue with our simplifying assumption that the price level remains constant.

Changes in National Income

Since the *AE* curve plays a central role in our explanation of the equilibrium value of national income, you should not be surprised to hear that the behavior of the *AE* curve also plays a central role in explaining why national income changes. To understand this influence we must recall an important distinction first encountered in Chapter 4.

Suppose desired aggregate expenditure rises. This may be either a response to a change in national income or the result of an increased desire to spend at each level of national income. A change in national income causes a *movement along* the aggregate expenditure function. An increased desire to spend at each level of national income causes a *shift in* the aggregate expenditure function. Figure 28-6 illustrates this important distinction.

Shifts in the Aggregate Expenditure Function

For any specific aggregate expenditure function there is a unique level of equilibrium national income. If the aggregate expenditure function shifts, the equilibrium will be disturbed and national income will change. Thus if we wish to find causes of changes in national income, we must look for causes of shifts in the *AE* function.

The aggregate expenditure function shifts when one of its components shifts, that is, when there is a shift in the consumption function, in desired investment expenditure, in desired government expenditure, or in desired net exports. Such shifts were defined earlier as changes in *autonomous* aggregate expenditure.

Increases in Autonomous Expenditure

What will happen if households permanently increase their levels of consumption spending at each level of disposable income? If the Ford Motor Company increases its rate of annual investment by $25 million

FIGURE 28-6 Movements Along and Shifts of the *AE* Curve

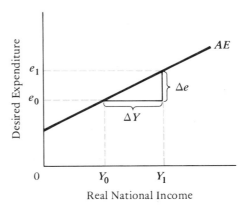

(i) A movement along the *AE* function

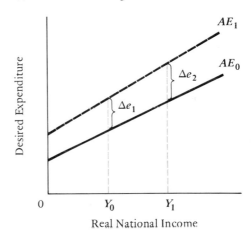

(ii) A shift of the *AE* function

A movement along the aggregate expenditure function occurs in response to a change in income; a shift of the *AE* function indicates a different level of desired expenditure at each level of income. In part (i) a change in income of ΔY, from Y_0 to Y_1, changes expenditure by Δe, from e_0 to e_1. In part (ii) a shift in the expenditure function from AE_0 to AE_1 raises the amount of expenditure associated with *each* level of income. At Y_0, for example, desired aggregate expenditure is increased by Δe_1; at Y_1, it is increased by Δe_2. (If the shift is a parallel one, $\Delta e_1 = \Delta e_2$.)

in order to meet the threat from imported cars? If the government increases its defense spending? Or if grain exports soar? (In considering these questions, remember that we are dealing with continuous flows measured as so much per period of time. An upward shift in the expenditure function means that expenditure rises to and stays at a higher amount.)

Because any such increase shifts the entire aggre-gate expenditure function upward, the same analysis applies to all of the changes mentioned. Two types of shift in *AE* occur. First, if the same addition to expenditure occurs at all levels of income, the *AE* curve shifts parallel to itself, as shown in Figure 28-7(i). Second, if there is a change in the propensity to spend out of national income, the slope of the *AE* curve changes, as shown in Figure 28-7(ii). (Recall

---

FIGURE 28-7   Shifts in the *AE* Function

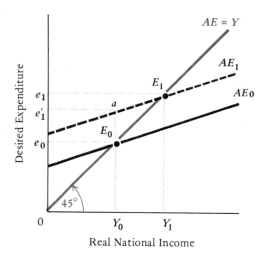

(i) A parallel shift in *AE*

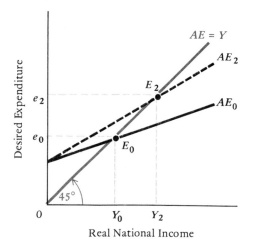

(ii) A change in the slope of *AE*

Upward shifts in the *AE* function increase equilib-rium income; downward shifts decrease equilibrium income. In both part (i) and part (ii) the aggregate ex-penditure function is initially AE_0, with national income Y_0.

In part (i) a parallel upward *shift* in the *AE* curve from AE_0 to AE_1 means that desired expenditure has in-creased by the same amount at each level of national in-come. For example, at Y_0 desired expenditure rises from e_0 to e_1' and therefore exceeds national income. Equilib-rium is reached at E_1, where income is Y_1 and expendi-ture e_1. The increase in desired expenditure from e_1' to e_1, represented by a *movement along AE_1*, is an induced re-sponse to the increase in income from Y_0 to Y_1.

In part (ii) a nonparallel upward shift in the *AE* curve, say, from AE_0 to AE_2, means that the marginal propensity to spend at each level of national income has increased. This leads to an increase in equilibrium na-tional income. Equilibrium is reached at E_2, where the new level of expenditure e_2 is equal to income Y_2. Again, the initial *shift* in the *AE* curve induces a *movement along* the new *AE* curve.

Downward shifts in the *AE* function, from AE_1 to AE_0 or from AE_2 to AE_0, would lead to a fall in equilib-rium income to Y_0.

that the slope of the *AE* curve is *z*, the marginal propensity to spend.)

Figure 28-7 shows that upward shifts in the aggregate expenditure function increase equilibrium national income. There we see that an upward *shift* of the *AE* curve will induce a *movement along* the new *AE* curve. This will not stop until a new equilibrium occurs. At the new, higher equilibrium level of national income, the flow of desired aggregate expenditure again equals national income. (We continue to assume that the price level is constant.)

Decreases in Autonomous Expenditure

What will happen to national income if consumption, investment, government spending, or exports decrease? All these changes shift the aggregate expenditure function downward. A constant reduction in expenditure at all levels of income shifts *AE* parallel to itself. A fall in the propensity to spend out of national income reduces the slope of the *AE* function.

Changes in Tax Rates

If tax rates change, the relationship between disposable income and national income changes.[3] For the same level of national income there will be a different level of disposable income and thus a different level of consumption. This is illustrated in Table 28-7. Consequently, *z*, the marginal propensity to spend out of national income, will have changed.

Consider a decrease in tax rates. If the government decreases its rate of income tax so that it collects 10 cents less out of every dollar of national income, disposable income rises in relation to national income. Thus consumption also rises at every level of national income. This results in a (nonparallel) upward shift of the *AE* curve, that is, a change in the slope of the curve, as shown in Figure 28-7(ii). The result of this shift will be a rise in equilibrium national income, as is also shown in Figure 28-7(ii).

A rise in tax rates has the opposite effect. It reduces disposable income and hence less consumption

[3] Effective tax rates can be changed either by changes in the percent of taxable income that is taken in taxes or by changes in the percent of national income that is taxable. For simplicity, in the text we have assumed that all national income is taxable.

expenditure at each level of national income. This results in a (nonparallel) downward shift of the *AE* curve and thus decreases the level of equilibrium national income. This, too, is illustrated in Figure 28-7(ii).

The results restated.   We have now derived two important general predictions of the elementary theory of national income.

1. **A rise in the amount of desired consumption, investment, government, or export expenditure associated with each level of national income will increase equilibrium national income.**
2. **A fall in the amount of desired consumption, investment, government, or export expenditure associated with each level of national income will lower equilibrium national income.**

A change in desired consumption in relation to national income can arise, as we have seen, either because the consumption function shifts or because the relation between disposable income and national income is altered.

The Multiplier

We now know the *direction* of the changes in national income that occur in response to various shifts in the aggregate expenditure function. But what about the *magnitude* of these changes?

Economists need an answer to this question to determine the effects of changes in expenditures in both the private and public sectors. During a recession the government often takes measures to stimulate the economy. If these measures have a larger effect than estimated, demand may rise too much and full employment may be reached with demand still rising. This outcome will have an inflationary impact on the economy. If the government greatly overestimates the effect of its measures, the recession will persist longer than is necessary. In this case there is a danger that the policy will be discredited as ineffective, even though the correct diagnosis is that too little of the right thing was done.

TABLE 28-7   Tax Changes Shift the Function Relating Consumption to National Income (*billions of dollars*)

(1) National income (Y)	Disposable income equal to 80 percent of national income		Disposable income equal to 90 percent of national income	
	(2) Disposable income ($Y_d = 0.8Y$)	(3) Consumption ($C = 100 + 0.8Y_d$)	(4) Disposable income ($Y_d = 0.9Y$)	(5) Consumption ($C = 100 + 0.8Y_d$)
100	80	164	90	172
500	400	420	450	460
1,000	800	740	900	820

The consumption function shifts if the relation between disposable and national income changes. The table is based on the simplified hypothetical consumption function from Table 28-1 combined with the assumption that Y_d is a constant fraction of Y. Initially, $Y_d = 0.8Y$. This yields a schedule relating consumption to national income that is given in columns 1 and 3 and is described by the equation $C = 100 + 0.64Y$. Income tax rates are then decreased so that now 90 percent of national income becomes disposable income. Column 4 indicates the Y_d that corresponds at the decreased tax rate to each level of Y shown in column 1. With an unchanged consumption function, consumption at the new tax rate is given by column 5. Columns 1 and 5 give the new schedule relating consumption to national income, described by the equation $C = 100 + 0.72Y$.

Definition. A measure of the magnitude of changes in income is provided by the multiplier. We have just seen that a shift in the aggregate expenditure curve will cause a change in equilibrium national income. Such a shift will be caused by a change in any autonomous component of aggregate expenditure, for example, an increase or decrease in investment or government spending. An increase in desired aggregate expenditure increases equilibrium national income by a multiple of the initial increase in autonomous expenditure. The **multiplier** is the ratio of changed income to changed expenditure, that is, the change in national income divided by the change in autonomous expenditure that brings it about.

Why the multiplier is greater than unity. What will happen to national income if, with unchanged tax rates, the government increases its spending on road construction by $1 billion per year?

Initially the road program will create $1 billion worth of new national income and a corresponding amount of employment for households and firms on which the initial billion dollars is spent. But this is not the end of the story. The increase in national income of $1 billion will cause an increase in disposable income, which will cause an induced rise in consumption expenditure. Road crews and road contractors, who gain new income directly from the government's road program, will spend some of it on food, clothing, entertainment, cars, television sets, and other consumption commodities. When output expands to meet this demand, employment will increase in all the affected industries. New incomes will then be created for workers and firms in these industries. When they in turn spend their newly earned incomes, output and employment will rise further. More income will be created and more expenditure induced. Indeed, at this stage you could wonder whether the increases in income will ever come to an end. To deal with this concern, we need to consider the multiplier in more precise terms.

The simple multiplier. Consider an increase in autonomous expenditure of ΔA, which might be, say, $1 billion per year. Remember that ΔA stands for *any* increase in autonomous expenditure; this could be an increase in investment, in government purchases, in exports, or in the autonomous component of consumption. The new autonomous expenditure shifts the aggregate expenditure function upward by that amount. National income is no longer in equilibrium at its original level since desired aggregate

FIGURE 28-8   The Simple Multiplier

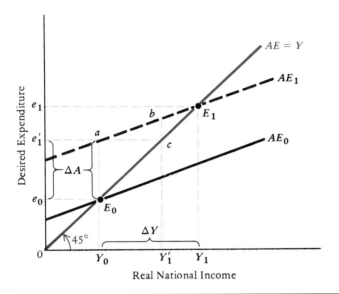

An increase in desired aggregate expenditure increases equilibrium national income by a multiple of the initial increase in autonomous expenditure. The initial equilibrium occurs at E_0 where AE_0 intersects the 45° line. At this point, desired expenditure e_0 is equal to national income Y_0. An increase in autonomous expenditure of ΔA then shifts the desired expenditure function upward to AE_1. If national income stays at Y_0, desired expenditure at point a is e_1'. Since this level of desired expenditure is greater than income, national income will rise. If income rises only by ΔA, it rises to Y_1' (point c, where $e_1' = Y_1'$). But at Y_1' desired expenditure still exceeds income by the amount bc.

Equilibrium occurs when income rises to Y_1. Here desired expenditure e_1 equals income Y_1. The extra expenditure of $e_1'e_1$ represents the induced increases in expenditure. It is the amount by which the final increase in income, ΔY, exceeds the initial increase in autonomous expenditure, ΔA. Since ΔY is greater than ΔA, the multiplier is greater than unity.

expenditure now exceeds income. Equilibrium is restored by a *movement along* the new AE curve.

The **simple multiplier** measures the change in equilibrium national income that occurs in response to a change in autonomous expenditure *at a constant price level*. We refer to it as simple because we have simplified the situation by assuming that the price level is constant. Figure 28-8 illustrates the simple multiplier and makes clear that it is greater than unity. Box 28-1 (p. 605) provides a numerical example.

The Size of the Simple Multiplier

The size of the multiplier depends on the slope of the AE function, that is, on the marginal propensity to spend, z. This is illustrated in Figure 28-9.

A high marginal propensity to spend means a steep AE curve. The expenditure induced by any initial increase in income is large, with the result that the final rise in income is correspondingly large. By contrast, a low marginal propensity to spend means a relatively flat AE curve. The expenditure induced by the initial increase in income is small, and the final

rise in income is not much larger than the initial rise in autonomous expenditure that brought it about.

The larger the marginal propensity to spend, the steeper the aggregate expenditure function and the larger the multiplier.

The precise value of the simple multiplier can be derived by using elementary algebra. The derivation is given in Box 28-2 (p. 606). The result is that the simple multiplier, which we call K, is

$$K = \Delta Y/\Delta A = 1/(1 - z)$$

where z is the marginal propensity to spend out of national income. (As we have seen, z is the slope of the aggregate expenditure function.)

As we saw earlier, the term $1 - z$ stands for the marginal propensity not to spend out of national income. For example, if $0.80 of every $1.00 of new national income is spent ($z = 0.80$), then $0.20 is the amount not spent. The value of the multiplier is then calculated as $K = 1/0.20 = 5$.

The simple multiplier can be written as the reciprocal of the marginal propensity not to spend.

FIGURE 28-9   The Size of the Simple Multiplier

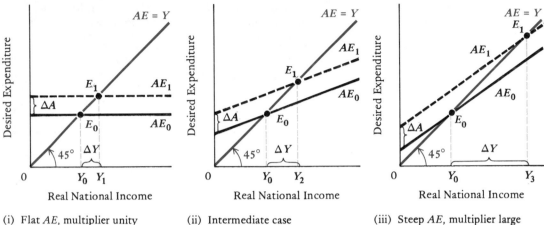

(i) Flat *AE*, multiplier unity   (ii) Intermediate case   (iii) Steep *AE*, multiplier large

The larger the marginal propensity to spend out of national income (z), the steeper the AE curve and the larger the multiplier. In each part of the figure the aggregate expenditure function is AE_0, equilibrium is at E_0, with income Y_0. The AE curve then shifts upward to AE_1 as a result of an increase in autonomous expenditure of ΔA. ΔA is the same in each part. The new equilibrium is at E_1.

In part (i) the AE function is horizontal, indicating a marginal propensity to spend of zero ($z = 0$). The change in income ΔY is only the increase in autonomous expenditure since there is no induced expenditure by those who receive the initial increase in income. The simple multiplier is then unity, its minimum possible value.

In part (ii) the AE curve slopes upward but is still relatively flat (z is low). The increase in national income to Y_2 is only slightly greater than the increase in autonomous expenditure that brought it about.

In part (iii) the AE function is quite steep (z is high). Now the increase in income to Y_3 is much larger than the increase in autonomous expenditure that brought it about. The simple multiplier is quite large.

From this we see that if $1 - z$ is very small, the multiplier will be very large (because extra income induces much extra spending). The largest possible value of $1 - z$ is unity, when z equals zero, indicating that all extra national income is not spent. In this case the multiplier itself has a value of unity, indicating that the increase in equilibrium national income is confined to the initial increase in autonomous expenditure. This is illustrated in Figure 28-9.

To estimate the size of the multiplier in an actual economy, we need to estimate the value of the marginal propensity not to spend out of national income in that economy. Evidence suggests that the Cana-dian value is larger than the 0.2 we used in our example.

The various elements of national income that are "not spent," that is, that are in $1 - z$, include income taxes, savings, and import expenditures. For the Canadian economy in the 1980s this leads to a realistic estimate of about 0.5 for z and thus also about 0.5 for $1 - z$. Thus the simple multiplier is approximately equal to 2, not 5 as in the example.

The simple multiplier is a useful starting point for understanding the effects of expenditure shifts on national income; however, many complications will arise in subsequent chapters.

BOX 28-1

The Multiplier: A Numerical Example

Consider an economy that has a marginal propensity to spend out of national income of 0.80. Suppose that autonomous expenditure increases by $1 billion per year because the government spends an extra $1 billion per year on new roads. National income initially rises by $1 billion. But that is not the end of it. The factors of production involved in road building that received the first $1 billion spend $800 million. This second round of spending generates $800 million of new income. This new income in turn induces $640 million of third-round spending. And so it continues,

with each successive round of new income generating 80 percent as much in new expenditure. Each additional round of expenditure creates new income and yet another round of expenditure.

The table carries the process through 10 rounds. Students with sufficient patience (and no faith in mathematics) may compute as many rounds in the process as they wish; they will find that the sum of the rounds of expenditures approaches a limit of $5 billion, which is five times the initial increase in expenditure. [38] The graph of the cumulative expenditure increases shows how quickly this limit is approached. The multiplier is thus 5, given the assumption about the marginal propensity to spend. Had the marginal propensity to spend been lower, say, 0.667, the process would have been similar, but it would have approached a limit of three instead of five times the initial increase in expenditure.

Spending Round

Round of spending	Increase in expenditure (millions of dollars)	Cumulative total (millions of dollars)
Initial increase	1,000.0	1,000.0
2	800.0	1,800.0
3	640.0	2,440.0
4	512.0	2,952.0
5	409.6	3,361.6
6	327.7	3,689.3
7	262.1	3,951.4
8	209.7	4,161.1
9	167.8	4,328.9
10	134.2	4,463.1
11 to 20 combined	479.3	4,942.4
All others	57.6	5,000.0

BOX 28-2

The Multiplier: An Algebraic Approach

High school algebra is all that is needed to derive the exact expression for the multiplier. Readers who feel at home with algebra may want to follow this derivation. Others can skip it and rely on the graphical and numerical arguments given in the text.

First we derive the equation for the *AE* curve. Aggregate expenditure is divided into autonomous expenditure, *A*, and induced expenditure, *N*.* So we write

$$AE = N + A \qquad [1]$$

Since *N* is expenditure that varies with income, we can write

$$N = zY \qquad [2]$$

where *z* is the marginal propensity to spend out of national income. (It is a positive number between zero and unity.) Substituting Equation 2 in Equation 1 yields the equation of the *AE* curve.

$$AE = zY + A \qquad [3]$$

Now we write the equation of the 45° line,

$$AE = Y \qquad [4]$$

* In simple models *N* is mainly consumption expenditure, but in other models it may include other types of expenditure. All that matters is that there is one class of expenditure, *N*, that varies with income and another class, *A*, that does not.

which states the equilibrium condition that aggregate desired expenditure must equal national income. Equations 3 and 4 are two equations with two unknowns, *AE* and *Y.* To solve we substitute Equation 3 in Equation 4 to obtain

$$Y = zY + A$$

Subtracting *zY* from both sides yields

$$Y - zY = A$$

Factoring out *Y* yields

$$Y(1 - z) = A$$

Dividing through by $1 - z$ yields

$$Y = A/(1 - z)$$

This tells us the equilibrium value of *Y* in terms of autonomous expenditures *A* and the propensity not to spend out of national income $(1 - z)$. The expression $Y = A/(1 - z)$ tells us that if *A* changes by ΔA, the change in *Y,* which we call $\Delta Y,$ will be

$$\Delta Y = \Delta A/(1 - z)$$

Dividing through by ΔA gives the value of the multiplier, which we designate by *K*:

$$K = \Delta Y/\Delta A = 1/(1 - z)$$

Summary

1. When the price level is fixed, national income depends on desired aggregate expenditure.
2. Desired aggregate expenditure includes desired consumption, desired investment, and desired government expenditures plus desired net exports. It is the amount that decision makers want to spend on purchasing the national product.
3. A change in disposable income leads to a change in consumption and saving. The responsiveness of these changes is measured by the marginal propensity to consume (*MPC*) and the marginal propensity to save (*MPS*), which are both positive and sum to one.
4. A change in wealth tends to cause a change in the allocation of

disposable income between consumption and saving. The change in consumption is positively related to the change in wealth, while the change in saving is negatively related to this change.

5. Since desired imports increase as national income increases, desired net exports decrease as national income increases, other things being equal. This gives rise to a negatively sloped net export function.

6. At the equilibrium level of national income, purchasers wish to buy neither more nor less than what is being produced. At incomes above equilibrium, desired expenditure falls short of national income, and output will sooner or later be curtailed. At incomes below equilibrium, desired expenditure exceeds national income, and output will sooner or later be increased.

7. Equilibrium national income is represented graphically by the point at which the aggregate expenditure curve cuts the 45° line, that is, where total desired expenditure equals total output.

8. Equilibrium national income is increased by a rise in the desired consumption, investment, government, or export expenditure associated with each level of the national income. Equilibrium national income is decreased by a fall in desired expenditures.

9. Equilibrium national income is decreased by a rise in the taxes associated with each level of national income, and increased by a fall in taxes.

10. The magnitude of the effect on national income of shifts in autonomous expenditure is given by the multiplier. It is defined as $K = \Delta Y / \Delta A$, where ΔA is the change in autonomous expenditure.

11. The simple multiplier is the multiplier when the price level is constant. It is equal to $1/(1 - z)$, where z is the marginal propensity to spend out of national income. Thus the larger z is, the larger is the multiplier. It is a basic prediction of national income theory that the simple multiplier is greater than unity.

Topics for Review

Desired expenditure
Consumption function
Average and marginal propensities to consume and to save
Aggregate expenditure function
Marginal propensities to spend and not to spend
Equilibrium national income at a given price level
Shifts of and movements along expenditure curves
Effect on national income of changes in desired expenditures
Effect on national income of a change in tax rates
The simple multiplier and the slope of the AE curve

Discussion Questions

1. "The concept of an equilibrium level of national income is useless because the economy is never in equilibrium. If it ever got there, no economist would recognize it anyway." Discuss.

2. Interpret each of the following statements either in terms of the shape of a consumption function or the values of *MPC* and *APC*.
   a. "Tom Green has lost his job, and his family is existing on its past savings."
   b. "The Grimsby household is so rich that they used all the extra income they earned this year to invest in a wildcat oil-drilling venture."
   c. "The widow Hammerstein can barely make ends meet by clipping coupons on the bonds left to her by dear Henry, but she would never dip into her capital."
   d. "We always thought Harris was a miser, but when his wife left him he took to wine, women, and song."
   e. "When the Schultzes' rich aunt died and left them some money, they stopped putting $10 a week to their account with the trust company."

3. Why might an individual's marginal propensity to consume be higher in the long run than in the short run? Why might it be lower? Is it possible for an individual's average propensity to consume to be greater than unity in the short run? In the long run? Can a country's average propensity to consume be greater than unity in the short run? In the long run?

4. Explain carefully why national income changes when aggregate desired expenditure does not equal national income. Sketch scenarios that fit the cases of too much and too little desired expenditure.

5. Predict whether each of the following events will, other things being equal, increase, decrease, or leave unchanged the size of the multiplier.
   a. Shift from foreign travel to holidays at home
   b. Increase in expenditures on highways
   c. Decisions by corporations to decrease the percentage of earnings they pay out in dividends and to increase their bank balances whenever national income falls
   d. Widespread adoption by cities of a city income tax
   e. Large increase in the percentage of disposable income saved by households

6. Explain how a sudden unexpected fall in consumer expenditure would initially cause an increase in investment expenditure by firms.

7. State the implied impact on the *AE* curve, and hence on equilibrium national income, relating to each of the following headlines.
   a. "Ottawa's planned spending up 10.5%."
   b. "Soviet Union agrees to buy more Canadian wheat."
   c. "Major Canadian companies expected to cut capital outlays."
   d. "Tax Reform Promises Lower Personal Tax Rates."
   e. "Ottawa Considers Major Cut in Old Age Security Payments."
   f. "Decrease in Spending on Foreign Travel Reflected in Increase in Saving."
   g. "Import cars boom spell trouble for Canadian Auto Industry."

8. Homer Hardcrust, chairman of the Economic Council of Canada, proposes that because of the current heavy unemployment, government should prepare an austerity program and cut down government expenditures to set an example for private households. What do you think the effects of his policy would be?

29

National Income and the Price Level in the Short Run

In Chapter 28 we treated the price level as constant. This was a reasonable simplification, on the principle that it is easier to study things one at a time than all at once. It allowed us to focus on the questions of how equilibrium national income is determined and why it changes. However, the assumption that the price level is constant is obviously unrealistic, and the time has now come to drop it.

We make the transition to a variable price level in two steps. First, we study the consequences for national income of exogenous changes in the price level—changes that happen for reasons that are not explained by our theory. Then we elaborate our theory to make the price level endogenous so that we can use our theory to study and explain movements in *both* national income and the price level.

Exogenous Changes in the Price Level

What happens to equilibrium national income when the price level changes for some exogenous reason, such as a rise in the prices of imported raw materials? To find out we need to understand how a change in the price level affects the desired aggregate expenditure curve.

Desired Aggregate Expenditure

The important result that we now wish to establish is that the price level and desired aggregate expenditure are negatively related to each other. In other words, a rise in the price level shifts the aggregate expenditure curve downward, while a fall in the price level shifts it upward. The explanation lies in two effects: what the change in the price level does to imports and exports, and what it does to the real value of wealth and hence to desired consumption expenditure. It is sufficient to look only at the implications of an increase in the price level in detail, since a decrease merely reverses everything.

Changes in international relative prices. When the domestic price level rises, Canadian goods become more expensive relative to foreign goods. As we saw in Chapter 28, this change in relative prices causes Canadians to reduce their purchases of Canadian goods, which have now become relatively more expensive, and to increase their purchases of foreign goods, which have now become relatively less expensive. At the same time consumers in other countries reduce their purchases of the now relatively expensive Canadian goods. We saw in Chapter 28 that these changes can be summarized as a downward shift in the net export function.

A rise in the domestic price level shifts the net export function downward, which in turn implies a downward shift in the desired aggregate expenditure curve. A fall in the domestic price level shifts the net export and desired aggregate expenditure curves upward.

Changes in the real value of wealth.   Much of the private sector's total wealth is held in the form of assets with a fixed nominal money value. One obvious example is money itself—cash and bank deposits. Other examples are provided by many kinds of debt, including treasury bills and bonds. When a bill or a bond matures, the owner is repaid a stated sum of money. What that money can buy—its real value—depends on the price level. For this reason, a rise in the domestic price level lowers the real value of all assets denominated in money units and hence lowers the wealth of their owners.

How does a fall in the real value of the private sector's wealth affect the aggregate expenditure curve?[1] As we saw in Chapter 28 (see Figure 28-2 on page 591), there is a direct link between wealth and consumption. Because households have less wealth, they increase their saving so as to restore their wealth to the level they desire for such purposes as retirement. An increase in saving of course implies a reduction in consumption.

A rise in the domestic price level lowers the real value of total wealth, which leads to a fall in desired consumption; this in turn implies a

downward shift in the desired aggregate expenditure curve. A fall in the domestic price level leads to a rise in wealth and desired consumption and thus to an upward shift in the desired aggregate expenditure curve.**

We have concentrated here on the direct effect of the change in wealth on desired consumption expenditure. There is also an indirect effect that operates through the interest rate. Although this effect is potentially very powerful, we cannot study it until we have studied the macroeconomic role of money and interest rates. Further discussion of this point must therefore be postponed until Chapter 34.[2]

Effects on Equilibrium National Income

Both because of a fall in the net export function and because of a fall in desired consumption, a rise in the price level causes the aggregate desired expenditure curve to shift downward. This is shown in Figure 29-1. The figure also allows us to reconfirm what we already know from Chapter 28: when the *AE* curve shifts downward, the equilibrium level of national income falls.

A rise in the price level causes the *AE* curve to shift down and thus leads to a fall in equilibrium national income.

Now suppose that there is a fall in the price level. Since this is the opposite of the case just studied, we can summarize the two key effects briefly. First, Canadian goods become relatively cheaper internationally, so net exports rise. Second, the purchasing power of some existing assets that are denominated in money terms is increased, so households spend more. The resulting increase in desired expenditure on Canadian goods causes the *AE* curve to shift up

---

[1] It is worth noting that all changes in the real value of a person's wealth do not change the total wealth of the private sector. In many cases the change in wealth of a creditor is exactly offset by the change in wealth of a debtor. For example, a rise in the price level lowers the real wealth of a bond holder but raises the real wealth of the bond issuer, who will have to part with less purchasing power when the bond is redeemed. However, many assets held by individuals are government debt, and hence any change in the price level causes a net change in the wealth of the private sector.

[2] Here is a brief summary of what is involved. When the price level rises, firms and households need to cover their increased money expenses between one payday and the next. This means they need to hold more money on average. The increased demand for money bids up the price that must be paid to borrow money (the interest rate). Firms that borrow money to build plants and to purchase equipment, and households that borrow money to buy durable goods and housing, respond to rising interest rates by choosing to spend less. This means a decrease in the aggregate demand for the nation's output.

FIGURE 29-1   Aggregate Expenditure and the Price Level

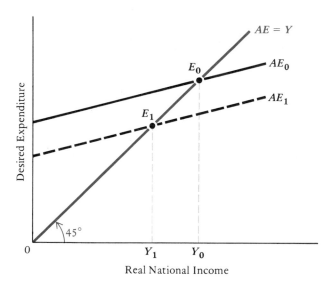

Changes in the price level cause the *AE* curve to shift and thus cause equilibrium national income to change. At the initial price level, the *AE* curve is given by the solid line AE_0 and hence equilibrium national income is Y_0. An increase in the price level reduces desired aggregate expenditure and thus causes the *AE* curve to shift down to the dashed line AE_1. As a result equilibrium national income falls to Y_1.

Starting with the dashed line AE_1, a fall in the price level would increase desired aggregate expenditure, shifting the *AE* curve up to AE_0 and raising equilibrium national income to Y_1.

and hence raises equilibrium national income. This is also shown in Figure 29-1.

A fall in the domestic price level leads to a rise in net exports and desired consumption expenditure; this causes the aggregate expenditure curve to shift up and equilibrium national income to rise.

The Aggregate Demand Curve

We now know from the behavior underlying the aggregate expenditure curve that the price level and real national income are negatively related to each other; that is, a change in the price level changes equilibrium national income in the opposite direction. This negative relationship can be shown in an important new concept called the *aggregate demand curve*.

Recall that the *AE* curve relates equilibrium national income to desired expenditure for a given price level, plotting national income on the horizontal axis. The **aggregate demand (*AD*) curve** relates equilibrium national income to the price level, again plotting national income on the horizontal axis. Because the horizontal axes of both the *AE* and the *AD* curves measure real national income, the two curves can be placed one above the other so that the level of national income on each can be compared directly. This is shown in Figure 29-2.

Now let us see how the *AD* curve is derived. Given a value of the price level, equilibrium national income is determined in part (i) of the figure by the now familiar condition that the *AE* curve crosses the 45° line. In part (ii) of the figure, the combination of the equilibrium level of national income and the corresponding value of the price level is plotted, giving one point on the *AD* curve.

When the price level changes, the *AE* curve shifts, for the reasons just seen. The new position of the *AE* curve gives rise to a new equilibrium level of national income that is associated with the new price level. This determines a second point on the *AD* curve in Figure 29-2(ii).

Any change in the price level leads to a new *AE* curve and hence to a new level of equilibrium income. Each combination of equilibrium income and its associated price level becomes a particular point on the *AD* curve.

Note that since the *AD* curve relates equilibrium national income to the price level, changes in the price level that cause shifts in the *AE* curve cause movements along the *AD* curve. A movement along the *AD* curve thus traces out the response of equilibrium income to a change in the price level.

The Slope of the AD Curve

We already know enough to establish that the *AD* curve is negatively sloped.

FIGURE 29-2   The *AD* Curve and the *AE* Curve

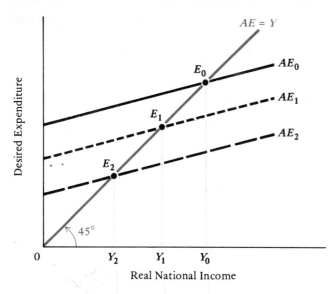

(i) Aggregate expenditure

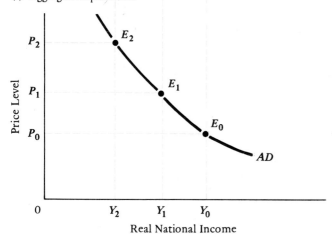

(ii) Aggregate demand

Equilibrium income is determined by the *AE* curve for each given price level; the level of income and its associated price level are then plotted to yield the *AD* curve. When the price level is P_0, the *AE* curve is AE_0 and hence equilibrium national income is Y_0, as shown in part (i). (This reproduces the initial equilibrium from Figure 29-1.) Plotting Y_0 against P_0 yields the point E_0 on the *AD* curve in part (ii).

An increase in the price level to P_1 causes AE_0 in part (i) to shift down to AE_1 and thus causes equilibrium national income to fall to Y_1. Plotting this new lower level of national income Y_1 against the higher price level P_1 yields a second point, E_1, on the *AD* curve in part (ii). A further increase in the price level to P_2 causes the *AE* curve in part (i) to shift down further, to AE_2, and thus causes equilibrium national income to fall further, to Y_2. Plotting Y_2 against P_2 yields a third point, E_2, on the *AD* curve in part (ii).

Thus a change in the price level causes a shift in the *AE* curve in part (i) and a movement along the *AD* curve in part (ii).

1. **A rise in the price level causes the aggregate expenditure curve to shift down and hence leads to a movement up and to the left along the *AD* curve, reflecting a fall in the equilibrium level of national income.**
2. **A fall in the price level causes the aggregate expenditure curve to shift up and hence leads** to a movement down and to the right along the *AD* curve, reflecting an increase in the equilibrium level of national income.

Early in our study (Chapter 4) we saw that demand curves for individual goods such as carrots or automobiles are also negatively sloped. However, the reasons for the negative slope of the *AD* curve are very different from the reasons for the negative slope of individual demand curves used in microeconomics; this important point is discussed further in Box 29-1.

Equilibrium National Income and Price Level

So far we have explained the equilibrium level of national income that arises *when the price level is taken as given*. We have also seen how that equilibrium level of national income would change if the price level were to change. What we have not yet done is explain what would cause the price level to change. We are now ready to take the important step of adding to our story an *explanation* of the behavior of the price level.

The equilibrium condition we have used so far is that desired aggregate expenditure be the same as national income, and thus our focus has been on spending decisions. To see how we might add an explanation of the price level to the model, let us briefly re-examine the aggregate demand curve.

Another Look at the Aggregate Demand Curve

The *AD* curve shows, for any given price level, the level of national income at which desired aggregate expenditure will equal national income. If that level of output were produced, purchasers would just be prepared to buy it. If a lower level were produced, desired purchases would exceed output. If a larger level were produced, desired purchases would be less than output.

Thus the *AD* curve only describes a demand equilibrium·

Any point on the *AD* curve is such that *if* the level of national income given by that point is produced, *then* at the corresponding price level desired aggregate expenditure will equal national income.

This is illustrated in Figure 29-3 (p. 615). A point on the *AD* curve thus indicates the equilibrium level of national income as long as we can take the price level as given and as long as we can assume that the associated level of national income will in fact be produced.

By treating the price level as given and by assuming that the quantity of output produced will equal whatever is demanded, we have been able to ignore supply decisions. Now, in order to *explain* the price level, we need to incorporate the supply decisions of firms into our analysis.

Aggregate Supply

Aggregate supply refers to the total output of goods that firms wish to produce.[3] Aggregate supply thus reflects decisions of firms to hire workers in order to produce goods and services to sell to households, governments, and other firms.

Suppose that firms wish to increase output above current production levels. For the moment, suppose further that the prices of all the inputs that firms use—labor, capital, and so forth—remain constant. Constant factor prices do not, however, mean that either the per unit costs that firms incur or the output prices they charge will remain unchanged as they expand output.

Increasing output may require that less efficient standby machines and plants are used, that less efficient workers are employed, and that existing workers are given overtime hours at premium wages. Thus even with the restriction that input prices remain constant, higher output is associated with increased costs because it requires the use of more and more costly methods of production. This increase in cost per unit of output is referred to as rising **unit costs.**

Since expanding output often means incurring higher unit costs, firms will generally expand output only if the higher output can be sold at higher prices.

Now consider what happens when firms wish to reduce their output. The forces just mentioned work

[3] Recall from Chapter 27 that total output equals national income.

BOX 29-1

The Shape of the Aggregate Demand Curve

In Chapter 4 we studied the demand curves for individual products. It is tempting to think that the properties of the aggregate demand curve arise from the same behavior that gives rise to those individual demand curves. Unfortunately, life is not so simple. Let us see why we cannot take such an approach.

If we assume that we can obtain a downward-sloping aggregate demand curve in the same manner that we derived downward-sloping individual market demand curves, we would be committing the *fallacy of composition*. This is to assume that what is correct for the parts must be correct for the whole.

Consider a simple example of the fallacy. Any art collector can go into the market and add to her private collection of nineteenth century French paintings provided only that she has enough money. But to assume that because any one person can do this, everyone could do so simultaneously is plainly wrong. The world's stock of nineteenth century French paintings is totally fixed. All of us cannot do what any one of us with enough money can do.

How does the fallacy of composition relate to demand curves? An individual demand curve describes a situation in which the price of one commodity

changes while the prices of all other commodities and consumers' money incomes are constant. Such an individual demand curve is negatively sloped for two reasons. First, as the price of the commodity rises, each consumer's given money income will buy a smaller *total* amount of goods, so a smaller quantity of the commodity will be bought. Second, as the price of the commodity rises, consumers buy less of it and more of the now relatively cheaper substitutes.

The first reason has no application to the aggregate demand curve, which relates the total demand for all output to the price level. All prices and total output are changing as we move along the *AD* curve. Since the value of output determines income, there is no reason to expect consumers' money incomes to be constant along this curve.

The second reason does have some, but very limited, application to the aggregate demand curve. A rise in the price level entails a rise in all domestic commodity prices. Thus there is no incentive to substitute among domestic commodities. But it does give rise, as we saw in Chapter 28, to some substitution between domestic and foreign goods.

---

in reverse. There will be cost savings as overtime hours are reduced, the least efficient labor is laid off, and the least efficient capital is put on standby. For these reasons the lower output will be associated with somewhat lower unit costs and hence with lower output prices.

Since reducing output means reducing unit costs, firms will contract output when the price at which their output can be sold falls.

The Short-Run Aggregate Supply Curve

We can summarize the supply decisions of firms in terms of the implied relation between desired output and the price level, which we call the **aggregate**

supply (*AS*) curve. For the moment we maintain the assumption that *input prices are constant,* and refer to the *AS* curve as a *short-run aggregate supply curve.* The **short-run aggregate supply (*SRAS*) curve** shows the relation between the price level and the total output that firms wish to produce and sell, with input prices given.

Slope of the *SRAS* curve.   For the reasons just given, the *SRAS* curve will usually be positively sloped, indicating that the higher the price level, the more output will be produced. This is illustrated in Figure 29-4 (p. 616).

The positive slope of the *SRAS* curve shows that with input prices constant, higher output is associated with higher prices because unit costs of

FIGURE 29-3 The Relation Between the *AE* and *AD* Curves

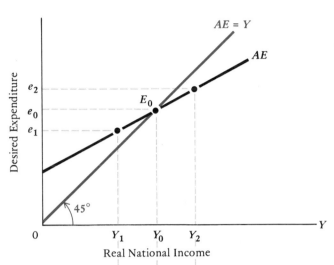

(i) Aggregate expenditure

(ii) Aggregate demand

The *AD* curve plots the price level against the level of national income consistent with expenditure decisions at that price level. In the figure the price level is constant at P_0. The *AE* curve in part (i) is drawn for that price level. The equilibrium level of national income is Y_0, as shown in part (i) by the intersection of the *AE* curve with the 45° line at E_0. At Y_0 national income is equal to desired aggregate expenditure, given by e_0. Y_0 is then plotted against P_0 in part (ii) to yield point E_0 on the *AD* curve.

Consider a level of national income of Y_1, less than Y_0. As can be seen in part (i), if national income were equal to Y_1, desired aggregate expenditure would be e_1, which is greater than Y_1. Hence Y_1 is not an equilibrium level of national income when the price level is P_0, and the combination (P_0, Y_1) is not a point on the *AD* curve in part (ii)—as shown by point X.

Now consider a level of national income of Y_2, greater than Y_0. As can be seen in part (i), if national income were equal to Y_2, desired aggregate expenditure would be e_2, less than Y_2. Hence Y_2 is not an equilibrium level of national income when the price level is P_0, and the combination (P_0, Y_2) is not a point on the *AD* curve in part (ii)—as shown by point Z.

production increase as the level of output increases.

The possibility of a horizontal *SRAS* curve, which gives rise to the level of national income being demand determined as in Figure 29-3, is discussed in Box 29-2 (p. 617).

The relation described by the *SRAS* curve holds only in the short run. This is because it is based on the assumption that input prices are constant, and changes in economic conditions will eventually cause input prices to change. Later we will examine the effects of changing input prices. For the moment let us see how the *SRAS* curve helps us explain the equilibrium values of national income *and* the price level.

**FIGURE 29-4   A Short-Run Aggregate Supply
Curve**

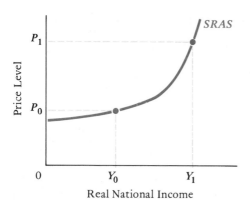

The *SRAS* curve is positively sloped. The positive
slope of the *SRAS* curve shows that with the prices of
labor and other inputs given, total desired output and the
price level will be positively associated. Thus a rise in the
price level from P_0 to P_1 will be associated with a rise in
the supply of total output from Y_0 to Y_1.

Macroeconomic Equilibrium

The equilibrium values of national output and the
price level occur at the intersection of the *AD* and
SRAS curves, as shown by the pair Y_0 and P_0 that
arise at point E_0 in Figure 29-5. We describe the
combination of national income and price level that
is on both the *AD* and the *SRAS* curves as a *macroeconomic equilibrium*.

To see why this pair is the only macroeconomic
equilibrium, consider what would happen if the price
level were below P_0. At that lower price level, the
desired output of firms, as given by the *SRAS* curve,
is less than the level of output consistent with expenditure decisions, as given by the *AD* curve. If
firms were to produce their desired level of output,
desired expenditure would exceed the amount of
goods supplied. Hence there can be no macroeconomic equilibrium when the price level is below P_0.

Similarly, when the price level is above P_0, the
behavior underlying the *SRAS* and *AD* curves are
not consistent. In this case producers will wish to
supply more than the level of income that is consis-

FIGURE 29-5   Macroeconomic Equilibrium

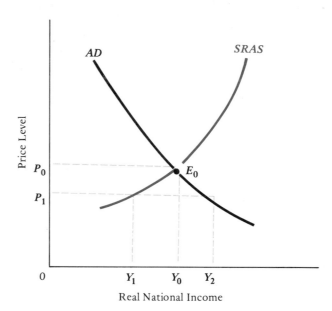

**Macroeconomic equilibrium occurs at the intersec-
tion of the *AD* and *SRAS* curves and determines the
equilibrium values for national income and the
price level.** Given the *AD* and *SRAS* curves in the figure, macroeconomic equilibrium occurs at E_0, with national income equal to Y_0 and the price level equal to P_0.
At P_0 the desired output of firms, as given by the *SRAS*
curve, is equal to the level of national income consistent
with expenditure decisions, as given by the *AD* curve.

If the price level were equal to P_1, less than P_0, the
desired output of firms, given by the *SRAS* curve,
would be Y_2. But at P_1 the level of output consistent
with expenditure decisions, given by the *AD* curve,
would be Y_1, greater than Y_2. Hence when the price level
is P_1, or at any other level less than P_0, the desired output of firms will be less than the level of national income
consistent with expenditure decisions.

Similarly, for any price level above P_0, the desired
output of firms given by the *SRAS* curve would exceed
the level of output consistent with expenditure decisions
given by the *AD* curve. Hence the only price level where
the supply decisions of firms are consistent with desired
expenditure is at macroeconomic equilibrium.

BOX 29-2

The Keynesian SRAS Curve

In this box we consider an extreme version of the *SRAS* curve that is horizontal over some range of national income. This curve is called the **Keynesian short-run aggregate supply curve,** after the English economist John Maynard Keynes, who in his famous book *The General Theory of Employment, Interest and Money* (1936) pioneered the study of the behavior of economies under conditions of high unemployment.

The behavior that gives rise to the Keynesian *SRAS* curve can be described as follows. When real national income is below potential national income, individual firms are operating at less than normal capacity output. Firms respond to cyclical declines in demand by holding their prices constant at the level

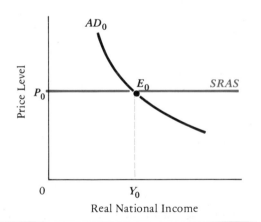

that would maximize profits if production were at normal capacity. They then respond to demand variations below that capacity by altering output. In other words, they will supply whatever they can sell at their existing prices as long as they are producing below their normal capacity. This means that the firms have horizontal supply curves and that their output is *demand determined.**

Under these circumstances, the economy has a horizontal aggregate supply curve, indicating that any output up to some level below or equal to potential output will be supplied at the going price level. The amount that is actually produced is then determined by the position of the aggregate demand curve, as shown in the figure. Thus we say that real national income is demand-determined.

If demand rises enough so that firms are trying to squeeze more than normal output out of their plants, their costs will rise, and so will their prices. Thus the horizontal Keynesian *SRAS* curve applies only to national incomes below potential income.

* The evidence is strong that firms, particularly in the manufacturing sector, do behave like this in the short run. One possible explanation is that changing prices frequently is too costly, so firms set the best possible (profit-maximizing) prices when output is at normal capacity and then do not change prices in the face of normal cyclical fluctuations in demand. This is discussed further in Chapter 15.

tent with demand at that price level. If firms were to produce their desired level of output, desired expenditure would not be large enough to purchase all output produced.

Only at the combination of national income and price level given by the intersection of the SRAS and AD curves are spending behavior and supply behavior consistent.

When the price level is less than its equilibrium value, expenditure behavior is consistent with a level of national income greater than the desired output of

firms. When the price level is greater than its equilibrium value, expenditure behavior is consistent with a level of national income less than the desired output of firms.

Macroeconomic equilibrium thus requires that two conditions be satisfied. The first is familiar from Chapter 28: At the prevailing price level, desired aggregate expenditure must be equal to national income. The second is introduced by consideration of aggregate supply: At the prevailing price level, firms must wish to produce the prevailing level of national income.

Changes in National Income and the Price Level

The aggregate demand and aggregate supply curves can now be used to show why national income and the price level change.

Shifts in the Aggregate Curves

A shift in the *AD* curve is called an **aggregate demand shock.** A *rightward* shift in the *AD* curve is an *increase* in aggregate demand; it means that at any given price level, expenditure decisions will now be consistent with a *higher* level of real national income. Similarly, a *leftward* shift in the *AD* curve is a *decrease* in aggregate demand; it means that at any given price level, expenditure decisions will now be consistent with a *lower* level of real national income.

A shift in the *SRAS* curve is called an **aggregate supply shock.** A *rightward* shift in the *SRAS* curve is an *increase* in aggregate supply; at any given price level, *more* real national income will be supplied. A *leftward* shift in the *SRAS* curve is a *decrease* in aggregate supply; at any given price level, *less* real national income will be supplied.[4]

What happens to real national income and to the price level when one of the aggregate curves shifts?

A shift in either the *AD* or the *SRAS* curve leads to changes in the equilibrium values of the price level and real national income.

Aggregate Demand Shocks

Figure 29-6 shows the effects of an increase in aggregate demand. This increase could have occurred because of, say, increased investment or government

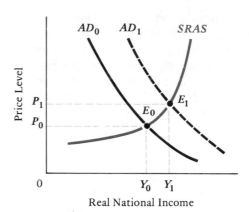

FIGURE 29-6   Aggregate Demand Shocks

Shifts in aggregate demand cause the price level and real national income to move in the same direction. An increase in aggregate demand shifts the *AD* curve to the right, say, from AD_0 to AD_1. Macroeconomic equilibrium moves from E_0 to E_1. The price level rises from P_0 to P_1, and real national income rises from Y_0 to Y_1, reflecting a movement along the *SRAS* curve.

A decrease in aggregate demand shifts the *AD* curve to the left, say, from AD_1 to AD_0. Equilibrium moves from E_1 to E_0. Prices fall from P_1 to P_0, and real national income falls from Y_1 to Y_0, again reflecting a movement along the *SRAS* curve.

spending; it means that more national output would be demanded at any given price level. For now we are not concerned with the source of the shock; we are interested in its implications for the price level and real national income.[5]

As is shown in the figure, following an increase in aggregate demand both the price level and real national income rise. Figure 29-6 also shows that both the price level and real national income fall as the result of a decrease in aggregate demand.

Aggregate demand shocks cause the price level and real national income to change in the same direction; both rise with an increase in aggregate demand, and both fall with a decrease.

---

[4] The distinction between movements along and shifts of curves encountered in Chapter 4 and again in Chapter 28 is also relevant here. Recall that the phrase "a change in quantity demanded" refers to a *movement along* a demand curve, whereas "a change in demand" refers to a *shift of* the demand curve. A similar distinction applies to the supply curve.

Note that for either the *AD* or the *SRAS* curve, a shift to the right means an increase and a shift to the left a decrease. If we speak of upward and downward shifts, however, the meaning differs for the two curves. An upward shift of the *AD* curve reflects an increase in aggregate demand, but an upward shift in the *SRAS* curve reflects a decrease in aggregate supply.

[5] Later (starting in Chapter 32) we will study how government policy can influence these variables.

An aggregate demand shock means a shift in the AD curve (for example, from AD_0 to AD_1 in the figure). Adjustment to the new equilibrium following an aggregate demand shock involves a movement along the $SRAS$ curve (for example, from point E_0 to point E_1).

Causes of Aggregate Demand Shocks

We have seen that the AD curve plots equilibrium national income as a function of the price level. Thus anything that alters equilibrium national income at a given price level must shift the AD curve; that is, any change other than a change in the price level that causes the AE curve to shift will also cause the AD curve to shift. (Recall that a change in the price level causes a *movement along* the AD curve.) This allows us to restate the conclusions on page 601 as follows:

A rise in the amount of desired consumption, investment, government, or net export expenditure associated with each level of national income shifts the AD curve to the right. A fall in any of these expenditures shifts the AD curve to the left.

Another Look at the Simple Multiplier

We have seen that the simple multiplier measures the magnitude of the change in equilibrium national income when the price level is constant. It follows that the simple multiplier gives the magnitude of the *horizontal* shift in the AD curve in response to a change in autonomous expenditure. This is shown in Figure 29-7.

The simple multiplier measures the horizontal shift in the AD curve in response to a change in autonomous expenditure.

If the $SRAS$ curve were horizontal, indicating that firms will supply everything that is demanded at the going price level, the simple multiplier also tells us the change in equilibrium income that will occur in response to a change in autonomous expenditure. The case of a horizontal $SRAS$ curve is discussed in Box 29-2 on page 617.

What happens in the more usual case where the aggregate supply curve slopes upward? In this case a rise in national income caused by an increase in autonomous expenditure will be associated with a rise in the price level. But we have seen that a rise in the price level (by reducing net exports and by lowering the real value of household wealth) shifts the AE curve downward, which tends to lower national income. The outcome of these conflicting forces is easily seen using aggregate demand and aggregate supply curves.

The Multiplier When the Price Level Varies

As can be seen in Figure 29-6, when the $SRAS$ curve is positively sloped, the change in national income caused by a change in autonomous expenditure is no longer equal to the size of the horizontal shift in the AD curve. A shift to the right of the AD curve causes the price level to rise, which in turn causes the rise in national income to be less than the horizontal shift of the AD curve. Part of the expansionary impact of an increase in demand is dissipated by a rise in the price level, and only part is transmitted to a rise in real output. Of course, there still is an increase in output, so a multiplier may still be calculated—but its value is less than the simple multiplier.

When the $SRAS$ curve is positively sloped, the multiplier is smaller than the simple multiplier.

Why is the multiplier smaller when the $SRAS$ curve is positively sloped? The answer lies in the behavior that is summarized by the AE curve. To understand this, it is useful to think of the final change in national income as occurring in two stages, as shown in Figure 29-8 (p. 621).

First, with prices constant, an increase in autonomous expenditure shifts the AE curve up and therefore shifts the AD curve to the right. This is shown by a shift up of the AE curve in part (i) of the figure and a shift to the right of the AD curve in part (ii). The horizontal shift in the AD curve is measured by the simple multiplier. But this cannot be the final equilibrium position because firms are unwilling to produce enough to satisfy the extra demand at the existing price level.

Second, we take account of the rise in the price level that occurs due to the positive slope of the $SRAS$ curve. As we have seen, a rise in the price

FIGURE 29-7   The Simple Multiplier and Shifts in the *AD* Curve

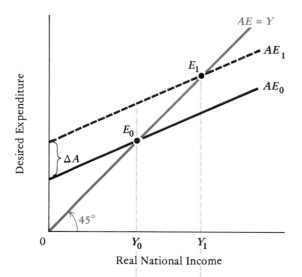

(i) Aggregate expenditure

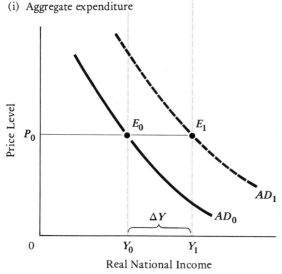

(ii) Aggregate demand

A change in autonomous expenditure changes equilibrium national income for any given price level, and the simple multiplier measures the resulting horizontal shift in the aggregate demand curve. The original desired expenditure function is AE_0 in part (i). Equilibrium is at E_0, with national income Y_0 at price level P_0. This yields point E_0 on the curve AD_0 in part (ii).

The AE curve in part (i) then shifts upward from AE_0 to AE_1 due to an increase in autonomous expenditure of ΔA. Equilibrium income now rises to Y_1, with the price level still constant at P_0. Thus the AD curve in part (ii) shifts to the right to point E_1, indicating the higher equilibrium income Y_1, associated with the same price level P_0. The magnitude of the shift, ΔY, is given by the simple multiplier.

A fall in autonomous expenditure can be analyzed by shifting the AE curve from AE_1 to AE_0, which shifts the AD curve from AD_1 to AD_0 at the price level of P_0. The equilibrium value of national income falls from Y_1 to Y_0.

level, via its effect on net exports and on wealth, leads to a downward shift in the *AE* curve. This second shift of the *AE* curve partially counteracts the initial rise in national income and so reduces the size of the multiplier. The second stage shows up as a shift down of the *AE* curve in part (i) of Figure 29-8 and a movement up and to the left along the *AD* curve in part (ii).

The Importance of the Shape of the SRAS Curve

We have now seen that the shape of the *SRAS* curve has important implications for how the effects of an aggregate demand shock are divided between changes in real national output and the price level. Figure 29-9 (p. 622) highlights this by considering

FIGURE 29-8 The *AE* Curve and the Multiplier When the Price Level Varies

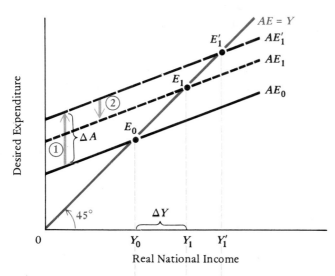

(i) Aggregate expenditure

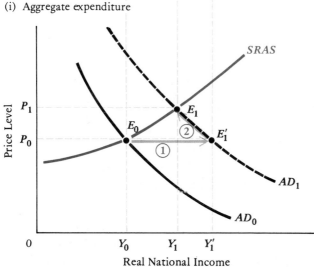

(ii) Aggregate demand

An increase in autonomous expenditures causes the *AE* curve to shift up, but the rise in the price level causes it to shift part of the way down again. Hence the multiplier effect on income is smaller than when the price level is constant. Originally, equilibrium is at point E_0 in both part (i) and part (ii), with real national income Y_0 and price level P_0. Desired aggregate expenditure then shifts by ΔA to AE_1', taking the aggregate demand curve to AD_1, as shown by arrow 1 in both parts. If the price level had remained constant at P_0, the new equilibrium would have been E_1' and real income would have risen to Y_1'. The amount Y_0Y_1' is the change called for by the simple multiplier.

Instead, however, the shift in the *AD* curve raises the price level to P_1 because the *SRAS* curve is positively sloped. The rise in the price level shifts the aggregate expenditure curve down to AE_1, as shown by arrow 2 in part (i). This is shown as a movement along the *AD* curve, as shown by arrow 2 in part (ii). The new equilibrium is thus at E_1. The amount Y_0Y_1 is ΔY, the actual increase in real income, whereas the amount Y_1Y_1' is the shortfall relative to the simple multiplier due to the rise in the price level.

The multiplier adjusted for the effect of the price increase is the ratio of $\Delta Y/\Delta A$ in part (i).

AD shocks in the presence of an *SRAS* curve that exhibits three distinct ranges.

Over the *flat* range, from 0 to Y_0, any change in aggregate demand leads to little change in prices and, as seen earlier, a response of output nearly equal to that predicted by the simple multiplier.

Over the *intermediate* range along which the *SRAS* curve is positively sloped, from Y_1 to Y_4, a shift in the *AD* curve gives rise to appreciable changes in both real income and the price level. As we saw earlier in this chapter, the change in the price level means that real income will change by less in response to a change in autonomous expenditure than it would if the price level were constant.

Over the *steep* range, for output above Y_4, virtually nothing more can be produced, however large

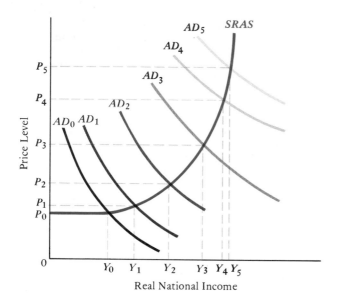

FIGURE 29-9   **The Effects of Increases in Aggregate Demand**

Increases in aggregate demand will have their major impact on increases in real income, increases in prices, or increases in both income and prices, depending on the shape of the SRAS curve. Because of the increasing slope of the *SRAS* curve, increases in aggregate demand up to AD_0 have virtually no impact on price. When aggregate demand increases from AD_0 to AD_1, there is a relatively small increase in price, from P_0 to P_1, and a relatively large increase in output, from Y_0 to Y_1. Successive further increases bring larger price increases and relatively smaller output increases. By the time aggregate demand is at AD_4 or AD_5, virtually all of the effect is on the price level.

the demand. This range depicts an economy near its capacity constraints. Any change in aggregate demand leads to a sharp change in the price level and to virtually no change in real national income. The multiplier in this case is nearly zero. Box 29-3 explores the reasons for such an increasing slope of the *SRAS*.

Let us consider the nearly vertical range in more detail using Figure 29-10 (p. 624) and in so doing look again at the *AE* curve. An increase in autonomous expenditure shifts the *AE* curve upward, thus raising the amount demanded. But a nearly vertical

SRAS curve means that output cannot be expanded to satisfy the increased demand. Instead, the extra demand merely forces prices up, and as prices rise, the *AE* curve is shifted down once again. The rise in prices continues until the *AE* curve is nearly back to where it started. Thus the rise in prices offsets the expansionary effect of the original shift and, as a result, leaves both real aggregate expenditure and equilibrium real income virtually unchanged.

The discussion of Figures 29-9 and 29-10 illustrates a general proposition:

The effect of any given shift in aggregate demand will be divided between a change in real output and a change in the price level, depending on the conditions of aggregate supply. The steeper the SRAS curve, the greater the price effect and the smaller the output effect.

For reasons discussed in Boxes 29-2 and 29-3, many economists think that the *SRAS* curve is shaped like that in Figure 29-9, relatively flat for low levels of income and becoming steeper as the level of national income increases. This shape of the *SRAS* curve implies that at low levels of national income (below potential), shifts in aggregate demand affect mainly output, and at high levels of national income (above potential), shifts in aggregate demand affect mainly prices.

Of course, as we have already noted, treating wages and other factor prices as constant is appropriate only when the time period under consideration is short. Hence the *SRAS* curve is used only to analyze short-run, or *impact,* effects. In the next chapter we see what happens in the *long run* when factor prices respond to changes in national income and the price level. But first, to conclude this chapter and set the stage for that long-run analysis, we consider the short-run effects of aggregate supply shocks.

Aggregate Supply Shocks

A decrease in aggregate supply is reflected in a shift to the left in the *SRAS* curve and means that less national output will be supplied at any given price level. An increase in aggregate supply is reflected in a shift to the right in the *SRAS* curve and means that more national output will be produced at any given price level. As with the discussion of aggregate

BOX 29-3

Another Look at the Shape of the SRAS Curve

The *SRAS* curve relates the price level to the quantity of output that producers are willing to sell. Such an *SRAS* curve is reproduced in Figure 29-3. Notice two things about its shape: In general it has a positive slope, and the slope increases as output rises.

Positive slope.   The positive slope of the *SRAS* curve indicates that a higher price level is associated with a higher volume of real output, other things being equal. Since the prices of all of the factors of production are being held constant along the *SRAS* curve, why is the curve not horizontal, indicating that firms would be willing to supply as much output as might be demanded with no increase in the price level?

You have already encountered an answer to this question. Even though *input prices* are constant, *unit costs of production* rise as output increases because of the bottlenecks that are likely to arise as firms in the economy approach full use of their capacity. Thus a higher price level for increasing output—rising short-run aggregate supply—is generally necessary to compensate firms for rising costs. (Recall the particular circumstances noted in Box 29-2 where this might not occur, and hence the *SRAS* curve might be flat.)

The preceding paragraph addresses the question "What has to happen to the price level if national output increases, with input prices held constant?" One may ask a different question: "What will happen to firms' willingness to supply output if product prices rise with no increase in input prices?" If there is an increase in the prices of products that firms sell, while the prices of everything that firms use to make their products remain constant, production becomes more profitable. Since firms are interested in making profits, when production becomes more profitable, they will usually produce more.* Thus when the price level of

final output rises while input prices are held constant, firms are motivated to increase their outputs. This is true for the individual firm and also for firms in the aggregate. This increase in the amount that will be produced leads to an upward slope of the *SRAS* curve.

Thus whether we look at how the price level will respond in the short run to increases in output or how the level of output will respond to an increase in the price level with input prices held constant, we find that the *SRAS* curve has a positive slope.

Increasing slope.   A somewhat less obvious but nevertheless important property of a typical *SRAS* curve is that its slope *increases* as output rises. It is rather flat to the left of potential output and rather steep to the right. Why? Below potential output, firms typically have unused capacity—some plant and equipment are idle. When firms are faced with unused capacity, only a small increase in the price of their output may be needed to induce them to expand production, at least up to normal capacity.

Once output is pushed far beyond normal capacity, however, unit costs tend to rise quite rapidly. Many higher cost expedients may have to be adopted. Standby capacity, overtime, and extra shifts may have to be used. Such expedients raise the cost of producing a unit of output. These higher-cost methods will not be used unless the selling price of the output has risen enough to cover them. The further output is expanded beyond normal capacity, the more rapidly unit costs rise and hence the larger the rise in price needed to induce firms to increase output even further.

This increasing slope is sometimes called the *first important asymmetry* in the behavior of aggregate supply. (The second important asymmetry, "sticky wages," is discussed in the next chapter.)

---

* Those who have already studied microeconomics can understand this in terms of price-taking firms being faced with higher prices and thus expanding output *along* their marginal cost curves until marginal cost is once again equal to price.

FIGURE 29-10 Demand Shocks When the SRAS Curve Is Nearly Vertical

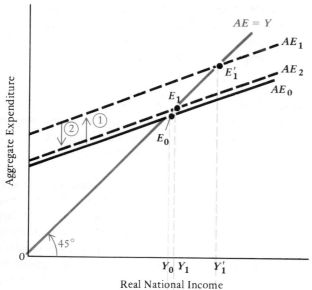

(i)

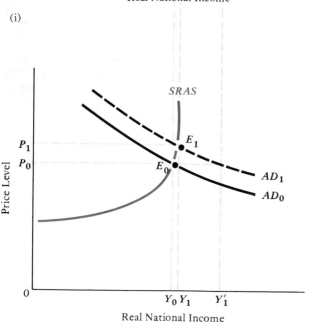

(ii)

When the *SRAS* curve is nearly vertical, the effect of an increase in autonomous expenditure is mainly a rise in the price level. An increase in autonomous expenditure shifts the *AE* curve up from AE_0 to AE_1, as shown by arrow 1 in part (i). Given the initial price level P_0, equilibrium would shift from E_0 to E'_1, and real national income would rise from Y_0 to Y'_1. (We use primes on these variables because these results cannot persist, since real national income cannot rise to Y'_1.) But the price level does not remain constant. This is shown by the *SRAS* curve in part (ii). Instead, the price level rises to P_1. This causes the *AE* curve to shift back down to AE_2, as shown by arrow 2 in part (i), and equilibrium income increases only to Y_1. If the *SRAS* curve were completely vertical, equilibrium income would return all the way to Y_0.

FIGURE 29-11   Aggregate Supply Shocks

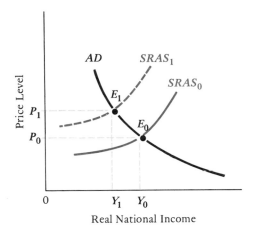

Shifts in aggregate supply cause the price level and real national income to move in opposite directions. A decrease in aggregate supply shifts the SRAS curve to the left, say, from $SRAS_0$ to $SRAS_1$. Equilibrium moves from E_0 to E_1. The price level rises from P_0 to P_1, but real national income falls from Y_0 to Y_1, reflecting a movement along the AD curve.

An increase in aggregate supply shifts the SRAS curve to the right, say, from $SRAS_1$ to $SRAS_0$. Equilibrium moves from E_1 to E_0. The price level falls from P_1 to P_0, but real national income rises from Y_1 to Y_0, again reflecting a movement along the AD curve.

demand shocks, we are not now concerned with the source of the aggregate supply shock.

Figure 29-11 illustrates the effects on the price level and real national income of aggregate supply shocks. As can be seen from the figure, following the decrease in aggregate supply, the price level rises and real national income falls. This combination of events is called **stagflation,** a rather inelegant word derived by combining *stagnation* (a term sometimes used to mean less than full employment) and *inflation.*

Figure 29-11 also shows that an increase in aggregate supply leads to an increase in real national income and a decrease in the price level.

Aggregate supply shocks cause the price level and real national income to change in opposite directions; with an increase in supply, the price level falls and income rises; with a decrease in supply, the price level rises and income falls.

An aggregate supply shock means a shift in the SRAS curve (for example, from $SRAS_0$ to $SRAS_1$ in the figure). Adjustment to the new equilibrium following the shock involves a movement along the AD curve (for example, from E_0 to E_1).

Causes of Aggregate Supply Shocks

The SRAS curve can shift for many reasons. Two sources of shift are of particular importance.

Changes in input prices. The fact that input prices are held constant along the SRAS curve suggests an important reason for the SRAS curve to shift. If input prices rise, firms will find that the profitability of their current production has been reduced. For any given level of output to be produced, an increase in the price level will be required. If prices did not rise, firms would react by decreasing production.[6] For the economy as a whole this would mean less output at each price level than before the input price increases. Thus if input prices rise, the SRAS curve shifts upward. This is what we have called a decrease in supply, as illustrated in Figure 29-11.

Similarly, a fall in input prices will cause the SRAS curve to shift downward (or, what is the same thing, to the right), reflecting what we have called an increase in supply.

Increases in productivity. If labor productivity rises, meaning that each worker can produce more, the unit costs of production will fall as long as wage rates remain constant. Lower costs generally lead to lower prices. Competing firms cut prices in attempts to raise their market shares, and the net result of such competition is that the fall in production costs is accompanied by a fall in prices.

Since the same output is sold at a lower price, this causes a shift to the right in the SRAS curve. This shift is an increase in supply, as illustrated in Figure 29-11.

[6] Students who have already studied microeconomics will recognize that such an upward shift in a firm's marginal cost curve leads to a decrease in the output that is profitable for the firm to produce. This is discussed in Chapter 12.

A change in either input prices or productivity will shift the *SRAS* curve because any given output will be supplied at a different price level than previously. An increase in input prices shifts the *SRAS* curve to the left; an increase in productivity or a decrease in input prices shifts it to the right.

A leftward shift in the *SRAS* curve, brought about, for example, by an increase in the price of basic raw materials and imported oil as occurred during the 1970s, lowers real national income and raises the price level. Stagflation, the unhappy combination of rising prices and falling real national income, can result from such supply shocks, as it did during the 1970s.

A rightward shift in the *SRAS* curve, brought about, for example, by an increase in productivity with no increase in factor prices, raises real national income and lowers the price level. This happier combination is the object of government policies seeking to encourage productivity increases. As we shall see in the next chapter, it has proved hard to achieve in practice.

Summary

1. The *AE* curve shows desired aggregate expenditure for each level of income, at a particular price level. Its intersection with the 45° line determines equilibrium national income for that price level. A change in the price level shifts the *AE* curve and leads to a new equilibrium level of national income.
2. The *AD* curve plots the equilibrium level of income against the corresponding price level. A change in the equilibrium level of income following a change in the price level is shown by a movement along the *AD* curve.
3. The short-run aggregate supply *(SRAS)* curve, drawn for given factor prices, is positively sloped because unit costs rise with increasing output and because rising product prices make it profitable to increase output.
4. A macroeconomic equilibrium refers to equilibrium values of national income and the price level, as determined by the intersection of the *AD* and *SRAS* curves.
5. Shifts in the *AD* and *SRAS* curves, called aggregate demand shocks and aggregate supply shocks, respectively, cause the equilibrium values of national income and the price level to change.
6. An aggregate demand shock can be caused by a change in autonomous expenditure. The simple multiplier measures the size of the resulting horizontal shift in the *AD* curve. It measures the actual size of the change in equilibrium real national income only if the price level is constant.
7. When the *SRAS* curve is positively sloped, part of the effect of an aggregate demand shock is dissipated in a change in the price level, and only part goes to change real income. Thus an aggregate demand shock causes the price level and national income to move in the same direction. The division of the effects between a change in national income and a change in the price level are easily discovered from *AD* and *AS* curves.
8. The steepness of the *SRAS* curve determines how the impact of a

shift in the *AD* curve is divided between a change in output and a change in the price level. When the *SRAS* curve is flat, shifts in the *AD* curve affect mainly real national income. When the *SRAS* curve is steep, shifts in the *AD* curve affect mainly the price level.

9. An aggregate supply shock can be caused by a change in factor costs or a change in productivity. The resulting shift in the *SRAS* curve will lead to a movement along the *AD* curve. Thus an aggregate supply shock causes the price level and national income to move in opposite directions.

10. A decrease in aggregate supply—a shock that shifts the *SRAS* curve to the left—can lead to stagflation—rising prices and falling national income. An increase in aggregate supply—a shift to the right of the *SRAS* curve—leads to an increase in real national income and a fall in the price level.

Topics for Review

Effects of a change in the price level
Relation between the *AE* and *AD* curves
Negative slope of the *AD* curve
Positive slope of the *SRAS* curve
Macroeconomic equilibrium
Aggregate demand shocks
The multiplier when the price level varies
Aggregate supply shocks
Stagflation

Discussion Questions

1. Explain the following by shifts in either or both the aggregate demand and aggregate supply curves. Pay attention to the initial position before the shift(s) occurs.
   a. Output and unemployment rise, while prices hold steady.
   b. Prices soar, but employment and output hold steady.
   c. Inflation accelerates even as the recession in business actively deepens.
2. A survey of private economic forecasters in mid 1986 showed that the consensus economic outlook for 1987 was cautiously optimistic—most thought that inflation and real growth would both remain roughly constant at their then 4.0 percent levels while unemployment would fall slightly. Explain what predictions about factors underlying the *AD* and *SRAS* curves would give rise to such a forecast. In retrospect, how accurate were these forecasts? What happened to the underlying determinants to cause actual events to differ from the forecasts?
3. In 1979–1980 the British government greatly reduced income taxes, but restored the lost government revenue by raising excise and sales taxes. This led to a short burst of extra inflation and a fall in employment. Explain this in terms of shifts in the aggregate demand and/or supply curves.
4. Indicate whether each of the following events is the cause or the

consequence of a shift in aggregate demand or supply. If it is a cause, what do you predict will be the effect on the price level and on real national income?

a. Unemployment decreases in 1984.

b. OPEC raises oil prices in 1979.

c. OPEC is forced to accept lower oil prices in 1982–1983.

d. In the late 1960s and early 1970s Canada experiences a rapid inflation under conditions of approximately full employment.

e. In country X income and employment continue to fall while the price level is quite stable.

f. Defense Minister Perrin Beatty promises a large increase in defense spending in 1988–1991.

5. A number of economists argued that as a result of the major tax reform introduced in 1987 by the Canadian government, a number of "disincentives to work" were being removed, and hence there would be an improvement in productivity and an increase in labor-force participation. If this proves true, what would you expect to be the effects on national income and the price level?

6. What would happen to American employment and income if, in an attempt to lower American unemployment, the American Congress enacted large increases in American tariff rates? What would happen if, in the face of a worldwide recession, all countries did the same?

7. Using your understanding of the chapter, analyze the following recent statements made by business people.

a. "We must be successful; our sales have increased every year for the past ten years."

b. "I can see why prices may rise in boom times, but rising prices and falling output just don't make sense."

c. "I can't understand why there is so much unemployment; our business is booming."

8. Interpret each of the following news items in terms of *AD* and *SRAS* curves.

a. "Management representative says union wage demands are irresponsible in the face of current high unemployment rates."

b. "Government spokesman says that although the recovery is expected to be vigorous, it will witness only modest reductions in the unemployment rate."

c. "Inflation in the U.S. fell quickly in 1982 due to the 'lucky break' of reduced union strength in the automobile and steel sectors."

d. "Wage increases have failed to keep up with inflation during the current boom."

e. "Innovations in microelectronic technology will lead to an increase in both national output and unemployment."

f. "Reagan's tough stance with public sector unions has vastly improved the inflation outlook for the U.S. over the next few years."

30

National Income and the Price Level in the Long Run

In Chapter 29 we studied how national income and the price level are determined in the short run, where the short run was taken to mean a period of time short enough that wages and other factor costs could be taken as given. We also examined the impact effects on national income and the price level of an aggregate demand shock or an aggregate supply shock.

We now need to see what happens in a longer-term setting when changes in national income and the price level in turn *induce* changes in factor prices.

Induced Changes in Factor Prices

We start by briefly reconsidering two concepts that we first encountered in Chapter 26—potential income and the output gap.

Another Look at Potential Income and the Output Gap

We saw in Chapter 26 that actual national income often diverges from potential national income, the difference being called the output gap (see Figure 26-3 on page 560 and Figure 26-4 on page 562).

Since potential income can be viewed as the level of total output that would be produced if factors of production were being efficiently used at their normal rates of utilization, potential income can be assumed constant for the purposes of this chapter.[1]

Determination of the output gap is illustrated in Figure 30-1. The actual level of national income is determined by the intersection of the *AD* and *SRAS* curves. Since potential national income is a constant, it is shown by the vertical line at Y^*. In part (i), potential income Y^* exceeds actual income Y_0, so there is a positive output gap of Y^*Y_0. In part (ii), Y^* is less than actual income Y_1, thus giving rise to a negative output gap of Y_1Y^*.

---

[1] In Chapter 38 we shall see that economic growth gives rise to a steady increase in potential national income over time. In this chapter we ignore the effects of growth on potential income. (Recall our discussion on page 563.)

FIGURE 30-1   Actual Income, Potential Income, and the Output Gap

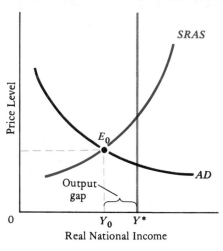

(i) A positive output gap

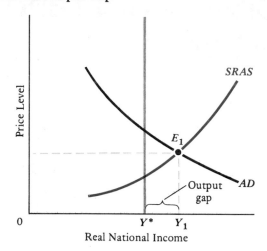

(ii) A negative output gap

The output gap is the difference between potential national income, Y^*, and actual national income, Y. Potential income is shown by a vertical line because it refers to a given, constant level of national income. Actual national income is determined by the intersection of the aggregate demand (AD) and short-run aggregate supply ($SRAS$) curves.

In part (i) the AD and $SRAS$ curves are such that there is a positive output gap. This is because equilibrium is at E_0, so actual national income is given by Y_0, less than potential income. The output gap is thus $Y^* - Y_0$.

In part (ii) the AD and $SRAS$ curves are such that there is a negative output gap. Although potential income is unchanged at Y^*, equilibrium is now at E_1, so actual national income is given by Y_1, greater than potential income. The output gap is thus $Y^* - Y_1$.

Wage Adjustments and the Output Gap

The output gap is a measure of the actual level of national income relative to potential. As such, it provides a convenient measure of the actual state of demand in markets for factor services relative to "normal rates of utilization." Although this applies to all factor services, for simplicity and ease of exposition in what follows, we focus on labor as the key factor of production and hence on its price, the wage rate, as the key factor price.

When there is a negative output gap—that is, when actual national income exceeds potential—the demand for labor services will be relatively high. When there is a positive output gap—that is, when actual national income is less than potential—the de-

mand for labor services will be relatively low. Each of these situations will have implications for wages. Before turning to a detailed analysis of each, we first consider a benchmark for the behavior of wages.

Upward and downward wage pressures.   In what follows we consider *upward* and *downward* pressure on wages caused by the output gap. Upward or downward in relation to what? One answer would be in relation to zero—upward pressure would be for wages to rise and downward pressure would be for wages to fall. However, most wage bargaining starts from the assumption that, other things being equal, workers should get the benefit of increases in their own productivity by receiving higher wages. Because of this, when there is neither upward nor downward pressure on wages emanating from the labor market, we would expect wages to be rising at the same rate as productivity is rising.[2] When wages and productivity change proportionately, labors cost per unit of output, which we have earlier called *unit labor costs,* remain unchanged. For example, if each worker produces 4 percent more and earns 4 percent more, unit labor costs will remain constant.

This, then, is our benchmark:

When there is neither excess demand nor excess supply in the labor market, wages will tend to be rising as fast as labor productivity; in this case unit labor costs will remain constant.

Note that with unit labor costs constant, there is no pressure coming from the labor market for the *SRAS* curve to shift, and hence no pressure for the price level to rise or fall.

In comparison with this benchmark, upward pressure on wages means pressure for wages to rise faster than productivity is rising. When this occurs, unit labor costs will also be rising. For example, if money wages rise by 8 percent while productivity rises by only 4 percent, labor cost per unit of output will be rising by about 4 percent. In this case the *SRAS* curve will be shifting leftward, and hence there will be upward pressure—emanating from the labor market on the price level.

Downward pressure on wages means pressure for wages to rise less fast than productivity. When this occurs, unit labor costs will be falling. For example, if productivity rises by 4 percent while money wages rise by only 2 percent, labor costs per unit of output will be falling by about 2 percent. In this case the *SRAS* curve will be shifting rightward, and hence there will be downward pressure—emanating from the labor market—on the price level.

A negative output gap. Consider a situation in which the *AD* and *SRAS* curves are such that actual output exceeds potential, as illustrated in part (ii) of Figure 30-1. Firms are producing beyond their normal capacity output, so there is an unusually large demand for all factor inputs, including labor. Labor shortages will emerge in some industries and among many groups of workers, particularly the skilled. Firms will try to bid workers away from other firms in order to maintain the high levels of output and sales made possible by the boom conditions.

As a result of tight labor market conditions, workers will find that they have considerable bargaining power with their employers, and they will put upward pressure on wages.[3] Firms, recognizing that demand for their goods is strong, will be anxious to maintain a high level of output. Thus to prevent their workers from either striking or quitting and moving to other employers, firms will be willing to accede to some of these upward pressures.

The boom associated with a negative output gap generates a set of conditions—high profits for firms and unusually large demand for labor—that puts sharp upward pressure on wages.

A positive output gap. Now consider a situation where the *AD* and *SRAS* curves are such that actual output is less than potential, as illustrated in part (i) of Figure 30-1. In this situation firms will be producing below their normal capacity output, so there is an unusually low demand for all factor inputs, including labor. The general conditions in the market for labor will be the opposite of those when actual output exceeds potential. There will now be labor surpluses in some industries and among some groups of workers. Firms will have below normal sales and will not only resist upward pressures on wages but will also tend to offer wage increases below productivity increases and may even seek reductions in wages.

---

[2] Ongoing inflation would also influence the normal pattern of wage changes. Wage contracts often allow for changes in prices that are expected to occur during the life of the contract. For now we maintain the simplifying assumption that the price level is expected to be constant; hence changes in money wages are also expected to be changes in real wages. The distinction between changes in money wages and real wages and the important role that expectations of price level changes play are discussed in Chapters 36 and 39.

[3] Additional upward pressures on the level of wages may be created by the fact that the price level, P_1, will be higher than P^*, the price level that would have prevailed had output attained its potential level.

The slump associated with a positive output gap generates a set of conditions—low profits for firms, unusually low demand for labor, and a desire on the part of firms to resist wage demands and even to push for wage concessions—that puts downward pressure on wages.

Adjustment asymmetry.   At this stage we encounter an important asymmetry in the economy's aggregate supply behavior. Boom conditions with severe labor shortages do cause wages to rise rapidly. In conditions of strong excess demand for labor, wage increases will bear little relation to productivity increases. Money wages may be rising 10 or 15 percent while productivity is rising at only 2 or 3 percent. This means that unit labor costs will be rising rapidly.

The experience of many economies suggests, however, that downward pressures on wages during slump conditions are not nearly so effective as are upward pressures during booms. Even in quite severe slumps, wages may continue to rise although their rate of increase falls below that of productivity. For example, productivity might be rising at, say, 3 percent while money wages were rising at 2 percent. In this case unit labor costs would be falling at only about 1 percent per year, and the leftward shift in the *SRAS* and downward pressure on the price level would be correspondingly slight.[4]

The inflationary and recessionary gaps.   We have seen that a negative output gap puts upward pressure on wages and prices while a positive output gap puts downward pressure on wages and prices. Box 30-1 (p. 634) discusses the same wage adjustment process in terms of the famous *Phillips curve*.

As we saw in Chapter 29 (see especially Figure 29-11), the increases in unit costs that occur when upward pressure on wages cause them to rise faster than productivity cause the *SRAS* curve to shift leftward. A leftward shift in the *SRAS* curve—a decrease in supply—causes the equilibrium price level to rise. Thus because a negative output gap induces large shifts in the *SRAS* curve that drive up the price

level, any excess of actual output Y above potential Y^* is often called an **inflationary gap.**

We also know that when wages rise less fast than productivity, unit costs fall, and this shifts the *SRAS* curve to the right. As a result of this increase in supply, the equilibrium price level will fall. However, to stress the asymmetry just discussed—which means that the potential for wage-induced reductions in the price level is quite weak—any shortfall of actual output relative to potential is called a **recessionary gap** (rather than a deflationary gap).

The induced effects on unit labor costs and consequent shifts in the *SRAS* curve play an important role in our analysis of the long-run consequences of aggregate demand shocks, to which we now turn.

The Long-Run Consequences of Aggregate Demand Shocks

We can now add to the preceding chapter's study of impact effects. We do this by considering the longer-run consequence of an aggregate demand shock. Shifts in the *AD* curve cannot be expected to leave input prices unchanged in the long run. However, we need to examine the effect of aggregate demand shocks on input prices separately for expansionary and for contractionary shocks, since the behavior of the economy is not symmetrical for the two. In what follows we make the simplifying assumption that labor productivity is constant, so that all changes in wages are also changes in unit labor costs and hence cause the *SRAS* to shift.

Expansionary AD Shocks

Suppose that the economy starts off in a position of full employment, so that actual national income equals potential. Further suppose that the price level is stable at the level consistent with income being at its potential level. This is shown by the initial equilibrium at E_0 in Figure 30-2(i).

Now suppose that this happy situation is disturbed by an increase in autonomous expenditure,

---

[4] This is the second asymmetry in aggregate supply that we have encountered. The first refers to the changing slope of the *SRAS* curve, as discussed in Box 29-3.

FIGURE 30-2   Demand-Shock Inflation

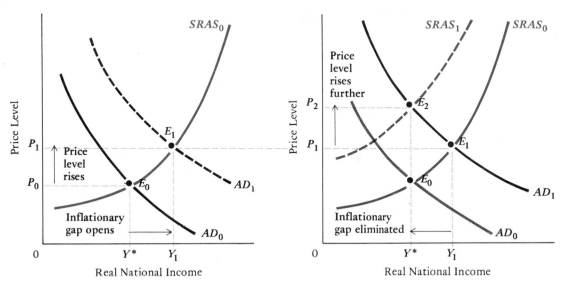

(i) Autonomous increase in aggregate demand

(ii) Induced shift in aggregate supply

A rightward shift of the *AD* curve first raises price and output along the *SRAS* curve. It then induces a shift of the *SRAS* curve that further raises prices but lowers output along the *AD* curve. In part (i) the economy is in equilibrium at E_0, at its level of potential output Y^* and price level P_0. The *AD* curve then shifts to AD_1. This moves equilibrium to E_1, with income Y_1 and price level P_1, and opens up an inflationary gap of Y^*Y_1.

In part (ii) the inflationary gap results in an increase in wages and other input costs, shifting the *SRAS* curve leftward. As this happens, income falls and the price level rises along AD_1. Eventually, when the *SRAS* curve has shifted to $SRAS_1$, income is back to Y^* and the inflationary gap has been eliminated. However, the price level has risen to P_2.

perhaps caused by a sudden boom in consumption spending. As also shown in part (i) of Figure 30-2, the impact effects of this aggregate demand shock are that the price level and national income both rise. Thus following the shock actual national income exceeds potential, creating an inflationary gap.

As we have just seen, an inflationary gap leads to an increase in wages. Sharp rises in wages mean sharp rises in costs. These lead to leftward shifts of the *SRAS* curve as firms seek to pass on their increases in input costs by increasing their output prices. For this reason the initial increases in the price level and in real national income shown in Figure 30-2(i) are *not* the final effects of the demand shock. As seen in

part (ii) of the figure, the leftward shift of the *SRAS* curve causes a further rise in the price level, but this time the price rise is associated with a fall in output.

The cost increases (and the consequent leftward shifts of the *SRAS* curve) go on until the inflationary gap has been removed, that is, until income returns to Y^*, its potential level. Only then is there no abnormal demand for labor, and only then do wages and costs, and hence the *SRAS* curve, stabilize.

This important expansionary demand-shock sequence can be summarized as follows:

1. Starting from full employment, a rise in aggregate demand raises the price level and raises income

BOX 30-1

The Phillips Curve and the Shifting SRAS Curve

In the early 1950s Professor A. W. Phillips of the London School of Economics was doing pathbreaking research on macroeconomic policy. He included in his early models an equation relating the rate of inflation to the difference between actual and potential income, $Y - Y^*$. Later he investigated the empirical underpinnings of this equation by studying the relation between the rate of increase of wage costs and the level of unemployment. In 1958 he reported that a stable relation had existed between these two variables for 100 years in the United Kingdom.

The relation, which came to be called the *Phillips curve,* is illustrated in the figure on the left. The curve shows money wages rising when unemployment is below the natural rate of unemployment, U_N, and falling when unemployment is above that critical level. It illustrates the effect that an output gap has on wages.

Recall that the rate of unemployment is related negatively to national income: The higher is national income, the lower is unemployment. Thus the Phillips curve can also be drawn with national income on the horizontal axis, as in the figure on the right.

Both figures show the same information. Inflationary gaps (which correspond to low unemployment rates) are associated with *increases* in wages, while recessionary gaps (which correspond to high unemployment rates) are associated with slow *decreases* in wages.

The Phillips curve must be clearly distinguished from the *SRAS* curve. The *SRAS* curve has the *price level* on the vertical axis while the Phillips curve has the *rate of wage inflation.* Therefore the Phillips curve tells us how fast the *SRAS* curve is shifting when actual income does not equal potential income.

Only when $Y = Y^*$ is the *SRAS* curve not shifting on account of demand pressures. When income is at its potential level, aggregate demand for labor equals aggregate supply; the only unemployment would thus be frictional unemployment. There would be neither upward nor downward pressure of demand on wages. Thus the Phillips curve cuts the axis at potential income Y^* and at the corresponding level of unemployment U_N.

The Phillips curve soon became famous. It provided a link between national income models and labor markets. This link allowed macroeconomists to drop the uncomfortable assumption, which they had

---

above its potential level as the economy expands along a given *SRAS* curve.

2. The expansion of income beyond its normal capacity level puts heavy pressure on factor markets; factor prices begin to rise, shifting the *SRAS* curve to the left.
3. The shift of the *SRAS* curve causes income to fall along the *AD* curve. This process continues *as long as* actual income exceeds potential income. Therefore, actual income eventually falls back to its potential level. The price level is, however, now higher than it was after the initial impact of the increased aggregate demand, but inflation will have come to a halt.

The ability to wring more output and income from the economy than its underlying potential output (as in point 2) is only a short-term possibility. National income greater than Y^* sets up inflationary

pressures that tend to push national income back to Y^*.

There is a self-adjustment mechanism that brings any inflation caused by a one-time demand shock to an eventual halt by returning output to its potential level and thus removing the inflationary gap.

Contractionary AD Shocks

Let us return to that fortunate economy with full employment and stable prices. It appears again in part (i) of Figure 30-3 (p. 636), which is similar to Figure 30-2(i). Now assume a *decline* in aggregate demand, perhaps due to a major reduction in consumption expenditure.

The impact of the decline is a fall in output and

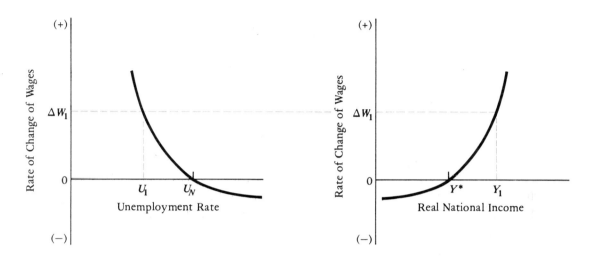

often been forced to use in many of their earlier formal models, that money wages were rigidly fixed and neither rose nor fell as national income varied. The Phillips curve relation between money wages and national income determines (in conjunction with productivity changes) the speed at which the *SRAS* curve shifts.

Consider, for example, the situation shown in part (ii) of Figure 30-1, where the level of income determined by the *AD* and *SRAS* curves is Y_1. Plotting Y_1 on the Phillips curve in the figure on the right tells us that wage costs will be rising at ΔW_1. Then the *SRAS* curve in Figure 30-1(ii) will be shifting upward by that amount. The same information can be seen in the figure on the left, where national income of Y_1 corresponds to unemployment of U_1.

some downward adjustment of prices, as shown in part (i) of the figure. As output falls, unemployment rises. The difference between potential output and actual output is, as we have seen, the output gap. When the output gap is positive, as in Figure 30-3, it is a recessionary gap.

Flexible wages. Consider what would happen if severe unemployment caused wage rates to fall sharply. Falling wage rates would lower costs for firms and cause a rightward shift of the *SRAS* curve. As shown in Figure 30-3(ii), the economy would move along its fixed *AD* curve with falling prices and rising output until full employment was restored at potential national income Y^*. We conclude that *if* wages were to fall whenever there was a recessionary gap, the resulting fall in the *SRAS* curve would restore full employment.

Flexible wages that fell when there was a recessionary gap would provide an automatic adjustment mechanism that would push the economy back toward full employment whenever output fell below potential.

Sticky wages. Boom conditions with severe labor shortages do cause wages to rise rapidly, shifting the *SRAS* curve upward. But as we noted earlier (see page 632, where we encountered the second asymmetry of aggregate supply behavior), the experience of many economies suggests that wages are sticky—that is, they are not very flexible—in a downward direction. If wages are sticky, unemployment has a weak and slow-acting downward effect on wages. The adjustment mechanism that depends on rightward shifts of *SRAS* is, therefore, weak and sluggish.

FIGURE 30-3   Demand-Shock Deflation with Flexible Wages

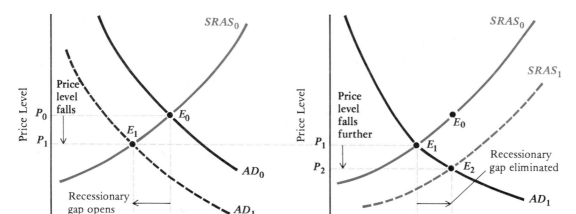

(i) Autonomous fall in aggregate demand   (ii) Induced shift in aggregate supply

A leftward shift of the *AD* curve first lowers price and output along the *SRAS* curve and then induces a (slow) shift of the *SRAS* curve that further lowers prices but raises output along the *AD* curve. In part (i) the economy is in equilibrium at E_0, at its level of potential output Y^* and price level P_0. The *AD* curve then shifts to AD_1, moving equilibrium to E_1, with income Y_1 and price level P_1, and opens up an output (or recessionary) gap of Y_1Y^*.

Part (ii) shows the adjustment back to full employment that would occur from the supply side of the economy if wages were sufficiently flexible downward. The fall in wages would shift the *SRAS* curve to the right. Real national income would rise, and the price level would fall further along the *AD* curve. Eventually, the *SRAS* curve would reach $SRAS_1$, with equilibrium at E_2. The price level would stabilize at P_2 when income had returned to Y^*, eliminating the recessionary gap.

The weakness of the automatic adjustment mechanism does not mean that slumps will last indefinitely. What it means is that speedy recovery back to full employment must be generated mainly from the demand side. If the economy is to avoid a lengthy stagnation, the force leading to recovery must be a rightward shift of the *AD* curve rather than a rightward drift of the *SRAS* curve.

The *SRAS* curve shifts to the left fairly rapidly when national income exceeds Y^*, but it shifts to the right only slowly when national income falls short of Y^*.

The asymmetry.   This difference in speed of adjustment is a consequence of the important asymmetry in the behavior of aggregate supply noted earlier in this chapter. This asymmetry helps explain two key facts about our economy. First, unemployment *can* persist for quite long periods without causing large decreases in wages and prices (which, if they did occur, would help to remove the unemployment). Second, booms, with labor shortages and production beyond normal capacity, cannot persist for long periods without causing large increases in wages and prices.

The Long-Run Aggregate Supply (*LRAS*) Curve

The possibility of automatic adjustments gives rise to an important concept: the **long-run aggregate** supply (*LRAS*) curve. This curve relates the price level to real national income *after wage rates and all other input costs have been fully adjusted to eliminate any difference between actual and purely frictional unemployment.*[5]

Shape of the *LRAS* curve. Once all the adjustments required have occurred, the economy will have eliminated any excess demand or excess supply of labor. In other words, full employment will prevail, and output will necessarily be at its potential level Y^*. It follows that the aggregate supply curve becomes a vertical line at Y^* as shown in Figure 30-4.[6]

Notice that the vertical *LRAS* curve does not represent the same thing as the vertical portion of the *SRAS* curve (see Figure 29-9). Over the vertical range of the *SRAS* curve, the economy is at its utmost limit of productive capacity, when no more can be squeezed out, as might occur in an all-out war effort. The vertical shape of the *LRAS* curve is due to the workings of an adjustment mechanism that is assumed always to bring the economy back to its level of potential output, even though it may stray away in the short run. It is called the *long-run* aggregate supply curve because it refers to adjustments that take a substantial amount of time.

Along the *LRAS* curve all the prices of *all outputs* and *all inputs* have been fully adjusted to eliminate any excess demands or supplies. Proportionate changes in money wages and the price level (which, by definition, will leave real wages unaltered) will also leave equilibrium employment and output unchanged. The key concept is this: If the price of absolutely everything (including labor) doubles, nothing real changes. When the price of everything bought *and* sold doubles, neither workers nor firms gain any advantage and hence neither has any incentive to alter their behavior. Output, therefore, is unchanged. The level of output will be what can be produced in the economy when all factors of pro-

[5] Students who have studied microeconomics will notice that this use of the term *long run* appears different from its meaning in microeconomics. Note, however, the key similarity that the long run has more flexibility for adjustment than does the short run.

[6] The *LRAS* curve is sometimes called the classical aggregate supply curve because the classical economists were mainly concerned with the behavior of the economy in long-run equilibrium.

FIGURE 30-4   The Long-Run Aggregate Supply (*LRAS*) Curve

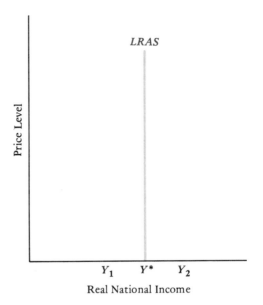

The long-run aggregate supply curve is a vertical line drawn at the level of national income equal to potential income, Y^*. It is a vertical line because the total amount of goods that the economy produces when all factors are efficiently used at their normal rate of utilization does not vary with the price level. If the price level were to rise from P_1 to P_2 *and* wages and all other factor prices were to rise by the same proportion, the desired output of firms would remain at Y^*.

If income were Y_1, less then Y^*, wages would be falling and the *SRAS* curve would be shifting right; hence the economy would not be on its *LRAS* curve. If income were Y_2, greater than Y^*, wages would be rising and the *SRAS* curve would be shifting left; hence the economy would not be on its *LRAS* curve.

duction, including labor, are utilized at "normal" levels of their capacity.

The vertical *LRAS* curve shows that given full adjustment of input prices, potential income, Y^*, is compatible with *any* price level.

Long-Run Equilibrium

Figure 30-5 shows the equilibrium output and the price level determined by the intersection of the *AD*

FIGURE 30-5   Long-Run Equilibrium and Aggregate Supply

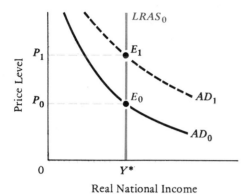

(i) A rise in aggregate demand

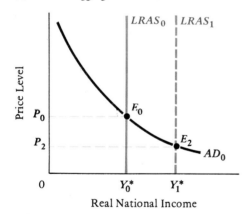

(ii) A rise in long-run aggregate supply

When the *LRAS* curve is vertical, aggregate supply determines the long-run equilibrium value of national income at Y^*. Given Y^*, aggregate demand determines the long-run equilibrium value of the price level. In both parts of the figure the initial long-run equilibrium is at E_0, so the price level is P_0 and national income is Y_0^*.

In part (i) a shift in the AD curve from AD_0 to AD_1 with the *LRAS* curve unchanged moves the long-run equilibrium from E_0 to E_1. This raises the price level from P_0 to P_1 but leaves national income unchanged at Y_0^* in the long run.

In part (ii) a shift in the *LRAS* curve from $LRAS_0$ to $LRAS_1$ with the aggregate demand curve constant at AD_0 moves the long-run equilibrium from E_0 to E_2. This raises national income from Y_0^* to Y_1^* but lowers the price level from P_0 to P_2.

curve and the vertical *LRAS* curve. Because the *LRAS* curve is vertical, shifts in aggregate demand change the price level but not the level of equilibrium output, as shown in part (i). In contrast, a shift in aggregate supply changes both output and the price level, as shown in part (ii). For example, a rightward shift of the *LRAS* curve increases national income and leads (eventually) to a fall in the price level.

With a vertical *LRAS* curve, output is determined solely by conditions of supply, and the role of aggregate demand is simply to determine the price level.

Of course, these are only long-term tendencies. To see the short-term impact of demand and supply shocks, we need to use the short-run aggregate supply curve. Because of wage stickiness, downward adjustments of wages and prices may take a long time, and so there may be long periods when the economy is not at, or even near, long-run equilibrium.[7]

Supply-Side Economics

Both of Ronald Reagan's U.S. presidential campaigns featured a theory of economic policy that came to be known as *supply-side economics*. To some the policy promised a quick cure for both high inflation and low growth in real national income. To others it seemed an exercise in wishful thinking.

The theoretical tools developed in this chapter can be used to explore both the theory and the doubts. Although supply-side economics has many aspects, we are here concerned specifically with the effects of supply-side policies on the price level and on real national income, starting from a situation with a large inflationary gap. When Ronald Reagan became president in January 1981, the inflation rate was about 10 percent and unemployment about 7 percent; any policy that would decrease them both would have been welcomed.

[7] The rest of this chapter may be omitted without loss of continuity.

How It Was Supposed to Work

The theory of supply-side economics called for adopting measures that would shift the *LRAS* curve to the right far enough and fast enough to eliminate the inflationary gap. In the most favorable case there would be no offsetting demand-side effects. This case is illustrated in Figure 30-6.

A major part of supply-side economics was the provision of tax incentives that were to increase potential national income by increasing the nation's supplies of labor and capital. Incentives were to be given to firms to increase their investment, thus increasing national productive capacity. Personal taxes were to be cut across the board to give everyone an incentive to work more. It was argued that people already employed would be more inclined to work

longer and harder when they were able to keep a larger fraction of their pre-tax earnings, and people outside of the labor force would be drawn in as a result of the higher after-tax wages. Extra tax incentives were to be given to persons at high income levels so as to increase the incentives for work and risk taking on the part of the most productive people. It was anticipated that the resulting increases in productive capacity and increases in productivity would shift the *LRAS* curve to the right.

It was also assumed that no budget deficits would result from the cuts in tax rates and increases in tax exemptions. The increase in national income, it was argued, would create a larger tax base so that even at the lower tax *rates*, total tax *revenues* (which would fall initially) would be restored. For example, if a 10 percent cut in tax rates were followed by a 10 percent

FIGURE 30-6   The Theory of Anti-inflationary Supply-Side Economics

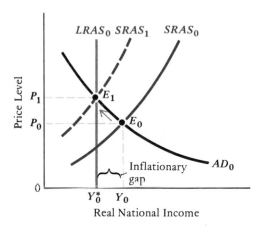

(i) An inflationary situation

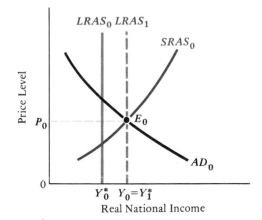

(ii) Supply-side success

Supply-side economics seeks to eliminate an inflationary gap by shifting the *LRAS* curve to the right without changing aggregate demand. Part (i) shows an economy in short-run equilibrium at E_0 on AD_0 and $SRAS_0$, with income Y_0 and price level P_0. As a result of the inflationary gap of $Y_0^*Y_0$, the *SRAS* curve will shift upward, taking the equilibrium along AD_0 (as shown by the arrow), with falling national income and rising price level. Other things being equal, the inflation will come to a halt once the curve has reached $SRAS_1$ and equilibrium is established at E_1, with price level P_1, and national income at its potential level Y_0^*.

Part (ii) shows the same economy after supply-side measures shift the *LRAS* curve to $LRAS_1$. This makes Y_1^* the new level of potential income and removes the inflationary gap. The fall of income and rise in the price level shown in part (i) are both prevented.

increase in real national income, it would leave tax revenues approximately the same.[8]

Doubts About the Theory

One major worry of critics of the theory was that demand-side effects would swamp any supply-side effects for at least the first several years. Whatever the long-term effects on the supply side, economic theory is clear about the short-term effects of these measures on the demand side. Cuts in personal tax rates that are intended to be permanent leave households with an increase in their current and expected future disposable income. As a result they spend more, causing a rightward shift in the aggregate demand curve. Also we know that an increase in investment increases aggregate demand. In the short run the extra expenditure on capital goods creates new incomes for the factors of production that produce these goods and, through the multiplier process, new incomes for others as well.

Thus the short-run effect of supply-side measures would surely be to shift the aggregate *demand* curve to the right. In the least favorable situation, if all the demand-increasing effects were to occur and none of the favorable aggregate supply effects, the result would surely be an increase in the inflationary gap. This possibility is illustrated in Figure 30-7.

Neither of the extreme cases illustrated in Figures 30-6 or 30-7 is likely to occur. Supply-side measures will lead to shifts to the right of both the *LRAS* and *AD* curves, and the effects of the policies will depend on the magnitude and timing of the two shifts. For example, if the effects on demand occur first but are followed by large increases in long-run aggregate supply, the initial effect would be to increase inflation, but the long-run effect would be for prices to come back down and for output to rise.

Supply-siders with training in economics surely knew that the short-term effects via aggregate demand would occur. But they believed that the supply-side shifts of long-run aggregate supply would be large enough, and quick enough, to dominate them. Critics not only doubted this view as to timing, but they also questioned whether the tax changes

[8] Students who have read Chapter 24 and encountered the Laffer curve (see page 498) will be familiar with this argument.

FIGURE 30-7   Demand Effects of Supply-Side Measures

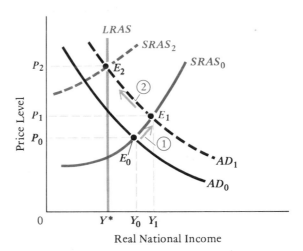

The effect of supply-side measures on aggregate demand is inflationary. The figure shows the economy in the same short-run initial equilibrium at E_0 as in Figure 30-6(i). However, it assumes that demand-side effects of the policy measures occur and are fully felt before any supply-side effects come into play. The AD curve shifts to the right to AD_1, and the economy moves toward equilibrium at E_1, as shown by arrow 1. This gives a temporary increase in output to Y_1 at the cost of an immediate rise in the price level to P_1. But the inflationary gap is also increased, to Y^*Y_1. Now the $SRAS$ curve starts to shift upward, taking the equilibrium along AD_1 in the direction shown by arrow 2, with falling output and rising prices. If nothing else happens, the inflation will finally come to an end at price level P_2 and output Y^*. As a result of the supply-side measures, the rise in the price level, from P_0 to P_2, is *greater* than it would have been without the measures, that is, from P_0 to P_1.

proposed would have the desired effects even in the long run. Economic theory makes no definite prediction about the effects of tax cuts on how much people will work. It might make them work more, because they earn more for each additional hour that they work. But it might make them work less, because the tax cut means that they can, if they wish, have both more disposable income and more leisure. For example, if in response to a 10 percent tax cut they worked 5 percent less, they would have approximately 5 percent more disposable income and 5 percent more leisure. (This is discussed in greater detail in Box 18-2 on page 350.)

Evaluating the Theory

It is difficult to resolve all the factual matters at issue in the supply-side debate on the basis of the Reagan administration's experiences. First, the proposed measures were never fully implemented. Second, the inflationary conditions postulated in the theory were changed by other policies, especially monetary policies, which will be examined in Chapter 34. It is clear, however, that aggregate *demand* effects did dominate in the short run.

Beyond this, most economists would agree on at least two aspects of the experience. First, policymakers and economists are much more alert to the supply-side effects of economic policies than many of them used to be. This is an important achievement.

Second, the timing of effects is such that measures that do succeed in shifting both aggregate demand and long-run aggregate supply will likely have their initial effects through a rapid shift in the *AD* curve. Their effects through a shift in the *LRAS* curve will occur only gradually. Thus the view of a number of Reagan supporters that supply-side measures would provide a *quick* fix to inflationary pressures is, simply, discredited. Such measures may, however, have contributed to the sustained recovery of 1983–1987.

Summary

1. Potential income is treated as given and thus can be represented by a vertical line at Y^*. The output gap is equal to the horizontal distance between Y^* and the actual level of income as determined by the intersection of the *AD* and *SRAS* curves.

2. A negative output gap means that demand in the labor market is relatively high. As a result, wages rise, the *SRAS* curve shifts leftward, and the price level rises. Thus any excess of actual national income over potential national income is called an inflationary gap.

3. A positive output gap means that demand in the labor market is relatively low. While there is some resulting tendency for wages to fall, asymmetrical behavior means that the strength of this force will be much weaker than that indicated in summary point 2. There will be very little deflation while the output gap will persist; thus any shortfall of actual national income relative to potential is called a recessionary gap.

4. An expansionary demand shock will create an inflationary gap that will induce factor price increases. These will shift the *SRAS* curve to the left, resulting in a higher level of prices, with output eventually decreasing to its potential level.

5. A contractionary demand shock will work in the opposite direction. If, however, factor prices are sticky, the automatic adjustment process may be slow, and a recessionary gap may not be quickly eliminated.

6. The long-run aggregate supply (*LRAS*) curve relates the price level and national income after all wages and other costs have been fully adjusted to long-run equilibrium. The *LRAS* curve is vertical at the level of potential income, Y^*.

7. Because the *LRAS* curve is vertical, output in the long run is determined by the position of the *LRAS* curve, and the only long-run role of the *AD* curve is to determine the price level.

8. Supply-side economics in an inflationary situation seeks to reduce an

inflationary gap and increase output by tax cuts and other incentive measures designed to shift the *LRAS* curve to the right and thus increase potential output. Whether or not this will work in the long run is a matter of current debate. In the short run such measures increase aggregate demand, thus adding to inflationary pressures.

Topics for Review

The output gap and the labor market
Asymmetry of wage adjustment
Inflationary gap
Recessionary gap
Aggregate-demand shocks and induced wage changes
Long-run aggregate supply (*LRAS*) curve
Supply-side economics

Discussion Questions

1. Discuss the following in terms of the *AD*, *SRAS*, and *LRAS* curves:
   "The best way to combat inflation is to promote economic growth."
2. "Starting from a full-employment equilibrium, an increase in government spending can produce more output and employment at the cost of a once-and-for-all rise in the price level."
   "Increased spending can never lead to a permanent increase in output above its full employment level."
   Discuss these two statements in terms of short- and long-run aggregate supply curves.
3. Identify the effects of each of the following events on the *SRAS* and *LRAS* curves.
   a. Increase in the price of imported raw materials used in key manufacturing industries
   b. Increase in the price of imported consumption goods such as coffee or bananas
   c. An attempt to combat acid rain by tightening restrictions on pollution emissions
   d. Projections of increased federal government deficits over the next five years
   e. An improved economic outlook leading to an investment boom
   f. Increased labor force participation rate of key sectors of the population
4. Discuss the following 1986 quotation:
   "Wages are surely sticky since unemployment during the recovery has remained above 9 percent, but wages have continued to grow at more than 4 percent."
5. Show the effects on the price level and output of income tax cuts that induce people to work more in an economy currently experiencing an inflationary gap.
6. Discuss the reasoning behind the statement of the government critic who argued that:
   "There is no sense in the government trying to stimulate demand since all that will do is cause inflation; it won't help reduce unemployment."

31

Business Cycles: The Ebb and Flow of Economic Activity

Changing, always changing; this is the dominant characteristic of the GDP for as far back as we have records. Long-term growth (which is studied in Chapter 38) appears in the upward trend in potential GDP. Short-term fluctuations are seen in oscillations of actual GDP around potential GDP. Such oscillations are caused by changes in aggregate demand and aggregate supply. They lead to changes in total real output and hence in the amount of employment and unemployment. They also affect living standards since the total amount of goods and services available varies as total output varies.

Cyclical Fluctuations

As we saw in Chapter 26, most economic series exhibit two types of change. The first is the long-term trend. In the case of GDP, there is an upward trend throughout the twentieth century associated with economic growth. In the case of unemployment, the series for the twentieth century is trend-free, exhibiting no long-term tendency for the unemployment rate to rise or fall.

The second type of change is fluctuation around the long-term trend. These fluctuations are far from random; they exhibit a systematic pattern. A year of relatively high output is likely to occur in conjunction with other years of high output, and such groups are likely to be separated by groups of years of relatively low output. This pattern of a sequence of highs followed by a sequence of lows followed again by another sequence of highs is the source of the term *cyclical* used to describe such economic fluctuations.

The Concept of the Business Cycle

The **business cycle** refers to the continual ebb and flow of business activity that occurs around any long-term trend after seasonal adjustments have been made.[1] Such cyclical fluctuations can be seen in many economic series. For example, continual oscillations in GDP are apparent in Figure 26-3 on page 560.

[1] When economists wish to analyze monthly or quarterly data, they often try to remove fluctuations that can be accounted for by a regular seasonal pattern. This *seasonal adjustment* is made because many economic series show a marked seasonal pattern over the year. For example, logging activity tends to be low in the winter months and high in the summer, while fuel oil sales tend to have the reverse seasonal pattern.

FIGURE 31-1   Three Indicators of Economic Activity in Canada, 1950–1986

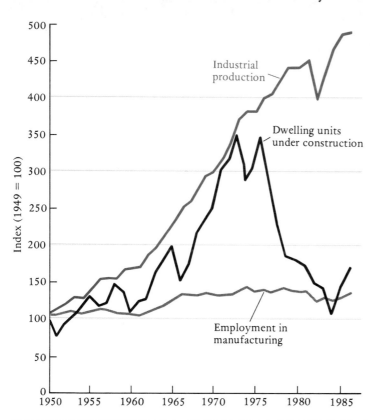

Short-term variability and a long-term upward trend characterize many indexes of Canadian economic activity. All three series are index numbers with 1949 = 100, so all pass through 100 at 1949. All series exhibit differing degrees of short-term variability and differing trend rates of growth. Dwelling starts under construction vary greatly from year to year. Employment in manufacturing does not fluctuate greatly because even a large change in unemployment, say from 4 percent to 8 percent of the labor force, makes a relatively small percentage change in employment. The serious recession of 1981–82 and the sustained recovery of 1983–86 are apparent in all three series. (*Source:* Statistics Canada, 11-003E.)

But the concept of the business cycle refers to fluctuations in the general pace of economic activity. This cannot be fully caught by a single statistic, even one as important as GDP. Figure 31-1 shows three other economic series. Each of these, as well as a dozen others that might be studied, tells us something about the general variability of the economy. It is clear that some series vary more than others and that they do not all move exactly together.

The picture suggested by Figures 26-3 and 31-1 is not one of occasional sharp shifts in the aggregate demand and supply curves. If it were, we would expect national income to show occasional sharp changes followed by long periods of little or no change. Instead the short-term situation is one of continual change at varying rates.

Evidently there are factors at work causing economic activity to display continual short-term fluctuations around the economy's long-term growth trend.

While all cycles are not alike in duration or intensity, each appears to have tendencies toward cumulative movements that eventually reverse themselves. This was true long before governments attempted to intervene to stabilize their economies, and it is true still.

The late Alvin Hansen, a distinguished American authority on business cycles, once reported that there were 17 cycles in the U.S. economy between 1795 and 1937, with an average duration of 8.35 years. A shorter "inventory cycle" of 40 months' duration was also found, as well as longer cycles associated with building booms (15 to 20 years). The Russian economist Kondratieff thought he could identify long waves of 40 to 50 years associated with the introduction of major innovations. Some economists have argued that in many Western democracies there exists a political business cycle associated with the pattern of elections.

Though the evidence is diverse, it is nevertheless possible to identify some basic characteristics of the pattern of business cycles:

1. **A common pattern of variation more or less pervades all economic series.**
2. **Economic series differ in their particular patterns of fluctuations.**
3. **Cycles differ substantially in the length and the size of the swings involved.**

The Terminology of Business Fluctuations

Although recurrent fluctuations in economic activity are neither smooth nor regular, a vocabulary has developed to denote their different stages. Figure 31-2 shows stylized cycles that illustrate some terms.

Trough.   A trough is, simply, the bottom. A trough is characterized by high unemployment of labor and a level of consumer demand that is low in relation to the capacity of industry to produce goods for consumption. There is thus a substantial amount of unused industrial capacity. Business profits are low; for some individual companies they are negative. Confidence in the future is lacking, and firms are consequently unwilling to risk making new investments. If a trough is deep enough, it may be called a *slump* or a **depression.**

Recovery.   When something sets off a recovery, the lower turning point of the cycle has been reached. The symptoms of a recovery (or expansion) are many: Worn-out machinery is replaced; employment, income, and consumer spending all begin to rise; expectations become more favorable as a result of increases in production, sales, and profits. Investments that once seemed risky may now be undertaken as the climate of business opinion starts to change from pessimism to optimism. As demand expands, production can be expanded with relative ease merely by re-employing the existing unused capacity and unemployed labor.

Peak.   A peak is the top of the cycle. At the peak there is a high degree of utilization of existing capacity; labor shortages may be severe, particularly in key skill categories; and shortages of essential key

---

FIGURE 31-2   A Stylized Business Cycle

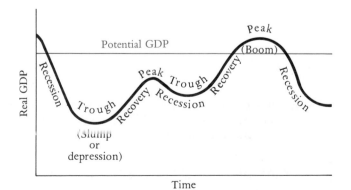

Although the phases of business fluctuations are described by a series of commonly used terms, no two cycles are the same. Starting from a lower turning point, a cycle goes through a phase of recovery, or expansion, reaches an upper turning point, and then enters a period of recession. Cycles differ from one another in the severity of their troughs and peaks and in the speed with which one phase follows another. Severe troughs are called *depressions*; extreme peaks are called *booms.*

raw materials may develop. Output can be raised further only by investment that increases capacity. Because such investment takes time, further rises in demand are now met more by increases in prices than by increases in production. As shortages develop in more and more markets, a situation of general excess demand for factors develops. Costs rise, but prices rise also, and business remains generally very profitable. A peak that exceeds the level of potential output may be referred to as a **boom.**

Recession.   A **recession,** which often follows a peak, is a sustained fall in the level of economic activity. Demand falls off, and as a result production and employment fall. As employment falls, so do households' incomes; falling income causes demand to fall further. Profits drop and more and more firms get into difficulties. Investments that looked profitable on the expectation of continual rising demand suddenly appear unprofitable, and investment is reduced to a low level. It may not even be worth replacing capital goods as they wear out because unused capacity is increasing steadily.

Turning points.   The point at which a recession begins is often called the **upper turning point.** The point at which a recovery begins is referred to as the **lower turning point**.

Explaining Business Cycles

An explanation of the business cycle must answer two questions: (1) What are the factors that cause GDP and other key macro variables to fluctuate? (2) What are the factors that cause those fluctuations to form a cyclical pattern? These two questions are taken up in the two main sections that follow.

Why Do Income and Employment Fluctuate?

Figure 31-3 presents an explanation of the fluctuations of GDP in terms of a fluctuating AD curve and a stable $SRAS$ curve.

FIGURE 31-3   A Demand-driven Business Cycle

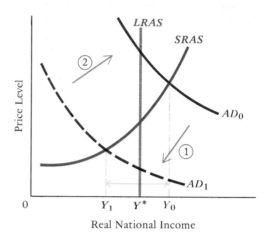

Fluctuations in aggregate demand can cause fluctuations in income and employment. Assume that over the course of the business cycle aggregate demand oscillates regularly. The economy starts with a high level of aggregate demand, AD_0, and income at its peak, Y_0. The AD curve then falls continuously, as shown by arrow 1, until it reaches AD_1. Income falls through Y^* and reaches its trough at Y_1.

The AD curve then rises continuously, as shown by arrow 2. Income is taken back through Y^* and reaches Y_0 at the next peak.

There is general agreement that over the course of Canadian economic history, the business cycle has been driven mainly by fluctuations in aggregate demand. Nevertheless, particular cycles can sometimes be explained in part by aggregate supply shocks. Indeed, events of the mid 1970s made the citizens of advanced industrial countries acutely aware of supply-side causes.

Aggregate demand shocks are a major historical source of fluctuations in GDP; aggregate supply shocks are another source.

Sources of Aggregate Demand Shocks

To say that cycles are caused mainly by fluctuations in aggregate demand only pushes the need for explanation one stage back. What are the sources of the continual disturbances to aggregate demand? The theory of income determination suggests four main candidates: shifts in each of the four main components of aggregate expenditure. Some key facts are illustrated in Figure 31-4.

Changes in Consumption

Consumption is the largest single component of aggregate expenditure, about two-thirds of the total. When searching for the causes of income changes, we are not concerned with changes in consumption *in response* to changes in income but instead with *shifts* in the function relating consumption to income. Such shifts can have many causes.

Changes in tastes. In the mid 1980s there was a significant increase in the demand for North American cars. If enough of the money that was spent on automobiles would have been saved instead, there would be a significant rightward shift in the aggregate demand curve. Jobs and incomes would first be gained in the auto industry. The induced increase in spending by workers in that industry would then set up a multiplier effect as increases in output, income, and spending spread throughout the economy.

Changes in expectations and interest rates. Expectations of future inflation may lead to a burst of spending to buy now while goods are cheap. By contrast, a wave of uncertainty about the future may lead to a rise in saving and hence a cut in spending. High interest rates can be a powerful incentive to postpone buying durable goods. For example, in 1981 rates of over 20 percent helped to depress the markets for automobiles and other consumer durables, and subsequent declines in interest rates led to a boom in those markets.

In an inflationary world it is important to distinguish between the real and the nominal rate of interest. The *nominal* rate of interest is the ratio of the *amount of money* repaid to the amount of money borrowed. The *real* rate of interest is the ratio of the *purchasing power of the money* repaid to the purchasing power of the money borrowed. The real rate of interest is the difference between the nominal rate of interest and the rate of inflation. It is this real interest rate that matters for most expenditure decisions. This distinction is further elaborated in Box 31-1 (page 649).

Changes in taxes. As we saw in Chapter 28, tax changes can also shift the aggregate consumption function. Income tax cuts mean that more *total* income becomes *disposable* income, leading to an increase in consumer spending. Tax increases have the opposite effect.

Changes in transfer payments. Government transfer payments amount to roughly one-eighth of personal income. Sharp changes in transfer payments could influence aggregate expenditure through their effects on personal consumption and investment.

Changes in Government Expenditures

As Figure 31-4 shows, World War II brought a rapid expansion of economic activity. Government spending was a major contributing factor. Wars generally result in an enormous increase in federal governmental expenditures as men and materials are shifted from civilian to military purposes, a shift that is then reversed in the postwar period. For example, federal government purchases of goods and services rose from $683 million in 1939 to $4,978 million in 1944 and fell back to $1,541 million by 1947. Changes in government purchases of goods and services from 1940 to 1946 were the dominant influence on GDP, and they had a substantial effect during the Korean War at the beginning of the 1950s.

Aside from periods of major wars, government expenditures have not often been destabilizing. For peacetime periods before 1940, government expenditures were both small and relatively stable. Since 1955 they have been large and stable and growing rather steadily. Thus whatever their potential for being a major source of cyclical instability, they have not proven to be such except during wars.

As Figure 31-4 shows, the shocks caused by changing government expenditure have been much smaller on average than the shocks caused by either changing net exports or changing private investment expenditure.

FIGURE 31-4   Changes in GDP and Selected Components, 1927–1986

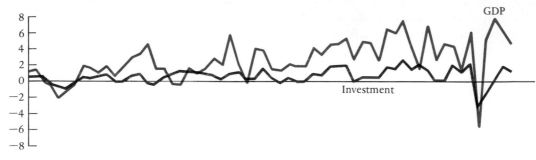

(i) Changes in GDP and investment

(ii) Changes in GDP and government purchases

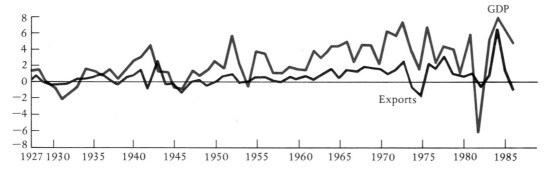

(iii) Changes in GDP and exports

Changes in GNP have been closely related to changes in investment expenditure. The year-to-year fluctuations in GNP correlate closely to changes in investment except during World War II and its aftermath, when changes in government expenditures were the dominant influence. Changes in merchandise exports have reinforced the destabilizing influence of the other two expenditure categories. (*Source*: Statistics Canada, 13–531, 13–201, 11–003 E.)

BOX 31-1

Real and Nominal Interest Rates: An Important Distinction

If you pay me $8 interest for a $100 loan for one year, the nominal rate is 8 percent. The real rate that I earn, however, depends on what happens to the overall level of prices in the economy.

If the price level remains constant over the year, the real rate that I earn would also be 8 percent, because I can buy 8 percent more goods and services with the $108 that you repay me than with $100 that I lent you. However, if the price level rises by 8 percent, the real rate would be *zero*, because the $108 you repay me buys the same quantity of goods as the $100 that I gave up. If I am unlucky enough to lend money at 8 percent in a year in which prices rise by 10 percent, the real rate I earn would be -2 percent.

If lenders and borrowers are concerned with real costs measured in terms of purchasing power, the nominal rate of interest will be set at the rate they want as return on their money plus an amount to cover any expected rate of inflation. Consider a one-year loan that is meant to earn a real return to the lender of 5 percent. If the expected rate of inflation is zero, the nominal rate set for the loan will be 5 percent. If a 10 percent inflation is expected, the nominal interest rate will be 15 percent.

To provide a given expected real rate of interest, the nominal rate will be set at the desired real rate of interest plus the expected annual rate of inflation.

Because they overlook this point, people are often surprised at the high nominal rates of interest that exist during periods of rapid inflation. For example, when the nominal interest rates rose drastically in 1979, many commentators expressed shock at the "unbearably" high rates. Most of them failed to notice that with inflation running at about 12 percent, an interest rate of 15 percent represented a real rate of only 3 percent. Had the government given in to the pressure to hold interest rates to the more "reasonable" level of 10 percent, it would have been imposing a negative real rate of interest. Lenders would then have been "rewarded" for lending their money by receiving less purchasing power in interest plus prin-

cipal than the purchasing power of the principal they parted with initially.

Concern about the burden of borrowing should be directed at the real, not the nominal, rate of interest.

For example, a nominal rate of 8 percent combined with a 2 percent rate of inflation is a much greater real burden on borrowers than a nominal rate of 16 percent combined with a 14 percent rate of inflation.

Cash Flow Problems

Some of the effects of inflation can be compensated for by changes in the nominal interest rate, but not all. The inflation premium on interest rates represents an early repayment of capital and hence causes cash flow problems for borrowers. Consider a simple example. A firm borrows $1,000 for 10 years at 4 percent when the price level is constant. The firm will pay $40 of interest per year, and at the end of 10 years it must repay in one lump sum the capital of $1,000.

Now assume that the same bargain is struck except that a 5 percent rate of inflation will occur *and is fully expected* over the period of the loan. In this case the nominal rate of interest is set at 9 percent, and annual interest payments will be $90.

In one sense the real situation is unchanged, but in another important sense it is different. The firm is now paying an annual inflation premium of $50. This compensates the lenders for the loss of purchasing power on the principal of their loans. But for the borrowers it constitutes an early repayment of capital. Note that the $1,000 repaid at the end of the 10-year period has a much smaller real value in the second (inflationary) situation.

So the stream of real payments is very different when a 4 percent interest rate is combined with a zero inflation rate and when a 9 percent interest rate is combined with a 5 percent inflation rate.

BOX 31-2

Fluctuations in National Income and the Balance of Trade

Exports are an important source of demand for domestically produced goods. A key determinant of a country's exports is the level of activity in its major trading partners. When the United States experiences a boom, as it did in the period 1983–1986, there is a large American demand for Canadian exports. In turn, via the multiplier process, the increase in exports will cause an expansion in Canadian national income. Similarly, when the United States experiences a recession, as it did in 1981–1982, American demand for Canadian goods will be low. Again the change in exports causes a multiplier effect, this time leading to a reduction in Canadian national income.

As a result of this *export multiplier,* the business cycles of major trading partners tend to be closely correlated.

Imports and the Size of the Multiplier

As we saw in Chapter 28, expenditure on imports will grow as domestic national income grows. Since imports represent spending on other countries' outputs, they raise the economy's marginal propensity not to spend, and hence, as we saw in Chapter 28, they reduce the size of the multiplier. [**39**] Of course this has both desirable and undesirable consequences. It is undesirable because it reduces the effectiveness of domestic policies that attempt to change the level of domestic income. It is desirable because it reduces the impact on national income of fluctuations in such

autonomous expenditure items as investment and exports.*

Net Exports and Domestic Absorption

The model of national income determination outlined in Chapter 28 provides an important perspective on the determination of net exports. Recall the basic condition for equilibrium national income:

$$Y = C + I + G + (X - M)$$

The sum of $C + I + G$ corresponds to total expenditure on all goods and services (domestic and foreign) for use *within* the economy; this total is often referred to as **domestic absorption (A).** The equilibrium relationship can therefore be rewritten as

$$Y = A + (X - M)$$

The right-hand side of this equation is desired aggregate expenditure on Canadian goods and services, represented as the sum of expenditure for *internal* use (domestic absorption) plus expenditure due to net *external* demand (net exports). Subtracting A from both sides, we get

$$Y - A = X - M$$

---

* The consequence of the latter effect is that imports act as a *built-in stabilizer.* We encounter built-in stabilizers again in Chapter 32 in our analysis of fiscal policy.

Changes in Net Exports

A country such as Canada, in which foreign trade plays a large role, is subject to destabilizing influences from foreign demand. Since about one-half of all goods produced in Canada are exported, fluctuations in the national income of other countries can be transmitted to our economy through fluctuations in their demand for our exports. As Figure 31-4 shows, changes in merchandise exports played an important role during the Great Depression. The fall in export

demand triggered by the depression in the economies of our major trading partners led to a fall in our exports, thereby reinforcing the early stages of the recession in Canada. Similarly, during World War II exports boomed at the same time that the domestic economy was expanding.

Similar influences of exports on the domestic economy can be seen throughout the period. One notable episode was the boom in the economy during the early 1970s followed by the decline in the mid 1970s. Exports rose sharply from 1971 to 1973 and

This makes it clear that net exports can be positive only if national income exceeds domestic absorption—that is, only if total demand for goods and services to be used in Canada is less than total output of goods and services in Canada. And if net exports are positive, it must be the case that national income exceeds the absorption of goods and services within Canada.†

Absorption Versus Component Approaches to the Trade Balance

Organizing the theory of income determination in this way has led economists to view the trade balance as an aggregate phenomenon: It must equal the difference between the two aggregates, *national income* and *domestic absorption.*

The trade balance, by definition, is also equal to the sum of all exports minus the sum of all imports. This makes it tempting to try to explain changes or trends in the trade account by "counting" the changes in particular exports and imports. Since both this "component" definition and the absorption definition are correct as *definitions* of the trade balance, either is valid as a framework that can be used to organize information in order to *analyze* the trade account.

† Note that foreigners can influence the demand for Canadian goods and services in two ways: by demanding exports and by investing in Canada.

The danger with the component approach is that the analyst may ignore the interaction between the items included in the trade balance and other variables such as national income. The absorption approach tends to draw attention to such interactions.

In order to compare the approaches, consider the effect on the trade balance of an exogenous increase in the foreign demand for one particular Canadian export. An increase in a particular export, *other things being equal,* will lead to an increase in national income. This increase in national income will lead in turn to increased expenditure on some imports. If one takes the component approach to analyzing the trade account, one may miss this induced effect. For example, if exports of wheat rose by $20 million in a given year, one might conclude that the trade balance would improve by $20 million. But the increased wheat exports would be reflected in higher incomes for farmers and the producers of transportation services who ship the wheat. These groups will spend some of their increased incomes on imports and some on domestic goods. The latter will lead to a multiplier effect on national income and result in further increases in spending on imports.

Clearly the net effect on the trade balance of the increased wheat exports must include the induced increases in imports. By relating the trade balance to the difference between total income and total spending in the domestic economy, this is exactly what the absorption approach does. [40]

---

then fell sharply in the years 1973 to 1975. More recently, the strength of the U.S. recovery over the 1982–1987 period stimulated Canadian exports and contributed to the recovery of the Canadian economy.

Factors other than foreign incomes also affect Canadian exports. One of the most important is the ability of Canadian firms to compete in international markets, as influenced in the short run by changes in the exchange rate and more directly by changes in domestic costs relative to foreign costs. Labor costs as reflected in wages are important, as are the costs of material inputs and energy.

In an open economy, fluctuations in exports exert an important influence on cyclical fluctuations.

Some further aspects of the relationship of net exports to cyclical movements in income are discussed in Box 31-2.

Changes in Investment

An important source of disturbance is investment expenditure. Consider the period 1929–1932. In 1929 total investment expenditure of firms and households in the Canadian economy was $1.2 billion, almost double the amount of expenditure needed to replace the capital goods that we used up that year in the process of producing a GDP of $6.1 billion. The Canadian economy in 1929, then, was adding rapidly to its stock of capital equipment. Four years later, in 1933, total investment expenditure was $145 million. This was less than one-third of the amount needed merely to keep the stock of capital intact. The Canadian economy in 1933, with its GDP reduced to $3.5 billion, was rapidly reducing its stock of capital equipment.

As Figure 31-4 shows, investment expenditure is quite volatile. Quite large shocks due to changes in investment expenditure hit the economy frequently. On average the change in investment from one year to the next has been about three times the average change in government expenditure.

Changes in investment are also quite closely correlated with changes in national income, as also shown in Figure 31-4. Rising investment tends to be associated with rapidly rising GDP, while falling investment tends to be associated with slowly rising or falling GDP. This is consistent with the view that investment shocks are a major cause of changes in national income.

Investment expenditures play a key role in most theories of cyclical fluctuations.

Why Does Investment Change?

The three major components of total investment expenditure are inventories, business fixed investment, and residential housing. Changes in investment are one of the prime causes of short-term fluctuations, but we do not have the whole story unless we know why investment fluctuates. In discussing the theory of income determination in Chapters 28 and 29 we talked simply of shifts in investment, not of the underlying causes of such shifts.

The Interest Rate and Investment

Empirical evidence shows that investment responds to many influencing factors. One of the most important is the rate of interest. Other things being equal, the higher the interest rate, the higher the cost of borrowing money for investment purposes and the less the amount of investment expenditure. Although in basic theory we talk of "the" interest rate, reality is not so simple; a few of these complications are discussed in Box 31-3 (see pages 654–655).

While each dollar of investment has the same consequences for aggregate demand, different types of investment respond to different sets of causes. Thus it is useful to discuss separately the determinants of the three major types of investment expenditures, both to see why the interest rate is such an important influence on investment and to determine what other factors are important.

Inventories.   Inventory changes represent only a small fraction of private investment in a typical year, but their average size is not an adequate measure of their importance. They are one of the more volatile elements of total investment and therefore have a major influence on shifts in investment expenditure.

Studies show that the stock of inventories held tends to rise as production and sales rise. Because the size of inventories is related to the level of sales, the *change* in inventories (which is current investment) is related to the *change* in the level of sales.

A firm may decide, for example, to hold inventories of 10 percent of its sales. If sales are $100,000, it will wish to hold inventories of $10,000. If sales increase to $110,000, it will want to hold inventories of $11,000. Over the period during which its stock of inventories is being increased, there will be a total of $1,000 new inventory investment.

The higher the level of production and sales, the larger the desired stock of inventories. Changes in the rate of production and sales cause temporary bouts of investment (or disinvestment) in inventories.

When a firm ties up funds in inventories, those same funds cannot be used elsewhere to earn income. At the very least the money could be lent out at the going rate of interest. Thus the higher the real rate of interest, the higher will be the cost of holding an inventory of a given size. And the higher that rate of interest, the more firms will try to lower their inventories. By causing firms to change the inventory levels that they desire to hold, a change in the rate of interest can lead to a flurry of investment or disinvestment in inventories.

The higher the real rate of interest, the lower the desired stock of inventories. Changes in the rate of interest cause temporary bouts of investment (or disinvestment) in inventories.

Residential housing construction. Since 1970 spending on residential construction has varied between one-fifth and one-third of all gross private investment and between 3.5 percent and 6.5 percent of GDP. Because expenditures for housing construction are both large and variable, they have a major impact on the economy.

Many influences on residential construction are noneconomic and depend on demographic or cultural considerations such as new family formation. But households must not only want to buy houses; they must also be able to do so. Periods of high employment and high average family earnings tend to lead to increases in house building and those of unemployment and falling earnings to decreases in such building.

Almost all houses are purchased with money borrowed on mortgages. Interest on the borrowed money typically accounts for over one-half of the purchaser's annual mortgage payments; the remainder is repayment of principal. It is for this reason that sharp variations in interest rates exert a substantial effect on the demand for housing.

Box 31-4 (see page 656) provides an illustration of the importance of interest rates for housing expenditures. This importance was borne out by experiences from 1979 to 1982. During this period mortgage rates rose from less than 11 percent to just over 15 percent and housing starts fell from 197,000 units to a mere 126,000 in 1982. (Since inflation fell from 1980, the increased nominal interest rates also meant increased real rates.) The construction industry itself and its major suppliers, such as the cement

and the lumber industries, felt the blow of a dramatic fall in demand. Conversely, in the mid 1980s interest rates fell sharply and there was a boom in the demand for new housing.

Expenditures for residential construction tend to vary positively with changes in average income and negatively with interest rates.

Business fixed investment. Investment in plant and equipment is the largest component of domestic investment. Much of it is financed by firms' retained profits (profits *not* paid out to its shareholders). This means that current profits are an important determinant of investment.

A second major determinant is the rate of interest. Much investment is financed by borrowed money. As became abundantly clear in the early 1980s, very high interest rates greatly reduce the volume of investment as more and more firms find their expected profits from investment do not cover the interest on borrowed investment funds.

A third major determinant is changes in national income. If there is a rise in aggregate demand that is expected to persist and cannot be met by existing capacity, investment in new plant and equipment will be needed. Once the new plants have been built and put into operation, however, the rate of new investment will fall.

This further illustrates an important characteristic of investment already encountered in the case of inventories: *If the desired stock of capital goods increases, there will be an investment boom while the new capital is being produced.* But if nothing else changes, even though business conditions continue to look rosy enough to justify the increased stock of capital, investment in new plant and equipment will cease once the larger capital stock is achieved. This aspect of investment leads to the *accelerator* theory of investment, which requires a closer look.

The Accelerator Theory of Investment

According to the accelerator theory, usually called the **accelerator,** investment is related to the rate of change of national income. When income is increasing, investment is needed to increase the capacity to

BOX 31-3

Many Rates of Interest

In the real world there are many different rates of interest. Speaking in terms of a single interest rate can be a valid simplification for many purposes because the whole set of rates *tends* to move upward or downward together. For some purposes, however, it is important to take into account the different rates that prevail at any one time.

At the same time that you receive an interest rate of 6 or 7 percent on deposits at a trust company you may have to pay 11 or 12 percent to borrow from that same trust company to finance your purchase of a house. Interest rates on consumer installment credit of 16 percent and 20 percent are common. A small firm pays a higher rate on funds it borrows from banks than does a giant corporation. Different government bonds pay different rates of interest, depending on the length of the period for which the bond runs. Corporation bonds tend to pay higher interest than treasury bills, and there is much variation among bonds of different companies.

Considering the extreme mobility of money, why do such differences exist? Why do funds not flow between different uses to eliminate these differences? The answer is that money *does* flow quite rapidly between alternative assets in response to interest differentials, but differences nevertheless pre-vail because quoted interest rates reflect many factors.

Differences in risk.   Corporation bonds generally have higher interest rates than government bonds because they have a greater degree of risk. For example, in mid 1986 many corporate issues were yielding more than 10 percent, while federal government bonds were paying less than 9 percent. Why? Investors were sure of the ability of the government to pay both the interest and the principal on their bonds, but they were less sure about the financial condition of private corporations.

Secured loans, where the borrower pledges an asset as collateral, tend to have lower interest rates than unsecured loans, other things being equal. Loans secured by houses (mortgages) tend to have lower interest rates than loans secured by automobiles, in part because it is harder to run away with a house than with a car and in part because a car can depreciate much more rapidly and unpredictably than a house.

Differences in duration.   The *term,* or duration, of a loan also affects its price. The same bank will usually pay a higher rate of interest on a certificate of deposit

---

produce consumption goods; when income is falling, it may not even be necessary to replace old capital as it wears out, let alone to invest in new capital.

The main insight the accelerator theory provides is the emphasis on net investment as *disequilibrium* behavior—the situation in which the actual stock of capital goods differs from what firms and households would like it to be. Anything that changes the desired size of the capital stock can generate investment. The accelerator focuses on one such source of change, changing national income. This gives the accelerator its particular importance in connection with *fluctuations* in national income. As we shall see, it can itself contribute to those fluctuations.

How the accelerator works.   To see how the theory works, suppose that there is a particular capital stock needed to produce each given level of an industry's output. The ratio of the value of capital to the annual value of output is called the **capital-output ratio.** Suppose that the industry is producing at capacity and the demand for its product increases. If the industry is to produce the higher level of output, its capital stock must increase. This necessitates new investment.

Table 31-1 (see page 657) provides a simple numerical example of the accelerator. Working through the data step by step leads to three conclusions:

1. **Rising rather than high levels of sales are needed to call forth net investment.**
2. **For net investment to remain constant, sales must rise by a constant amount per year.**
3. **The amount of net investment will be a mul-**

that cannot be redeemed at the bank (without penalty) for at least one year than on a straight savings account from which funds can be withdrawn in a matter of minutes. Yet many savers prefer savings accounts because they want to be able to withdraw their money on short notice. Except when interest rates are thought to be temporarily abnormally high, borrowers are usually willing to pay more for long-term loans than for short-term loans because they are certain of having use of the money for a longer period. Lenders usually require a higher rate of interest the longer is the time before the borrower must repay. Other things being equal, the shorter the term of a loan, the lower the interest rates.

Differences in costs of administering credit. There is great variation in the cost of different kinds of credit transactions. It is almost as cheap (in actual dollars) for a bank to lend an airline $1 billion that the airline agrees to pay back with interest after one year as it is for the same bank to lend you $14,000 to buy a new car that you agree to pay back over two years in 24 equal installments.

The installment loan to you requires many more bookkeeping entries than the loan to the airline. In addition, it is easier, and therefore less costly, to check

the airline's credit rating than it is to check yours. The difference in the cost *per dollar* of each loan is considerable. The bank may very well make less profit per dollar on a $14,000 loan at 20 percent per year than on a $1 billion loan at 10 percent per year. In general, the bigger the loan and the fewer the payments, the less the cost per dollar of servicing the loan. Why, then, do banks and finance companies usually insist that you repay a loan in frequent installments? They worry that if you do not pay regularly, you will not have the money when the loan comes due.

In the market for borrowed funds there is a structure of various interest rates for credit transactions of different kinds.

Individual rates will be set that take into account such factors as risk premiums, duration of loan, and costs of administration. Nevertheless, it is useful and usual to talk about movements of interest rate structures up and down as changes in "the" interest rate. This simplification is appropriate when the entire structure of rates moves up or down together such that changes in a single rate can capture changes in all rates.

tiple of the increase in sales because the capital-output ratio is greater than one.[2]

The data in Table 31-1 are for a single industry, but if many industries behave in this way, one would expect aggregate net investment to bear a similar relation to changes in national income. This is what the accelerator theory predicts. **[41]**

The accelerator theory says nothing directly about replacement investment, but it does have im-

plications for such investment. When sales are constant (no net investment required), replacement investment will be required to maintain the capital stock at the desired level. When sales are increasing from a position of full capacity, both net investment and replacement investment will be required. When sales are falling, not only will net investment be zero, but there will be a tendency to forgo replacement investment as well.

Limitations of the accelerator. Taken literally, the accelerator posits a rigid response of investment to changes in sales (and thus, aggregatively, to changes in national income). In fact, the relation is more subtle.

Changes in sales that are thought to be temporary will not necessarily lead to new investment. It is

---

[2] In the example in the table the capital-output ratio is 5:1. Why should anyone spend $5 on capital stock to get $1 of output? It is not unreasonable to spend $5 to purchase a machine that produces only $1 of output *per year,* provided that the machine will last enough years to repay the $5 plus a reasonable return on this investment.

BOX 31-4

The Cost of Buying a House on Time

Few people who buy a house can pay cash. Most purchases are financed by borrowing money on a *mortgage*. A mortgage is a loan to the house purchaser (sometimes of as much as 85 or 90 percent of the purchase price, but 60 to 75 percent is common). In return, the borrower promises to make fixed monthly payments that cover interest on the money borrowed and repay the amount borrowed (the principal) over some agreed period, commonly 20 or 30 years. (The monthly payments often include an amount to cover insurance and taxes, but this is ignored in what follows.) The house itself acts as security for the loan. Loans of this type are said to be *amortized,* which means that fixed payments over a stated period gradually repay the principal and cover the interest on the principal outstanding.

Because the loan stretches over a long period, a great deal of the total amount paid by the borrower is interest on the outstanding loan. For example, on a 20-year mortgage for $50,000 at a nominal annual interest rate of 8 percent per year (a monthly rate of 8/12 of 1 percent), a total of $100,375 would be paid in 240 monthly installments of $418.23 each. This is $50,000 to repay the principal of the loan and $50,375 in interest. At a 12 percent nominal annual rate (a monthly rate of 1 percent), the total payments would be $132,130, making $82,130 total interest on top of the $50,000 to repay the principal.

The interest on a mortgage is calculated on the amount of the loan still outstanding. After each payment the amount outstanding is reduced so that, with fixed annual payments, most of the total amount paid goes to paying interest in the early years and to repaying principal in later years. It follows that the purchaser's equity in the house (the down payment plus the total amount of the loan that has been repaid over the years) builds up slowly at first, then more and more rapidly as the terminal date approaches.

Note in the table that when half the life of the mortgage has passed, only about a quarter of the principal has been repaid. In the first year of the mortgage, $4,965 goes as interest and only $825 to reduce the principal on the loan. In the last year, only $300 is interest and $5,490 goes to repay the principal.

Breakdown of Payments in Selected Years on a 20-Year Mortgage for $50,000 at 10 Percent (*all figures to the nearest dollar*)

Year	Payments made over the year	Interest paid over the year	Principal repaid over the year	Equity (cumulative total over all the years)*
1	5,790	4,965	825	825
2	5,790	4,875	915	1,745
5	5,790	4,560	1,230	5,100
10	5,790	3,765	2,025	13,490
15	5,790	2,455	3,335	27,290
19	5,790	820	4,970	44,510
20	5,790	300	5,490	50,000

* In addition to equity due to down payment.

usually possible to increase the level of output for a given capital stock by working overtime or extra shifts. While this solution would be more expensive per unit of output in the long run, it is usually preferable to making investments in new plant and equipment that would lie idle after a temporary spurt of demand had subsided. Thus expectations about what the required capital stock will be may lead to

TABLE 31-1 An Illustration of the Accelerator Theory of Investment

(1) Year	(2) Annual sales	(3) Change in sales	(4) Required stock of capital[a]	(5) Net investment: increase in required capital stock
1	$10	$0	$ 50	$ 0
2	10	0	50	0
3	11	1	55	5
4	13	2	65	10
5	16	3	80	15
6	19	3	95	15
7	22	3	110	15
8	24	2	120	10
9	25	1	125	5
10	25	0	125	0

[a] Assuming a capital-output ratio of 5:1.

With a fixed capital-output ratio, net investment occurs only when it is necessary to increase the stock of capital in order to change output. Assume that it takes $5 of capital to produce $1 of output per year. In years 1 and 2 there is no need for investment. In year 3 a rise in sales of $1 requires investment of $5 to provide the needed capital stock. In year 4 a further rise of $2 in sales requires an additional investment of $10 to provide the needed capital stock. As columns 3 and 5 show, the amount of net investment is proportional to the *change* in sales. When the increase in sales tapers off in years 7–9, investment declines. When sales no longer increase in year 10, net investment falls to zero because the capital stock of year 9 is adequate to provide output for year 10's sales.

a much less rigid response of investment to income than the accelerator suggests.

Another limitation of the accelerator theory is that it takes a limited view of what constitutes investment. The fixed capital-output ratio emphasizes investment in what economists call **capital widening,** the investment in additional capacity that uses the same ratio of capital to labor as existing capacity. It does not explain **capital deepening,** which is the increase in the amount of capital per unit of labor that occurs, say, in response to a fall in the rate of interest. Neither does the theory say anything about investments brought about as a result of new processes or new products. Furthermore, it does not allow for the fact that investment in any period is likely to be limited by the capacity of the capital-goods industry.

For these and other reasons, the accelerator does not by itself give anything like a complete explanation of variations in business fixed investment. It

should not be surprising that a simple accelerator theory provides a relatively poor overall explanation of changes in investment. Yet accelerator-like influences do exist, and empirical evidence continues to suggest that they play a role in the cyclical variability of investment.

Theories of the Cycle

There are several main theories about the cycle. They do not have to be regarded as competing. Indeed, each one captures some of the forces that contribute to the cycle.

Systematic Spending Fluctuations

The most commonly accepted theory looks to systematic fluctuations in aggregate expenditure brought about by systematic alterations in spending behavior as the cause of the cycle. Several influences can cause such alterations.

The Multiplier-Accelerator Mechanism

The combination of the multiplier and the accelerator can make upward or downward movements in the economy cumulative. Imagine that the economy is settled into a depression with heavy unemployment. Then a revival of investment demand occurs. Orders are placed for new plant and equipment, which creates new employment in the capital-goods industries. The newly employed workers spend most of their earnings. This creates new demand for consumer goods. A multiplier process is now set up, with new employment and incomes created in the consumer-goods industries.

The spending of the newly created incomes in turn means further increases in demand. At some stage the increased demand for consumer goods creates, through the accelerator process, an increased demand for capital goods. Once existing equipment is fully employed in any industry, extra output requires new capital equipment, and the accelerator theory takes over as the major determinant of investment expenditure. Such investment increases or at least maintains demand in the capital-goods sector of the economy. So the process goes on, the multiplier-accelerator mechanism continuing to produce a rapid rate of expansion in the economy.

The upper turning point.   A rapid expansion can continue for some time, but it cannot go on forever. Eventually the economy will run into bottlenecks in terms of certain resources. For example, investment funds may become scarce, and as a result interest rates rise. Firms now find new investments more expensive than anticipated, and thus some become unprofitable. Or suppose that what limits the expansion is exhaustion of the reservoir of unemployed labor. The full-employment ceiling guarantees that any sustained rapid growth rate of real income and employment will eventually be slowed.

At this point the accelerator again comes into play. A slowing in the rate of increase of production leads to a decrease in business fixed investment. This decrease causes a drop in employment in the capital-goods industries and, through the multiplier, a fall in consumer demand. As consumer demand falls, investment in plant and equipment is reduced to a low level because firms already have more productive capacity than they can use. Unemployment rises, and the upper turning point has been passed.

The lower turning point.   A contraction, too, is eventually brought to an end. Consider the worst depression imaginable, one in which every postponable expenditure of households, firms, or governments is postponed. Even then aggregate demand does not fall to zero. Figure 28-1 on page 590 shows that as aggregate disposable income falls, households spend a larger and larger fraction of that falling income. Finally, should income fall to the break-even level, all disposable income is spent (and none is saved).

Neither does government spending fall in proportion to the fall in government tax revenues. Government expenditures on most programs continue even if tax revenues sag to low levels.

Finally, even investment expenditures, in many ways the most easily postponed component of aggregate expenditure, does not fall to zero. Industries providing basics still have substantial sales and need replacement investment. Even in the worst depression some new processes and new products appear, and these require new investment.

Taken together, the minimum levels of consumption, investment, and government expenditure will assure a minimum equilibrium level of national income that, although well below the full-employment level, will not be zero. There is a floor below which income will not fall.

Sooner or later, an upturn begins. If nothing else causes an expansion of business activity, there will eventually be a revival of replacement investment because as existing capital wears out, the capital stock eventually falls below the level required to produce current output. At this stage new machines are bought to replace those that are worn out.

The rise in the level of activity in the capital-goods industries causes, by way of the multiplier, a further rise in income. The economy turns the corner. An expansion, once started, triggers the sort of cumulative upward movement that has already been discussed.

Other Endogenous Forces

The multiplier-accelerator is one endogenous force contributing to cyclical fluctuations. Two others are inventories and construction.

Inventory cycles. As we have seen, there are good reasons to suppose that the required size of inventories is related to the level of firms' sales and that sales are related to the level of national income. If firms maintain anything like a rigid inventory-to-sales ratio, this will cause an accelerator-like linkage between investment in inventories and *changes* in national income.

Many observers believe that these sharp and somewhat periodic fluctuations lead to an "inventory cycle" of roughly 40 months' average duration.

Construction cycles. Economists have noted some long-run, wave-like movements of roughly 20 years' duration in the statistics for expenditures on residential construction. These are sometimes referred to as "building cycles." Some economists suggest an accelerator-like explanation that runs from external events to demographic changes, to changes in the demand for housing and other buildings, and thence to changes in construction activity.

A major war, by taking males away from home, tends to retard family formation and thereby tends to depress the demand for private housing. When the war ends, there is typically an increase in marriages and household formation, an increase in the demand for housing, and a boom in the construction industry.

Depending on the capacity of the building industry, the boom may last many years before the desired increases in the stock of buildings of various kinds are achieved, but eventually it ends. Then, approximately 20 years after the end of the war that triggered the boom, there is likely to be a further boom in the number of marriages and births as the new generation starts its process of family formation. Wars are not the only source of such population-induced

cycles; a severe depression will lead to a similar postponement of family formation.

The evidence concerning construction spending over the past century is thought by many economists to support the theory just outlined, a theory very much like the accelerator, though with changes in demographic factors, rather than changes in income, providing the impetus.

Random Shocks and Long Lags

One other model of the cycle does not assume cyclical behavior from firms and households. It suggests instead that random shifts in expenditure are transformed into systematic cycles of output and employment.

This theory begins with lags. For example, if a fall in the rate of interest makes an investment in a new project profitable, it may take 6 months to plan it, 3 months to let contracts, 6 months before spending builds up to its top rate, and another 24 to complete the project. These lags mean that changes in the rate of interest will cause reactions in investment expenditure that are distributed over quite a long period of time.

These lags have important implications for key macro variables. Although the disturbances might be random or erratic, income and employment both follow a cyclical path.

Each major component of aggregate expenditure has sometimes undergone shifts large enough to disturb the economy significantly. Long lags can convert such shifts into cyclical oscillations in national income.

A recent controversy in economics has emerged in response to research that shows that most of the cyclical patterns in the American economy can be explained by the effects of unpredictable technological disturbances that buffet the economy. These models argue that uncertainty about those shocks mean that when they do occur, households and firms react to them in a manner that spreads their effects out over several time periods. Thus, these *real business cycle* models predict that sporadic random shocks will give rise to smooth cyclical behavior of key macroeconomic variables.

While these models are able to explain many business cycle facts, many economists remain skeptical about them. In particular, they are doubtful about the nature and source of the shocks that play such a central role in the models, and in the limited role they assign to economic policies in either causing business cycles or in offsetting the effects of other disturbances.

Policy-induced Cycles

Yet another theory of the cycle is based on the allegation that government-induced demand shocks have sometimes caused cyclical fluctuations. Government expenditure has not often been the cause of major shocks due to sudden large changes. But government tax policy and monetary policy have both been shifted enough to cause significant demand shocks. Why should the government administer such potentially disturbing demand shocks? Several reasons have been suggested.

A political business cycle.   As early as 1944 Polish-born Keynesian economist Michael Kalecki warned of a political business cycle. He argued that once governments had learned to manipulate the economy, they would engineer an election-geared business cycle. In pre-election periods they would raise spending and cut taxes. The resulting expansionary demand shock would create high employment and good business conditions, which would bring voters' support for the government. But the resulting inflationary gap would lead to a rising price level. So after the election was won, the government would depress demand to remove the inflationary gap and provide some slack for expansion before the next election.

This theory invokes the image of a cynical government manipulating employment and national income solely because it wants to stay in office. Few people believe that governments deliberately do this all the time, but the temptation to do it some of the time, particularly before elections, may prove irresistible.

Alternating policy goals.   A variant of the policy-induced cycle does not require a cynical government and an easily duped electorate. Instead both sides need only be rather shortsighted and have rather narrow vision.

In this theory, when there is a recession and relatively stable prices, the public and the government identify unemployment as the number one economic problem. The government then engineers an expansionary policy shock through some combination of tax cuts and spending increases. This, plus such natural cumulative forces as the multiplier-accelerator, expands economic activity. Unemployment falls and income rises, but as income rises above potential national income, the price level begins to rise. It first rises along the stable *SRAS* curve and then rises further as boom conditions raise factor prices and shift the *SRAS* curve upward (see Figure 30-2 on page 633).

At this point the unemployment problem is declared cured. Now inflation is seen as the nation's number one economic problem. A contractionary demand shock is engineered. The natural cumulative forces again take over, causing a recession. The inflation subsides but unemployment rises, setting the stage once again for an expansionary shock to cure the unemployment problem.

Many economists have criticized government policy over the past few decades as sometimes causing fluctuations by alternately pushing expansion to cure unemployment and then contraction to cure inflation. We shall see in Chapter 39 that this charge is particularly strong against monetary policy. But whatever the policy, the charge is that policymakers have sometimes been too shortsighted in alternating their concern between unemployment and inflation.

Misguided stabilization policy.   In a variant of the theory just expounded, the government tries to hold the economy at potential national income by countering fluctuations in private-sector expenditure with offsetting changes of its own spending and taxes. The government can in principle dampen such cyclical fluctuations by its stabilization policies. But unless it is very sophisticated, bad timing may accentuate rather than dampen fluctuations. We return to this possibility in subsequent chapters.

Securities Markets (Stock Markets)

It is commonplace to observe that stock market values have sometimes displayed cumulative upward movements and at other times cumulative downward movements. The first are called *bull markets* and the second *bear markets*. Most people also know that the Great Depression of the 1930s was preceded by the great stock market crash of 1929.

The association between fluctuations in the stock market and in the economy is there, but is there a causal connection? Do stock market booms help to cause business cycle booms, and do stock market slumps help to cause business cycle slumps? Before we can answer this question, we need to learn a bit about such markets.

The Function of Securities Markets

When a household buys shares newly issued by a company, it becomes one of the firm's owners. The company will not return the household's money, except in the rare event that the firm is liquidated. If the household wishes to get its money back, it can only persuade someone else to buy its shares in the company.

Similarly, when a household buys a bond from a company, it cannot get its money back from the company before a specified date. If I bought a 2007 bond in 1987, the bond will be redeemed by the company (i.e., the loan will be paid back) only in 2007. If I wish to get my money back sooner, all I can do is sell the bond to someone who is willing to become one of the company's creditors.

An organized market where stocks and bonds are bought and sold is called a **securities market,** or a **stock market.** Two of the best known are the New York Stock Exchange and the Toronto Stock Exchange. The trading of existing shares on the stock market indicates that ownership is being transferred; it does not indicate that companies are raising new money from the public.

Securities markets are important because by providing for the ready transfer of corporate securities, they make it possible for individuals to save without having to commit themselves for long periods.

Securities markets allow people to put their savings into stocks and bonds that are not themselves directly or quickly redeemable. For example, if I want to invest in a particular stock that pays an attractive yield, I may do so even though I know that I will want my money back after only a year. Given a securities market, I can be confident of my ability to sell the security a year from now. But while securities markets provide for the quick sale of stocks and bonds, they do not guarantee that securities can be sold at the same price at which they were bought. The price at any time is the one that equates the demand and supply for a particular security, and rapid fluctuations in stock prices are common.

Prices on the Stock Market

Figure 31-5 shows the wide swings in a well-known index of stock market prices, the Toronto Stock Exchange (TSE) Industrial Composite Index. The most recent swing in the period covered in the figure began from a trough in September 1982 when the index was about 1500. The index then rose, almost without interruption, until in mid 1987 it passed through 3800, a rise of 150 percent in just 50 months. Then in October 1987 it suffered a dramatic fall, tumbling 25 percent in less than two weeks to below 2900. It will probably have again changed significantly since then.

This was only one in a series of "booms" and "busts" that have periodically interrupted the long-term trend for stock market prices to rise slowly but steadily over the years. There had also been two large swings in the mid 1970s. Between 1979 and May 1981 the average stock price rose by 80 percent, yielding large gains for people who were wise or lucky enough to have bought at the beginning and sold at the end of this upswing. But then a downward movement occurred, with stock prices losing more than 30 percent of their value within a little over a year. Just a little earlier, in 1973, stocks lost 20 percent of their value and then recovered quite rapidly.

FIGURE 31-5   Fluctuations in an Index of Stock Prices, 1960–1986

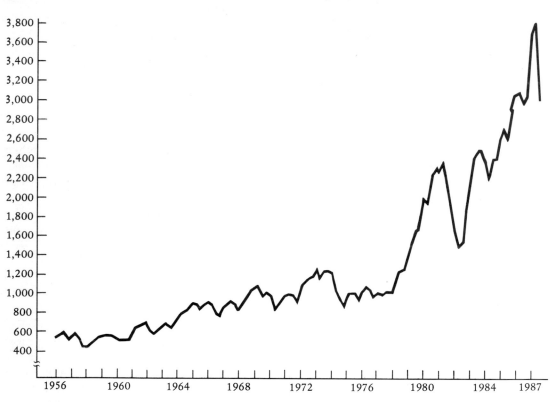

Stock market fluctuations are very sharp and irregular, and have witnessed a sharp increase. The chart shows quarterly variations in the Toronto Stock Exchange Industrial Composite Index. The index grew steadily from 1962 to 1972 and then displayed very little trend over the next 16 years. Over that period the index did, however, fluctuate sharply; it is these fluctuations that make large speculative gains and losses possible. Two notable falls in the index occurred during the economic downturns in 1970.

The market fell during the 1981–1982 recession, but the economic recovery of 1982 to 1986 was accompanied by a dramatic sustained increase in the TSE index; the index rose from about 1800 at the end of 1982 to over 3700 at the beginning of 1987, and then fell dramatically in late October to under 3000.

Measuring Stock Market Swings

Commentators are often careless about making the key distinction between the *number of points* by which the index changes over some period and the *percentage change* in that index over the same period. For example, when the TSE Industrial Composite fell by just over 500 points from a value of over 3800 in one week in October 1987, newspaper reporters were quick to point out that this was one of the largest one-week falls ever, measured by the number of points. But was it the greatest loss of stock values in any meaningful sense?

The answer is no. To see the significance for wealth holders of changes in stock market prices, we need to deal not in index points but in percentages. When we do this, the dramatic collapse of 1987 is put into perspective. Serious though it was, the loss of 25 percent in stock values was by no means un-precedented. As noted, in 1973–1974 stocks lost 20 percent of their value and then recovered; in 1975–1976 they lost 15 percent of their values before re-covering. These losses, as well as those of September 1986, remain dwarfed by the loss everyone hopes will never be repeated: Over 80 percent of the value of stocks was lost over the three-year period from 1929 to 1933!

Causes of Stock Market Swings

What causes such rapid gains and losses, and what do they have to do with business cycles?

When investors buy a company's stocks, they are buying rights to share in the stream of div-idends to be paid out by that company. They are also buying an asset that they can sell in the future at a gain or loss.

The value of that stock depends on two things: first, what people expect the stream of future dividend payments to be, and second, what capital gain or loss people expect to realize when the stock is sold.

Both things make dealing in stocks an inherently risky operation. Will the company in which you are investing pay more or less in dividends in future years? Will the company's value rise or fall so that you can sell your share in it for more or less than what you bought it for? While dividend policies of most established companies tend to be fairly stable, stock prices are subject to wide swings.

The Influence of Present and Future Business Conditions

We have observed that many influences act on stock market prices; these include the state of the business cycle and the stance of government policies.

Cyclical forces.   If investors expect a firm's earnings to increase, the firm will become more valuable, and the price of its stock will rise. Such influences cause stock prices to move with the business cycle, being high when current profits are high and low when current profits are low. It also causes stock prices to vary with a host of factors that influence expectations of future profits. A poor crop, destruction of trees by acid rain, announcement of new defense spend-ing, a change in the foreign-exchange value of the dollar, or a change in the political complexion of the administration can all affect profit expectations and hence stock prices.

Policy factors.   We shall see later in this book that major alterations in monetary policy can cause major changes in interest rates. Such changes, or just the expectations of them, will have major effects on stock prices. Say, for example, that interest rates rise rapidly. Investors will see that they can now earn an increased amount by purchasing government bonds. As a result, they will wish to alter their investment portfolios to hold more bonds and fewer stocks. But everyone cannot do this, since only so many stocks and so many bonds are available to be held at any given time. As all investors try to sell their stocks, prices fall. The fall will only stop when the expected rate of return to investment in stocks, based on their lower purchase price, makes stocks equally attractive as bonds. Then investors will no longer try to shift out of bonds *en masse*.

Speculative Booms

In addition to responding to a host of factors that can reasonably be expected to influence the absolute and relative earnings of companies, stock prices often develop an upward or downward movement of their own, propelled by little more than speculation that feeds on itself.

In major stock market booms, people begin to expect rising stock prices and hurry to buy while stocks are cheap. This action bids up the prices of shares and creates the capital gains that justify the original expectations. This is an example of the phe-nomenon of *self-realizing expectations*. Investors get rich on paper in the sense that the market value of their holdings rises. Money-making now looks easy to others, who also rush in to buy, and new purchases push up prices still further. At this stage attention to current earnings all but ceases. If a stock can yield, say, a 50 percent capital gain in one year, it does not matter much if the current earnings represent only a small percentage yield on the purchase price of the stocks. Everyone is "making money," so more people become attracted by the get-rich-quick opportunities. Their attempts to buy bid up prices still further. In such speculative booms, current earnings represent an ever-diminishing percentage yield on the current price of the stocks.

Capital gains can be so attractive that investors may buy stocks on margin—that is, borrow money to buy them, using the stocks themselves as security for the loans. In doing this, many investors may be borrowing money at a rate of interest considerably in excess of the yield from current dividends. Even if $50,000 is borrowed at 10 percent (interest payments are $5,000 per year) to buy stocks yielding a current dividend return of only 4 percent (dividend receipts are $2,000 per year), never mind, says the investor's logic; the stocks can be sold in a year or so for a handsome capital gain that will more than repay the $3,000 of interest not covered by dividends. Some people have the luck or good judgment to sell out near the top of the market, and they actually make money. Others wait eagerly for ever-greater capital gains, and in the meantime they get richer and richer—on paper.

Eventually something breaks the period of unrestrained optimism. Some investors may begin to worry about the very high prices of stocks in relation not only to current yields but also to possible future yields, even when generous allowances for growth are made. Or it may be that the prices of stocks become depressed slightly when a sufficiently large number of persons try to sell out in order to realize their capital gains. As they offer their securities on the market, they cannot find purchasers without some fall in prices. Even a modest price fall may be sufficient to persuade others that it is time to sell. But every share that is sold must be bought by someone. A wave of sellers may not find new buyers at existing prices, causing prices to fall. Panic selling may now occur.

A household that borrowed $50,000 to buy stocks near the top of the market may find the paper value of its holdings sliding below $50,000. How will it repay its loan? Even if it does not worry about the loan, its broker will. The household may sell now before it loses too much, or its broker may "sell the

customer out" to liquidate the loan. All this causes prices to fall even further and provides another example of self-realizing expectations. If enough people think prices are going to come down, their attempt to sell out at the present high prices will create the fall in prices the expectations of which caused the selling.

This is a very simple and stylized description of a typical speculative cycle, yet it describes the basic elements of market booms and busts that have recurred throughout stock market history. The biggest boom of all began in the mid 1920s and ended on Black Tuesday, October 29, 1929. The collapse was dramatic, with stocks losing about half of their value in about two months. Nor did it stop there. For three long years stock prices continued to decline until the average value of stock sold on the New York Stock Exchange had fallen from its 1929 high of $89.10 a share to $17.35 a share by late 1933. It also happened, although less dramatically, in the booms and busts of the 1970s and 1980s discussed earlier in this section.

Stock Market Swings: Cause or Effect of Business Cycles?

Stock markets tend often to lead, and sometimes to follow, booms and slumps in business activity. In both cases the causes usually run from real business conditions, whether actual or anticipated, to stock market prices. This is the dominant theme, the stock market as reflector.

It is also possible for the stock market to be a causal factor in the business cycle. For example, some people held that the wild boom of the late 1920s tied up funds in speculative uses that would otherwise have gone to the real investment spending needed to sustain the boom into the 1930s. Such circumstances are possible, but they are only a minor theme.

Stock market fluctuations are more typically a consequence than a cause of the business cycle.

In many cases the stock market and the business cycle both reflect the common influence of other factors. For example, stock markets often react to changes in interest rates that may be caused by government policy; as we have seen, such interest-rate changes can also play a causal role in cyclical fluctuations in the economy. Typically the stock market responds quicker than does the economy to such influences, and for this reason many observers look to it as a "leading indicator" of likely future economic developments.

The relationship between the stock market and the economy is further complicated by the existence of occasional speculative booms and busts. There are often real economic forces influencing expectations of stock prices, but at least for a while the prices may become dominated by speculative psychology. Unfortunately, speculative behavior causes the stock market to react to many events that turn out to have little or no enduring implications for the economy. As one wag put it, the stock market has predicted seven out of the last two recessions!

As an example, consider the long upswing that took stock prices up by about 85 percent in less than three years between early 1984 and early 1987. At the time Canada enjoyed a very strong recovery, and the rising stock prices no doubt reflected the resulting favorable profit outlook of Canadian companies. Added onto all that may have been a speculative component. Certainly many doubted that the full increase in stock values of over 85 percent in less than four years was justified by underlying business opportunities. Only time can tell how much, if any, of the rise in values was due to transitory speculative behavior. Certainly the fall of over 25 percent in October 1987 indicated that much of the run-up in values was a result of a speculative form.

Stock Markets: Investment Marketplaces or Gambling Casinos?

Stock markets fulfill many important functions. It is doubtful that the great aggregations of capital needed to finance modern firms could be raised under a private ownership system without them. There is no doubt, however, that they also provide an unfortunate attraction for many naive investors whose get-rich-quick dreams are more often than not destroyed by the fall in prices that follows the occasional speculative booms they help to create.

To some extent public policy has sought to curb the excesses of stock market speculation through supervision of security issues. This is an area of complex overlap between federal and provincial jurisdiction. Policy seeks, among other things, to prevent both fraudulent or misleading information and trading by "insiders" (those in a company with confidential information). Moreover, the regulators can limit the ability of speculators to trade on margin.

All in all, the stock market is both a real marketplace and a place to gamble. As in all gambling situations, players who are less well informed and less clever than the average tend to be losers in the long term.

Causes of Business Cycles: A Consensus View?

Economists once argued long and bitterly about which was the best explanation of the recurrent cyclical behavior of the economy.

Today most economists agree that there is not a single cause or class of causes governing business cycles.

In an economy that has tendencies for both cumulative and self-reversing behavior, any large shock, whether from without or within, can initiate a cyclical swing. Wars are important; so are major technical inventions. A rapid increase in interest rates and a general tightening of credit can cause a sharp decrease in investment. Expectations can be changed by a political campaign or a development in another part of the world. The list of possible initial impulses, autonomous or induced, is long. It is probably true that the characteristic cyclical pattern involves many outside shocks that sometimes initiate, sometimes reinforce, and sometimes dampen the cumulative tendencies that exist within the economy.

Cycles differ also in terms of their internal structure. There are variations in timing, duration, and amplitude. In some cycles full employment of labor may be the bottleneck that determines the peak. In others high interest rates and shortages of investment funds may nip an expansion and turn it into a recession at the same time that the unemployment of labor is still an acute problem. In some cycles the recession phase is short; in others a full-scale period of stagnation sets in. In some cycles the peak develops into a severe inflation; in others the pressure of excess demand is hardly felt, and a new recession sets in before the economy has fully recovered from the last trough. Some cycles last long; others are short.

In this chapter we have suggested reasons why an economy that is subjected to periodic external shocks will tend to generate a continually changing pattern of fluctuations, as cumulative and then self-reversing forces alternatively come into play. In the next chapter we study how governments seek to influence the cycle and remove some of its extremes through the use of fiscal policy.

Summary

1. The economy experiences continual fluctuations. A self-reinforcing cumulative process leads to a cyclical pattern of fluctuations.

2. Economists break a stylized cycle into four phases: trough, recovery, peak, and recession. These phases have certain characteristic features, although no two real-world cycles are exactly the same.

3. Short-term fluctuations in GDP are usually, though not always, the result of variations in aggregate demand. Overall, these fluctuations show a fairly clear pattern that is described as cyclical. Despite the overall pattern, the evidence is that the cycles are irregular in amplitude, in timing, in duration, and in the way they affect particular industries and sectors of the economy.

4. Any explanation of the business cycle must explain both *why* income fluctuates and *how* those fluctuations get transformed into cycles.

5. Shifts in consumption, government, and export expenditures can cause major fluctuations in Canadian national income and employment.

6. Investment expenditure causes fluctuations in aggregate demand. The three principal components of private investment are changes in business inventories, residential construction, and business fixed investment. The interest rate is an important determinant of investment spending.

7. Changes in business inventories, the smallest of the three major components of investment expenditure, often account for an important fraction of the year-to-year changes in the level of investment. They respond both to changes in the level of production and sales and to the rate of interest.

8. Residential construction shows a cyclical pattern of its own. House building responds to economic (as well as noneconomic) influences, varying directly with the level of national income and inversely with the rate of interest. The rate of interest is important because interest payments are a large fraction of the mortgage payments that greatly affect a household's ability to purchase a house.

9. Business fixed investment depends on a number of variables. These include innovation, expectations about the future, level of profits, rate of interest, and changes in national income.

10. The accelerator theory relates net investment to changes in national

income on the assumption of a fixed capital-output ratio. Its central prediction is that rising income is required to maintain a given level of investment. Its central insight is that net investment is a disequilibrium phenomenon that occurs when the actual capital stock is different from the desired capital stock.

11. There are several explanations of the cyclical pattern of economic fluctuations. Among these are (1) that expenditure shifts themselves are systematic; (2) that lags in the system transform random expenditure shifts into systematic cyclical changes in income; and (3) that in part the cycle is either the conscious or the accidental result of government policy.

12. Securities (stock) markets allow firms to raise new capital from the sale of newly issued securities and allow the holders of existing securities to sell their securities to other investors. Prices on the stock market tend to reflect the public's expectations both of firms' future earnings and of future changes in prices (for whatever reason). This necessarily puts a strong speculative dimension into security prices, and large speculative swings do occur. Such swings are accentuated by the phenomenon of self-realizing expectations.

Topics for Review

Business cycles and economic fluctuations
Phases of the cycle
Causes of cyclical fluctuations
Components of investment
The accelerator
Interactions of the multiplier and the accelerator
Political business cycle
The stock market

Discussion Questions

1. How and in what direction might each of the following shift the function relating consumption expenditure to disposable income?
   a. Introduction of user-fee charges for medical care
   b. A change in attitudes so that we become a nation of conspicuous conservers rather than conspicuous consumers, taking pride in how little we eat or spend for housing, clothing, and so on
   c. Increases in income taxes
   d. News that due to medical advances everyone can count on more years of retirement than ever before
   e. A spreading belief that all-out nuclear war is likely within the next 10 years
   f. Sharp increases in the down payments required on durable goods
2. Suppose the government wished to reduce private investment in order to reduce an inflationary gap. What policies might it adopt? If it wished to do so in such a way as to have a major effect on residential housing and a minor effect on business fixed investment expenditures, which measures might it use?

3. What effect on total investment—and on which categories of investment—would you predict as a result of each of the following?
   a. Widespread endorsement of zero population growth by young couples
   b. A sharp increase in the frequency and duration of strikes in the transportation industries
   c. Forecasts of very low growth rates of real national income over the next five years
   d. Tax reform that eliminates deductions for property taxes in computing taxable personal income

4. When interest rates rose sharply in the early 1980s, home construction fell dramatically, but sales of mobile homes increased. How does the rise in the sale of mobile homes relate to the notion that investment responds to the rate of interest?

5. Empirical studies show that as the volume of a firm's sales increases, the size of its inventories of raw materials tends to increase in proportion. It is common for business firms to speak of such inventories in terms of "a 20-day supply of coal" rather than "52,000 tons of coal" or "$280,000 worth of coal." Why should relative size be more important than absolute quantity or dollar value?

6. Which "cause" of business investment is being relied on in each of the following quotes?
   a. An aluminum industry spokesman, justifying a $0.50 a pound increase in aluminum prices: "We must have it to build the new capacity we need."
   b. A major steel company, in a newspaper ad: "We need lower taxes, not cheaper money or government deficits, to help lower barriers to capital formation."
   c. "The government used a credit crunch to bring on a recession and reduce inflation."

7. Since different series behave differently, does it make sense to talk about a business cycle? Predict the comparative behavior of the following pairs of series in relation to fluctuations in the GDP.
   a. Purchases of food, purchases of consumer durables
   b. Tax receipts, bankruptcies
   c. Unemployment, birth rates
   d. Employment in Montreal, employment in Oshawa
   Check your predictions against the facts for the past decade.

8. The highest interest rates in Canadian history occurred in 1981–1982. The deepest recession since the 1930s occurred in 1982. How might these facts be related? What has happened to interest rates and economic activity since?

32

Fiscal Policy

As we have seen, national income fluctuates continually due to shifts in aggregate demand and short-run aggregate supply. **Fiscal policy** involves the use of government spending and tax policies to influence the *AD* curve and, to a lesser degree, the *SRAS* curve in order to damp fluctuations in the economy.

Since government expenditure increases aggregate demand and taxation decreases it, the *direction* of the required changes in spending and taxation is generally easy to determine once we know the direction of the desired change in national income. But the *timing, magnitude,* and *mixture* of the changes pose more difficult issues.

Any policy that attempts to stabilize national income at or near a desired level (usually potential national income) is called **stabilization policy.** This chapter deals first with the theory of fiscal policy as a tool of stabilization policy and then with the experience of using it.

There is no doubt that the government can exert a major influence on national income. Prime examples are the massive military spending during major wars. During World War II the Canadian government's defense expenditures rose from 1.2 percent of national income in 1939 to 36 percent in 1944. At the same time the unemployment rate fell from 11.4 percent to 1.4 percent. Economists agree that the increase in government spending helped bring about the fall in unemployment and the associated rise in GDP. Similar experiences occurred in the United States and most European countries before or immediately following the outbreak of the war in 1939.

When used appropriately, fiscal policy can be an important tool for stabilizing the economy. In the heyday of fiscal policy, from 1945 to late 1965, many economists were convinced that the economy could be adequately stabilized just by varying the size of the government's taxes and expenditures. That day is past. Today most economists are aware of the limitations of fiscal policy.

The Theory of Fiscal Policy

Fiscal policy is often referred to as the government's budgetary policy or simply as the budget.

The Budget Balance

The **budget balance** is the difference between all government revenue and all government expenditures. In this definition *government expenditure* includes both transfer payments and purchases of currently produced goods and services. Thus the budget balance is the difference between all the money the government takes in as revenue and all the money it pays out. These are called its *budget receipts* and *outlays,* respectively.

Changes in either government spending or tax policies influence the budget balance. If receipts are exactly equal to outlays, the government has a **balanced budget.** If receipts exceed outlays, there is a **budget surplus;** if receipts fall short of outlays, there is a **budget deficit.** If the government raises its outlays without raising taxes, the extra expenditure is said to be *deficit-financed.* If the extra outlays are accompanied by an equal increase in tax rates that yields an equal increase in receipts, we speak of a *balanced budget change in spending.*

Financial Implications of Deficits and Surpluses

When the government spends more than it raises, where does the money come from? If the government raises more than it spends, where does the money go? The difference between expenditure and current revenue shows up as changes in the government's debt.

A deficit requires an increase in borrowing, for which there are two main sources: the central bank and the private sector. The government borrows money from these sources by selling treasury bills and bonds. A **treasury bill,** or note, is a promise to repay a stated amount at some specified date between 90 days and one year from the date of issue. A government *bond* is also a promise to pay a stated sum of money in the future, but in the more distant future than a bill—as much as 25 years from the date of issue.[1]

When the government borrows from the private sector, this action merely shifts funds between the

two sectors. When the government "borrows" from the central bank, however, the central bank creates new money. Since the central bank can create as much money as it likes, there is no limit to what the government can "borrow" from it.

A surplus allows the government to reduce its outstanding debt. Treasury bills and bonds may be redeemed from the excess tax revenue.

The Paradox of Thrift

When a government follows a balanced budget policy, as most governments tried to do during the Great Depression of the 1930s, its spending becomes pro-cyclical. It must restrict its spending during a recession because its tax revenue will necessarily be falling at that time. During a recovery, when its revenue is rising, it must increase its spending. In other words, it rolls with the economy, raising and lowering its spending in step with everyone else.

Not long ago people generally accepted, and indeed many still fervently believe, that a prudent government should always balance its budget. This belief is based on an analogy with what seems prudent behavior for the individual household. It is a foolish household whose current expenditure consistently exceeds its current revenue so that it goes steadily further into debt. From this commonsense observation some people argue that if avoiding an ever-rising debt is good for the individual, it must also be good for the nation. But the *paradox of thrift* suggests that the analogy between the government and the household may be misleading.

The theory of national income developed in Chapters 26 through 30 predicts that if all spending units in the economy simultaneously try to increase the amount that they save, the combined increase in thriftiness will *reduce* the equilibrium level of income. The contrary case, a general decrease in thriftiness and increase in expenditure, increases national income. This prediction has come to be known as the paradox of thrift.[2]

---

[1] Bills carry a promise to return a fixed amount at maturity. Interest arises because they are initially sold at a discount; the difference between their current price and their redemption value represents interest. Bonds carry a fixed "coupon rate of interest" on their redemption value. They guarantee not only the repayment of a fixed sum on the redemption date but also the periodic payment of fixed sums between sale and redemption.

[2] The prediction is not actually a paradox. It is a straightforward implication of the theory of the determination of income. The expectations that lead to the "paradox" are based on the fallacy of composition, the belief that what is true for the parts is necessarily true for the whole.

The policy implication of this prediction is that substantial unemployment is correctly combated by encouraging governments, firms, and households to spend more, *not* to save more. In times of unemployment and depression, frugality will only make things worse. This prediction goes directly against the idea that we should tighten our belts when times are tough. The concept that it is not just possible but acceptable to spend one's way out of a depression touches a sensitive nerve in people raised on the belief that success is based on hard work and frugality and not on prodigality; as a result, the idea often arouses great emotional hostility.

Applications.   As discussed in Box 32-1, the implications of the paradox of thrift were not generally understood during the Great Depression. However, by the middle of the 1930s, many economists had concluded that the government was not making the most of its potential to control the economy in a beneficial manner. Why, they asked, should not the government try to stabilize the economy by doing just the opposite of what everyone else was doing—by increasing its demand when private demand was falling and lowering its demand when private demand was rising? At best this policy could hold aggregate demand constant even though its individual components were fluctuating.

When Milton Friedman said, "We are all Keynesians now," he was referring to (among other things) the general acceptance of the view that the government's budget is much more than just the revenue and expenditure statement of a very large organization. Whether we like it or not, the sheer size of the government's budget inevitably makes it a powerful tool for influencing the economy.

Limitations.   The paradox of thrift concentrates on shifts in aggregate demand caused by changes in saving (and hence spending) behavior. Thus it applies only in the short run, when the *AD* curve plays an important role in the determination of national income.

In the long run, when the economy is on its *LRAS* curve and hence aggregate demand is not important for the determination of national income (see Figure 30-5), the paradox of thrift ceases to apply.

The more people save, the larger the supply of funds available for investment. The more people invest, the greater the growth of potential income. Increased potential income causes the *LRAS* curve to shift to the right.

These longer-term effects are taken up in Chapter 38 in the discussion of economic growth. In the meantime we concentrate on the short-run demand effects of saving and spending.

The paradox of thrift is based on the short-run effects of changes in saving and investment on aggregate demand.

Fiscal Policy with Stable Private Expenditure Functions

A relatively easy problem faces fiscal policymakers when private-sector expenditure functions for consumption, investment, and net exports are given and unchanging. What is needed then is a once-and-for-all fiscal change that will remove any existing inflationary or recessionary gap.

Changes in tax rates or expenditure.   The necessary policies were explained in Chapter 29. A reduction in tax rates or an increase in government expenditure shifts the *AD* curve to the right, leading to an increase in national income. An increase in tax rates or a cut in government expenditure shifts the *AD* curve to the left, leading to a decrease in national income.

The key proposition in the theory of fiscal policy follows these results.

Government taxes and expenditure, by shifting the *AD* curve, can be used to remove output gaps.

Balanced budget changes.   Another policy available to the government is to make a balanced budget change by changing spending and taxes equally. Say the government increases tax rates enough to raise an extra $1 billion that it then uses to purchase goods and services. Aggregate expenditure would remain unchanged if, and only if, the $1 billion that the government takes from the private sector would otherwise have been spent by the private sector. If

BOX 32-1

Fiscal Policy and the Great Depression

Failure to understand the implication of the paradox of thrift led many countries to adopt policies during the Great Depression that were disastrous. Failure to understand the role of built-in stabilizers has also led many observers to conclude, erroneously, that fiscal expansion had been tried in the Great Depression but had failed. Let us see how these two misperceptions are related.

The Paradox of Thrift in Action

In Canada, Prime Minister R. B. Bennett said in 1932, in the worst recession in recorded history, "We are now faced with the real crisis in the history of Canada. To maintain our credit we must practice the most rigid economy and not spend a single cent." His government that year brought down a budget based on the principle of trying to balance revenues and expenditures, and it included *increases* in tax rates.

U.S. President Franklin D. Roosevelt, in his first inaugural address (1933), urged: "Our great primary task is to put people to work. . . . [This task] can be helped by insistence that the Federal, State and local governments act forthwith on the demand that their costs be drastically reduced. . . . There must be a strict supervision of all banking and credits and investments."

Across the Atlantic, King George V told the British House of Commons in 1931, "The present condition of the national finances, in the opinion of His Majesty's Ministers, calls for the imposition of additional taxation and for the effecting of economies in public expenditure."

As the paradox of thrift predicts, these policies reduced aggregate demand and hence tended to worsen, not cure, the depression.

Interpreting the Deficit in the 1930s

Government deficits did increase in the 1930s, but they were not the result of a program of deficit-financed public expenditure. They were the result of the fall in tax yields brought about by the fall in national income as the economy sank into depression. The various governments did not advocate a program of massive deficit-financed spending to shift the *AD* curve to the right. Instead, they hoped that a small amount of government spending plus numerous policies designed to stabilize prices and to restore confidence would lead to a recovery of private investment expenditure that would substantially shift the aggregate demand curve. To have expected a massive revival of private investment expenditure as a result of the puny increase in aggregate demand instituted by government now seems hopelessly naive.

When we judge these policies from the viewpoint of modern multiplier theory, their failure is no mystery. Indeed, Professor E. Cary Brown of MIT, after a careful study, concluded, "Fiscal policy seems to have been an unsuccessful recovery device in the 'thirties—not because it did not work, but because it was not tried."

The performance of the North American economies from 1930 to 1945 is quite well explained by modern national income theory. It is clear that the governments did not effectively use fiscal measures to stabilize their economies. War cured the depression because war demands made acceptable a level of government expenditure sufficient to remove the recessionary gap. Had the Canadian and American administrations been able to do the same, they might have ended the waste of the Depression many years sooner.

---

that is the case, the government's policy would reduce private expenditure by $1 billion and raise its own spending by $1 billion. Aggregate demand, and hence national income and employment, would remain unchanged.

But this is not the usual case. When an extra $1

billion in taxes is taken away from households, they usually reduce their spending on domestically produced goods by less than $1 billion. If the marginal propensity to consume out of disposable income is, say, 0.75, consumption expenditure will fall by only $750 million. If the government spends the entire $1 billion on domestically produced goods, aggregate expenditure will increase by $250 million. In this case the balanced budget increase in government expenditure has an expansionary effect because it shifts the aggregate expenditure function upward and hence shifts the *AD* curve to the right.

A balanced budget increase in government expenditure will have an expansionary effect on national income, and a balanced budget decrease will have a contractionary effect.

The **balanced budget multiplier** measures these effects. It is the change in income divided by the balanced budget change in government expenditure that brought it about. Thus if the extra $1 billion of government spending financed by the extra $1 billion of taxes causes national income to rise by $500 million, the balanced budget multiplier is 0.5; if income rises by $1 billion, it is 1.0.

Now compare the sizes of the multipliers for a balanced budget and a deficit-financed increase in government spending. With a deficit-financed increase in expenditure, there is no increase in tax rates and hence no consequent decrease in consumption expenditure to offset the increase in government expenditure. With a balanced budget increase in expenditure, however, the offsetting increase in tax rates and decrease in consumption does occur. Thus the balanced budget multiplier is much lower than the multiplier that relates the change in income to a deficit-financed increase in government expenditure with tax rates constant.

Fiscal Policy with Shifting Private Expenditure Functions

As we saw in Chapter 31, private expenditure functions are constantly changing. Investment expenditure shifts a great deal with business conditions, and consumption functions sometimes shift upward as the public goes on a spending spree or downward as people become cautious and increase their saving. This makes stabilization policy much more difficult than it would be if it were possible simply to identify a stable inflationary or recessionary gap and then take steps to eliminate it once and for all.

What can the government reasonably expect to achieve by using fiscal policy when private expenditure functions are shifting continually? Fiscal policy might be altered often in an effort to stabilize the economy completely, or it might be altered less frequently, responding only to gaps that appear to be large and persistent while ignoring small, transitory fluctuations.

Fine Tuning

In the heyday of Keynesian fiscal policy in the 1950s and 1960s, many economists advocated the use of fiscal policy to remove even minor fluctuations in national income around its full-employment level. Fiscal policy was to be altered frequently and by relatively small amounts to hold national income almost precisely at its full-employment level. This is called **fine tuning** the economy.

A necessary condition for fine tuning is a relatively short **decison lag,** the period of time between perceiving a problem and making the desired reaction to it. Many things contribute to the length of this lag. Experts must study the economy and agree among themselves on what fiscal changes are most desirable; they must then persuade the government to initiate the action they endorse.

In countries where political institutions keep the decision lag short, fine tuning has been attempted. Careful assessment of the results shows that their successes, if any, have fallen far short of what was hoped. One basic reason lies in the complexity of any economy. Although economists and policymakers can identify broad and persistent trends, they do not have detailed knowledge of what is going on at any particular moment, of all the forces that are operating to cause changes in the immediate future, or of all the short-term effects of small changes in the various government expenditures and tax rates.

Further difficulties for fine tuning also arise because of an **execution lag,** the time it takes to put policies in place after the decision is made, and because of lags between the introduction of a given policy measure and its effects being felt in the economy. Often by the time the effects of a given policy decision are felt, circumstances in the economy have changed and the policy is no longer appropriate.

Fine tuning often has done as much to encourage fluctuations in the economy as to remove them.

As a result of these experiences, fine tuning is currently out of favor.

Removal of Persistent Gaps

In addition to more or less continual fluctuations, the economy occasionally develops severe and persistent output gaps. For example, an inflationary gap developed in the United States in the late 1960s as Vietnam War expenditures accelerated, while a recessionary gap developed between 1981 and 1983 when Canada, along with many Western countries, experienced the deepest and longest-lasting recession since the 1930s. Gaps such as these may persist long enough for their major causes to be studied and understood and for fiscal remedies to be carefully planned and executed.

A persistent recessionary gap. The removal of a recessionary gap is illustrated in Figure 32-1. There are three possible ways in which the gap may be removed.

First, wages and other factor prices may eventually be forced down enough to shift the *SRAS* curve to the right by enough to reinstate full employment and potential income (at a lower price level). The evidence is, however, that this process takes a long time.

Second, the natural cyclical forces of the economy could induce a demand-side recovery for the reasons spelled out in Chapter 31. This would cause a shift to the right of the *AD* curve, moving the economy back to full employment and potential income. The evidence is that such recoveries do occur. Sometimes they happen quickly; often, however, a recession can be both deep and prolonged.

Third, government expenditure can be increased or taxes cut in an effort to shift the *AD* curve to the right. The advantage of using fiscal policy is that it may substantially shorten the length of what would otherwise be a long recession. The disadvantage is that it may stimulate the economy just before private-sector spending recovers due to natural causes.

If it does, the economy may overshoot its potential output, and a serious inflationary gap may open up.

A persistent inflationary gap. Figure 32-2 (see page 676) shows the three ways in which an inflationary gap can be removed.

First, wages and other factor prices may be forced upward by the excess demand. This will shift the *SRAS* curve to the left, eventually eliminating the gap, reducing income to its potential level, and raising the price level.

Second, a cyclical reduction in aggregate demand may occur for the reasons outlined in Chapter 31. This might reduce income to its potential level without the rise in the price level associated with a shift of the *SRAS* curve. But unless aggregate demand declines quickly, rising wages and other input prices will lead to a shift to the left of the *SRAS* curve and hence to rising prices.

Third, the government, by raising taxes or cutting spending, may force aggregate demand down sufficiently to remove the inflationary gap. The advantage of this approach is that it avoids the inflationary increase in prices that accompanies the first method. The disadvantage is that if private-sector expenditures fall off to their more normal level, national income may be pushed below potential, thus opening up a recessionary gap.

Policy. Many economists who do not believe in the value of fine tuning do feel that fiscal policy can aid in removing persistent output gaps. Others believe that even with persistent gaps, the risks that fiscal policy will destabilize the economy are still too large. They would have the government abandon any attempt at stabilization policy, instead setting its budget solely in relation to such long-term considerations as the desirable size of the public sector and the need to obtain a satisfactory long-term balance between revenues and expenditures.

Tools of Fiscal Policy

The major fiscal tools can be classified in many ways; one important classification is the division between automatic and discretionary tools.

FIGURE 32-1   Removal of a Recessionary Gap

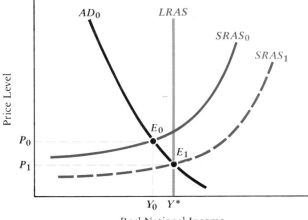

(i) A recessionary gap removed by a rightward shift in **SRAS**

A recessionary gap may be removed by a (slow) rightward shift of the *SRAS* curve, a natural revival of private-sector demand, or a fiscal policy-induced increase in aggregate demand. Initially equilibrium is at E_0, with national income at Y_0 and the price level at P_0. The recessionary gap is Y_0Y^*.

As shown in part (i), the gap might be removed by a shift in the *SRAS* curve to $SRAS_1$. This increase in aggregate supply could occur as a result of reductions in wage rates and other input prices. The shift in the *SRAS* curve causes a movement down and to the right along AD_0. This establishes a new equilibrium at E_1, achieving potential income, Y^*, and lowering the price level to P_1.

As shown in part (ii), the gap might also be removed by a shift of the *AD* curve to AD_1. This increase in aggregate demand could occur either because of a natural revival of private-sector expenditure or because of a fiscal policy-induced increase in expenditure. The shift in the *AD* curve causes a movement up and to the right along $SRAS_0$. This shifts the equilibrium to E_2, taking income to Y^* and the price level to P_2.

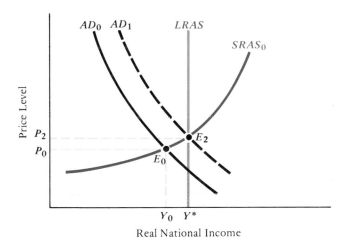

(ii) A recessionary gap removed by a rightward shift in *AD*

Automatic Fiscal Tools: Built-In Stabilizers

For reasons discussed in Chapter 31, the *AD* curve is continually fluctuating. A stabilization policy for fine tuning the economy would thus require a policy that was itself ever changing. If such a conscious fine tuning policy is impossible, must we say that nothing can be done through fiscal policy except to reduce major, long-lived output gaps?

Fortunately, this is not so. Much of the adjustment of fiscal policy to an ever-changing economic environment is done automatically by what are called built-in stabilizers. A **built-in stabilizer** is anything

FIGURE 32-2   Removal of an Inflationary Gap

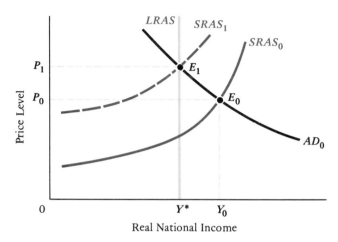

(i) An inflationary gap removed by a leftward shift in *SRAS*

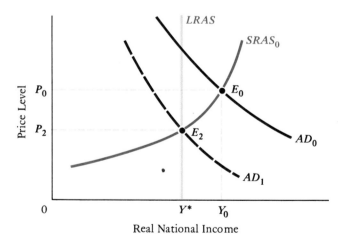

(ii) An inflationary gap removed by a leftward shift in *AD*

An inflationary gap may be removed by a leftward shift of the *SRAS* curve, a natural reduction in private-sector demand, or a policy-induced reduction in aggregate demand. Initially equilibrium is at E_0, with national income at Y_0 and the price level at P_0. The inflationary gap is Y^*Y_0.

As shown in part (i), the gap might be removed by a shift in the *SRAS* curve to $SRAS_1$. This decrease in aggregate supply could occur as a result of increases in wage rates and other input prices. The shift in the *SRAS* curve causes a movement up and to the left along AD_0. This establishes a new equilibrium at E_1, reducing income to its potential level, Y^*, and raising the price level to P_1.

As shown in part (ii), the gap might also be removed by a shift in the *AD* curve to AD_1. This decrease in aggregate demand could occur either because of a natural fall in private spending or because of contractionary fiscal policy. The shift in the *AD* curve causes a movement down and to the left along $SRAS_0$. This shifts the equilibrium to E_2, taking income to Y^* and the price level to P_2.

---

that reduces the marginal propensity to spend out of national income and hence, as we saw on page 606, reduces the multiplier. Built-in stabilizers lessen the magnitude of the fluctuations in national income caused by autonomous changes in such expenditures as investment. Furthermore, they do so without the government's having to react consciously to each change in national income as it occurs.

The three principal built-in stabilizers are taxes, government expenditure on goods and services, and government transfer payments.

Taxes

Direct taxes act as a built-in stabilizer. If there were no taxes, every change in national income of $1.00

would cause a change in disposable income of nearly a dollar.[3] With a marginal propensity to consume out of disposable income (*MPC*) of, say, 0.8, consumption would change by $0.80. With taxes, however, disposable income changes by less than $1.00; hence consumption expenditure will change by less than $0.80 when national income changes by $1.00 (even though the *MPC* is still 0.8).

Consider, for example, the extreme case in which the marginal personal income-tax rate is 100 percent. If there is an autonomous rise of $1 billion in investment expenditure, none of the $1 billion that accrues to households will be disposable income. There are no induced rounds of secondary expenditure; the rise in national income is limited to the initial $1 billion in new investment, and the multiplier is unity.

Similarly, a drop in investment expenditure of $1 billion reduces incomes earned in the investment industry by $1 billion and hence reduces government tax revenue by $1 billion. But it does not affect disposable income. Thus there are no secondary rounds of induced contractions in consumption experience to magnify the initial drop in national income caused by the investment decline.

Table 32-1 illustrates the principle by comparing the effects of two different marginal tax rates on the marginal propensity to spend out of national income in otherwise identical situations. The general proposition can be stated as follows.

Direct taxes reduce the magnitude of fluctuations in disposable income associated with any given fluctuation in national income. Hence, for a given marginal propensity to consume out of disposable income, they reduce the marginal propensity to spend out of national income.

Tax rates have increased greatly over this century. Although citizens complain about the burden of high taxes—perhaps with good reason—few are aware that high taxes have helped to reduce the large swings

in national income and employment that would have otherwise plagued all industrial economies.

Government Purchases

Government purchases of goods and services tend to be relatively stable in the face of cyclical variations in national income. Much spending is already committed by earlier legislation, so only a small proportion can be varied at the government's discretion from one year to the next. And even this small part is slow to change. In contrast, private consumption and investment expenditure tend to vary with national income.

Thus the higher the share of government spending in the economy, the lower the cyclical instability of total expenditure. The twentieth century rise in the importance of the government's role in the economy may be a mixed blessing. One benefit, however, has been to put a large built-in stabilizer into the economy.

Social insurance and welfare services. Welfare payments rise with the unemployment that accompanies falling national income. Many welfare schemes are financed by taxes based on payrolls or earnings, and these taxes yield less when income is low. Thus welfare schemes act to make net additions to disposable income in times of slumps. They also make net subtractions in times of boom, when payments are low and revenues high.

The Canada Pension Plan is financed by taxes (called *contributions*) paid jointly by employers and employees. Unemployment insurance is financed by a payroll tax on employers and employees. During recessions these tax collections decrease while payments to the unemployed rise.[4]

Agricultural support policies. When there is a slump in the economy, there is a general decline in the demand for all goods, including agricultural prod-

---

[3] Undistributed profits and other minor items would still hold disposable income below national income. We ignore these in the text because taxes are the major source of the discrepancy between national income and disposable income.

[4] The Unemployment Insurance Act requires the federal government to adjust the payroll tax (referred to as the unemployment insurance premiums) annually so as to finance some of the changes in benefits paid out. This greatly reduces the automatic stabilizing influence of the unemployment insurance scheme.

TABLE 32-1 **The Effect of Tax Rates on the Marginal Propensity to Spend out of National Income**

Marginal rate of tax	Change in national income (millions) ΔY	Change in tax revenue (millions) ΔT	Change in disposable income (millions) ΔY_d	Change in consumption (millions) ΔC	Marginal propensity to spend out of national income $\Delta C/\Delta Y$
0.2	$1,000	$200	$800	$640	0.65
0.4	1,000	400	600	480	0.48

The higher the marginal rate of tax, the lower the marginal propensity to spend out of national income. When national income changes by $1,000, disposable income changes by $800 when the tax rate is 20 percent and by $600 when the tax rate is 40 percent. Although the *MPC* out of disposable income is 0.8 in both examples, consumption changes by $640 in the first case and by only $480 in the second. Although that households' *MPC* out of their disposable income is unchanged, an increase in tax rates lowers the marginal propensity to spend out of national income on which the size of the multiplier depends.

---

ucts. The free-market prices of agricultural goods fall, and government agricultural supports come into play. This means that government transfers, which support agricultural disposable income, rise as national income falls.

Transfer payments, which act as built-in stabilizers, tend to stabilize disposable income, and hence consumption expenditure, in the face of fluctuations in national income.

To illustrate this important proposition suppose that investment expenditure falls by $10 billion. In the absence of transfer payments, this would reduce disposable income by $6 billion. With an *MPC* out of disposable income of 0.8, this $6 billion reduction would cause an initial induced fall in consumption expenditure of $4.8 billion. Now assume instead that the fall in national income is accompanied by an increase in transfer payments of $4 billion. Instead of falling by $6 billion, disposable income now falls by only $2 billion. With the *MPC* out of disposable income still at 0.8, the initial induced fall in consumption expenditure is only $1.6 billion instead of $4.8 billion.

The Role of Built-In Stabilizers

Most built-in stabilizers are fairly new phenomena. Sixty years ago high marginal tax rates, high and

stable government expenditures, farm stabilization policies, and large unemployment and other transfer payments were unknown in Canada. Each of these built-in stabilizers was the unforeseen by-product of policies originally adopted for other reasons. The progressive income tax arose out of a concern to make the distribution of income less unequal. Social insurance and agricultural support programs were adopted more because of a concern with the welfare of the individuals and groups involved than with preserving the health of the economy. But unforeseen or not, they work. (Even governments can be lucky.)

No matter how lucky governments have been in finding built-in stabilizers, these cannot reduce fluctuations to zero. Stabilizers work by producing stabilizing reactions to changes in income. But until income changes, the stabilizer is not even brought into play.

Discretionary Fiscal Policy

Short-term, minor fluctuations that are not removed automatically by built-in stabilizers cannot, given present knowledge and techniques, be removed by consciously fine tuning the economy. We have already seen, however, that larger and more persistent gaps sometimes appear. In these cases there may be time for the government to operate a discretionary fiscal policy, that is, to institute changes in taxes and spending that are designed to offset gaps. To do this effectively an administration must periodically make conscious decisions to alter fiscal policy. The Department of Finance must study current economic trends and predict the probable course of the economy. If the predicted course is unsatisfactory, the cabinet must be persuaded to adopt the appropriate fiscal stance.

In considering discretionary fiscal policy, we shall deal with two related questions. First, is it important that the fiscal change be easily reversible? Second, does it matter whether households and firms regard the government's fiscal changes as temporary or as long-lived?

The Need for Reversibility

To see what is involved in the issue of reversibility, assume that national income is normally at or near potential. A *temporary* slump in private investment then opens up a large recessionary gap. If the gap persists, eventually the government decides to adopt some combination of tax cuts and spending increases to push the economy back toward full employment. If private investment recovers to its pre-slump level and the government does not quickly reverse this policy, an inflationary gap will open up as the combination of rising investment expenditure and continuing fiscal stimulus takes national income into the inflationary range. The process is illustrated in Figure 32-3.

Alternatively, assume that starting from the same situation of approximately full employment, a temporary investment boom opens up an inflationary gap. Rather than let the inflation persist, the government reduces expenditure and raises taxes to remove the gap. If, when the investment boom is over and investment expenditure returns to its original level, the government does nothing, a recessionary gap will open up and a slump may ensue. This, too, is analyzed in Figure 32-3.

Fiscal policies designed to remove persistent output gaps resulting from abnormal levels of private expenditure will destabilize the economy unless the policies can be rapidly reversed once private expenditure returns to its more normal level.

FIGURE 32-3   Effects of Fiscal Policies That Are Not Reversed

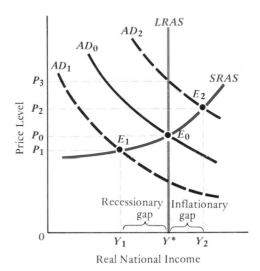

Fiscal policies that are initially appropriate may become inappropriate when private expenditure shifts. The normal level of the aggregate demand function is assumed to be AD_0, leaving income normally at Y^* and the price level at P_0. Suppose a slump in private investment shifts aggregate demand to AD_1, lowering national income to Y_1 and causing a recessionary gap of Y^*Y_1.

The government now introduces fiscal expansion to restore aggregate demand to AD_0 and national income to Y^*. Suppose that private investment recovers, raising aggregate demand to AD_2. If fiscal policy can be quickly reversed, aggregate demand can be returned to AD_0 and income stabilized at Y^*. If the policy is not quickly reversed, equilibrium will be at E_2 and an inflationary gap Y^*Y_2 will open up. This will cause wages to rise and thus shift the $SRAS$ curve leftward and eventually restore Y^* at a price level P_3.

Now suppose that starting from equilibrium E_0 a persistent investment boom takes AD_0 to AD_2. To stop the price level from rising in the face of the newly opened inflationary gap, the government introduces fiscal restraint, thereby shifting aggregate demand back to AD_0. Further assume, however, that the investment boom soon comes to a halt so that the aggregate demand curve shifts down to AD_1. Unless the fiscal policy can be rapidly reversed, a recessionary gap will open up and equilibrium income will fall to Y_1.

Even if the output gaps persist long enough for fiscal changes to be agreed on and to be made, subsequent rapid changes in private expenditure may require a quick reversal of the fiscal stance—a reversal that cannot always be made easily. As a result, many economists argue that caution dictates responding only to large output gaps that are expected to persist and even then attempting to close only part of the gap in anticipation of some stabilizing change in private expenditure.

"Temporary" Versus "Long Lasting" Changes

Consider the attempt to remove a persistent output gap through changes in tax rates. Such a gap, though persistent, is unlikely to be a permanent feature of the economy. The relevant tax changes should therefore be advocated only "for the duration," that is, for as long as the government thinks the gaps would persist without the tax changes. A discretionary fiscal policy designed to remove such a gap might take the form, say, of a surcharge on income taxes for a two-year period. Similarly, a recession might be fought by temporary tax rebates.

Such tax changes cause changes in household disposable income and, according to the theory of the consumption function encountered in Chapter 28, would cause changes in consumption expenditure. Consumption expenditure would increase as tax rebates rose in times of recessionary gaps and would decrease as tax surcharges rose in times of inflationary gaps. This theory of the effects of short-term tax changes relies on the assumption that household consumption depends on current disposable income.

Permanent-income theories.   Many recent theories of the consumption function have emphasized what is called a household's expected **permanent income** or **lifetime income** as the major determinant of consumption. According to such theories, households have expectations about their lifetime incomes and adjust their consumption to those expectations. When temporary fluctuations in income occur, households maintain their long-term consumption plans and use their stocks of wealth as buffers to absorb income fluctuations. Thus when there is a

purely temporary rise in income, households will save all the extra income; when there is a purely temporary fall in income, households will maintain their long-term consumption plans by using up part of their wealth accumulated through past saving.

To the extent that such behavior occurs, it will have serious consequences for short-lived tax changes. A temporary tax rebate raises households' disposable income, but households, recognizing it as temporary, would not revise their expenditure plans and instead save the extra money. Thus the hoped-for increase in aggregate expenditure would not occur. Similarly, a temporary rise in tax rates reduces disposable income, but that might merely cause a drop in saving. Thus total expenditure is again unchanged, and a temporary surcharge fails to reduce the inflationary gap.

If households' consumption expenditure is more closely related to lifetime income than to current income, tax changes that are known to be of short duration will have relatively small effects on current consumption.[5]

The advantage of having households perceive tax rate changes as long lasting conflicts with the need for the reversibility of cuts and surcharges if they are not to destabilize the economy at a later date. This conflict reduces the usefulness of changes in tax rates as a stabilizing tool.

Judging the Stance of Fiscal Policy

Governments seek to shift aggregate demand by consciously changing their fiscal policy stance. The *stance of fiscal policy* refers to its expansionary or contractionary effects on the economy. An expansionary fiscal policy increases aggregate demand and thus tends to increase national income; a contractionary fiscal policy reduces aggregate demand and tends to lower national income.

In Chapter 31 and earlier in this one, we looked separately at taxes, purchases of goods and services, and transfer payments as means of influencing ag-

---

[5] The permanent-income theory is not as devastating for fiscal policy as it may seem. This important matter is discussed further in the appendix to this chapter.

gregate demand. But people want a summary measure, one number to express the government's effect on the economy.

The Inadequacy of the Deficit As a Measure

Not surprisingly, people tend to focus on the government's budget deficit to judge the stance of fiscal policy. A rising government deficit is often taken to indicate an expansionary fiscal policy, and a falling deficit is often taken to indicate a contractionary policy. But a number of problems make the deficit an unreliable guide to judging the fiscal stance.

The deficit is the difference between the government's outlays and receipts, its receipts being largely tax revenue. But tax revenue is the result of the interaction of tax rates, which the government sets, and the level of national income, which is influenced by many forces beyond the government's control.

The major tools of fiscal policy are government expenditure and tax *rates*. The budget deficit or surplus is the relation between government expenditure and tax *revenues*.

Assume, for example, that government expenditure is constant at $100 billion and that at current tax rates the government takes 20 percent of national income in taxes. Suppose that national income is $500 billion, so tax revenues are also $100 billion. Now assume that tax revenues sink to $75 billion, opening up a $25 billion budget deficit. This could be the result of a discretionary cut in tax rates so that they now yield only 15 percent of an unchanged national income. It could also be the result of a fall in national income itself to $375 billion, with tax rates constant. In the first case a conscious change in the government's fiscal policy causes the fall in tax revenues. In the second case a fall in national income that is not the result of fiscal policy causes tax revenue to fall; the increase in the deficit simply reflects the operation of the automatic stabilizers discussed earlier in this chapter.

This example illustrates why judging changes in the stance of fiscal policy from changes in the government's budget balance can be misleading. Doing so confuses changes in the deficit due to fluctuations in national income, which may not be the result of shifts in fiscal policy, with changes in the deficit that are the result of shifts in fiscal policy.

Cyclically Adjusted Deficit

When measuring changes in the stance of fiscal policy, it is common to calculate changes in the estimated budget balance on the assumption that national income is constant at some base level. Holding income constant ensures that measured changes in the budget balance are due to changes in policy. The base most commonly used is potential national income. Because estimating the budget balance for a given level of national income controls for cyclically induced fluctuations in expenditures and tax revenues, it is referred to as making the *cyclical adjustment;* the resulting measure is referred to as the *cyclically adjusted budget balance,* or **cyclically adjusted deficit (CAD).**[6] It is an estimate of government expenditure minus government tax revenues, not as they actually are but as they would be if national income had been at its potential level. Table 32-2 shows the actual and cyclically adjusted deficit on an annual basis since 1970.

Changes in the cyclically adjusted deficit are an indicator of changes in the stance of fiscal policy.

Box 32-2 (see page 683) introduces the concept of the *budget deficit function* and discusses how it, along with the cyclically adjusted deficit, can avoid the errors that arise from using the current budget balance as an indicator of the stance of fiscal policy.[7]

---

[6] This concept used to be called the full-employment surplus. The change from *full-employment* to *cyclically adjusted* came when the amount of unemployment associated with potential income rose rapidly in the 1970s, and referring to so much unemployment as full employment became embarrassing. The change from *surplus* to *deficit* occurred because in the 1960s people were trying to stress the depressing effects of surpluses whereas in the 1980s people wanted to stress the alleged harmful effects of deficits.

[7] The cyclically adjusted deficit is vastly superior to the actual budget deficit for estimating year-to-year changes in the stance of fiscal policy. But the balanced budget multiplier indicates one reason why even the cyclically adjusted deficit is not a completely reliable measure of the fiscal stance. The balanced budget multiplier suggests that a dollar of spending will increase aggregate demand by more than a dollar of tax revenue will decrease it. Therefore, to measure the effect of fiscal actions on aggregate demand properly a more sophisticated measure that takes account of these differential effects is required. Such a measure, called the *weighted cyclically adjusted deficit,* is often used by economists in detailed empirical work assessing fiscal policy.

TABLE 32-2   Measured, Cyclically Adjusted, and Structural Budget Balances for the Federal Government, 1970–1986
(billions of dollars)

Year	Measured budget deficit[a]	Cyclically adjusted budget deficit[a]	Structural budget deficit (cyclically and inflation adjusted)
1970	−0.3	−0.5	−0.9
1971	0.1	0.0	−0.3
1972	0.6	0.7	0.2
1973	−0.4	0.6	−0.5
1974	−1.1	0.5	−0.9
1975	3.8	3.9	3.0
1976	3.4	4.1	3.0
1977	7.3	6.8	5.8
1978	10.7	9.9	8.3
1979	9.3	8.9	4.8
1980	10.1	8.2	3.6
1981	8.0	6.2	0.0
1982	21.1	11.8	5.0
1983	24.0	13.3	8.2
1984	30.5	21.3	18.4
1985	32.3	24.3	19.2
1986	24.9	18.3	13.2

Source: Department of Finance, *Economic Review.*

[a] A minus sign indicates a surplus.

Changes in the measured budget balance reflect both changes in output and inflation. The cyclically adjusted deficit controls for the influences of the level of output, while the last column adds to this an adjustment for the effect of the inflation rate. Changes in the last column thus give a measure of changes in fiscal policy. Several things can be noted about the adjustments. First, the inflation adjustment is always negative, so column 3 is always smaller than column 2 (if column 2 shows a deficit, column 3 will show a smaller deficit or even a surplus). Second, because the economy has operated at less than full employment since 1975, the cyclical adjustment has also been negative, so column 2 has been smaller than column 1. Actual budget deficits have been growing rather dramatically. Part of this is due to persistent slack in the economy and to high inflation, but column 3 indicates that fiscal policy was expansionary in the early 1980s before turning contractionary in 1986.

The cyclical adjustment just discussed distinguishes between changes in the budget balance that arise due to the operation of *automatic* stabilizers and those that arise due to *discretionary* policy. To judge the stance of fiscal policy, it is necessary to make a second adjustment to the measured budget balance—one that focuses on a component of the budget that has (virtually) no impact on aggregate demand. This component is the inflation premium included in the nominal interest payments made by the government to service the national debt.

As we saw in Box 31-1, nominal interest rates can be divided into a real component and an inflation premium. Debt-service payments made by the government thus also have a real and an inflation premium component. Whereas the real component constitutes a transfer from the government to holders of the government debt as payment for use of the principal, the inflation premium does not. This is because the inflation premium is exactly offset by a reduction in the real value of the principal.

Suppose that the current value of the government's debt is $200 billion. Suppose also that in the current year the government runs a deficit of $20 billion and that the current inflation rate is 10 percent. On crude measures the government has a deficit of $20 billion; this corresponds to the increase in the nominal value of the government's indebtedness. On an inflation-adjusted basis, the deficit is zero. This is because the real value—or purchasing power—of the debt is unchanged, even though the nominal stock of debt has risen by $20 billion (10 percent) from $200 billion to $220 billion. Because the real value of the government's indebtedness is unchanged, the "effective," or inflation-adjusted, deficit is zero. The *inflation adjustment* is equal to the inflation premium component of government debt-service payments.

This makes it clear why the inflation premium component of the deficit contributes little or nothing to aggregate demand. The private sector receives the payment but suffers an equivalent reduction in the real value of its holdings of government bonds. To maintain their asset position, recipients of the government interest payments must save the entire inflation premium component. Hence the net effect of this component on aggregate demand will be approximately zero—the government's demand will be

BOX 32-2

The Budget Deficit Function

The distinction between changes in the budget balance due to changes in the fiscal stance and those due to cyclical changes in the economy is easily seen in what is called the government's *budget deficit function*.

The budget deficit function (curve *B* in the figure) expresses the difference between the government's expenditures and its tax revenues at each level of national income for given levels of government expenditure and tax rates. The curve in part (i) shows that deficits are associated with low levels of income and surpluses with high levels of income; this is because at a given tax *rate,* tax *revenue* rises with national income.

Changes in the government's budget balance induced by changes in national income are shown by *movements along* a given budget deficit function. Changes in the budget balance due to policy-induced changes in the level of government expenditure or tax rates are shown by *shifts* in the budget function. Such shifts indicate a different budget balance at each level of national income.

In part (ii), a fall in national income from Y_0 to Y_1 causes the actual budget to go from a surplus of D_0 to a deficit of D_1. Government expenditure and tax rates are unchanged; that is, the fiscal policy stance is unchanged. The unchanged fiscal stance is correctly captured by the constant cyclically adjusted deficit, *CAD*, measured at the (constant) potential level of national income, Y^*.

Part (iii) illustrates a contractionary change in the stance of fiscal policy. A government expenditure cut or a tax rate increase shifts the budget deficit function from B_0 to B_1. Now there is a smaller budget deficit *at each level of national income.* This change is correctly captured by the fall in the cyclically adjusted deficit from *CAD* to *CAD'*.

To see the misleading effects of judging changes in the policy stance from changes in the measured deficit, suppose that national income had fallen from Y_0 to Y_1 at the same time that the budget deficit function shifted from B_0 to B_1. In that case the mea-

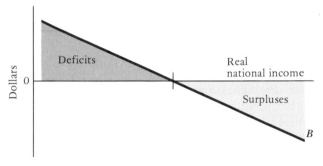

(i) The budget deficit function

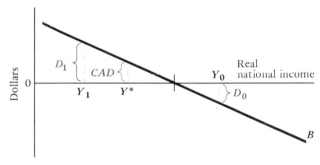

(ii) Changes in the measured deficit

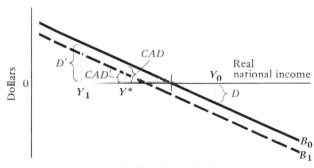

(iii) Changes in the cyclically adjusted deficit

sured balance would have gone from surplus (*D*) to deficit (*D'*) despite the fall in the cyclically adjusted deficit from *CAD* to *CAD'*. Thus the measured balance would have indicated an expansionary fiscal policy when the fiscal stance was in fact contractionary.

offset by a fall in private-sector demand as households raise their saving in order to recoup some of the inflation-induced fall in their real wealth.

Hence to measure the net influence of the government on aggregate demand, it is necessary to subtract the inflation premium component of nominal interest payments from the measured budget balance.

The structural balance.   When the cyclical and inflation adjustments are made to the government's budget balance, a useful measure of discretionary fiscal policy is obtained. This is called the *structural balance,* or, more commonly, the structural deficit. This is shown in the third column in Table 32-2.

The Experience of Fiscal Policy

The 1930s saw massive unemployment that persisted through nearly a decade. This experience left many people with the misconception that discretionary fiscal policy cannot solve an unemployment problem. The facts, as reviewed in Box 32-1, show that fiscal policy contributed little to recovery from the depression not because it failed to work but because it was not used. Most of the increase in the deficit that occurred was due to the decline in national income rather than to any shift in the high-employment deficit that would have signaled the adoption of a more expansive policy stance. When Keynesian fiscal policy was finally tried under the impetus of the wartime emergency, it proved spectacularly successful.

An important legacy of World War II was a radically altered view of the role of government expenditures and taxes as instruments of government policy. The 1945 White Paper on Employment and Income established the principle that the federal government had a responsibility to maintain high and stable levels of employment and income.

The implementation of this policy was greatly complicated by the unsettled state of federal-provincial relations. As early as 1940 a proposal to widen federal jurisdiction had been made by the Rowell-Sirois Commission, but the division of powers has continued to be a contentious issue to the present day. Through a succession of temporary agreements (see Chapter 24), the federal government has retained sufficient power to operate a flexible fiscal policy,

and consideration of the desired degree of fiscal stimulus or restraint has become an important element in the budgets presented to Parliament.

The 1960s and 1970s

In comparison with earlier and later periods, the quarter century following World War II was one of prosperity and steady growth. One prolonged slump occurred in 1958–1963. By 1965 the recessionary gap had been virtually eliminated, but in retrospect it appears that policymakers misjudged the situation and allowed the economy to develop an inflationary gap. Tax increases and some expenditure cuts were imposed in the years 1966–1968, but the effects of the fiscal restraint came too late to prevent the buildup of inflationary forces. At the end of the 1960s tight monetary policy reinforced the fiscal restraint, and unemployment rose in 1969 and 1970.

The 1970s began with a substantial recessionary gap. Expansionary policies were put into place. But the situation was misread because of a leftward shift in the long-run aggregate supply curve. (The reasons for this are discussed in Chapter 37.) Looking back we now see that the shift in the *LRAS* curve created an inflationary gap, which the government's expansionary policy inadvertently served to widen.

In late 1974 a series of shocks caused a downturn in the world economy. In response, an expansionary budget was brought down late in the year. As Table 32-2 shows, the federal budget moved to a deficit position in 1975, and the deficit grew steadily through the rest of the decade. In part this reflects discretionary fiscal policy, because the structural balance also moved into substantial deficit. However, the actual deficit also reflects the influence of other factors, including more generous unemployment insurance provisions and a relatively high rate of inflation. The latter caused outlays to grow rapidly because many federal transfer payments such as old-age pensions were indexed to inflation. Tax revenues also rose due to inflation, although not as quickly as they would have had the income tax system not been indexed. Since both expenditures and revenues grew, the difference between them also grew. (See Box 32-3 on page 686 for further discussion of indexation of the tax system.)

Tax cuts were introduced in 1977 and 1978 when, despite steady but gradual growth, the economy was thought to be operating below capacity. In December 1979 the minority Conservative government introduced a budget that aimed to reduce the size of the deficit. But the government fell on the issue of the budget, and the Liberals were returned to power in the election of February 1980. Just two months later a Liberal minibudget reintroduced two of the tax measures proposed in the defeated Conservative budget.

The 1960s and 1970s were thus years of fiscal activism, if not fiscal fine tuning. Discretionary tax and expenditure changes were constantly used in an attempt to stabilize the economy. Much of the reason active fiscal policy was so much in vogue was the dramatic success of tax cuts introduced in the United States in 1964. This episode, still cited by proponents of fiscal activism, is discussed in Box 32-4 (see page 688).

The overall evidence from the period, however, suggests that the record of fiscal activism was quite mixed: Sometimes fiscal policy moderated cyclical swings, and sometimes it accentuated them. As a result, fiscal activism fell from favor in most circles.[8]

The 1980s

In the early 1980s fiscal policy was complicated by two major problems. First, as already noted (see Table 32-2), the federal budget deficit had become so large that worries were emerging about its implications. Second, the rate of inflation was unacceptably high despite an (also unacceptable) high rate of unemployment. (Inflation was about 10 percent and unemployment was over 8 percent at the beginning of 1980.) For the first time since the government has accepted responsibility for stabilizing the economy, the direction—not simply the extent—of desirable

changes in the stance of fiscal policy was at issue. Reducing the recessionary gap called for an expansionary fiscal stance; reducing inflation and concern about the deficit called for a contractionary fiscal stance. Successive budgets in the 1980s introduced small changes in the overall fiscal stance, being pulled one way and the other by the two competing objectives.[9]

In late 1981 a major worldwide downturn set in, turning 1982 into the worst recession since the Great Depression. Still caught on the horns of the dilemma, the budget of 1982 made little change in the fiscal stance.

In 1983 the budget tried to resolve the dilemma with short-term measures aimed at unemployment and longer-term measures aimed at the deficit. The budget introduced moderate stimulus—about $6 billion phased in over two years—combined with a series of measures, including tax increases, to offset this stimulus later. This *tilt*—stimulus now, restraint later—was widely viewed as an appropriate way to stimulate the economy without increasing the future cyclically adjusted deficit.

In 1983 there was a strong recovery. Real output grew by over 6 percent and inflation slowed dramatically. The budget introduced in February 1984 maintained a steady course, giving rise to very little change in the stance of fiscal policy. It also did very little to address the persistent budget deficit.

A Conservative government was elected in fall 1984. The new government had strong support in the business and financial communities and appeared committed to reversing the trend of rising government deficits. In November 1984 it published an Agenda Paper that laid out a number of "fundamental principles" to guide fiscal policy, including these:

1. To achieve sizable year-over-year reductions in the deficit
2. To ensure that the majority of the reduction in

[8] The fall from favor of fiscal policy activism was given a further push with the election of U.S. President Ronald Reagan, an avowed fiscal conservative, in 1980. Ironically, despite the Reagan administration's disavowal of fiscal *policy,* its actions had significant fiscal *effects*. Many economists believe that the dramatic increase in the deficit under him played a major role in stimulating the economy and ending the 1982 recession. It also stimulated an extensive public debate about the consequences of persistent budget deficits, and Congress debated and passed legislation (the Gramm-Rudman-Hollings Bill) to try to reduce the deficit.

[9] One important feature of the October 1980 budget was the introduction of the National Energy Program, designed to increase the federal government's share of the revenues from petroleum production mainly at the expense of the industry. Also, to help increase Canadian participation in the industry, a series of grants for exploration and development that would increase with the Canadian ownership of a firm were introduced. The NEP was dismantled by the Conservative government in 1984.

BOX 32-3

Inflation Indexing of Income Taxes

In Canada, marginal tax rates rise with income, as Table 24-2 on page 497 shows. Many economists believe that beyond some point high marginal tax rates provide strong disincentives to the supply of effort. A steelworker with a high marginal tax rate is less inclined to work overtime in periods of boom, and a lawyer or a highly trained technical consultant is less likely to accept one more case, the higher his or her marginal tax rate.

In inflationary situations, when an individual's money income rises, the purchasing power of this income does not necessarily rise. For example, a secretary who gets a 10 percent raise is no better off when the prices of everything she purchases also rise by 10 percent *and* the fraction of income she pays in taxes does not change. However, with marginal tax rates that rise with money income, the fraction of income she pays in taxes will rise; as a result, her *after-tax money income* will rise by less than 10 percent. Even though her *before-tax real income* remains unchanged (prices and before-tax money income both rise by 10 percent), her *after-tax real income* will fall because she now pays in taxes a larger fraction of her income.

This is because inflation, by increasing the dollar value of the taxpayer's money income, moves the taxpayer into a tax bracket with a higher marginal tax rate. Unless the growth of before-tax nominal (money) income exceeds the rate of inflation, the increase in taxes will necessarily reduce after-tax real income.

Indexation of income tax prevents this automatic increase in tax rates in response to inflation. When a tax system is indexed, the rate of taxation at any given level of *real* income remains constant. The tax schedule—that is, the tax bracket at which a particular marginal rate applies—is adjusted each year to allow for the effects of inflation on nominal incomes. If inflation has averaged 10 percent in the economy but average real income is unchanged, the average person's nominal income will go up by 10 percent. If before the inflation there was a $30,000 cutoff for a 40 percent marginal tax rate, the cutoff would now move up by 10 percent, to $33,000. People whose initial incomes were under $30,000 and whose real income remained unchanged would now have money income under $33,000 and would not move to a higher tax bracket. People whose income before the inflation was $30,000 and whose *real* income grew would, by definition, have nominal incomes that grew in excess of the 10 percent inflation rate; they would move to a

---

the deficit is achieved through better management and expenditure restraint
3. To reduce the growth rate of the national debt to less than that of national income by the end of the decade[10]

Finance Minister Michael Wilson brought down three budgets over the following 2½ years. How did they stack up against the fundamental principles?

The first fiscal principle was clearly honored—as shown in Figure 32-4 (see page 690), the trend of rising deficits was reversed. Each of the Wilson

[10] The paper also included a commitment to reduce the government's financial requirements, the amount the government actually borrows on financial markets, equal to the deficit less the government's net revenues on "off-budget" items, the major component of which is the money it collects from its employees' contributions to the public service pension plan.

budgets received some vote of confidence from financial markets, although the vote was in most cases reserved rather than enthusiastic; the deficit cuts were in fact smaller than many market participants had hoped for. Further, as we shall discuss shortly, his third budget, delivered in February 1987, caused concern that the deficit was not firmly on a downward track.

There was also progress on the commitment to achieve some expenditure restraint; approximately 70 percent of the deficit reductions came on the expenditure side of the budget. Total program spending (all spending exclusive of interest payments on the national debt) declined not only as a share of GDP but also in absolute terms in fiscal 1985–1986, the first such decline in 25 years. Nevertheless, these budgets involved substantial tax increases. Personal

higher tax bracket. Similarly, people whose real income fell would move to a lower tax bracket.

In an indexed tax system, average and marginal tax rates depend only on real income.

In his 1973 budget John Turner, then minister of finance, indexed the Canadian income tax system. In the very high inflation of the 1970s indexation held Canadian tax burdens below what they would have been had the tax schedule of 1972 remained in force in terms of money income. By the same token it has reduced the tax revenues of the federal government over the same period.

There are arguments against indexing the tax system. For example, some people think that indexation is inflationary because it reduces the public's resistance to inflation. With an unindexed tax system, inflation leads to higher taxes and people will therefore resist inflation. Indexation of the tax system, it is argued, reduces public opposition to inflation and thus makes it easier for governments to justify inflationary policies. Others argue that indexation will reduce inflation because it reduces the payoff to governments from pursuing inflationary policies. The increased tax

bite that arises from an unindexed tax system in the presence of inflation provides a great incentive for governments to follow inflationary policies; real resources can be transferred from the private sector to the public purse simply by inflating people into higher tax brackets. Thus it is not clear whether indexation leads to more or less inflationary policies.

Politicians do not necessarily like inflation-indexed tax systems. In the United States the tax system has not been indexed. However, since 1975 the U.S. Congress has passed a series of tax cuts that can be understood as an attempt to undo the automatic increases in taxes that would have resulted from inflation. Politicians were in reality indexing the tax system each year, and they were doing it in a manner that gave them political credit for passing tax cuts. This option has not been available to Canadian politicians until the last few years as a number of the indexation provisions in the Canadian tax system have been eliminated or restricted. (Ironically, in 1981 the Reagan administration committed itself to eventual indexation of the U.S. tax system, while the Canadian tax reform of 1987 did nothing to restore indexation to the Canadian tax system.)

income taxes and the federal sales tax—both highly visible—were increased. Less widely known was that less visible corporate and energy tax revenues fell as a share of GDP. (Some of these tax measures, in particular changes in the corporate tax system and the broadening of the federal sales tax base, could be interpreted as the first stages of the comprehensive tax reform package introduced in June 1987. See the discussion in Box 24-2 on page 506.)

Mr. Wilson's third principle—reducing the rate of growth of debt to below that of GDP—appeared also to be within grasp in his first two budgets. But events subsequent to the February 1986 budget suggested that the goal would not be achieved before the end of the decade.

In the summer of 1986 the Canadian economy suffered from two major international shocks—a dra-

matic fall in the world price of oil and a collapse in the international markets for Canadian agricultural exports. Automatic stabilizers in the form of increased payments under the terms of various agricultural support programs and reduced tax revenue from the energy sector were thus triggered, and in addition the government decided to provide farmers with an additional $1 billion in discretionary funds. As a result the deficit and debt projections made in the February 1986 budget had to be revised; the 1986–1987 deficit was no longer expected to fall below $30 billion, and the rate of growth of the debt was no longer expected to be below that of GDP by the end of the decade.

Thus while progress in controlling the federal deficit was certainly visible, the reductions were judged quite modest. After four years of sustained

BOX 32-4

Fiscal Drag and the 1964 U.S. Tax Cuts: A Fiscal Policy Success

Fiscal drag, first diagnosed in the early 1960s, is the problem produced by economic growth acting on stable government expenditure and fixed tax rates. In normal circumstances, growth leads to a falling cyclically adjusted budget deficit. (In terms of the figure in Box 32-2, the drag is due to a movement along the budget deficit function as potential income grows.)

Throughout the 1950s potential output rose 2 to 3 percent per year because of economic growth. With tax rates constant, rising national income causes rising tax revenues. But because in the 1950s government expenditure was relatively stable, rising tax revenues exerted a drag on the growth of aggregate demand by taking income away from households, who would have spent it, and transferring it to governments, who did not. There was thus a falling cyclically adjusted deficit.

This is illustrated in the figure, where we start with the curves AD_0, $LRAS_0$, and $SRAS_0$. These yield equilibrium at E_0 and potential income Y_0^*. Economic growth now shifts the supply curves to $LRAS_1$ and $SRAS_1$. As a result of fiscal drag, however, the aggregate demand curve shifts only to AD_1 rather than to AD_2, which would have been required to sustain full employment. An output gap of $Y_1Y_2^*$ is thus created.

To prevent the exertion of an ever-stronger depressing effect on national income by a falling CAD, it is necessary periodically either to increase government spending or to reduce tax rates. This problem

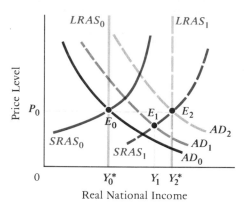

Real National Income

arose in the American economy during the 1950s. Economic growth was producing a declining CAD. As a result each cyclical upswing was weaker than the one before it, and the average level of unemployment over the cycle was creeping upward. By the beginning of the 1960s many economists were calling for a tax cut to remove the drag and restore full employment. Their concern was not with cyclical stabilization of the economy but with solving a problem associated with long-term economic growth.

When the 1964 tax cut was enacted, the predicted effects occurred. The tax cuts were perceived to be permanent and the increased (current and expected future) disposable income caused an increase in consumption expenditure that in turn caused an increase in national income and employment.

---

economic growth, and after three federal budgets that focused on deficit reduction, government deficits remained historically very large. Many commentators felt that deficits would soon start to grow again, given that a federal election was on the horizon. The various parties were gearing up to articulate expenditure programs and tax reductions that they felt would help their popularity with the electorate but could only serve to maintain or enlarge the deficit and thus continue to add to the growing stock of public debt.

In the mid 1980s a new phenomenon began to emerge as a source of concern—provincial government deficits. We take this up below when we discuss the implications of persistent large government deficits and consequent growth of the national debt.

The Economics of Budget Deficits

The average Canadian has some idea of the size of the federal budget deficit (or at least a sense that it is too big). The average West German is not likely to have any idea of the size of the government's budget deficit or a strong opinion on whether it is too large. Why is our budget deficit so large? Why do we worry so much about it? Is it really such a big problem?

Facts About the Deficit

The recent emergence of record federal budget deficits is shown in Figure 32-4. Part (i) shows total federal spending (on goods and services and transfers) and total federal revenues since 1970 as a share of GDP. Over the period 1975–1980 expenditures were a relatively constant fraction of GDP, while tax revenues fell sharply. This is the basis for the Department of Finance view that discretionary tax cuts introduced in the 1970s were responsible for the growing deficit. Other analysts, however, argue that it was the failure to constrain expenditure in the face of the tax cuts that is responsible and that there was also a switch toward delivering some transfers through tax concessions rather than direct expenditure.

If the source of the growth in the deficit in the 1970s was unclear, it was less so in the 1980s. The increase in the deficit that occurred in the 1981–1983 period reflect the combined effects of the severe recession in 1982, some mild discretionary fiscal expansion, and increased interest payments on the government's debt. The latter was due to both the sharp rise in interest rates that occurred and the cumulative effect of the persistent deficits on the size of the government debt.

Part (ii) shows the deficit, again measured as a share of GDP—this is the shaded area between the two lines in part (i). The government budget had been in deficit prior to 1982, although as a percentage of GDP the deficit had not been unusually large by historical standards. After 1982, however, the deficit increased dramatically as a share of GDP. As can be seen from Table 32-2, the cyclically adjusted deficit grew even more than the actual deficit over the period 1982–1985.

So far we have focused on the federal government budget balance. We could also consider the deficit on a total government basis; the difference between that and the federal deficit is due to the net deficit position of the provincial and municipal governments. For most of the past two decades, provincial and municipal governments combined have experienced only relatively small budget imbalances, and hence most of the concern about budget deficits in Canada has been focused on the federal government. In fact, for most of the last two decades, the total government deficit was smaller than the federal government deficit, reflecting the combined surpluses of the other two levels of government. But in 1986 the total government deficit was larger.

The reduction in the deficit of the federal government has been offset by the increase in the deficits of provincial and municipal governments.

In 1986 *all* 10 provincial governments were running deficits. Although deficits had been the order of the day in certain provinces, they had traditionally been offset by surpluses in other provinces. In 1986 a deficit emerged in Alberta, which had typically been a surplus province due to large oil revenues. It began running a deficit in response to depressed economic conditions brought about by adverse shocks to the agricultural and energy sectors. Most worrisome, perhaps, was the deficit in Ontario, a province that had been experiencing a sustained economic boom since 1983.

Why Worry About Deficits?

It is possible to identify a set of conditions whereby neither government deficits nor the public debt would matter in the economy. However, the required conditions (discussed in more detail in Appendix B to Chapter 39) are so stringent that most economists believe that the deficit does exert important influences on the economy.

One such influence is the short-run stabilizing or destabilizing role in the economy emphasized earlier in this chapter. A second is a potential adverse long-run effect on income and welfare, to which we now turn. People worry about the long-run effects of persistent deficits for many reasons. We will look at four.

FIGURE 32-4 **Federal Revenues, Expenditures, and Budget Balances,**
1967–1986 (*percentage of GDP, national accounts basis*)

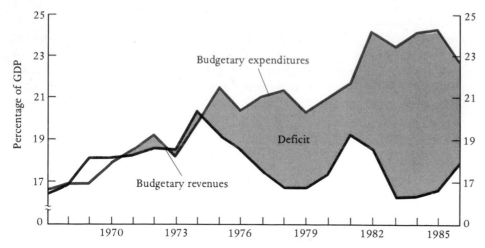

(i) Revenues and expenditures

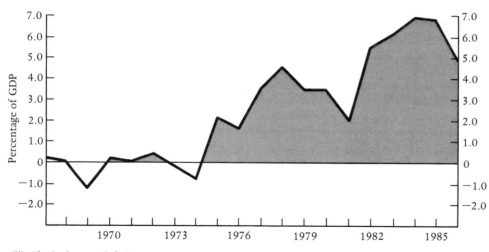

(ii) The budgetary deficit

The deficit has grown sharply in recent years, reflecting rapid increases in expenditures relative to revenues. Part (i) shows expenditures and revenues of the federal government, both as a percentage of national income. The difference is the federal deficit, shown in part (ii).

From 1967 though 1973 expenditures grew steadily while revenue fluctuated around a rising trend; as a result the budget balance fluctuated between deficit and surplus positions but showed no significant trend. Persistent deficits emerged in the next five years as expenditures remained roughly constant while revenues fell.

In the 1980s the deficit increased dramatically. In the early part of this decade the growth in the deficit reflected the effects of the recession; as can be seen in Table 32-2, the cyclical adjustment grew sharply in this period. Revenues fell sharply and have recovered only slowly since. Expenditures rose rapidly, in part reflecting the operation of automatic stabilizers. More recently, government restraint curtailed growth in program spending, but this was more than offset by the rapid growth in interest payments on the national debt, so that, as shown, total expenditure continued to rise. In 1986 the deficit fell both in absolute terms and as a percentage of GDP. (*Source:* Department of Finance, *Budget Papers*, February 1987.)

Will a deficit cause inflation?   Neither economic theory nor the available evidence suggests that deficits by themselves are sufficient to cause inflation.

The worry that persistent deficits may cause inflation arises out of the fear that a continuous deficit will lead to a continuous expansion in the money supply, that is, that it would eventually lead to pressure in the Bank of Canada to expand the money supply and thus cause inflation. This case cannot be studied in detail until Chapter 36. For now we merely observe that if a deficit is financed by "borrowing" from the Bank, the money supply will be increased every year. (In effect the Bank *creates* the money to finance the deficit.) If this increase is too rapid, it will cause inflation.

Deficits financed by the continual creation of new money may cause inflation.

No one believes that this is desirable.

Will the deficit crowd out private investment?   People fear that deficit spending may lead to a more or less equivalent reduction in private-sector investment spending. Government borrowing to finance its deficit can absorb a significant proportion of private savings. In 1986, for example, the federal deficit was equal to about 52 percent of household savings and fully 24 percent of total private-sector savings by households and firms. The fear is that heavy government borrowing drives up the interest rate and that the higher interest rate reduces private investment expenditure. This "crowding out" process is illustrated in Figure 32-5.

If government borrowing to finance the deficit drives up the interest rate, some private investment expenditure will be crowded out.

However, interest rates in an open economy such as Canada are closely tied to those prevailing in international markets. Hence the scope for increases in the interest rate and crowding out of investment is quite limited. By and large, the budget deficit will result in increased foreign borrowing (not necessarily by the government, but by other borrowers in the economy who are forced to borrow abroad since the government deficit has absorbed most of the available domestic saving). Domestic interest rates and investment will remain relatively unchanged.[11]

Will the debt harm future generations?   To the extent that government borrowing to finance current expenditures crowds out private investment, there will be a smaller stock of capital to pass on to future generations. Less capital means less output; this is the long-term burden of the debt.

However, we have seen that investment in an open economy will not be reduced much by a government deficit. Does this mean there is no burden of the debt in an open economy? Unfortunately, the answer is no. While private investment can be maintained, foreign lenders will supply much of the funds. Future generations may well inherit a capital stock that is not significantly reduced as a result of the deficit, but they will also inherit an increased stock of foreign liabilities. Future payments of interest and dividends to foreigners will lower GNP (income owned by Canadians) in relation to GDP (output produced in Canada) since some income generated by the output will accrue to foreigners. These will also lower GNP relative to what it would have been in the absence of the deficits.

Attracting funds from abroad entails a transfer of purchasing power to domestic residents when the funds enter the country and a transfer back to foreigners when interest and dividend payments and repayments of principal occur.

The alternative view, that the debt does not matter because we largely owe it to ourselves, is taken up in Box 32-5 (see pages 694–695).

This argument is dramatically illustrated by recent experience in the United States. The United States slowly built up a net creditor position over the six decades before 1980. That position was completely dissipated as a result of massive foreign borrowing during Ronald Reagan's presidency. Most econo-

---

[11] The crowding-out debate is closely related to debates about the effectiveness of fiscal policy, a debate we take up in Chapter 39. In an open economy a government deficit does not always crowd out investment because interest rates don't rise. Instead, the increased foreign borrowing may cause the currency to appreciate and thus crowd out net exports. We discuss this possibility in Chapter 42.

FIGURE 32-5   Crowding Out Private Investment by Government Borrowing

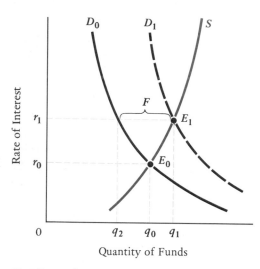

(i) Effects of government borrowing
     with constant national income

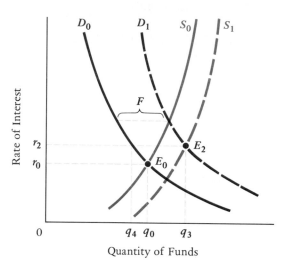

(ii) Effects of government borrowing
      with increased national income

Government borrowing may crowd out private-sector borrowing and investing. Part (i) of the figure shows a supply of funds available to be lent, S, that is fairly insensitive to the interest rate. Initially the demand to borrow funds is D_0, giving an equilibrium interest rate of r_0 and a quantity of funds borrowed for all purposes of q_0.

Government spending now increases by F, all of which is borrowed. This shifts the demand for funds to the right, from D_0 to D_1, taking equilibrium to E_1. The interest rate rises to r_1, and the quantity of funds borrowed rises to q_1. But q_2q_1 of these go to the government, so the private sector borrows only q_2, which is q_2q_0 less than it was able to borrow, and hence invest, before the deficit forced the government into the market.

If, however, the extra government expenditure increases national income, it will boost saving. The savings function will then shift to the right, say, from S_0 to S_1 in part (ii) of the figure. Crowding out will then be lessened. At equilibrium E_2 the interest rate rises to r_2, and private borrowing is only q_4q_0 less than before the government entered the market.

---

mists attribute this foreign borrowing to the enormous government budget deficits that occurred. As a result of these large deficits, the United States has become one of the world's largest debtor nations.

Does the size of the debt hamper the operation of policy?   The large interest bill on the national debt puts a strain on the budget process. For example, in 1986 a full 28 percent of all tax revenues went to pay interest on the national debt! The government's freedom of fiscal maneuver is obviously hampered by

such a large and rising claim on the national tax revenues. When the government's interest obligations grow, it can, of course, incur an even larger deficit, at least for a while, but eventually interest on the stock of debt must be paid from new revenues.[12] Eventually the government must either reduce its expenditure on other programs or raise taxes.

---

[12] Of course for a while interest on current debt can be paid by incurring new debt, but this is an explosive process. The interest demands on old and new debt would soon absorb the whole of government tax revenue and eventually all of national income.

Although interest payments on the national debt have not yet reached crisis proportions, the large claim on existing government revenues is a cause for concern.

Deficits and the National Debt

The foregoing indicates that much of the concern about government budget deficits arises from their *cumulative* effect on the national debt and therefore on the government's interest obligations.

Facts About the Debt

The national debt in December 1986 was over $200 billion, about $8,000 for every man, woman, and child in the country. About 10 percent of the debt was held by the government itself and by the Bank of Canada; interest payments on this part of the debt are only bookkeeping transactions.[13]

The national debt of over $200 billion represents money that the federal government has borrowed by selling bonds to Canadian and foreign households, firms, and financial institutions.

In this sense the national debt is owed by all of us to some of us and to foreigners.

The debt in relation to GDP. The figures for debt per person, which are often quoted in an attempt to shock the reader, require interpretation. For a government, as for a household, the significance of debt depends on what it represents and on whether the income is available to pay the interest. No one would be shocked, for example, to find that a Canadian family of four earning $60,000 a year had a mortgage of $50,000 on a $100,000 home.

It is useful in evaluating the national debt and the government's interest payments on it to consider them *relative* to the size of the economy. Worries about the debt arise primarily when the debt grows

[13] The Bank of Canada buys government bonds in the course of operating monetary policy (see Chapter 35). Government departments sometimes acquire government bonds when they have funds that they do not need for short, or even long, periods of time.

faster than the economy; it is really the debt-to-GDP ratio that matters. A national debt of $200 billion clearly has different implications when GDP is $50 billion and when it is $500 billion.

Figure 32-6 (see page 696) shows historical data for the debt and interest payments on it as a proportion of GDP.

Part (i) shows that national debt as a proportion of GDP started to fall at the end of World War II and continued to fall until 1976. The debt rose relative to GDP after 1977, and by 1986 the debt had reached almost 50 percent of GDP. That figure is still much less than the more than 100 percent at the postwar peak. Nevertheless, the trend is worrisome, and medium-term projections suggest that the debt-to-GDP ratio will continue to rise.

Consider next the interest payments on the debt, often called the *debt-service payments,* shown in part (ii) of the figure. Clearly, there is genuine cause for worry here. If the trend continues, interest payments could eventually put an intolerable burden on the government's taxing capacity. Ever-bigger deficits would occur, and with them even more borrowing.

In view of the costs imposed by a rising debt-to-GDP ratio, many economists and others have argued that the government's fiscal policies are imprudent and have called for a commitment to control the deficit.

Proposals to Control the Deficit

As we have seen, government deficits contribute to aggregate demand and hence can play a useful role in damping cyclical fluctuations in the economy. As we have also seen, government deficits contribute to increases in the national debt and hence in the long term might lead to a reduction in living standards. This conflict between the short-term stabilization role of deficits and the long-term adverse effects of a large public debt has long been a subject of debate among economists and others.

Views range from those who dismiss the long-run costs of the national debt and hence are not concerned about the deficit to those who wish to eschew the short-term stabilization role for the deficit entirely and impose a virtual straitjacket on the government, requiring it always to balance its budget.

BOX 32-5

Does the National Debt Matter? The Owe-It-to-Ourselves View

A few economists have argued that since the national debt simply involves a debt of some Canadians payable to other Canadians, it imposes no net burden on the country. Of course these economists recognize that the debt is a burden to taxpayers in general who must ultimately provide the funds for the government to make interest payments on the debt. But, the "owe-it-to-ourselves" argument holds, that burden is exactly offset by the interest payments that are made to those Canadians who own government bonds.

The owe-it-to-ourselves view thus argues that the major effect of the national debt is that interest payments on it merely redistribute income from the general taxpayer towards bond-holders. Since the ownership of government bonds is widely held, being a major component of most public and private pension funds, the argument holds that even this redistribution of income is not a serious matter.

This contention raises several issues.

Crowding Out. First, suppose that the basic facts alleged in the owe-it-to-ourselves view are true—that is, that virtually all Canadian government debt is in fact held by Canadians. Even in this case, it does not follow that there is no net burden to the Canadian economy arising from the government debt.

A good deal of economic theory and evidence suggests that government bonds are held in place of claims on income streams produced by real capital. That is, if the debt did not exist, people would still wish to hold assets to provide for future consumption; in the absence of the government debt they would have invested in corporations engaged in producing goods and services. Thus the bonds, which on net contribute nothing to the economy but merely redistribute income from one group to another, crowd out investment in real capital that would have created wealth and income for Canadians.

On this argument, it is the very fact that the government debt only redistributes income between Canadians that means that it gives rise to a net burden to the economy. By crowding out investment in physical capital, it leads to a lower capital stock and hence to reduced levels of income and wealth for Canadians.

International Capital Mobility. The basic contention that the debt is merely owed-to-ourselves is not completely true. While the vast majority of Canadian government bonds (90 percent) is held by Canadian citizens, government bonds are also sold on international markets so that the remaining 10 percent is held by foreigners. Accordingly, the interest

---

We now look at some of the specific proposals that have been put forward; some of the general options are illustrated in Figure 32-7 (see page 697).

An annually balanced budget?   Much current rhetoric of fiscal restraint calls for a balanced budget. In the United States, the Gramm-Rudman-Hollings bill, passed in late 1985, was an attempt to eliminate the federal deficit by 1991 by mandating expenditure cuts.

The discussion earlier in this chapter suggests that an annually balanced budget would be extremely difficult, perhaps impossible, to achieve. With fixed tax rates, tax revenues fluctuate as national income

fluctuates. Much government expenditure is fixed by past commitments, and most of the rest is hard to change quickly.

But suppose that an annually balanced budget, or something approaching it, were feasible. What would its effects be? Would they be desirable?

We saw earlier that a larger government sector whose expenditures on goods and services are not very sensitive to the cyclical variations in national income is a major built-in stabilizer. To insist that annual government expenditure be tied to annual tax receipts would be to abandon the present built-in stability provided by government. Government expenditure would then become a major *destabilizing*

payments on these bonds, which must be financed by Canadian taxpayers, accrue to foreign nationals.

The fact that some Canadian government debt is held abroad is enough to refute the owe-it-to-ourselves myth. But in fact the situation is even more complicated—and more damaging to the owe-it-to-ourselves view.

Suppose a large Canadian corporation wishes to float a new debt issue in order to finance an expansion in its existing capacity. While it might expect to sell a large fraction of the new bonds on the Canadian market, the fact that the Canadian government is flooding that market with debt of its own in order to finance its budget deficit means that the Canadian corporation will have to sell its debt abroad. (Ontario Hydro and Quebec Hydro are examples of two organizations that have found themselves in exactly this position in recent years.)

Again there will be a burden to the national debt, not in the form of a reduced capital stock in Canada, but nevertheless in the form of reduced income and wealth for Canadians. Foreign nationals will now own claims to the income from the new Canadian investment projects, and some of the income from these Canadian projects will accrue to those foreign nationals who acquired these financial claims.

In this case the burden to the national debt arises *indirectly* because of the need that it creates for Canadian firms to finance their investment by selling bonds and equities abroad. Once this indirect effect is recognized, simply looking at the share of foreign ownership of the national debt does not give a good indication of how much is owed-to-ourselves and how much is actually owed-to-foreign-nationals.

What Limits the Acceptable Size of the Deficit? The arguments given in the text provide a basis for balancing the need for short-run fiscal stabilization with the longer-run concerns for fiscal prudence. But the owe-it-to-ourselves view is not helpful in this regard.

If the owe-it-to-ourselves view were correct, why would we not want a $200 billion deficit, or even a $500 billion one, rather than the controversial $30-plus billion one we have now? Surely the politicians would like that, as it would allow them to avoid many of the hard decisions involved in restraining expenditures and raising taxes. Of course, no one would seriously advocate such a deficit. But if the owe-it-to-ourselves view were correct, there would be no reason for objecting to such a deficit.

force. Tax revenues necessarily rise in booms and fall in slumps; an annually balanced budget would force government expenditure to do the same. Changes in national income would then cause induced changes not only in household consumption expenditure but also in government expenditure. This would greatly increase the economy's marginal propensity to spend and hence increase the value of the multiplier.

An annually balanced budget would accentuate the swings in national income that accompany changes in such autonomous expenditure flows as investment and exports.

A further problem is that the goal of budget *balance* is in fact stricter than is required to avoid a rising debt-to-GDP ratio. Growth in GDP means that some growth in the debit, and hence a (small) deficit, is consistent with a stable debt-to-GDP ratio. In the rest of this chapter, we shall assume that the term *budget balance* allows for this possibility.

A zero structural balance? The concept of the structural balance was designed to assess changes in the stance of fiscal stabilization policy. It was not intended to help assess the long-term viability of fiscal policy. Yet it has often been used in this way by people who have argued that the national debt is

FIGURE 32-6   Relative Significance of the National Debt

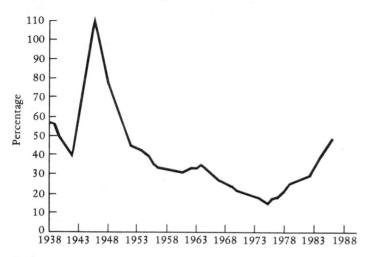

(i) Net government debt as a percentage of GDP

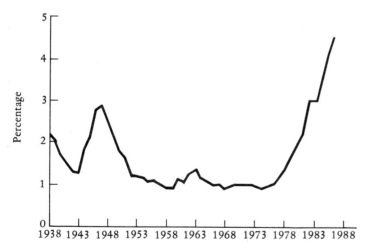

(ii) Net interest on government debt as a percentage of GDP

After falling for 30 years, the national debt and interest payments on it have both started to rise as a share of national income. Part (i) plots net federal government debt while part (ii) plots net interest payments made by the federal government, both as a percentage of GDP.

The national debt, after rising sharply through World War II, was a declining fraction of GDP until 1975. Since 1975 there has been a continuing rise, with the rise being quite sharp in the last few years shown. In 1986 the ratio reached 48.7 percent.

Interest payments on the national debt have followed a similar pattern; since interest rates rose in the late 1970s and early 1980s, the upturn in interest payments was sharper and occurred sooner than with the debt. Interest payments on the debt reached 2.9 percent of national income in 1948 and remained under three percent for the next 33 years. In 1983 they rose to 3.3 percent, and in 1986 they reached 4.6 percent. (*Source: Public Accounts,* Department of Finance.)

not a long-term problem as long as the structural balance is not in deficit.

A zero structural balance is not, however, a good target for long-run fiscal prudence because the economy usually is expected to operate at or below potential income. Thus a budget that is balanced at potential income will produce deficits whenever output is below potential, a balance at potential income,

and a surplus only in the rare event that output exceeds potential.

A second problem with the structural deficit as an indicator of fiscal imprudence arises from the inflation adjustment. In arriving at a measure of the structural deficit, the inflation adjustment is typically made using the *actual* stock of government debt. Thus the larger the stock of debt, the larger the

FIGURE 32-7   Balanced and Unbalanced Budgets

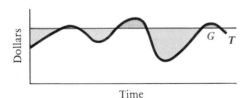

Time
(i) A cyclically unbalanced budget

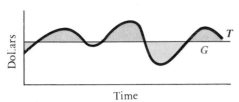

Time
(ii) A cyclically balanced budget

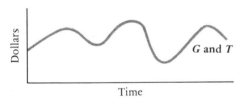

Time
(iii) A constantly balanced budget

An annually (constantly) balanced budget is a destabilizer; a cyclically balanced budget is a stabilizer. The flow of tax receipts, T, is shown varying over the business cycle, while in parts (i) and (ii) government expenditure, G, is shown at a constant rate.

In part (i) deficits (dark areas) are common and surpluses (light areas) are rare because the average level of expenditure exceeds the average level of taxes. Such a policy will tend to stabilize the economy against cyclical fluctuations, but the average fiscal stance of the government is expansionary.

In part (ii) government expenditure has been reduced until it is approximately equal to the average level of tax receipts. The budget is now balanced cyclically. The policy still tends to stabilize the economy against cyclical fluctuations because of deficits in slumps and surpluses in booms. But the average fiscal stance is neither strongly expansionary nor strongly contractionary.

In part (iii) a balanced budget has been imposed. Deficits have been prevented, but government expenditure now varies over the business cycle, tending to destabilize the economy by accentuating the cyclical swings in aggregate expenditure.

inflation adjustment will be, and the smaller will be the structural component of any given measured deficits. Thus small structural deficits can hide the very problem fiscal imprudence is concerned with: a too rapidly rising stock of debt.

A cyclically balanced budget?   An alternative policy, one that would prevent continual deficits (and could also inhibit the growth in the size of the government sector), would be to balance the budget over the business cycle. This would be more feasible than the annually balanced budget, and it would not make government expenditure a destabilizing force.

Although more attractive in principal than the annually balanced budget, a cyclically balanced budget would carry problems of its own. Government might well spend in excess of revenue in one year, leaving an obligation to spend less than current revenue in following years. Could such an obligation to balance over a period of years be made binding? What a government commits itself to in one year does not necessarily restrict what it (or its successor) does the next year.

Perhaps even more of a problem is that there is always room for some disagreement about the current state of the business cycle. Critics of the cyclically balanced budget proposal argue that many governments have often misinterpreted long-term factors such as demographic changes that lead to an increase in the measured unemployment rate or structural change that leads to a fall in the measured rate of income growth as short-term cyclical factors that call for fiscal stimulus. Thus the critics argue that while governments can appear to accept the need for balance over the cycle, this has not in fact stopped them from running persistently large deficits and hence imprudently running up the national debt.

Although a budget balanced over the course of the business cycle is in principle an acceptable way of reconciling short-term stabilization and long-term prudence, the business cycle may not be well enough defined in practice to make the proposal operational.

The medium-term fiscal plan.   In a study published in 1984, Professors Neil Bruce and Douglas Purvis of Queen's University addressed the issue of fiscal prudence by evaluating the government's medium-term fiscal plan. That plan gives projections for the key economic variables such as output, inflation, interest rates, and unemployment as well as for government revenues and expenditures.

Bruce and Purvis defined the *imprudent deficit* as the part of projected deficits that contributes to growth in the debt-to-GDP ratio above some target level. Thus they allow for trend growth in the economy and for projected inflation. The imprudent deficit nets out cyclical and inflation adjustments in much the same manner as calculations of the structural deficit do. The crucial difference is that the inflation adjustment is applied only to the level of debt consistent with the target debt-to-GDP ratio rather than to the actual stock of debt. This means that current deficits, which contribute to the actual debt, do not also automatically lead to an increase in the inflation adjustment applied to future deficits.

Their calculation showed the imprudent deficit to be significant. They concluded that there was cause for concern about the long-term implications of projected deficits and that some concerted but systematic phasing-in of budget cuts was in order. Further, they argued that even though the actual cuts could be implemented gradually, the process had to be started quickly so that the program for re-establishing fiscal prudence be flexible enough that the short-term objectives of fiscal stabilization need not be abandoned.

Summary.   The need for fiscal prudence is accepted by virtually everyone. How to evaluate it and enforce it, however, is still subject to controversy. Indeed, there is serious doubt that the idea of a balanced budget over any time period is operational.

Many economists believe that a superior alternative to insisting on a precise balance is to pay attention to the balance without making a fetish of never adding to the national debt.

The Political Economy of the Debt

Almost all economists accept that if the debt got so large that it could not be serviced without either putting a crushing burden on taxpayers or forcing

the government to create new money to service it, there would be serious problems. But many think we are still a long way from that point. To them the overriding principle is that the debt should be changed according to the needs of stabilization policy.

An alternative view is what has come to be called *fiscal conservatism*. The conservative view takes a broad historical perspective. It says that in the eighteenth century spendthrift European rulers habitually spent more than their tax revenues and so created harmful inflation. By the end of the nineteenth century the doctrine was well established that a balanced budget was the citizen's only protection against profligate government spending and consequent wild inflation. Thus the conservatives hold that the balanced budget doctrine was not silly and irrational, as Keynes made it out to be. Instead it was the symbol of the people's victory in a long struggle to control the spendthrift proclivities of their nations' rulers.

The Keynesian revolution swept away that view. Budget deficits became, according to Keynesians, the tool by which benign and enlightened governments sought to ensure full employment. But, say the conservatives, deficit spending let the tiger out of the cage. Inflationary gaps, recessionary gaps, or full employment notwithstanding, governments spent and spent and spent. Deficits accumulated, national debt rose, and inflation became the rule.

The main premise of the conservative view is that governments are not passive agents who do what is necessary to create full employment and maximize social welfare. Governments are composed of individuals—elected officials, legislators, and civil servants—who, like everyone else, seek mainly to maximize their own well-being. Their welfare is best served by a big government role and a satisfied electorate. Thus they tend to favor spending and to resist tax increases. This creates a persistent tendency toward deficits that is quite independent of any consideration of a sound fiscal policy.

The debate reflects deeply held views about the role of government, the nature and motivation of public officials, and the desirability of stabilization. Keynesians tend to regard government officials as well meaning, and substantial government intervention as essential to an effective and humane society.

Fiscal conservatives regard public officials as self-serving and of limited competence. They see public intervention, however well motivated, as probably inept and ultimately destabilizing. Both recognize that an interventionist government will play a large role in economic affairs. Conservatives regard that prospect with concern, Keynesians with relative equanimity.

Summary

1. Fiscal policy uses government expenditure and tax policies to influence the economy by shifting the aggregate demand curve. Changes in either government spending or tax policies also influence the budget balance.

2. The so-called paradox of thrift is not a paradox at all. It applies to the short-run effects of saving and investment on aggregate demand. It predicts that severe recessions can be combated by encouraging an increase in spending.

3. When private expenditure functions are fixed, it is a relatively simple matter to increase expenditure, to cut tax rates, or to make a balanced budget increase in expenditure in order to remove a recessionary gap (and to make the opposite changes to remove an inflationary gap).

4. Fiscal policy is more difficult when, as is almost always the case, private expenditure functions are continually shifting. Fine tuning, the attempt to hold the aggregate expenditure function virtually constant by offsetting even small fluctuations in private expenditure, has been largely discredited. Many economists still believe, however, that large and persistent gaps can be offset by fiscal policy.

5. Short-term stabilization by fiscal policy operates largely through such automatic stabilizers as tax revenues, which vary directly with national income; expenditures on goods and services, which do not vary with national income; and transfer payments, which vary negatively with national income.

6. Discretionary fiscal policy is also used sometimes to attack large and persistent gaps. It must be reversible; otherwise the economy may overshoot its target once private investment recovers from a temporary slump or falls back from a temporary boom. However, tax changes need to be perceived as relatively long-lived if they are to induce major changes in household spending patterns. (Temporary changes may merely affect the current saving rate and not expenditure.) The need to have tax changes perceived as long-lived, however, conflicts with the need to have fiscal policy easily reversible.

7. Changes in the stance of fiscal policy may be reasonably judged by changes in the structural deficit. This is the balance between revenues and expenditures as they would be if full employment prevailed and with the inflation premium component of interest payments on the national debt netted out.

8. Canadian national debt and debt-service payments have risen and

fallen as a percentage of national income, but they have not shown a long-term trend to grow inexorably. Recent increases in these ratios reflect the cumulative effect of recent large deficits. Persistent deficits are a cause for concern for several reasons, including inflation, crowding out of investment, and reducing national income in the long run.

9. An annually balanced budget would be unfeasible; even if it were possible, it would destabilize the economy. A cyclically balanced budget would act as a stabilizer while also curbing the growth of the government sector. Growth of GDP and some minimal acceptable inflation rate both create room for the average budget balance over the course of the business cycle to show some deficit; a deficit persistently in excess of this can be viewed as imprudent.

10. Keynesians take a relatively sanguine view of the national debt. As long as it does not grow wildly as a proportion of national income, they view its short-term fluctuations and its long-term upward trend in absolute terms as a stabilizing device. Fiscal conservatives mistrust government and view insistence on a balanced budget as the only effective means of curtailing reckless government spending, which wastes scarce resources and feeds the fires of inflation. In an open economy, deficits can cause foreign borrowing and therefore lead to a reduction in living standards in the long run when interest payments are made to foreigners.

Topics for Review

Fiscal policy
Budget balance, balanced budget, budget surplus, and budget deficit
Fine tuning
Built-in stabilizers
Discretionary fiscal policy
The stance of fiscal policy
Actual, cyclically adjusted, and structural budget balances
National debt and debt service
Keynesian and fiscal conservative views of debt

Discussion Questions

1. In 1986, falling world energy prices and collapsing world agricultural markets caused a slowdown in the Canadian economy. The operation of automatic stabilizers in the face of these adverse shocks meant that the deficit would be larger than anticipated, and in addition the government announced an additional one billion dollar discretionary expenditure program to assist farmers. Write a brief critique of the government's decision to let the deficit rise relative to its target path in these circumstances.

2. The Gramm-Rudman-Hollings bill, called the Balanced Budget Act of 1985, passed in the United States Congress, stipulates annual reductions in the federal deficit through 1991, when the budget

must balance. If the targets are not met, the bill mandates specific spending cuts that must be made. It was criticized as arbitrary, unbalanced, mechanical, inflexible, and not credible. On the basis of the analysis in this chapter, write a brief defense of or attack on the bill.

3. As the recovery from the 1982 recession entered its fifth year in 1987, government deficits remained historically large, and concern over them was widespread. Another concern, however, was that in the event of a downturn, emphasis on the deficit might lead to procyclical fiscal policy. Explain how this might happen. Focus on what measure might allow it to be avoided. Should it be avoided?

4. "Fiscal policy has been a relatively weak instrument in Canada because of our heavy dependence on foreign trade and because of the wide regional disparities in employment opportunities." Discuss.

5. Arrange the following in order in terms of the expected size of their effect on aggregate demand and employment.
    a. Government subsidies to farmers of $100 million, financed by an increase in income taxes of $100 million
    b. Government deficit expenditure of $100 million during a recession
    c. Government deficit expenditure of $100 million near the end of a recovery
    d. A general tax cut, costing $100 million in lost revenue to the government

6. Which of the following would be built-in stabilizers?
    a. Food stamps for the needy
    b. Cost of living escalators in government contracts and pensions
    c. Income taxes
    d. Free college tuition for unemployed workers after six months of unemployment, provided that they are under 30 years old and have had five or more years of full-time experience since high school

7. The U.S. Employment Act of 1946 made no explicit mention of price stability as an objective of macroeconomic policy. Why do you suppose this was so? What is the relationship between fiscal policy and the price level?

8. Consider the typical annual expenditures and revenues of the organizations listed below. Comment on the appropriate debt policy for each, taking into account their respective goals, life span, and resources.
    a. Family household
    b. Two private corporations, one growing rapidly and the other a mature firm
    c. A village of 5,000 inhabitants
    d. The Canadian government
    e. The United Nations

9. President Reagan said in 1982, "I don't place very much faith in those various deficit forecasts." Why would the president of the United States be skeptical about deficit forecasts? Does the evidence suggest that this skepticism was misplaced?

10. In his first inaugural address President Franklin D. Roosevelt expounded the doctrine of "sound finance"—that the government's budget should always be balanced. During his term, however, government spending rose faster than taxes, and deficits resulted. How would the effectiveness of the New Deal on employment have been changed if Roosevelt had been successful in keeping the budget balanced throughout his first term?

The Permanent-Income and Life-Cycle Hypotheses of Household Consumption

In the Keynesian theory of the consumption function, current consumption expenditure is related to current income—either current disposable income or current national income. Recent research has produced hypotheses that relate consumption to some longer-term concept of income than the income that the household is currently earning.

The two most influential theories of this type are the **permanent-income hypothesis (PIH)**, developed by 1976 Nobel Laureate Milton Friedman, and the **life-cycle hypothesis (LCH)**, developed by 1985 Nobel Laureate Franco Modigliani and his collaborators. Although there are differences between these hypotheses, it is their similarities that are important. In particular, we note that in both the PIH and the LCH household behavior tends to smooth the time pattern of consumption relative to that of disposable income.

In discussing this "consumption smoothing" issue, it is important to ask: What variables do these theories seek to explain? What assumptions do they make? What are the major implications of these assumptions?

Variables

Three variables need to be considered: consumption, saving, and income. Keynesian-type theories seek to explain the amounts that households spend to purchase goods and services for consumption. This concept is called *consumption expenditure*. Permanent-income theories seek to explain the actual flows of consumption of the *services* that are provided by the commodities that households buy. This concept is called *actual consumption*.[1]

With services and nondurable goods, expenditure and actual consumption occur more or less at the same time, and the distinction between the two concepts is not important. Consumption of a haircut, for example, occurs at the time it is purchased, and an orange or a package of corn flakes is consumed very soon after it is purchased. Thus if we knew purchases of such goods and services at some time, say, last year, we would also know last year's consumption of those goods and services.

But this is not the case with durable consumer goods. A house is purchased at one point in time, but it yields its services over a long time, possibly as long as the purchaser's lifetime. The same is true of a personal computer and a watch and, over a shorter period of time, a car and a dress. For such products, if we know purchases last year, we do not necessarily know last year's consumption of the services that the products yielded.

Thus one important characteristic of durable goods is that *expenditure* to purchase them is not necessarily synchronized with *consumption* of the stream of services that the goods provide. If in 1988 Alice Smith buys a car for $12,000, runs it for six years, and then discards it as worn out, her expen-

---

[1] Because Keynes' followers did not always distinguish carefully between the concepts of consumption expenditure and actual consumption, the word *consumption* is often used in both contexts. We follow this normal practice, but where there is any possible ambiguity in the term, we will refer to *consumption expenditure* or *actual consumption*.

diture on automobiles is $12,000 in 1988 and zero for the next five years. Her consumption of the services of automobiles, however, is spread out at an average annual rate of $2,000 for six years. If everyone followed Alice Smith's example by buying a new car in 1988 and replacing in in 1993, the automobile industry would undergo wild booms in 1988 and 1993 with five intervening years of slump, even though the actual consumption of automobiles would be spread more or less evenly over time. This example is extreme, but it illustrates the possibilities, where consumers' durables are concerned, of quite different time paths of *consumption expenditure*, which is the subject of Keynesian theories of consumption, and *actual consumption*, which is the subject of permanent-income theories.

Now consider saving. The change in emphasis from consumption expenditure to actual consumption implies a change in the definition of saving. Saving is no longer income minus consumption expenditure; it is now income minus the value of actual consumption. When Alice Smith spent $12,000 on her car in 1988 but used only $2,000 worth of its services in that year, she was actually consuming $2,000 and saving $10,000. The purchase of a consumers' durable is thus counted as saving, and only the value of its services actually consumed is counted as consumption.

The third important variable is income. Instead of using current income, the theories use a concept of long-term income. The precise definition varies from one theory to another, but basically it is related to the household's expected income stream over a fairly long planning period. In the LCH it is the income that the household expects to earn over its lifetime, called its *lifetime income*.

Every household is assumed to have a view of its lifetime income. This is not as unreasonable as it might seem. Students training to be doctors have a very different view of expected lifetime income than those training to become schoolteachers. Both expected income streams will be different from that expected by an assembly line worker or a professional athlete. One possible lifetime income stream is shown in Figure 32A-1.

The household's expected lifetime income is then converted into a single figure for *annual* **permanent income**. In the LCH this permanent income is the

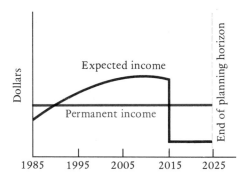

FIGURE 32A-1   Current Income and Permanent Income

Expected current income may vary greatly over a lifetime, but expected permanent income is defined to be the constant annual equivalent. The graph shows a hypothetical expected income stream from work for a household whose planning horizon was 40 years from 1985. The current income rises to a peak, then falls shwoly for a while, and finally falls sharply on retirement. The corresponding permanent income is the amount the household could consume at a steady rate over its lifetime by borrowing early against future earnings (as do most newly married couples), then repaying past debts, and finally saving for retirement when income is at its peak without either incurring debt or accumulating new wealth to be passed on to future generations.

maximum amount the household could spend on consumption each year without accumulating debts that are passed on to future generations. If a household were to consume a constant amount equal to its permanent income each year, it would add to its debts in years when current income was less than permanent income and reduce its debts or increase its assets in years when its current income exceeded its permanent income. Over its lifetime, however, it would just break even, leaving neither accumulated assets nor debts to its heirs. If the interest rate were zero, permanent income would be just the sum of all expected incomes divided by the number of expected years of life.[2] With a positive interest rate,

[2] In the PIH the household has an infinite time horizon and the relevant permanent-income concept is the amount the household could consume forever without increasing or decreasing its present stock of wealth.

permanent income will diverge from this amount because of the costs of borrowing and the extra income that can be earned by investing savings.

Assumption

The basic assumption of this type of theory, whether PIH or LCH, is that the household's actual consumption is related to its permanent rather than its current income. Two households that have the same permanent income (and are similar in other relevant characteristics) will have similar consumption patterns even though their current incomes may behave differently.

Implications

The major implication of these theories is that changes in a household's current income will affect its actual consumption only so far as they affect its permanent income. Consider two income changes that could occur in a household with a permanent income of $20,000 per year and an expected lifetime of 30 or more years. In the first case suppose that the household receives an unexpected extra income of $2,000 *this year only*. The increase in the household's permanent income is small. If the rate of interest were zero, the household could consume an extra $66.66 per year for the rest of its expected life span; with a positive rate of interest, the extra annual consumption would be more because money not spent this year could be invested and would earn interest.[3] In the second case the household gets a toally unforeseen increase of $2,000 a year *for the rest of its life*. In this event the household's permanent income has risen by $2,000 because the household can actually consume $2,000 more every year without accumulating new debts. Although in both cases current income rises by $2,000, the effect on permanent income is very different.

Keynesian theory assumes that *consumption expenditure* is related to current income and therefore predicts the same change in this year's consumption expenditure in each of the cases just discussed. Permanent-income theories relate *actual consumption* to permanent income and therefore predict different changes in actual consumption in each case. In the first case there would be only a small increase in actual annual consumption; in the second there would be a large increase.

In the LCH and the PIH any change in current income that is thought to be temporary will have only a small effect on permanent income and hence on actual consumption.

Implications for the Behavior of the Economy

According to the PIH and the LCH, actual consumption is not much affected by temporary changes in income. Does this mean that aggregate expenditure, $C + I + G + (X - M)$, is not much affected? *Not necessarily.* Consider what happens when households get a temporary increase in their incomes. If actual consumption is not greatly affected by this, households must be saving most of this increase. But from the point of view of these theories, households save when they buy a durable good just as much as when they buy a financial asset such as a stock or a bond. In both cases actual current consumption is not changed.

Thus spending a temporary increase in income on bonds or on new cars is consistent with both the PIH and the LCH. But it makes a great deal of difference to the short-run behavior of the economy which is done. If households buy stocks and bonds, aggregate expenditure on currently produced final goods will not rise when income rises temporarily.[4] If households buy automobiles or any other durable consumer good, aggregate expenditure on currently produced final goods will rise when income rises temporarily. Thus the PIH and the LCH leave unsettled the question that is critical in determining the size of the multiplier: What is the reaction of household *expenditures* on currently produced goods and services, particularly durables, to short-term, temporary changes in income?

---

[3] If the rate of interest were 7 percent, the household could invest the $2,000, consume an extra $161 a year, and have nothing left at the end of 30 years.

[4] Except for such indirect effects as changes in interest rates, or in a dozen other ways.

The PIH and LCH leave unanswered the critical question of the ability of short-term changes in fiscal policy to remove inflationary and recessionary gaps.

Assume, for example, that a serious recessionary gap emerges and that the government attempts to stimulate a recovery by giving tax rebates and by cutting tax rates—both on an announced temporary basis. This will raise households' current disposable incomes by the amount of the tax cuts, but it will raise their permanent incomes by only a small amount. According to the PIH, the flow of actual current consumption should not rise much. Yet it is quite consistent with the PIH that households should spend their tax savings on durable consumer goods, the consumption of which can be spread over many years.

In this case, even though actual consumption this year would not respond much to the tax cuts, expenditure would respond a great deal. Since current output and employment depend on expenditure rather than on actual consumption, the tax cut would be effective in stimulating the economy. However, it is also consistent with both the LCH and the PIH that households spend only a small part of their tax savings on consumption goods and seek to invest the rest in bonds and other financial assets. In this case the tax cuts may have only a small stimulating effect on the economy. It is important to note that the PIH and the LCH do *not* predict unambiguously that changes in taxes that are announced to be only short-lived will be ineffective in removing inflationary or deflationary gaps.

PART NINE

Money, Banking, and Monetary Policy

33

The Nature of Money and Monetary Institutions

What is the significance of money to the economy, and why are economists concerned about it? Indeed, what is money, and how did it come to play its present role?

Many people believe that money is one of the more important things in life and that there is never enough of it. Yet economists argue that increasing the world's money supply would not make the average person better off. The reason is that although money allows its owners to buy someone else's output, the total amount of goods and services available for everyone to buy depends on the total output that is produced, not on the total amount of money that people possess. Increasing the world's money supply would not change the total quantity of goods produced and hence available for consumption, although it would likely cause an inflation.

The Real and Monetary Sectors of the Economy: The Classical Dichotomy

Early in the history of economics, changes in the quantity of money were seen to be associated with changes in the price level. Eighteenth century economists developed the first comprehensive theories in which the economy was conceived of as being divisible into a "real" part and a "monetary" part.

The real sector. In such theories the allocation of resources is determined in the real sector of the economy by demand and supply. This allocation depends on *relative* prices. For example, whether a lot of beef is produced relative to pork depends on the relative prices of beef and pork, not on the money price of either. If the price of beef is higher than the price of pork and both commodities cost about the same to produce, there is an incentive to produce beef rather than pork. At prices of $1 a pound for pork and $3 for beef, the *relative* incentive is the same as it would be at $2 for pork and $6 for beef. As with beef and pork, so it is with all other commodities:

The allocation of resources among different production activities depends on relative prices.

The monetary sector. According to the early economists the price *level* is determined in the monetary sector of the economy. An increase in the money supply leads to an increase in all money prices. In the beef and pork example, an increase in the total money available might raise the price of pork from $1 to $2 a pound and the price of beef from $3 to $6, but in equilibrium it would leave their relative prices unchanged. Hence it would have no effect on the real part of the economy, that is, on the amount of resources allocated to beef and to pork production (or to anything else). If the quantity of money were doubled, the prices of all commodities would double, and money income would also double, so everyone earning an income would be made no better or worse off by the change.

Thus, in equilibrium, the real and the monetary parts of the economy were believed to have no effect on each other. The doctrine that the quantity of money influences the level of money prices but has no effect on the real part of the economy is called the doctrine of the **neutrality of money.**

Because early economists believed that the most important questions—How much does the economy produce? What share of it does each group in the society get?—were answered in the real sector, they spoke of money as a "veil" behind which occurred the real events that affected material well-being.

The modern view.   Modern economists still accept the insights of the early economists that relative prices are a major determinant of the allocation of resources and that the quantity of money has a lot to do with determining the absolute level of prices. They accept the neutrality of money in long-run equilibrium when all forces causing change have fully worked themselves out. We shall see in Chapter 34, however, that most do not accept the neutrality of money when the economy is undergoing change from day to day, that is, when the economy is not in a state of long-run equilibrium.

In this chapter we look first at the experience of price level changes—one aspect of the importance of money—and then at the nature of money itself and the operation of the modern institutions that comprise the monetary system of our economy.

Historical Experience

In Chapter 26 (on pages 552–553) we discussed some important introductory material related to the price level and changes in it (inflations and deflations). That material should be reviewed at this stage. In the figures in this chapter we present some further details of the behavior of the price levels over very long periods of time. Figure 33-1 shows the course of producer (or wholesale) prices in Canada from 1867 through 1986. Considerable year-to-year fluctuations are apparent. Despite large fluctuations in the nineteenth century, the price trend during that period was neither upward nor downward. In contrast, so far the twentieth century has seen both large fluctuations *and* a distinct rising trend in the price level.

Although admittedly a long time, even two centuries may still not be enough to give a clear perspective of very long term price fluctuations. The experience of the period since 1946 looks much more dramatic and unusual when compared only with the nineteenth century than when considered in longer perspective. For an indication of the longer-term course of price levels, we can look across the Atlantic. Figure 33-2 (page 711) shows the course of the price level in England over seven centuries. It shows that there was an overall inflationary trend but that it was by no means evenly spread over the centuries.

The Nature of Money

Inflation is a monetary phenomenon in the sense that a rise in the general level of prices is the same thing as a decrease in the purchasing power of money. But what exactly is money? Probably more folklore and general nonsense are believed about money than about any other aspect of the economy. In this section we describe the functions of money and briefly outline its history. One purpose of this account is to remove some of these misconceptions. In addition, the recent revival of interest in the gold standard makes some discussion of early monetary systems relevant.

What Is Money?

Traditionally in economics **money** has been defined as any generally accepted medium of exchange. A **medium of exchange** is anything that will be accepted by virtually everyone in a society in exchange for goods and services. But money is more than that.

FIGURE 33-1   Index of Canadian Wholesale Prices, 1867–1986

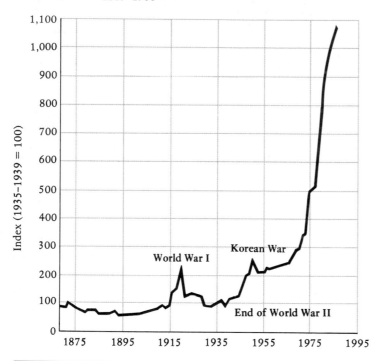

Persistent peacetime inflation is only a recent problem in Canada. Although the price level has fluctuated throughout Canadian history, no long-term trend was visible during the period from confederation to 1940. From the time of World War II to the present, the price level has shown a consistent upward trend. (*Source:* Statistics Canada, Industrial Price Index, 62–0112.)

Money has several functions. It acts as a medium of exchange, as a store of value, and as a unit of account.

Different kinds of money vary in the degree of efficiency with which they fulfill these functions, and different definitions of money may be required for different purposes.

A Medium of Exchange

If there were no money, goods would have to be exchanged by barter, one good being swapped directly for another. We discussed this cumbersome system in Chapter 3. The major difficulty with barter is that each transaction requires a *double coincidence of wants.* For an exchange to occur between A and B, not only must A have what B wants, but B must have what A wants. If all exchange were restricted to barter, anyone who specialized in producing one commodity would have to spend a great deal of time searching for satisfactory transactions.

The use of money as a medium of exchange removes these problems. People can sell their output for money and subsequently use the money to buy what they wish from others. The double coincidence of wants is unnecessary when a medium of exchange is used.

Without money the economic system, which is based on specialization and the division of labor, could not function, and we would have to return to primitive forms of production and exchange. It is not without justification that money has been called one of the great inventions contributing to human freedom.

To serve as an efficient medium of exchange, money must have a number of characteristics. It must be readily acceptable. It must have a high value relative to its weight (otherwise it would be a nuisance to carry around). It must be divisible, because

FIGURE 33-2 A Price Index of Consumables in Southern England, 1275–1959

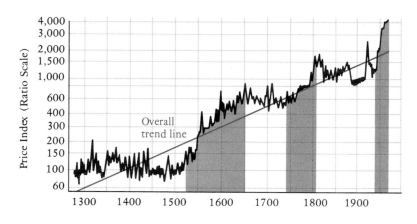

Over the past seven centuries long **periods of stable prices have alternated with long periods of rising prices.** This remarkable price series shows an index of the prices of food, clothing, and fuel in southern England from 1275 through 1959. The trend line shows that the average change in prices over the whole period was 0.5 percent per year. The shaded areas indicate periods of unreversed inflation. The series also shows that even the perspective of a century can be misleading because long periods of stable or gently falling prices tended to alternate with long periods of rising prices. (*Source: Lloyds Bank Review*, No. 58, October 1960.)

money that comes only in large denominations is useless for transactions having only a small value. It must not be readily counterfeitable, because if money can be easily duplicated by individuals, it will lose its value.

A Store of Value

Money is a convenient way to store purchasing power; goods may be sold today and money stored until it is needed. The money provides a claim on someone else's goods that can be exercised at a future date. The two sides of the transaction can be separated in time with the obvious increase in freedom that this confers.

To be a satisfactory store of value, however, money must have a relatively stable value. When the price level is stable, the purchasing power of a given sum of money is also stable. When the price level changes, this is not so. Such changes undermine the usefulness of money as a store of value. An extreme example is discussed in Box 33-1.

Although money can serve as a satisfactory store of accumulated purchasing power for a single individual, it cannot do so for the society as a whole. If a single individual accumulates a pile of dollars, he or she will, when the time comes to spend it, be able to command the current output of some other individual. The whole society cannot do this. If all individuals were to save their money and then retire simultaneously to live on their savings, there would be no current production to purchase and consume. The society's ability to satisfy wants depends on goods and services being available; if some of this want-satisfying capacity is to be stored up for the whole society, goods that are currently producible must be left unconsumed and carried over to future periods.

A Unit of Account

Money may also be used purely for accounting purposes without having a physical existence of its own. For instance, a government store in a truly communist society might say that everyone had so many "dollars" to use each month. Goods could then be assigned prices and each consumer's purchases recorded, the consumer being allowed to buy until the allocated supply of dollars was exhausted. These dollars need have no existence other than as entries in the store's books, yet they would serve as a perfectly satisfactory unit of account.

Whether they could also serve as a medium of exchange between individuals depends on whether

BOX 33-1

Hyperinflation

Can the price level ever rise so rapidly that money loses its usefulness either as a medium of exchange or as a store of value? The answer appears to be that very occasionally this has happened. Inflation rates of 50, 100, and even 200 percent or more a year have occurred year after year and proven manageable as people adjust their contracts to real terms. While there are strains and side effects, the evidence shows such situations to be possible without causing money to become useless.

Does this mean that there is no reason to fear that rapid inflation will turn into hyperinflation that will destroy the value of money completely? The historical record is not entirely reassuring. There have been a number of instances where prices began to rise at an ever-accelerating rate until the nation's money ceased to be a satisfactory store of value even for the short period between receipt and expenditure and hence ceased also to be useful as a medium of exchange.

Consider the index of wholesale prices in Germany during and after World War I given in the table. The index shows that a good purchased with one 100-mark note in July 1923 would have required *10 million* 100-mark notes for its purchase only four months later! While Germany had experienced substantial inflation during World War I, averaging more than 30 percent per year, the immediate postwar years of 1920 and 1921 gave no sign of an explosive inflation. Indeed, during 1920 price stability was experienced. But in 1922 and 1923, the price level exploded. On November 15, 1923, the mark was officially repudiated, its value wholly destroyed. How could this happen?

When an inflation becomes so rapid that people lose confidence in the purchasing power of their currency, they rush to spend it. But people who have goods become increasingly reluctant to accept the rapidly depreciating money in exchange. The rush to spend money accelerates the increase in prices until people finally become unwilling to accept money on any terms. What was once money ceases to be money.

Date		German wholesale price index (1913 = 1)
January	1913	1
January	1920	13
January	1921	14
January	1922	37
July	1922	101
January	1923	2,785
July	1923	74,800
August	1923	944,000
September	1923	23,900,000
October	1923	7,096,000,000
November	1923*	750,000,000,000

* The mark was repudiated on November 15, 1923.

The price system can then be restored only by repudiation of the old monetary unit and its replacement by a new unit. This destroys the value of monetary savings and of all contracts specified in terms of the old monetary units. It wipes out many people's savings by destroying the value of assets denominated in money terms.

There are about a dozen documented hyperinflations in world history, among them the collapse of the continental during the American Revolution, the ruble during the Russian Revolution, the drachma during and after the German occupation of Greece in World War II, the pengö in Hungary during 1945 and 1946, and the Chinese national currency during 1946–1948. Every one of these hyperinflations was accompanied by great increases in the money supply; new money was printed to give governments purchasing power they could not or would not obtain by taxation. And every one occurred in the midst of a major political upheaval in which grave doubts existed about the stability and future of the government itself.

Is hyperinflation likely in the absence of civil war, revolution, or collapse of the government? Most economists think not. And it is clear that high inflation rates over a period of time do not mean the inevitable or even likely onset of a hyperinflation, however serious the distributive and social effects of such rates may be.

the store would agree to transfer dollar credits from one customer to another at the customer's request. Banks will transfer dollars credited to demand deposits in this way, and thus a bank deposit can serve as both a unit of account and a medium of exchange. Notice that the use of *dollars* in this context suggests a further sense in which money is a unit of account. People think about values in terms of the monetary unit with which they are familiar.

Another related function of money is sometimes distinguished. It can be used as a standard of deferred payments. Payments that are to be made in the future, on account of debts and so on, are reckoned in money. Money is used as a unit of account with the added dimension of time because the account will not be settled until later.

The Origins of Money

The origins of money are lost in antiquity; most primitive tribes known today make some use of it. The ability of money to free people from the cumbersome necessity of barter must have led to its early use as soon as some generally acceptable commodity appeared.

Metallic Money

All sorts of commodities have been used as money at one time or another, but gold and silver proved to have great advantages. They were precious because their supply was relatively limited, and they were in constant demand by the rich for ornament and decoration. Also, they do not easily wear out. Thus they tended to have a high and stable price. They were easily recognized and generally known to be commodities that, because of their stable price, would be readily accepted. They were also divisible into extremely small units.

Precious metals thus came to circulate as money and to be used in many transactions. Before the invention of coins it was necessary to carry the metals in bulk. When a purchase was made, the requisite quantity of the metal was carefully weighed on a scale. A sack of gold and a highly accurate set of scales were the common equipment of the merchant and trader.

The invention of coinage eliminated the need to weigh the metal at each transaction. The prince or ruler weighed the metal and made a coin out of it to which he affixed his own seal to guarantee the amount of precious metal it contained. If a coin was certified to contain exactly 1/16 of an ounce of gold and a commodity was priced at 1/8 of an ounce of gold, two coins could be given over without weighing the gold. This was clearly a great convenience as long as traders knew they could accept the coin at its "face value." The face value was nothing more than a statement that a certain weight of metal was contained therein.

Abuses of metallic money. The ruler's subjects, however, could not let a good opportunity pass. Someone soon had the idea of clipping a thin slice off the edge of the coin. If he collected a coin stamped as containing half an ounce of gold, he could clip a slice off the edge and pass the coin off as still containing half an ounce of gold. ("Doesn't the stamp prove it?" he would argue.) If he got away with this, he would have made a profit equal to the market value of the clipped metal.

Whenever this practice became common, even the most myopic traders noticed that things were not what they seemed in the coinage world. It became necessary to weigh each coin before accepting it at its face value; out came the scales again, and most of the usefulness of coins was lost. To get around this problem, the idea arose of minting the coins with a rough edge. The absence of the rough edge would immediately be apparent and would indicate that the coin had been clipped. The practice, called milling, survives on some coins as an interesting anachronism to remind us that there were days when the market value of the metal in the coin (if it were melted down) was equal to the face value of the coin.

Debasement of metallic money. Not to be outdone by the cunning of their subjects, the rulers were quick to seize the chance of getting something for nothing. The power to mint placed rulers in a good position to work a *really* profitable fraud. When faced with debts that could not be paid or repudiated, rulers merely used some suitable occasion—a marriage, an anniversary, an alliance—to remint the coinage. Subjects would be ordered to bring their gold coins into the mint to be melted down and coined afresh with a new stamp. The subjects could then go away with one new coin for every old coin they had brought in. Between the melting down and the re-coining, however, the rulers had only to toss some inexpensive base metal in with the molten gold to earn a handsome profit. If the coinage were debased by adding, say, 1 pound of new base metal to every 4 pounds of old coins, five coins would be made for every four turned in. For every four coins brought in, the rulers could return four and have one left as profit with which to pay off debts.

Since gold and silver are softer and more malleable than most base metals, an experienced trader could usually tell if a coin had been seriously debased by testing its hardness. This is why, in films depicting ancient markets, you will often see a merchant biting a coin to see how easily it could be bent.

The result of debasement was inflation. The subjects had the same number of coins as before and hence could demand the same quantity of goods. When rulers paid their bills, however, the recipients of the extra coins could be expected to spend some or all of them, and this caused a net increase in demand. The extra demand would bid up prices. Debasing the coinage thus led to a rise in prices.

It was the experience of such inflations that led early economists to propound the *quantity theory of money and prices*. They argued that there was a relation between the average level of prices and the quantity of money in circulation, such that an increase in the quantity of money would lead to a proportionate increase in the price level. (We shall have more to say about this theory in Chapter 34.)

Gresham's law.   The early experience of currency debasement led to the observation known as **Gresham's law** after the Elizabethan financial expert Sir Thomas Gresham. Gresham's hypothesis that "bad money drives out good" has stood the test of time.

When Queen Elizabeth I of England first came to the throne in the middle of the sixteenth century, the coinage had been severely debased. Seeking to help trade, Elizabeth minted new coins containing their full face value in gold. But as fast as she fed these new coins into circulation, they disappeared.

Why? Gresham reasoned as follows to the young queen.

Suppose that you possessed one new and one old coin, each with the same face value, and had a bill to pay. What would you do? Clearly, you would pay the bill with the debased coin and keep the undebased one. You part with less gold that way. Suppose that you wanted to obtain a certain amount of gold bullion by melting down the gold coins (as was frequently done). Which coins would you use? Clearly, you would use new, undebased coins because you would part with less "face value" that way. The debased coins would thus remain in circulation and the undebased coins would disappear. Whenever people got hold of an undebased coin, they would hold on to it; whenever they got a debased coin, they would pass it on. The example in Box 33-2 shows that Gresham's law is as applicable in the twentieth century as it was in the sixteenth century.

Paper Money

The next important step in the history of money was the evolution of paper currency. Artisans who worked with gold required secure safes, and the public began to deposit their gold with such goldsmiths for safekeeping. Goldsmiths would give their depositors receipts promising to hand over the gold on demand. When any depositor wished to make a large purchase, she could go to her goldsmith, reclaim some of her gold, and hand it over to the seller of the goods. If the seller had no immediate need for the gold, he would carry it back to the goldsmith for safekeeping.

If people knew the goldsmith to be reliable, there was no need to go through the cumbersome and risky business of physically transferring the gold. The buyer need only transfer the goldsmith's receipt to the seller, who would accept it, secure in the knowledge that the goldsmith would pay over the gold whenever it was needed. If the seller wished to buy a good from a third party, who also knew the goldsmith to be reliable, this transaction, too, could be effected by passing the goldsmith's receipt from the buyer to the seller. The convenience of using pieces of paper instead of gold is obvious.

Thus, when it first came into being, paper money

BOX 33-2

Where Has All the Coinage Gone?

Tourists traveling in Chile in the 1970s (and in other countries with rapid inflation) often wondered aloud why paper currency was used even for transactions as small as the purchase of a newspaper or a pack of matches. Metallic currency in such places was scarce and sometimes nonexistent. Similarly, the silver dollar, silver half-dollar, silver quarter, and silver dime have disappeared from circulation in North America. The reason for these things is an example of Gresham's law.

Consider a country that has three different "tokens," each of them legal tender in the amount of $0.25. One is a silver quarter with $0.10 worth of recoverable silver in it; a second is made of cheaper metals with $0.05 worth of recoverable metal in it; the third is a $0.25 bill, a brightly colored piece of paper money that says plainly on its face "legal tender for all debts public and private."

If prices are stable and the government produces all three forms of money, there is no reason why they should not all circulate freely and interchangeably. Each is legal tender, and each is worth more as money than as anything else.

However, suppose an inflation starts and prices—including, proportionally, the prices of silver and other metals—begin to rise sharply. By the time prices have tripled, the silver quarters will have disappeared because the silver in each one is now worth $0.30, and people will hoard them or melt them down rather than spend them to buy goods priced at only $0.25. While not everyone will do this, coins passing from hand to hand will eventually reach someone who withdraws them from circulation.

What about the coins made of cheaper metal? Since prices have tripled, they now contain metal worth $0.15, still less than their face value. Will they too disappear? They will if there is further inflation of, say, 100 percent. This raises the market value of the metal in the coin above its face value. The coins will disappear as they are melted down. By that time, only the paper money will be in circulation. The "bad" paper money will have driven out the "good" metal money.

Thus inflation may make some money "good" and some "bad" in Gresham's sense. If it does, the bad will displace the good.

---

was a promise to pay on demand so much gold, the promise being made first by goldsmiths and later by banks. Banks, too, became known for their vaults ("safes") where the precious gold was stored and protected. As long as the institutions were known to be reliable, their pieces of paper would be "as good as gold." Such paper money was *backed* by precious metal and was *convertible* on demand into this metal. When a country's money is convertible into gold, the country is said to be on a *gold standard.*

In nineteenth century Canada private banks operating initially under provincial charters commonly issued paper money nominally convertible into gold. **Bank notes** represented banks' promises to pay. They remained an important part of the money supply well into the current century, and they were not completely supplanted by government-issued paper money until 1950.

Fractionally backed paper money. For most transactions individuals were content to use paper currency. It was soon discovered that it was not necessary to keep an ounce of gold in the vaults for every claim to an ounce circulating as paper money. It was necessary to keep some gold on hand because paper would not do for some transactions. If someone wished to make a purchase from a distant place where her local bank was not known, she might have to convert her paper into gold and ship the gold. Further, she might not have perfect confidence in the bank's ability to honor its pledge to redeem the notes in gold at a future time. Her alternative was to exchange her notes for gold and store the gold until she needed it.

For these and other reasons, some holders of notes demanded gold in return for their notes. However, some of the bank's customers received gold in various transactions and stored it in the bank for safekeeping. They accepted promises to pay (i.e., bank notes) in return. At any one time, then, some of the bank's customers would be withdrawing gold, others would be depositing it, and most would be trading in the bank's paper notes without any need or desire to convert them into gold. Thus the bank was able to issue more money redeemable in gold than the amount of gold held in its vaults. This was good business, because the money could be profitably invested in interest-earning loans to households and firms.

This discovery was made by the early goldsmiths. From that time to the present, banks have had many more claims outstanding against them than they actually had in reserves available to pay those claims. We say that the currency issued in such a situation is *fractionally backed* by the reserves.

In the past the major problem of a fractionally backed, convertible currency was maintaining its convertibility into the precious metal backing it. The imprudent bank that issued too much paper money found itself unable to redeem its currency in gold when the demand for gold was even slightly higher than usual. It would then have to suspend payments, and all holders of its notes would suddenly find the notes worthless. The prudent bank, which kept a reasonable relation between its note issue and its gold reserve, found that it could meet a normal range of demand for gold without any trouble.

If the public lost confidence and en masse demanded redemption of their currency, the banks would be unable to honor their pledges. The history of nineteenth and early twentieth century banking on both sides of the Atlantic is full of examples of banks ruined by "panics," sudden runs on their gold reserves. When this happened the banks' depositors and the holders of their notes would find themselves with worthless pieces of paper.

Central banks were a natural outcome of this sort of banking system. Where were the commercial banks to turn when they had good investments but were in temporary need of cash? If they provided loans for the public against reasonable security, why should not some other institution provide loans to them against the same sort of security? Central banks evolved in response to such needs.

Fiat currencies.   As time went on, note issue by private banks became less common and central banks took control of the currency. Central banks in turn became governmental institutions. In time *only* central banks were permitted to issue notes.

Originally the central banks issued currency that was fully convertible into gold. In those days gold would be brought to the central bank, which would issue currency in the form of "gold certificates" that asserted the gold was available on demand. The gold supply thus set some upper limit on the amount of currency. But central banks could issue more currency than they had gold because not all of the currency was presented for payment at any one time. Thus even under a gold standard, central banks had substantial discretionary control over the quantity of currency outstanding.

During the period between World Wars I and II, almost all the countries of the world abandoned the gold standard; their currencies were no longer convertible into gold. Money that is not convertible by law into anything valuable depends on its acceptability for its value. Money that is declared by government order, or fiat, to be legal tender for settlement of all debts is called a **fiat money.** Some issues raised by the abandoning of the gold standard are discussed in Box 33-3.

Today almost all currency is fiat money.

Some countries (including the United States until 1968) preserve the fiction that their currency is backed by gold, but no country allows its currency to be converted into gold on demand. Gold backing for Canadian currency was eliminated in 1940, although note issues continued to carry the traditional statement "will pay to the bearer on demand" until 1954. The holder of a $20 bill who took this seriously and demanded $20 could hand over the $20 bill and receive in return a different but identical $20 bill! Today's Bank of Canada notes simply say, "This note is legal tender." It is, in other words, fiat money pure and simple.

Legal tender is anything that by law must be accepted when offered either for the purchase of goods or services or to discharge a debt. If you are offered something that is legal tender in payment for

BOX 33-3

Should Currency Be Backed by Gold?

The gold standard imposed an upper limit on the quantity of convertible currency that could be issued. Now that the system has been abandoned, does it matter that the central bank is not limited to its ability to issue currency?

Gold derives its value because it is scarce relative to the demand for it (the demand being derived from its monetary and its nonmonetary uses). Tying a currency to gold meant that the quantity of money in a country was determined by such chance occurrences as the discovery of new gold supplies. This was not without advantages, the most important being that it provided a check on governments' ability to cause inflation. Gold cannot be manufactured at will; paper currency can.

There is little doubt that in the past, if the money supply had been purely paper, many governments would have attempted to pay their bills by printing new money rather than by raising taxes. Such increases in the money supply, in periods of full employment, would lead to inflation in the same way that the debasement of metallic currency did.

Thus the gold standard provided some check on inflation by making it difficult for the government to change the money supply. Periods of major gold discoveries, however, brought about inflations of their own. In the 1500s, for example, Spanish gold and silver flowed into Europe from the New World, bringing inflation in their wake.

A major problem caused by a reliance on gold is that although it is usually desirable to increase the money supply when real national income is increasing, this cannot be done on a gold standard unless, by pure chance, gold is discovered at the same time. The gold standard took discretionary powers over the money supply out of the hands of government. Whether or not one thinks this is a good thing depends on how one thinks governments would use this discretion.

In general, a gold standard is probably better than having the currency managed by an ignorant or irresponsible government, but it is worse than having the currency supply adjusted by a well-informed and intelligent one. *Better* and *worse* in this context are judged by the criterion of having a money supply that varies adequately with the needs of the economy but does not vary so as to cause violent inflations or deflations.

---

a debt and you refuse to accept it, the debt is no longer legally collectible.

Not only is our modern currency fiat money, so is our coinage. Modern coins, unlike their historical ancestors, contain a value of metal that is characteristically a minute fraction of the value of the coin. Modern coins, like modern paper money, are merely tokens.

Why Is Fiat Money Valuable?

Today paper money and coinage are valuable because they are generally accepted. Because everyone accepts them as valuable, they *are* valuable; the fact that they can no longer be converted into anything has no effect on their functioning as a medium of exchange.

In the early days of the gold standard, paper money was valuable because everyone believed it was convertible into gold on demand. Experience during periods of crisis, when there was often a temporary suspension of convertibility into gold, and of panic, when there were bank failures, served to demonstrate that the mere *promise* of convertibility was not sufficient to make money valuable. Gradually the realization grew that neither was convertibility necessary.

Fiat money is valuable when it will be accepted in payment for goods and for debts.

Many people are disturbed to learn that present-day paper money is neither backed by nor convertible into anything more valuable—that it consists of nothing but pieces of paper whose value derives from common acceptance and from confidence that it will continue to be accepted in the future. Most people believe their money should be more substantial than that; after all, what of "dollar diplomacy" and the "bedrock solidity" of the Swiss franc? But money is in fact made of nothing more than pieces of paper. There is no point in pretending otherwise.

If paper money is acceptable, it is a medium of exchange; if its purchasing power remains stable, it is a satisfactory store of value; and if both of these things are true, it will also serve as a satisfactory unit of account.

Modern Money

By the twentieth century private banks had lost the authority to issue bank notes. Yet they did not lose the power to create deposit money.

Deposit Money

Banks' customers frequently deposit coins and paper money with the banks for safekeeping, just as in former times they deposited gold. Such a deposit is recorded as an entry on the customer's account. A customer who wishes to pay a debt may come to the bank and claim the money in dollars, then pay the money to another person. This person may then redeposit the money in a bank.

Like the gold transfers, this is a tedious procedure, particularly for large payments. It is more convenient to have the bank transfer claims to this money on deposit. The common cheque is an instruction to the bank to make the transfer. Such transfers soon became easy and inexpensive, and cheques soon became widely accepted in payment for commodities and debts. The deposits became a form of money called **deposit money,** defined as money held by the public in the form of deposits in banks that can be withdrawn on demand.

When individual A deposits $100 in a bank, the bank credits A's account with $100. This is the bank's promise to pay $100 cash on demand. If A pays B $100 by writing a cheque that B then deposits in the same bank, the bank merely reduces A's account by $100 and increases B's by the same amount. Thus the bank still promises to pay on demand the $100 originally deposited, but it now promises to pay it

to B rather than to A. What makes all this so convenient is that B can actually deposit A's cheque in any bank, and the banks will arrange the transfer of credits.

Cheques are in some ways the modern equivalent of old-time bank notes issued by commercial banks. The passing of a bank note from hand to hand transferred ownership of a claim against the bank. A cheque on a deposit account is similarly an order to the bank to pay the designated recipient, rather than oneself, money credited to the account. Cheques, unlike bank notes, do not circulate freely from hand to hand; thus cheques themselves are not currency. The balance in the demand deposit *is* money; the cheque transfers money from one person to another. Because cheques are easily drawn and deposited and because they are relatively safe from theft, they are widely used. Over 6 billion cheques a year are now drawn in Canada. During the past decade the number of cheques drawn increased at about 7 percent per year.

Thus, when chartered banks lost the right to issue notes of their own, the form of bank money changed but the substance did not. Today banks have money in their vaults (or on deposit with the central banks) just as they always did. Once it was gold; today it is the legal tender of the times—fiat money. It is true today, just as in the past, that most of the bank's customers are content to pay their bills by passing among themselves the bank's promises to pay money on demand. Only a small proportion of the transactions made by the bank's customers is made in cash.

Bank deposits are money. Today, just as in the past, banks can create money by issuing more promises to pay (deposits) than they have cash reserves available to pay out.

The Banking System

Many types of institutions make up a modern banking system such as exists in Canada today. The **central bank** is the government-owned and -operated institution that serves to control the banking system. Through it, the government's monetary policy is conducted. In Canada the central bank is the Bank of Canada; we study it in detail in Chapter 35. *Financial intermediaries* are privately owned institutions that serve the general public. They are called intermediaries because they stand between savers, from whom they accept deposits, and investors, to whom they make loans. In this chapter we focus on an important class of financial intermediaries, the *chartered banks*.

Modern commercial banking systems are of two main types. One type has a small number of banks, each with a large number of branch offices; the other consists of many independent banks. The banking systems of Britain and Canada are of the first type, with only a few banks accounting for the overwhelming bulk of the business. The American system is of the second type. The functioning of the banking system is, however, essentially the same in both systems.

The Canadian System

The Canadian banking system is controlled by the provisions of the Bank Act, first passed in 1935 and revised several times since. Under the Bank Act charters can be granted to financial institutions to operate as banks, and up until 1980 there were only a few chartered banks, most of which were very large and each of which operated under identical regulatory provisions. (In 1980 there were only 11 chartered banks, and the five largest together held more than 90 percent of total chartered bank assets.)

The 1980 revisions to the Bank Act allowed for foreign banks to commence operations in Canada, although it limited severely the scale and scope of their activity. Subsequent revisions have altered some of these restrictions and made it easier to obtain new banking charters, but the revisions have maintained the distinction between these newer institutions and banks operating under what are essentially the pre-1980 provisions of the Bank Act. The original provisions, in slightly modified form, are now known as Schedule A of the Bank Act; the foreign banks and the new, smaller domestic banks operate under Schedules B and C. The term **chartered banks** is used to refer to the Schedule A banks.

The chartered banks have common attributes:

They hold deposits for their customers; they permit certain deposits to be transferred by cheque from an individual account to other accounts held in any bank branch in the country; they make loans to households and firms; and they invest in government securities.

Banks are not the only financial institutions in the country. Many other privately owned, profit-seeking institutions, such as trust companies, mortgage loan companies, and credit unions, accept savings deposits and grant loans for specific purposes. Finance companies make loans to households for practically any purpose—sometimes at very high effective interest rates. The post office and the telegraph system will transfer money, and credit card companies will extend credit so that purchases can be made on a buy-now, pay-later basis.

The chartered banks (including Schedule B and C banks) are subject only to federal regulations and are required to hold reserves with the Bank of Canada against their deposit liabilities. Other institutions do not face reserve requirements, but most are subject to various federal and provincial regulations concerning ownership and control and the types of financial activities they are allowed to engage in. Thus there are differences among all types of financial institutions, not just between banks and others.

The chartered banks have historically been such a stable and dominant group that the terms *chartered banks* and *banking system* have been considered virtually synonymous. However, recent events may serve to break this identification. First, there have been dramatic changes in the makeup of the chartered banks—in 1985 two relatively new, regionally based chartered banks failed, and in 1986 two other chartered banks merged and yet two others were taken over by foreign banks. Second, the federal government and several provincial governments have recently proposed extensive changes in regulations, including the abolition of reserve requirements for the chartered banks, that would further blur the distinction between the chartered banks and other financial institutions.

Interbank Activities

Chartered banks have a number of interbank cooperative relationships. For example, banks often share loans. Even the biggest bank cannot meet all the credit needs of a giant corporation, and often a group of banks will offer a "pool loan," agreeing on common terms and dividing the loan up into manageable segments.

Another form of interbank cooperation is the bank credit card. Visa and MasterCard are the two most widely used credit cards, and each is operated by a group of banks.

Probably the most important form of interbank cooperation is cheque clearing and collection. Bank deposits are an effective medium of exchange only because banks accept each other's cheques. If a depositor in bank X writes a cheque to someone who deposits it in bank Y, bank X now owes money to bank Y. This creates a need for the banks to present cheques to each other for payment.

There are millions of such transactions in the course of a day, and they result in an enormous sorting and bookkeeping job. Multibank systems make use of a **clearing house** where interbank debts are settled. At the end of the day, all the cheques drawn by bank X's customers and deposited in bank Y are totaled and set against the total of all the cheques drawn by bank Y's customers and deposited in bank X. It is necessary only to settle the difference between the two sums. The actual cheques are passed through the clearing house back to the bank on which they were drawn. Both banks are then able to adjust the individual accounts by a set of book entries. A flow of cash between banks is necessary only when there is a net transfer of cash from the customers of one bank to those of another. This flow of cash is accomplished by a transfer of deposits held by the chartered banks with the Bank of Canada.

Profit Seeking

Banks are private firms that start with invested capital and seek to "earn money" in the same sense as firms making neckties or bicycles. A chartered bank provides a variety of services to its customers: a safe place to store money; the convenience of demand deposits that can be transferred by personal cheque; a safe and convenient place to earn a modest but guaranteed return on savings; and often financial advice and estate management services. The bank earns

some revenue by charging for these services, but such fees are a small part of the bank's total earnings. The largest part (typically about five-sixths) of a bank's earnings is derived from the bank's ability to invest profitably the funds placed with it.

Principal Assets and Liabilities

Table 33-1 is the combined balance sheet of the chartered banks in Canada. The bulk of a bank's liabilities are deposits owed to its depositors. The principal assets of a bank are the *securities* it buys (including government bonds), which pay interest or dividends, and the *loans* it makes to individuals and to businesses. A bank loan is a liability to the borrower (who must pay it back) but an asset to the bank. The bank expects not only to have the loan repaid but also to receive interest that more than compensates for the paperwork involved and the risk of nonpayment.

Most money deposited with banks is "at work," having been invested in loans or securities. Deposits are the lifeblood of a chartered bank. Without them the bank has nothing to lend or invest except the small amount of its initial capital. Banks attract deposits by paying interest to depositors and by providing them, for a fee that does not cover the banks' full cost, with services such as clearing cheques and providing regular monthly statements. Banks earn profits by lending and investing money deposited with them for more than they pay their depositors in terms of interest and other services provided.

Reserves

The Need for Reserves

All bankers would as a matter of convenience and prudence keep sufficient cash on hand to be able to meet depositors' day-to-day requirements for cash. But just as the goldsmiths of old discovered that only a fraction of the gold they held was ever withdrawn at any given time, and just as banks of old discovered that only a fraction of convertible bank notes were actually converted, so, too, have modern banks discovered that only a fraction of their deposits will be

TABLE 33-1   Consolidated Balance Sheet of Canadian Chartered Banks, December 31, 1986 *(billions of dollars)*

Assets		Liabilities	
Reserves (including deposits with Bank of Canada)	8	Deposits: Demand	19
Loans (determined in Canadian dollars)	182	Savings	129
Government of Canada securities	20	Time	46
Foreign-currency assets	207	Foreign-currency liabilities	207
Other assets	51	Other liabilities	46
	468	Capital account	21
			468

Source: Bank of Canada Review.

Reserves are only a small fraction of deposit liabilities. If all the bank's customers who held demand deposits tried to withdraw them in cash, the banks could not meet this demand without liquidating $11 billion of other assets. This would be impossible without assistance from the Bank of Canada.

withdrawn in cash at any one time. Most deposits of any individual bank remain on deposit with it; thus an individual bank need keep only fractional reserves against its deposits.

The reserves needed to assure that depositors can withdraw their deposits on demand is quite small in normal times.

In abnormal times, however, nothing short of 100 percent might do the job if the commercial banking system had to stand alone. When a few bank failures cause a general loss of confidence in banks' ability to redeem their deposits, the results can be devastating. Until relatively recent times, such an event—or even the rumor of it—could lead to a "run" on banks as depositors rushed to withdraw their money. Faced with such a panic, banks would have to close until they had borrowed funds or liquidated enough assets to meet the demand or until the demand subsided. But banks could not instantly turn their loans into cash since the borrowers had the money tied up in such things as real estate or business enterprises. Neither could the banks obtain cash by selling their securities to the public since payments would be made by cheques, which would not provide cash with which to pay off depositors.

To avoid panics reserves must be large enough to meet extraordinary demands for cash.

The need of the banking system for reserves against depositors' panics has been diminished by government policies. First, the central bank can provide chartered banks with needed cash either by lending them money or by buying the securities they want to sell. Second, the government provides insurance that guarantees that depositors will get their money back even if a bank fails completely. Such insurance decreases the likelihood of a widespread panic because one bank's failure is much less likely to lead to a run on other banks. Most depositors will not withdraw their money as long as they are *sure* they can get it when they need it.

Actual and Required Reserves

As Table 33-1 shows, in 1986 only a fraction of the total major assets of the chartered banks consisted of cash and interest-earning assets that could quickly be converted into cash. Cash reserves are held in the form of deposits in the Bank of Canada and notes. All banks need to keep some reserves of cash to satisfy their depositors' day-to-day requirements. The Canadian banking system is a **fractional reserve system,** with banks holding reserves of only a fraction of their deposits. The size of the reserve reflects not only the judgment of bankers but also the legal requirements imposed by the Bank Act.

A bank's **reserve ratio** is the fraction of its deposits that it holds as reserves either as currency in its vaults or as deposits with the central bank. Reserves that the banks are required to hold under the Bank Act are called **required reserves.** Any reserves that a bank holds over and above required reserves are called **excess reserves.** Since 1980 the required reserve ratios have been 10 percent for demand deposits and 4 percent for term deposits.

Most liquid assets are held in the form of bonds and treasury bills (government securities with usual terms to maturity of three or six months) issued by the government of Canada. These assets generally yield a lower rate of return than loans, but they act as **secondary reserves** that can be used to replenish cash holdings should they be run down.

Central Banks

All advanced free-market economies have a central bank. Many of the world's early central banks were private, profit-making institutions that provided services to ordinary banks. Their importance, however, led them to develop close ties with the government. Central banks soon became instruments of the government, though not all of them were publicly owned. The Bank of England (the "Old Lady of Threadneedle Street"), one of the world's oldest and most famous central banks, began to operate as the central bank of England in the seventeenth century but was not "nationalized" until 1947. In the United States the central bank is called the Federal Reserve System (popularly known as the Fed), and in this country it is the Bank of Canada.

The similarities of central banks in the functions they perform and the tools they use are much more important than their differences in organization. Although our attention is focused on the operations of the Bank of Canada, the basic situation is not different for the Bank of England, the Bank of Greece, or the Federal Reserve System.

Organization of the Bank of Canada

The Bank of Canada is a publicly owned corporation; all profits accruing from its operations are remitted to the government of Canada. The responsibility for the bank's affairs rests with a board of directors composed of the governor, the senior deputy governor,

the deputy minister of finance, and 12 directors. The governor is appointed by the directors, with the approval of the cabinet, for a seven-year term. In January 1987, John Crow was appointed governor, replacing Gerald Bouey, who retired after serving two seven-year terms.

The organization of the Bank of Canada is designed to keep the operation of monetary policy free from day-to-day political influence. Thus the Bank is not responsible to Parliament for its day-to-day behavior in the way that the Department of Finance is for the operation of fiscal policy. Nonetheless, the governor of the Bank and the minister of finance consult regularly. Furthermore, in the case of fundamental disagreement over policy, the governor must resign or acquiesce to the cabinet's desired policy as enunciated by the minister.[1]

Basic Functions of the Bank of Canada

A central bank serves four main functions: as a banker for private banks, as a bank for the government, as the controller of the nation's supply of money, and as a supporter of financial markets. The first three functions are revealed by a study of Table 33-2, which shows the balance sheet of a central bank.

Banker to the chartered banks. The central bank accepts deposits from the chartered banks and will, on order, transfer them to the account of another bank. In this way the central bank provides the chartered banks with the equivalent of a chequing account and with a means of settling debts to other banks. The deposits of the chartered banks with the central bank appear in Table 33-2. Notice that the cash reserves of the chartered banks deposited with the central bank are *liabilities* of the central bank (because it promises to pay them on demand), just as the money reserves of an individual or corporation deposited with a chartered bank are the liabilities of the chartered bank.

Historically, one of the earliest services provided by central banks was that of "lender of last resort"

[1] In 1962, when James Coyne was governor, such a fundamental disagreement arose and Coyne was eventually forced to resign. This incident is discussed further in Box 42-3.

TABLE 33-2   Assets and Liabilities of the Bank of Canada, December 1986 *(millions of dollars)*

Assets		Liabilities	
Government of Canada securities	$18,211	Notes in circulation	$17,911
Advances to banks	868	Government of Canada deposits	49
Foreign-currency assets	323	Deposits of chartered banks	2,446
Other assets	1,543	Foreign-currency liabilities	87
	$20,945	Other liabilities and capital	1,452
			$20,945

Source: Bank of Canada Review, April 1987.

The balance sheet of the Bank of Canada shows that it serves as banker to the chartered banks and the government and as issuer of our currency; it also suggests the bank's role as regulator of money markets and the money supply. The principal liabilities of the Bank are the basis of the money supply. Bank of Canada notes are currency, and the deposits of the chartered banks give them the reserves they use to create deposit money. The bank's holdings of Government of Canada securities arise from its operations designed to regulate the money supply and financial markets.

---

to the banking system. Central banks would lend money to private banks that had sound investments (such as government securities and safe loans to individuals) but were in urgent need of cash. If such banks could not obtain ready cash, they might be forced into involvency because they could not meet the demands of their depositors, in spite of their being basically sound. Today's central banks continue to be the lender of last resort.

U.S. banks borrow extensively from the Federal Reserve System in order to maintain their reserves, but the corresponding institutional arrangement that Canadian banks use is somewhat more complicated. Some Bank of Canada holdings of government securities, shown in Table 32-2, are held under **purchase and resale agreements (PRA).** Rather than rely on loans from the Bank of Canada, the chartered banks meet their immediate cash requirements by varying the amount of **day-to-day loans** they make available to a group of investment dealers who carry inventories of Government of Canada securities. When necessary, these dealers can obtain financing from the Bank of Canada under PRA; that is, they can sell securities to the Bank of Canada and agree to buy them back at a later date. Thus when the chartered banks reduce their day-to-day loans, they induce an increase in PRA. The result is the same as if the banks had borrowed from the Bank of Canada directly.

Banker to the government. Governments, too, need to hold their funds in an account into which they can make deposits and on which they can write cheques. The government of Canada keeps its chequing deposits at the Bank of Canada, replenishing them from much larger accounts kept at the chartered banks. When the government requires more money, it too needs to borrow, and it does so by printing bonds. Most are sold directly to the public, but occasionally the government raises funds by selling securities (mostly short-term) to the central bank, which "buys" them by crediting the government's account with a deposit for the amount of the purchase. In December 1986 the Bank of Canada held over $18 billion in Government of Canada securities. These securities play an important role in the monetary system.

Controller and regulator of the money supply. One of the most important functions of a central bank is to control the money supply. From Table 33-2 it is clear that the overwhelming proportion of a central bank's liabilities (its promises to pay) are either notes (money) or the reserves of the chartered banks, which underlie the deposits (money) of households and firms.

The central bank can change the levels of its assets and liabilities in many ways, and as its liabilities rise and fall, so does the money supply. Consider a single example. Suppose the central bank buys $100 million worth of newly printed bonds from the government of Canada. The bank's assets (government bonds) rise by $100 million, and so do its liabilities (Government of Canada deposits). The government has an extra $100 million of purchasing power to spend. As easy as printing money, you say. Indeed, it is the same thing.

Regulator and supporter of money markets. Central banks usually assume a major responsibility to support the country's financial system and to prevent serious disruption by wide-scale panic and resulting bank failures. Various institutions are in the business of borrowing on a short-term and lending on a long-term basis. To some extent the chartered banks do this when they take in demand (or savings) deposits and lend money for various terms. But trust and mortgage loan companies are the major institution for this kind of transaction. They receive deposits from the public and lend the money on long-term mortgages.

Large, unanticipated increases in interest rates tend to squeeze these institutions. The average rate they earn on their investments rises only slowly as old contracts mature and new ones are made, but they must either pay higher rates to hold on to their deposits or accept wide-scale withdrawals that could easily bring about insolvency. To prevent such financial disasters, central banks often buy and sell government bonds either to slow the rate of change in interest rates or to narrow the range over which the rates are allowed to fluctuate.

Money Creation by the Banking System

The fractional reserve system provides the leverage that permits chartered banks and other financial institutions to create new money. The process is important, so it is worth examining in some detail.

Some Simplifying Assumptions

To focus on the essential aspects of how banks create money, assume that banks can invest in only one kind of asset, loans, and that there is only one kind of deposit, a demand deposit.

Three other assumptions are provisional. When we have developed the basic ideas concerning the bank's creation of money, these assumptions will be relaxed.

1. *Fixed required reserve ratio.* It is assumed that all banks have the same required reserve ratio, which does not change. In our numerical illustration we shall assume that the required reserve ratio is 20 percent (i.e., 0.20), that is, at least $1 of reserves for every $5 of deposits.
2. *No excess reserves.* It is assumed that all banks want to invest any reserves they have in excess of the legally required amount. This implies that they always believe there are safe investments to be made when they have excess reserves.
3. *No cash drain from the banking system.* It is assumed that the public holds a fixed amount of currency in circulation. Thus changes in the money supply will take the form of changes in deposit money.

The Creation of Deposit Money

A typical bank's balance sheet is shown in Table 33-3. The Canadian Immigrants Bank of Commerce (CIBC) has assets of $200 of reserves (all figures are in thousands of dollars), held partly as cash on hand and partly as deposits with the central bank, and $900 of loans outstanding to its customers. Its liabilities are $100 to those who initially contributed capital to start the bank, and $1,000 to current depositors. The bank's ratio of reserves to deposits is 200/1,000 = 0.20, exactly equal to its minimum requirement.

TABLE 33-3   Initial Balance Sheet of the Canadian Immigrants Bank of Commerce *(thousands of dollars)*

Assets		Liabilities	
Cash and other reserves	$ 200	Deposits	$1,000
Loans	900	Capital	100
	$1,100		$1,100

The CIBC has a reserve of 20 percent of its deposit liabilities. The chartered bank earns money by finding profitable investments for much of the money deposited with it. In this balance sheet loans are its earning assets.

**TABLE 33-4 Balance Sheet of CIBC
After an Immigrant Deposits $100**
(thousands of dollars)

Assets		Liabilities	
Cash and other reserves	$ 300	Deposits	$1,100
Loans	900	Capital	100
	$1,200		$1,200

The immigrant's deposit raises deposit liabilities and cash assets by the same amount. Since both cash and deposits rise by $100, the cash reserve ratio, formerly 0.20, increases to 0.27. The bank has more cash than it needs to provide a 20 percent reserve against its deposit liabilities.

**TABLE 33-5 Monopoly Bank Balance
Sheet After Making a $400 Loan**
(thousands of dollars)

Assets		Liabilities	
Cash and other reserves	$ 300	Deposits	$1,500
Loans	1,300	Capital	100
	$1,600		$1,600

The loan restores the reserve ratio of 0.20. By increasing its loans by a multiple of its new cash deposit, the bank restores its reserve ratio of 0.20.

An immigrant arrives in the country and opens an account by depositing $100 with the CIBC. This is a wholly new deposit for the bank, and it results in a revised balance sheet (Table 33-4). As a result of the immigrant's new deposit, both cash assets and deposit liabilities have risen by $100. More important, the reserve ratio has increased from 0.20 to 0.27 (300/1,100). The bank now has excess reserves; with $300 in reserves it could support $1,500 in deposits.

A Single Monopoly Bank

If the CIBC were the only bank in the system, it would know that any loans that it made would eventually give rise to new deposits of an equal amount. It would then be in a position to say to the next business executive who comes in for a loan, "We will lend your firm $400 at the going rate of interest." The bank would do so by adding that amount to the firm's deposit account. Table 33-5 shows what would happen in this case. The new immigrant's deposit initially raised cash assets and deposit liabilities by $100. The new loans created an additional $400 of deposit liabilities. This restored the reserve ratio to its legal minimum (300/1,500 = 0.20), and no further expansion of deposit money is possible. As the bank's customers do business with one another, settling their accounts by cheques, the ownership of the deposits will be continually changing. But what matters to the bank is that its total deposits will remain constant.

The extent to which a monopoly bank could in-

crease its loans *and thus its deposits* depends on the reserve ratio. Because in this case the ratio is 1/5 (= 0.20), the bank would be able to expand deposits to five times the original acquisition of money. In general, if the reserve ratio is r, a monopoly bank can increase its deposits by $1/r$ times any new reserves. As we shall see, this relation holds for *any* banking system, not just for one with a single bank. [42]

Many Banks

Deposit creation is more complicated in a multibank system than in a single-bank system, but *the end result is exactly the same.* It is more complicated because when a bank makes a loan, the recipient of the loan may pay the money to someone who deposits it in another bank.

To follow the sequence by which a multibank system creates deposits, we first return to Tables 33-3 and 33-4. The CIBC is shown in equilibrium in Table 33-3. After it has received a new cash deposit as shown in Table 33-4, it is no longer in equilibrium. Whereas the monopoly bank could immediately create $400 of new deposits, one of many banks in a multibank system cannot do this because many of the new deposits that it creates will end up in other banks, causing a cash drain to these other banks. What now happens is most easily seen under an extreme assumption. We assume that every new borrower immediately uses the borrowed funds to pay people who deal with a different bank.

With its present level of deposits at $1,100, the bank needs only $220 of reserves (0.20 × $1,100 = $220), so it can lend the $80 excess that it has on

TABLE 33-6   CIBC Balance Sheet After a New Loan and Cash Drain of $80
(thousands of dollars)

Assets		Liabilities	
Cash and other reserves	$ 220	Deposits	$1,100
Loans	980	Capital	100
	$1,200		$1,200

The bank lends its surplus cash and suffers a cash drain. The bank keeps $20 as a reserve against the immigrant's new deposit of $100. It lends $80 to a customer who writes a check to someone who deals with another bank. When the check is cleared, the CIBC suffers an $80 cash drain. Comparing Tables 33-3 and 33-6 shows that the bank has increased its deposit liabilities by the $100 deposited by the new immigrant and increased its assets by $20 of cash reserves and $80 of new loans. It has also restored its reserve ratio of 0.20.

TABLE 33-7   Changes in the Balance Sheets of Second-Generation Banks
(thousands of dollars)

Assets		Liabilities	
Cash and other reserves	+$16	Deposits	+$80
Loans	+ 64		
	+$80		+$80

Second-generation banks receive cash deposits and expand loans. The second-generation banks gain new deposits of $80 as a result of the loan granted by the CIBC, which is used to make payments to customers of the second-generation banks. These banks keep 20 percent of the cash they acquire as their reserve against the new deposit, and they can make new loans using the other 80 percent. When the customers who borrowed the money make payments to the customers of third-generation banks, a cash drain occurs.

hand. Table 33-6 shows the position after this has been done and after the proceeds of the loan have been withdrawn to be deposited to the account of a customer of another bank. The CIBC once again has a 20 percent reserve ratio.

So far deposits in the CIBC have increased by only the initial $100 of the new immigrant's money with which we started, as shown in Table 33-4. (Of this, $20 is held as a cash reserve against the deposit and $80 has been lent out in the system.) But other banks have received new deposits of $80 as the persons receiving payment from those who borrowed the $80 from the CIBC deposited those payments in their own banks. The receiving banks are sometimes called *next-generation banks* or, more specifically according to the situation, *second-generation, third-generation,* and so on. In this case the second-generation banks receive new deposits of $80, and when the checks clear, they have new reserves of $80. Because they require an addition to their reserves of only $16 to support the new deposit, they have $64 of excess reserves. They now increase their loans by $64. After this money is spent by the borrowers and has been deposited in other, third-generation banks, the balance sheets of the second-generation banks will have changed, as in Table 33-7.

The third-generation banks now find themselves with $64 of new deposits. Against these they need hold only $12.80 in cash, so they have excess reserves

of $51.20 that they can immediately lend out. Thus there begins a long sequence of new deposits, new loans, new deposits, and new loans. The stages are shown in Table 33-8. The series in the table should look familiar, for it is the same convergent process underlying the multiplier encountered in Chapter 28.

The banking system has created new deposits and thus new money, although each banker can honestly say, "All I did was invest my excess reserves. I can do no more than manage wisely the money I receive."

If r is the reserve ratio, the ultimate effect on the deposits of the banking system of a new deposit will be $1/r$ times the new deposit. [43] This is exactly the same result in the monopoly bank case.[2]

Many Deposits

The two cases just discussed, the monopoly bank and a single new deposit in a multibank situation, show that under either set of opposite extreme assumptions, the result is the same. So it is, too, in intermediate situations. A far more realistic picture of deposit creation is one in which new deposits accrue simultaneously to all banks, perhaps because

[2] The "multiple expansion of deposits" that has just been worked through applies in reverse to a withdrawal of funds. Deposits of the banking system will fall by $1/r$ times any amount withdrawn from the bank and not redeposited at another.

TABLE 33-8   Many Banks, a Single New Deposit (*thousands of dollars*)

Bank	New deposits	New loans	Addition to reserves
CIBC	$100.00	$ 80.00	$ 20.00
Second-generation bank	80.00	64.00	16.00
Third-generation bank	64.00	51.20	12.80
Fourth-generation bank	51.20	40.96	10.24
Fifth-generation bank	40.96	32.77	8.19
Sixth-generation bank	32.77	26.22	6.55
Seventh-generation bank	26.22	20.98	5.24
Eighth-generation bank	20.98	16.78	4.20
Ninth-generation bank	16.78	13.42	3.36
Tenth-generation bank	13.42	10.74	2.68
Total first 10 generations	446.33	357.07	89.26
All remaining generations	53.67	42.93	10.74
Total for banking systems	$500.00	$400.00	$100.00

The banking system as a whole can create deposit money whenever it receives new reserves. The table shows the process of the creation of deposit money on the assumptions that all the loans made by one set of banks end up as deposits in another set of banks (the next-generation banks), that the required reserve ratio (r) is 0.20, and that there are no excess reserves. Although each bank suffers a cash drain whenever it grants a new loan, the system as a whole does not, and the system ends up doing in a series of steps what a monopoly bank would do all at once; that is, it increases deposit money by $1/r$, which in this example is five times the amount of any increase in reserves that it obtains.

---

of changes in the monetary policy of the government.

Say, for example, that the community contains 10 banks of equal size and that each received new deposits of $100 in cash. Now each bank is in the position shown in Table 33-4, and each can begin to expand deposits based on the $100 of excess reserves. (Each bank does this by granting loans to customers.)

Because each bank does one-tenth of the total banking business, an average of 90 percent of any newly created deposit will find its way into other banks as the customer pays other people in the community by cheque. This will represent a cash drain from the lending bank to the other banks. However, 10 percent of each new deposit created by every other bank should find its way into this bank. All banks receive new cash, and all begin creating deposits simultaneously; no bank should suffer a significant cash drain to any other bank.

Thus all banks can go on expanding deposits without losing cash to each other; they need only

worry about keeping enough cash to satisfy those depositors who will occasionally withdraw cash. The expansion can go on with each bank watching its own ratio of cash reserves to deposits, expanding deposits as long as the ratio exceeds 1/5 and ceasing when it reaches that figure. The process will come to a halt when each bank has created $400 in additional deposits, so that for each initial $100 cash deposit, there is now $500 in deposits backed by $100 in cash. Now *each* of the banks will have entries in its books similar to those shown in Table 33-5.

The general rule, if there is no cash drain, is that a banking system with a reserve ratio of r can change its deposits by $1/r$ times any change in reserves.

Excess Reserves and Cash Drains

Two of the simplifying assumptions made earlier can now be relaxed.

Excess reserves. If banks do not choose to invest excess reserves, the multiple expansion discussed will not occur. Turn back to Table 33-4. If the CIBC had been content to hold 27 percent reserves, it might well have done nothing more. Other things being equal, banks will choose to invest excess reserves because of the profit motive. But there may be times when they believe the risk is too great. It is one thing to be offered a good rate of interest on a loan, but if the borrower defaults on the payment of interest and principal, the bank will be the loser. Similarly, if the bank expects interest rates to rise in the future, it may hold off making loans now so that it will have reserves available to make more profitable loans after the interest rate has risen.

There is nothing automatic about deposit creation; it rests on the decisions of bankers. If banks do not choose to use excess reserves to expand their investments, there will not be an expansion of deposits.

The money supply is thus at least partially determined by the chartered banks in response to such forces as changes in national income and interest rates. However, the upper limit of deposits is determined by the required reserve ratio and by the reserves available to the banks, both of which are under the influence of the central bank.

Cash drain. Suppose that firms and households find it convenient to keep a fixed *fraction* of their money holding in cash (say, 5 percent) instead of a fixed *amount* of dollars. In that case an extra $100 in money supply will not all stay in the banking system; only $95 will remain on deposit, while the rest will be added to money in circulation. In such a situation any multiple expansion of bank deposits will be accompanied by a cash drain to the public that will reduce the maximum expansion below what it was when the public was content to hold all its new money as bank deposits. Table 33-9 shows the position of a typical bank after a credit expansion of $400 and a cash drain of $20.

The story of deposit creation when all banks receive new deposits and there is a cash drain to the public goes like this. Each bank starts creating de-

---

TABLE 33-9 Monopoly Bank Balance Sheet After a Credit Expansion and an Accompanying Cash Drain
(*thousands of dollars*)

Assets		Liabilities	
Cash and reserves	$ 280	Deposits	$1,480
Loans	1,300	Capital	100
	$1,580		$1,580

The limit to the amount of deposit expansion is reduced by a cash drain. This example differs from that shown in Table 33-5 because, after a new deposit of $100 and a new loan of $400, 5 percent of the newly created money is withdrawn as cash to be held by the public. Cash and deposits each fall by $20 and the reserve ratio falls below 20 percent.

---

posits and suffers no significant cash drain to other banks. But because approximately 5 percent of newly created deposits is withdrawn to be held as cash, each bank suffers a cash drain to the public. The expansion continues, each bank watching its own ratio of cash reserves to deposits, expanding deposits as long as the ratio exceeds 1/5 and ceasing when it reaches that figure. Because the expansion is accompanied by a cash drain, it will come to a halt with a smaller deposit expansion than in the case of no cash drain.[3]

The Money Supply

The total stock of money in the economy at any moment is called the **money supply.** Economists and financial analysts use several different definitions for the money supply, most of which are regularly reported in the *Bank of Canada Review*. Typically the definitions involve the sum of currency in circulation plus some types of deposit liabilities of financial institutions. Definitions vary in terms of what deposits are included. Different definitions come into or go out of favor as the importance of different types of deposits changes.

---

[3] It can be shown algebraically that the percentage of cash drain must be added to the reserve ratio to determine the maximum possible expansion of deposits. [44]

Kinds of Deposits

Most of the deposits held by the average person are either demand deposits or savings deposits.

Demand Deposits

A **demand deposit** means that the customer can withdraw the money on demand (i.e., without giving any notice of intention to withdraw). Demand deposits are transferable by cheque. A cheque instructs the bank to pay without a delay a stated sum of money to the person to whom the cheque is made payable.

Savings Deposits

Prior to recent changes in the Bank Act, a **savings deposit** was an interest-bearing deposit legally withdrawable only after a certain notice period. (Hence another word for savings deposit used to be *time* deposit.) In practice, although it was impossible to pay a bill by writing a cheque on a savings deposit, such deposits were always quickly convertible into a medium of exchange. A depositor wishing to use a savings deposit to pay a bill had to withdraw money from a savings account and then either pay the bill in cash or deposit the funds in a demand account and write a cheque on the demand account.

The Disappearing Distinction

For decades interest rates on savings deposits amounted to only a few percent, and people were content to keep most of their money in savings deposits and their reserves of cash for ordinary transactions in demand deposits. Then, interest rates available on savings deposits and other safe liquid investments grew, and it became more and more expensive (in terms of lost interest) to keep cash in demand deposits, even for a week or two. Starting in the early 1970s, several devices were invented that tended to make it easier to convert interest-bearing deposits into demand deposits transferable by cheque.

Chequable savings accounts are now common, and some banks even offer a service whereby fixed sums are automatically transferred from a customer's savings account to his or her demand account when funds in the demand account become insufficient to meet newly presented cheques. The effective distinction is no longer between demand and savings accounts but rather between a multitude of types of accounts, each offering different combinations of interest payments, service provided, and service charges levied. The deposit that is genuinely tied up for a period of time now takes the form of a **term deposit (TD),** which is purchased with a statement of a particular withdrawal date, a minimum of 30 days into the future, and which pays a much reduced interest rate in the event of early withdrawal.

Demand deposits offer other services to compensate for the lack of interest earnings. These include free traveler's cheques, detailed monthly statements, and return of canceled cheques.

Definitions of the Money Supply

The definition of the money supply varies with the type of deposits considered. The narrowly defined money supply, called **M1,** includes currency and demand deposits. Broader definitions such as **M2** and **M3** add in savings accounts and term deposits, which serve the temporary store-of-value function and are in practice quickly convertible into a medium of exchange at a known price ($1 on deposit in a savings account is always convertible into a $1 demand deposit or $1 in cash). Table 33-10 shows the principal elements in the money supply.

Near Money and Money Substitutes

Over the past two centuries what has been accepted by the public as money has expanded from gold and silver coins to include first bank notes and then bank deposits subject to transfer by cheque. Until recently, most economists would have agreed that money stopped at that point. No such agreement exists today, and an important debate centers on the definition of money appropriate to present circumstances.

If we concentrate only on the medium-of-exchange function of money, there is little doubt about what is money in Canada today. Money consists of notes, coins, and deposits subject to transfer by

TABLE 33-10   Canadian Money Supply, January 1987 *(billions of dollars)*

Currency	$ 14.8
Plus: Demand deposits	17.8
Equals M1	32.6
Plus: Daily interest chequable savings deposits and nonpersonal notice deposits	40.2
Equals M1A	72.8
Plus: Other personal savings deposits and personal fixed-term deposits at the chartered banks	103.0
Equals M2	175.8
Plus: Nonpersonal fixed-term deposits and foreign-currency deposits	40.5
Equals M3	216.3

Source: Bank of Canada Review, April 1987.

The money supply can be defined in a variety of ways: M1, M1A, M2, and M3 figures are all published regularly by the Bank of Canada. M1 is the narrowly defined money supply that includes items that serve directly as a medium of exchange. M1A also includes nonpersonal notice and chequable savings deposits. M2 includes additional categories of bank deposits that serve the store-of-value function and can be readily converted into demand deposits or currency. M3 adds in bank term deposits that cannot be converted easily because the funds must remain on deposit for a fixed term and foreign-currency deposits whose value in terms of Canadian dollars varies with the exchange rate. (Series called M2+ and M3+ add to M2 and M3, respectively, related deposits with trust companies, credit unions, and Quebec savings institutions called *caisses populaires.*)

TABLE 33-11   The Dollar As a Store of Value Since 1962

$1 put aside in	Had the purchasing power 5 years later of	Its average annual loss of value over the 5-year period was
1962	$.86	2.8%
1967	.79	4.2%
1972	.47	10.7%
1977	.37	12.6%
1982	.76	4.3%

The dollar has become an increasingly less satisfactory store of value since the 1960s. The second column shows the purchasing power, measured by the Consumer Price Index, of $1 five years after it was saved (assuming it earned no interest). In order for it to have maintained its real purchasing power, it would have had to earn the annual percentage return shown in the last column. The increase in the required return explains the growing use of near money and money substitutes that (unlike currency and demand deposits) earn interest.

cheque or cheque-like instruments. No other asset constitutes a generally accepted medium of exchange; indeed, even notes and cheques are not universally accepted—as you will discover if you try to buy a pack of cigarettes with a $1,000 bill (or even a $100 bill in a corner grocery store). But such exceptions are unimportant.

The problem of deciding what is money arises because some media of exchange—currency, which carries no interest yield, and demand deposits, whose interest yield tends to be quite low—may provide relatively poor ways to meet the store-of-value function (see Table 33-11). Assets that earn a higher-interest return will do a better job of meeting this function of money than will currency or demand

deposits. At the same time, however, these other assets are less capable of filling the medium-of-exchange function.

Near Money

Assets that fulfill adequately the store-of-value function and are readily converted into a medium of exchange but are not themselves a medium of exchange are sometimes called **near money.** Deposits at a trust company are a characteristic form of near money. When you have such a deposit, you know exactly how much purchasing power you hold (at current prices), and, given modern banking practices, you can turn your deposit into a medium of exchange—cash or a chequing deposit—at a moment's notice. Additionally, your deposit will earn some interest during the period that you hold it.

Why then does not everybody keep their money in such deposits instead of in demand deposits or currency? The answer is that the inconvenience of continually shifting money back and forth may outweigh the interest that can be earned. One week's interest on $100 (at 5 percent per year) is only about $.10, not enough to cover carfare to the bank or the cost of mailing a letter. For money that will be needed soon, it would hardly pay to shift it to a time deposit.

In general, whether it pays to convert cash or demand deposits into interest-earning savings deposits for a given period will depend on the inconvenience and other transaction costs of shifting funds and on the amount of interest that can be earned.

There is a wide spectrum of assets in the economy that pay interest and also serve as reasonably satisfactory temporary stores of value. The difference between these assets and savings deposits is that their capital values are not quite as certain as those of savings deposits. If I elect to store my purchasing power in the form of a treasury bill that matures in 30 days, its price on the market may change between the time I buy it and the time I want to sell it, say, 10 days later. If the price changes, the purchasing power available to me changes. But because of the short horizon to maturity, the price will not change very much. (After all, the government will pay the face value in a few weeks.) Such a security is thus a reasonably satisfactory short-run store of purchasing power. Indeed, any readily salable capital asset whose value does not fluctuate significantly with the rate of interest will satisfactorily fulfill this short-term store-of-value function.

Money Substitutes

Things that serve as a temporary medium of exchange but are not a store of value are sometimes called **money substitutes.** Credit cards are a prime example. With a credit card, many transactions can be made without either cash or a cheque. The evidence of credit, the credit slip you sign and hand over to the store, is not money because it cannot be used to make other transactions. Furthermore, when your credit card company takes advantage of an arrangement to have your bank pay each bill as it is presented or when it sends you a bill, you have to use money to pay for the original transaction. The credit card serves the short-run function of a medium of exchange by allowing you to make purchases even though you have no cash or bank deposit currently in your possession. But this is only temporary; money remains the final medium of exchange for these transactions when the credit account is settled.

Conclusion

Since the eighteenth century, economists have known that the amount of money in circulation is an important economic variable. As theories became more carefully specified in the nineteenth and early twentieth centuries, they included a variable called "the money supply." But for theories to be useful, we must be able to identify real-world counterparts of these theoretical magnitudes.

What is an acceptable enough medium of exchange to count as money has changed and will continue to change over time. New monetary assets are continually being developed to serve some, if not all, the functions of money, and they are more or less readily convertible into money. There is no single, timeless definition of what is money and what is only near money or a money substitute. Indeed, as we have seen, our monetary authorities use several definitions of money, and these definitions change from year to year.

Summary

1. Early economic theorists regarded the economy as divided into a real part and a money part. The real sector is concerned with production, allocation of resources, and distribution of income—determined by relative prices. The level of prices at which all transactions take place is determined by the monetary sector, that is, by the demand for and supply of money. With the demand for money constant, an increase in the money supply would cause all equilibrium money prices to increase, but relative prices, and hence everything in the real sector, would be left unaffected.

2. Traditionally in economics, money has referred to any generally accepted medium of exchange. A number of functions of money may be distinguished. The major ones are serving as a medium of exchange, a store of value, and a unit of account.

3. Money arose because of the inconvenience of barter, and it developed in stages from precious metal, to metal coinage, to paper money convertible to precious metal, to token coinage and paper money fractionally backed by precious metals, to fiat money, and to deposit money. Societies have shown great sophistication in developing monetary instruments to meet their needs.

4. The banking system in Canada consists of two main elements: chartered banks and the central bank, the Bank of Canada. Each has an important effect on the money supply.

5. Chartered banks are profit-seeking institutions that allow their customers to transfer demand deposits from one bank to another by means of cheques. They create and destroy money as a by-product of their commercial operations—by making or liquidating loans and various other investments.

6. Because most customers are content to pay their accounts by cheque rather than by cash, banks need only small reserves to back their deposit liabilities. Consequently, banks are able to create deposit money. When the banking system receives a new cash deposit, it can create new deposits to some multiple of this amount. The amount of new deposits created depends on the legal minimum reserves the Bank of Canada enforces on the banks, the amount of cash drain to the public, and whether the banks choose to hold excess reserves.

7. All advanced free-market economies have a central bank that serves as banker for private banks, banker for the government, controller and regulator of the money supply, and regulator and supporter of money markets.

8. The money supply—the stock of money in the country at a specific moment—can be defined in various ways. M1 is currency plus demand deposits plus chequable substitutes, the narrowest definition now in use. (M1 was about $32 billion in 1986.) M3, the widest commonly used definition, adds in all time and savings deposits. (M3 was about $216 billion in 1986.)

9. Near money includes interest-earning assets that are convertible into money on a dollar-for-dollar basis but are not currently included in the definition of money. Money substitutes such as credit cards temporarily serve as a medium of exchange but are not money.

Topics for Review

Real and monetary sectors of the economy
Functions of money
Gresham's law
Fully backed, fractionally backed, and fiat money

The banking system and the central bank
Creation and destruction of deposit money
Reserve ratio, required reserves, and excess reserves
Demand and savings deposits
The money supply
Near money and money substitutes

Discussion Questions

1. "For the love of money is the root of all evil" (I Timothy 6:10). If a nation were to become a theocracy in which money was illegal, would you expect the level of national income to be affected? How about the productivity of labor?

2. Consider each of the following with respect to its potential use as a medium of exchange, a store of value, and a unit of account. Which would you think might be regarded as money?
   a. A $100 Bank of Canada note
   b. An American Express credit card
   c. A painting by Picasso
   d. A treasury bill payable in three months
   e. A savings account with a trust company in London, Ontario
   f. One share of General Motors stock
   g. A lifetime pass to the Art Gallery of Ontario

3. When the Austrian government minted a new 1,000-shilling gold coin—worth $78 face value—the 1-inch-diameter coin came into great demand among jewelers and coin collectors. By law, the number of such coins to be minted each year is limited. Lines of people eager to get the coins formed outside the government mint and local banks. "There is exceptional interest in the new coin," said a Viennese banker. "It's a numismatic hit and a financial success." It has disappeared from circulation, however. Explain why.

4. A Canadian who receives a U.S. coin has the option of spending it at face value or taking it to the bank and converting it to Canadian money at the going rate of exchange. When the rate of exchange was near par, so that $1 Canadian was within $0.03 of $1 U.S., American and Canadian coins circulated side by side, exchanging at their face values. Use Gresham's law to predict which coinage disappeared from circulation in Canada when the Canadian dollar fell to $0.75 U.S. Why did a $0.03 differential not produce this result?

5. Some years ago a strike closed all banks in Ireland for several months. What do you think happened during the period?

6. During hyperinflations in several foreign countries after World War II, American cigarettes were sometimes used in place of money. What made them suitable?

7. Assume that on January 1, 1986, a couple had $25,000 that they wished to hold for use one year later. Calculate, using library sources, which of the following would have been the best store of value over that period. Will the best store of value over that period necessarily be the best over the next 24 months?
   a. The dollar
   b. Stocks whose prices moved with the Toronto Stock Exchange Industrial 300 average

    c. A Labatts 11¾ percent 2005 bond

    d. Gold

    e. Silver

8. If all depositors tried to turn their deposits into cash at once, they would find that there are not sufficient reserves in the system to allow all of them to do this at the same time. Why then do we not still have panicky runs on the banks? Would a 100 percent reserve requirement be safer? What effect would such a reserve requirement have on the banking system's ability to create money? Would it preclude any possibility of a panic?

9. What would be the effect on the money supply of each of the following?

    a. Declining public confidence in the banks

    b. A desire on the part of banks to increase their levels of excess reserves

    c. Monopolizing of the banking system into a single superbank

    d. Increased use of credit cards

    e. Transfer of deposits from banks to new nonbank institutions

34

The Role of Money in Macroeconomics

At one time or another most of us have known the surprise of opening our wallet to discover that we had either more or less money than we thought. There can be pleasure in deciding how to spend an unexpected windfall in the first case, just as there can be pain in deciding what expenditure to eliminate in the second.

What determines how much money people hold in their wallets and how much they keep in the bank? What happens when people discover that they are holding more, or less, money than they believe they need to hold? These turn out to be key questions for our study of the influence of money on output and prices.

Financial Assets

At any one moment households have a given stock of wealth. This wealth is held in many forms. Some of it is money in the bank or in the wallet; some is in short-term securities such as term deposits or treasury bills; some is in long-term bonds; and some is in real capital, which may be held directly (in the form of family businesses) or indirectly (in the form of shares of stock that indicate ownership of a corporation's assets).

Kinds of Assets

These ways of holding wealth may be grouped into three main categories: (1) assets that serve as a medium of exchange, that is, paper money, coins, and bank deposits on which cheques may be drawn, (2) financial assets, such as bonds earning a fixed rate of interest, that will yield a fixed money value at some future date (called the *maturity date*) and can usually be sold before maturity for a price that fluctuates on the open market, and (3) claims on real capital (physical objects such as factories and machines).

To simplify our discussion, we will regroup wealth into just two categories: money and bonds. By money we mean M1 as defined in Chapter 33, and by bonds we mean all other forms of wealth. Money therefore includes currency, demand deposits, and chequable savings deposits. Bonds include all other interest-earning financial assets *plus* claims in real capital.[1]

The Rate of Interest and the Price of Bonds

A bond is a promise by the issuer to pay a stated sum of money as interest each year and to repay the face value of the bond at some future maturity date, often many years distant. The time until the date is called the **term to maturity,** often simply the **term,** of the bond. Some bonds, called perpetuities, pay interest forever and never repay the principal.

The **present value (*PV*)** of a bond, or of any asset, refers to the value now of the future payment, or payments, to which the asset represents a claim. The present value is thus the amount someone would be willing to pay now to secure the right to the future stream of payments conferred by ownership of the asset.

This amount depends critically on the rate of interest as is most easily seen in the case of a perpetuity. Assume that such a bond will pay $100 per year to its holder. The *present value* of this bond depends on how much $100 per year is worth, and this in turn depends on the rate of interest.

A bond that will produce a stream of income of $100 a year forever is worth $1,000 at 10 percent interest because $1,000 invested at 10 percent per year will yield $100 interest per year forever. But the same bond is worth $2,000 when the interest rate is 5 percent per year because it takes $2,000 invested at 5 percent per year to yield $100 interest per year. The lower the rate of interest obtainable on the market, the more valuable is a bond paying a fixed amount of interest.

Similar relations apply to bonds that are not perpetuities, though the calculation of present value must allow for the lump-sum repayment of principal at maturity.[2]

The present value of any asset that yields a stream of money over time is negatively related to the interest rate.

This proposition has two important implications: (1) If the rate of interest falls, the value of an asset producing a given income stream will rise, and (2) a rise in the market price of an asset producing a given income is equivalent to a decrease in the rate of interest earned by the asset. Thus a promise to pay $100 one year from now is worth $92.59 when the interest rate is 8 percent and only $89.29 when the interest rate is 12 percent: $92.59 at 8 percent interest ($92.59 × 1.08) and $89.29 at 12 percent interest ($89.29 × 1.12) are both worth $100 in one year's time.

The present value of bonds that are not perpetuities becomes increasingly dominated by the fixed redemption value as the maturity date approaches. Take an extreme case. The present value of a bond that is redeemable for $1,000 in a week's time will be very close to $1,000 no matter what the interest rate. Thus its value will not change much even if the rate of interest leaps from 5 percent to 10 percent during that week.

The sooner the maturity date of a bond, the less the bond's value will change with a change in one the rate of interest.

For example, a rise in the interest rate from 8 to 12 percent will lower the value of $100 payable in one year's time by 3.6 percent, but it will lower the value of $100 payable in 10 years' time by 37.9 percent.[3] (Although some assets that we included in our definition of money do earn interest, they are so short-term that their values remain unchanged when the interest rate changes.)

The discussion should make it clear that the pres-

---

[1] This simplification can take us quite a long way. However, for some problems it is necessary to treat debt and equity as distinct assets so that three categories—money, debt (bonds), and equity stocks—are used.

[2] Further details on the calculation of present value are given in Chapter 18, pages 356–357.

[3] The example assumes annual compounding. The first case can be calculated from the numbers of the previous example: (92.59 − 89.29)/92.59. The 10-year case uses the formula

$$\text{Present value} = \frac{\text{Principal}}{(1 + r)^n}$$

which gives $46.30 with 8 percent and $28.75 with 12 percent. The percentage fall in value is thus (46.30 − 28.75)/46.30 = 0.379.

ent value of an asset determines its market price. If the market price of any asset is greater than the present value of the income stream it produces, no one will want to buy it; if the market value is below its present value, there will be a rush to buy it. These facts lead to the following conclusions:

In a free market the equilibrium price of any asset will be the present value of the income stream it produces.

Supply of Money and Demand for Money

The Supply of Money

The money supply is a stock. (It is so many billions of dollars, *not* a flow of so much per unit of time.) In January 1987 M1 was approximately $33 billion.

We saw in Chapter 33 that deposit money is created by the commercial banking system, but only within limits set by their reserves. We also saw in Chapter 33 that the reserves of the commercial banking system are under the control of the Bank of Canada, ultimate control of the money supply is also in the hands of the Bank. In this chapter we shall assume that the money supply can be precisely controlled by the Bank of Canada.

The Demand for Money

The amount of wealth everyone in the economy wishes to hold in the form of money balances is called the **demand for money.** Because households have only one decision to make on how to divide their given stock of wealth between money and bonds, it follows that if we know the demand for money, we also know the demand for bonds. With *a given level of wealth* a rise in the demand for money necessarily implies a fall in the demand for bonds; if people wish to hold $1 billion more money, they must wish to hold $1 billion less of bonds. It also follows that if households are in equilibrium with respect to their money holdings, they are in equilibrium with respect to their bond holdings.

When we say that on January 1, 1987, the demand for money was $33 billion, we mean that on that date the public wished to hold money balances that totaled $33 billion. But why do firms and households wish to hold money balances at all? There is a cost to holding any money balance. The money could instead be used to purchase bonds; it would then earn more interest.[4]

The opportunity cost of holding any money balance is the extra interest that could have been earned if the money had instead been used to purchase interest earning assets.

Clearly, money will be held only when it provides services that are valued at least as highly as the opportunity cost of holding it. The services provided by money balances are, first, to finance purchases and sales; second, to provide a cushion against uncertainty about the timing of cash flows; and third, to provide a hedge against uncertainty over the prices of other financial assets.

The desire to hold money to obtain each of these services is summarized by the transactions, precautionary, and speculative motives for holding money. We now examine each of these motives in detail.

The Transactions Motive

Most transactions require money. Money passes from households to firms to pay for the goods and services produced by firms; money passes from firms to households to pay for the factor services supplied by households to firms. Money balances that are held to finance such flows are called **transactions balances.**

In an imaginary world, where the receipts and

[4] As we saw in Chapter 33 (see especially Table 33-10), some definitions of the money supply (even narrow definitions like M1A) include some interest-bearing chequable deposits. This complicates but does not fundamentally alter the analysis of the demand for money. In particular, it means that the opportunity cost of holding those interest-bearing components of M1A is not the *level* of interest rates paid on bonds but the *differential* between that rate and the rate paid on M1A assets. For simplicity, we treat the interest rate on all M1A assets as being zero so that we can identify the *level* of the interest rate on bonds as the opportunity cost of money.

disbursements of households and firms were perfectly synchronized, it would be unnecessary to hold transactions balances. If every time a household spent $10 it received $10 as part payment of its income, no transactions balances would be needed. In the real world, however, receipts and disbursements are not perfectly synchronized.

Consider, for example, the balances held because of wage payments. Assume, for purposes of illustration, that firms pay wages every Friday and that households spend all their wages on the purchase of goods and services, with the expenditure spread out evenly over the week. Thus on Friday morning firms must hold balances equal to the weekly wage bill; on Friday afternoon households will hold these balances.

Over the week, households' balances will be drawn down as a result of purchasing goods and services. Over the same period, the balances held by firms will build up as a result of selling goods and services until, on the following Friday morning, firms will again have amassed balances equal to the wage bill that must be met on that day.

On the average over the week firms will hold balances equal to half the wage bill and so will households. Thus, in this example total money balances held will be equal to the total weekly wage bill. Notice that while the money circulates so that each group holds a varying balance over the week, the combined demand for balances summed over the two groups remains constant.

Our argument has been conducted in terms of the wage bill, but a similar analysis holds for all receipts and payments of households and firms. Because their receipts and payments are not perfectly synchronized, they must hold money balances to bridge the gap.

The transactions demand for money arises because of the nonsynchronization of payments and receipts.

What determines the size of the transactions balances to be held? It is clear that in our example total transactions balances vary with the value of the wage bill. If the wage bill doubles for any reason (e.g., because twice as much labor is hired at the same

wage rate or because the same amount of labor is hired at twice the wage rate), the transactions balances held by firms and households on this account will also double. As it is with wages so it is with all other transactions: The size of the balances held is positively related to the value of the transactions.

Next we ask how the total value of transactions is related to national income. Because of the "double counting" problem first discussed in Chapter 27, the value of all transactions exceeds the value of the economy's final output. When the flour mill buys wheat from the farmer and when the baker buys flour from the mill, both are transactions against which money balances must be held, although only the value added at each stage is part of national income. Typically, the total value of transactions is many times as large as the total value of final output, which is national income.

We now make an added assumption that there is a stable, positive relation between transactions and national income. If a rise in aggregate expenditure leads to a rise in national income, it also leads to a rise in the total value of all transactions and hence to an associated rise in the demand for transactions balances. This allows us to relate transactions balances to national income. [45]

The larger the value of national income, the larger the value of transactions balances that will be held.

The Precautionary Motive

Many goods and services are sold on credit. The seller can never be certain when payment will be made, and the buyer can never be certain of the day of delivery and thus when payment will fall due. As a precaution against cash crises when receipts are abnormally low or disbursements are abnormally high, firms and households carry money balances. These are called **precautionary balances.** The larger such balances, the greater the protection against running out of money because of temporary fluctuations in cash flows.

How serious this risk is depends on the penalties for being caught without sufficient money balances.

A firm is unlikely to be pushed into insolvency, but it may incur considerable costs if it is forced to borrow money at high interest rates in order to meet a temporary cash crisis.

The precautionary motive arises because households and firms are uncertain about the degree to which payments and receipts will be synchronized.

The protection provided by a given quantity of precautionary balances depends on the volume of payments and receipts. A $100 precautionary balance provides a large cushion for a household whose volume of payments per month is $800 and a small cushion for a firm whose monthly volume is $10,000. Fluctuations of the sort that create the need for precautionary balances tend to vary directly with the size of the firm's cash flow. To provide the same degree of protection as the value of transactions rises, more money is necessary.[5]

The precautionary motive also causes the demand for money to vary positively with the money value of national income.

The Speculative Motive

Firms and households hold some money in order to avoid the risks inherent in fluctuating prices of bonds. Money balances held for this purpose are called **speculative balances.** This motive was first analyzed by Keynes, and modern analysis is the work of Professor James Tobin of Yale University.[6]

When a household or firm holds money balances, it foregoes the extra interest income that it could earn if it held bonds instead. But market interest rates fluctuate, and so do the market prices of existing

[5] Institutional arrangements affect precautionary demands. In the past, for example, a traveler would have carried a substantial precautionary balance in cash, but today a credit card covers most unforeseen expenses that may arise while traveling.

[6] Professor Tobin was awarded the Nobel Prize in economics in 1981 for his research in monetary economics and the analysis of financial markets.

bonds (since their present values depend on the interest rate). Because their prices fluctuate, bonds are a risky asset. Many households and firms do not like risk; they are said to be *risk-averse.*

In choosing between holding money or holding bonds, wealth holders must balance the extra interest income that they could earn by holding bonds against the risk that bonds carry. At one extreme, if a household or a firm holds all its wealth in the form of bonds, it earns extra interest on its entire wealth, but it also exposes its entire wealth to the risk of changes in the price of bonds. At the other extreme, if the household or firm holds all its wealth in the form of money, it earns less interest income, but it does not face the risk of unexpected changes in the price of bonds. Wealth holders usually do not take either extreme position. They hold part of their wealth as money and part as bonds; that is, they *diversify* their holdings.

Influence of wealth. The motivation to hold money in order to diversify wealth holdings means that the demand for money varies positively with wealth. For example, Ms. B. O'Reiley might elect to hold 5 percent of her wealth in money and the other 95 percent in bonds. If her wealth is $50,000, her demand for money will be $2,500. If her wealth increases to $60,000, her demand for money will rise to $3,000.

Although an individual's wealth may rise or fall rapidly, the total wealth of a society changes only slowly. For the analysis of short-term fluctuations in national income, the effects of changes in wealth are fairly small, and we shall ignore them for the present. (Over the long term, however, variations in wealth can have a major effect on the demand for money.)

Influence of interest rates. Wealth held in cash earns no interest; hence the reduction in risk involved in holding more money carries a cost in terms of interest earnings forgone.

The speculative motive leads households and firms to add to their money holdings until the reduction in risk obtained by the last dollar added is just balanced (in each wealth holder's

view) by the cost in terms of the interest forgone on that dollar.

When the rate of interest falls, the opportunity cost of holding money falls. This leads to more money being held both for the precautionary motive (to reduce risks caused by uncertainty about the flows of payments and receipts) and for the speculative motive (to reduce risks associated with fluctuations in the market price of bonds). When the rate of interest rises, the cost of holding money rises. This leads to less money being held for speculative and precautionary motives.

The demand for money is negatively related to the rate of interest.[7]

Real and Nominal Money Balances

In referring to the demand for money, it is important to distinguish real from nominal values. Real values are measured in purchasing power units, nominal values in money units.

First, consider the demand for money in real terms. This means the number of units of purchasing power the public wishes to hold in the form of money balances. In an imaginary one-product wheat economy, this would be measured by the number of bushels of wheat that could be purchased with the money balances held. In a more complex economy it could be measured in terms of the number of weeks of national income; for example, the real value of the amount of money demanded might be equal to one month's national income.

When we come to measure the real demand for money, we measure the amount demanded in constant dollars. This means that the real demand is the nominal quantity demanded divided by an index of price level (where the base year is given a value of 1 rather than 100).

The real demand for money is the nominal quantity demanded divided by the price level.

For example, in the decade from 1976 to 1986 the nominal quantity of M1 balances held in Canada rose by 175 percent from $18.6 billion to $32.6 billion. Over the same period, however, the price level, as measured by the CPI, roughly doubled—if we let the price level be 1 in 1976, it was 2.1 in 1986. This tells us that the real quantity of M1 held actually fell slightly, from $18.6 billion to $15.5 billion measured in constant 1976 dollars.

From real demand to nominal demand. Our discussion has identified the determinants of the demand for real money balances as real national income, real wealth, and the interest rate. Notice that the real demand for money depends, among other things, on real national income; it is not influenced by the price level. Now suppose that, with the interest rate, real wealth, and real national income constant, the price level doubles. The demand for real money balances will be unchanged. For this to be true, however, the demand for nominal balances must double. If the public used to demand $30 billion worth of nominal money balances, they must now demand $60 billion worth. This keeps the real demand unchanged at $60/ 2 = $30. The constancy of the level of demand for real balances is shown in this example by the fact that $60 billion at the new, higher price level represents exactly the same purchasing power as did $30 billion at the old price level.

Other things being equal, the nominal demand for money balances varies in proportion to the price level; doubling the price level doubles desired nominal money balances.

This is a central proposition of the quantity theory of money, discussed further in Box 34-1.

Total Demand for Money: Recapitulation

Figure 34-1 (see page 742) summarizes the influences of national income, the rate of interest, and the price level, the three variables that account for most of the

---

[7] When the price level is changing continually, it is necessary to distinguish the real from the nominal rate of interest. This was discussed in Box 31-1 on page 649. For now, there is no need to distinguish these two concepts of the interest rate since they are the same when the price level is constant, and they are measured by the market rate of interest.

BOX 34-1

The Quantity Theory of Money and the Velocity of Circulation

The basic quantity theory of money can be set out formally in terms of the following four equations. Equation 1 states that the demand for money balances depends on the value of transactions as measured by nominal income, which is real income multiplied by the price level, *PY.*

$$M^D = kPY \qquad [1]$$

Equation 2 states that the supply of money, *M,* is set by the central bank.

$$M_S = M \qquad [2]$$

Equation 3 states the equilibrium condition that the demand for money must equal its supply.

$$M^D = M_S \qquad [3]$$

Substitution produces the basic relation among *P, M,* and *Y,* as shown in Equation 4.

$$M = kPY \qquad [4]$$

The original form of the classical quantity theory assumes that *k* is a constant given by the transactions demand for money and that *Y* is constant because full employment is maintained. Thus *M* and *P* move proportionally. Increases or decreases in the money supply lead to proportional increases or decreases in prices.

Often the quantity theory is presented using the concept of the velocity of circulation, *V,* instead of the proportion of the money income that people wish to hold in cash, *k.* The **velocity of circulation** is defined as national income divided by the quantity of money.

$$V = PY/M \qquad [5]$$

Rearranging gives what is called the *equation of exchange.*

$$MV = PY \qquad [6]$$

Velocity may be interpreted as showing the average amount of "work" done by a unit of money. Thus, if the annual national income is $400 billion and the stock of money is $100 billion, on average each dollar's worth of money is used four times to create the values added that compose the national income.

There is a simple relation between *k* and *V.* One is the reciprocal of the other, as may be seen immediately by comparing Equations 4 and 6. Thus it makes no difference whether we choose to work with *k* or *V.* Further, if *k* is assumed to be constant, this implies that *V* must also be treated as being constant. An example may help to illustrate the interpretation of each.

Assume that the stock of money people wish to hold is equal to one-fifth of the value of total transactions. Thus *k* is 0.2 and *V,* the reciprocal of *k,* is 5. This indicates that if the money supply is to be one-fifth of the value of annual transactions, the average unit of money must account for $5 worth of transactions; that is, each dollar must be used on average five times.

Modern versions of the quantity theory do not assume that *k* is exogenously fixed but nevertheless argue that it will not change in response to a change in the quantity of money.

---

short-term variations in the nominal quantity of money demanded. The function relating money demand to the rate of interest is often called the **liquidity preference (LP) function.** Whatever name is used, the relation describes how the quantity of money people wish to hold varies as the rate of interest varies.

Monetary Forces and National Income

We are now in a position to examine the relationship between monetary forces and the equilibrium values of national income and the price level. The first step

---

FIGURE 34-1   Demand for Money As a Function of Interest Rates, Income, and Price Level

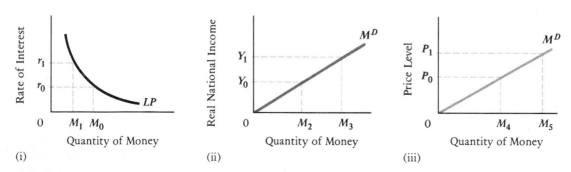

(i)   (ii)   (iii)

The quantity of money demanded varies negatively with the rate of interest and positively with both national income and the price level. In part (i) the demand for money is shown varying negatively with the interest rate along the liquidity preference function. When the interest rate rises from r_0 to r_1, households and firms reduce the quantity of money demanded from M_0 to M_1.

In part (ii) the demand for money is shown varying positively with national income. When national income rises from Y_0 to Y_1, households and firms increase the quantity of money demanded from M_2 to M_3.

In part (iii) the demand for money is shown varying positively with the price level. When the price level rises from P_0 to P_1, households and firms increase the quantity of money demanded from M_4 to M_5.

---

in explaining this relationship is a new one: the link between monetary equilibrium and aggregate demand. The second is familiar from earlier chapters: the effects of shifts in aggregate demand on equilibrium values of national income and the price level.

Monetary Equilibrium and Aggregate Demand

Monetary equilibrium occurs when the demand for money equals the supply of money. In Chapter 4 we saw that in a competitive market for some commodity such as carrots, the price will adjust so as to ensure equilibrium. The rate of interest does the same job with respect to money demand and money supply.

The Liquidity Preference Theory of Interest

Figure 34-2 shows how the interest rate will change in order to equate the demand for money with its supply. When a single household or firm finds that

it has less money than it wishes to hold, it can sell some bonds and add the proceeds to its money holdings. This transaction simply redistributes given supplies of bonds and money among individuals; it does not change the total supply of either money or bonds.

Now assume that all the firms and households in the economy have an excess demand for money balances. They all try to sell bonds to add to their money balances. But what one person can do, all persons cannot do. At any moment the economy's total supplies of money and bonds are fixed; there are just so much money and so many bonds in existence. If everyone tries to sell bonds, there will be no one to buy them. Instead the price of bonds will fall.

We saw that a fall in the price of bonds means a rise in the rate of interest. As the interest rate rises, people economize on money balances because the opportunity cost of holding such balances is rising. This is what we saw in Figure 34-1(i), where the quantity of money demanded falls along the liquidity

**FIGURE 34-2   The Liquidity Preference Theory
of Interest**

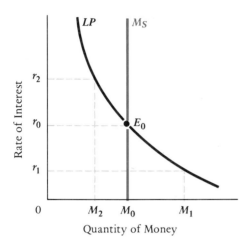

The interest rate rises when there is an excess demand for money and falls when there is an excess supply of money. The fixed quantity of money, M_0, is shown by the completely inelastic supply curve M_S. The demand for money is LP; its negative slope indicates that a fall in the rate of interest causes the quantity of money demanded to increase. Equilibrium is at E_0, with a rate of interest of r_0.

If the interest rate is r_1, there will be an excess demand for money of M_0M_1. Bonds will be offered for sale in an attempt to increase money holdings. This will force the rate of interest up to r_0 (the price of bonds falls), at which point the quantity of money demanded is equal to the fixed available quantity of M_0. If the interest rate is r_2, there will be an excess supply of money M_2M_0. Bonds will be demanded in return for excess money balances. This will force the rate of interest down to r_0 (the price of bonds rises), at which point the quantity of money demanded has risen to equal the fixed supply of M_0.

preference curve in response to a rise in the rate of interest. Eventually the interest rate will rise enough that people will no longer be trying to add to their money balances by selling bonds. At that point there is no longer an excess supply of bonds, and the interest rate will stop rising. The demand for money again equals the supply.

Assume next that firms and households hold larger money balances than they would like. A single household or firm would purchase bonds with its excess balances, achieving monetary equilibrium by reducing its money holdings and increasing its bond holdings. But just as in the example, what one household or firm can do, all cannot do. At any moment the total quantity of bonds is fixed, so everyone cannot simultaneously add to personal bond holdings. When all households enter the bond market and try to purchase bonds with unwanted money balances, they bid up the price of existing bonds, and the interest rate falls. Hence households and firms become willing to hold larger quantities of money; that is, the quantity of money demanded increases along the liquidity preference curve in response to a fall in the rate of interest. The rise in the price of bonds continues until firms and households stop trying to convert bonds into money. In other words, it continues until everyone is content to hold the existing supply of money and bonds.

Monetary equilibrium occurs when the rate of interest is such that the existing supply of money is willingly held, that is, when the demand for money equals its supply.

The determination of the interest rate depicted in Figure 34-2 is often described as the *liquidity preference theory of interest* and sometimes as the *portfolio balance theory.*

As we shall see, a shift either in the demand for money or in the supply will lead to a change in the interest rate. But, as we saw in Chapter 31, desired investment expenditure is sensitive to changes in the interest rate. Here, then, is a link between monetary factors and real expenditure flows.

The Transmission Mechanism

The mechanism by which changes in the demand for and the supply of money affect aggregate demand is called the **transmission mechanism.** The transmission mechanism operates in three stages: first, the link between monetary equilibrium and the interest rate; second, the link between the interest rate and investment expenditure; and third, the link between investment expenditure and aggregate demand.

From monetary disturbances to changes in the interest rate.   The interest rate will change if the supply of money changes or if there is a shift in the demand for money. For example, as shown in Figure 34-3(i), an increase in the supply of money, with an unchanged liquidity preference function, will give rise to an excess supply of money at the original interest rate. As we have seen, an excess supply of money will cause the interest rate to fall. As also shown in part (i) of the figure, a decrease in the supply of money will cause the interest rate to rise.

As shown in Figure 34-3(ii), an increase in the demand for money, with an unchanged supply of money, will give rise to an excess demand for money

at the original interest rate and cause the interest rate to rise. As also shown in part (ii) of the figure, a decrease in the demand for money will cause the interest rate to fall.

Monetary disturbances, which can arise due to either changes in the demand for or the supply of money, cause changes in the interest rate.

From changes in the interest rate to shifts in aggregate expenditure. The second link in the transmission mechanism relates interest rates to expenditure.

FIGURE 34-3   Monetary Disturbances and Interest-Rate Changes

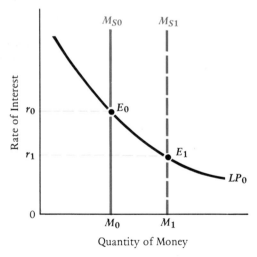

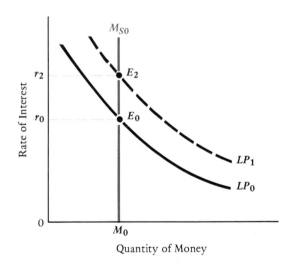

(i) A change in the supply of money

(ii) A change in the demand for money

Shifts in the supply of money or in the demand for money cause the equilibrium interest rate to change. In both parts of the figure the money supply is shown by the vertical curve M_{S0} and the demand for money is shown by the negatively shaped curve LP_0 The initial equilibrium is at E_0 with corresponding interest rate r_0.

In part (i) an increase in the money supply causes the money supply curve to shift to the right from M_{S0} to M_{S1}. The new equilibrium is at E_1, where the interest rate is r_1, less than r_0. Starting at F_1 with M_{S1} and r_1, it can be seen that a decrease in the money supply to M_{S0} leads to an increase in the interest rate from r_1 to r_0.

In part (ii) an increase in the demand for money causes the LP curve to shift to the right from LP_0 to LP_1. The new equilibrium occurs at E_2, and the new equilibrium interest rate is r_2, greater than r_0. Starting at E_2, we see that a decrease in the demand for money from LP_1 to LP_0 leads to a decrease in the interest rate from r_2 to r_0.

FIGURE 34-4   Effects of Changes in the Money Supply on Investment Expenditure

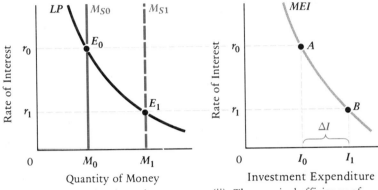

(i) Money demand and supply

(ii) The marginal efficiency of investment

Increases in the money supply reduce the rate of interest and increase desired investment expenditure. Equilibrium is at E_0, with a quantity of money of M_0 (shown by the inelastic money supply curve M_{S0}), an interest rate of r_0, and an investment expenditure of I_0 (point A). The Bank of Canada then increases the money supply to M_1 (shown by the money supply curve M_{S1}). This lowers the rate of interest to r_1 and increases investment expenditure by ΔI to I_1 (point B). A reduction in the money supply from M_1 to M_0 raises interest rates from r_1 to r_0 and lowers investment expenditure by ΔI, from I_1 to I_0.

We saw in Chapter 31 that investment, which includes expenditure on inventory accumulation, residential construction, and business fixed investment, responds to changes in the rate of interest. Other things being equal, a decrease in the rate of interest makes borrowing cheaper and generates new investment expenditure.[8] This negative relation between investment and the rate of interest is called the **marginal efficiency of investment (*MEI*)** function.

The first two links in the transmission mechanism are shown in Figure 34-4. We concentrate for the moment on changes in the money supply, although, as we have already seen, the process can also be set in motion by changes in the demand for money. In part (i) we see that a change in the money supply causes the rate of interest to change in the opposite direction. In part (ii) we see that a change in the interest rate causes the level of investment expenditure to change in the opposite direction. Therefore, changes in the money supply cause investment expenditure to change in the same direction.

An increase in the money supply leads to a fall in the interest rate and an increase in investment expenditure. A decrease in the money supply leads to a rise in the interest rate and a decrease in investment expenditure.

From shifts in aggregate expenditure to shifts in aggregate demand.   Now we are back on familiar ground. In Chapter 29 we saw that a shift in the aggregate expenditure curve can lead to a shift in the *AD* curve. This is shown again in Figure 34-5.

A change in the money supply, by causing a change in investment expenditure and hence a shift in the *AE* curve, causes the *AD* curve to shift.

An increase in the money supply causes an increase in investment expenditure and therefore an increase in aggregate demand. A decrease in the money supply causes a decrease in investment expenditure and therefore a decrease in aggregate demand.

The transmission mechanism connects monetary forces and real expenditure flows. It works from a change in the demand for or the supply

---

[8] In Chapter 31 we saw that purchases of durable consumer goods also respond to changes in interest rates. In this chapter we concentrate on investment expenditure, which may be taken to stand for *all interest-sensitive expenditure.*

FIGURE 34-5   Effects of Changes in the Money Supply on Aggregate Demand

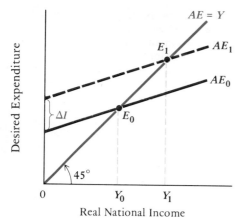

(i) Shift in aggregate expenditure

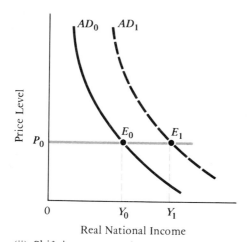

(ii) Shift in aggregate demand

Changes in the money supply cause shifts in the aggregate expenditure and aggregate demand functions. In Figure 34-4 an increase in the money supply increased desired investment expenditure by ΔI. In part (i) of the present figure the aggregate expenditure function shifts up by ΔI (which is the same as ΔI in Figure 34-4), from AE_0 to AE_1. At the fixed price level P_0, equilibrium income rises from Y_0 to Y_1, as shown by the horizontal shift in the aggregate demand curve from AD_0 to AD_1 in part (ii).

When the supply of money falls (from M_{S1} to M_{S0} in Figure 34-4), investment falls by ΔI, thereby shifting aggregate expenditure in the above figure from AE_1 to AE_0. At the fixed price level P_0, this reduces equilibrium income from Y_1 to Y_0.

of money to a change in bond prices and interest rates, to changes in investment expenditure, to a shift in the aggregate demand curve.

This is illustrated in Figure 34-6 for the case of an expansionary monetary shock, that is, a shift in money demand or money supply that tends to increase aggregate demand.

The Strength of Monetary Forces

How much will a given change in the money supply cause the AD curve to shift? The size of the shift in

FIGURE 34-6   Transmission Mechanism for an Expansionary Monetary Shock

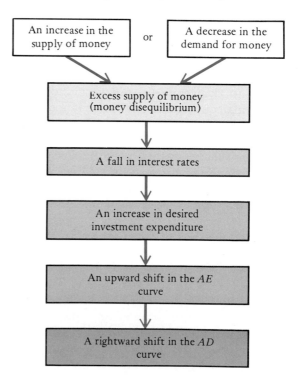

An increase in the supply of money or a decrease in the demand for money leads to an increase in aggregate demand. The excess supply of money following an expansionary monetary disturbance leads to a fall in the interest rate and an increase in investment. This causes an upward shift in the AE curve, and thus a rightward shift in the AD curve.

aggregate demand in response to an increase in the money supply depends on the size of the increase in investment expenditure. This in turn depends on two factors that play a key role in the transmission mechanism.

The first factor is how much interest rates fall in response to the increase in the money supply. The more interest-sensitive the demand for money, the less interest rates will have to fall to induce firms and households willingly to hold the increase in the money supply.

The second is how much investment expenditure increases in response to the fall in interest rates. The more interest-sensitive investment expenditure, the more it will increase in response to any given fall in the interest rate.

It follows that the size of the shift in aggregate demand in response to a change in the money supply depends on the shapes of the liquidity preference and marginal efficiency of investment curves. The influence of the shapes of the two curves is shown in Figure 34-7 below and may be summarized as follows:

FIGURE 34-7   Two Views on the Strength of Monetary Changes

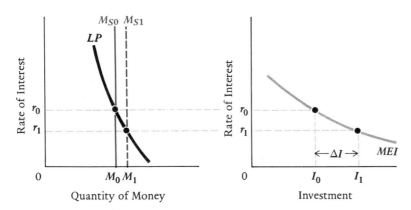

(i) Changes in the money supply effective

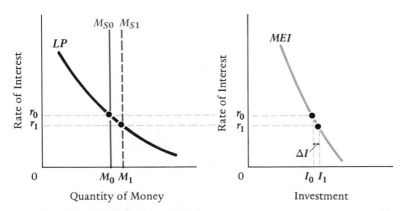

(ii) Changes in the money supply ineffective

The strength of the effect of a change in the money supply on investment and hence on aggregate demand depends on the interest elasticity of both the demand for money and desired investment expenditure. Initially the money supply is M_{S0}, and the economy is in equilibrium with an interest rate of r_0 and investment expenditure of I_0.

In both parts of the figure the central bank expands the money supply from M_{S0} to M_{S1}. The rate of interest thus falls from r_0 to r_1, as shown in each of the left panels. This causes an increase in investment expenditure of ΔI, from I_0 to I_1 as shown in each of the right panels.

In part (i) the demand for money is highly interest-inelastic, so the increase in the money supply leads to a large fall in the interest rate. Further, desired investment expenditure is highly interest-elastic, so the large fall in interest rates also leads to a large increase in investment expenditure. Hence in this case the change in the money supply will be effective in stimulating aggregate demand.

In part (ii) the demand for money is interest-elastic, so the increase in the money supply leads only to a small fall in the interest rate. Further, desired investment expenditure is highly interest-inelastic, so the small fall in interest rates also leads only to a small increase in investment expenditure. Hence in this case the change in the money supply will not be effective in stimulating aggregate demand.

1. **The steeper (the less interest-sensitive) the** *LP* **function, the greater the effect a change in the money supply will have on interest rates.**
2. **The flatter (the more interest-sensitive) the** *MEI* **function, the greater the effect a change in the interest rate will have on investment expenditure and hence on aggregate demand.**

The combination that produces the largest effect on aggregate demand for a given change in the money supply is a steep *LP* function and a flat *MEI* function. This combination is illustrated in Figure 34-7(i). It accords with the view, which we shall see later is often associated with so-called monetarists, that monetary policy is relatively effective as a means of influencing the economy. The combination that produces the smallest effect is a flat *LP* function and a steep *MEI* function. This combination is illustrated in Figure 34-7(ii). It accords with the view, which we shall see later is often associated with some so-called Keynesians, that monetary policy is relatively ineffective.

Aggregate Demand, the Price Level, and National Income

Effect of a change in the money supply. We have just seen that a change in the money supply shifts the aggregate demand curve. If we want to know what it does to real national income and to the price level, we need to know the slope of the aggregate supply curve. This step, which is familiar from earlier chapters, is recalled in Figure 34-8.[9]

The key result is that the increase in equilibrium real income is less than the horizontal shift in the *AD*

---

[9] Since the demand for money in general will depend on the level of national income, as shown in Figure 34-1(ii), our analysis at this stage is incomplete. The induced change in equilibrium national income will lead to a shift in the liquidity preference function in Figure 34-2. For simplicity we have assumed in the text that the liquidity preference function does not shift in response to a change in national income. The Appendix to Chapter 39 presents a formal analysis in which this effect is allowed for and in which equilibrium levels of the interest rate and national income are determined simultaneously.

FIGURE 34-8   Effects of Changes in the Money Supply

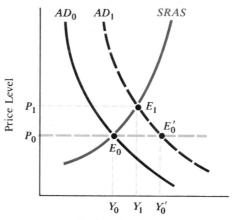

A change in the money supply leads to a change in national income that is smaller than the horizontal shift in the *AD* curve. An increase in the money supply causes the *AD* curve to shift to the right, from AD_0 to AD_1. With the price level constant, national income would rise from Y_0 to Y_0'. With the upward-sloping *SRAS* curve, income rises only to Y_1, and the price level rises to P_1.

---

curve. This is because part of this shift is dissipated by a rise in the price level. If the aggregate demand curve were vertical, the rise in the price level would not diminish the effect on real output; real output would rise by an amount equal to the horizontal shift of the *AD* curve. But because the *AD* curve is negatively sloped, the rise in real output is smaller.

Effect of a change in the price level. We can now use the transmission mechanism to explain the negative slope of the *AD* curve, that is, to explain why equilibrium national income is negatively related to the price level.

In Chapter 29 when we explained the negative slope of the *AD* curve, we mentioned three reasons but relied on the wealth effect (real balance effect) because it was simple and direct. Now that we have developed a theory of money and interest rates, we are able to understand the indirect effect that works through the transmission mechanism.

The essential feature of this indirect effect is that a rise in the price level raises the money value of transactions. This leads to an increased demand for money, which brings the transmission mechanism into play. People try to sell bonds to add to their money balances, but collectively all they succeed in doing is forcing up the interest rate. The rise in the interest rate reduces investment expenditure and so reduces equilibrium national income.

This effect is important because, empirically, the interest rate is the most important link between monetary factors and real expenditure flows. Box 34-2 is for readers who wish to study the reasons for the negative slope of the *AD* curve in more detail.

The Monetary Adjustment Mechanism

Suppose that an economy in equilibrium with real national income equal to its potential level were disturbed by an increase in the money supply. Since real national income would increase, there would be an inflationary gap, as shown in Figure 34-9(i). Let us now examine the mechanism by which such an inflationary gap is eliminated. This involves an important but subtle implication of the theory.

A sufficiently large rise in the price level will eliminate any inflationary gap, *provided the nominal money supply remains constant.*

Operation of the monetary adjustment mechanism. Because it causes excess demand in factor markets,

---

FIGURE 34-9 The Monetary Adjustment Mechanism

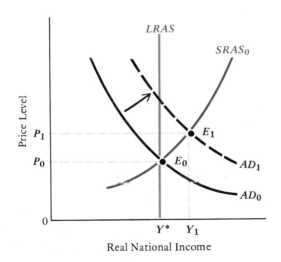

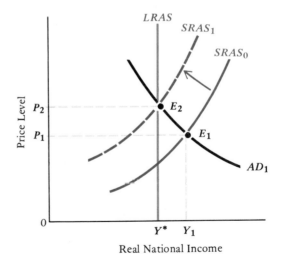

(i) Inflationary gap created

(ii) Inflationary gap eliminated

A rise in the price level will eliminate an inflationary gap. The economy is initially in long-run equilibrium at E_0 with price level P_0 and real income Y^*. In part (i) some disturbance shifts the *AD* curve to the right, leading to equilibrium E_1 with a higher price level P_1 and an inflationary gap of Y^*Y_1.

E_1 is also shown in part (ii). The inflationary gap causes wages to rise, shifting the *SRAS* curve to the left so that the price level starts to rise. The monetary adjustment mechanism (working through a rising interest rate and falling investment) lowers aggregate expenditure so that the economy moves upward along the *AD* curve. Eventually, the inflationary gap is eliminated and equilibrium reached at E_2 with income at Y^* and price level P_2.

BOX 34-2

The Slope of the Aggregate Demand Curve

The *AD* curve relates the price level to the equilibrium level of real national income. It is negatively sloped because the higher the price level, the lower the equilibrium national income. The main reason for this negative slope is found in the transmission mechanism.

Let us look at this process in detail. Although the argument contains nothing new, it does require that you follow carefully through several steps.

We start with an initial position depicted in part (i) of the figure. The liquidity preference schedule is LP_0, and the money supply is M_S. Equilibrium is at E_0 with the interest rate at r_0. The *MEI* schedule given in part

(ii) shows that at the rate of interest r_0, desired investment expenditure is I_0. In part (iii) the aggregate expenditure curve AE_0 is drawn for that level of investment (I_0). Equilibrium is at E_0 with a real national income of Y_0. Plotting Y_0 against the initial price level (P_0) yields point A on the aggregate demand curve in part (iv).

An increase in the price level to P_1 raises the money value of transactions and increases the quantity of money demanded at each possible value of the interest rate. As a result, the liquidity preference function shifts from LP_0 to LP_1. This raises interest rates to r_1 and lowers investment expenditure by ΔI_1 to I_1.

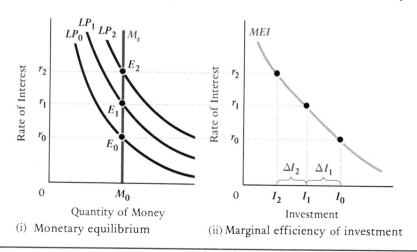

(i) Monetary equilibrium   (ii) Marginal efficiency of investment

the inflationary gap will cause factor prices to rise. This will shift the *SRAS* curve up and take the price level with it. This raises the money value of transactions, and the resulting increase in the demand for money raises interest rates. Hence at any level of real income, desired real expenditure falls. The fall in real expenditure as the price level rises is shown by a movement upward to the left *along* the *AD* curve. This reduces the inflationary gap. When the price level has risen enough, the inflationary gap disappears and the price level stops rising.

This mechanism, illustrated in Figure 34-9(ii), may be called the *monetary adjustment mechanism*. It works through the transmission mechanism.

The monetary adjustment mechanism will eliminate any inflationary gap, provided that the nominal money supply is held constant.

Thus inflationary gaps tend to be self-correcting as long as the money supply does not increase. They will cause the price level to increase, but those increases set in motion a chain of events in the markets for financial assets that will eventually remove the inflationary gap.

The self-correcting mechanism is one reason why price levels and the money supply have been linked for so long in economics. Many things can cause the price level to rise for some time. Yet whatever the

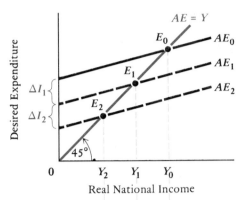

(iii) Equilibrium national income

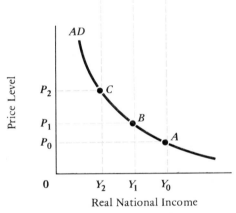

(iv) The aggregate demand curve

The fall in investment causes the AE curve in part (iii) to shift down by an equal amount to AE_1. Equilibrium income falls to Y_1. Plotting Y_1 against P_1 produces point B on the AD curve in part (iv).

A further increase in the price level to P_2 shifts the liquidity preference function to LP_2, raises the interest rate to r_2, and lowers investment expenditure to I_2. The fall in investment shifts the AE curve in part (iii) to AE_2, and equilibrium income falls to Y_2. Plotting Y_2 against P_2 produces point C on the AD curve in part (iv).

The negative relation between the price level and equilibrium real income shown by the AD curve occurs because, other things being equal, a rise in the price level raises the *demand* for money. Notice the qualification "other things being equal." It is important for this process that the nominal money *supply* remain constant. The transmission mechanism operates because the demand for money increases when the price level rises, while the money supply remains constant. The attempt to add to money balances by selling bonds is what drives the interest rate up and reduces desired expenditure, thereby reducing equilibrium national income. (This argument is conducted in terms of the nominal supply and demand for money. Arguing in terms of the real demand and supply of money leads to identical results.) [46]

reason for the rise, unless the money supply is expanded, the price level increase itself sets up forces that will remove the initial inflationary gap and so bring demand inflation to a halt.

Frustration of the monetary adjustment mechanism. The self-correcting mechanism for removing an inflationary gap can be frustrated indefinitely if the money supply is increased at the same rate that prices are rising. Say the price level is rising 10 percent a year under the pressure of a large inflationary gap. Demand for nominal money balances will also be rising at about 10 percent per year. Now suppose that the Bank of Canada increases the money supply

at 10 percent per year. No excess demand for money will develop, since the extra money needed to meet the rising demand will be forthcoming. The real interest rate will not rise, and the inflationary gap will not be reduced. This process is analyzed in Figure 34-10.

If the money supply increases at the same rate as the price level rises, the real money supply and hence the real interest rate will remain constant, and the monetary adjustment mechanism will be frustrated.

An inflation is said to be *validated* when the money supply is increased as fast as the price level

FIGURE 34-10   Frustration of the Monetary Adjustment

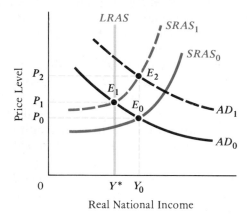

Real National Income

An inflationary gap can persist indefinitely if the money supply increases as fast as the price level. Suppose the economy is at E_0, with income Y_0 and price level P_0. Since potential income is Y^*, there is an inflationary gap of Y^*Y_0. The price level now rises; this tends to shift the economy upward along the AD curve, thereby tending to reduce the excess aggregate demand. But the Bank of Canada increases the money supply so that the AD curve shifts outward, thereby tending to increase excess aggregate demand. If the two forces just balance each other, by the time the price level has risen to P_2 the curve will have shifted to AD_1, leaving the inflationary gap unchanged, with equilibrium at E_2.

so that the monetary adjustment mechanism is frustrated. A validated inflation can go on indefinitely, although, as we shall see in Chapter 37, possibly not at a constant rate.

A recessionary gap.   In principle, the monetary adjustment mechanism will operate to eliminate a recessionary gap. If the recessionary gap led to a fall in factor prices, the *SRAS* curve would shift to the right, causing the price level to fall and national income to rise. However, as we saw in Chapter 30, many economists argue that wages and other factor costs are quite rigid in the face of a recessionary gap. (This was referred to as the second asymmetry of aggregate supply—see page 632.) In this circumstance the monetary adjustment mechanism will not be very effective in causing national income to return quickly to its potential level. Thus many economists argue that aggregate demand should be stimulated in the face of a recessionary gap, either through fiscal policy, which we studied in Chapter 32, or through monetary policy, which we study in the next chapter.

Summary

1. For simplicity we divide all forms in which wealth is held into money, which is a medium of exchange, and bonds, which earn a higher interest return than money and can be turned into money by selling them at a price that is determined on the open market.

2. The price of bonds varies negatively with the rate of interest. A rise in the interest rate lowers the prices of all bonds. The longer its term to maturity, the greater the change in the price of a bond for a given change in the interest rate.

3. The value of money balances that the public wishes to hold is called the *demand for money*. It is a stock (not a flow), measured as so many billions of dollars.

4. Money balances are held, despite the opportunity cost of bond interest forgone, because of the transactions, precautionary, and speculative motives. They have the effect of making the demand

for money vary positively with real national income, the price level, and wealth and vary negatively with the rate of interest. The nominal demand for money varies proportionally with the price level.

5. When there is an excess demand for money balances, people try to sell bonds. This pushes the price of bonds down and the interest rate up. When there is an excess supply of money balances, people try to buy bonds. This pushes the price of bonds up and the rate of interest down. Monetary equilibrium is established when people are willing to hold the fixed stocks of money and bonds at the current rate of interest. The liquidity preference (*LP*) function is the relation between money demand and the interest rate.

6. A change in the interest rate causes desired investment to change along the marginal efficiency of investment (*MEI*) function. This shifts the aggregate desired expenditure function and causes equilibrium national income to change. This means that the aggregate demand curve shifts.

7. Points 5 and 6 together describe the transmission mechanism that links money to national income. A decrease in the supply of money tends to reduce aggregate demand. An increase in the supply of money tends to increase it.

8. The steeper the *LP* curve and the flatter the investment curve, the greater the effect of a given change in the money supply on aggregate demand.

9. The negatively sloped aggregate demand curve indicates that the higher the price level, the lower equilibrium national income. The explanation lies with the monetary adjustment mechanism: The higher the price level, the higher the demand for money, the higher the rate of interest, the lower the aggregate expenditure function, and thus the lower equilibrium income.

10. The monetary adjustment mechanism that causes the aggregate demand curve to have a negative slope means that a sufficiently large rise in the price level will eliminate any inflationary gap. However, this mechanism can be frustrated if the Bank of Canada validates the price rise by increasing the money supply as fast as the price level is rising.

Topics for Review

Discussion Questions

1. "Central banker says using monetary policy to lower interest rates now would only cause inflation to rise and lead to higher interest rates in the future." Explain how this might be so.

2. "Bond prices pressed downward by news of M1's sharp rise, economy's rebound." Does this *Wall Street Journal* headline necessarily contradict our theory about the direct link between money supply and bond prices?

3. The Governor of the Bank of Canada recently expressed concern about the record government deficit and the growing level of public debt in the economy. Why should these things concern him?

4. Describing a possible future "cashless society," a public report recently said, "In the cashless society of the future, a customer could insert a plastic card into a machine at a store and the amount of the purchase would be deducted from his 'bank account' in the computer automatically and transferred to the store's account. No cash or cheques would ever change hands." What would such an institutional change do to the various motives for holding money balances? What functions would remain for commercial banks and for the central bank if money as we now know it disappeared in this fashion? What benefits and disadvantages can you see in such a scheme?

5. What motives do you think explain the following holdings?
   a. Currency and coins in the cash register of the local supermarket at the start of each working day
   b. The payroll account of the Ford Motor Company in the local bank
   c. Certificates of deposit that mature after one's retirement
   d. Government bonds held by private individuals

6. What would be the effects on the economy if Parliament were to vote a once-and-for-all universal social dividend of $5,000 paid to every Canadian over the age of 17, to be financed by the creation of new money?

7. Suppose that you alone know that the Bank of Canada is going to engage in policies that will decrease the money supply sharply, starting next month. How might you make speculative profits by purchases or sales of bonds now?

8. What would happen if, starting from a situation of 10 percent rates of inflation and of monetary expansion, the Bank of Canada cut the rate of monetary expansion to 5 percent?

9. Trace the full sequence of events by which the monetary adjustment mechanism would work if, in the face of a constant money supply, workers and firms insisted on actions that raised prices continually at a rate of 10 percent per year. "Sooner or later in this situation something would have to give." What possible things could "give"? What would be the consequence of each "giving"?

35

Monetary Policy

The Bank of Canada conducts monetary policy in order to influence such key macroeconomic variables as real national income, employment and unemployment, inflation, interest rates, and the exchange rate. The primary way in which it seeks to influence these variables is through control of the money supply.

Later in this chapter we study in detail how the Bank chooses to conduct monetary policy . . . and what is involved in choosing between different operating procedures and deciding how much emphasis to place on each of the potential policy targets.

Control of the Money Supply

The Bank Act requires each chartered bank to maintain reserves in the form of Bank of Canada notes and deposits at the Bank of Canada, and it permits the central bank to buy and sell various financial assets. The provisions enable the central bank to vary the amount of cash reserves available to the banking system and thus to regulate the money supply.

Open-Market Operations

The most important tool the central bank has for influencing the supply of money is the purchase or sale of government securities on the open market. In a typical year the Bank of Canada buys and sells over $7 billion worth of government securities. What is the effect of these purchases and sales?

Central-bank purchases and sales of government securities in financial markets are known as **open-market operations.** Just as there are stock markets, there are active and well-organized markets for government securities. You or I, General Motors, the Bank of Montreal, or the Bank of Canada can enter this market and buy or sell negotiable government securities at whatever price supply and demand establishes.

Purchases on the Open Market

When the Bank of Canada buys a security from someone in the nonbank private sector, it pays for it with a cheque drawn on the central bank and payable to the seller. The seller deposits this cheque in a chartered bank, which then presents the cheque to the Bank of Canada for payment. The central bank makes a book entry increasing the deposit of the chartered bank at the central bank.

At the end of these transactions, the central bank has acquired a new asset in the form of a security and a new liability in the form of a deposit by the chartered bank. The seller has reduced its security holdings and increased its deposits. The chartered bank has a new deposit equal to the amount paid for the security by the central bank. The chartered bank's reserves and its deposit liabilities have increased by an equal amount.

When the central bank buys securities on the open market, the reserves of the chartered banks are increased. These banks in turn can expand deposits, thereby increasing the money supply.

Table 35-1 shows the changes in the balance sheets of the several parties in response to a central-bank purchase of $100 in government securities from the nonbank private sector. After these transactions, the chartered banks have excess reserves and are in a position to expand their loans and deposits. Indeed, the chartered banks are in precisely the position studied on page 725 (see Table 33-4). The new deposit made by the immigrant might just as well have been made by someone who had sold a security to the Bank of Canada.

If the central bank buys many securities in the open market, the entire banking system will gain new reserves. Whether the seller is a household, a firm, or a bank, the Bank of Canada's purchase of securities on the open market sets in motion a series of book transactions that increase the banking system's reserves and thus make possible a multiple expansion of credit.[1]

Sales on the Open Market

When the central bank sells a $100 security to a household or firm, it receives in return the buyer's cheque drawn against its own deposit in a chartered

---

TABLE 35-1   Balance Sheet Changes Caused by an Open-Market Purchase from a Household

Private household

Assets		Liabilities	
Bonds	−$100	No change	
Deposits	+ 100		

Chartered banks

Assets		Liabilities	
Reserves (deposits with central bank)	+ $100	Demand deposits	+ $100

Central bank

Assets		Liabilities	
Bonds	+ $100	Deposits of chartered banks	+ $100

The money supply is increased when the Bank of Canada makes an open-market purchase from the nonbank private sector. When the Bank of Canada buys a $100 bond from a household, the household gains money and gives up a bond. The chartered banks gain a new deposit of $100 and thus new reserves of $100. Chartered banks can now engage in a multiple expansion of deposit money of the sort analyzed in Chapter 33.

---

bank. The central bank presents the cheque to the chartered bank for payment. Payment is made by a book entry that reduces the chartered bank's deposit at the central bank.

The changes in this case are the opposite of those shown in Table 35-1. The central bank has reduced its assets by the value of the security it sold and reduced its liabilities in the form of the deposits of chartered banks. The household or firm has increased its holdings of securities and reduced its cash on deposit with a chartered bank. The chartered bank has reduced its deposit liability to the household or firm and reduced its reserves (on deposit with the central bank) by the same amount. Each of the asset changes is balanced by a liability change. Indeed, everything balances.

But the chartered bank finds that the equal change in its reserves and deposit liabilities causes its ratio of reserves to deposits to fall. Consider, for example,

---

[1] In Chapter 33 we studied a case in which the Bank sold a bond to a household or a non-bank firm. If instead the purchaser was a chartered bank, the end result would have been the same. In this case the chartered bank gives up one asset (a bond) and gains another (cash or a deposit with the central bank). But now the chartered bank has excess reserves (liabilities unchanged, cash reserves increased) on the basis of which it can engage in the expansion of deposits.

a bank with $10 million in deposits backed by $1 million reserves in fulfillment of a 10 percent reserve ratio. As a result of the Bank's open-market sales of $100,000 worth of bonds, the bank loses $100,000 of deposits and reserves. Reserves are now $900,000 while deposits are $9.9 million, a reserve ratio of only 9.09 percent.

Banks whose reserve ratios are driven below the minimum requirement must take immediate steps to restore their reserve ratios. The necessary reduction in deposits can be accomplished by not making new investments when old ones are redeemed (e.g., by not granting new loans when old ones are repaid) or by selling (liquidating) existing investments.

When the central bank sells securities on the open market, the reserves of the chartered banks are decreased. These banks in turn are forced to contract deposits, thereby decreasing the money supply.

But what if the public does not wish to buy the securities the Bank of Canada wishes to sell? Can it force the public to do so? The answer is that there is always a price at which the public will buy. In its open-market operations, the Bank must be prepared to have the price of the securities fall if it insists on suddenly selling a large volume of them. As we have seen, a fall in the price of securities is the same thing as a rise in interest rates, so if the Bank wishes to curtail the money supply by selling bonds, it may well drive up interest rates. This process was illustrated in Figure 34-4 on page 745.

Notice in Table 33-2 on page 723 that the Bank's holdings of government securities are large relative to the reserves of chartered banks. By selling securities it can contract those reserves very sharply if it chooses. Similarly, by buying securities it can expand reserves. Open-market operations are a potent weapon for affecting the size of bank reserves—and thus for affecting the money supply.

Tools Other Than Open-Market Operations

The major tool the Bank of Canada uses in conducting monetary policy is its open-market opera-

tions. But other tools are available and have on occasion been used extensively.

Reserve Requirements

One way that a central bank can control the money supply is by altering the required minimum reserve ratios. Suppose the banking system is loaned up; that is, it has no excess reserves. If the Bank increases the required reserve ratio (say from 20 percent to 25 percent), the reserves held by the chartered banks will no longer be adequate to support their outstanding deposits. Chartered banks will then be forced to reduce their deposits until they achieve the new, higher required reserve ratio.[2] This decrease in deposits is a decrease in the money supply. This process is illustrated in Table 35-2.

A reduction in reserve requirements immediately provides banks with excess reserves. Of course, if banks choose not to increase their loans, they will not need to respond to a decrease in required reserves, since those are only minimum requirements. In normal times the profit motive will lead most banks to respond by increasing loans and deposits—and thus lead to an increase in the money supply.

Increases in required reserve ratios force banks with no excess reserves to decrease deposits and thus reduce the money supply. Decreases in required reserve ratios permit banks to expand deposits, which increases the money supply.

This method of controlling the money supply has been used in the United States but not in Canada. Given the small margin of excess reserves held by the chartered banks, increases in the required reserve ratios would force abrupt adjustments in bank assets. An equivalent contraction in the money supply can be brought about by using the more flexible tool of open-market operations, which can be spread out over time to induce a more orderly adjustment. Changes in reserve requirements are occasionally made, but this is usually done for purposes other

[2] They will do this by gradually decreasing their loans and/or selling some of their securities. In the short term they may undertake purchase and resale agreements to give themselves time to meet the increased reserve requirements without disrupting financial markets.

TABLE 35-2   Balance Sheet for a Loaned-Up Banking System

(a) Before: 20 percent reserve ratio				(b) After: 25 percent reserve ratio			
Assets		Liabilities		Assets		Liabilities	
Reserves	$1,000	Deposits	$5,000	Reserves	$1,000	Deposits	$4,000
Loans	4,100	Capital	100	Loans	3,100	Capital	100
	$5,100		$5,100		$4,100		$4,100

Increasing the required reserve ratio forces a loaned-up bank to reduce its deposits and thus decreases the supply of deposit money. The banking system in part (a) has a ratio of reserves to deposits of 0.20. If the Bank of Canada raises the required reserve ratio to 0.25, the reserves of $1,000 will support deposits of only $4,000. As shown in part (b), the banking system can reduce its deposits by reducing its loans. A reduction in reserve requirements from 0.25 to 0.20 would permit a banking system in the position of (b) to expand its loans and deposits to those of (a) with no increases in its dollar reserves.

than stabilizing the economy. For example, reforms of the Bank Act in 1980 reduced the reserve requirement on demand deposits from 12 to 10 percent.

Changes in the Bank Rate

The rate of interest at which the Bank of Canada makes loans to the chartered banks is called the **bank rate.** In some countries, commercial banks that find themselves short of reserves borrow from the central bank. A rise in the bank rate in such countries will cause the commercial banks to be more prudent in their lending activities. If they lend so much out that they have insufficient reserves, they will have to pay a higher rate to borrow from the central bank. However, this mechanism is not very important in Canada because the chartered banks rarely borrow from the Bank of Canada.

Prior to March 1980 the bank rate was simply set by the Bank of Canada. Changes in the rate had an "announcement effect"—such changes were widely interpreted as a signal of changes in the stance of monetary policy, which would cause market interest rates quickly to move in the same direction. Since March 1980 the bank rate itself has become a "market rate." It is now set at a premium of one-quarter of a percentage point over the average rate determined in the weekly Thursday auction of three-month treasury bills.

Most observers believed that a market-determined bank rate would lessen the role played by the

bank rate by eliminating the announcement effect; however, the financial press now gives more attention to changes in the bank rate, and it is not at all clear that it is less important as a signal about monetary policy. The Bank of Canada is a major participant in the market for treasury bills, and its purchases or sales clearly influence the bank rate by influencing the treasury bill rate. But its purchases and sales also influence the money supply. Hence the bank rate now signals actual rather than intended monetary policy.

Secondary Reserve Requirements

When the central bank attempts to restrain inflationary forces, it may wish to dampen expenditures not only through higher interest rates but also through some form of direct control over the expansion of bank loans. Restricting the supply of cash reserves will not restrain the banks from extending credit if they have substantial quantities of liquid assets that can be sold off to finance new loans. The Bank of Canada is empowered to restrict the ability of the chartered banks to expand their loans through the imposition of a required minimum secondary reserve ratio within the range of 0 to 12 percent of deposits. Secondary reserves are defined as holdings of treasury bills, day-to-day loans, and excess cash reserves. A required minimum ratio of 8 percent was in effect from the end of 1971 until the end of 1974, when it was lowered to 7 percent. Further reductions were made during 1975 and 1977; at the beginning of 1978, the required ratio was 5 percent. It has not changed since.

Moral Suasion

The term *moral suasion* is generally used to describe attempts by the central bank to enlist the cooperation of private financial institutions in the pursuit of some objective of monetary policy. In a country such as Canada, where there are only a few banks, the central bank can easily communicate its view to the chartered banks. In some cases moral suasion involves general discussions aimed at improving understanding of the current financial situation and the objectives of policy. In other cases specific requests have been issued to the banks. For example, on a number of occasions in recent years the Bank of Canada has attempted to restrain the growth of term deposits by requesting the observance of ceilings either on the interest rates offered or on the volume of deposits.

Effects of Changes in the Money Supply: A Review

We have now seen how the Bank of Canada can alter the money supply. Before turning to a more detailed discussion of the Bank's operating procedure and the policy choices it faces, we review the analysis in Chapter 34 of the effects of changes in the money supply.

Suppose that initially the economy is in equilibrium at less than potential income. The Bank then increases the money supply. Firms and households now hold excess money balances, and they try to buy bonds. This action forces up the price of bonds, which implies a fall in the rate of interest.

The resulting increase in desired investment expenditure shifts the aggregate demand curve rightward, thus raising equilibrium national income. This process is shown in Figures 34-4 and 34-5 on pages 745 and 746.

When the Bank decreases the money supply, this creates an excess demand for money because firms and households no longer have the money balances they wish to hold at the existing level of interest rates. In an effort to replenish their inadequate holdings of money, firms and households seek to sell bonds, causing an increase in the interest rate. The increased interest rate causes a reduction in investment expenditure. This in turn shifts the aggregate demand curve leftward and lowers equilibrium income.

Monetary policy works through the transmission mechanism to shift the aggregate demand curve and so to change equilibrium national income. An increase in the money supply is expansionary, a decrease contractionary.

As a result, changes in the money supply will cause real national income and the price level to change in the same direction, as shown in Figure 34-8 on page 748.

Instruments and Objectives of Monetary Policy

The Bank of Canada conducts monetary policy in order to influence real national income and the price level. These ultimate objectives of the Bank's policy are called **policy variables.** The variables that it controls *directly* in order to achieve these objectives are called its **policy instruments.** Variables that are neither policy variables nor policy instruments but nevertheless can play a key role in the execution of monetary policy are called **intermediate targets;** their importance lies in the influence they exert on the policy variables.

Policy Variables

The Bank's twin policy variables are real national income and the price level. In practice the two are often lumped into a single variable, nominal national income.

Nominal national income as a policy variable. Changes in nominal national income arise from changes in both real national income and the price level. In principle the central bank will be concerned about how a given change in nominal national income is divided between these two components.

We saw in Chapter 34 that monetary policy operates by influencing aggregate demand. In the short run the effects of a monetary policy that shifts the *AD* curve will be divided between the price level and real output in a manner determined by the slope of the *SRAS* curve. Thus, while the central bank cares about the price level and real output, there is little it can do in the short run to achieve separate goals with respect to each. For any price-level response that is achieved, the real output consequence must be accepted. Alternatively, for any real output response that is achieved, the price-level consequence must be accepted. Monetary policy is not capable of pursuing two objectives of pushing the price level (P) and national income (Y) toward independently determined targets. For this reason we choose to focus on nominal national income (PY) as the target for monetary policy in the short run.

Price level as the policy variable in the long run. We have seen that in the long run, when the level of wages is fully adjusted to the price level, the *LRAS* curve is vertical and hence the major impact of monetary policy will be on the price level.

Although monetary policy influences both real output and the price level in the short run, its main effects in the long run are only on the price level.

Policy Instruments

Having selected its policy variables and formulated targets for their behavior, the Bank must decide how to achieve these targets. How can the policy variables be made to perform in the way that the Bank wishes? Since the Bank can control neither income nor the price level directly, it must employ its policy instruments, which it does control directly, to influence aggregate demand in the desired manner.

The primary instrument used by the Bank of Canada to conduct monetary policy is open-market operations.

Open-market operations change the size of the Bank's monetary liabilities, which are the currency in circulation plus reserves of the chartered banks. Chartered bank reserves are held on deposit with the Bank and are the Bank's liability because it must redeem them on demand. The Bank of Canada's monetary liabilities, as we saw in Chapter 33, form the *base* on which chartered banks can expand and create deposits. For this reason their liabilities are often referred to as the **monetary base.**

The central bank cannot expect to be able to use its open-market operations to control both the interest rate and the monetary base independently. This is because of the liquidity preference function, which relates the quantity of money to the rate of interest.

The Bank must therefore choose between two alternative procedures in conducting its open-market operations. It may set the *price* (and hence the interest rate) at which it sells or buys bonds on the open market. In this case the quantity of bonds sold or purchased is determined by market demand. If the Bank wishes to change its policy, it must change the price at which it is willing to buy and sell bonds. This approach is called **interest-rate control**, and here the interest rate is properly viewed as a policy instrument.

Alternatively, the Bank may choose to set the *quantity* of open-market sales or purchases. It does this in order to set the reserves of the chartered banks. In this case it is the price of bonds, and hence the interest rate, that is determined by market demand. If the Bank wishes to change its policy, it changes the amount of its open-market purchases or sales. (Of course, this means that the interest rate at which these transactions are made may also change.) In this case, where the Bank chooses to set the quantity of its open-market operations, it is directly deciding how much the monetary base will change. For this reason it is said to be using **base control**, and the monetary base is properly viewed as the policy instrument.

Intermediate Targets

Major changes in the direction or method of monetary policy are usually made only infrequently. Decisions regarding the implementation of policy must, however, be made almost daily. Given the values that the Bank wishes its policy variables to take on, and given the current state of the economy, is a purchase or a sale in the open market called for? How big a purchase or sale? At what interest rate? Such questions must be answered continually by the Bank in its day-to-day operations.

Daily information about the policy variables, however, is rarely available. Inflation and unemployment rates are available only on a monthly basis and with a considerable lag. National income figures are available even less frequently; they appear on a quarterly basis. Thus the policymakers do not know exactly what is happening to the policy variables when they make decisions about their policy instruments.

How, then, does the Bank of Canada make decisions? Central banks have typically used *intermediate targets* to guide them when implementing monetary policy in the very short run. To serve as an intermediate target, a variable must satisfy two criteria. First, information about it must be available on a frequent basis, daily if possible. Second, its movements must be closely correlated with those of the policy variable so that changes in it can reasonably be expected to indicate that the policy variable is also changing.

The two most commonly used intermediate targets have been the money supply and the interest rate. Since the two are not independent, it is important that the central bank not choose a target for one that is inconsistent with the other. By the same token, since the two are closely related, it might appear not to matter much which one is used.

For example, if the Bank wishes to remove an inflationary gap by forcing interest rates up, it will sell securities and thus drive their prices down. These open market sales will also contract the money supply. It is largely immaterial whether the Bank seeks to force interest rates up or to contract the money supply; doing one accomplishes the other. Similarly, driving interest rates down by open-market purchases of government securities will tend to expand the money supply as the public gains money in return for the securities it sells to the Bank.

Nevertheless, there are differences between a monetary regime where interest rates are taken as the intermediate target and a regime that uses the money supply as target.

Choice of intermediate targets. Over the years there has been controversy over which intermediate target the Bank should rely on most. In the earlier part of the postwar period, many central banks relied mainly on interest rates.

A majority of economists, including most monetarists, have long been critical of the practice of using the interest rate as an intermediate target. These economists pointed out that since interest rates tended to vary directly with the business cycle, rising on the upswing and falling on the downswing, it was difficult for the central bank to determine the impact of its monetary policy by observing the interest rate alone. Historical examples were pointed to where central banks, trying to restrain a boom, thought their restrictive policies were working because interest rates were rising sharply. In retrospect it was concluded, however, that interest rates were rising because of rapidly expanding national income and, hence, increasing demand for money.

As a result of such criticisms, many central banks, including the Bank of Canada, turned to rely almost exclusively on the narrow monetary aggregate M1 as their intermediate target. When M1 turned out to be a less than completely reliable guide, broader monetary aggregates were used.

Today, however, after more than a decade's experience with such aggregates, similar criticisms can be levied at exclusive concentration on them. The reason is that changes in the money supply are reliable indicators of the direction of monetary policy *only* if the demand for money is relatively stable. Recent experience suggests that the demand for money can change quite substantially and that a central bank can discover what is happening to this demand only after much time-consuming research. Critics of the use of monetary aggregates as intermediate variables can point to historical circumstances in which a central bank incorrectly thought it was exerting a restraining force on the economy through a restrictive monetary policy because monetary aggregates were growing slowly. In retrospect, however, it turned out that monetary policy had been expansionary. There was an excess supply rather than an excess demand for money, the reason being that the demand for money had fallen more than had been appreciated at the time.

TABLE 35-3   Assignment of Variables Under Alternative Operating Regimes of Monetary Policy

Regime	Policy instrument	Intermediate target	Policy variable
1. Monetary targeting—base control	Open-market operations: regulate volume of open-market sales and purchases	Quantity of money (M1) via money supply process	
2. Monetary targeting—interest-rate control	Open-market operations: regulate price at which open-market sales and purchases are made (i.e., regulate interest rate)	Quantity of money (M1) via liquidity preference	1. Real national income and the price level *or* 2. Nominal national income
3. Interest-rate targeting	Open-market operations: regulate intermediate target directly	Interest rates	

Even with a given set of policy variables, central banks might adopt a variety of operating regimes. The central bank could use either the quantity of money or the interest rate as its intermediate target.

When the central bank opts for monetary targeting, it can influence its target only indirectly. Through its open-market operations it can control directly either the size of the monetary base or the level of interest rates. If it controls the monetary base (regime 1), the quantity of money is influenced via the money supply process, while the interest rate is determined via monetary equilibrium as in Figure 34-2. If the central bank controls the interest rate (regime 2), the influence on the quantity of money operates via the liquidity preference function.

Should the central bank choose to use the interest rate as an intermediate target (regime 3), it can achieve its target directly by using open-market operations to control the interest rate. Although this appears to be a simpler process (and in terms of operation, it is simpler), many economists favor monetary targeting.

Other variables, such as the interest rate and the exchange rate, might also appear as policy variables. The interest rate could then appear as a policy instrument, an intermediate target, or a policy variable, depending on the policy regime.

Today some central banks still try to target on a money supply figure while others, including the Bank of Canada, use no single target but try to assess their monetary stance by looking at interest rates, various money supply measures, and other targets.

Operating Regime

A central bank's **operating regime** refers to the combination of intermediate targets and the policy instruments it selects to achieve those targets.

Table 35-3 illustrates some possible operating regimes for the central bank. If the Bank chooses the interest rate as its intermediate target, it can achieve that target directly by using interest rate control as its instrument. In this case the distinction between intermediate target and policy instrument is superfluous. If the Bank chooses the money supply as its intermediate target, it can achieve its target indirectly by means of either base control or interest-rate control. The somewhat confusing multiple roles that can be played by the various economic variables are clarified in the table and summarized as follows.

Nominal national income is a policy variable. The money supply can be an intermediate target or a policy instrument. The interest rate can be a policy variable, an intermediate target, or a policy instrument.

Whichever operating regime is adopted, attempts to use monetary policy to fine-tune the economy remain fraught with dangers. The problems come mainly from the lags between a change in the policy instruments and the reaction of the policy variables that the Bank wishes to control. The way in which long lags can make stabilization policy become destabilizing has already been discussed in Chapter 32 in the context of fiscal policy, and it is further discussed in Box 35-1 in the context of monetary policy.

Monetary Policy in Action

Having studied its objectives and instruments, we now consider how monetary policy has actually operated since World War II.

Throughout the 1950s and 1960s, the Bank of Canada used interest rates as its main intermediate target. In spite of difficulties in judging the stance of monetary policy by observing interest rates in some periods, in others the stance was clear. For example, there is little doubt that monetary policy was contractionary in 1968 and 1969 when the Bank tried to stop Canada from importing the U.S. inflation.[3]

There is also little doubt that monetary policy was quite expansionary in the early 1970s. By 1974 inflation was close to the double-digit level. Then the first OPEC supply-side shock sent oil prices, and then the general price level, soaring. Inflation accelerated, output fell, and unemployment grew.

Monetary Gradualism: 1975–1980

In 1975 the Bank of Canada announced a policy of "monetary gradualism." The rate of increase in the money supply (narrowly defined as M1) was to be reduced gradually in an effort to reduce the inflation rate gradually. To accomplish this, a target range for money supply growth was to be stated publicly and periodically revised downward.

The first target range was set at 10 to 15 percent growth per year. The first reduction, to a range of 8 to 12 percent, came in August 1976. Successive steps

---

[3] The attempt was frustrated by the Bank's commitment to a fixed rate of exchange between the Canadian dollar and the U.S. dollar. As we shall see in Chapter 42, monetary policy cannot simultaneously control the money supply and the exchange rate.

further reduced the range; in mid February 1981 the target range was 4 to 8 percent. The Bank was quite successful at keeping actual money growth inside the target range, although there was considerable movement within that range. But after some reduction during the early periods of gradualism, the inflation rate again accelerated, and by the end of the decade it was not far below the rate prevailing when the policy was introduced in 1975. This was because the restraint sought through money supply control was offset by shifts in the demand for money, many of which were caused by the very inflation the policy was attempting to curb.

Inflation raises the cost of holding non-interest-bearing M1 balances, since one consequence of rapid inflation is a high nominal rate of interest. This provides an incentive to economize on M1 balances and invest the funds instead in interest-earning assets.

A series of spectacular institutional changes showed just how adaptive the financial system can be to changes in the needs of its users; many of these changes were noted in Chapter 33. Firms learned how to reduce their M1 balances by careful cash management. In some countries funds were even moved to banks in remote areas where cheques were cleared once rather than twice a day, so that once cheques were cleared, cash managers knew they had the use of their remaining balances for a whole 24 hours! Banks introduced automatic transfer systems where money could be held in interest-earning accounts and transferred to chequing accounts only when needed. As a result of such changes, the demand for M1 balances often fell faster than the supply was being restricted. Thus M1 control did not always create the desired conditions of tight money.

In 1982 the Bank of Canada formally abandoned monetary targeting, although many commentators felt that it had really abandoned the policy in mid 1981 when it allowed the money supply to fall well below the target range and focused considerable attention on propping up the exchange rate. The Bank remained committed to trying to control the economy through aggregate demand. It stated, however, that no observed relation between M1 or any other monetary magnitude on the one hand and national income on the other hand was stable enough to make complete reliance on monetary targets useful.

BOX 35-1

How Monetary Policy Can Be Destabilizing

In the real world the full effects of monetary policy occur only after quite long time lags. *Execution lags,* lags that occur after the decision is made to implement the policy, can have important implications for the conduct of monetary policy.

Sources of Execution Lags

1. Open-market operations affect the reserves of the chartered banks. The full increase in the money supply occurs only when the banks have granted enough new loans and made enough investments to expand the money supply by the full amount permitted by existing reserve ratios. This process can take quite a long time.
2. The division of all assets into just two categories, money and bonds, is useful for showing the underlying forces at work in determining the demand for money. In fact, however, there is a whole series of assets— from currency and demand deposits to term deposits, to treasury bills and short-term bonds, to long-term bonds and equities. When households find themselves with larger money balances than they require, a chain of substitution occurs, with short-term and long-term interest rates falling as households try to hold less money and more interest-earning assets. The change in longer-term interest rates in turn affects interest-sensitive expenditures. These adjustments along a chain of interest rates can take considerable time to work out.
3. It takes time for new investment plans to be drawn up, approved, and put into effect. It may easily take up to a year before the full increase in investment expenditure builds up in response to a fall in interest rates.
4. The increased investment expenditures set off a multi-

plier process that increases national income by some multiple of the initiating increase in investment expenditure. This, too, takes some time to work out.

Similar considerations apply to contractionary monetary policies that seek to shift the aggregate expenditure function downward.

Furthermore, although the end result is fairly predictable, the speed with which the entire expansionary or contractionary process works itself out can vary from time to time in ways that are hard to predict.

Monetary policy is capable of exerting expansionary and contractionary forces on the economy, but it operates with a time lag that is long and unpredictably variable.

Implications of Execution Lags

To see the significance of execution lags for the conduct of monetary policy, assume that the execution lag is 18 months. If on December 1 the Bank of Canada decides that the economy needs stimulus, it can be increasing the money supply within days, and by the end of the year a significant increase may be registered.

But because the full effects of this policy take time to work out, the policy may prove to be destabilizing. By the fall of next year a substantial inflationary gap may have developed due to cyclical forces unrelated to the Bank's monetary policy. The Bank

Monetary Stringency: 1981–1983

The early 1980s saw an extremely restrictive monetary policy, one that reduced inflation to low levels, but at the cost of a very severe recession. Since during this period the Bank of Canada was mainly following the lead of the U.S. Federal Reserve System (the Fed), the period is best studied by observing the forces operating in the United States.

The United States Experience

In 1980 the Fed embarked on a policy of monetary restraint aimed at fighting inflation. As a result, interest rates rose sharply, as shown in Figure 35-1[4]

[4] In 1980 the Fed switched from a regime of interest-rate control to a regime of base control. Although this policy requires that interest rates be free to find their own level, many economists did not expect the degree of interest rate volatility shown in Figure 35-1.

may then call for a contractionary policy, but the full effects of the monetary expansion initiated nine months earlier are just being felt, so an expansionary monetary stimulus is adding to the existing inflationary gap. If the Bank now applies the monetary brakes by contracting the money supply, the full effects of this move will not be felt for another 18 months. By that time a contraction may have already set in because of the natural cyclical forces of the economy. If so, the delayed effects of the monetary policy may turn a minor downturn into a major recession.

The long execution lag of monetary policy makes monetary fine tuning difficult, and it may make it destabilizing.

If the execution lag were known with certainty, it could be built into the Bank's calculations. But the fact that the lag is highly variable makes this nearly impossible. Of course, when a persistent output gap has existed and is predicted to continue for a long time, monetary policy may be stabilizing even when its effects occur after a long time lag.

A Monetary Rule?

The poor record of monetary policy as a short-run stabilizer has lent force to the monetarists' persistent criticisms of monetary fine tuning. Monetarists argue that (1) monetary policy is a potent force of expansionary and contractionary pressures; (2) monetary policy works with lags that are both long and variable; and (3) central banks are often given to sudden and sharp reversals of policy stance. Consequently, monetary policy has a destabilizing effect on the economy, the policy itself accentuating rather than dampening the economy's natural cyclical swings.

Monetarists argue from this position that the stability of the economy would be much improved if the central bank stopped trying to stabilize it. What then should the central bank do? Since growth of population and of productivity lead to a rising level of output, the central bank ought to provide the extra money needed to allow the holding of additional desired money balances as real income and wealth rise over time.

According to the monetarists, the central bank should expand the money supply year in and year out at a constant rate equal to the rate of growth of real income. When the growth rate shows signs of long-term change, the central bank can adjust its rate of monetary expansion. It should not, however, alter this rate with a view to stabilizing the economy against short-term fluctuations.

This reasoning led a number of central banks, including the Bank of Canada, to focus on the growth of the money supply in formulating their policies. As we shall see, the results have been mixed. Experience has shown that the demand for money can sometimes shift quite substantially. A stable money supply rule in the face of demand instability guarantees monetary shocks rather than monetary stability.

(see page 766). The sharp rise in interest rates in late 1980 helped choke off the recovery that had just started. A further rise in rates in early 1982 fed the downturn and helped make it the most serious recession since the 1930s.

These interest rates, and the recession they wrought, were more severe than might have been expected from the monetary policy that was intended. What happened to cause the high interest rates and the severe recession in the face of this moderate showdown in the rate of growth of the money supply? Once again, the key to the puzzle lay in the relation between the demand for money and national income.

As a result of an unanticipated surge in the demand for money, there was a severe money shortage—that is, monetary policy was much tighter than the Fed had expected. This was not because money

FIGURE 35-1   Short-Term Interest Rates, Canada and the United States, 1979–1986

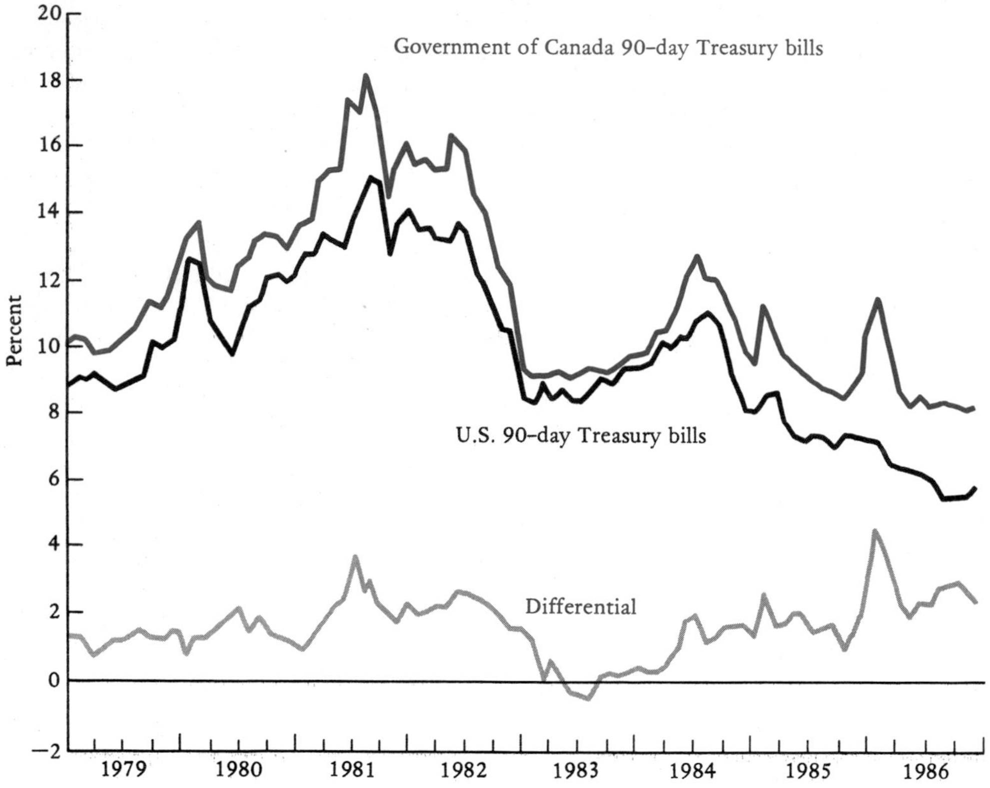

Short-term interest rates have moved together in Canada and the United States, both rising until mid 1982 and both falling since. During 1979 and 1980 interest rates displayed an upward trend, reflecting increases in inflation. Tight monetary policy then led to sharp increases in interest rates in 1981. Subsequent declines in inflation then led to declines in nominal interest rates.

The interest differential shows that Canadian interest rates were typically a little higher than American interest rates. The differential was especially large in 1981 and 1982 when sharp increases in U.S. rates were more than matched by increases in Canadian rates, and in late 1985 and early 1986 when sharp decreases in U.S. rates were not matched by decreases in Canadian rates. (*Source: Bank of Canada Review*, several issues.)

supply targets were missed—in fact, M1 rose above its target range in this period. Rather, monetary policy was tight because money demand was again misestimated—this time it was underestimated.[5]

[5] Note that this was the opposite of the shift that disrupted Canadian monetary policy in the 1970s.

In part the Fed's reaction was to raise the rate of monetary growth. But basically the Fed stuck to its monetary targets, and as a result it pursued very restrictive monetary policy. This created a heated controversy in the financial press and caused many critics to attack the Fed's policies.

By June 1982 M1 was back in its target range.

But the serious weakness in the economy and the "room for monetary ease" created by the return of M1 to its target range led to a loosening of monetary policy in the second half of 1982.

Why did the Fed allow this severely contractionary policy to persist so long? One possibility is that the Fed was actually quite happy to have a very contractionary policy. Many observers had come to the view that only a sharp monetary contraction would lower inflationary expectations and so allow the actual inflation rate to fall. Another possibility is that having announced its targets for monetary growth, the Fed had to adhere to them in order to maintain its own credibility. Failure to meet the targets, this argument runs, would undermine belief in the Fed's commitment to reducing inflation. Such a loss of confidence would in turn work to make interest rates and the actual inflation rate respond sluggishly to the Fed's policies.

The Canadian Reaction

The very tight monetary policy in the United States led to similar monetary restraint in Canada. As in the United States, there is a question about why this was done. Two reasons are probably important. One is that the high degree of integration of capital markets means there is not very much scope for Canadian interest rates to be held far below U.S. rates. (This matter is discussed further in Chapter 39.) Insofar as the Bank of Canada had some freedom to hold rates below those in the United States, it did not exercise its freedom (see Figure 35-1). The second reason suggested is that, discouraged by the failure of gradualism to control inflation, the Bank of Canada welcomed the opportunity to follow the United States in a more severe bout of monetary restraint. By the early 1980s many commentators had begun to wonder if the problem of inflation was intractable. If it could be solved, the failure of gradualism suggested that a severe jolt of very restrictive policy might be needed to do the job.

The severe monetary restraint did have powerful effects on the Canadian economy—in fact, the effects were more powerful than many economists predicted at the time. As we have already noted (see Figure 35-1), interest rates soared and a severe reces-

sion occurred. Real output growth was *negative* throughout 1982, and by the end of that year the unemployment rate reached 12.8 percent, its highest level since the Great Depression of the 1930s. The monetary restraint also had a strong restraining effect on inflation—the rate of change of the CPI fell from its peak of 12.7 percent in the third quarter of 1981 to 4.6 percent at the end of 1983. The fall in inflation brought with it a fall in nominal interest rates; for example, the 90-day commercial paper rate fell from a peak of just over 17 percent in mid 1982 to 9.3 percent by the end of 1983.[6]

Low Inflation and Economic Recovery: 1983–1987

In early 1983 a sustained recovery began, and by mid 1987 national income had moved back toward potential. Much of the growth was centered in the export-oriented manufacturing industries in Ontario and Quebec. Although painfully slow for those who remained unemployed, the first four years of the recovery saw a record 990,000 jobs created and cumulative output growth of 15.7 percent.

The main challenge for monetary policy in this period was to create a sufficient increase in the money supply to accommodate the recovery without triggering a return to the high inflation rates that prevailed at the start of the decade.

This task was not as simple as it may appear. The transition from high inflation to low inflation led to what has become known as the *re-entry problem* for monetary policy. The combination of falling nominal interest rates and rising national income led to a sharp increase in the demand for real money balances. Since an increase in real balances can be achieved by either relatively slow growth in the price level or a rapid increase in the nominal money supply, the Bank of Canada basically had two alternatives.

It could continue its policy of maintaining a low growth rate of the nominal money supply. This

---

[6] Real interest rates did not fall as much, if indeed they fell at all, as inflation fell to an equal or greater extent than nominal interest rates.

would restrain aggregate demand and thus guard against the risk of a resurgence of inflation, but at the cost of slowing the pace of the recovery. With this policy real balances would begin to increase only when the rate of price increase fell below the rate of monetary growth. For that to occur, national income would have to be kept below potential for a prolonged period.

Alternatively, the Bank could allow a short but rapid burst of growth in the nominal money supply, thus generating the desired increase in real money balances. Once the new level of real balances was achieved, money growth could again be cut back to a rate consistent with low inflation, allowing for the underlying rate of growth in real income. But the trick with this policy was to avoid triggering expectations of renewed inflation—essentially the Bank had to generate a one-shot increase in the level of the money supply without creating the impression that it was raising the rate of growth of the money supply.

Most economists agreed that the second policy was preferable *in principle*. But there was wide disagreement over the size and duration of the required monetary expansion and hence whether the Bank's actual policy was appropriate. In late 1983 and early 1984, when growth in monetary aggregates first started to surge, many voiced the fear that the Bank was being overly expansionary and was risking a return to higher inflation. As the re-entry problem came to be more widely understood and as inflation pressures failed to re-emerge, these criticisms subsided and the consensus appeared to be that the Bank had done a commendable job of handling the re-entry problem.

Recently some critics have suggested that perhaps the Bank was too cautious in expanding liquidity during the re-entry problem. Professor Peter Howitt of the University of Western Ontario has argued that excessive caution by the Bank caused the recovery to be slower than necessary.[7] Howitt argues that the Bank erred in focusing almost exclusively on the narrowly defined money supply. The declines in interest rates that occurred as inflation fell caused a substitution out of interest-bearing deposits into de-

mand deposits. Hence the demand for M1 grew rapidly. The demand for broader money aggregates did not grow nearly as fast since the broader aggregates include both demand deposits (which were growing) and interest-bearing deposits (which were falling). If the Bank had focused more on a broader aggregate, the argument goes, it would have seen that the relevant rate of monetary expansion was not excessive.

It is true that Canadian monetary expansion was slower during this period than American monetary expansion. But it is also true that inflation fell more slowly in Canada than in the United States. If the Bank did err in following a monetary policy that was too tight, it was probably because of a commitment not to relax monetary restraint before inflation had unquestionably fallen to the lower, more acceptable range that the Bank was striving for.

Whatever the judgment of monetary policy in that period, many observers now worry that Canadian policymakers have been too complacent in accepting the current 4 percent range Canadian inflation seems to have settled into.[8] In 1987 the question of whether monetary policy should be tightened in an attempt to lower inflation even further was widely debated. Some economists argued that if that were not done, Canada would experience gradually increasing inflation until once again a severe monetary restriction would be necessary. We return to this debate in Chapter 36.

Some Tentative Conclusions

The search for a single monetary aggregate to be *the* correct intermediate target was slowly abandoned. Gradually, it became accepted that the economy was too complicated for a single magnitude to provide all the information that the Bank needed in developing an effective monetary policy. The high degree of substitutability among M1, M2, and M3 meant that all three magnitudes needed to be surveyed for the information that they could provide. Furthermore, institutional developments meant that the de-

[7] *Monetary Policy in Transition* (Toronto: C. D. Howe Institute, 1986).

[8] In 1974, when inflation rose to the "unprecedented peak" of 4 percent, it was considered a national emergency that led to the introduction of wage and price controls in the United States and their serious consideration in Canada!

gree of substitutability was subject to continual change so that no one magnitude could be taken as an appropriate intermediate target in all circumstances.

The behavior of interest rates conveyed information that might not be available from monetary aggregates alone. For example, in the mid 1980s real interest rates were high by historical standards. A goal of monetary policy, therefore, became to create the stable conditions that would allow interest rates to return to more normal levels, but to do this without rekindling inflationary expectations. The important lesson was also drawn from the earlier period of the 1970s that even if all the monetary aggregates are only increasing slowly, real interest rates that are low or negative, as they often were, cannot be the symptom of a tight monetary policy. Thus the combination of low rates of growth of monetary aggregates and unusually low interest rates probably indicates major reductions in the demand for money and, hence, that monetary policy is more expansionary than the behavior of any monetary aggregate would reveal.

New goals of monetary policy in addition to the traditional ones of income and price level have emerged. The two new goals of greatest importance are the health of the financial system and the behavior of exchange rates.

1. The enormous debt that third world countries, particularly oil exporters, piled up in the 1970s became unsustainable in the 1980s. Much of this debt was owed to banks in the developed countries, the United States and Canada being important creditors. As oil revenues fell, the oil-exporting countries found it impossible to pay the interest on their debt without further loans, let alone trying to repay any of the principal. Central banks became acutely aware that a sudden default of these debtor countries could cause a financial crisis in the banking system. It also became aware that every time the interest rate rose 1 percent, the burden on these debtor countries was measured in billions of dollars of extra payments. There is little hope that these countries can ever generate the revenues necessary to repay the principal of these loans. What the banking community of the developed world could at most try to do was to delay the final day of reckoning by re-

scheduling some of the loans and lending some of the money needed to repay the remaining interest until the major banks could adjust their portfolios sufficiently to write off enormous amounts of loans without going into insolvency.

2. The exchange rate has always been important in Canada, and it became an important variable for the United States in the mid 1980s. Central banks in the developed countries can no longer worry only about domestic variables. The behavior of the exchange rate influences the health of domestic industries that either export or compete with imports and therefore has an important influence on domestic economic performance.

The Bank of Canada seems to have come more and more to take nominal national income as its target variable. In the past the Bank has often concentrated on real national income as its goal of stabilization policy (remove recessionary or inflationary gaps) and the price level as its traditional goal of preserving the purchasing power of the nation's currency. Recently, however, the understanding has spread that the Bank can, at best, influence the *AD* curve, and how this influence divides itself between income and the price level depends on the shape of the *SRAS* curve, which is beyond the Bank's control. The Bank is still concerned with the long-term trend in the price level as its most important goal, but in the shorter term it seems to accept that it can influence nominal national income and adjust its policies to the behavior of that variable, which is a composite of changes in real income and the price level.

As the enormous federal budget deficit is reduced, there may be a need for the Bank to adopt a compensating monetary policy. The reduction in the deficit means some combination of tax increases and expenditure decreases on the part of the government. As we saw in Chapter 32, both of these changes reduce aggregate demand and tend to contract economic activity. To offset these forces, the Bank could engage in a once-and-for-all monetary expansion. As we saw in Chapter 34, this increases aggregate demand. There is no reason in theory why a change in the *mix* of macroeconomic policy to a more restrictive fiscal policy and a more expansionary monetary policy cannot leave the level of aggregate demand unchanged. This would mean that the policy changes did not significantly affect either national income or the price level. This shift in policy mix requires that the Bank be willing to play a more sophisticated role than merely following blind rules for the growth of monetary aggregates. This is a role that some would say is fraught with dangers of trying to do things that are beneficial in theory but that, given the imperfections of practical policy, may turn out to be harmful in practice—harmful in the specific way of increasing inflationary pressures. Whether or not this is a serious worry should become apparent by the end of the decade.

Summary

1. The major tool the Bank of Canada uses to control the supply of money is open-market operations. Purchases of bonds on the open market expand the money supply because they create new deposits that permit (but do not force) a multiple expansion of bank credit. Sales on the open market reduce bank reserves and force a multiple contraction of bank credit on the part of all banks that do not have excess reserves.

2. Other policies at the Bank of Canada's disposal include changing the reserve requirements of the chartered banks, changing the bank rate, and using moral suasion.

3. The ultimate objectives of monetary policy are called policy variables. In principle these include real national income and the rate of change of the price level. However, in practice nominal income is often taken to be the policy variable in the short term since the Bank of Canada cannot expect to be able to influence the composition of changes in nominal income between real growth and inflation.

4. Where the Bank of Canada cannot influence its policy variables directly, it must work through policy instruments that it can control and that will in turn influence its policy variables. Intermediate targets are used to guide decisions about policy instruments. The money supply and the interest rate may both be either intermediate targets or policy instruments.

5. National income can be influenced by open-market operations. Since it cannot control both independently, the Bank must choose between the interest rate and the money supply as the intermediate target of such operations. To reduce national income the Bank sells bonds on the open market, thereby reducing bank reserves, driving up the rate of interest, and shifting the *AD* curve to the left. To increase national income the Bank buys bonds on the open market, thereby increasing reserves, driving down the rate of interest, and shifting the *AD* curve to the right.

6. In the period up to 1975, the Bank of Canada used interest rates as its main intermediate target. In 1975 the Bank converted to monetarism and based its monetary policy on targets for the rate of increase of the money supply (defined as M1).

7. In the period of monetary gradualism from 1975 to 1980, the stance

of monetary policy was meant to be restrictive by gradually reducing the rate of increase of the money supply. However, due to innovations in banking practices, the demand for M1 often fell faster than the supply, making monetary policy expansive rather than restrictive.

8. In the period of stringency (1981–1983) the Fed, followed by the Bank of Canada, adopted a policy of severe monetary restraint. Interest rates soared to unprecedented heights, and the aggregate demand curves of both countries were driven sharply to the left. This led to a severe recession and a sharp fall in inflation.

9. During the long recovery from the recession that broke the inflation, the Bank largely accommodated the increase in the demand for real balances that resulted from the fall in the inflation rate and the rise in national income.

10. It is generally agreed that rapid changes in the money supply and interest rates can have large effects on the economy. There is disagreement, however, on how much monetary policy can and should be used as a device for stabilizing national income at its potential level or coping with temporary bouts of rising prices.

Open-market operations
The Bank rate
Policy variables, policy instruments, and intermediate targets
Variability of monetary policy and monetary rules
Appropriateness of monetary targets when money demand is shifting

Topics for Review

Discussion Questions

1. Professor Peter Howitt has recently argued that the Bank of Canada pursued an overly restrictive monetary policy during the recovery of 1983–1985. Describe the basic policy problem facing the Bank in this period and evaluate the basis for Howitt's view. On the basis of evidence available to it at the time, was it unreasonable for the Bank to be concerned about a resurgence of inflation? What has been the experience of inflation since that time?

2. During the recovery of the Canadian economy from 1983 to 1985, two different views were often expressed. Some analysts said that adherence to a long-run constant growth rate was particularly important for monetary growth lest inflationary expectations be rekindled by an overly fast rate of monetary expansion. Others said that encouraging the recovery required a temporary burst of monetary expansion. Discuss these two views.

3. The Federal Reserve Board runs a facility in Culpeper, Virginia, that costs $1.8 million per year to maintain and to guard against robbery, according to Senator William Proxmire of Wisconsin. Inside this "Culpeper switch," a dugout in the side of a mountain, the government has hidden $4 billion in new currency for the purpose, it says,

of "providing a hedge against any nuclear attack that would wipe out the nation's money supply." Comment on the sense of this policy.

4. Describe the chief instruments of monetary policy available to the Bank of Canada, and indicate whether they might be used for each of the following purposes and, if so, how.

   a. To create a mild tightening of bank credit
   b. To signal that the Bank favors a sharp curtailment of bank lending
   c. To permit an expansion of bank credit with existing reserves
   d. To supply banks and the public with a temporary increase of currency for Christmas shopping

5. It is often said that an expansionary monetary policy is like "pushing on a string." What is meant by such a statement? How does this contrast with a contractionary monetary policy?

6. In what situations might the following pairs of objectives come into conflict?

   a. Lowering the cost of government finance and using monetary policy to change aggregate demand
   b. Ending a deep recession and maintaining a currently achieved target for monetary growth
   c. Maintaining stable interest rates and controlling inflation

7. Writing in 1979, Nobel Laureate Milton Friedman accused the Fed of following "an unstable monetary policy," arguing that while the Fed "has given lip service to controlling the quantity of money . . . it has given its heart to controlling interest rates." Why might the desire to stabilize interest rates create an "unstable" monetary policy?

8. In 1982 the Bank of Canada stopped formally announcing and trying to attain precise target rates of growth for some monetary aggregate. Discuss the reasons behind this, and indicate whether you agree with the Bank's decision.

PART TEN

Issues and Controversies in Macroeconomics

36

Inflation

If you look again at Figure 26-1 on page 553 you will see that for 20 years following World War II inflation remained low. The only exceptions were the "bubbles" immediately following World War II and the Korean War. During the second half of the 1960s, the inflation rate slowly inched upward. It reached the double-digit range in the mid 1970s. By then inflation had been declared public enemy number one. Even more worrisome, it fell only slightly in the face of a concerted anti-inflationary attack during the late 1970s, rose again to the double-digit level in 1980, then remained quite stubborn during the recession of 1981–1982. At last, in 1983 inflation fell dramatically, then drifted down slowly to around 4 percent, where it remained through 1987. Although this was an improvement over the double-digit inflation rates experienced earlier, 4 percent is historically a very high inflation rate with which to emerge from a serious recession.

What are the causes of inflation? How was the great anti-inflationary battle of the early 1980s fought? Can inflation be prevented from sky-rocketing into the double-digit range again? Can inflation ever be eliminated altogether?

Inflationary Shocks

We start by noting a key distinction.

It is important to distinguish between the forces that cause a once-and-for-all increase in the price level and the forces that can cause a continuing (or sustained) increase.

Some terms that are sometimes used to stress this distinction are further discussed in Box 36-1.

Any event that tends to drive the price level upward is called an *inflationary shock*. To examine the causes and consequences of such shocks, we begin with an economy in long-run equilibrium: The price level is stable, and national income is at its potential level. We then study the economy as it is buffeted by different types of inflationary shocks.

Supply Shocks

Suppose there is a decrease in short-run aggregate supply, that is, that the *SRAS* curve shifts up and to the left. This might be caused, for example, by a rise in the costs of imported raw materials or a rise in domestic wage costs per unit of output. The price level rises and output

BOX 36-1

Inflation Semantics

The distinction between *once-and-for-all* and *continuing* rises in the price level is important. Some economists have sought to emphasize it by reserving the term *inflation* for a continuing or sustained rise in the price level and using other expressions such as *a rise in the price level* for a once-and-for-all increase.

One difficulty with this is that it is counter to ordinary usage, where inflation refers to any rise in the price level. Indeed, using the restricted definition causes difficulty when communicating with the public. If we were to use it, we would have to keep saying such things as "only some of the current rise in prices is an inflation, while the rest is merely a rise in the price level" and "we won't know whether or not the current rise in the price level is an inflation or not until we see if it is sustained."

In this book we use the term *inflation* as it is commonly used to mean any rise in the price level. We then make the distinction by referring to *temporary* or *once-and-for-all* inflations on the one hand and to *continuing* or *sustained* inflations on the other.

No matter of substance turns on the terms that we use to refer to clearly defined concepts. We use the expressions *temporary inflation* and *once-and-for-all rise in the price level* interchangeably. We use *sustained inflation* where some other economists, using the more restricted meaning, might merely talk of an inflation.

This discussion is important because students need to guard against being confused by different usages. Our selection of terms reflects only a desire to keep our language as close as possible to everyday usage.

---

falls. The rise in the price level shows up as a temporary burst of inflation.

What happens next depends on whether the shock to the *SRAS* curve is an isolated event or one of a series of recurring shocks. We choose import price increases as an example of an isolated supply shock because such shocks have occurred during the past two decades. We choose continued wage-cost push as an example of a repeated supply shock because, as we shall see later in this chapter and again in Chapter 39, this possibility has worried many economists ever since governments accepted responsibility for maintaining full employment.

What happens also depends on how the Bank of Canada reacts. If the Bank responds by increasing the money supply, we say that the supply shock has been *accommodated*. If the Bank holds the money supply constant, the shock is not accommodated. (Notice that our terminology distinguishes between the Bank's response to a supply shock, which we describe as accommodating the shock, and its response to a demand shock, which we describe in Chapter 34 and again later in this chapter, as validating the shock.)

Isolated Supply Shocks

Suppose that the leftward shift in the *SRAS* curve is an isolated event; say it is caused by a once-and-for-all increase in the cost of imported raw materials. How does monetary policy affect the economy's response to such an isolated supply shock?

No monetary accommodation. The leftward shift in the *SRAS* curve causes the price level to rise and pushes income below its full-employment level, opening up a recessionary gap. Pressure now mounts for wages and other factor costs to fall. When they do, the *SRAS* curve shifts downward, causing a return of income to full employment and a fall in the price level. In this case the period of inflation accompanying the original supply shock is eventually followed by a period of deflation, that is, a fall in the average level of all prices. The deflation continues until the original long-run equilibrium is re-established. This is discussed in the second paragraph of the caption to Figure 30-3. Given that wages and prices fall slowly, the recovery to full employment takes a long time.

Monetary accommodation.   Now let us see what happens if the money supply is changed in response to the isolated supply shock. Suppose the Bank reacts to the fall in national income by increasing the money supply. This shifts the *AD* curve to the right and causes both the price level and output to *rise*. When the recessionary gap is eliminated, the price level, rather than falling back to its original value, has risen further. The effects are illustrated in Figure 36-1.

Monetary accommodation of a supply shock causes the initial rise in the price level to be followed by a further rise, resulting in a higher price level than if the recessionary gap were relied on to reduce costs and prices.

FIGURE 36-1   Monetary Accommodation of a Single Supply Shock

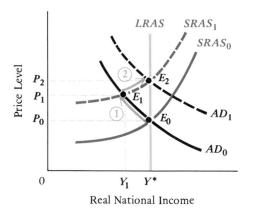

Monetary accommodation of a single supply shock causes costs, the price level, and money supply all to move in the same direction. A supply shock causes the *SRAS* curve to shift leftward from $SRAS_0$ to $SRAS_1$, as shown by arrow 1. Equilibrium is established at E_1.

If there is no monetary accommodation, the unemployment would put downward pressure on wages and other costs, causing the *SRAS* curve to shift slowly back to the right to $SRAS_0$. Prices would fall and output would rise until the original equilibrium was restored.

If there is monetary accommodation, the *AD* curve shifts from AD_0 to AD_1, as shown by arrow 2. This re-establishes full employment equilibrium at E_2 but with a higher price level, P_2.

The monetary authorities might decide to accommodate the supply shock because relying on cost deflation to restore full employment forces the economy to suffer through an extended slump. Monetary accommodation can return the economy to full employment quickly, but at the cost of a once-and-for-all increase in the price level.

Repeated Supply Shocks

We have been assuming that a recessionary gap would be associated with downward pressure on wages. This implies that labor markets behave much like commodity markets, so that wages fall when there is excess supply and rise only when there is excess demand.

As an example of a repeated supply shock, assume that powerful unions are able to raise wages in the absence of excess demand for labor and even in the face of significant excess supply. Large manufacturing firms pass these higher wages on in the form of higher prices. This type of supply shock causes what is called **wage-cost push inflation:** an increase in the price level due to increases in money wages that are not associated with excess demand for labor.

No monetary accommodation.   Suppose the Bank does not accommodate these supply shocks. The initial effect of the leftward shift in the *SRAS* curve is to open up a recessionary gap, as shown in Figure 36-1. If unions continue to negotiate increases in wages, subjecting the economy to further supply shocks, prices continue to rise and output continues to fall. Eventually the trade-off between higher wages and unemployment will become obvious to everyone.

Might not really powerful unions continue to force wages up despite this realization? As long as they did so, the recessionary gap would go on growing until, finally, unemployment reached 100 percent. Of course, this would not happen because long before everyone is unemployed, unions would cease forcing up wages in order to maintain jobs for those who are still employed.

Once the wage-cost push ceases, there are two possible scenarios. First, the unions may succeed in holding on to their high wages but not push for further increases. The economy then comes to rest with a stable price level and a large recessionary gap. Second, the persistent unemployment may eventually erode the power of the unions so that wages begin to fall. In this case the supply shock is reversed, and the *SRAS* curve shifts downward until full employment is eventually restored.

Non-accommodated wage-cost push tends to be self-limiting because the rising unemployment that it causes tends to restrain further wage increases.

Monetary accommodation. Now suppose that the Bank accommodates the shock with an increase in the money supply, thus shifting the *AD* curve to the right, as shown in Figure 36-1. In the new full-employment equilibrium both money wages and prices have risen. The rise in wages has been offset by a rise in prices. Workers are no better off than they were originally, although those who remained in jobs were temporarily better off in the transition after wages had risen (taking equilibrium to E_1 in Figure 36-1) but before the price level had risen (taking equilibrium to E_2).

The stage is now set for the unions to try again. If they succeed in negotiating further increases in money wages, they hit the economy with another supply shock. If the Bank again accommodates the shock, full employment is maintained, but at the cost of a further round of inflation. If this process goes on repeatedly, it can give rise to a continual wage-cost push inflation. The wage-cost push tends to cause a stagflation, with rising prices and falling output. Monetary accommodation tends to reinforce the rise in prices but to offset the fall in output. This case is illustrated in Figure 36-2.

Two things are required for wage-cost push inflation to continue. First, powerful groups, such as industrial unions or government employees, must press for and employers must grant increases in money wages, even in the absence of excess demand for labor and goods. Second, governments must accommodate the resulting inflation by increasing the money supply and so prevent the unemployment that would otherwise occur. The process set up by this sequence of wage-cost push and monetary accommodation is often called a *wage-price spiral*.

FIGURE 36-2 Monetary Accommodation of a Repeated Supply Shock

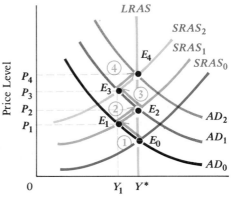

Real National Income

Monetary accommodation of a repeated supply shock causes a continuous inflation in the absence of excess demand. The initial equilibrium is at E_0. A supply shock then takes equilibrium to E_1, just as in Figure 36-1. This is the stagflation phase of rising prices and falling output; it is indicated by arrow 1.

The Bank of Canada then accommodates the supply shock by increasing the money supply, taking the *AD* curve to AD_1 and equilibrium to E_2. This is the expansionary phase of rising prices and output (arrow 2).

A second supply shock followed by monetary accommodation takes equilibrium to E_3 (arrow 3) and then to E_4 (arrow 4). As long as the supply shocks and the monetary accommodation continue, the inflation continues.

Is monetary accommodation desirable? Once started, a wage-price spiral can be halted only if the Bank stops accommodating the supply shocks that are causing the inflation. The longer the Bank waits to do so, the more entrenched will be the expectations that it will continue its policy of accommodating the shocks. These entrenched expectations may cause wages to continue to rise after accommodation has ceased. Because employers expect prices to rise, they go on granting wage increases. If expectations are firmly enough entrenched, the wage push can continue for quite some time in spite of the downward pressure caused by the rising unemployment associated with the growing recessionary gap.

Because of this possibility, some economists argue that the process should not be allowed to begin. One way to ensure this is to refuse to accommodate any supply shock whatsoever.

To some people, caution dictates that no supply shocks be accommodated lest a wage-price spiral be set up. Others are willing to risk accommodating isolated shocks in order to avoid the severe, though transitory, recessions that otherwise accompany them.

This key issue is discussed further in Chapter 39.

Demand Shocks

Now suppose that an initial equilibrium is disturbed by a rightward shift in the aggregate demand curve. This causes the price level and output to rise, as shown in Figures 36-3 and 36-4. The shift in the AD curve could have been caused by either an increase in autonomous expenditure or an increase in the money supply.[1] As with a supply shock, it is important to distinguish between the case in which the Bank reacts and that in which it does not. As we have seen, when the Bank reacts to the demand shock by increasing the money supply, it is said to be validating the shock.

No monetary validation.   This case is shown in Figure 36-3. Because the initial AD shock takes output above the full-employment level, an inflationary gap opens up. The pressure of excess demand soon causes wages and other costs to rise, shifting the $SRAS$ curve up and to the left. As long as the Bank holds the money supply constant, the rise in the price level brings into play the monetary adjustment mechanism (discussed in detail in Chapter 34): The economy moves up and to the left along the fixed AD curve, and the rise in the price level acts to reduce the inflationary gap. Eventually the gap is eliminated as equilibrium is established at a higher but stable price level and with income at its potential level. In this

[1] As we saw in Chapter 34, an increase in the money supply works through the transmission mechanism—excess supply of money, higher price of bonds, lower interest rates, increased investment expenditure—to shift the AD curve to the right.

FIGURE 36-3   An Unvalidated Demand-Shock Inflation

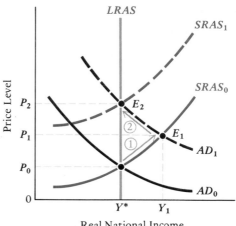

An unvalidated demand shock raises the equilibrium price level but leaves equilibrium income unchanged. The initial equilibrium is at E_0, with full-employment income Y^* and the price level P_0. A demand shock shifts the AD curve from AD_0 to AD_1, shifting equilibrium from E_0 to E_1, as shown by arrow 1. At E_1 income is Y_1 and the price level is P_1. The inflationary gap of Y^*Y_1 causes wages to rise, shifting the $SRAS$ curve to the left. Equilibrium moves along AD_1 to E_2, as shown by arrow 2. At E_2, income has returned to Y^*, removing the inflationary gap, while the price level has risen to P_2.

---

case the initial period of inflation is followed by further inflation that lasts only until the new equilibrium is reached.

Monetary validation.   Next, suppose that after the demand shock has created an inflationary gap, the Bank frustrates the monetary adjustment mechanism by increasing the money supply when output starts to fall. This is the case illustrated in Figure 36-4.[2] Two forces are now brought into play. Spurred by

[2] Although we distinguish between a single supply shock and a continuing one, we do not make a similar distinction with a demand shock. This is because the accommodation of a single supply shock restores full-employment equilibrium, whereas the validation of a demand shock perpetuates the disequilibrium.

FIGURE 36-4   A Validated Demand-Shock Inflation

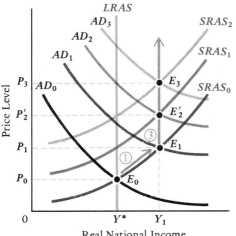

Monetary validation will cause the *AD* curve to shift rightward, offsetting the leftward shift in the *SRAS* curve and so leaving an inflationary gap in spite of the ever-rising price level. As in Figure 36-3, an initial demand shock shifts equilibrium from E_0 to E_1, taking income to Y_1 and the price level to P_1. The resulting inflationary gap then causes the *SRAS* curve to shift to the left. This time, however, the money supply is increased, shifting the *AD* curve to the right. By the time the aggregate supply curve has reached $SRAS_1$, the aggregate demand curve has reached AD_2. Now instead of being at E_2 in Figure 36-3, equilibrium is at E_2'. Income remains constant at Y_1, leaving the inflationary gap constant at Y^*Y_1, while the price level rises to P_2'.

The persistent inflationary gap continues to push the *SRAS* curve to the left, while the continued monetary validation continues to push the *AD* curve to the right. By the time the aggregate supply reaches $SRAS_2$, the aggregate demand has reached AD_3. The price level has risen still further to P_3, but because of the frustration of the monetary adjustment mechanism, the inflationary gap remains unchanged at Y_1Y^*. As long as this monetary validation continues, the economy moves along the vertical path of arrow 3.

the inflationary gap, the wage increases cause the *SRAS* curve to shift to the left. Fueled by the expansionary monetary policy, the *AD* curve shifts to the right. As a result of both of these shifts, the price level rises, but output need not fall. Indeed, if the

shift in the *AD* curve exactly offsets the shift in the *SRAS* curve, the inflationary gap will remain constant.

Validation of a demand shock turns what would have been a transitory inflation into a sustained inflation fueled by monetary expansion.

Because of the validation process, all subsequent shifts in the *AD* curve that perpetuate the inflation are caused by monetary forces.

Inflation As a Monetary Phenomenon

There has been heated debate among economists about the extent to which inflation is a monetary phenomenon. Does it have purely monetary causes—changes in the demand for or the supply of money? Does it have purely monetary consequences—only the price level is affected? One slogan stating an extreme position on this issue was made popular by Milton Friedman: "Inflation is *everywhere* and *always* a monetary phenomenon."

To consider these issues, let us summarize what we have already learned. First, look at causes.

1. Many forces can cause the price level to rise. On the demand side, anything that shifts the *AD* curve to the right will cause the price level to rise. This includes such expenditure changes as an autonomous increase in investment or government expenditure and such monetary changes as an increase in the money supply or a decrease in money demand. On the supply side, anything that increases costs of production will shift the *SRAS* curve to the left and cause the price level to rise.
2. Such inflations can continue for some time without any increases in the money supply.
3. The rise in prices must eventually come to a halt, unless monetary expansion occurs.

Points 1 and 2 provide the sense in which, looking at causes, a temporary burst of inflation need not be a monetary phenomenon. It need not have monetary causes, and it need not be accompanied by monetary expansion. Point 3 is the sense in which, looking at causes, a sustained inflation must be a monetary phenomenon. If a rise in prices is to continue, it must be accompanied by continuing increases in the money supply (or decreases in money demand). This is true regardless of the cause that set the rise in motion.[3]

Second, let us summarize the consequences of an inflation on the assumption that we begin from a situation where actual national income is at its potential level ($Y = Y^*$).

1. In the short run a demand-shock inflation tends to be accompanied by an increase in national income.
2. In the short run a supply-shock inflation tends to be accompanied by a decrease in national income.
3. When all adjustments have been fully made (so that the relevant supply-side curve is the *LRAS* curve), shifts in either the *AD* or *SRAS* curve leave national income unchanged and affect only the price level.

Points 1 and 2 provide the sense in which, looking at consequences, inflation is not, in the short run, a purely monetary phenomenon. Point 3 provides the sense in which, looking at consequences, inflation is a purely monetary phenomenon from the point of view of long-run equilibrium.

We have now established three important conclusions.

1. Without monetary accommodation, supply shocks cause temporary bursts of inflation accompanied by recessionary gaps. The gaps are removed if and when wages fall, restoring equilibrium at potential income and at the initial price level.
2. Without monetary validation, demand shocks cause temporary bursts of inflation accompanied by inflationary gaps. The gaps are removed as wages rise, returning income to its potential level, but at a higher price level.
3. With an appropriate response from the Bank, an

inflation, initiated by either supply or demand shocks, can continue indefinitely; an ever-increasing money supply is necessary for an ever-continuing inflation.

Sustained Inflation

The price level has risen in almost all years since the end of the Second World War. The decade from 1972 to 1982 was one of sustained inflation, often at rates of over 10 percent per year. In the mid 1980s the inflation rate was around 4 percent. Although this was lower than had been achieved in the previous 20 years, the rate would have been judged unsatisfactory at any time in the twentieth century before 1975. Four percent is a rate of inflation that will halve the purchasing power of money in about 18 years, less than the life expectancy of most people who retire in their sixties.

Why do we have sustained inflations of either the rapid sort, as in the 1970s, or the more gradual sort, as in the 1980s? What are the costs and benefits of reducing or eliminating such inflations?

Before we can deal with these questions, we must look in greater detail at what is involved in a sustained inflation. We have already stressed the role of monetary validation in allowing the *AD* curve to shift up continually. We now focus on the forces that cause the *SRAS* curve to shift upward.

Upward Shifts in the *SRAS* Curve

A rise in the cost of producing each unit of output, which is called unit cost, will cause the *SRAS* curve to shift upward. What is it then that causes unit costs to rise?

Influence of wage rates and productivity. Does every rise in wage rates force up unit costs? The answer is no, because what happens to unit costs depends on what happens to the cost of labor in relation to what happens to the productivity of labor (output per unit of labor input).

Although wages are usually the largest single element of production costs, a rise in wages is not by itself enough to raise unit costs. This is because pro-

[3] The statement that inflation is everywhere and always a monetary phenomenon depends on a restricted and specific definition of the term *inflation*. To justify the statement, a temporary burst of inflation with nonmonetary causes must be called a rise in the price level, and the term *inflation* must be reserved for increases in the price level that are sustained for long enough that they must be accompanied by monetary expansion. Variations in the use of these terms are discussed in Box 36-1.

ductivity—output per unit of labor input—is usually rising as well. For example, if wages and productivity both rise by 3 percent, each unit of labor earns 3 percent more, but it also produces 3 percent more. Thus costs per unit of output remain unchanged.

If wage increases are to cause a rise in unit costs, money wage rates must rise by more than productivity has risen.

In what follows, it is simplest to assume that productivity does not change so that a rise in money wages causes a rise in unit costs. To apply the analysis to cases where productivity is changing, the statement "wages rise" needs only to be replaced by the statement "wages rise by more than productivity rises."

Why Wages Change

Let us now ask what we know about the behavior of money wages and hence of the *SRAS* curve. Up to now it has been enough to say that an inflationary gap implies excess demand for labor, low unemployment, upward pressure on wages, and, hence, an upward-shifting *SRAS* curve.

But now we need to look in more detail at three forces that can cause wage costs to change and thus shift the *SRAS* curve upward. These are demand for labor, expectations, and random forces. Much of what we say in the case of demand forces is a recapitulation, but the points are important enough to bear repeating.

Demand Forces

The excess demand for labor associated with an inflationary gap puts upward pressure on wages. Wages rise more rapidly than they otherwise would.

The excess supply of labor associated with a recessionary gap puts downward pressure on wages. Wages rise less rapidly (or fall more rapidly) than they otherwise would.

The absence of either an inflationary or a recessionary gap means that there is no demand pressure on wages. Demand forces do not exert any pressure on wages either to rise or to fall.

Natural rate of unemployment. We saw in Chapter 26 that when current national income is at its potential level ($Y = Y^*$), unemployment is not zero. Instead there may be a substantial amount of frictional unemployment caused by the movement of people between jobs. The amount of unemployment (all of it frictional) that exists when national income is at its potential level is called the **natural rate of unemployment (U_N)**. It follows from this definition that when current national income exceeds full-employment income ($Y > Y^*$), current unemployment will be less than the natural rate ($U < U_N$). When current national income is less than full-employment income ($Y < Y^*$), current unemployment will exceed the natural rate ($U > U_N$).

We can now use the natural rate terminology to restate the three results about the pressure that is put on wage rates, and through them on the *SRAS* curve, by inflationary and recessionary gaps.

When the unemployment rate is below the natural rate, demand forces put upward pressure on wages.

When the unemployment rate is above the natural rate, demand forces put downward pressure on wages.

When unemployment is at its natural rate, demand forces exert neither upward nor downward pressure on wages.

The influence of demand forces on wages is shown by the *Phillips curve*, discussed in Box 30-1 on pages 634–635.

Expectational Forces

A second force that can influence wages is *expectations*. Suppose, for example, that both employers and employees expect a 4 percent inflation next year. Unions will start negotiations from a base of a 4 percent increase in money wages, which would hold their real wages constant. Firms may also be inclined to begin bargaining by conceding at least a 4 percent increase in money wages, since they expect that the prices at which they sell their products will rise by 4 percent. *Starting from that base*, unions will attempt to obtain some desired increase in their real wages.

At this point such factors as profits, productivity, and bargaining power become important.

The general expectation of an x percent inflation creates pressures for wages to rise by x percent and hence for the *SRAS* curve to shift by x percent.

Other Random Forces

Wage changes are also affected by forces that are associated with neither excess demand nor expected inflation. These forces can be positive, pushing wages higher than they otherwise would go, or negative, pushing wages lower than they otherwise would go. Furthermore, they are assumed to be many in number and independent of one another, so that they exert an overall random influence on wages—sometimes speeding wage increases up a bit, sometimes slowing them down a bit, but having a net effect that more or less cancels out when taken over several years. Over the long term they may be regarded as random events and are referred to as *random shocks*.

One example of such forces occurs when an exceptionally strong union or an exceptionally weak management comes to the bargaining table and produces a wage increase that is a percentage point or two *above* what would have occurred under more typical bargaining conditions. Another example is when a new government policy that is favorable to management causes this year's negotiated wage rates to be a percentage point or two *below* what they would have been.

Random shocks may be important causes of temporary bursts of inflation, but they are less important for sustained inflations. Although they may have a large positive or negative effect in any one year, over the period of a sustained inflation positive shocks in some years will tend to be offset by negative shocks in other years so that, in total, they contribute little to the long-term trend of the price level.

Overall Effect

The overall change in wage costs is a result of the three basic forces just studied. We express this as:

$$\begin{array}{c}\text{percentage}\\\text{increase in}\\\text{money}\\\text{wages}\end{array} = \begin{array}{c}\text{demand}\\\text{effect}\end{array} + \begin{array}{c}\text{expectational}\\\text{effect}\end{array} + \begin{array}{c}\text{random}\\\text{shock}\\\text{effect}\end{array}$$

It is important to realize that what happens to wage costs is the net effect of all three of these forces. Consider two examples. Assume that both labor and management expect a 3 percent inflation next year and are willing on this account to allow wages to increase by 3 percent. This would leave the relation between wages and other prices unaltered. Next assume that there is a significant inflationary gap with an associated labor shortage. The demand pressure causes wages to rise by 2 percentage points more than they otherwise would have risen. Finally, assume a shock, in the form of a temporary concern on the part of labor unions with foreign competition, that moderates wage claims by 1 percentage point this year. The final outcome is that wages rise by 4 percent, which is the net effect of +3 from expectations, +2 from demand forces, and −1 from the random shock.

For the second illustration, assume that there is once again a 3 percent expected inflation but that this time there is a recessionary gap. The associated heavy unemployment puts downward pressure on wage bargains, and hence the demand effect now works to moderate wage increases, say, to the extent of 2 percentage points. Finally assume that some unusual cost-plus government contracts reduce employer resistance to wage rises to the extent of contributing an upward pressure on wage bargains of 1 percentage point. The net effect is for wages to rise by 2 percent, which is the net effect of +3 from expectations, −2 from demand forces, and +1 from shock effects.

The overall effect of the three forces acting on wage costs—demand, expectations, and random shocks—determines what happens to the *SRAS* curve.

Inflationary gaps, expectations of inflation, and positive random shocks put pressure on wage rates to rise and hence on the *SRAS* curve to shift upward. Recessionary gaps, expectations of deflation, and negative random shocks put pressure on wage rates to fall and hence on the *SRAS* curve to shift down. What happens to the *SRAS* curve in any one year is the overall effect of all of these forces.

Accelerating Inflation

One of the reasons that policymakers worry so much about inflation is their concern that even a moderate inflation may be hard to keep under control. They worry that inflation often has a tendency to accelerate. They fear that if the Bank of Canada relaxes and is willing to accept, say, 4 percent inflation, 4 percent may soon become 5 percent, and once 5 percent becomes accepted, 5 percent may become 6 percent, and so on.

In this section we first consider the reasons for worrying that the inflation rate will tend to drift upward unless it is held rigidly in check.

Look again at Figure 36-4, which represents a continuing inflation. The *SRAS* curve is shifting up due to the inflationary gap, and the *AD* curve is shifting up because the inflation is being validated by increases in the money supply. What this analysis shows is that if income is held above potential, the price level will be rising. We know that inflation is positive, but we do not know whether the rate of inflation is rising, falling, or constant.

One of the most important results in the theory of inflation concerns what happens to the rate of inflation when a central bank takes steps to perpetuate an inflationary gap. This is the *acceleration hypothesis* to which we now turn. The argument is in several steps.

Initial pure demand inflation. Suppose that initially prices are rising in the presence of neither random shocks nor expectations of inflation. This means that the inflation is due solely to the existence of excess demand. Suppose also that the level of output is held constant. For this to happen, the upward shift in the *SRAS* curve has to be accompanied by an increase in the money supply such that the *AD* curve shifts up by the same amount. When the *SRAS* and the *AD* curves are shifting up at the same speed, the inflationary gap remains unchanged.

Expectational effects. Eventually people will begin to expect that monetary validation, and hence infla-

tion, will continue. As these inflationary expectations emerge, additional upward pressure will be put on wages as the inflationary effect comes into play. Now that the demand effect on wages has been augmented by an expectational effect, the *SRAS* curve will begin to shift upward more rapidly.

More rapid monetary validation required. If the Bank still wishes to hold the level of output constant, it must increase the rate at which the money supply is growing. This is because, to hold *Y* constant, the *AD* curve must be shifted more rapidly to compensate for the more rapid shifts in the *SRAS* curve.

An increasing rate of inflation. As a result of the increasingly rapid upward shifts in both the *AD* and *SRAS* curves, the rate of inflation must now be increasing. The rise in the actual inflation rate will in turn cause an increase in the expected inflation rate. This will then cause the actual inflation rate to increase, which will in turn increase the expected inflation rate, and so on. The net result is a *continually increasing rate of inflation.*

Conclusion. The foregoing analysis of the response of inflationary expectations to a persistent inflationary gap leads to what is called the **acceleration hypothesis.**

According to the acceleration hypothesis, as long as an inflationary gap persists, expectations of inflation will be rising, and this will lead to increases in the actual rate of inflation.

The tendency for inflation to increase is discussed further in Box 36-2.

Constant Inflation

Must a sustained inflation always accelerate? Or is it possible for an inflation to go on at a constant rate indefinitely?

The answer is that not all sustained inflations must accelerate. When the demand effect is absent and all inflation is thus expectational, inflation can persist indefinitely at a constant rate. Let us see why this is so.

BOX 36-2

The Phillips Curve and Accelerating Inflation

Professor Phillips was interested in studying the short-run behavior of an economy subjected to cyclical fluctuations (see Box 30-1 on pages 634–635). Others, however, treated the curve as establishing a long-term trade-off between inflation and unemployment.

Let the government fix income at Y_1 (and thus unemployment at U_1) in the figures and validate the ensuing wage inflation of ΔW_1 per year. By doing this

the government is apparently able to choose a particular combination of inflation and unemployment, with lower levels of unemployment being attained at the cost of higher rates of inflation.

In the 1960s Phillips curves were fitted to the data for many countries, and governments made decisions about where they wished to be on the trade-off between inflation and unemployment. Then, in the late 1960s, in country after country, the rate of wage and

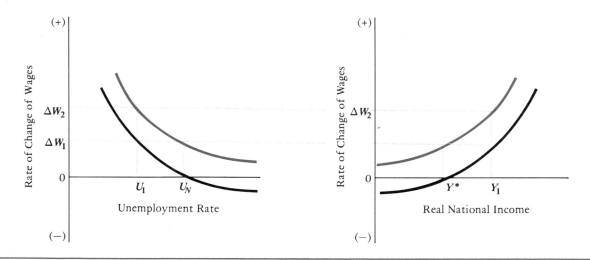

When national income is at its potential level, there is neither an inflationary nor a recessionary gap. In this case there is no demand effect operating on wage bargains. Leaving random shocks aside, the only force operating on wages is expectations. Say, for example, that both workers and employers expect a 4 percent inflation and employers are prepared to raise wages by 4 percent per year to keep wages in line with everything else. Wages will rise by 4 percent per year, and the *SRAS* curve will shift upward by that amount each year. If the Bank accommodates the resulting inflation by increasing the money supply by 4 percent each year, the *AD* curve will also be shifting up by that amount.

This case is illustrated in Figure 36-5 (see page 786). Here wage costs are rising due to expectations of inflation, and these expectations are being fulfilled.

Steady inflation with full employment results when the rate of monetary growth, the rate of wage increase, and the expected rate of inflation are all consistent with the actual inflation rate.

The key point about a pure expectational inflation at a constant rate is that there is no demand effect operating on wage bargains. Wages rise at the expected rate of inflation and that is just enough to preserve the existing relation between wages and all other prices. If there were a labor shortage, there would be pressure for wages to rise relative to other prices, and this would push the rate of wage increase above the expected rate of inflation. If there were more unemployment than the normal frictional amount, there would be a tendency for wages to fall

price inflation associated with any given level of unemployment began to rise. Instead of being stable, the Phillips curves were shifting upward. The explanation lay primarily in a shifting relation between the pressure of demand and wage increases due to expectations, as discussed in the text.

In the text we noted that two important influences on wages are demand and expectations. It was gradually understood that the original Phillips curve concerned only the influence of demand and left out inflationary expectations. This proved to be an important and unfortunate omission. An increase in expected inflation shows up as an upward shift in the original Phillips curve drawn in Box 30-1.

The importance of expectations can be shown by drawing what is called an **expectations-augmented Phillips curve,** as in the figures. The heights of the Phillips curves above the axis at Y^* and at U_N show the expected inflation rate. This is the amount that wages will rise when there is neither excess demand nor excess supply pressure in labor markets. The actual wage increase is shown by the augmented curve, with the increase in wages exceeding expected inflation when $Y > Y^*$ ($U < U_N$) and falling short of expected inflation when $Y < Y^*$ ($U > U_N$). *The de-*

mand component shown by the simple Phillips curve tells us by how much wage changes will deviate from the expected inflation rate.

Now we can see what was wrong with the idea of a stable inflation-unemployment trade-off. Targeting on income Y_1 or unemployment U_1 in the figure is fine as long as no inflation is *expected.* But once some particular rate of inflation comes to be expected, people will demand that much just to hold their own. The Phillips curve will shift upward to the position shown in the figure. Now there is inflation ΔW_2 because of the combined effects of expectations and excess demand.

But this higher rate is above the expected rate. Once that higher rate comes to be expected, the Phillips curve will shift upward once again. *The expectations-augmented Phillips curve shows that the actual rate of inflation exceeds the expected rate whenever there is an inflationary gap.* Sooner or later this will cause inflationary expectations to be shifted upward. The inflation rate associated with any given level of Y or U rises over time. This is the theory of accelerating inflation that is further studied in the appendix to this chapter.

relative to other prices, and this would hold wage increases below the expected rate of inflation.

The negative demand effect of a recessionary gap is rather weak. Thus when the recessionary gap is relatively small, the demand effect may be swamped by the expectational and random shock effects so that an approximately stable inflation rate is the net result. This is what seems to have occurred in the mid 1980s, when a fairly stable inflation rate persisted for several years in spite of a modest recessionary gap.

Breaking an Entrenched Inflation

When an inflation has been going on for a long time, can it be reduced without inflicting major hardships in terms of unemployment and lost output?

This question greatly worried policymakers in the early 1980s when they set out to break the existing two-digit inflation. It also worried those who, later in the 1980s, were unsatisfied with the 4 percent inflation rate that had persisted for several years. The issue was then, and still is, how to reduce inflation when people have come to accept the existing rate as normal and have adapted their behavior to the belief that the rate will continue.

Our analysis begins with a situation of a continuing, fully validated inflation, with actual income at its potential level ($Y = Y^*$). The inflation has been going on for some time, and people expect it to continue. Firmly held expectations of a continuation of the current inflation rate are what leads to the concept of an *entrenched inflation.*

Now suppose that the Bank decides to reduce the

FIGURE 36-5   Steady Inflation at the Natural Rate of Unemployment

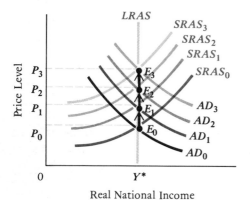

When income equals Y^* (and hence unemployment equals U_N) there is no demand effect on wages, and steady inflation can proceed at a rate consistent with inflationary expectations. With no demand effect the SRAS curve shifts upward at the expected rate of inflation. If the Bank raises the money supply at the same rate, the upward shift in the AD curve will match that of the SRAS curve. Output will stay at Y^*, unemployment will be at the natural rate, and inflation will be steady. The steady inflation is shown by the rising price level as equilibrium moves along the arrows from E_0 to E_1 to E_2 to E_3 in the figure.

inflation rate by reducing its rate of monetary validation. The events that follow generally fall into three phases.

Phase 1: Removing the inflationary gap.   The first phase, shown in Figure 36-6(i), consists of slowing the rate of monetary expansion below the current rate of inflation. This slows the rate at which the AD curve is shifting upward. To illustrate, we take an extreme case: the "cold turkey approach," where the rate of monetary expansion is cut to zero so that the upward shift in the AD curve is halted abruptly.

Under the combined influence of an inflationary gap and expectations of continued inflation, wages continue to rise, and the SRAS curve thus continues to shift upward. Eventually the gap is removed. If the only influence on wages were demand, that would be the end of the story. At Y^* there is no

upward demand pressure on wages. Wages would stop rising, the SRAS curve would be stabilized, and the economy would remain at full employment with a stable price level.

Phase 2: Stagflation.   Governments around the world have many times wished that things were really that simple. However, wages depend not only on excess demand but also on inflationary expectations. Once inflationary expectations have been established, it is not always easy to get people to revise them downward, even in the face of changed monetary policies. Thus the SRAS curve continues to shift upward, causing the price level to continue to rise and income to fall further.

Expectations may cause inflation to persist after its original causes have been removed. What was initially a demand inflation due to an inflationary gap becomes an expectational inflation.

This is phase 2, shown in Figure 36-6(ii).

The emerging recessionary gap has two effects. First, there is rising unemployment. Thus the demand influence on wages becomes negative. Second, as the recession deepens and monetary restraint continues, people revise their expectations of inflation downward. When they have no further expectations of inflation, there are no further increases in wage costs, and the SRAS curve stops shifting. The stagflationary phase is over. The inflation has come to a halt, but a large recessionary gap now exists.

Keynesians tend to be pessimistic and to expect a severe and long lasting slump in phase 2. Monetarists tend to be optimistic and to expect a relatively mild and short-lived recession in phase 2. These opposing views are investigated in Box 36-3 (pages 788–789).

Phase 3: Recovery.   The final phase is the return to full employment. When the economy comes to rest at the end of the stagflation, the situation is exactly the same as when the economy is hit by an isolated supply shock (see Figure 36-1). The move back to full employment can be accomplished in either of two ways. First, the recessionary gap can be relied on to reduce wages, thus shifting the SRAS curve down. Second, the money supply can be increased to shift the AD curve to a level consistent with full

FIGURE 36-6   Eliminating an Entrenched Inflation

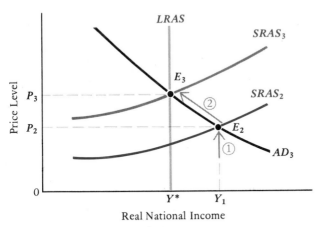

(i) Phase 1: removing the inflationary gap

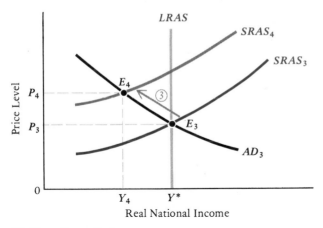

(ii) Phase 2: stagflation

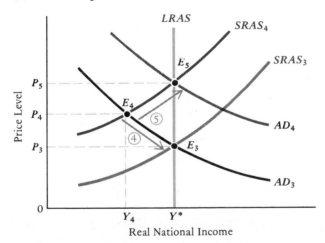

(iii) Phase 3: recovery

(i) Phase 1: The elimination of an entrenched inflation begins with a demand contraction to remove the inflationary gap. A fully validated inflation of the type shown in Figure 36-4 is taking the economy along the path shown by arrow 1 here. When the curves reach $SRAS_2$ and AD_3, the Bank stops expanding the money supply, thus stabilizing aggregate demand at AD_3. Wages continue to rise, taking the $SRAS$ curve leftward. The economy moves along arrow 2 with income falling and the price level rising. When aggregate supply reaches $SRAS_3$, the inflationary gap is removed and equilibrium is established at income Y^* and price level P_3.

(ii) Phase 2: Expectations and wage momentum lead to a stagflation, with falling output and continuing inflation. The economy moves along the path shown by arrow 3. The driving force is now the $SRAS$ curve, which continues to shift because inflationary expectations cause wages to continue to rise. The recessionary gap grows as income falls. The inflation continues, but at a diminishing rate. If wages stop rising when income has reached Y_4 and the price level P_4, the stagflation phase is over, with equilibrium at E_4.

(iii) Phase 3: After expectations are reversed, recovery takes income to Y^* and the price level is stabilized. There are two possible scenarios for recovery. In the first the recessionary gap causes wages to fall (slowly), taking the $SRAS$ curve back to $SRAS_3$ (slowly) as shown by arrow 4. The economy retraces the path originally followed in part (ii) back to E_3. In the second scenario, the Bank increases the money supply sufficiently to shift the AD curve to AD_4. The economy then moves along the path shown by arrow 5. This restores potential income at the cost of a further temporary inflation that takes the price level to P_5. Full employment and a stable price level are now achieved.

BOX 36-3

Controversies over the Length of the Stagflation Phase Needed to Break an Entrenched Inflation

Keynesian View

Keynesians cite two reasons for believing that the phase 2 stagflation in the process of breaking a sustained inflation will often tend to be long and painful. The first has to do with wage momentum and the second with expectations.

Keynesians allege the existence of a self-perpetuating momentum to wage increases. According to this view, workers are concerned about their own wage rates *relative* to rates in closely related occupations and industries. Because wage contracts fix wage rates for periods of one to three years, any particular wage will be negotiated in a situation where many related wage rates are already fixed for some time into the future (until existing contracts expire). Assume, for example, that excess demand caused many existing wages to be raised by, say, 10 percent in contracts negotiated in the recent past. As a result, people currently negotiating new wage contracts will tend to hold out for something close to 10 percent, even if the pressure of excess demand has weakened greatly.

This concern over wage comparability tends to give momentum to rounds of wage increases. The process is sometimes called a *wage-wage spiral*:

Once started, wages tend to chase each other in a rising spiral as bargainers seek to avoid falling behind increases that have already been agreed on for other workers.

The second main reason concerns expectations. In its simplest version, this reason is based on the so-called extrapolative theory, according to which people tend to believe that recent trends will continue. They require much new evidence before they conclude that an established inflationary trend has changed. The argument is that unless a deviation from the trend persists, people tend to dismiss a deviation—say, a fall in the inflation rate—as a transitory change and do not let it influence their long-term wage- and price-setting behavior.

The combination of the momentum of wage increases, even in the face of large recessionary gaps, and slowly adjusting expectations means that phase 2 will be long.

Monetarist View

Monetarists expect phase 2 to be over rapidly. Some say that under ideal circumstances it may never occur at all. They offer two reasons.

First, monetarists deny that significant wage-wage

employment. These two possibilities are illustrated in Figure 36-6(iii).

Economists who worry about waiting for wages and prices to fall fear that the process will take a very long time. The worry about a temporary burst of monetary expansion is that expectations of inflation may be rekindled when the Bank increases the money supply. If inflationary expectations are revived, the Bank will then have an unenviable choice. Either it must let another severe recession develop to break these new inflationary expectations, or it must validate the inflation in order to reduce unemployment. In the latter case it is back where it started, with a validated inflation on its hands.

Inflation in the 1970s

In the late 1960s Canadian inflation began to creep up toward the 4 to 5 percent range. This caused great concern and led to the adoption of tight monetary and fiscal policies. These in turn led to a downturn in the economy in late 1969, and inflation started to fall by mid 1970. However, the early 1970s witnessed quite expansionary policies, and inflation again began to rise. Expansion continued until early 1974, and inflation rose throughout that period. Then a recession set in. As a recessionary gap began to open up, the normal expectation was for a moderation of inflation. Just then, the first OPEC shock hit, and

momentum exists. They believe that new wage bargains respond to current market conditions. Thus a large recessionary gap with unemployment above the natural rate will lead quickly to new wage settlements well below the expected rate of inflation. The only lag in the adjustment of wage costs to current demand conditions is caused by the length of wage contracts. Thus it will take time for *all* wages to adjust to depressed market conditions.

Second, many monetarists argue that expected inflation falls rapidly during phase 2. They accept one version of the theory of **rational expectations**, according to which people look to the government's *current* macroeconomic policy when forming their expectations of future inflation. People are assumed to understand how the economy works and to form their expectations about future inflation rates by predicting the outcome of the monetary policies currently being followed. Their expectations need not always be correct, but the rational expectations hypothesis assumes that people do not continue to make systematic errors in forming their expectations.

Rational expectations have the effect of shortening the deflationary period. Instead of being strongly influenced by past inflation rates, people act in anticipation of the outcome of current government policies.

Once they realize that the Bank has stopped validating the inflation, they will quickly revise their inflationary expectations downward, and their consequent wage- and price-setting behavior will produce a rapid slowdown in the actual inflation rate. Expected inflation falls quickly to zero, and there is no further upward push to wages arising from expectations.

This happy result occurs only if people believe the Bank is going to stick to its restrictive policies. If they are skeptical about the Bank's resolve, they may expect the inflation to continue. They will then increase wages and prices in anticipation of the inflation, and their actions will generate the very inflation that they expected. Thus monetarists lay heavy stress on the credibility of the Bank's monetary policy.

Keynesians argue in response that sophisticated financial market operators may understand the underlying monetary causes of inflation, but the general public and most labor leaders and business managers hold different, sometimes crude, theories of inflation. They will tend, so the Keynesians argue, to extrapolate from past experiences and will not even know what the Bank is doing to the money supply, let alone base their expectations on it.

The experience of the early 1980s, and its relation to this debate, is discussed later in this chapter.

inflation jumped into the double-digit range. The result was stagflation.

1975–1980: Wage and Price Controls and Monetary Gradualism

By the summer of 1975 Canadian policymakers were concerned about the accelerating rate of inflation. They thought they perceived an accelerating wage-push inflation in a time of world recession. Having failed in an attempt to secure agreement of labor in a voluntary incomes policy, the Canadian cabinet decided in the autumn of 1975 to impose wage and price controls. The Anti-Inflation Board (AIB) was

set up and given power to control wages and prices for three years. At roughly the same time, the Bank of Canada adopted a policy of "monetary gradualism" by announcing its intention to reduce gradually the rate at which the money supply was growing.

Whether by accident or design, the two policies made a coherent package. The monetary policy was meant to reduce the speed with which the *AD* curve was shifting upward. Wage-price controls were meant to reduce the speed with which the *SRAS* curve was shifting upward. If the upward rush of the two curves could be slowed at the same rate, the inflation rate could be reduced without having to endure the stagflation phase (phase 2 in Figure 36-6), which occurs when the upward rush of the *AD* curve is checked faster than that of the *SRAS* curve.

The AIB's targets for wage increases were 10 percent in 1976, 8 percent in 1977, and 6 percent in 1978. The very modest targets for reduction in wage inflation given by the AIB in its first year were probably at or above the rates the market would have produced in any case. In 1977–1978, however, the targets were reduced on schedule, and there seems little doubt that some restraint on wages was exercised. The AIB had perhaps its clearest and strongest impact on the rate of increase of wages in the public sector. The government had found it increasingly difficult to restrain public-sector wages since the growth of unionization in that sector in the late 1960s. In the private sector, some wage restraint was also clearly achieved, although less than in the public sector and perhaps in part in response to the public-sector slowdown.

The AIB attempted to influence inflation by acting through the cost side, acting on the aggregate supply curve. Monetary gradualism, which we discussed in Chapter 35, attempted to influence inflation primarily by acting on the *AD* curve. At first all seemed to go well. The inflation rate fell in successive years starting in 1975. Then in 1979 and in 1980 it rose, taking it back to where it had been at the peak of the 1975 "crisis." Developments in early 1981 were no more encouraging; inflation was over 10 percent in mid 1981. Had five years of gradualism accomplished nothing?

The problem was that the demand-for-money function had become a major source of economic disturbances. As we saw in Chapter 35, major innovations in monetary institutions led to sharp reductions in the demand for M1 balances over that period. Instead of a gradually tightening money supply, money was becoming more plentiful *relative to demand*.

As we noted in Chapter 35 and earlier in this chapter, the proposition that a loose monetary policy stimulates the economy and leads to inflation and that a tight monetary policy does the opposite remains valid. The problem is that it is not always possible to identify a tight or loose policy by the rate of growth of the money supply.

The failure of gradualism did not upset any basic economic theory. What it did upset was the proposition that aggregate demand could be precisely controlled by merely controlling the supply of money.

Indeed, if central banks had paid more attention to the interest rate—which had been discredited as an intermediate target—they might have realized that monetary policy was not restrictive. Several times during this period the real interest rate (the money rate corrected for the rate for inflation) was negative.

In retrospect, although a case can be made that the AIB should never have been created, it is a shame that once it was created, a more severe attack on inflation was not attempted. If over three years the rate of monetary expansion had been reduced to amounts consistent with inflation in the range of 0–2 percent and wage inflation forced to that range by the AIB, the inflation might have been halted.

Inflation in the 1980s

We have seen that the 1970s was a period of a rising inflationary trend. By the turn of the decade inflation was firmly entrenched, and a major controversy arose over how to reduce it. Everyone agreed on the goal of returning to a much lower inflation rate, but there was disagreement as to the means of achieving the goal.

Monetarists advocated breaking the inflation with monetary restraint in the manner analyzed earlier in this chapter. Since they felt that there would be a short phase 2, they were willing to rely exclusively on monetary policy to bring about the transition from a high to a low inflationary environment.

Keynesians agreed that a low rate of monetary growth was a necessary condition for returning to a low rate of inflation. However, because they felt that phase 2 would be long—some talked in terms of five to ten years—they were reluctant to use monetary policy alone during the transition. As a result, many Keynesians advocated using **incomes policies,** a term that covers any direct government intervention used to affect wage and price setting. They hoped that such intervention would shorten phase 2 by helping to break inflationary expectations. This and other possible uses of incomes policies are discussed in Box 36-4.

The Reduction of Inflation

After some minor policy vacillations, a severe anti-inflationary monetary policy was initiated in the United States in 1981. For a variety of reasons, the Bank of Canada chose to follow the U.S. lead and also adopted a more restrictive policy. In the budget of June 1982, the Canadian government felt that fiscal restraint was not appropriate in the face of the recession, but it tried to contribute to the disinflation process by introducing a package of controls on civil service compensation—the so-called *6&5 Program.*

There is still debate over the effects of the program. Some feel it stiffened the resistance of private-sector firms to continued inflationary wage increases. Be that as it may, serious recession, falling sales, and falling profits eventually had to have an effect in moderating wage increases. When it came, the fall in inflation was dramatic: from a peak of 13 percent in mid 1981 to around 5 percent by early 1984.

By 1984 the restrictive policies had succeeded in reducing inflation to a level not seen since the early 1960s, but it had also produced a major recession with all its attendant costs, including unemployment, lost output, business bankruptcies, and foreclosed mortgages.

The results came out somewhere between the extremes that had been predicted. Keynesians were right in predicting that the anti-inflationary policies would induce a severe recession. But the inflation rate came down much faster than Keynesians had predicted. Jobs rather than wages quickly became the focus of many contract settlements. Not only were new wage agreements moderated in response to the excess supply of labor, but also some existing contracts were reopened and lower wages agreed on.

Thus, as so often happens with great debates, neither the extreme pessimists nor the extreme optimists were right. The truth lay somewhere in between. Whatever the reasons, during the early 1980s inflation fell faster than many Keynesians had expected, and the slump was deeper and more prolonged than many monetarists had expected.

A Stable Inflation Rate

For several years following 1984, the Canadian inflation rate stabilized at a figure around 4 percent, and it was a time of low inflation in the world as a whole. How is it that a relatively steady inflation rate persisted for several years with no clear tendency toward acceleration? The answer is that there was no inflationary gap in the economy. Thus the inflation was purely expectational and so fulfilled the conditions for a stable, rather than an accelerating, rate.

But since there clearly was a recessionary gap, why did inflation not decelerate further? The answer here seems to be that the weak demand forces that work toward deceleration when there is excess supply were swamped by the forces of expectational inflation and random shocks. (Recall from Chapter 30 the second asymmetry of the *SRAS* curve: It shifts rapidly upward when there is excess demand but only slowly downward when there is excess supply.)

As the recovery proceeded through the late 1980s, concern grew that inflation could accelerate if the economy moved into the range of an inflationary gap. This concern was mitigated to some extent, however, by the collapse in oil prices in 1986, which, by reducing costs of production, helped to shift the *SRAS* curve downward.

The unfortunate inflationary experience of the 1970s and early 1980s is still fresh in the memories of policymakers, and there is a clear resolution to prevent a high rate of inflation from returning, let alone becoming entrenched in people's expectations. So it is likely that any outbreak of demand inflation in the near future would be met by contractionary fiscal and monetary policies designed to remove the inflationary gap. However, as time passes and the memory of inflation dims, the risk of inflation's being rekindled increases.

BOX 36-4

Incomes Policies

In the past Keynesian economists have often recommended the use of incomes policies as an anti-inflationary device. There is a wide range of such policy measures. Voluntary guidelines for wage and price increases can be set, as they were in the United States under the Kennedy administration in the 1960s. The government may consult labor and business leaders with a view to moderating their wage demands and price hikes, as has often been done in European countries. More drastically, compulsory controls may be imposed on wage, price, and profit increases. A proposal commonly made in the 1970s and early 1980s was for a **tax-related incomes policy (TIP),** which would operate through the tax system to provide penalties for "excessive" wage and price hikes and rewards for moderate ones.

Incomes policies might be used for three quite distinct purposes: (1) to suppress a demand inflation, (2) to break an expectational inflation, and (3) to control a permanent wage-cost push inflation. We discuss the first two purposes in this box and the third in Chapter 39.

Demand Inflation

One reason incomes policies have such a bad reputation throughout the world is that they have often been used, as they were in the United States during Richard Nixon's presidency, in a futile attempt to stop a demand inflation. To see why such an attempt is futile, consider the situation shown at E_1 in Figure 36-3 on page 778. If nothing else is done, the inflationary gap will cause the price level to rise to P_2. Wage and price controls could be used to hold the price level at P_1, but once the controls are removed, the excess demand will cause prices to rise.

The conclusion that using incomes policy in an attempt to control a demand inflation will be ineffective (while the cost in terms of social stress and economic disruption can be enormous) is borne out not only by the U.S. experience of the early 1970s but by the experience of Britain and a number of other European countries as well.

Expectational Inflation

When an entrenched inflation exists, incomes policies may help to break expectations. If successful, incomes policies will greatly reduce the stagflation phase. This could happen if, once phase 1 is over and the inflationary gap has been eliminated, incomes policies were used to stop wages and prices from rising because of the expectational effect. The *SRAS*

Are Full Employment and Stable Prices Compatible?

A debate has raged on both sides of the Atlantic for many decades: Are full employment and a low, stable inflation rate compatible in the long term? As long as the *SRAS* curve shifts only because of demand, expectational, and random shock effects, as we assumed earlier in this chapter, the answer is yes. But what worries some observers is the possibility of a cost push that pushes wages up faster than productivity once the fear of unemployment is reduced by the continued achievement of potential income. As far back as the 1940s many Keynesians were worried that once the government was committed to maintaining full employment, much of the discipline of

the market would be removed from wage bargains. The scramble of every group trying to get ahead of every other group would lead to a wage-cost push inflation. The commitment to full employment would then lead to accommodating increases in the money supply.

There is evidence that something like this has happened periodically over the last 40 years in Britain and in many of the countries of continental Europe. Most economists are more skeptical that it has been a serious force in North America. Nonetheless, some observers still worry that full employment and a low, stable inflation rate may in the end prove incompatible. They argue for some permanent form of incomes policy. (See Box 36-4.)

curve would not continue to shift upward and thereby open up a recessionary gap. Once expectations have adjusted to the new anti-inflationary monetary policy and to the existing stable price level, the controls could be removed. The economy would then be at a position of stable prices and full employment.

The sequence of events seems almost too good to be true. The stagflation phase is eliminated, and the economy goes directly from phase 1, with an inflationary gap, to the final situation of an equilibrium at Y^*. If such a policy had been tried as many advocated during the early 1980s, *and if it had worked*, the recession of the early 1980s, with all of its consequent unemployment and lost output, would have been avoided.

Controls were used when the AIB formed part of a package to counter the explosive double-digit inflation of the 1974–1975 period. It seems probable, however, that the rapid rates of inflation of around 10 percent did not persist long enough to build up strongly felt or uniformly held expectations of continued inflation at those rates. The underlying or *core* rate of inflation was still widely perceived to be in the 6 to 7 percent range that had persisted throughout most of the decade. The rise in inflation above this core rate was fairly easily reversed.

What Can We Conclude?

Opponents of incomes policies believe that the costs of using incomes policies will exceed the alleged benefits. First, they argue that the benefits, in terms of shortening the stagflation phase, would be small because the policies would not be wholly successful in restraining wage and price increases. Second, they argue that the costs, in terms of direct administrative burdens and indirect frustration of the workings of the price system, would be large.

Although most experience internationally is with incomes policies used in a futile attempt to control a demand inflation, the evidence about the costs of using such policies may be relevant, even where the objective is not futile. The evidence suggests that when prices are set by government administrators rather than market forces, the allocation of resources becomes increasingly arbitrary, with serious consequences for the efficient working of the economic system.

An interesting argument presented by some economists is that the best way to ensure that the two objectives can be obtained most of the time is for governments to make clear that a stable price level, rather than full employment, is their overriding commitment and that whenever the two come into short-run conflict, price stability will be given priority over full employment! They argue that once this message has been accepted by the public, there will be two benefits. First, wage-cost push inflations may not occur, even at full employment. Second, incipient inflations of the supply or the demand-shock variety will be easy to quell with only minor recessions because inflationary expectations and inertias will never have a chance to become strongly entrenched.

In this environment major policy-induced recessions would not be required to control an outbreak of inflation. Paradoxically, by abandoning its full-employment commitment, the government might make the maintenance of something close to full employment much more likely—at least, that is how the argument goes.

Throughout the history of economics, inflation has been recognized as a harmful phenomenon. This view was given renewed strength as a result of the worldwide experiences of high inflation rates since the 1960s. The resolve is there, at least in advanced industrial countries, to prevent another outbreak of rapid inflation and, should one occur for reasons of unavoidable supply-side shocks, to prevent the inflation from continuing long enough to become firmly entrenched in people's expectations. The resolve is a matter settled in the past decade; the success in ful- filling this resolve is a matter to be tested in the coming decade.

Summary

1. Either supply shocks or demand shocks can cause a temporary inflation. For either to lead to sustained inflation, it must be accompanied by a continuing expansion of the money supply so that the *AD* curve is shifting upward.

2. A sustained price inflation will also be accompanied by a closely related growth in wages and other factor costs, so that the *SRAS* curve is shifting up.

3. Factors that influence shifts in the *SRAS* curve can be divided into three main categories: demand, expectations, and random shocks.

4. The influence of demand can be expressed in terms of the inflationary and recessionary gaps, which relate national income to potential income, or in terms of the difference between the actual and natural rates of unemployment.

5. Expectations of inflation tend to cause wage settlements that preserve the expected real wage and hence lead to nominal wage increases.

6. It is impossible to have a sustained, steady inflation when income exceeds its potential level. As expectations constantly catch up to the existing inflation rate, that rate, which is the sum of the expectations and demand effects, must accelerate.

7. It is possible to have a sustained inflation at potential national income (and hence at the natural rate of unemployment). There is then no demand pressure on prices, but expectations can cause wages and hence prices to grow at the same rate as the money supply.

8. Stopping an inflation through restrictive monetary policy will lead to a recession that lasts while inflation only gradually falls to a rate consistent with the new lower rate of money growth. The length and depth of the recession will depend on the strength of the downward pressure on wages and on the speed with which inflationary expectations adjust.

9. In the early 1980s the rate of monetary expansion was reduced dramatically in an attempt to bring inflation down rapidly. This resulted in a larger recession than most monetarists had predicted, but also in a faster reduction in inflation than most Keynesians had predicted.

10. Some economists believe zero inflation is an achievable goal of the policy of price stability; others believe a gradual upward drift of the price level on the order of 1 to 2 percent per year must be accepted.

11. Some observers doubt that continued full employment is compatible with stable prices. They advocate permanent incomes policies to

control wage inflation and so make the two objectives compatible. Many economists are skeptical that such policies are needed and see no compelling evidence why full employment and stable prices cannot coexist in a flexible market economy.

Topics for Review

Temporary and sustained inflations
Monetary accommodation of supply shocks
Monetary validation of demand shocks
Demand inflation
Expectational inflation
Natural rate of unemployment
Accelerating inflation
Entrenched inflation
Incomes policies

Discussion Questions

1. In the period 1984–1986, Canada's underlying inflation rate appeared to stabilize in the 4 percent range. What has happened to inflation since? Why? How does the 4 percent rate compare to (i) the average since World War II, (ii) the average over the past decade, (iii) inflation in other periods when unemployment was 9 percent, and (iv) inflation when monetary growth was over 15 percent? Do you think that the Bank of Canada should allow inflation to rise in order to reduce unemployment, or maintain the inflation rate at or below 4 percent.
2. On what source or sources of inflation do the following statements focus attention?
   a. "The one basic cause of inflation is the government's spending more than it takes in. The cure is a balanced budget."
   b. "Wage bargains currently being negotiated in autos and several other basic industries will soon cause inflation to accelerate."
   c. "Canadians have become so accustomed to 4 percent inflation that it would be difficult for the Bank of Canada to induce the transition to 1 or 2 percent inflation."
   d. Newspaper editorial in Manchester, England: "If American unions were as strong as those in Britain, American inflationary experience would have been as disastrous as has Britain's."
   e. Study issued in 1980 by the Worldwatch Institute: "The nation's spiraling inflation reflects a global depletion of physical resources and therefore cannot be cured by traditional fiscal and monetary tools."
   f. Article in the London *Economist*: "Oil price collapse will reduce 1986 inflation rate."
3. When OPEC radically increased the price of oil in 1974, the world was hit with a severe supply shock. The Bank of Canada decided to accommodate this with a rapid burst of monetary expansion, while the U.S. Central Bank decided on a policy of non-accommodation.

What do you think happened to the inflation rate and the national incomes of the two countries over the following two years?

4. When the entrenched inflation of the early 1980s was broken, the economies of many industrial countries came to rest with a relatively stable price level and high unemployment. People who feared the outbreak of inflation opposed even a temporary increase in the rate of monetary expansion. Use aggregate demand and aggregate supply analysis to show why some people felt that a *temporary* burst of monetary expansion might bring increases in employment without increases in inflation.

5. Discuss the following views expressed in 1986.
   a. "Now that inflation has been beaten to the ground, we can get on with reducing unemployment."
   b. "Eternal vigilance is the price of a low inflation rate."

6. Inflations cannot long persist, whatever their initiating causes, unless they are validated by increases in the money supply. Why is this so? Does it not imply that control of inflation is merely a matter of not allowing the money supply to rise faster than the rate of increase of real national income?

7. Discuss the following views on the effects of inflation.
   a. "The beast [of inflation] is a luminescent specter, a killer, a threat to society, public enemy No. 1."
   b. "In the early 1980s inflation became the national obsession, . . . the catchall scapegoat for individual and societal economic difficulties, the symptom that diverts attention from the basic maladies."

8. In an article on the harmful effects of inflation written early in the 1980s, a reporter wrote: "With the rise in mortgage interest rates to 11 percent, heaven only knows the price of what was once idealized as 'the $100,000 house.' " At the time the inflation rate was 8 percent. Did the 11 percent interest rate represent a heavy burden of inflation on the new homeowner? What do you think the mortgage interest rate would have been if the inflation rate had been zero? Which situation would have meant a heavier real burden on the purchaser of a new house?

9. Discuss the apparent conflict between the following views. Can you suggest how they might be reconciled using aggregate demand and aggregate supply analysis?
   a. "A rise in interest rates is deflationary, since business investment and household demand for durables both fall when interest rates rise."
   b. "A rise in interest rates is inflationary, since interest is a major business cost, and as with other costs, a rise in interest will be passed on by firms in terms of higher prices."

Sustained Inflation and the Phillips Curve

In this appendix we use the Phillips curve, introduced in Chapter 30, to analyze sustained inflations.

The Price Phillips Curve

The Phillips curve shown in Box 30-1 on pages 634–635 described a relationship between the rate of change of *wages* and the state of demand, as measured by the level of national income. As we saw, changes in wages cause the *SRAS* curve to shift, giving rise to changes in the price level. These two steps are commonly combined to produce a new curve relating the rate of change of the *price level* and the level of national income. Such a curve, often referred to as a *price Phillips curve*, is shown in Figure 36A-1.

The conditions under which it is possible to derive a price Phillips curve from the original relation between wages and national income are fairly complicated.[1] But the curve is commonly used, and we shall focus on it in this appendix. (We shall henceforth refer to the price Phillips curve simply as the Phillips curve.) The key simplification is that once the level of income has been determined—by the intersection of the *SRAS* and *AD* curves, as before—the rate of inflation can be read *directly* from the Phillips curve.

Notice that the Phillips curve in Figure 36A-1 has the *rate of change of prices* on the vertical axis. The *SRAS* curve that appears so frequently in the text has the *level of prices* on the vertical axis. Since both curves have real national income on the horizontal axis, they might be easily confused. They must therefore be carefully distinguished.

[1] For example, at any given level of income the relationship between the rate of change of wages given by the figure in Box 30-1 and the rate of change of prices given by Figure 36A-1 depends on what is assumed about how fast the central bank is causing the *AD* curve to shift.

Components of Inflation

Recall the three influences that cause the *SRAS* curve to shift upward and hence the price level to rise: demand, expectations, and random shocks. In this appendix we continue to use the terms *demand* and *shock*, but we introduce the term *core inflation* as a generalization of the term *expectations* used in the text. The rate of increase of prices can now be written as the sum of the three components:

$$\Delta p = C + DE + SE$$

where Δp is the annual percentage rate of changes of prices (i.e., the rate of inflation), C refers to core inflation, DE to demand effect, and SE to shock effect. We now look at these components one at a time.

Demand Inflation

Demand inflation refers to the influence on the price level of inflationary and recessionary gaps. We have seen that an inflationary gap involves upward pressure on wages and hence on the price level, while a recessionary gap involves downward pressure. This is shown in Figure 36A-1 by the vertical distance between the Phillips curve and the horizontal axis.

The Phillips curve in Figure 36A-1 is merely a novel way of expressing relations we have used many times before. (It is important to remember, however, that Figure 36A-1 does not tell the whole story of inflation; it describes only the effects of *demand*.) These relations include the following.

1. There is neither upward nor downward pressure of demand on the price level when national income is at its potential level. Graphically, the Phillips curve cuts the axis at Y^*.
2. When there is an inflationary gap, wages and

FIGURE 36A-1   Price Phillips Curve

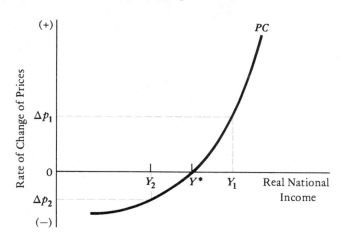

The price Phillips curve shows the positive relationship between the level of national income and rate of increase in the *price level.* An increase in national income leads to an increase in the rate of change of wages and, other things being equal, to an increase in the rate of change of prices. A fall in income leads to a decrease in the rate of change of wages and, other things being equal, to a decrease in the rate of change of prices.

With zero core inflation and output at its capacity level Y^*, inflation is zero as shown. When output is above Y^* at, say, Y_1, inflation is positive at Δp_1. When output is below Y^* at, say, Y_2, inflation is negative at Δp_2.

other costs will rise. As we have seen, this shifts the *SRAS* curve and causes the price level to rise. The inflation continues as long as the gap persists. Graphically, the Phillips curve lies above the axis where Y exceeds Y^*.

3. When there is a recessionary gap, wages and other costs will fall. This shifts the *SRAS* curve downward and causes the price level to fall. The deflation continues as long as the gap persists. Graphically, the Phillips curve lies below the axis when Y is less than Y^*.

4. The speed of the upward adjustment of the price level in the face of an inflationary gap exceeds the speed of the downward adjustment in the face of a recessionary gap. Graphically, the Phillips curve gets steeper the further to the right one moves along it. [47]

Core Inflation

The demand component cannot be the whole explanation of inflation since, if it were, inflation would only occur if national income exceeded Y^* and inflation could be quickly removed by forcing income back to Y^*. This behavior is emphatically rejected by the recent experiences of Canada and other Western economies. To explain what we observe about inflation we add the concept of core inflation. Core inflation refers to the underlying trend of inflation,

and it is referred to by several different names: *core* inflation, *expectational* inflation, *inertial* inflation, and the *underlying rate* of inflation.

In the text we singled out expectations as a main influence on the price level in addition to demand. But we also saw that how expectations are formed is a major source of controversy among economists. The controversy actually runs deeper than that; some analysts question whether it is explicit expectations about the future or inertia based on past experience that really dominates wage settlements. For example, past experience may matter if recent wage increases have failed to keep up with price increases; in such circumstances current wage settlements may have a "catch-up" component.

For these and other reasons, we use the general term *core inflation* to describe persistent effects that do not depend on current demand conditions. These include expectations and other elements that stem from both forward- and backward-looking behavior. Some elements may change quickly, others only slowly. Their total influence at any point in time is summarized in the term *core inflation.*

Core inflation operates on the *SRAS* curve through the effects of wages and other costs.[2] Core

[2] Some variations in net profit margins can and do occur. These cause price inflation to diverge temporarily from cost inflation and are included in shock inflation.

inflation may also be related to *expected future changes* in wage and capital costs, since firms who plan to change prices only infrequently must set prices on the basis of their expected costs over their planning period. If that is the case, to make our concept of core inflation operative, we need a theory of how firms form their expectations of the future movement of costs. Some of the theories on how the expectations that determine the core inflation rate are formed are discussed in Chapter 39.

Graphically, the core inflation rate is added to the demand effect by shifting the Phillips curve upward by the amount of the core rate. This gives rise to a *core-augmented Phillips curve,* or more commonly an *expectations-augmented Phillips curve,* as shown in Figure 36A-2. At any given level of income, the height of the core-augmented Phillips curve is given by the sum of the demand effect and the core rate of inflation. For example, at $Y = Y^*$, when demand inflation is zero, the height of the Phillips curve is given by the core rate. At any other level of income the rate of inflation differs from the demand effect by an amount equal to the core rate.

Short-run Phillips curve.   Because the Phillips curve shifts upward or downward as the core rate of inflation rises or falls, it is called a **short-run Phillips curve (SRPC)** when it is drawn at any particular height above Y^* (that is, for any given level of core inflation).

The short-run Phillips curve is drawn for a given rate of core inflation.

Shock Inflation

Shock inflation refers to once-and-for-all changes that give a temporary upward or downward jolt to the price level. These included changes in indirect taxes, changes in profit margins, changes in import prices, and all kinds of other factors often referred to as *supply shocks.* Shock inflation includes everything that is not included in demand and core inflation.

Summary

Putting all of this together, the current inflation rate depends on the influence of (1) demand as indicated by the inflationary or recessionary gap, demand inflation; (2) expected increase in costs, core inflation; and (3) a series of exogenous forces coming mainly from the supply side, shock inflation. These three components of inflation may be illustrated both numerically and graphically.

For a numerical example, assume that in the absence of any demand pressure, prices would rise by 10 percent because firms expect underlying costs to rise by 10 percent; that this price rise is moderated by 1 percentage point because costs only rise by 9 percent due to heavy unemployment; and that the price rise is augmented by 3 percentage points because large increases in indirect taxes force prices up. The final inflation is 12 percent, made up of 10 percent core inflation minus 1 percent demand inflation plus 3 percent shock inflation.

Graphically, the components of inflation are illustrated in Figure 36A-3 (see page 801) for two cases with a common positive core inflation component. The curve labeled *SRPC* is the expectations-augmented Phillips curve, that is, the Phillips curve shifted up by the core inflation rate. Its height above the axis at Y^* thus indicates core inflation. Points along *SRPC* where Y does not equal Y^* indicate how much the pressures of excess or deficient demand cause inflation to deviate from the core rate. The amount by which actual inflation lies above or below the *SRPC* shows the amount by which shocks cause the actual inflation rate to deviate from the sum of the core and the demand effects.

Expectations and Changes in Inflation

Originally the Phillips curve of Figure 36A-1 was thought to provide the whole explanation of inflation. When it was realized that the short-run Phillips curve shifted upward or downward, the concept of core inflation was added to explain this. Changes in the core rate cause shifts in the short-run Phillips curve. As a result we have the following conclusion.

There is a family of short-run Phillips curves, one for each core rate of inflation.

This is illustrated in Figure 36A-4 (see page 802). Let us now see what governs changes in the core rate and hence shifts in the *SRPC.*

FIGURE 36A-2   Core Inflation and the Short-Run Phillips Curve

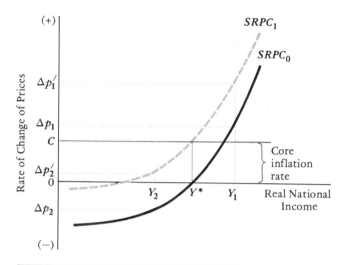

Core inflation shifts the price Phillips curve and so changes the rate of inflation that corresponds to any given level of national income. The curve $SRPC_0$, which reproduces the Phillips curve from Figure 36A-1, corresponds to a zero core inflation rate. When core inflation rises to, say, C, the Phillips curve shifts up to $SRPC_1$. The rate of inflation at Y^* rises from 0 to C. At Y_1, which is greater than Y^*, inflation rises from Δp_1 to $\Delta p_1'$. At Y_2, which is less than Y^*, inflation was initially negative at Δp_2 but now becomes positive at $\Delta p_2'$.

Look at point Z on $SRPC_1$ in Figure 36A-5 (see page 803), which is $SRPC_1$ reproduced from Figure 36A-4 and corresponds to a core inflation rate of C_1. At the point Z shock inflation is zero and demand inflation is positive (since $Y_1 > Y^*$), so the actual inflation rate is above the core rate of C_1. Sooner or later this excess will come to be expected, the core rate will then rise, and the $SRPC$ will shift upward. As long as national income is held above Y^*, the actual inflation rate will exceed the core rate, and as a result sooner or later the core rate will rise. This means that the short-run Phillips curve will sooner or later shift upward, as indicated by the arrow above point Z.

Now look at point W in Figure 36A-5 where again core inflation is C_1 and shock inflation is zero. At W demand inflation is negative (since $Y_2 < Y^*$), so the actual inflation rate is below the core rate of C_1. Sooner or later this difference will influence expectations, and the core rate will fall. As long as national income is held below Y^*, the actual inflation rate will be less than the core rate, and sooner or later the core rate will fall. This means that sooner or later the short-run Phillips curve will begin to

shift downward, as indicated by the arrow below W.

So we have a basic prediction of the theory:

A persistent inflationary gap will sooner or later cause the inflation rate to accelerate, whereas a persistent recessionary gap will sooner or later cause the inflation rate to decelerate.

This, of course, is the acceleration hypothesis that we encountered in the text. Let us now examine it in more detail.

Accelerating Inflation

Consider an economy with a core inflation of C_1 that has just experienced an increase in aggregate demand so that output is above Y^* as at point Z in Figure 36A-5. There is an inflationary gap with a positive inflation rate; the $SRAS$ curve will be shifting upward, while monetary validation by the central bank is shifting the AD curve upward. (It may be worth

FIGURE 36A-3 The Components of Inflation Illustrated

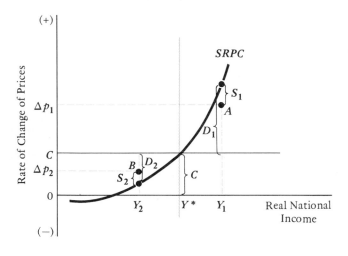

The inflation rate can be separated into three components: core inflation, demand inflation, and shock inflation. The Phillips curve is drawn for a given core rate of inflation and hence is labeled as a short-run Phillips curve. The given core rate, C, is shown by the height of the horizontal colored line.

Point A indicates a national income of Y_1 combined with an inflation rate of Δp_1. This rate is composed of the following: a core rate, C; a positive demand component, D_1 (determined by the shape of *SRPC*); and a negative shock component, S_1.

Point B indicates a national income of Y_2 combined with an inflation rate of Δp_2. This rate is composed of the following: core inflation, once again given by C; the demand component, D_2, which is now negative (since income Y_2 is less than Y^*); and a positive shock component, S_2.

reiterating what is happening here: Core inflation produces the rise in prices that results from firms' expectations about the long-run trend in costs; the demand component produces the addition to inflation due to what are thought to be transitory demand factors; shock inflation is still treated as zero.)

Is this situation sustainable? Only if the Phillips curve remains stable. If the short-run Phillips curve stayed put, policymakers could conclude that they had achieved a pretty good trade-off. They would have gained a permanent increase in output of Y^*Y_1 at the cost of a permanent increase in inflation from C_1 to Δp_1.

But as we have seen, this is not all that is happening. The persistence of a demand inflation will eventually cause the core inflation rate to rise and hence cause the *SRPC* to shift upward. In turn, this increases the rate at which the *SRAS* curve is shifting upward. Let us trace this process in detail.

At point Z prices and costs are rising at Δp_1 per year, and sooner or later firms and workers will stop believing that this increase from the old rate C_1 is a transitory phenomenon. They will come to expect

some of this increase to persist and incorporate it into core inflation. Let us say that after a passage of time firms come to expect wages and other costs to rise at the rate C_2 each period. This will produce a core inflation at a rate of C_2 per annum in Figure 36A-5. The short-run Phillips curve now shifts up to $SRPC_2$ in the figure. The rise in the core rate of inflation increases the actual inflation rate corresponding to each possible level of national income. If national income is maintained at Y_1 so that demand inflation remains positive, the actual inflation rate rises above Δp_1.

Now the *SRAS* curve will be shifting upward more rapidly. If output is to be maintained at Y_1, the central bank will have to increase the rate of monetary expansion. This will cause the *AD* to shift up more rapidly to match the more rapid upward shift in *SRAS*. This is illustrated in terms of the *SRAS* and *AD* curves in Figure 36-3.

The actual inflation rate, Δp_2, is well above the core rate, C_2. Sooner or later this will cause the core rate to rise again, and the short-run Phillips curve will again shift upward. As long as output is main-

FIGURE 36A-4   A Family of Short-Run Phillips Curves

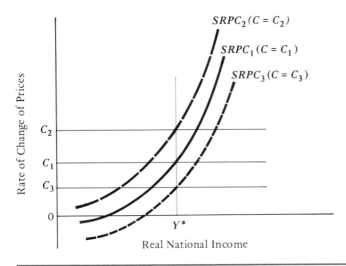

There is a separate short-run Phillips curve for each core rate of inflation. The Phillips curve of Figure 36A-3, shown here as $SRPC_1$, relates national income to inflation on the assumption that core inflation is C_1. The actual rate of inflation depends on both the core rate and the level of national income (as well as on shock inflation, assumed here to be zero).

For each positive core rate of inflation there is a short-run Phillips curve that lies above the axis at $Y = Y^*$ by the particular core rate to which it relates. If the core rate were C_2, greater than C_1, the Phillips curve would lie above $SRPC_1$, as shown by $SRPC_2$. If the core rate were C_3, less than C_1, the curve would lie below $SRPC_1$, as shown by $SRPC_3$.

tained at Y_1 so that demand inflation is positive, this process of growing core inflation will continue.

From this an important conclusion follows.

If the central bank validates any rate of inflation that results from Y being held above Y^*, the inflation rate itself will accelerate continuously *and* the rate of monetary expansion required to frustrate the monetary adjustment mechanism will also accelerate.

The Long-Run Phillips Curve

Is there any level of income in this model that is compatible with a constant actual rate of inflation? The answer is yes, potential income. When income is at Y^*, the demand component of inflation is *zero*, as shown in Figure 36A-1. This means that, still letting shock inflation be zero, actual inflation equals core inflation. Since the core rate is determined by what people expect the inflation rate to be when actual inflation equals core inflation, the actual inflation rate is equal to the expected rate. There are no surprises. No one's plans are upset, so no one has any incentive to alter plans as a result of what actually happens to inflation.

Providing that the inflation rate is fully validated and shock inflation is zero, any rate of inflation can persist indefinitely as long as income is held at its potential level.

We now define the **long-run Phillips curve (LRPC)** as the relation between *national income* and *stable rates of inflation* that neither accelerate nor decelerate. This occurs when the core and actual inflation rates are equal. According to the theory just described, the long-run Phillips curve is vertical. This is illustrated in Figure 36A-6 on the facing page.

Maintaining a point on the *LRPC* leads to steady inflation at the core rate. This is illustrated in Figure 36A-7 (see page 804), where we show a situation with a positive core inflation rate and where there is full accommodation by the central bank. In part (i) the intersection of the *SRAS* and *AD* curves determines Y at Y^*. In part (ii) the Phillips curve shows the rate of inflation. There is no demand effect on inflation, so the actual and core inflation rates are equal. As a result the situation is sustainable (as long as the central bank continues to validate the core inflation). The increasing price level in part (i) reflects the positive inflation rate indicated in part (ii). Note

FIGURE 36A-5   Shifts in the Short-Run Phillips Curve

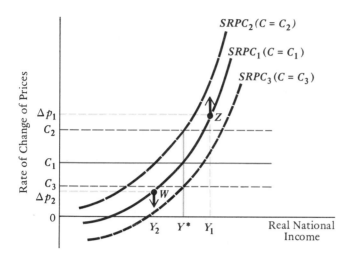

Changes in the core rate of inflation, which arise when actual inflation differs from the core rate, cause the short-run Phillips curve to shift. With a core inflation rate of C_1, the short-run Phillips curve is $SRPC_1$, reproduced from Figure 36A-4.

If income is maintained at Y_1, greater than Y^*, actual inflation will be Δp_1, greater than the core rate, as indicated by point Z. Eventually, this excess of the actual inflation rate over the core rate will cause the core rate to rise, from C_1, say, to C_2, shifting the short-run Phillips curve to $SRPC_2$, as indicated by the arrow above point Z.

If income is maintained at Y_2, less than Y^*, actual inflation will be Δp_2, less than the core rate, as indicated by point W. Eventually, the shortfall of actual inflation below the core rate will cause the core rate to fall below C_1, say, to C_3, causing the short-run Phillips curve to shift down to $SRPC_3$, as indicated by the arrow below W.

---

that in part (ii), since the core rate is not changing, the $SRPC$ will be stable, which means we are also on the $LRPC$.

We can now state a general conclusion.

The long-run Phillips curve is vertical at Y^*; only Y^* is compatible with a stable rate of inflation, and any stable rate is, if fully validated, compatible with Y^*.

The Natural Rate of Unemployment

We have talked about variations of Y from Y^*, but for every level of national income there is an associated level of unemployment. Recasting these conclusions in terms of unemployment we have the following: As before, call the unemployment associated with Y^* the natural rate of unemployment. Note that unemployment can be pushed below the natural rate, but only at the cost of opening up an inflationary gap. If the government seeks to maintain this lower rate of unemployment, the inflation rate will accelerate and will have to be validated by ever-increasing rates of monetary expansion.

FIGURE 36A-6   Vertical Long-Run Phillips Curve

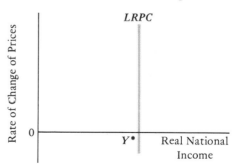

When actual inflation equals expected inflation, there is no trade-off between inflation and unemployment. In long-term equilibrium the actual rate of inflation must remain equal to the expected rate (otherwise expectations would be revised). This can only occur at potential income Y^*, that is, along the $LRPC$.

At Y^* there is no demand pressure on the price level; hence the only influence on actual inflation is expected inflation. Any stable rate of inflation (provided it is validated by the appropriate rate of monetary expansion) is compatible with Y^* and its associated natural rate of unemployment.

FIGURE 36A-7   Monetary Accommodation and Steady Inflation

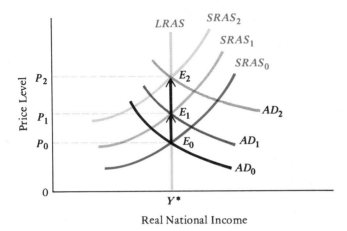

(i) Upward shifting *AD* and *SRAS* curves

Positive core inflation means that wage costs will be rising even when output is just at its capacity level; monetary accommodation can keep output constant and sustain the inflation rate. Core inflation is shown in part (ii) by C, the height of the short-run Phillips curve above the axis at Y^*. This translates into an upward-shifting *SRAS* curve from $SRAS_0$ to $SRAS_1$ to $SRAS_2$ in part (i). Monetary accommodation means that the *AD* curve in part (i) also shifts upward, from AD_0 to AD_1 to AD_2. As drawn, the monetary accommodation just keeps output constant at Y^*, so inflation persists at the core rate C.

The positive wage inflation in part (ii) is reflected in an equal rate of price increase from P_0 to P_1 to P_2 in part (i). Since we are on the *LRPC*, core inflation is constant and the *SRPC* is stable.

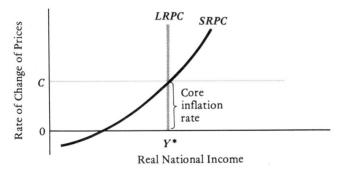

(ii) Steady inflation

The lowest rate of unemployment that can be maintained without a tendency for the rate of inflation to accelerate is the natural rate.

Implications for Monetary Policy

The foregoing analysis has three major implications for the understanding and conduct of monetary policy.

First, the interaction among money, inflation, and output is complex. In particular, it depends on how expectations are formulated. Monetary policies may affect expectations differently. at different times.

Therefore, it would be wrong to expect a simple, mechanical relationship between the money supply and the behavior of output and the price level.

Second, differences between the expected rate of inflation and the rate that is being validated by monetary policy lead to changes in the level of output and in the actual rate of inflation. Hence changes in the rate of monetary expansion can have powerful though not entirely predictable effects on the economy.

Third, in the long run GDP will move to the level indicated by the long-run aggregate supply curve and the long-run Phillips curve. This means that changes in the rate of monetary expansion will cause only temporary changes in the level of output. In the long run changes in the rate of monetary expansion have their only influence on the rate of inflation.

Some Extensions

Shock inflation. All of the foregoing analysis has been done on the assumption that shock inflation is zero. In today's world many shocks hit the price level. What we see is a much less regular experience than the simple combination of core plus demand inflation. The inflation rate varies quite substantially from period to period due to the action of the many shocks that impinge on it. When such shocks occur, the economy's output-inflation combination will lie off the current expectations-augmented Phillips curve—above it for a positive shock and below it for a negative shock.

Asymmetrical speeds of reaction. The shape of the Phillips curve means that it is easier to raise the core rate than to lower it. The change in the core rate from period to period depends on the discrepancy between the actual rate and the core rate. The steepness of the short-run Phillips curve above Y^* means that it is easy to create a substantial gap between the actual rate and the core rate by increasing the inflationary gap. This will tend to drag up the core rate fairly quickly. The flatness of the short-run Phillips curve below Y^* means that only a small discrepancy between the actual and the core rates can be created by even a large recessionary gap. Therefore, the core rate can be depressed only slowly by creating recessionary gaps.

It is an important prediction of this theory that the core rate of inflation can accelerate fairly quickly but will decelerate only slowly.

Summary

We now summarize the key points of the theory of the expectations-augmented Phillips curve and indi-cate where there is substantial agreement and where there is controversy with competing theories.

1. *The rate of price inflation must follow the trend rate of cost inflation quite closely.* There is little disagreement over this relation, which defines the core rate of inflation. Notice, however, that it is just a matter of simple arithmetic that the major determinant of price inflation is cost inflation. This says nothing about causes. Costs could be rising because of the pressure of excess demand in factor markets or because of the exercise of arbitrary power on the part of unions.
2. *The influence of demand on inflation is asymmetrical.* Inflationary gaps cause inflation to rise well above the core rate, whereas recessionary gaps force the actual rate only slightly below the core rate. The evidence for this asymmetry is strong, although some economists deny it.
3. *The core inflation rate falls slowly even in the face of large recessionary gaps.* There is a substantial disagreement over this point, for some economists believe that the core rate can fall quite rapidly. This key controversy underlies many differences in policy recommendations.
4. *Shocks caused by such influences as changes in indirect taxes, agricultural crop failures, or increases in import prices temporarily affect the inflation rate.* Economists do not always agree on this point; at the time of the first OPEC oil-price shocks in 1974, some said that if oil-related prices rose, other prices would fall, keeping the price level constant. As a result of the evidence of the OPEC shocks, most economists now agree that supply shocks affect the price level, causing temporary deviations in the rate of inflation from what it would otherwise be. Another example of a clear supply-shock inflation was the rise in the price level that occurred in Britain in 1979 and 1980 after income taxes were cut and value-added taxes raised by the new Conservative government.
5. *Demand-induced rises in the inflation rate yield only temporary increases in national income.* Any departure of national income from Y^* sets in motion forces that cause a return to Y^*. Output in excess of Y^* causes an inflation that sets in motion the monetary adjustment mechanism. Frustration of the monetary adjustment mechanism by monetary expansion can sustain output above Y^*, but only if the rate of increase of wages, prices, and money is continually accelerating.

37

Employment and Unemployment

In the early 1980s worldwide unemployment rose to high levels. It remained high in many advanced industrial countries and only began to come down, and then very slowly, during the latter half of the decade. Canada's experience reflects rather closely these international developments. From a high of 12.8 percent in late 1982, Canada's unemployment rate fell to 9.4 percent at the start of 1987.

As we shall see later in this chapter, those overall figures hide large variations in rates for specific groups. For example, in 1986 the unemployment rate was 8 percent for males over 25 years of age and 16.5 percent for males between the ages of 15 and 24.

Many social policies designed to alleviate the short-term economic consequences of unemployment have been instituted since the 1930s, and their success may be counted as a real triumph of economic policy. Being unemployed, even for some substantial period of time, is no longer the economic disaster that it once was. But the longer-term effects of high unemployment rates in terms of the disillusioned who have given up trying to make it within the system and who contribute to social unrest should be a matter of serious concern to the haves as well as the have-nots.

Many Canadians believe that unemployment is the most serious macroeconomic problem facing the nation. Is this so? What policies might be effective in reducing the problem?

Kinds of Unemployment

The unemployed can be classified in various ways. They can be grouped by personal characteristics, such as age, sex, degree of skill or education, and ethnic group. They can also be classified by geographic location, occupation, duration of unemployment, or reasons for their unemployment.

In this chapter we are concerned mainly with the reasons for unemployment. Although it is not always possible to say why a particular unemployed person has no job, it is often possible to gain some idea of the total numbers of people unemployed for each major cause.

In Chapter 26, we distinguished two types of unemployment: *deficient-demand* unemployment, which is unemployment due to a recessionary gap, and *frictional* unemployment, which was used to account for the unemployment that exists when national income is at its potential level and hence there is neither a recessionary nor an inflationary gap.

For our more detailed study we will now distinguish a second reason why there is unemployment at potential income. We call this second reason *structural* unemployment. We also discuss an additional type, *real-wage* unemployment.

Frictional Unemployment

Frictional unemployment results from the normal turnover of labor. Young people enter the labor force and look for jobs. People leave jobs for many reasons. Some quit because they are dissatisfied with the working conditions; others are fired. Whatever the reason, they must search for new jobs, which takes time. Persons who are unemployed while searching for jobs are said to be frictionally unemployed.

Frictional unemployment would persist even if the structure of jobs in terms of skills, industries, occupations, and location was unchanging.

Normal turnover of labor will always produce a pool of persons who are frictionally unemployed. The search aspect of frictional unemployment is emphasized in a branch of modern theory that studies the rational behavior of people searching for jobs.

In looking at causes of unemployment, Keynes made a basic distinction between voluntary and involuntary unemployment. *Voluntary* unemployment occurs when there is a job available, but the unemployed person is not willing to accept it at the going wage rate. *Involuntary* unemployment occurs when a person is willing to accept a job at the going wage rate but cannot find one. In Box 37-1, where we discuss search unemployment in more detail, we see that the distinction between voluntary and involuntary unemployment is not as clear as Keynes suggested.

Structural Unemployment

Structural adjustments can cause unemployment. When the pattern of demand for goods changes, the pattern of demand for labor also changes. Until labor adjusts fully, structural unemployment develops.

Structural unemployment may be defined as unemployment caused by a mismatch between the structure of the labor force—in terms of skills, occupations, industries, or geographic location—and the structure of the demand for labor. In Canada today, structural unemployment exists, for example, in the oil and gas industry in Alberta and in many of the older foundry and mill towns in Ontario.

Natural causes. Economic growth can cause structural unemployment. As growth proceeds, the mix of required inputs changes, as do the proportions in which final goods are demanded. These changes require considerable economic adjustment. Structural unemployment occurs when such adjustments are slow enough that severe pockets of unemployment develop in areas, industries, and occupations in which the demand for factors of production is falling faster than the supply.

Changes that accompany economic growth shift the structure of the demand for labor. Demand rises in such expanding areas as Ontario and industrial Quebec and falls in such contracting areas as the western resource-based provinces. Demand rises for workers with certain skills, such as computer programming and electronics engineering, and falls for workers with other skills, such as stenography and bookkeeping. Demand rises, say, for airline pilots and short-order cooks and falls for lumberjacks and riggers and for crew members on transatlantic passenger liners. To meet changing demands, the structure of the labor force must change. Some existing workers can retrain, and some new entrants can acquire fresh skills.

Structural unemployment will increase if there is either an increase in the speed at which the structure of the demand for labor is changing or a decrease in the speed at which labor is adapting to these changes.

Policy causes. Government policies can influence the economy's ability to adapt.

Policies that discourage movement of labor among regions, industries, and occupations also raise structural unemployment.

BOX 37-1

Search Unemployment

Some frictional unemployment is involuntary: No acceptable job in the person's occupational and skill category has yet been located. Often, however, it is voluntary. The unemployed person is aware of available jobs but is searching for better options. Voluntary frictional unemployment is often called **search unemployment.**

The existence of search unemployment shows that the distinction between voluntary and involuntary unemployment is not as clear as it might seem at first sight. How, for example, should we classify an unemployed woman who refuses to accept a job at a lower skill level than the one for which she feels she is qualified? What if she turns down a job for which she is trained because she hopes to get a higher wage offer for a similar job from another employer?

In one sense people in search unemployment are voluntarily unemployed because they could find some job; in another sense they are involuntarily unemployed because they have not yet succeeded in finding the job for which they feel they are suited at a rate of pay that they believe exists.

Workers do not have perfect knowledge of all available jobs and rates of pay, and they may be able to gain information only by searching the market.

Faced with this uncertainty, it may be sensible to refuse a first job offer, for the offer may prove to be a poor one in light of further market information. Too much search—for example, holding off while being supported by others in the hope of finding a job better than that for which one is really suited—is an economic waste. Thus search unemployment is a gray area: Some is useful, some wasteful.

It is socially desirable for there to be sufficient search unemployment to give unemployed people time to find an available job that makes the best use of their skills.

How long it will pay to remain in search unemployment depends on the economic costs of being unemployed. By lowering the costs of being unemployed, unemployment insurance tends to increase the amount of search unemployment. This is not necessarily undesirable. If the amount of search unemployment would otherwise be too little, the insurance scheme can increase economic efficiency. If, however, the amount of search unemployment is already too much, unemployment insurance will lower economic efficiency.

Policies that discourage firms from replacing human labor with machines may protect employment in the short term. If, however, such policies lead to the decline of an industry because it cannot compete effectively with innovative foreign competitors, structural unemployment can result in the long run.

One further cause of structural unemployment is the persistence of a disequilibrium structure of relative wages. Typical causes of such a structure are minimum wages, union agreements that narrow wage differentials, nationally negotiated wage structures that take no account of local market conditions, and equal pay laws that apply in situations where the groups concerned do not in fact all contribute equally to the profitability of the enterprise. Such policies cause particular groups to lose employment because

their relative wages are above their equilibrium value.

For example, an elderly person may be prepared to work for $100 a week as a caretaker of an apartment. Further, the owner may believe that this person is capable of doing what is needed. But suppose the minimum wage is $150 a week. If there were no minimum wage, the elderly person would get the job. But because of the minimum wage, the owner either goes without a caretaker or hires someone else who can provide her with more services than she needs. She reasons that since she has to pay more, she might as well get something for it.

The same considerations apply to an inexperienced worker just out of school who would accept $100 a week for a first job. A potential employer is willing to pay this wage, but the minimum wage is $150. Once again the employer hires someone else who is overqualified for the job. A further unfortunate effect is that such young workers do not get the on-the-job training and experience that would equip them to hold down a stable, higher-paying job a year or two later.

Much empirical research supports the conclusion that imposed wage structures such as minimum wages tend to transfer employment from those whose relative wages are raised by the intervention to those whose relative wages are lowered. But do imposed wages affect overall employment? That is a difficult question, but, as we discussed in Chapter 19, the evidence suggests that overall employment falls as a result of minimum wages. If such policies lead to an increase in the average wage paid, they may contribute to what we will call real-wage unemployment.

The Distinction Between Frictional and Structural Unemployment

As with many distinctions, the one between structural and frictional unemployment becomes blurred at the margin. In a sense structural unemployment is really long-term frictional unemployment. For illustration, consider a change that requires labor to reallocate from one sector to another. If the reallocation occurs quickly, we call the unemployment frictional; if the reallocation occurs slowly, we call the unemployment structural.

The major characteristic of both frictional and structural unemployment is that there is a job available—that is, an unfilled vacancy—for each unemployed person.

In the case of pure frictional unemployment, the job vacancy and the searcher are matched. The only problem is that the searcher has not yet located the vacancy. In the case of structural unemployment, the job vacancy and the searcher are mismatched in one or more relevant characteristics such as occupation, industry, location, or skill requirements.

The sum of frictional plus structural unemploy-

ment is what we have earlier called the *natural rate of unemployment.*

Deficient-Demand Unemployment

We have called unemployment that occurs because total demand is insufficient to purchase all the output that could be produced by a fully employed labor force *deficient-demand unemployment*. It is the unemployment that exists because there is a recessionary gap. As a result there are fewer available jobs than there are unemployed persons. Deficient-demand unemployment can be measured as the number of persons currently employed minus the number of persons who would be employed at potential income. (It is thus the employment counterpart of the output gap.) When deficient-demand unemployment is zero, there is some job available for every person unemployed. In this situation unemployment persists either for structural or frictional reasons. This is the natural rate of unemployment.

National income theory seeks to explain the causes of and cures for unemployment in excess of frictional and structural unemployment. *Full employment* does not mean zero unemployment; it means that all unemployment is frictional or structural.

National income theory thus seeks to explain the deficient-demand unemployment associated with variations in the nation's total national income around its potential income.

Real-Wage Unemployment

Unemployment due to too high a real wage is called **real-wage unemployment** or sometimes **Classical unemployment.** This latter term is used because many economists, whom Keynes dubbed the Classical economists, believed that unemployment in the 1930s was caused by high real wages. The remedy they suggested for unemployment was to reduce wages. Keynes argued that the unemployment was due to too little aggregate demand, and his remedy was to raise demand, not cut wages. Keynesians won that debate, and there is now general agreement that the unemployment of the 1930s was caused by deficient aggregate demand rather than excessive real wages.

Because the debates of the 1930s aroused strong emotions, many modern Keynesians have refused to believe that *any* unemployment could be caused by high real wages. There is concern, however, that some current unemployment in Western Europe and elsewhere (including Canada) may be traced to excessive real wage levels.

So far in this book we have used the term *real wages* to mean the purchasing power of money wages. This is measured by deflating the money wage by the Consumer Price Index. In this section we are concerned with the real cost to the employer of hiring a worker. We call this the **real product wage.** The nominal cost to the employer includes the pre-tax wage rate, any extra benefits such as pension plan contributions, and any government payroll taxes such as employers' contributions to social insurance. The real product wage is the nominal cost for a specific time period, say, per hour of labor employed, divided by the value of the output produced by labor during the same time period. Thus, for example, if it costs $20 to employ labor that produces output valued at $30, the real product wage is 0.666, which says that labor costs absorb two-thirds of the value of output.

Too high a real product wage can affect employment through forces operating both in the short run and in the long run. Consider the short run first. At any moment in time many industries have an array of plants, ranging from those that embody the oldest technologies in use and can do little more than cover their variable costs to those that embody the latest technology and can make a handsome return over variable costs. A rise in the real product wage of 10 percent will mean that some plants can no longer cover their variable costs and so will close down. If, for example, a plant had wages of $0.70 and other variable costs of $0.25 for every $1 of sales, production would be worthwhile, since $0.05 of every $1 of sales would be available as a return on already invested capital. If the product wage rose so that $0.77 for every $1 of sales was paid in wages, the plant would be shut down, since it would not even be covering its variable costs. The plant's employees

would then lose their jobs. This also applies to the economy as a whole.

An economy-wide rise in real product wages, other things being equal, means that some plants and firms will no longer be able to cover their variable costs and will shut down. When they do, the unemployment rate will rise.

Now consider a period of time long enough for the demand for labor to be adjusted to the real product wage by replacing old plant and equipment with new capital that requires different capital-labor ratios. In the long run firms will adopt technologies that replace expensive labor with less expensive capital, and this will increase the amount of real-wage unemployment. Thus when the real wage is too high across the whole economy, a structural mismatch will develop between the labor force and the capital stock. This mismatch will show up as unemployment; when the capital stock is working at full capacity, there is still unemployed labor. The unemployment will continue until one of two things happens. Unemployment may force down the real wage until it pays firms to employ all of the existing labor. Alternatively, new technologies may be invented that make profitable use of the unemployed labor in spite of its high real product wage.

One approach to distinguishing between the various types of unemployment empirically is discussed in Box 37-2.

Experience of Unemployment

Measured and Nonmeasured Unemployment

The number of unemployed persons is estimated from a sample survey conducted each month by Statistics Canada. Persons who are currently without a job but say they have actively searched for one during the sample period are recorded as unemployed. The total number of estimated unemployed is then expressed as a percentage of the labor force (employed plus unemployed) to obtain the figure for percentage unemployment.

BOX 37-2

Distinguishing Types of Unemployment

One useful measure of the natural rate of unemployment is the percentage of the labor force unemployed when the number of unfilled job vacancies is equal to the number of persons seeking jobs. When these two are equal, there is a job opening for every person seeking a job. Any unemployment that remains must be either frictional or structural.

This measure is illustrated in the figure, which plots the number of unfilled vacancies (v) against the number of unemployed (u). The 45° line is the locus of points where $u = v$. On that line there is some job available to match every unemployed person, so there is no deficient-demand unemployment. The uv curve shows the actual relationship between unemployment and vacancies that is suggested by empirical evidence. In an economy with the relation uv_1, zero deficient-demand unemployment occurs at the point x, with frictional plus structural unemployment given by the amount a measured on either axis.

When a boom occurs, employers seek to hire more workers, so more vacancies open up. Since there are more jobs available, the unemployed spend less time searching before finding an acceptable job. Thus the pool of unemployed falls. A boom therefore takes the economy to some point such as y, where there are more vacancies than unemployed. A slump takes the economy to some point such as z, where there are fewer vacancies than unemployed.

A change in structural plus frictional unemployment shifts the uv curve. For example, if people lose their jobs in Alberta while more jobs are created in Toronto, there may be a rise in the number of unemployed (in Alberta) and a rise in the number of unfilled job vacancies (in Toronto). Hence both u and v increase. In the diagram a shift to uv_2 indicates a rise in frictional plus structural unemployment from a to b.

In most countries where reliable vacancy data are available the uv relation shifted outward in the late 1960s and early 1970s. This indicated a rise in the natural rate of unemployment.

Deficient-Demand Unemployment

We can measure deficient-demand unemployment as total unemployment minus estimated frictional plus structural unemployment. Graphically it is actual unemployment minus the unemployment where the uv relation cuts the 45° line. If the economy is at point z, this measure is ac in the figure.*

Real-Wage Unemployment

Unemployment due to excessive increases in the real wage will show up in the figure approximately as a movement along the existing uv curve, say from point x to w, rather than as a shift of that curve. There will be a large rise in unemployment and a small fall in vacancies (which would otherwise have resulted from the normal turnover of labor in the now-closed plants). A general rise in the real product wage can lead to a general rise in unemployment that looks like deficient-demand unemployment because there is a rise in unemployment with no corresponding rise in unfilled vacancies.

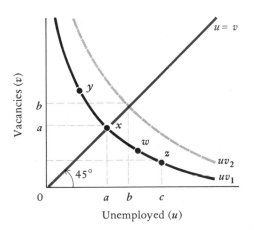

* Notice that the measure is not current unemployment minus current vacancies but current unemployment minus the vacancies that would exist were there no output gap.

The measured figure for unemployment may overstate or understate the number of people who are involuntarily unemployed.

On the one hand, the measured figure overstates unemployment by including people who are not involuntarily unemployed. For example, unemployment insurance benefits provide protection against genuine hardship, but they also induce some people to stay out of work and collect benefits for as long as they last. Such people have in fact voluntarily withdrawn from the labor force, but they are usually included in the ranks of the unemployed because, for fear of losing their benefits, they report to the survey that they are actively looking for a job.

On the other hand, the measured figure understates involuntary unemployment by omitting some people who would accept a job if one were available but who did not actively look for one in the sample week. For example, people who have not found jobs by the time their unemployment benefits are exhausted may become discouraged and stop seeking work. Such people have withdrawn from the labor force and will not be recorded as unemployed. They are, however, truly unemployed in the sense that they would willingly accept a job if one were available.

People in this category are referred to as **discouraged workers.** They have voluntarily withdrawn from the labor market because they believe they cannot find a job under current conditions.

In addition there is part-time unemployment. If some workers are working six hours a day instead of eight hours because there is insufficient demand for the product they manufacture, that group is suffering 25 percent unemployment even though no individual is reported as unemployed. Twenty-five percent of the potential manpower is going unused. Involuntary part-time work is a major source of unemployment of labor resources not reflected in the overall unemployment figures reported in the press.

For example, in mid 1983 some 425,000 workers were in part-time unemployment, accounting for 23 million hours per month of unrecorded unemployment—equivalent to 138,000 full-time unemployed persons. Between 1981 and 1984 the number of part-time jobs rose by 16 percent, while the number of full-time jobs *fell* by 3 percent.

The Overall Unemployment Rate

Figure 26-2 (see page 557) shows the behavior of the unemployment rate since the end of World War II. Until 1970 the rate fluctuated cyclically but showed no clear rising or falling trend. During the 1950s the average rate was 4.4 percent, and during the 1960s it was 5.0 percent—not a significant difference.[1] From 1970, however, the cyclical fluctuations appear to be superimposed on a rising trend. The *low* figure of 5.3 percent unemployment for the post-1970 period was above the *average* of 4.7 percent for the previous two decades, and the high figure of 12.8 percent was the highest since the Great Depression of the 1930s. The low figure was achieved during the boom of 1972–1973; the high occurred in 1982. The average rate of unemployment was 6.6 percent during the 1970s and 10.1 percent during the first six years of the 1980s. The sustained recovery that Canada experienced in the mid 1980s still left unemployment at 9.4 percent at the beginning of 1987.

Figure 37-1 presents one estimate of the natural rate of unemployment, prepared by Professor Pierre Fortin of Laval University.[2] This estimate takes into account the effects of variables measuring demographic, policy, institutional, and sectoral changes. His estimate shows the natural rate of unemployment rising steadily in the early 1960s to a peak in 1978. After 1978 it declines steadily through to 1985. Below we discuss some of the reasons for these movements in the natural rate.

The excess of actual unemployment over the natural rate, called *cyclical unemployment,* is equal to deficient demand unemployment plus real-wage unemployment. Fortin's estimate thus indicates that at the start of 1987 cyclical unemployment was around 3 percent. Other researchers, including those whose

---

[1] Yearly figures in this section are based on annual averages for unemployment.

[2] "How Natural Is Canada's High Unemployment Rate?" *Eastern Economic Journal,* 1987.

**FIGURE 37-1   Actual and Natural Unemployment
                 Rates, 1966–1985**

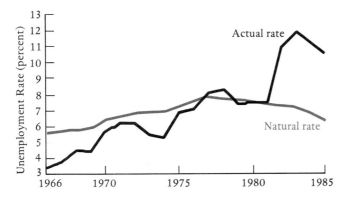

**Fluctuations in aggregate unemployment reflect
cyclical movements around a slowly changing natural rate of unemployment.** The natural unemployment
rate rose gradually from 5.3 percent in 1966 to 7.8 percent in 1978. It then fell gradually to 6.2 percent in 1985.

The actual unemployment rate fluctuated much more
but also reflected some of the trend movements in the
natural rate. The actual rate showed a distinct upward
trend over the early part of the period, starting out at 3.4
percent, below the natural rate, in 1966 and reaching 8.1
percent, above the natural rate, in 1978. The actual rate
then rose sharply in the early 1980s, reaching 11.9 percent in 1983, showing that the effects of the recession far
outweighed the gradual decline in the natural rate. Since
1983 the actual rate has fallen steadily, reflecting the combined effects of the recovery and the fall in the natural
rate.

research was reflected in the final report of the Macdonald Royal Commission in 1985, have estimated
the natural rate to be somewhat higher, and hence
would argue that cyclical unemployment was perhaps as low as 1.0 percent at the start of 1987. Nevertheless, most researchers agree that:

**The rise in the actual unemployment rate over
the late 1960s and most of the 1970s was accompanied by a rise in the natural unemployment
rate; since then the natural rate has probably
fallen somewhat.**

Expressed as percentage points, the difference between 1.5 percent and 3.5 percent cyclical unemployment may not seem very big, but a reduction of
two percentage points in the unemployment rate
means that over a quarter of a million more people
have jobs.

It is important to know how much deficient-demand unemployment exists. Raising aggregate demand when national income is already at its potential
level, and hence when there is no deficient-demand
unemployment, would open up an inflationary gap.
This would accelerate inflation while achieving only
a transitory fall in unemployment. We return to this
below.

The Relative Importance of the Various Kinds of Unemployment

At the beginning of 1987 there were about 1.3 million unemployed in Canada, about 9.4 percent of the
labor force. According to the most widely accepted
estimates, most of this unemployment was frictional
and structural, with deficient-demand accounting for
something between 200,000 and 500,000.

Most of the deficient-demand unemployment
that existed at the end of the recession in 1982 was
eliminated by the subsequent recovery, and the remainder will be eliminated *if* the recovery takes the
economy all the way to its potential income. But
what of the more than a half million unemployed
who will remain after deficient-demand unemployment is eliminated? To study them further we look
at some of the characteristics of the unemployed.

Figure 37-2 gives some idea of the current duration of the spells of unemployment.[3] Data are given
for 1982, a year of severe recession, and for 1986,
when the economy was much closer to its potential
income. The differences between the two sets of
figures are due mainly to the reduction in deficient-demand unemployment over the period.

[3] The figures are based on the Labor Force Survey, which asks
currently unemployed individuals how long they have been out
of work. Notice that this gives us the duration of *currently uncompleted* bouts of unemployment. It gives different and shorter figures than the duration of *completed bouts* of unemployment, which
is obtained by asking people who have just found a job how long
they were out of work.

In 1986 some 28 percent of the unemployed had been out of work for 13 weeks or less. Long-term unemployment accounted for only 41 percent of the unemployed in that year. These figures represent some improvement over the recession year 1982, when only 18 percent of the unemployed had been without jobs for 4 weeks or less and 52 percent for more than 13 weeks. But the 1986 figures were not yet back to the more favorable ones for 1979, probably the last year when national income was at its potential level. In that year just less than one-third of the unemployed had been out of work for more than 13 weeks.

Three facts stand out about the unemployed. First, there is a group of marginal workers who move in and out of jobs, sometimes several times a year, and who account for a significant fraction of the total spells of unemployment. Second, most spells of unemployment are of short duration. Third, the bulk of total unemployment is accounted for by those in long-term unemployment. The consistency of the second and third points can be seen by a simple example. Consider four people, each unemployed for a week, and a fifth who is unemployed for nine months. For this group of five people, 80 percent of the spells of unemployment are short-term, but the long-term bout counts for 90 percent of the total weeks of unemployment.

It seems that the potentially soul-destroying bouts of prolonged periods without a job are confined to a relatively small part of the labor force, but a part that rises significantly in recessions.

Figures 37-3 and 37-4 document some of the inequalities in unemployment rates. Males and females, the young and the experienced have very different unemployment experiences, as Figure 37-3 shows. Equally dramatic are the differences between sectors, as shown in Figure 37-4.

Why Does the Natural Rate of Unemployment Change?

Structural unemployment can increase because the pace of change accelerates or the pace of adjustment to change slows down. An increase in the rate of growth, for example, usually speeds up the rate at which the structure of the demand for labor is chang-

FIGURE 37-2   Duration of Unemployment

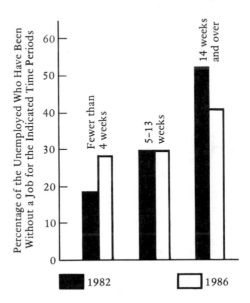

In recession years, the average duration of unemployment rises. In 1982, which was a year of severe recession and high overall unemployment, over half of the unemployed were without jobs for more than 13 weeks, while less than one-fifth were without jobs for less than 5 weeks. In 1986, a year of relative prosperity, only 41 percent of the unemployed were without jobs for more than 13 weeks, while over a quarter were without jobs for less than 5 weeks. (*Source:* Statistics Canada, *The Labour Force.*)

ing. The adaptation of labor to the changing structure of demand may be slowed by such diverse factors as a decline in education and new regulations that make it harder for workers in a given occupation to take new jobs in other states. Any of these changes will cause the natural rate of unemployment to rise. Changes in the opposite direction will cause the natural rate to fall.

Demographic changes.   Because people usually try several jobs before settling into one for a longer period of time, young or inexperienced workers have higher unemployment rates than experienced workers. The proportion of inexperienced workers in the

FIGURE 37-3 Variations in Experience of Unemployment, 1982 and 1986

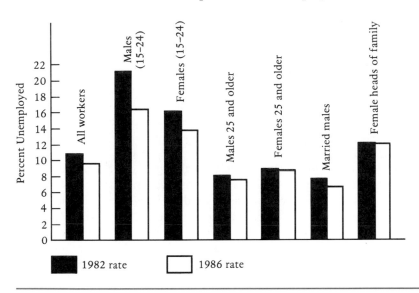

Unemployment is very unevenly divided among sex and skill groups. The overall unemployment rates of 11.0 and 9.6 percent in 1982 and 1986, respectively, concealed large variations in the unemployment rates of different groups. The recession of 1982 led to higher unemployment rates for most groups, but the difference between the 1982 rate and the 1986 rate varied considerably from group to group, with the largest decline being experienced by males between 15 and 24. The unemployment rate for this group fell from 21.2 percent in 1982 to the still high rate of 16.5 percent in 1986. (*Source: Canadian Statistical Review.*)

labor force rose significantly as the baby boom generation of the 1950s entered the labor force along with an unprecedented number of women who elected to work outside the home. It is estimated that these demographic changes added nearly a percentage point to the natural rate of unemployment. Since

FIGURE 37-4 Unemployment Rates by Sector, 1982 and 1986

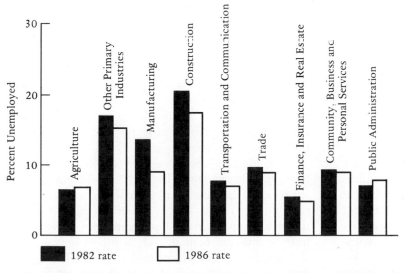

Unemployment rates vary greatly across sectors in both recessions and booms. Unemployment was highest in construction and lowest in finance, insurance, and real estate in both the recession year 1982 and the relatively prosperous year 1986. The ranking of unemployment rates by sector was unchanged between the two years, but there were considerable changes in the differences between sectors. (*Source:* Statistics Canada, *The Labour Force.*)

birthrates were low in the 1960s and a further increase in the percentage of females entering the labor force is unlikely, some demographically induced fall in this type of unemployment has been occurring recently and will continue over the next decade.

Although the natural rate of unemployment, and youth unemployment in particular, should fall as the baby boom generation passes on to middle age, many worry that although the brighter, the more energetic, and the luckier of that generation will do well, many others will not. Learning by on-the-job experience is a critical part of developing marketable labor skills. Many who are in the ranks of youth unemployment have been denied that experience early in their working careers. They may be condemned to remain at best marginal workers taking temporary jobs with low current pay and little future job security.

Other significant changes include the large increase in female participation rates and the related increase in the number of households with more than one income earner. In 1960 only 30 percent of females 20 years and older were in the labor force; in 1972 the figure was 38 percent; by 1986 it had jumped to almost 50 percent. When both husband and wife work, it is possible for one to support both while the other looks for "a really good job" rather than accepting the first job offer that comes along.

Wage and price rigidity.   Recent research suggests that the speed with which wages and prices adjust to changing market conditions may have slowed over the years. Anything that slows the speed of adjustment to the economy's ever-changing conditions will create a larger pool of structural unemployment.

Social insurance programs.   Minimum-wage laws are of real help to those who keep their jobs when their wages are forced up. They hurt those who lose their jobs as a result of the higher wage rates. They may also have a longer-term harmful effect. Employers are discouraged from hiring young people at low wages while providing on-the-job training. During a period of training, employees acquire marketable skills that allow them subsequently to command a higher wage. By discouraging such practices, minimum-wage laws create a pool of people without skills who alternate between low-paid jobs and bouts

of unemployment, thus raising the number of people who are in structural or frictional unemployment at any one time.

Enriched unemployment insurance benefits will, as discussed in Box 37-1, make it easier for the unemployed to maintain living standards while searching for a new job. As a result they can afford to turn down job offers in anticipation of potential better offers. This serves to increase the amount of search unemployment and probably played a role in the increase in the natural rate in the 1970s.

Increasing structural change.   The amount of resource reallocation across industries and areas appears to have increased in the 1970s. In part this is the result of the increasing integration of the Canadian economy with that of the rest of the world. Most observers feel that on balance this integration has been beneficial. But one less fortunate consequence is that changes in demand or supply conditions anywhere in the world requiring adjustments throughout the world's trading sectors increasingly affect Canada.

Internationally, one of the most significant demand changes for North America in the 1970s was the emergence of the Eastern bloc countries as major food importers. The failure of their system of collective agriculture to meet domestic demand led them to become large importers of grain. To pay for these imports, they had to become major exporters of other commodities such as natural gas.

A further demand change was the input price shocks that buffeted the world in the 1970s and early 1980s: two enormous oil price increases in the 1970s and an increase of over 200 percent in average basic materials prices in the early 1970s. Such changes have shifted competitive advantages in industrial production, leading to growth in some areas and countries and decline in others.

Changing prices have also caused changes in quantities demanded. The high cost of gas and oil led to a shift to small cars, an enormous investment program to retool North American industry, and major car imports from Japan and Germany that cut heavily into the demand for North American cars and for their major inputs such as steel. The results were all too evident in the unemployment figures. At the beginning of 1983, when the overall unemployment rate was just below 12 percent, unemployment was estimated to be more than double that rate in the auto industry and in primary metals. Some of these workers were recalled as output recovered, but many had to find jobs in other industries and areas where new skills were required. Rising oil prices also led to a shift to natural gas for home heating, a large demand for insulation, and alterations in typical designs of new houses.

In the mid 1980s another set of changes more or less reversed the ones just discussed. These entailed a new and equally dramatic set of adjustments. More than a decade of high oil prices had led to a reduction in demand for oil and a great increase in its supply. Finally the OPEC countries were no longer able to control the price of oil, which tumbled in a few months during 1985–1986 to about one-third of its earlier value. The immediate effects were felt by the world's oil producers, Canada among them. A rash of business bankruptcies and bank difficulties (including two bank failures) were brought on by the sudden loss of prosperity among both oil producers and organizations that sold to them or had lent to them. Oil users benefited greatly. Just as the high price of oil set in motion a series of adjustments that economized on oil, the low price set in train the opposite series of adjustments. Once again the pattern of advantage of different technologies, products, and geographic areas changed, and major adaptations occurred.

The world food shortages in the 1970s and the accompanying high prices of foodstuffs caused a number of supply reactions to occur throughout that decade. Many countries, including a number of less-developed countries, expanded their food production enormously. They were aided by technological developments that greatly increased crop yields per acre. By the mid 1980s food shortages were threatening to turn into surpluses for many products. Difficult times for Canadian farmers were already evident by the mid 1980s—although these were to some extent due to overborrowing during the earlier period of expansion. Serious slumps in world agricultural markets could have serious consequences for Canadian agriculture and would entail further major readjustments in the Canadian economy, among both farmers and all who depend on farm income for their own sales.

A further factor on the cost side has been the increased use of robots in factories and computer-based processes in offices. These changes have eliminated many assembly line and clerical jobs and forced their former holders to look elsewhere for new jobs.

Another major set of forces leading to structural change arises from the shifting pattern of demand. As a result of rising income and changing social patterns, people spend a higher proportion of their income on services than they used to and a correspondingly smaller proportion on manufactured goods. Restaurant meals and day-care facilities for children are two services with rising demands. This shift is dramatically illustrated by the fact that the *increase* in employment in the North American fast food industry during the past two decades exceeded the total combined employment in the automobile and steel industries!

The pace of technological change since the start of the 1970s has contributed greatly to an increase in the level of structural unemployment.

Future outlook. Certain factors may work to reduce the natural rate of unemployment in the future. First, the proportion of youths and females newly entering the labor force will diminish as the baby boom generation ages and the female participation rate stabilizes. Second, educational systems in some or all provinces may be revamped to give students better job-related training. Third, governments may become more aware of the importance of structural changes in the economy and of the need for policies to encourage rather than inhibit adaptability and flexibility in the economy.

Unemployment Policies

All kinds of unemployment have costs in terms of the output that could have been produced by the unemployed workers. Yet reducing unemployment is also costly. For example, retraining and reallocation schemes designed to reduce structural unemployment use scarce resources.

BOX 37-3

Difficulties in Using Demand Management to Reduce Unemployment

Deficient demand unemployment represents an unnecessary waste of human resources and causes serious economic and social costs. Macroeconomics explains how monetary and fiscal policies can be used to reduce such unemployment. But the issues encountered in this chapter suggest that it may be difficult to identify the extent of deficient demand unemployment, and hence to identify the appropriate policy stance.

Changes in the Natural Unemployment Rate

Policy errors can result from a failure to distinguish between changes in the natural rate of unemployment and cyclical fluctuations around the natural rate.

If the actual unemployment rate rises because the natural rate has risen, stimulating aggregate demand would not be an appropriate response. Increased demand will have little effect on unemployment but will lead to increased inflation. Most observers agree that this is what happened in Canada in the early 1970s.

Similarly, pursuing contractionary policies because the actual unemployment rate is falling may cause a recessionary gap to open up if the natural rate is also falling. Many observers warn that this may be a problem for the late 1980s and early 1990s when the natural rate is expected to fall.

Real-Wage Unemployment

Even if the natural rate of unemployment, and hence the cyclical component of actual unemployment, are correctly measured, the correct policy stance may be difficult to determine. As we also saw in the text, cyclical unemployment includes both deficient demand and real-wage unemployment. Stimulating aggregate demand in the face of real-wage unemployment may cause inflation without reducing unemployment.

We saw in Chapter 36 (see especially Figure 36-1 on page 776) that a real-wage shock opens up a recessionary gap, and hence increases unemployment. If the real-wage shock is temporary, monetary accommodation reduces the recessionary gap at the cost of a once-and-for-all rise in the price level. If, however, the real-wage shock was permanent, so that nominal wages increase in response to the rise in the price level, monetary accommodation would trigger a wage-price spiral with little or no effect on the unemployment rate.

The Natural Rate Revisited

Recently some economists have argued that the natural rate of unemployment itself may have a cyclical component.

The argument is that business cycles are often accompanied by large swings in key relative prices. The international terms of trade, the price of raw materials and resources relative to manufactures, and the relative price of services are examples of relative prices that change substantially in the face of cyclical fluctuations. As a result, the relative profitabilities of different firms, sectors, and regions change, and workers laid off in declining sectors seek employment in other sectors. For all the reasons discussed in the text, this "mismatch" of workers with job opportunities, which occur as a result of aggregate cyclical fluctuations, will temporarily increase the level of structural unemployment in the economy.

A related reason for structural unemployment to respond to cyclical fluctuations lies in the operation

---

It would be neither possible nor desirable to reduce unemployment to zero. The causes of unemployment could never be removed completely, and reducing the amount of unemployment stemming from those causes is costly.

Unemployment insurance is one method of helping people cope with unemployment. Certainly, it has reduced significantly the human costs of the bouts of unemployment that are inevitable in a changing society. Nothing, however, is without cost.

of Canada's Unemployment Insurance Act. The regional extended benefits provisions of the Unemployment Insurance Act allow for extended benefits to accrue to workers in regions with unusually high unemployment rates. During the 1982–1983 recession many Canadian regions suffered high enough unemployment to qualify for these extended benefits. The increased generosity of benefits not only provided for more support for the unemployment during the deep recession, it also allowed for increased search and hence increased structural unemployment during the recovery. As a result, the actual unemployment rate in these regions fell only slowly during the recovery. But this slow decline was because of the persistent structural unemployment, not because of continued deficient demand unemployment.

Economists who stress the importance of these cyclical movements in structural unemployment argue that estimates of the natural rate of unemployment, such as those reported in Figure 37-1, *understate* the extent of structural unemployment following a major recession such as occurred in Canada in the early 1980s.

Implications for Policy

The estimates presented in Figure 37-1 suggest that cyclical unemployment in 1986 stood at about 3 percent. Many economists—including the author of those estimates, Professor Pierre Fortin of Laval University—argue that there is little real wage unemployment, so that the entire 3 percent represents deficient demand unemployment. Not surprisingly, these economists call for substantial demand stimulus to eliminate what they perceive to be an enormous recessionary gap.

At the other extreme, some economists argue that the natural rate is currently much larger than the 6.2 percent of Figure 37-1, and hence that cyclical unemployment is smaller than indicated by the figure. They also argue that there is considerable real wage unemployment in Canada, so that the remaining deficient demand unemployment is negligible. As a result these economists oppose the introduction of any demand stimulus on the grounds that such stimulus will only create an inflationary gap.

A third group of economists believe that deficient demand unemployment in 1986 was somewhere between the two extremes identified above but were nevertheless opposed to the use of demand stimulus. Their argument was that the deficient demand unemployment was the necessary price of combatting inflation—indeed, creating deficient demand was an explicit goal of policy. These economists argue that in order to maintain the credibility of the government's commitment to fighting inflation, it was necessary to wait for the automatic adjustment mechanism to reduce the recessionary gap, rather than to reverse the stance of aggregate demand policies.

A further lesson arises from the inherent uncertainty attached to identifying the amount of deficient demand unemployment. One view is that because of the uncertainty, demand management should be used cautiously. While fine tuning may be ruled out, periods with persistent deficient demand unemployment can be identified and expansionary demand policy can then be safely used. Other economists argue, however, that the extent of the uncertainty makes any targeting of demand policy on unemployment ill-advised—they would argue that demand policies should focus only on controlling inflation.

While unemployment insurance alleviates the suffering caused by some kinds of unemployment, it can itself contribute to unemployment for, as we have observed, it encourages search unemployment.

Supporters of unemployment insurance empha-

size its benefits. Critics emphasize its costs. As with any policy, a rational assessment of the value of unemployment insurance requires a balancing of its undoubted benefits against its undoubted costs. Most Canadians seem convinced that when this calculation

BOX 37-4

Industrial Change: An Economist's Cautionary Tale

The audience hushed as the royal commissioners filed into the room. The chief forecasting wizard—behind his back some called him the economic soothsayer—began his report. "I have identified beyond reasonable doubt the underlying trends now operating," he declared to an expectant audience. "The nation's leading industry, industry X, is in a state of decline. From its current position of employing 50 percent of our work force it will, within the duration of one human lifetime, employ only 5 percent."

"Forty-five percent of the nation's jobs destroyed within one lifetime!" proclaimed the newspaper headlines.

"Where can new jobs possibly come from at so rapid a pace?" asked a labor leader.

"We must protect industry X; we just cannot let all these jobs go down the tubes," argued an employer.

"Perhaps we should identify and promote new 'sunrise industries,'" said a mandarin. Indeed, it was widely believed that a new high-tech product, product Y, would be the wave of a future new transportation revolution, and a call went out for subsidies and tax expenditures to back its development.

"Is there any hope that the private sector might provide the new jobs?" someone asked.

"Possibly," said a junior economist, more out of desperation than hope, "the new product Z that is being produced by a few people in backyard sheds might grow to be a significant employer."

He was immediately pounced on by a chorus of more realistic thinkers. "Product Z! It's noisy, it's smelly, and it's a plaything for the rich. Surely *it* will never provide significant employment."

All of the economic facts in the above tale are true; only the royal commission and the policy initiatives are fictitious.

The country was Canada.

The time was 1900.

Industry X, the employer of 50 percent of the work force, was agriculture.

Product Y, the sunrise industry, was zeppelins.

Product Z, the scorned plaything of the rich, was automobiles.

The decline of some traditional industries is a cause for concern. Some are suffering a temporary decline, and some are declining permanently. In either event, the hardships on those losing their jobs are severe. The tale does, however, have a serious message. Here are a few of the lessons that can be gleaned from a look at the Canadian economy of 1900:

1. The economy is constantly changing. Indeed, the motto of any market economy could be "nothing is permanent." New products appear continually, while others disappear.

At the early stage of a new product, total demand is low, costs of production are high, and many small firms are each trying to get ahead of their competitors by finding the twist that appeals to consumers or the

---

is made, the benefits greatly exceed the costs, although many also recognize the scope for reform of certain aspects of the program, as discussed in Chapter 25 (pages 535–538).

Deficient-Demand Unemployment

We do not need to say much more about this type of unemployment since its control is the subject of stabilization policy, which we have studied in several earlier chapters. A major recession that occurs due to natural causes can be countered by monetary and fiscal policy to reduce deficient-demand unemployment. Some potential pitfalls in using aggregate demand management to reduce perceived deficient demand unemployment are identified in Box 37-3 (see pages 818–819).

The 1970s and 1980s saw the emergence of *policy-induced* deficient-demand unemployment. This occurred when, in an attempt to combat inflation, the government adopted drastic contractionary policies that opened up large recessionary gaps. As we saw in Chapter 36, a temporary bout of deficient-demand unemployment was the price of reducing inflation.

technique that slashes costs. Sometimes new products never get beyond that phase—they prove to be passing fads. Others, however, do become items of mass consumption.

Successful firms in growing industries buy up, merge with, or otherwise eliminate their less successful rivals. Simultaneously, their costs fall, owing to scale economies. Competition drives prices down along with costs.

Eventually, at the mature stage, a few giant firms often control the industry. They become large, conspicuous, and important parts of the nation's economy. Sooner or later, new products arise to erode the position of the established giants. Demand falls off, and unemployment occurs as the few firms run into financial difficulties.

A large, sick, declining industry may appear to many as a national failure and a disgrace. At any moment, however, firms can be found in all phases—from small firms in new industries to giant firms in declining industries. Large declining industries are as much a natural part of a healthy changing economy as large stable industries and small growing ones.

2. The policy of shoring up the declining industries of the 1980s could be just as destructive of our living standards as the policy of protecting the agricultural sector from decline in 1900 would have been. (Policies that ease the human cost of the adjustment are, however, to be recommended.)

3. To tell where the new employment will come from requires the kind of crystal ball our young economist would have needed in 1900 to stick by his wild guess of identifying the new plaything of the rich as the massive automobile industry 30 years later.

Economists are continually asked, "Where will the new employment come from?" The answer "we don't know" is *wrongly* taken to mean "it won't come." In the past, the new jobs have come, and we see no new identifiable forces to prevent their coming in the future. For example, in the course of the current recovery, many people gaining employment are starting in *new* jobs—jobs with firms and in locations that did not exist or would not have been predicted even five years ago.

4. Picking winners and backing them by government policy is a sure way to waste public funds and inhibit the development of the real winners. People risking their own money and diversifying risks over many ventures are a surer route to employment creation than governments risking taxpayers' money and mesmerized by a few current fads and fashion.

5. The industrial policy we do need is one that encourages private initiatives and risk taking. Small businesses are often, if not always, the route to the creation of new employment. Risk taking and the growth of small firms should not be discouraged by such things as complicated regulatory rules and tax laws.

Real-Wage Unemployment

If this type of unemployment is a major problem, its cure is not an easy matter. Basically what is required is a fall in the real product wage combined with measures to increase aggregate demand so as to create enough total employment. But, as many European countries have discovered, the cure is slow and requires enough time to install new labor-using capital.

The steps might be as follows. First, the real product wage would have to fall substantially. Then, since wages enter into disposable income and disposable income determines consumer demand, the cut in wages would tend to reduce aggregate demand and hence reduce equilibrium national income. This deflationary force could then be countered by expansionary fiscal and monetary policy that would create sufficient aggregate demand to restore full employment.

Frictional Unemployment

The turnover that causes frictional unemployment is an inevitable part of the functioning of the economy.

Insofar as it is caused by ignorance, increasing the knowledge of workers about market opportunities may help. But such measures have a cost, and that cost has to be balanced against the benefits.

Some frictional unemployment is an inevitable part of the learning process. One reason that there is a high turnover rate, and hence high frictional unemployment, is that new entrants have to try jobs to see if they are suitable. They will typically try more than one job before settling into one that most satisfies, or least dissatisfies, them.

Structural Unemployment

The reallocation of labor among occupations, industries, skill categories, and regions that gives rise to structural unemployment is an inevitable part of growth. There are two basic approaches to reducing structural unemployment: First, try to arrest the changes that accompany growth, and, second, accept the changes and try to speed up the adjustments. Throughout history labor and management have advocated, and governments have tried, both approaches. Box 37-4 (see pages 820–821) gives a cautionary tale concerning the choice between the two.

Resisting change.   Since the beginning of the Industrial Revolution workers have often resisted the introduction of new techniques to replace the older techniques at which they were skilled. This is understandable. New techniques often destroy the value of the knowledge and experience of workers skilled in the displaced techniques. Older workers may not even get a chance to start over with the new technique. Employers may prefer to hire younger persons who will learn the new skills faster than older workers who are set in their ways of thinking. From society's point of view, new techniques are beneficial because they are a major source of economic growth. From the point of view of the workers they displace, new techniques can be an unmitigated disaster.

Here are two characteristic ways in which economic change has been resisted. First, a declining industry may be supported with public funds. If the market would support an output of X, but subsidies are used to support an output of $2X$, jobs are provided for, say, half the industry's labor force who

would otherwise become unemployed and have to find jobs elsewhere. Second, change may be accepted but agreement reached to continue to employ workers who would otherwise be made redundant by the new technology. Both these policies are attractive to the people who would otherwise become unemployed. It may be a long time before they can find another job, and when they do, their skills may not turn out to be highly valued in their new occupations.

In the long term, however, such policies are not beneficial. Agreements to hire unneeded workers raise costs and can hasten the decline of an industry threatened by competitive products. An industry that is declining due to economic change becomes an increasingly large burden on the public purse as economic forces become less and less favorable to its success. Sooner or later, public support is withdrawn, and an often precipitous decline then ensues.

In assessing these remedies for structural unemployment, it is important to realize that although they are not viable in the long run for the economy, they may be the best alternatives for the affected workers during their lifetimes.

There is often a genuine conflict between the workers threatened by structural unemployment, whose interests lie in preserving their jobs, and the general public, whose interest is served by economic growth, which is the engine of rising living standards.

Aiding adjustments to change.   Another policy to deal with structural change is to accept the decline of industries and the destruction of specific jobs that go with it and to try to reduce the cost of adjustment for those affected. Retraining and relocation grants make movement easier and reduce structural unemployment without inhibiting economic change and growth. Retraining programs exist in a number of countries but have met with mixed success at best. Relocation grants are used successfully in countries such as Sweden but have not played a role in Canada.

A number of policies have been introduced in Canada. These have focused on two sources of adjustment problems. One is imperfections in capital markets that make it difficult for workers to borrow funds in order to retrain or relocate. The other is the lack of good information about current and future job prospects.

A major aspect of labor market policies is education. Between 1960 and 1986, university enrollment rose from 107,000 to 467,000 and community college enrollment increased from 50,000 to 322,000. Over the same period, the number of persons undertaking technical training increased from fewer than 5,000 to over 350,000, partly under the stimulus of the Adult Occupational Training Act of 1967.

Policies to improve the flow of information include the creation of job banks and information centers and initial steps toward a nationwide computerized information system called Jobscan. Job creation programs such as the Local Employment Assistance Programme, Canada Community Services Projects, New Technology Employment Programme, and Summer Canada are also major labor market policies aimed at structural unemployment.

A number of programs that aid adjustment in a variety of ways exist under the National Training Act and the Labour Adjustment Benefits Act. The Canadian Mobility Programme, which finances relocation and travel assistance, spends about $8 million annually, and each year helps about 5,000 workers relocate permanently and another 20,000 temporarily. Women's employment counseling centers serve 5,000 women entering or re-entering the work force each year. Other services meet the special needs of such groups as the physically disabled, criminal offenders, and youths.

In 1985 the Conservative government introduced a Canadian Job Strategy. This strategy involved federal expenditures of about $1.4 billion annually toward six programs, the biggest of which were Job Development, Job Entry, and Skill Shortages. These programs were directed to groups such as women, aboriginal peoples, and disabled persons who were perceived as being "disadvantaged" in labor markets. The funds are allocated on a regional basis. The $1.4 billion does not, however, all represent new expenditures, as a number of existing labor market adjustment programs—including the Industry and Labour Adjustment Program and the Canadian Industrial Renewal Program—were discontinued.

Some of the changes appear to be merely window-dressing, but some real changes were effected. The government defended the changes on the grounds that the old programs provided only "short-term responses to labour market fluctuations," while the new programs concentrated on directing help to individuals who need it most. Critics of the changes argued that short-term assistance is all that is needed to promote adjustment, and that the changes in some cases replace pro-adjustment policies with disguised welfare payments, often distributed in a manner more geared to the political interests of the government than to the adjustment needs of the economy.

Summary

1. Unemployment may be voluntary or involuntary. Involuntary unemployment is a serious social concern both because it causes economic waste due to lost output and because it is a source of human suffering.
2. Looking at causes, it is useful to distinguish several kinds of unemployment: (a) frictional unemployment, which is due to the time it takes to find a first job and to move from job to job as a result of normal labor turnover; (b) structural unemployment, which is caused by the need to reallocate resources among occupations, regions, and industries as the structure of demands and supplies changes; (c) deficient-demand unemployment, which is caused by too low a level of aggregate demand; and (d) real-wage unemployment, which is caused by too high a real product wage. Together the amounts of

frictional unemployment and structural unemployment make up what is now called the natural rate of unemployment.

3. Measured unemployment figures may overestimate or underestimate the actual number of unemployed, for they may include some people who are voluntarily unemployed and omit discouraged workers who have left the labor force.

4. The natural rate of unemployment has risen in recent years. This is due in part at least to demographic changes in the work force, increasing wage and price rigidity in the economy, increasing generosity of unemployment compensation and other social insurance programs, and increasing structural change in the economy.

5. Unemployment insurance helps to alleviate the human suffering associated with inevitable unemployment. It also increases unemployment by encouraging voluntary unemployment.

6. Unemployment can be reduced by raising aggregate demand, by making it easier to move between jobs, by slowing down the rate of change in the economy, and by raising the cost of staying unemployed. However, it is neither possible nor desirable to reduce unemployment to zero.

Topics for Review

Voluntary and involuntary unemployment
Deficient-demand unemployment
Frictional unemployment
Structural unemployment
Real-wage unemployment
Effects of demographic and structural changes on unemployment

Discussion Questions

1. Interpret the following statements from newspapers in terms of types of unemployment
   a. Recession hits local factory, 2,000 laid off.
   b. "A job? I've given up trying," says mother of three.
   c. "We closed down because we could not stand the competition from Taiwan," says local manager.
   d. "When they raised the minimum wage, I just could not afford to keep all of these retired policemen on my payroll as security guards," says local shopping center owner.
   e. Slack demand puts local foundry on short time.
   f. "Of course, I could take a job as a dishwasher, but I'm trying to find something that makes use of my high school training," says local teenager in our survey of the unemployed.
   g. "Thank God for the minimum wage. Without it, I couldn't earn enough to feed the kids," says single father of four.
   h. Retraining main challenge in increased use of robots.
   i. Modernization may cut textile employment.
   j. Uneven upturn: signs of recovery hit Ontario, but B.C. and Alberta still in recession.

2. What differences in approach to unemployment are suggested by the following facts?
   a. Britain has spent billions on subsidizing firms that would otherwise have gone out of business in order to protect the jobs of the employees.
   b. Sweden has pioneered in spending large sums to retrain and relocate displaced workers.
3. Discuss the following views:
   a. "Canadian workers should resist automation, which is destroying their jobs," says a labor leader.
   b. "Given the fierce foreign competition, it's a case of automate or die," says an industrialist.
4. Discuss the following quotation: "There is nothing natural about the natural rate of unemployment; we should not let the inappropriate name 'natural' mislead us into believing that this amount of unemployment should be accepted as normal."
5. Use the latest *Bank of Canada Review* to compare the percentage of total long-term unemployment in the most recent year available with the figures for earlier years given in the text of this chapter. Can you think of any reasons why the figures have changed?
6. What theories can you suggest to explain why unemployment rates stay persistently above average for youths and below average for males over 25?
7. It is often argued that the true unemployment figure for Canada is much higher than the officially reported figure. What are possible sources of "hidden unemployment"? On the other side, are there reasons for expecting some exaggeration of the number of people reported as unemployed? Would the relative strength of these opposing forces change over the course of the business cycle? What would you expect if a short recession turned into a long and deep depression?
8. At a time when the Canadian unemployment rate stood at close to 10 percent, the press reported, "Skilled labor shortage plagues many firms—newspaper ads often draw few qualified workers; wages over time are up." What type of unemployment does this suggest to be important?

38

Economic Growth

Popular debate is bedeviled by confusion about the various causes of change in national income. Some commentators argue that governments can spend their way into a rising national income. Others argue that while expansionary government policies may stimulate the economy in the short run, they often have adverse effects on growth in the economy in the long run.

Causes of Increases in Real National Income

Figure 38-1 illustrates some of the most important possibilities. If there is a recessionary gap, raising aggregate demand will yield a once-and-for-all increase in national income. But once potential income is achieved, further increases in aggregate demand yield only transitory increases in real income but lasting increases in the price level.

Measures that reduce structural unemployment can also increase the employed labor force and thus increase potential income. The increase in income resulting from this change might not be very large. There would, however, be social gain resulting from the reduction in unemployment, especially the long-term unemployment that occurs when people are trapped in declining areas, industries, or occupations.

Over the long haul, however, what really raises national income is *economic growth*, that is, the increase in potential income due to changes in factor supplies (labor and capital) or in the productivity of factors (output per unit of factor input). The removal of a serious recessionary gap might raise national income by 10 percent, while the elimination of all structural unemployment might raise it by somewhat less. But a modest growth rate of 3 percent per year raises national income by 10 percent in 3 years and *doubles* it in about 24 years.

Over any long period of time, economic growth rather than variations in aggregate demand or in structural unemployment exerts the major effect on real national income.

Effects of Investment and Saving on National Income

Short-Run and Long-Run Effects of Investment

The theory of income determination that we studied in Part Eight is a short-run theory. It takes potential income as constant and concentrates

FIGURE 38-1   Ways of Increasing National Income

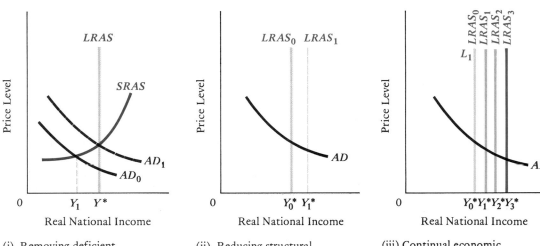

(i) Removing deficient
     demand unemployment

(ii) Reducing structural
      unemployment

(iii) Continual economic
      growth

A once-and-for-all increase in national income can be obtained by raising aggregate demand to remove a recessionary gap or by shifting the *LRAS* curve by cutting structural unemployment. Continued increases in national income are possible by shifting the *LRAS* curve through continued economic growth. In part (i), with the aggregate demand curve at AD_0, there is a recessionary gap of Y_1Y^*. An increase in aggregate demand from AD_0 to AD_1 takes equilibrium to E_1, achieving a once-and-for-all change in national income from Y_1 to Y^*.

In part (ii) potential output rises from Y_0^* to Y_1^* due to measures that reduce structural unemployment. The *LRAS* curve shifts from $LRAS_0$ to $LRAS_1$ because people who were formerly unemployed due to having the wrong skills or being in the wrong place are now available for employment.

In part (iii) increases in factor supplies and productivity lead to increases in potential income. This *continually* shifts the long-run aggregate supply curve outward. In successive periods it moves from $LRAS_0$ to $LRAS_3$, taking potential income from Y_0^* to Y_1^* to Y_2^* to Y_3^* *and so on, as long as growth continues*.

on the effect of investment expenditure on aggregate demand. Short-run national income theory concentrates on variations of actual national income around a given potential income. This short-term viewpoint is the focus of Figure 38-1(i).

In the long run, by adding to the nation's capital stock, investment raises potential income. This effect is shown by the continuing outward shift of the *LRAS* curve in Figure 38-1(iii).

The theory of economic growth is a long-run theory. It ignores short-run fluctuations of actual national income around potential income

and concentrates on the effects of investment in raising potential income.

The contrast between the short- and long-run aspects of investment is worth emphasizing. In the short run, any activity that puts income into people's hands will raise aggregate demand. Thus the short-run effect on national income is the same whether a firm invests in digging holes and refilling them or in building a new factory. The long-run growth of potential income, however, is affected only by the part of investment that adds to a nation's productive capacity, that is, by the factory but not by the refilled hole.

This point is important because some of what is classified as investment in the national income accounts is really consumption expenditure. Assume, for example, that a firm discards an adequate but dingy office building and "invests" in a lavish new head office building with superior facilities for its staff. This will count as investment in the national income data, and the expenditure will add to aggregate demand. In terms of growth, however, it is (at least in part) really disguised consumption for the firm's staff, not investment that will increase the productivity of its labor force.

Similar observations are true of public-sector expenditure. Any expenditure will add to aggregate demand and raise national income if there are unemployed resources. But only some expenditure adds to the growth of full-employment income. Indeed, public investment expenditure that shores up a declining industry in order to create employment may have an adverse effect on growth. Such expenditure may prevent the reallocation of resources in response to shifts both in the pattern of world demand and in the country's comparative advantage. Thus in the long run the country's capacity to produce commodities that are demanded on open markets may be diminished.

Short-Run and Long-Run Effects of Saving

The short-run effects of an increase in saving are to reduce aggregate demand. If, for example, households elect to save more, this means they spend less. The resulting downward shift in the consumption function lowers aggregate demand and thus lowers equilibrium national income.

In the longer term, however, higher savings are necessary for higher investment. Firms usually reinvest their own savings, while the savings of households pass to firms, either directly through the purchase of stocks and bonds or indirectly through financial intermediaries. If full employment is more or less maintained in the long run, the volume of investment will be strongly influenced by the volume of savings. The higher the savings, the higher the

investment—and the higher the investment, the greater the rate of growth due to the accumulation of more and better capital equipment.

In the long run there is no paradox of thrift; societies with high savings rates have high investment rates and, other things being equal, high growth rates.

The Cumulative Nature of Growth

Growth is a much more powerful method of raising living standards than removing either recessionary gaps or structural unemployment *because it can go on indefinitely.* For example, a growth rate of 2 percent per year may seem insignificant, but if it continues for a century, it will lead to a more than sevenfold increase in real national income!

The cumulative effect of small annual growth rates is large.

To appreciate the cumulative effect of what seems like very small differences in growth rates, examine Table 38-1. Notice that when one country grows faster than another, the gap in their respective standards widens progressively. If countries A and B start from the same level of income, and if country A grows at 3 percent per year while country B grows at 2 percent per year, A's income per capita will be twice B's in 72 years. You may not think it matters much whether the economy grows at 2 percent or 3 percent per year, but your children and grandchildren will! (A helpful approximation device is the "rule of 72." Divide 72 by the growth rate, and the result is approximately the number of years it will take for income to double.) [48]

To dramatize the powerful long-run effects of differences in growth rates, we included in early editions of this text a table showing students of the 1960s that if the then current growth trends continued, the United States would not long remain the world's richest nation, for Sweden, Canada, Japan, and others were growing at a much faster rate. Many readers of that era rejected the notion as a textbook gimmick; deep down they knew that the material

TABLE 38-1 The Cumulative Effect of Growth

| Year | Rate of growth per year | | | | |
	1%	2%	3%	5%	7%
0	100	100	100	100	100
10	111	122	135	165	201
30	135	182	246	448	817
50	165	272	448	1,218	3,312
70	201	406	817	3,312	13,429
100	272	739	2,009	14,841	109,660

Small differences in growth rates make enormous differences in levels of potential national income over a few decades. Assume that potential national income is 100 in year zero. At a rate of growth of 3 percent, it will be 135 in 10 years, 448 after 50 years, and over 2,000 in a century. Compound interest is a powerful force!

standard of living of the United States was and would remain the highest the world had ever known. Such a table is no longer even interesting, for by 1980 several industrial countries had indeed passed the United States in terms of per capita national income, and several more were within 10 percent of the U.S. level. Japan's experience is discussed in Box 38-1.

Growth, Efficiency, and Redistribution

Without any doubt, the most important single force leading to long-run increases in living standards is economic growth. To see this, let us compare the effects of growth with policies that increase economic efficiency or redistribute income. For the moment, we will consider a country with a constant population.

Making the economy more efficient can increase national income. But a once-and-for-all increase of between 5 and 10 percent would be an extremely optimistic estimate of what could be obtained by removing all economic inefficiencies.

Redistributing income can make lower-income people better off at the expense of higher-income people, but increasing the incomes of the bottom 20 percent of the people by, say, 10 percent above what they now are would be a very optimistic prediction

of what could be done with further redistribution policies. In any case, without growth the magnitude of the income gains that can be achieved for lower-income groups through redistribution is limited by the size of national income.

Economic growth, however, can go on raising national income for as long as growth continues, which can be for centuries. Even the modest rate of growth of 2 percent per year takes less than five years to make it possible to raise everyone's income by the 10 percent that was suggested as the maximum that could be achieved by policies that raise efficiency once and for all. It takes just over nine years for the 2 percent growth rate to raise the living standards of the poor (and everyone else) by 20 percent—which is a very high estimate of what might be obtained through redistribution policies. Furthermore, the gain continues beyond those time horizons as long as the growth persists. The 2 percent growth rate doubles average living standards about every 35 years, so average living standards will quadruple over one biblically allotted lifetime of three score years and ten.

The continued importance of efficiency and redistribution. When we say that over the long term by far the most potent force for raising living standards is economic growth rather than reducing inefficiencies or redistributing income, we are *not* asserting the unimportance of policies designed to increase economic efficiency or to redistribute income.

Consider efficiency first. If at any moment we could increase national income by removing certain inefficiencies, the gains would be valuable. After all, any increase in national income is welcome in a world where there is not enough to satisfy everyone's wants. Furthermore, inefficiencies may themselves serve to reduce the growth rate. For example, rent control, which we saw in Chapter 7 can be criticized for reducing the efficiency of the housing market, may also be criticized for reducing the geographic mobility of labor that is necessary for economic growth.

Now consider redistribution. It may be some consolation for the poor to know they are vastly better off, thanks to economic growth, than they

BOX 38-1

A Case Study of Rapid Growth: Japan, 1953–1973

The real national income of Japan was 5.4 times as large in 1973 as it was in 1953. Japan's economic growth rate was more than double the average rate in 10 North American and European countries and greatly exceeded the rate in any of them. What accounted for the extraordinarily rapid growth of Japan's economy?

To answer that question, two economists, Edward F. Denison and William K. Chung, analyzed and measured the sources of economic growth in Japan over two decades and compared the results with those for 10 Western countries. They also measured the difference between levels of output per worker in the United States and Japan in 1970 and identified its sources and magnitude. The results were published in 1976.*

They found that no single factor was responsible for Japan's high postwar growth rate. Rather, the Japanese economy benefited from several major sources of growth: an increase in quantity of labor, an increase in quantity of capital, improved technology in production, and economies of scale. Japan gained more in each of these respects than any of the 10 other countries studied. In addition, Japan had the greatest reallocation of labor from agriculture to industry of all the

countries studied except Italy. Since productivity is generally higher in industry than in agriculture, a shift of this kind raises average productivity and thereby contributes to growth even without an increase in output per person in either sector.

The overall growth record of Japan was high partly because of a low initial *level* of productivity. It is easier to improve from a low base than a high one. At the end of the period productivity was still more than 40 percent lower in Japan than in the United States, even after eliminating the effects of differences between the countries in working hours, in composition and allocation of the labor force, in amounts of capital and land, in size of markets, and in the cyclical positions of the two economies. There was thus an obvious potential for still further Japanese growth relative to the United States.

A question was, could Japan's growth rate be sustained? The authors stressed the probability of a decline in the growth rate as the various ways of securing fast growth by "catching up" are successively exhausted. Nevertheless, they considered a fairly high rate of long-term growth in Japan—between 5 and 8 percent per year—likely for the rest of this century. (This prediction proved accurate for the decade following the period covered by their study.) By the year 2000 Japan may well be enjoying the highest standard of living of any industrialized country in the world.

* Edward F. Denison and William K. Chung, *How Japan's Economy Grew So Fast: The Sources of Postwar Expansion* (Washington, D.C.: Brookings Institution, 1976).

---

would have been if they had lived 100 years ago. But this does not make it less upsetting if they cannot afford the basic medical treatment for themselves or schooling for their children that is available to higher-income citizens.

Interrelations among the policies.   One important implication of the foregoing discussion is that policies to reduce inefficiencies or redistribute income need to be examined carefully for any effects they may have on economic growth. Any policy that reduces the growth rate may be a bad bargain, even

if it increases the immediate efficiency of the economy or creates a more equitable distribution of income. Consider, for example, a hypothetical redistributive policy that raises the incomes of lower-income people by 5 percent but lowers the rate of economic growth from 2 to 1 percent. In 10 years, those who gained from the policy would be no better off than if they had not received the redistribution of income while the growth rate had remained at 2 percent (and, of course, everyone who did not gain from the redistribution would be worse off from the beginning). After 20 years' time, those who had gained from the redistribution would have 5 percent more of a national income that was 12 percent smaller than it would have been if the growth rate had remained at 2 percent.

Of course, not all redistribution policies have unfavorable effects on the growth rate. Some may have no effect, and others—by raising health and educational standards of ordinary workers—may raise the growth rate.

Theories of Economic Growth

In theoretical discussions of growth it is useful to have a measure of the ability of an economy to convert its resources into goods and services. One widely used measure is output per hour of labor, or *productivity*. Obviously, productivity depends not only on labor input but also on the amount and kind of machinery used, the raw materials available, and so on. The focus of this measure is explained by the special emphasis human beings place on labor.[1]

Economists today recognize that many different factors may contribute to or impede economic growth. Although our present knowledge of the relative importance of these factors is far from complete, modern economists look at the problems of growth more optimistically than did the classical economists of a century or more ago. Of particular importance is the nature and source of the investment opportunities that can lead to growth. The differences between the classical and contemporary points of view can best be understood by considering a revealing though extreme case.

Growth in a World with No Learning

Suppose that there is a known and fixed stock of projects that might be undertaken. Suppose also that nothing ever happens to increase either the supply of

such projects or knowledge about them. Whenever the moment is right, some of the investment opportunities are utilized, thereby increasing the stock of capital goods and depleting the reservoir of unutilized investment opportunities. Of course, the most productive opportunities will be used first.

Such a view of investment opportunities can be represented by a fixed marginal efficiency of capital (*MEC*) schedule of the kind presented in Chapter 18. Such a schedule is graphed in Figure 38-2. It relates the stock of capital to the productivity of an additional unit of capital. The productivity of a unit of capital is calculated by dividing the annual value of the additional output resulting from an extra unit of capital by the value of that unit of capital. Thus, for example, a marginal efficiency of capital of 0.2 means that $1 of new capital adds $0.20 per year to the stream of output.

The downward slope of the *MEC* schedule indicates that, with knowledge constant, increases in the stock of capital bring smaller and smaller increases in output per unit of capital. That is, the rate of return on successive units of capital declines. This shape is a consequence of the law of diminishing returns discussed on pages 194–195.

If, with land, labor, and knowledge constant, more and more capital is used, the net amount added by successive increments will diminish and may eventually reach zero. As capital is accumulated in a state of constant knowledge, the society will move down its *MEC* schedule.

In such a "nonlearning" world, where new investment opportunities do not appear, growth occurs only so long as there are unutilized opportunities to use capital effectively to increase output. Growth in a nonlearning world is a transitory phenomenon that occurs as long as the society has a backlog of unutilized investment opportunities.

So far we have discussed the *marginal* efficiency of capital. The *average* efficiency of capital refers to the average amount produced in the whole economy per unit of capital employed. It is common in discussions of the theory of growth to talk in terms of the *capital-output ratio,* which is the reciprocal of output per unit of capital. In a world without learning the capital-output ratio is increasing.

---

[1] The discussion of productivity on pages 208–210 of Chapter 11 is relevant here. It should be read now and treated as part of this chapter. (Indeed, the whole section on the very long run, pages 207–211, could be usefully read now.)

FIGURE 38-2   The Marginal Efficiency of Capital Schedule

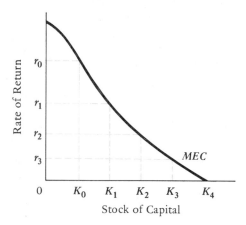

A declining *MEC* schedule shows that successive increases to the capital stock bring smaller and smaller increases in output and thus a declining rate of return. A fixed *MEC* schedule can represent the theory of growth in an economy with some unutilized investment opportunities but no learning. Increases in investment that increase the capital stock from K_0 to K_1 to . . . K_4 lower the rate of return from r_0 to r_1 to . . . zero. Because the productivity of successive units of capital decreases, the capital-output ratio rises.

In a world without learning the growth in the capital stock will have two important consequences:

1. Successive increases in capital accumulation will be less and less productive, and the capital-output ratio will be increasing.
2. The marginal efficiency of new capital will be decreasing and will eventually be pushed to zero as the backlog of investment opportunities is used up.

Consequences of Learning

The steady depletion of growth opportunities with constant knowledge results from the fact that new investment opportunities are never discovered or created. However, if investment opportunities are created as well as used up with the passage of time, the

MEC schedule will shift outward over time, and the effects of increasing the capital stock may be different. This is illustrated in Figure 38-3.

Such outward shifts can be regarded as the consequences of "learning" either about investment opportunities or about the techniques that create such opportunities. As shown in the figure, when learning occurs, what matters is how rapidly the *MEC* schedule shifts relative to the amount of capital investment being undertaken.

Gradual reduction in investment opportunities: The classical view.   If, as in Figure 38-3(i), investment opportunities are created, but at a slower rate than they are used up, there will be a tendency toward a falling rate of return and an increasing ratio of capital to output. The predictions in this case are the same as those given for the world without learning.

This figure illustrates the theory of growth held by most early economists. They saw the economic problem as one of fixed land, a rising population, and a gradual exhaustion of investment opportunities. These conditions, they believed, would ultimately force the economy into a static condition with no growth, high capital-output ratios, and the marginal return on additional units of capital forced down toward zero.

Constant or rising investment opportunities: The contemporary view.   The pessimism of the classical economists came from their failure to anticipate the possibility of really rapid innovation—of technological progress that could push investment opportunities outward as shown in parts (ii) and (iii) of Figure 38-3.

In a world with rapid innovation:

1. Successive increases in capital accumulation may prove highly productive, and the capital-output ratio may be constant or decreasing.
2. Despite large amounts of capital accumulation, the marginal efficiency of new capital may remain constant or even increase as new investment opportunities are created.

FIGURE 38-3   Shifting Investment Opportunities: Three Cases

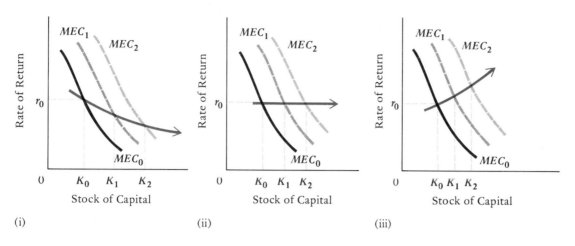

(i)   (ii)   (iii)

When both knowledge and the capital stock grow, the actual marginal efficiency of capital depends on their relative rates of growth. In each case the economy at period 0 has the MEC_0 curve, a capital stock of K_0, and a rate of return of r_0. In period 1 the curve shifts to MEC_1 and there is investment to increase the stock of capital to K_1. In period 2 the curve shifts to MEC_2 and there is new investment that increases the capital stock to K_2. It is the relative size of the shift of the MEC curve and the additions of the capital stock that are important.

In part (i) investment occurs more rapidly than increases in investment opportunities, and the rate of return falls along the black arrow. In part (ii) investment occurs at exactly the same rate as investment opportunities, and the rate of return is constant. In part (iii) investment occurs less rapidly than increases in investment opportunities, and the rate of return rises.

The historical record suggests that outward shifts in investment opportunities over time have led to the reality of sustained growth. Evidently modern economies have been successful in generating new investment opportunities at least as rapidly as old ones were used up. Modern economists devote more attention to understanding the *shifts* in the MEC schedule over time and less to its shape in a nonlearning situation.

Box 38-2 takes up some of the controversies surrounding government policies to promote learning and innovation.

A Contemporary View of Growth

The classical economists had a relatively simple theory of growth because they viewed a single mechanism—capital accumulation—as decisively impor-

tant. Contemporary theorists begin by recognizing a number of factors that influence growth, no one of which is necessarily dominant.

Quantity of Capital Per Worker

Human beings have always been tool users. It is still true that more and more tools tend to lead to more and more output. As long as a society has unexploited investment opportunities, productive capacity can be increased by increasing the stock of capital. The effect on output per worker of "mere" capital accumulation is so noticeable that it was once regarded as virtually the sole source of growth.

But if capital accumulation were the only source of growth, it would lead to movement down the MEC schedule and to a rising capital-output ratio and a falling rate of return on capital. The evidence

BOX 38-2

Should Canada Adopt Policies to Promote R&D Expenditure?

Various groups have regularly argued that Canada's expenditure on research and development is too low and that the government should adopt policies to promote R&D spending. However, many economists are skeptical.

First, they insist that the actual level of R&D spending is difficult to measure. Professor Kristian Palda of Queen's University argues that current estimates of Canadian R&D expenditure are in fact serious underestimates. He writes:

The leading edge of innovative industrial activity is widely found in small enterprises launched by engineers or scientists. . . . Their fairly high salaries are not carried on the R&D line of their corporate financial statements. In Canada, due to the heavy representation of the small-scale manufacturing firm, this undoubtedly leads to a substantial underestimate of industrial R&D effort and personnel.

In addition, "high technology" itself is difficult to define; it could mean "capital intensive," "value added per employee," or perhaps "skill level requirements per employee," depending on the circumstances. The blanket application of any one definition leads to ab-

surd results. Professor Palda notes that if, for example, high technology were defined as an industry where research expenditures make a large contribution to the productivity of that industry, then agriculture would be the most technology-intensive industry in North America. Yet most blanket statements about the state of R&D expenditure in Canada do not even consider agriculture.

There is the related question, given the presence of foreign-owned subsidiaries in the Canadian economy, of whether the percentage of R&D expenditure within Canada is a relevant measure of technical performance. One study conducted by the federal Ministry of State for Science and Technology estimated that in one year in the mid 1970s the cost of "invisible" R&D performed for Canadian subsidiaries by their parent firms was $688 million. Canada may or may not be backward in its research *performance,* but that it suffers in terms of *access* to R&D results seems implausible.

Nevertheless, some groups have lobbied actively for policies to encourage R&D expenditure in Canada. What strategies are involved?

---

does not support these predictions. The facts suggest that investment opportunities have expanded as rapidly as investments in capital goods, roughly along the pattern of Figure 38-3(ii). While capital accumulation has taken place and has accounted for much observed growth, it cannot have been the only source of growth.

Quality of Capital

New knowledge and inventions can contribute markedly to the growth of potential national income, even without capital accumulation. To see this, assume that the proportion of the society's resources devoted to the production of capital goods is just sufficient to replace capital as it wears out. Thus if

the old capital were merely replaced in the same form, the capital stock would be constant and there would be no increase in the capacity to produce. But if there is a growth of knowledge, so that as old equipment wears out it is replaced by different, more productive equipment, national income will be growing.

Increases in productive capacity that are intrinsic to the form of capital goods in use are called **embodied technical change.** The historical importance of embodied technical change is clear: The assembly line and automation transformed much of manufacturing, the airplane revolutionized transportation, and electronic devices now dominate the information technology industries. These innovations plus less well known but no less profound ones—for

One often quoted strategy is to "pick winners" and subsidize them. This approach raises two questions: Is the political will strong enough to let the losers sink, and is the political intellect bright enough to identify the potential winners? The evidence is that the answer to the first is often negative, and the answer to the second is that private investors making decisions about where to invest their own funds usually make better decisions.

Another proposal is to subsidize R&D directly. But it is possible that if governments actively promoted R&D, the private sector would reduce its R&D expenditure correspondingly. And giving R&D subsidies to firms that do not have a sufficient market may well be a waste of money: Technological improvements are of no advantage when they do not contribute to a marketable product; hence access to a large market is necessary.

A related proposal is to screen the import of foreign technology. Presumably this would stimulate R&D expenditure by keeping foreign technology out. Some would prefer to try to direct the import of technology into Canadian firms rather than to foreign subsidiaries. This would tend to reduce the role of foreign ownership in the Canadian economy, but it would result in a slower transmission of new technology and a higher price for what is transmitted.

Common to all these proposals is the advocacy of increased government involvement to promote "high technology" industries. But what are the costs of such intervention? Foreign experience tells us that the costs could be enormous. In examining the French experience with nuclear energy, aerospace computers, and electronics, Professor Palda shows that technology was ultimately imported from abroad only after expensive domestic programs had failed to be technically or economically successful.

Most economists remain rather skeptical about the need and the effectiveness of R&D policies. Professor Donald McFetteridge of Carleton University has argued that researchers have yet to produce any statistical evidence that the rate of return to industrial and R&D development in Canada is positive—let alone so high that it should be favored over alternative uses of scarce investment money.

example, improvements in the strength of metals, the productivity of seeds, and the techniques for recovering basic raw materials from the ground—create new investment opportunities.

Less obvious but nonetheless important changes occur through **disembodied technical change,** that is, changes in the organization of production that are not embodied in the form of the capital goods or raw materials used. One example is improved techniques of managerial control.

Most innovations involve both embodied and disembodied changes. But whatever the form of innovation, the nature of the goods and services consumed and the way they are made change continually as innovations occur. Major innovations of the past century have resulted from the development of the telephone, the linotype, the automobile, the airplane, plastics, the assembly line, coaxial cable, xerography, computers, transistors, and silicon chips. It would be hard for us to imagine life without them.

Quality of Labor

The "quality" of labor—or what is often called *human capital*—has several aspects. One involves improvements in the health and longevity of the population. Of course, these are desired as ends in themselves, yet they have consequences for both the size of the labor force and its productivity. There is no doubt that they have increased productivity per worker-hour by cutting down on illness, accidents, and absenteeism. At the same time the extension of the normal life span with no comparable increase in the working life span has created a larger group of nonworking aged that exercises a claim on total output. Whether health improvements alone have increased output per capita in the United States is not clear.

A second aspect of the quality of human capital concerns technical training, from learning to operate a machine to learning how to be a scientist. Training is clearly required to invent, operate, manage, and repair complex machines. More subtly, there are often believed to be general social advantages to an educated population. It has been shown that productivity improves with literacy and that, in general, the longer a person has been educated, the more adaptable he or she is to new and changing challenges and thus, in the long run, the more productive. But education may also increase feelings of alienation in a society that is thought to be arbitrary or unjust.

Quantity of Labor

The size of a country's population and the extent of its participation in the labor force are important in and of themselves, not merely because they affect the quantity of a factor of production. For this reason it is less common to speak of the quantity of people available for work as a source of or detriment to growth than it is to speak of the quantity of capital or iron ore in the same way. But clearly, for any given state of knowledge and supplies of other factors of production, the size of the population can affect the level of output per capita. Every child born has both a mouth and a pair of hands; over a lifetime each person will be both a consumer and a producer. Thus, on average, it is meaningful to speak of overpopulated or underpopulated economies, depending on whether the contribution to production of additional people would raise or lower the level of per capita income.

Because population size is related to income per capita, we can define a theoretical concept, *optimal population,* that maximizes income per capita.

Many countries have or have had conscious population policies. America in the nineteenth century sought immigrants, as did Australia until recently. Greece in the 1950s and 1960s tried to stem emigra-

tion to Western Europe. All are examples of countries that believed they had insufficient population, though the motives were not in every case purely economic. In contrast, many underdeveloped countries of South America, Africa, and Asia desire to limit population growth.

Structural Change

Changes in the economy's structure can cause large fluctuations in its growth rate. For example, an expansion in such low-productivity sectors as agriculture and a decline in such high-productivity sectors as manufacturing will temporarily lower the measured aggregate growth rate.

When one type of energy (say, solar) supplants another type (say, oil), much existing capital stock specifically geared to the original energy source may become too costly to operate and will be scrapped. New capital geared to the new energy source will be built. During the transition, investment expenditure is high, thus stimulating aggregate demand. But there is little if any expansion in the economy's output capacity because the old capital goods have been scrapped. Gross investment is high, but net investment is low since the capital expenditure *transforms* the capital stock, but does not *increase* it. Similarly, new pollution control laws will affect investment expenditure but will not lead to growth in capacity. (The reduction in pollution may nonetheless be socially desirable.)

A rise in the international price of *imported* energy will also lower productivity. Although the same volume of goods can be produced with a given input of labor, a smaller portion of the output's value now accrues as income to domestic workers and firms because more must be used to pay for the energy imports. The higher-priced imported energy input means that domestic *value added* falls, and with it GDP per worker. This shows up in the statistics as a decline in productivity and a temporary fall in growth rates.

These are some of the many factors that were operative in the 1970s and early 1980s. They worked to depress growth rates for some considerable period of time. But they are not permanent factors. When the structural adjustments are complete, their depressing effects will pass. Further, many of the effects were reversed when oil prices fell in early 1986, giving a boost to the productivity of many domestic factors of production.

Institutional Considerations

Almost all aspects of a country's institutions can foster or deter the efficient use of a society's natural and human resources. Social and religious habits, legal institutions, and traditional patterns of national and international trade are all important. So, too, is the political climate. In Chapter 22 many of these institutions were discussed as potential influences on development.

Is There a Most Important Source of Growth?

The modern theory of growth tends to reject a dominant source of growth and to recognize that several influences singly and in interaction affect the growth rate.

Among the major contributors to rapid economic growth are a capital stock that is steadily growing and improving in quality, a healthy and well-educated labor force, and a rate of population growth that is small enough to permit per capita growth in capital.

These factors are more likely to be used effectively in some institutional settings than in others.

A complete theory of growth would do more than list a series of influences that affect the growth rate. It would include assessments of their relative importance, the trade-offs involved in having more of one beneficial influence and less of another, and the interactions among the various influences. This poses a formidable program for further empirical research.

While much remains to be learned, an important tentative conclusion of initial research on growth is that improvements in *quality* of capital, human as well as physical, have played a larger role than increases in the *quantity* of capital in the economic growth of Canada since 1900. (This conclusion was first reached by Professor Robert Solow of MIT, who received the 1987 Nobel Prize in Economics.) Whether quality rather than quantity of capital is also the more important source of growth for countries with different cultural patterns, more acute population problems, or more limited natural resources is a matter of continuing research.

Benefits and Costs of Growth

In the remainder of this chapter, we shall outline some more general considerations concerning economic growth. We start by looking at the benefits and then the costs of growth. Boxes 38-3 and 38-4 outline the popular arguments on both sides of the growth debate.

Benefits of Growth

Growth in Living Standards

A country whose per capita output grows at 3 percent per year doubles its living standards about every 24 years.

A primary reason for desiring growth is to raise general living standards.

The extreme importance of economic growth in raising income can be illustrated by comparing the real income of a father with the real income of the son who follows in his father's footsteps. If the son neither rises nor falls in the relative income scale compared with his father, his share of the country's national income will be the same as his father's. If the son is 30 years younger than his father, he can expect to have a real income nearly twice as large as the one his father enjoyed when his father was the same age. These figures assume that the father and son live in a country such as Canada where the growth rate has been 2 or 3 percent per year. If they live in Japan, where growth has been going on at a rate of about 8 percent per year, the son's income will be about 10 times as large as his father's.

For those who share in it, growth is a powerful

BOX 38-3

An Open Letter to the Ordinary Citizen from a Supporter of the Growth-Is-Bad School

Dear Ordinary Citizen:

You live in a world that is being despoiled by a mindless search for ever higher levels of material consumption at the cost of all other values. Once upon a time, men and women knew how to enjoy creative work and to derive satisfaction from simple activities undertaken in scarce, and hence highly valued, leisure time. Today the ordinary worker is a mindless cog in an assembly line that turns out ever more goods that the advertisers must work overtime to persuade the worker to consume.

Statisticians and politicians count the increasing flow of material output as a triumph of modern civilization. Consider not the flow of output in general but the individual products that it contains. You arise from your electric-blanketed bed, clean your teeth with an electric toothbrush, open with an electric can opener a can of the sad remnants of a once-proud orange, and eat your bread baked from super-refined and chemically refortified flour; you climb into your car to sit in vast traffic jams on exhaust-polluted highways. And so it goes, with endless consumption of high-technology products that give you no more real satisfaction than the simple, cheaply produced equivalent products used by your great-grandfathers: soft woolly blankets, natural-bristle toothbrushes, real oranges, coarse but healthful bread, and public transport that moved on uncongested roads and gave its passengers time to chat with their neighbors, to read, or just to daydream.

Television commercials tell you that by consuming more you are happier. But happiness lies not in increasing consumption but in increasing the ratio of *satisfaction of wants* to *total wants*. Since the more you consume, the more the advertisers persuade you that you want to consume, you are almost certainly less happy than the average citizen in a small town in 1900 whom we can visualize sitting on the family porch, sipping a cool beer or a lemonade, and enjoying the antics of the children as they play with scooters made out of old crates and jump rope with pieces of old clothesline.

Today the landscape is dotted with endless factories producing the plastic trivia of the modern industrial society. They drown you in a cloud of noise, air, and water pollution. The countryside is despoiled by strip mines, petroleum refineries, acid rain, and dangerous nuclear power stations producing energy that is devoured insatiably by modern factories and motor vehicles.

Worse, our precious heritage of natural resources is being fast used up. Spaceship earth flies, captainless, in its senseless orgy of self-consuming consumption.

Now is the time to stop this madness. We must stabilize production, reduce pollution, conserve our natural resources, and seek justice through a more equitable distribution of existing total income.

A long time ago Malthus taught us that if we do not limit population voluntarily, nature will do it for us in a cruel and savage manner. Today the same is true of output: If we do not halt its growth voluntarily, the halt will be imposed on us by a disastrous increase in pollution and a rapid exhaustion of natural resources.

Citizens, awake! Shake off the worship of growth, learn to enjoy the bounty that is yours already, and reject the endless, self-defeating search for increased happiness through ever-increasing consumption.

Upward!

A. Nongrowthman

---

weapon against poverty. A family earning $9,500 today can expect an income of $14,000 within 10 years (in constant dollars) if it just shares in a 4 percent growth rate. The transformation of the lifestyle of blue-collar workers in North America (as well as in Europe and Japan) in a generation provides a notable example of the escape from poverty that growth makes possible.

BOX 38-4

An Open Letter to the Ordinary Citizen from a Supporter of the Growth-Is-Good School

Dear Ordinary Citizen:

You live in the world's first civilization that is devoted principally to satisfying *your* needs rather than those of a privileged minority. Past civilizations have always been based on leisure and high consumption for a tiny upper class, a reasonable living standard for a small middle class, and hard work with little more than subsistence consumption for the great mass of people. In the past the average person saw little of the civilized and civilizing products of the economy, except when toiling to produce them.

The continuing Industrial Revolution is based on mass-produced goods for you, the ordinary citizen. It ushered in a period of sustained economic growth that has raised consumption standards of ordinary citizens to levels previously reserved throughout history for a tiny privileged minority. Reflect on a few examples: travel, live and recorded music, art, good food, inexpensive books, universal literacy, and a genuine chance to be educated. Most important, there is leisure to provide time and energy to enjoy these and thousands of other products of the modern industrial economy.

Would any ordinary family seriously doubt the benefits of growth and prefer to go back to the world of 150 or 500 years ago in its same relative social and economic position? Surely, the answer is no. But we cannot say the same for those with incomes in the top 1 or 2 percent of the income distribution. Economic growth has destroyed much of their privileged consumption position. They must now vie with the masses when visiting the world's beauty spots and be annoyed, while lounging on the terrace of a palatial mansion, by the sound of charter flights carrying or-

dinary people to inexpensive holidays. Many of the rich resent the loss of exclusive rights to luxury consumption. Some complain bitterly, and it is not surprising that they find their intellectual apologists.

Whether they know it or not, the anti-growth economists are not the social revolutionaries they think they are. They are counterrevolutionaries who would set back the clock of material progress for the ordinary person. They say that growth has produced pollution and wasteful consumption of all kinds of frivolous products that add nothing to human happiness. But the democratic solution to pollution is not to go back to where so few people consume luxuries that pollution is trivial; it is to accept pollution as part of a transitional phase connected with the ushering in of mass consumption, and to learn to control the pollution it tends to create.

It is only through further growth that the average citizen can enjoy consumption standards (of travel, culture, medical and health care, etc.) now available to people in the top 25 percent of the income distribution—which includes the intellectuals who earn large royalties from the books they write denouncing growth. If you think that extra income confers little real benefit, just ask those in that top 25 percent to trade incomes with the average citizen. Or see how hard *they* struggle to reduce their income taxes.

Ordinary citizens, do not be deceived by disguised elitist doctrines. Remember that the very rich and the elite have much to gain by stopping growth and even more by rolling it back, but you have everything to gain by letting it go forward.

Onward!

A. Growthman

Growth and Income Redistribution

Not everyone benefits equally from growth. Many of the poorest are not even in the labor force and thus are least likely to share in the higher wages that, along with profits, are the primary means by which the gains from growth are distributed. For this reason, even in a growing economy redistribution policies will be needed if poverty is to be averted.

Economic growth makes many kinds of redistributions easier to achieve. For example, a rapid growth rate makes it more feasible politically to alleviate poverty. If existing income is to be redistributed, someone's standard of living will actually have to be lowered. However, when there is economic growth, and when the increment in income is redistributed (through government intervention), it is possible to reduce income inequalities without actually having to lower anyone's income. It is much easier for a rapidly growing economy to be generous toward its less fortunate citizens—or neighbors—than it is for a static economy.

Growth and Life-style

A family often finds that a big increase in its income can lead to a major change in the pattern of its consumption—that extra money buys important amenities of life. In the same way the members of society as a whole may change their consumption patterns as their average income rises. Not only do markets in a country that is growing rapidly make it profitable to produce more cars, but the government is led also to produce more highways and to provide more recreational areas for its newly affluent (and mobile) citizens. At yet a later stage, a concern about litter, pollution, and ugliness may become important, and their correction may then begin to account for a significant fraction of GDP. Such "amenities" usually become matters of social concern only when growth has assured the provision of the basic requirements for food, clothing, and housing of a substantial majority of the population.

National Defense and Prestige

When one country is competing with another for power or prestige, rates of growth are important. If our national income is growing at 2 percent, while another country's is growing at 5 percent, the other country will only have to wait for our relative strength to dwindle. Moreover, the faster its productivity is growing, the easier a country will find it to bear the expenses of an arms race or a program of foreign aid.

More subtly, growth has become part of the currency of international prestige. Countries that are engaged in persuading other countries of the might or right of their economic and political systems point to their rapid rates of growth as evidence of their achievements.

Costs of Growth

The benefits of growth suggest that it is a great blessing. It is surely true that, other things being equal, most people would regard a fast rate of growth as preferable to a slow one, but other things are seldom equal.

Social and Personal Costs of Growth

Industrialization can cause deterioration of the environment. Unspoiled landscapes give way to highways, factories, and billboards; air and water become polluted; and unique and priceless relics of earlier ages—from flora and fauna to ancient art and ruins—often disappear. Urbanization tends to move people away from the simpler life of farms and small towns and into the crowded, slum-ridden, and often darkly evil life of the urban ghetto. Those remaining behind in the rural areas find that rural life, too, has changed. Larger-scale farming, the decline of population, and the migration of children from the farm to the city all have their costs. The stepped-up tempo of life brings joys to some but tragedy to others. Accidents, ulcers, crime rates, suicides, divorces, and murders all tend to be higher in periods of rapid change and in more developed societies.

When an economy is growing, it is also changing. Innovation renders some machines obsolete and also leaves some people partially obsolete. No matter how well trained workers are at age 25, in another 25 years most will find that their skills are at least partially obsolete. A rapid growth rate requires rapid adjustments, which can cause much upset and misery to the individuals affected.

It is often argued that costs of this kind are a small price to pay for the great benefits that growth can bring. Even if that is true in the aggregate (which is a matter of debate), these personal costs are very unevenly borne. Indeed, many of those for whom growth is most costly (in terms of jobs) share least in the fruits of growth. Yet it is also a mistake to see only the costs—to yearn for the good old days while enjoying higher living standards that growth alone has made possible.

The Opportunity Cost of Growth

In a world of scarcity almost nothing is free. Growth requires heavy investments of resources in capital goods as well as in activities such as education. Often these investments yield no immediate return in terms of goods and services for consumption; thus they imply sacrifices by the current generation of consumers.

Growth, which promises more goods tomorrow, is achieved by consuming fewer goods today. For the economy as a whole this is the primary cost of growth.

An example will suggest the magnitude of this cost. Suppose the fictitious economy of USSA has full employment and is experiencing growth at the rate of 2 percent per year. Its citizens consume 85 percent of the GDP and invest 15 percent. The people of USSA know that if they are willing to decrease immediately their consumption to 77 percent, they will produce more capital and thus shift at once to a 3 percent growth rate. The new rate can be maintained as long as they keep saving and investing 23 percent of the national income. Should they do it?

Table 38-2 illustrates the choice in terms of time paths of consumption. How expensive is the "invest now, consume later" strategy? On the assumed figures, it take 10 years for the actual amount of consumption to catch up to what it would have been had no reallocation been made. In the intervening 10 years a good deal of consumption is lost, and the cumulative losses in consumption must be made up before society can really be said to have broken even. It takes an additional nine years before total consumption over the whole period is as large as it would have been if the economy had remained on the 2 percent path. **[49]**

A policy of sacrificing present living standards for a gain that does not begin to be reaped for a generation is hardly likely to appeal to any but the altruistic or the very young. The question of how much of its living standards one generation is prepared to sacrifice for its heirs (who are in any case likely to be richer) is troublesome. As one critic put it: Why should we sacrifice for them? What have they ever done for us?

TABLE 38–2   The Opportunity Cost of Growth

Year	(1) Level of consumption at 2% growth rate	(2) Level of consumption at 3% growth rate	(3) Cumulative gain (loss) in consumption
0	85.0	77.0	(8.0)
1	86.7	79.3	(15.4)
2	88.5	81.8	(22.1)
3	90.3	84.2	(28.2)
4	92.1	86.8	(33.5)
5	93.9	89.5	(37.9)
6	95.8	92.9	(40.8)
7	97.8	95.0	(43.6)
8	99.7	97.9	(45.4)
9	101.8	100.9	(46.3)
10	103.8	103.9	(46.2)
15	114.7	120.8	(28.6)
20	126.8	140.3	19.6
30	154.9	189.4	251.0
40	189.2	255.6	745.9

Transferring resources from consumption to investment goods lowers current income but raises future income. The example assumes that income in year zero is 100 and that consumption of 85 percent of national income is possible with a 2 percent growth rate. It is further assumed that to achieve a 3 percent growth rate, consumption must fall to 77 percent of income. A shift from (1) to (2) decreases consumption for 10 years but increases it thereafter. The cumulative effect on consumption is shown in (3); the gains eventually become large.

Many governments, particularly those seeking a larger role in world affairs, have chosen to force the diversion of resources from consumption to investment. The Germans under Hitler, the Russians under Stalin, and the Chinese under Mao Tse-tung adopted four-year and five-year plans that did just this. Many less-developed countries are using such plans today. Such resource shifts are particularly important when actual growth rates are small (say, less than 1 percent), for without some current sacrifice there is little or no prospect of real growth in the lifetimes of today's citizens. The very lowest growth rates are frequently encountered in the very poorest countries. This creates a cruel dilemma, often called the vicious circle of poverty.

Are There Limits to Growth?

Opponents of growth argue that sustained growth is undesirable; some even argue that it is impossible. Of course, all terrestrial things have an ultimate limit. Astronomers predict that the solar system itself will die as the sun burns out in another 6 billion or so years. To be of practical concern, a limit must be within some reasonable planning horizon. Best-selling books of the 1970s by Jay Forrester (*World Dynamics,* 1973) and D. H. Meadows et al. (*The Limits to Growth,* 1974) predicted an imminent growth-induced doomsday. Living standards were predicted to reach a peak about the year 2000 and then, in the words of Yale Professor William Nordhaus, a leading critic of these models, to "descend inexorably to the level of Neanderthal man." What lessons are there to be learned from this debate?

The Uncontroversial Fact of Increasing Pressure on Natural Resources

The years since World War II have seen a rapid acceleration in the consumption of the world's resources, particularly fossil fuels and basic minerals. World population has increased from under 2.5 billion to over 4 billion in that period, and this alone has increased the demand for all the world's resources. But the single fact of population growth greatly understates the pressure on resources.

Calculations by Professor Nathan Keyfitz of Harvard and others focus on the resources used by those who can claim a life-style of the level enjoyed by 90 percent of American families. This so-called middle class, which today includes about one-sixth of the world's population, consumes 15 to 30 times as much oil per capita and, overall, at least 5 times as much of the earth's scarce resources per capita as do the other "poor" five-sixths of the population.

The world's poor are not, however, content to remain forever poor. Whether they live in the USSR, Argentina, Korea, or Kenya, they have let their governments understand that they expect policies that generate enough growth to give *them* the higher consumption levels that all of *us* take for granted. This upward aspiration is being fulfilled to some degree in many countries. The growth of the middle class has been nearly 4 percent per year—twice the rate of population growth—over the postwar period. The number of persons realizing middle-class living standards is estimated to have increased from 200 million to 700 million between 1950 and 1980 and is predicted almost to double again by the turn of the century.

Growth is a major factor in the recently recognized or projected shortages of natural resources. Yet the 4 percent growth rate of the middle class, which is too fast for present resources, is too slow for the aspirations of the billions who live in underdeveloped countries and see the fruits of development all around them. Thus the pressure on world resources of energy, minerals, and food is likely to accelerate, even if population growth is reduced.

A Tentative Verdict

Most economists agree that conjuring up absolute limits to growth based on the assumptions of constant technology and fixed resources is not warranted. Most agree that any barrier can be overcome by technological advances—but not in an instant, and not automatically. Clearly there is a problem of timing: How soon can we discover and put into practice the knowledge required to solve the problems that are made ever more imminent by growth in the population, the affluence, and the aspirations of the billions who now live in poverty? There is no guarantee that a whole generation may not be caught in transition, with social and political consequences that promise to be enormous even if they are not cataclysmic. The nightmare conjured up by the doomsday models served its purpose by helping focus our attention on these problems.

Summary

1. National income can increase as a result of reduction in the recessionary gap, reduction in structural unemployment, or growth in the level of potential national income.

2. Investment has short-term effects on national income through aggregate demand and long-term effects through growth in potential national income. Such growth is frequently measured using rates of change of potential real national income per person or per hour of labor employed.

3. Savings reduce aggregate demand and therefore reduce national income in the short run, but in the long run savings finance the investment that leads to growth in potential income.

4. The cumulative effects of even small differences in growth rates become large over periods of a decade or more.

5. Understanding growth involves understanding both the utilization of existing investment opportunities and the process of creating new investment opportunities. The source of economic growth was once thought to be almost entirely capital accumulation and the utilization of a backlog of unexploited investment opportunities. Today most economists recognize that many investment opportunities can be created, and much attention is given to the sources of outward shifts in the *MEC* schedule through both embodied and disembodied technical change.

6. The most important benefit of growth lies in its contribution to the long-run struggle to raise living standards and escape poverty. It also makes more manageable the policies that would redistribute income among people. Growth also plays an important role in a country's national defense and its struggle for international prestige.

7. Growth, while often beneficial, is never costless. The opportunity cost of growth is the diversion of resources from current consumption to capital formation. For individuals who are left behind in a rapidly changing world the costs are higher and more personal. The optimal rate of growth involves balancing benefits and costs. Most people do not wish to forgo the benefits growth can bring, but neither do they wish to maximize growth at any cost.

8. In addition to mere increases in quantity of capital per person, any list of factors affecting growth includes the extent of innovation, the quality of human capital, the size of the working population, and the whole institutional setting.

9. The critical importance of increasing knowledge and new technology in sustaining growth is highlighted by the great drain on existing natural resources resulting from the explosive growth of the past two or three decades. Without continuing new knowledge, the present needs and aspirations of the world's population cannot come anywhere close to being met.

Topics for Review

Short-run and long-run effects of investment and saving
Cumulative nature of growth
Factors affecting growth
Effects of capital accumulation with and without new knowledge
Embodied and disembodied technical change
Benefits and costs of growth

Discussion Questions

1. We usually study and measure economic growth in macroeconomic terms. But in a market economy, who makes the decisions that lead to growth? What kind of decisions and what kind of actions cause growth to occur? How might a detailed study of individual markets be relevant to understanding economic growth?

2. Dr. David Suzuki has recently argued that despite the fact that "in the 20th century the list of scientific and technological achievements has been absolutely dazzling, the costs of such progress are so large that negative economic growth may be right for the future." Policies to achieve this include "rigorous reduction of waste, a questioning and distrustful attitude towards technological progress, and braking demands on the globe's resources." Identify some of the benefits and costs of economic growth, and evaluate Dr. Suzuki's position.

3. Why is rising productivity a more significant contributing factor for economic growth than simply increasing the quantity of productive resources? Define *productivity*. List all the factors that increase the productivity of labor and the productivity of capital. Comment on the differences and similarities of the two lists.

4. *Family Weekly* recently listed among "inventions that have changed our lives" microwave ovens, digital clocks, bank credit cards, freeze-dried coffee, tape cassettes, climate-controlled shopping malls, automatic toll collectors, soft contact lenses, tubeless tires, and electronic word processors.

   Which of them would you hate to do without? Which, if any, will have a major impact on life in the twenty-first century? If there are any that you believe will not, does that mean they are frivolous and unimportant?

5. The Overseas Development Council recently introduced "a new measure of economic development based on the physical quality of life." Its index, called PQLI, gives one-third weight to each of the following indicators: literacy, life expectancy, and infant mortality. While countries such as the United States and Canada rank high on either the PQLI or on an index of per capita real national income, some relatively poor countries, such as Sri Lanka, rank much higher on the PQLI index than much richer countries such as Algeria and Kuwait. Discuss the merits or deficiencies of this measure.

6. "The case for economic growth is that it gives man greater control over his environment, and consequently increases his freedom." Explain why you agree or disagree with this statement by Nobel Laureate W. Arthur Lewis.

7. Consider a developed economy that decides to achieve a zero rate

of growth for the future. What implications would such a "stationary state" have for the processes of production and consumption?

8. Suppose solar energy becomes the dominant form of energy in the twenty-first century. What changes will this make in the growth rates of Africa and Northern Europe?

9. Discuss the following newspaper headlines in terms of the sources, costs, and benefits of growth.

   a. "Stress addiction: 'Life in the fast lanes' may have its benefits"
   b. "Education: An expert urges multiple reforms"
   c. "Industrial radiation risk higher than thought"
   d. "Developments in the field of management design are looking ahead"
   e. "Ford urged by federal safety officials to recall several hundred thousand of its 1981–1982 front-drive vehicles because of alleged fire hazards"

10. In the late 1970s and early 1980s productivity growth was historically low, but it rebounded after 1983. How might you explain this?

39

Macroeconomic Controversies

How well do markets work? Can government improve market performance? In various guises these two questions are the basis of most disagreements over economic policy. We shall see that different answers to these questions imply big differences in macroeconomic policy prescriptions.

Alternative Views: Conservative and Interventionist

Macroeconomics is mainly concerned with the behavior of three important variables: employment (and unemployment), the price level, and the rate of economic growth. Macroeconomic policy suggests goals for each: full employment, stable prices, and a satisfactory growth rate. The advantages of full employment and a positive growth rate are obvious and not subject to serious dispute. Although most people agree that inflation is harmful, there is much debate about what can really be blamed on it.

Broadly speaking, we can identify a non-interventionist and an interventionist view with respect to each of the policy goals just specified. The non-interventionist view says that the unaided market economy can best achieve the goal. The interventionist view says that government policy can improve the economy's performance in terms of that goal. Since one can take a non-interventionist or an interventionist position with respect to each of these three goals, there are eight different possible policy combinations.[1]

Consider two extreme policy stances: *conservatives* are non-interventionist on all issues, while *interventionists* support government intervention at all times. A few people may actually be conservative or interventionist in this sense. Most, however, would favor intervention on some issues and oppose it on others. They might still identify themselves as conservative or interventionist because they were more often on one side than the other.

It is popular to equate monetarist with conservative and Keynesian with interventionist. It is true that many monetarists are on the conservative side and many Keynesians on the interventionist side. But it is not always so. For example, it is quite possible to be Keynesian in accepting the Keynesian macro model as a reasonable description of the economy's macroeconomic behavior but conservative in believing that the unaided market usually does the best job of allocating resources.

---

[1] Since each of the three issues breaks up into hundreds of different subissues, thousands of different policy stances are available on one side or the other of each issue.

The Conservative View

Conservatives believe that the free-market economy performs quite well on balance. Although shocks do hit the system, they lead rather quickly, and often painlessly, to the adjustments dictated by the market system. For example, relative prices in booming sectors rise, drawing in resources from declining sectors or regions. As a result, resources (and particularly labor) usually remain fully employed, so there is no need for full-employment policies.

Conservatives hold that macroeconomic performance will be most satisfactory if determined solely by the workings of the free market.

Of course, few believe that the market system functions perfectly, thereby ensuring *continuous* full employment. But the view is that the market system works well enough to preclude any constructive role for policy.

In addition, many conservatives believe that policy instruments are so crude that their use is often counterproductive. A policy's effects may be so uncertain, with regard to both strength and timing, that it may often impair rather than improve the economy's performance.

In a modern economy some government presence is inevitable. Thus a stance of no intervention is impossible; rather, what is advocated by conservatives is minimal direct intervention in the market system. This involves the government's bearing responsibility for providing a *stable environment* in which the private sector can function.

The Interventionist View

Interventionists believe that the functioning of the free-market economy is often far from satisfactory. Sometimes markets show weak self-regulatory forces, and the economy settles into prolonged periods of heavy unemployment. At other times markets tend to "overcorrect," causing the economy to lurch between the extremes of large recessionary and inflationary gaps.

This behavior can be improved, argue the interventionists. Even though interventionist policies

may be imperfect, they may be good enough to improve the functioning of the economy with respect to all three main goals of macro policy.

Macroeconomic Issues

Everyone agrees that the economy's performance is often less than perfectly satisfactory. Serious unemployment has been a recurring problem. Inflation was a serious problem throughout the 1970s and early 1980s. For most of that period growth rates were unsatisfactorily low. Conservatives and interventionists differ in diagnosing the causes of these economic ills.

The Business Cycle

We saw in Chapter 26 that cyclical ups and downs can be observed for as far back as records exist. Monetarists and Keynesians have long argued about the causes. As was noted in Chapter 34, monetarists often are identified with conservative views, and Keynesians with intervention.[2]

Monetarist views. Monetarists believe that the economy is inherently stable because private-sector expenditure functions are relatively stable. In addition, they believe that shifts in the aggregate demand curve are mainly due to policy-induced changes in the money supply.[3]

The view that business cycles have mainly monetary causes relies heavily on the evidence advanced by Milton Friedman and Anna Schwartz in their monumental study *A Monetary History of the United States, 1867–1960.* They establish a strong correlation between changes in the money supply and changes

---

[2] Appendix A to this chapter presents the widely used *IS/LM* model of the influence of monetary and fiscal policy. The *IS/LM* model expands on the theory developed in Chapter 34.

[3] The view that fluctuations often have monetary causes is not new. The English economist R. G. Hawtrey, the Austrian Nobel Laureate F. A. von Hayek, and the Swedish economist Knut Wicksell are prominent among those who have given monetary factors an important role in explaining the turning points in cycles and/or the tendency for expansions and contractions, once begun, to become cumulative and self-reinforcing. Modern monetarists carry on this tradition.

in the level of business activity. Major recessions have been associated with absolute declines in the money supply and minor recessions with the slowing of the rate of increase in the money supply below its long-term trend.

The correlation between changes in the money supply and changes in the level of business activity is now accepted by almost all economists. But there is controversy over how this correlation is to be interpreted. Do changes in money supply cause changes in the level of aggregate demand and hence of business activity, or vice versa?

Friedman and Schwartz maintain that changes in the money supply cause changes in business activity. They argue, for example, that the severity of the Great Depression was due to a major contraction in the money supply that shifted the aggregate demand curve far to the left. The Great Depression is discussed in Box 39-1.

According to monetarists, fluctuations in the money supply cause fluctuations in national income.

This leads the monetarists to advocate a policy of stabilizing the growth of the money supply. In their view this would avoid policy-induced instability of the aggregate demand curve.

Keynesian views.   The Keynesian view on cyclical fluctuations in the economy has two parts. First, it emphasizes variations in investment as a cause of business cycles and stresses the nonmonetary causes of such variations.[4]

Keynesians reject what they regard as the extreme monetarist view that only money matters in explaining cyclical fluctuations. Many Keynesians believe that both monetary and nonmonetary forces are im-

[4] Like the monetarists, the Keynesians are modern advocates of views that have a long history. The great Austrian (and later American) economist Joseph Schumpeter stressed such explanations early in the present century. The Swedish economist Wicksell and the German Speithoff both stressed this aspect of economic fluctuations before the emergence of the Keynesian school of thought.

portant in explaining the cyclical behavior of the economy. Although they accept serious monetary mismanagement as one potential source of economic fluctuations, they do not believe that it is the only or even the major source of such fluctuations. Thus they deny the monetary interpretation of business cycle history given by Friedman and Schwartz. They believe that most fluctuations in the aggregate demand curve are due to variations in the desire to spend on the part of the private sector and are not induced by government policy.

Keynesians also believe that the economy lacks strong natural corrective mechanisms that will always force it easily and quickly back to full employment. They believe that while the price level rises fairly quickly to eliminate *inflationary* gaps, the price level does not fall quickly to eliminate *recessionary* gaps. Keynesians stress the asymmetries noted in earlier chapters that imply that prices and wages fall only slowly in response to a recessionary gap. As a result, Keynesians believe that recessionary gaps can persist for long periods of time unless they are eliminated by an active stabilization policy.

The second part of the Keynesian view on cyclical fluctuations is that they accept the correlation between changes in the money supply and changes in the level of economic activity, but their explanation questions the causality suggested by the monetarists. Many Keynesians accept that changes in the money supply can be an important source of fluctuations in economic activity, but they argue that much of the evidence adduced by monetarists actually reflects causality in the other direction. These Keynesians argue that changes in the level of economic activity tend to cause changes in the money supply. They offer several reasons for this, but only the most important need be mentioned.

Keynesians point out that from 1945 to the early 1970s most central banks tended to stabilize interest rates as the target variable of monetary policy. To do this they had to increase the money supply during upswings in the business cycle and decrease it during downswings. When an expansion got under way, the demand for money tended to increase, and if there was no increase in the money supply, interest rates would rise. The central bank might prevent this rise in interest rates by buying bonds offered for sale at

BOX 39-1

Two Views on the Great Depression in the United States

The stock market crash of 1929, and other factors associated with a moderate downswing in American business activity during the late 1920s, caused the public to wish to hold more in cash and less in demand deposits. The banking system could not, however, meet this increased demand for liquidity without help from the Federal Reserve System. (As we saw in Chapter 33, banks are never able to meet from their own reserves a sudden demand to withdraw currency on the part of a large fraction of their depositors. Their reserves are always inadequate to meet such a demand.) The Fed had been set up to provide just such emergency assistance to banks that were basically sound but were unable to meet sudden demands by depositors to withdraw cash. However, the Fed refused to extend the necessary help, and successive waves of bank failures followed as a direct result. During each wave hundreds of banks failed, ruining many depositors and thereby worsening an already

severe depression. In the last half of 1931 almost 2,000 American banks were forced to suspend operations! One consequence of this was a sharp drop in the money supply; by 1932 the money supply was 35 percent below the level of 1929. To monetarists these facts seem decisive.

While Keynesians accept the argument that the Fed's behavior was perverse, they argue that the cyclical behavior of investment and consumption expenditure was the major cause of the Great Depression. In support of this view they point out that in Canada and the United Kingdom, where the central bank came to the aid of the banking system, bank failures were few during the Great Depression, and as a consequence the money supply did *not* shrink drastically as it did in the United States. Despite these markedly different monetary histories, the behavior of the recessionary gap, investment expenditure, and unemployment was very similar in the three countries.

current prices, but in so doing it would increase banks' reserves and thereby inject new money into the economy. Similarly, in a cyclical contraction interest rates would tend to fall unless the central bank stepped in and sold bonds to keep interest rates up. Generally it did so, thereby decreasing the money supply. This behavior created the positive correlation on which the monetarists rely.

According to Keynesians, fluctuations in national income are often caused by fluctuations in expenditure decisions. Further, they believe that fluctuations in national income cause fluctuations in the money supply.

Nevertheless, most Keynesians also agree that policy-induced changes in the money supply can cause national income to change.

The Price Level

As we saw in Chapter 36, sustained inflation requires a sustained expansion of the money supply.

Motives for such excessive monetary expansions have varied from time to time and place to place. Sometimes central banks have rapidly increased the money supply in an effort to end a recession. Then when the economy expanded due to its own natural recuperative forces, the increased money supply allowed a significant inflation during the boom phase of the cycle. At other times central banks have tried to hold interest rates well below their free-market levels. To do this they buy bonds to hold bond prices up. We have seen that these open-market operations increase the money supply and so fuel an inflation. At still other times central banks have helped governments finance large budget deficits by buying up the new public debt. These open-market operations provide what is popularly known as *printing press finance*. The steady increase in the money supply fuels a continuous inflation.

Monetarist views. As we have said, many monetarists hold that inflation is everywhere and always a monetary phenomenon. They thus focus on changes in the money supply as the key source of shifts in the *AD* curve.

According to monetarists, all inflations are caused by excessive monetary expansion and would not occur without it.

Keynesian views. Keynesians agree that a sustained rise in prices cannot occur unless it is accompanied by continued increases in the money supply. Keynesians also emphasize, however, that temporary bursts of inflation can be caused by shifts in the *AD* curve brought about by increases in private- or public-sector expenditure. If such inflations are not validated by monetary expansion, they are brought to a halt by the monetary adjustment mechanism.

Keynesians also accept the importance of supply-shock inflations. Again, they accept that such inflations cannot go on indefinitely unless accommodated by monetary expansion. But Keynesians argue that "temporary" inflation due to either *AD* or *SRAS* shifts can go on long enough to be a matter of serious policy concern.

Many Keynesians also take seriously the possibility of wage-cost push inflation that we studied in Chapter 36. This type of inflation, if it exists, makes full employment incompatible with a stable price level. Again, the central bank is faced with the agonizing choice of whether or not to accommodate.

Growth

Conservative views. Conservatives, and indeed most monetarists, feel that in a stable environment free from government interference growth will take care of itself. Large firms will spend much on research and development. Where they fail, or where they suppress inventions to protect monopoly positions, the genius of backyard inventors will come up with new ideas and will develop new companies to challenge the positions of the established giants. Left to itself, the economy will prosper as it has in the past, provided only that inquiring scientific spirit and the profit motive are not suppressed.

Interventionist views. Interventionists, and indeed most Keynesians, are less certain than conservatives

about the ability of market forces to produce growth. While recognizing the importance of invention and innovation, they fear the dead hand of monopoly and cautious business practices that choose security over risk taking. Therefore, the state needs at the very least to give a nudge here or there to help the growth process along.

The Role of Policy

The conservative and the interventionist diagnoses of the economy's ills lead, not surprisingly, to very different prescriptions about the appropriate role of economic policy.

Conservative Prescriptions

It is not necessary to distinguish conservative policies with respect to full employment and with respect to stable prices. This is because conservatives believe that both goals will be achieved by the same basic policy: provision of a stable environment in which the free-market system may operate.

Full Employment and Stable Prices: Providing a Stable Environment

Creating a stable environment, as the conservatives advocate, may be easier said than done. Let us focus on the prescriptions for establishing stable fiscal and monetary policies.

One major problem to keep in mind is that macro variables are interrelated. The stability of one may imply the instability of another. In such cases, a choice must often be made. How much instability of one aggregate can we tolerate to secure stability in another related aggregate?

Assume, for example, that the government decides to adopt the goal of stability in the budget balance as part of the stable environment. This "stability" would require great *instability* in tax and expenditure policy. Tax revenues depend on the interaction between tax rates and the level of national income. With given tax rates, tax revenues change with the ebb and flow of the business cycle. A stable budget balance would require that the government raise tax rates and cut expenditure in slumps and lower tax rates and raise expenditures in booms.

Not only does this squander the budget's potential to act as a stabilizer, but great instability of the fiscal environment is also caused by continual changes in tax rates and expenditure levels. A stable fiscal environment requires substantial stability in government expenditures and tax rates. Stability is needed so that the private sector can make plans for the future in a climate of known patterns of tax liabilities and government demand.

Any target budget balance must be some average over a period long enough to cover a typical cycle. Stability from year to year should be found in tax rates and expenditure programs, *not* in the size of the budget balance.

This in turn requires that the budget deficit vary cyclically, showing its largest deficits in slumps and its largest surpluses in booms.[5]

Advocates of a stable monetary environment are actually advocating stable inflation. Whether a *zero* rate is feasible or not is discussed in Box 39-2. The central bank is urged to set a target rate of increase in the money supply and hold it. To establish the target, the central bank estimates the rate at which the demand for money would be growing if actual income equaled potential income and the price level were stable. As a first approximation this can be taken to be the rate at which potential income itself is growing. This then becomes the target rate of growth of the money supply. The key proposition is that the money supply should be changing gradually along a stable path that is independent of short-term variations in the demand for money caused by cyclical changes in national income. This is referred to as a *k* **percent rule.**

Will the *k* percent rule really provide monetary stability? The answer is not necessarily.

Assuring a stable rate of monetary growth does not assure a stable monetary environment. Monetary shortages and surpluses depend on the

relation between the supply and the demand for money.

The *k* percent rule looks after supply, but what about demand?

Problems for the *k* percent rule arise when the demand for money shifts. For example, payment of interest on checking deposits increases the demand for M1. In this event, if the central bank adheres to a *k* percent rule, there will be an excess demand for money, and interest rates will rise. Thus contractionary pressure will be put on the economy.

Should the central bank commit itself to a specific *k* percent rule or merely work toward unannounced and possibly variable targets? The announced rule makes it easier to evaluate how well the central bank is doing its job. It also helps to prevent the central bank from succumbing to the temptation to fine tune the economy.

One disadvantage of the announced rule is that it sets up speculative behavior. Assume, for example, that when weekly money supply figures are announced there is too much money. Speculators then know that the central bank will sell more bonds in the future to reduce the excess. This will depress the price of bonds. Speculators are thus induced to sell bonds, hoping to rebuy them at bargain prices once the central bank acts.

Stable pre-announced M1 targets can introduce instability into interest-rate behavior.

A second disadvantage of such a rule is that the central bank, to preserve its credibility, may fail to take discretionary action that would otherwise be appropriate. For example, after an entrenched inflation is broken, the economy may come to rest with substantial unemployment and a stable price level (see Figure 36-6). There is then a case for a once-and-for-all discretionary expansion in the money supply to get the economy back to full employment. The *k* percent rule precludes this, condemning the economy to a slump.

Despite these problems, conservatives believe the *k* percent rule is superior to any known alternative. Some would agree that in principle the central bank

---

[5] Appendix B to this chapter takes up the recent debate that has emerged among economists over whether the deficit matters.

BOX 39-2

Is a Zero Inflation Rate a Feasible Policy Goal?

The 1950s were characterized by what would be regarded today as satisfactory price stability. But prices were not exactly steady. The inflation rate varied between 0.5 percent and 3 percent. Despite what appeared to most observers to be a slowly growing average recessionary gap throughout this period, the inflation rate never reached zero in any year. Between 1955 and 1961 there were only two years when the rate was below 1 percent: 1955 (0.2 percent) and 1961 (0.7 percent).

This creeping inflation worried observers at the time. An inflation, even a gradual one in the face of an obvious recessionary gap, seemed hard to understand.

The explanation in modern theory would likely come from the supply side. The combination of rising prices and recessionary gaps usually suggests a supply-shock inflation. The explanation that satisfied many observers at the time was the **structural rigidity theory** of inflation, which was indeed a supply-shock explanation.

The structural rigidity theory assumes that resources do not move quickly from one use to another and that it is easy to increase money wages and prices but hard to decrease them. Given these conditions, when patterns of demand and costs change due to such forces as economic growth, real adjustments occur slowly. Shortages appear in potentially expanding sectors, and prices rise because the slow movement of resources prevents these sectors from expanding rapidly enough. Factors of production

remain in contracting sectors on part-time employment or become unemployed because mobility in the economy is low. Wages and prices are slow to move downward, so there are few significant wage and price reductions in these contracting sectors.

Thus the mere process of adjustment in an economy with structural rigidities causes inflation to occur. Prices in the expanding sectors rise; prices in the contracting sectors stay about the same; on average, therefore, the price level rises.

The inflation of the late 1950s and early 1960s was mild, and the debate on its causes was inconclusive. However, this was the first suggestion of a force that later became a plaguing policy problem: inflations originating in shifts in the aggregate supply curve.

Although the structural rigidity theory cannot be a major part of the explanation of the high inflation rates of the 1970s and early 1980s, it suggests that a zero inflation rate may not be an achievable target. Of course, good luck—such as the fall in the world price of oil that occurred in early 1986, when the inflation rate was already low and perhaps still declining—can temporarily drive the inflation rate to zero or even below zero. But if there is anything in the structural rigidity theory, the minimum inflation rate compatible with a changing economy may be 1 percent to 2 percent rather than zero. A test of this theory might occur by the end of the 1980s; if inflation continues to fall, will it reach zero, or get stuck in the 1–2 percent range?

---

could improve the economy's performance by occasional bouts of discretionary monetary policy to offset such things as major shifts in the demand for money. But they also believe that once given any discretion, the central bank would abuse it in an attempt to fine tune the economy. The resulting instability would, they believe, be much more than any instability resulting from the application of a k percent rule in an environment subject to some change.

Long-Term Growth

Conservatives want to let growth take care of itself. They argue that governments cannot improve the workings of free markets and that their interventions can interfere with market efficiency. Thus they push for reducing the current level of government intervention.

Given the large web of government rules, regulations, and perverse tax incentives that has grown up over many years, the conservatives' agenda for reducing government intervention is usually a long one. Such an agenda was adopted by so-called supply siders during the later 1970s and early 1980s. The supply-side, conservative view that growth is best encouraged by reducing the present degree of government intervention has already caused some significant policy changes and will no doubt always find numerous supporters.

The agenda includes *eliminating* the following policies:

Supporting declining industries. This policy causes resources that could be more productively employed elsewhere to leave the industry more slowly. Most economists agree that such policies are costly, harmful to growth, and in the end self-defeating.

Encouraging monopolies and discouraging competition. Most economists tend to oppose such policies, although there is disagreement over how much competition is desirable in certain industries. For example, conservatives tend to support complete deregulation of fare and route setting by airlines, while interventionists tend to worry that cutthroat competition may reduce airline quality and safety.

Taxing income rather than consumption. Consider a woman in the 25 percent tax bracket who earns an extra $1,000 and pays $250 income tax. If she spends her after-tax income, she will be able to buy $750 worth of goods. If she saves the money, she will be able to buy a $750 bond. If the bond pays a 4 percent real return, she will earn $30 interest per year. But a 25 percent tax must then be paid on the interest earnings, leaving only a $22.50 annual income. This is a 3.0 percent after-tax return on the bond and *a 2.25 percent after-tax return on the original $100 income.* Conservatives allege that this "double taxing" of saving is a serious disincentive to saving. They argue for taxes on consumption, not on income, so that any income that is saved would be untaxed. A tax would be levied only when the interest earned on the savings was actually spent on consumption.

High rates of income tax. Conservatives allege that high taxes discourage work. But the effect of high taxes may actually be to make people work either more or less hard. Theory is silent on which is more likely, and no hard evidence has yet shown that lowering current tax rates makes people work harder. Many elements of tax reform, introduced in the United States in 1986 and proposed in Canada in June 1987, which saw tax bases broadened and tax rates reduced, were well received by conservatives.

"Double taxation" of business profits. Business profits are taxed first as income of firms and second as income of households when paid out as dividends. This and other policies that reduce business profits and hence discourage the return to investing in equities are alleged to discourage households from saving and investing in businesses that are the mainspring of economic growth.

All these policies are alleged to reduce the rate of growth below what it would otherwise be. Problems arise in assessing the existence and importance of the alleged harmful effects of each policy and also, since the government needs revenue, in finding alternative revenue sources that will have less harmful effects than the ones being criticized.

Interventionist Prescriptions

Interventionists call for different policies for the three policy goals of full employment, price stability, and growth. As we consider their prescriptions, we give their reasons for rejecting the conservative case.

Full Employment

Interventionists call for discretionary fiscal and monetary policies to offset significant inflationary and recessionary gaps. Some of the major problems associated with discretionary stabilization policy have been discussed in earlier chapters. The issues in the debate that is popularly known as "rules versus discretion" are discussed further in Box 39-3.

A Stable Price Level

Some interventionists, particularly a group called *post-Keynesians,* believe that the k percent rule may not be enough to achieve full employment and stable

BOX 39-3

Rules Versus Discretion

Three of the main issues involved in the rules versus discretion debate are problems created by lags, type of stabilization needed, and adequacy of information.

Lags. Economists hostile to discretionary policy emphasize the long and variable lags of both fiscal and monetary policy. Monetary policy can be put into effect quickly, but it takes 6 to 18 months for the full effects of a change in interest rates to be felt in terms of altered private-sector expenditures. It often takes a long time to put fiscal policy into effect since federal budgets are usually several months in the making. Once the changes are made, however, their effects spread quickly through the economy.

Conservatives feel that these lags destroy the presumption that discretionary full-employment policy will usually be stabilizing. Interventionists feel that although the lags are serious, discretionary policies can be effective in reducing persistent recessionary gaps. Few interventionists, however, now call for fine tuning.

A stable climate for planning. Supporters of rules emphasize the need for a stable climate for firms and households to plan for the future. They argue that continual changes in tax rates and the money supply designed to stabilize the economy are destabilizing because they create a climate of uncertainty that makes long-term planning difficult.

Supporters of discretionary policy argue that they want discretion exercised only when the occasional serious recession develops and that large fluctuations in income and employment can be as upsetting to long-term planning as the occasional changes in tax rates and expenditures required by stabilization policy.

Do we know enough? Discretionary stabilization policy requires that we forecast what the state of the economy will be in the absence of that policy. Generally, actual information is available only with a lag. Policymakers know approximately what GDP was last quarter and what unemployment was last month. (The first preliminary figures for many economic variables can be subject to substantial errors. Often these estimates are revised several times over subsequent months and even years.) On the basis of these data, projections of future behavior of the economy must be made and policy set.

Supporters of discretionary policy accept that errors in projections may be large in relation to the recessionary gaps created by minor recessions but believe that the errors are small in relation to major recessions. They argue that for major recessions policymakers will be in no doubt about the existence of a large recessionary gap or the need for some significant stimulus, even though its exact amount cannot be precisely determined.

---

prices simultaneously. This is because they accept the wage-cost push theory of inflation discussed in Chapter 36.

Some Keynesians call for incomes policies to restrain the wage-cost push and so make full employment compatible with stable prices. They believe that such policies should become permanent features of the economic landscape.

Wage-price controls might work as *temporary* measures to break inflationary inertias (see Chapter 36, pages 788–789), but as permanent features they would introduce inefficiencies and rigidities.

More permanent incomes policies might be of two types. The first type, commonly used in Europe

in past decades but now out of favor, is often called a *social contract*. Labor, management, and the government consult annually and agree on target wage changes. These are calculated to be non-inflationary, given the government's projections for the future and its planned economic policies. Such a scheme is most easily initiated in a centralized economy such as West Germany's, where a few giant firms and unions exert enormous power, or in a country such as Britain, where the party in power during much of the period in which social contracts were used had strong official links with the labor unions.

The other main type of incomes policy is **tax-related incomes policy (TIP),** which we first encountered in Chapter 36. TIPs provide tax incentives for management and labor to conform to government-established wage and price guidelines. For example, increases in wages and prices in excess of the guidelines would be taxed heavily. TIPs have not yet been tried, although they have been strongly advocated by some economists.

TIPs rely on tax incentives to secure voluntary conformity with wage and price guidelines, whereas wage and price controls try to impose conformity by law.

Advocates of TIPs argue that their great advantage is leaving decisions on wages and prices in the hands of labor and management while influencing behavior by altering the incentive system. Critics, however, argue that they would prove to be an administrative nightmare.

Growth

Policies for intervention to increase growth rates are of two sorts. Some policies seek to alter the general economic climate in a way favorable to growth. They typically include subsidization or favorable tax treatment for research and development, for purchase of plant and equipment, and for other profit-earning activities. Measures to lower interest rates temporarily or permanently are urged by some as favorable to investment and growth. Most interventionists support these general measures.

Some also support more specific intervention, usually in the form of what is called *picking and backing winners* in one way or another. Advocates of this view, such as Professor Lester Thurow of MIT, want governments to pick the industries, usually new ones, that have potential for future success and then back them with subsidies, government contracts, research funds, and all the other encouragements at the government's command.

Opponents argue that picking winners requires foresight and that there is no reason to expect the government to have better foresight than private investors. Indeed, since political considerations inevitably get in the way, the government may be less successful than the market in picking winners. If so,

channeling funds through the government rather than through the private sector may hurt rather than help growth rates. (This debate is continued in Box 38-2 on page 834.)

Rational Expectations and the Micro Foundations of Macroeconomics[6]

For many years Keynesian economics seemed successful both in explaining the overall behavior of the economy and in suggesting policies for controlling inflation and unemployment. As long as it appeared to work, few were interested in *how*. During the late 1960s and the 1970s, however, control of the economy by means of traditional fiscal and monetary policies seemed to become more difficult. This raised concerns about the foundations of Keynesian theory. The main question was, What behavior in the individual markets for goods and factors of production is implied by the Keynesian aggregate relationships? This question concerns what are called the *micro foundations,* or *micro underpinnings*, of macro models.

While these concerns about the Keynesian model were surfacing, the monetarist model seemed to provide an alternative for understanding the macro behavior of the economy and for prescribing appropriate policies. This elicited a debate about the merits of the two models, a debate that still rages today. Micro foundations are at the heart of the debate between monetarism and Keynesianism. The issues are important; because they are at the frontier of modern research, they are also difficult. The analysis depends on material that is treated in detail in more advanced courses. At this stage, therefore, we can discuss the issues only in broad outline.

Monetarist Micro Foundations

There is no single set of accepted monetarist micro foundations. Most monetarists, however,

---

[6] The rest of this chapter may be omitted without loss of continuity.

view markets as competitive.[7] One important characteristic of competitive markets is that prices and wages are flexible; they adjust to establish equilibrium at all times. When a competitive market is in equilibrium (see Chapter 4), the market is said to have *cleared*. This means that every purchaser has been able to buy all he or she wishes to buy at the going price and every seller has been able to sell all he or she wishes to sell at that price.[8] When each and every market is in equilibrium, there is full employment of all resources. The prices that clear markets are called **market-clearing prices**.

According to the monetarists, strong forces ensure that departures from full-employment equilibrium are quickly rectified. That is, monetarists believe that the *automatic adjustment mechanism* works quite efficiently.

We now consider two particular monetarist views.

Traditional Monetarism

The monetarist school of thought that evolved in the 1960s was led by Professor Milton Friedman of the University of Chicago. Economists of that school, often called *traditional monetarists*, hold that the economy, when left to its own, tends to stabilize at the full-employment level. They also hold that, historically, monetary policies have been erratic: We saw in Chapter 34 that monetarists believe that monetary policy exerts a powerful influence on the economy, so they reach the following conclusion:

Traditional monetarists believe that fluctuations in the money supply are a major source of fluctuations in output and the price level.

Although monetary policy has strong effects, it operates with a long and variable lag. According to

Friedman and his followers, these long and variable lags not only doom monetary policy to failure but make it counterproductive as well. In their view monetary policy has actually served to destabilize the economy in the past. The best course for monetary policy is held to be to follow the *k* percent rule, that is, to set the rate of increase of the money supply at some given value and hold it there.

New Classical Monetarism

The *new Classical monetarists* follow Professors Robert Lucas and Thomas Sargeant in holding that temporary departures from full employment occur mainly because people make mistakes. This viewpoint can be best understood in terms of the proposition derived from microeconomics that individual supply and demand behavior depends only on the structure of relative prices.

To follow their argument, let us start by assuming that each of the economy's markets is in equilibrium; there is full employment, prices are stable, and the actual and expected rates of inflation are zero. Now suppose the government increases the money supply by 5 percent. People find themselves with unwanted money balances, which they seek to spend.[9] For simplicity, assume that this leads to an increase in desired expenditure on all commodities; the demand for each commodity shifts to the right, and all prices, being competitively determined, rise. Individual decision makers see their selling prices go up and mistakenly interpret this increase as a rise in their own relative price. This is because they expect the overall rate of inflation to be zero. Firms will produce more and workers will work more; both groups think they are getting an increased *relative* price for what they sell. Thus total output and employment rise.

When both groups eventually realize that their own relative prices are in fact unchanged, output and employment fall back to their initial levels. The extra

---

[7] They realize, of course, that perfect competition does not exist everywhere in the economy, but they believe that the forces of competition are strong—strong enough that analysis based on the theory of perfect competition will be close to the real behavior of the economy.

[8] Competitive markets clear only at the equilibrium price. At any other price there are either unsatisfied purchasers (excess demand) or unsatisfied sellers (excess supply).

[9] Most monetarists accept the theory of the transmission mechanism (discussed in Chapter 34) according to which the excess money balances are used to buy financial assets, thus driving down interest rates and stimulating expenditure *indirectly*. However, most monetarists tend to stress the relative importance of the *direct* expenditure effects created by excess money balances.

output and employment occur only while people are being fooled. When they realize that *all* prices have risen by 5 percent, they revert to their initial behavior. The only difference is that now the price level has risen by 5 percent, leaving relative prices unchanged.

According to the new Classical theory, deviations from full employment occur only because people make mistakes that cause markets to clear at more or less than full-employment output. People are not prevented from selling as many commodities or as much labor as they wish; the contraction or expansion in output is voluntary.

New Classical monetarists focus on the role of changes in relative prices in signaling appropriate information in a world where tastes and technology are constantly changing. They hold that fluctuations in the money supply will lead to increased fluctuations in all prices. This makes it hard for households and firms to distinguish changes in relative prices, to which they do wish to respond, from changes in the price level, to which they do not wish to respond. Such confusion, created by fluctuations in the money supply, thus leads to mistakes in supply and demand decisions.

This discussion highlights the importance for firms and households of distinguishing the causes of any price changes. Consider, for example, what happens if there is an unexpected and unperceived increase in the money supply. This will lead to an increase in most, if not all, prices above what most agents had expected. Most firms perceive this as an increase in the relative price of their own output and hence increase their level of production above what it normally would have been. Consequently, national income rises above the full-employment level. A similar argument shows that an unanticipated and unperceived decrease in the money supply would cause output to fall below its full-employment level.

The Lucas aggregate supply curve.   The behavior just described gives rise to the **Lucas aggregate supply curve.**

The Lucas aggregate supply curve posits that national output will vary positively with the ratio of the actual to the expected price level.

This is often also referred to as the *surprises only* supply curve since it implies that only changes in the price level that are unexpected (surprises) will give rise to fluctuations in aggregate supply.

To see this, consider what happens if there is again an increase in the money supply, but this time suppose that it has been widely expected in advance by firms and households. Again prices will rise. Most firms will now take this to mean only that the *observed* change in the price of their own output has roughly matched the *expected* change in the average of all other prices. Hence they will not interpret it as a rise in the relative price of their own output and will maintain their production level at its normal level. National income will not rise above potential despite the rise in the general price level.

According to the new Classical theory, expected changes in the price level do not lead to fluctuations in aggregate supply.

New Classical policy views.   New Classical monetarists support the *k* percent rule, just like the traditional monetarists. They believe that firms and households make better decisions when monetary and fiscal policies are stable than when they are highly variable. They believe that active interventionist policies designed to stabilize the economy make it harder for people to interpret the signals generated by the price system and so lead them to make more errors in forming their expectations. This then increases rather than reduces the fluctuations of output around its full-employment level and increases rather than reduces the fluctuations of unemployment around the natural rate.

According to the new Classical theory, active use of monetary policy in an attempt to stabilize the economy will lead to confusion about relative and absolute prices. This will cause people to make mistakes in their output and purchasing decisions and therefore increase aggregate output fluctuations.

This conclusion depends on the particular view adopted by the new Classical monetarists about how people form predictions or expectations, a subject that has recently become an important part of macroeconomic debates.

The Theory of Rational Expectations

The new Classical model is augmented by the theory of *rational expectations*. People look to the government's current macroeconomic policy to form their expectations of future inflation. They understand how the economy works, and they form their expectations rationally by predicting the outcome of the policies being pursued. People learn fairly quickly from their mistakes; though random errors occur, systematic and persistent errors do not. In an obvious sense, such expectations are *forward-looking*.

According to the theory of rational expectations, people do not make persistent, systematic errors in predicting the overall inflation rate; they may, however, make unsystematic errors.

Policy invariance.   Rational expectations, combined with the Lucas aggregate supply curve, give rise to the new Classical *policy invariance*, or policy neutrality, with this result:

Systematic attempts to use monetary policy to stabilize the economy will lead to systematic changes in the price level but will not influence the behavior of output.

Thus, according to the new Classicists, monetary policy can do harm—by creating confusion about the source of price changes—but cannot do good, except by random chance. Thus even in the face of major recessions, laissez faire is the best conceivable stabilization policy.

Let us review how this follows from combining the monetarist micro foundations with the theory of rational expectations.

1. According to the new Classical theory's micro foundations, deviations from full employment occur only because of errors in predicting the price level (which cause workers and firms to mistake changes in the price level for changes in relative prices).
2. According to the theory of rational expectations, errors in predicting the price level are only random.
3. It follows from the first two points that there is no room for active government policy to stabilize the economy. The causes of fluctuations are random.[10] It is in the nature of random fluctuations that they cannot be foreseen and offset. Thus there is no room for stabilization policy to reduce the fluctuations in the economy by offsetting the disturbances that emanate from the private sector.

Not all monetarists accept the theory of rational expectations. For those who do, however, the contrast with the Keynesians is extreme.

The most extreme monetarist attack on stabilization policy has two parts. The first is a model of an economy where deviations from full employment occur only because of errors. The second is a theory of people's expectations that predicts that persistent, systematic errors—and hence systematic deviations from full employment—will not occur.

Monetarist Conclusions

The two monetarist schools obviously do not agree on everything. Both agree, however, that monetary policy should not be used actively to stabilize the economy. This is for two reasons: (1) Fluctuations in the money supply are the major source of fluctuations in output and inflation, and (2) there is no long-term trade-off between inflation and national income.[11]

Most economists accept the view that monetary forces are important in influencing inflation and unemployment, but many do not agree that monetary forces are the *most* important force. Most economists

---

[10] However, long lags may cause macro variables to display cyclical fluctuations, as discussed in Chapter 31.

[11] Recall that any attempt to hold income above its full-employment level will lead not to a constant rate of inflation but to a continuously accelerating inflation. This is just a restatement of the acceleration hypothesis and the natural rate hypothesis developed in detail in Chapter 36 and its appendix.

also agree that inflation will tend to accelerate if income is held permanently above its full-employment level.

One aspect of the monetarist model that is particularly controversial is the belief in downward flexibility of prices, which leads to the prediction that as long as national income is below its full-employment level, the price level would *fall* at an ever-accelerating rate. Keynesians say that the observed downward inflexibility of the price level refutes this view. They reject the prediction that the main cause of recessionary gaps is *voluntary* reductions in employment and output due to errors in reading the signals provided by the price system. Most Keynesians do not believe that output deviates from its potential level *only* because workers and firms make mistakes.

Keynesian Micro Foundations

The Keynesian micro foundations emphasize the noncompetitive nature of the economy. Most firms are seen as setting their own prices rather than accepting those set on competitive markets. Their per unit output costs tend to be fairly constant, and they set prices by adding a relatively inflexible markup to their costs.[12] They then sell what they can at the going price. Cyclical fluctuations in aggregate demand cause cyclical fluctuations in the demand for each firm's products, which in turn cause individual firms to make cyclical variations in output and employment rather than in price.

While in the monetarist model the main impact of fluctuations in aggregate demand is on prices, in the Keynesian model their main impact is on output and employment.

A similar argument holds for labor markets in the Keynesian model. Wages respond to the price level and productivity, but are relatively insensitive to short-term cyclical fluctuations in demand. (This is discussed in detail in Chapter 20.) A recent pro-

[12] Complete cyclical inflexibility of markup is not necessary. What matters is that firms do not adjust prices continually and as a result are willing to sell further units at the same price. This much price inflexibility need not imply an absence of profit maximization. Instead it may follow from profit maximization when it is costly to alter prices. This is discussed further in Chapter 15.

posal to change wage-setting arrangements is discussed in Box 39-4.

This short-term wage inflexibility can stem from rational behavior on the part of workers. If wage rates adjust to clear labor markets, wages will vary over the cycle. *All* workers will then bear the uncertainty associated with the cyclical movements in wages. However, if wages are set in response to long-term considerations but do not vary cyclically so as to clear labor markets, cyclical fluctuations in demand will cause employment to fluctuate. Since most layoffs and rehires are based on seniority, employment fluctuations are all borne by the 10 or 20 percent of workers who are the least senior. The majority of workers will then have little uncertainty in the face of cyclical fluctuations in demand, all the uncertainty having been placed on the minority with low seniority. Thus contracts that fix wages over the cycle and allow employment to vary may be preferable to the majority of workers compared to contracts that allow wages to vary in order to clear the labor market continually and thus prevent unemployment.

In Keynesian macroeconomics, the economy does not have a unique short-term equilibrium. Because firms would like to sell more and some workers would be willing to work more at current prices, fluctuations in aggregate demand cause output and employment to fluctuate in the short term.

The Keynesian macro model allows for systematic disturbances that can cause prolonged deflationary or recessionary gaps.

According to the Keynesians, stabilization policy can then be used to offset at least the gaps that are large and persistent.

Such policies seek to alter aggregate demand using both fiscal and monetary tools.

Differences Between the Two Models

There are many differences in the micro behavior that underlies the models. Probably the most impor-

BOX 39-4

The Share Economy

Several times in this text we have noted that wage rigidity is widely perceived to be a major impediment to the efficient functioning of the economy. In his important book *The Share Economy,* Professor Martin Weitzman of the Massachusetts Institute of Technology proposed a dramatic policy designed to restore flexibility of wages and thus enhance economic performance.

How the Share Economy Works

The basic idea is quite simple. Under Weitzman's proposal, part of the payment that any firm makes to labor would be tied directly to that firm's net revenues. This payment, which is like an annual bonus, is called the *share wage.* In addition, workers would also receive a *base wage,* which is fixed for the duration of the labor contract and is much lower than their wage under existing, traditional labor contracts.

When the firm is prosperous and net revenues are high, the share wage paid to workers would be correspondingly high. In these circumstances the total wage, equal to the base wage plus the share age, would exceed the initial wage that prevailed prior to the scheme's introduction. But when the firm's sales are down and thus net revenues are low, the share

wage would also be low. In these circumstances the total wage would be below the initial wage.

Consider, for example, a firm that is currently paying its workers a fixed wage of $20 an hour. Now suppose that under the share contract it pays them a base wage of only $10 an hour and that it also promises to pay workers a fixed percentage of its net revenues. Finally, suppose that this percentage is such that if net revenues are at their average or normal level, each worker will receive a combined base plus share wage of $20 an hour, just equal to the wage in the absence of the share contract.

If the firm's net revenues turn out to be above their normal level, the share wage will rise to reflect this; thus the total payment to workers will exceed $20 an hour, and the workers will share in the prosperity of the firm. If the firm's net revenues turn out to be below their normal level, the share wage will fall; in this case the total wage will be below $20 an hour, and the workers will "share" in the ill fortunes of the firm.

Implications of the Share Economy

Under traditional wage-setting arrangements, rigid wages mean that a firm will lay off workers in the face of a fall in demand for its output. Under a share

tant relates to the distinction between voluntary and involuntary unemployment.

In the monetarist model all unemployment and output below capacity are voluntary. Workers decide to be unemployed, and firms decide to produce less than capacity output as a result of errors they make in predicting the general price level (and therefore the relative price of what they sell). So if surveyed, the millions of unemployed around the world in the early 1980s would have said that they could have had a job at the going wage, but they refused to accept it because, given their expectations about inflation, the expected real wage was too low.

In the Keynesian model, prices and wages do not fluctuate to clear markets. Unemployment and production below capacity are involuntary in the sense

that unemployed workers would like jobs at the going wage rate but cannot find them, and firms would like to sell more at going prices, but customers are not forthcoming.[13] So if surveyed, the millions of unemployed around the world in the early 1980s would have said that they would have accepted a job at the going wage rate, but none was available.

Major current debate centers around these two prototype models and some of their subtler offshoots. Issues such as what determines the degree of wage and price flexibility in the economy, the conditions under which it can be expected that people can form accurate expectations and act on them, and

[13] Of course, one could still argue that this unemployment is voluntary because the workers had earlier voluntarily agreed to the contracts.

contract, firms will have a much smaller incentive to lay off workers during a downturn, since the total wage paid to each worker falls. Thus workers will face a more stable employment pattern with the share contract. However, workers will have to accept the risk of a fluctuating total wage compared to the initial situation in which they received a fixed wage of $20 *if they remained employed.*

Many observers feel that the situation under a share contract, where each worker bears a small part of the burden of the downturn, is more equitable than the situation under a fixed total wage, where those workers who keep their jobs bear none of the burden while the minority who get paid off bear the total burden. Further, many observers feel that the economy would operate more efficiently in the presence of the enhanced wage flexibility that the share contracts would generate.

Weitzman proposes that tax incentives be introduced to encourage firms to enter into such contracts. For example, share income could be subject to a special low tax rate, with regular tax rates still applying to any income from a fixed wage rate. Firms and workers would thus have an incentive to arrange for a large fraction of the total payment to labor to be share income.

This proposal is controversial. Some unions have criticized it, arguing that if the contract specifies a given fraction of net revenues is to be paid to all workers, firms will have an incentive to add to their work force and thus reduce each worker's share. This practice, the argument continues, will drive wages down to very low levels. Other unions reply that the expansion in employment is precisely one of the desirable features of the system, and there is no reason to expect *total* wages to fall. Some observers fear the impact on the deficit of the special tax incentives that might be required; others reply, using reasoning reminiscent of the Laffer curve (see page 498), that the improvement in the performance of the economy will be so great that total tax revenues will rise, not fall. Perhaps the highest praise of all came in a *New York Times* editorial in which *The Share Economy* was referred to as "the best idea since Keynes."

the potential for destabilizing the economy by pursuing an active stabilization policy are at the forefront of modern research. Views on how the economy behaves at both the micro and macro levels will be influenced by the progress of the debate. So will views on the place of fiscal and monetary policy as possible ways to eliminate inflationary or recessionary gaps.

The Progress of Economics

In this chapter we have discussed a number of current controversies about the behavior of the economy and the evidence that relates to them. General acceptance of the view that the validity of economic theories

should be tested by confronting their predictions with the mass of all available evidence is fairly new in economics.

Since 1936 when Keynes's *The General Theory of Employment, Interest, and Money* was published, great progress has been made in economics in relating theory to evidence. This progress has been reflected in the superior ability of governments to achieve their policy objectives. The financial aspects of World War II were handled far better than those of World War I. When President Roosevelt tried to reduce unemployment in the 1930s, his efforts were greatly hampered by the failure even of economists to realize the critical importance of budget deficits in raising aggregate demand and in injecting newly created money into the economy. When the Vietnam War forced the government to adopt expansive fiscal and monetary policies, economists had no trouble in predicting the outcome. More involvement abroad was obtained at the cost of heavy inflationary pressure at home.

The general propositions of theories are tested in such important policy areas as running wars, curing major depressions, and coping with inflations, even if all their specific predictions are not. In some sense, then, economic theories have always been subjected to empirical tests. When they were wildly at variance with the facts, the ensuing disaster could not but be noticed, and the theories were discarded or amended in the light of what was learned.

The advances of economics in the past 50 years reflect economists' changed attitudes toward empir-

ical observations. Today economists are much less likely to dismiss theories just because they do not like them and to refuse to abandon theories just because they do like them. Economists are more likely to try to base their theories as much as possible on empirical observation and to accept empirical relevance as the ultimate arbiter of the value of theories. As human beings, we may be anguished at the upsetting of a pet theory; as scientists, we should try to train ourselves to take pleasure in it because of the new knowledge gained thereby. It has been said that one of the great tragedies of science is the continual slaying of beautiful theories by ugly facts. It must always be remembered that when theory and fact come into conflict, theory, not fact, must give way.

Summary

1. Macroeconomic performance is judged in terms of the behavior of many variables. The key variables are (a) output, employment, and unemployment, (b) the rate of change of the price level, and (c) long-term growth.

2. Views about the role of policy in improving macroeconomic performance range between two extremes. The conservative view is that there is only a minimum role for policy; macroeconomic performance will be most satisfactory when the market system is allowed to function as freely as possible. The interventionist view is that active use of policy will improve macroeconomic performance. It is common to identify monetarists with conservatives and Keynesians with interventionists.

3. Monetarists believe that because the economy is inherently stable, the goal of damping the business cycle is best achieved by avoiding fluctuations in policy, especially monetary policy. Hence they advocate a k percent rule. Keynesians believe that the economy is inherently unstable in that expenditure functions shift regularly and the economy's self-corrective mechanisms are weak. Hence they believe in an active role for both monetary and fiscal policy to stabilize the business cycle.

4. Monetarists believe that inflation is everywhere and always a monetary phenomenon and so advocate the same conservative policies to avoid price instability as they advocate to minimize policy-induced cycles in output. They also argue that to control inflation, the long-term growth rate of the money supply must not be too high. Keynesians accept the view that monetary expansion is necessary for inflation to persist in the long term, but they take seriously the role of other factors in causing short-term but substantial infla-

tion. Hence they believe in an active role for policy to offset these factors in the short term.

5. Conservatives believe that long-term growth will be maximized when the incentives provided by the profit motive are strongest. Interventionists see a need for special government programs to channel resources into research and development and other investment expenditures designed to raise potential output.

6. Conservatives see a role for policy in terms of providing a stable environment for individual decision makers. This involves maintaining a consistent set of "fiscal rules of the game" in terms of expenditure and tax rates and providing a steady but gradual growth in the money supply.

7. Interventionists have specific prescriptions for each policy variable. They advocate active use of discretionary monetary and fiscal policy to stabilize output and employment. Despite imperfections caused by lags and incomplete knowledge, they believe such policies are helpful. Similar policies can be combined with incomes policies to stabilize the fluctuations in the price level that arise from various sources and are subject to an upward bias. They also support policies to promote growth through subsidization, tax favors, and more specific intervention.

8. Monetarists view markets as competitive and hence believe that departures from full-employment equilibrium are quickly rectified. As a result, they believe that fluctuations in aggregate demand lead primarily to fluctuations in the price level rather than in the level of output. They believe that the best course for monetary policy is to follow a k percent rule. For traditional monetarists, this is because they believe that long and variable lags in the effect of monetary policy mean that an interventionist monetary policy would destabilize output.

9. New Classical monetarists believe that departures from full-employment output occur only when people make mistakes in predicting the price level. When combined with the theory of rational expectations, this leads to the policy invariance proposition. New Classical monetarists support the k percent rule because they believe an interventionist monetary policy will not be effective in stabilizing output.

10. Keynesians emphasize the noncompetitive nature of the economy. As a result they believe that fluctuations in aggregate demand lead primarily to fluctuations in output rather than in the price level. In this view, an interventionist stabilization policy can be effective in stabilizing fluctuations in output.

Conservatives and interventionists
Micro foundations
k percent rule

Topics for Review

Traditional and new Classical monetarists
Lucas aggregate supply curve
Theory of rational expectations
Policy invariance proposition

Discussion Questions

1. To what extent is today's unemployment a serious social problem? If people could vote to choose between 10 percent unemployment combined with zero inflation and 2 percent unemployment combined with 10 percent inflation, which alternative do you think would win? Which groups might prefer the first alternative and which groups the second?

2. Some economists urge the government to fight inflation and combat unemployment by encouraging private-sector saving and investment. How might expanded saving and investment help to reduce inflation and combat unemployment?

3. Nobel Laureate Paul Samuelson quoted a "conservative economist friend" as saying in mid 1980, "If you're contriving a teensy-weensy recession for us, please don't bother. It won't do the job. What's needed is a believable declaration that Washington will countenance *whatever* degree of unemployment is needed to bring us back on the path to price stability, and a demonstrated willingness to *stick* to that resolution no matter how politically unpopular the short-run job-lessness, production cutbacks, and dips in profit might be." Discuss the "conservative friend's" view of inflation. Does experience since 1980 suggest that his advice was followed? If so, what was the consequence?

4. An ad that appeared in the *New York Times* in the early 1980s had this to say about inflation. "First [our politicians] blamed wage in-creases and price hikes for inflation. Then when 'voluntary guidelines' were established, the blame shifted to OPEC oil prices. Both expla-nations were wrong. Government policy is responsible for inflation—paying for deficit spending by 'creating money out of thin air.'" What theories of inflation are rejected and accepted by the writers of this ad?

5. In the mid 1980s a fervent national debate developed concerning the need to protect U.S. industries from foreign competition. How do the pro and con views of protectionism relate to the conservative and interventionist policies for promoting long-term growth?

6. A number of key microeconomic policy issues that were discussed earlier in this book are listed below. Go back and review the relevant discussion of some of them, and then present both the conservative case for "letting the market work" and the interventionist case in favor of a particular policy prescription. (Although the issues listed are "microeconomic" issues, their impact on the macroeconomic issues—in particular economic growth—can be important.)
   a. Rent controls (Chapter 6)
   b. De-industrialization (Chapter 17)
   c. Minimum-wage laws (Chapter 19)
   d. Increasing tariffs and other restrictions on imports (Chapter 21)
   e. Paying for social benefits (Chapter 25)
   f. Financing health care (Chapter 25)

Money in the National Income Model

We have studied the interaction of money, interest rates, and national income in terms of the apparatus in Figures 34-3 through 34-6. A loose end in that model can best be seen by considering the impact of an increase in the money supply. This leads to a fall in interest rates as shown in Figure 34-4(i), to increases in expenditure as shown in Figure 34-4(ii), and to increased national income as shown in Figure 34-5. But increased national income in turn leads to an increased need for transactions balances. This increased demand for money must then be added to the liquidity preference schedule in Figure 34-4. How is the increase in demand satisfied? Does accounting for it radically alter the conclusions of the analysis of Chapter 34?

The answer to the last question is no. This appendix provides a model that integrates monetary and expenditure factors and shows how they jointly determine the interest rate and the level of national income. The British economist Sir John Hicks (awarded the Nobel Prize in economics in 1972) suggested the approach in his famous review of Keynes' *General Theory,* "Mr. Keynes and the Classics: A Suggested Interpretation." It involves identifying the relationship between income and interest rates that is imposed first by goods market equilibrium and then by money market equilibrium. We then bring the two together to determine the one combination of real national income and interest rate that satisfies both equilibrium conditions simultaneously. Finally, we use the model to examine the effects of monetary and fiscal policy.

The Interest Rate and Aggregate Expenditure: The *IS* Curve

As we saw in going from Figure 34-4(ii) to Figure 34-5(i), a fall in the rate of interest is associated with a rise in the level of real national income, due to increased investment expenditures. Figure 34A-1 depicts this relationship between interest rate and na-

tional income as the negatively sloped *IS* curve.[1] The *IS* curve shows the combinations of national income and the rate of interest for which aggregate desired expenditure just equals total production in the economy. The negative relationship is derived for *given* values of the other variables influencing the aggregate expenditure function of Figure 34-5(i).

For given settings of the relationships underlying the aggregate expenditure function, the condition of goods market equilibrium—national income equals aggregate expenditure—means that the level of national income will vary negatively with the interest rate.

Fiscal Policy

Increases in the level of government expenditure raise the total level of aggregate expenditure *for any given interest rate.* As Figure 32-1 shows, this in turn leads to a multiplier effect on national income. In terms of the present model, an increase in government expenditure causes the *IS* curve to shift upward and to the right, as shown in Figure 39A-1. Combinations of national income and the interest rate that were on the original *IS* curve and hence were initially positions of equilibrium in the goods market are now positions of excess demand due to the increase in autonomous government demand. Hence output must rise to satisfy the increased demand (in the process leading to the now familiar multiplier effect), interest rates must rise to reduce investment demand, or, as IS_1 shows, some combination of both must occur.[2]

---

[1] *IS* stands for investment and saving, since the equilibrium condition is often expressed in terms of the equality between these two aggregates.

[2] A reduction in taxes, by altering the relationship between national income and disposable income, would also lead to a rightward shift in the *IS* curve.

**FIGURE 39A-1   Goods Market Equilibrium:
The *IS* Curve**

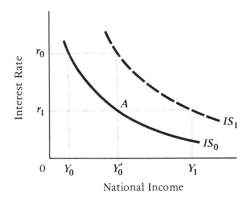

National Income

**The locus of combinations of national income and
the interest rate for which aggregate expenditure
equals output is called the *IS* curve.** The *IS* curve
slopes downward and to the right, indicating that a fall
in the interest rate from r_0 to r_1 leads, via increased investment, to an increase in the level of national income
from Y_0 to Y_0'. Expansionary fiscal policy creates excess
demand for output and causes the *IS* curve to shift to the
right to IS_1; from an initial position at *A*, the interest
rate must rise to r_0, national income must rise to Y_2, or
some combination of both along IS_1 must occur.

**Expansionary fiscal policy causes the *IS* curve
to shift upward and to the right, creating a new
locus of points at which aggregate expenditure
equals national income.**

By similar reasoning, cuts in government spending or tax increases shift the *IS* curve down to the
left. [50]

Liquidity Preference and National Income: The *LM* Curve

When the money supply is held constant, if the demand for and the supply of money are to be equal
the *total* demand for money arising from the transactions, speculative and precautionary motives must
also be constant. As we have seen, the demand for
money can be expected to vary positively with the

level of national income and negatively with the rate
of interest. If there is to be monetary equilibrium
with a given money supply, any increase in national
income must therefore be accompanied by an increase in the interest rate to keep total money demand
constant. This is depicted by the positively sloped
LM curve in Figure 39A-2. The *LM* curve shows the
combinations of national income and interest rate for
which total money demand is constant at the level
of a given money supply.[3]

**For a given money supply, the condition of
monetary market equilibrium means that the**

[3] The *L* stands for liquidity preference (or demand for money)
and the *M* for money supply.

**FIGURE 39A-2   Monetary Market Equilibrium:
The *LM* Curve**

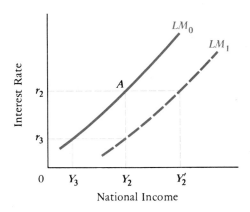

National Income

**The locus of combinations of national income and
the interest rate of which total money demand
equals a given money supply is called the *LM*
curve.** The *LM* curve slopes upward and to the right,
indicating that a fall in the rate of interest from r_2 to r_3,
which causes the demand for money to rise, must be accompanied by a fall in the level of national income, say,
from Y_2 to Y_3, in order to keep money demand equal to
the constant money supply. An open-market purchase
creates an excess supply of money and causes the *LM*
curve to shift to the right to LM_1; from an initial position at *A*, the interest rate must fall to r_3, national income must rise to Y_2', or some combination of both
along *LM* must occur.

level of national income will vary directly with the interest rate.

Monetary Policy

An increase in the supply of money resulting from an open-market purchase by the central bank causes the *LM* curve to shift downward and to the right, as in Figure 39A-2. The combinations of national income and interest rate that were on the original curve LM_0 and hence were initially positions of monetary equilibrium now correspond to excess supply due to the increase in the supply of money. To reestablish equilibrium, the demand for money must increase to match the larger money supply; hence national income must rise, the interest rate must fall, or, as LM_1 shows, some combination of both must occur.

An increase in the money supply causes the *LM* curve to shift downward and to the right, creating a new locus of points at which total money demand equals the money supply.

By similar reasoning, a decrease in the money supply causes the *LM* curve to shift upward to the left. [51]

Macroeconomic Equilibrium: Determination of National Income and the Interest Rate

The model is shown in Figure 39A-3. The intersection of the *LM* and *IS* curves indicates the only combination of national income and interest rate for which aggregate expenditure equals national income *and* the demand for money is equal to the supply.

The intersection of the *IS* and *LM* curves gives the equilibrium levels of national income and the rate of interest in a model that combines both expenditure and monetary influences.

Figure 39A-3 shows the effects of particular shifts in the *IS* and *LM* curves. This analysis leads to four general predictions.

1. A rightward shift in the *IS* curve raises national income and the rate of interest.
2. A leftward shift in the *IS* curve lowers national income and the rate of interest.
3. A rightward shift in the *LM* curve raises national income and lowers the rate of interest.
4. A leftward shift in the *LM* curve lowers national income and raises the rate of interest.

The Effects of Fiscal and Monetary Policy

Given our analysis of the effects of government expenditure on the *IS* curve and the effects of the money supply on the *LM* curve, we can summarize the analysis in our four basic predictions about the effects of monetary and fiscal policy.

1. An increase in government expenditure raises national income and raises the rate of interest.
2. An increase in the money supply raises national income and lowers the rate of interest.
3. A decrease in government expenditure lowers national income and lowers the rate of interest.
4. A decrease in the money supply lowers national income and raises the rate of interest.

These results represent what may be called the *Keynesian synthesis*, in which both monetary and fiscal policies have an effect on national income and interest rates.[4] [52]

At one time, debate in macroeconomics centered on the relative strengths of monetary and fiscal policy. *Monetarists* argued that monetary policy was powerful and fiscal policy was weak; *Keynesians* tended to argue that the opposite was the case. These views, and how they are related to the underlying behavioral relations, can be understood in terms of the *IS/LM* model.[5]

Consider first the strength of an increase in government spending. This increases expenditure directly and, as we have seen, shifts the *IS* curve rightward. The effect on national income is smaller than

---

[4] As we saw in Chapters 32 and 34, a cut in tax rates has effects similar to an increase in G, and a fall in the demand for money has effects similar to an increase in the money supply.

[5] This discussion expands on the analysis illustrated in Figure 34-7 on page 747.

FIGURE 39A-3   Effects of Shifts in the *IS* and *LM* Curves

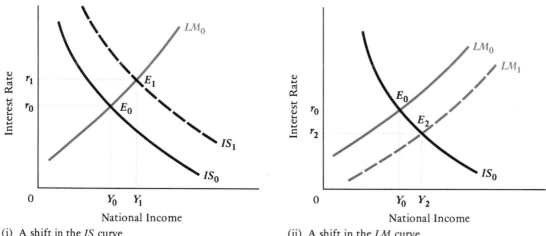

(i) A shift in the *IS* curve   (ii) A shift in the *LM* curve

Similar shifts in the *IS* and *LM* curves have similar effects on national income and opposite effects on the rate of interest. The initial levels of income and interest rate are Y_0 and r_0 in both parts of the figure. In part (i) a rightward shift in the *IS* curve from IS_0 to IS_1 raises national income from Y_0 to Y_1 and raises the rate of interest from r_0 to r_1. In part (ii) a rightward shift in the *LM* curve from LM_0 to LM_1 raises national income from Y_0 to Y_2 and lowers the rate of interest from r_0 to r_2. Part (i) shows the effect of an increase in government expenditure; part (ii) shows the effect of an increase in the money supply.

this rightward shift because (1) the conditions for monetary equilibrium summarized in the *LM* curve mean that an increase in national income must be accompanied by an increase in the interest rate, and (2) an increase in the interest rate gives rise to a fall in the level of interest-sensitive spending in the economy. The weaker either of these two effects is, the stronger the effects of the increase in government spending will be. The more interest-elastic the demand for money, the flatter will be the *LM* curve, and hence the less the interest rate will rise in response to the fiscal stimulus. The less interest-elastic desired expenditure is, the steeper will be the *IS* curve and the smaller the "crowding out" of private investment following a fiscal expansion.

Now consider monetary policy. An increase in the money supply causes the *LM* curve to shift to the right; this leads to a fall in the interest rate and an increase in interest-sensitive expenditure. As a

result there is a movement down and to the right along the *IS* curve, and national income rises. The rise in national income will be larger (1) the larger the fall in the interest rate and (2) the larger the induced increase in interest-sensitive expenditure. The less interest-elastic the demand for money is, the steeper will be the *LM* curve and the larger the fall in the interest rate following a monetary expansion. The more interest-elastic desired expenditure is, the flatter will be the *IS* curve and the larger the induced increase in interest-sensitive expenditure.

Monetarists, then, in this debate tended to think of the demand for money as relatively interest-insensitive and desired expenditure as relatively interest-sensitive; this gives rise to the combination of a steep *LM* curve and a flat *IS* curve with the implication of effective monetary policy and ineffective fiscal policy. Keynesians, by contrast, tended to think of the opposite combination of interest-sensitive money demand and interest-insensitive desired expenditure; this gives rise to a steep *IS* curve and a flat *LM* curve with the implication of effective fiscal policy and ineffective monetary policy.

The Price Level and Aggregate Demand

So far we have treated the price level as given and presumed that all changes in national income were changes in *real* output. Consider now what would happen to the analysis if the price level were allowed to vary.

Changes in the Price Level

As we saw in Box 34-2 on pages 750–751, an increase in the price level leads to an increase in liquidity preference. For money market equilibrium to be preserved, the interest rate must rise, the level of income must fall, or, since either leads to a reduction in money demand, some combination of both must occur. That is, the *LM* curve must shift upward and to the left.

A fall in the price level reduces liquidity preference, and the *LM* curve shifts down and to the right.

Increases in the price level cause the *LM* curve to shift upward to the left; decreases in the price level cause the *LM* curve to shift downward to the right.

But we know that the effect in the first case is to reduce national income, while the effect in the second case is to increase national income. This is illustrated in Figure 39A-4.

Equilibrium in the money and goods markets combined implies that the price level and national income are negatively related, as summarized in the downward-sloping aggregate demand curve.

The negative relationship between the price level and national income summarized in the aggregate demand curve is a straightforward extension of the transmission mechanism running from liquidity

FIGURE 39A-4   Derivation of Aggregate Demand

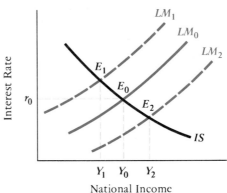

(i) *IS-LM* model

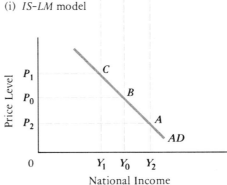

(ii) Aggregate demand

Changes in the price level shift the *LM* curve and thus change the equilibrium level of income. An increase in the price level increases the demand for money. Alternatively, it can be seen as reducing the real value of the existing money stock. The excess demand for money leads to a leftward shift in the LM_0 curve to LM_1 and a fall in national income. A fall in the price level creates an excess supply of money and a rightward shift in the LM_0 curve to LM_2. The price level and national income are inversely related, as shown by the *AD* curve in part (ii).

preference to the rate of interest to aggregate expenditure.

Shifts in the Aggregate Demand Curve

The *AD* curve was derived on the basis of a given money supply and given relationships underlying the

IS curve; it is a straightforward exercise to demonstrate that fiscal and monetary policies, by influencing the *IS* and *LM* curves, cause the *AD* curve to shift. [53]

An increase in the money supply means that the *LM* curve corresponding to any particular price level shifts downward to the right. Hence that price level now corresponds to a higher level of real national income; that is, the *AD* curve shifts to the right as a result of an increase in the money supply.

An increase in government expenditure causes the *IS* curve to shift upward to the right as before; it now intersects any given *LM* curve at a higher level of national income. Again, any given price level now corresponds to a larger real national income; that is, the *AD* curve shifts to the right as a result of an increase in government expenditure.

Does the Deficit Matter?

Analysts who focus on the deficit as a summary description of the government's influence on the economy presuppose that tax-financed government expenditure contributes less to aggregate demand than bond-financed government expenditure, since the latter leads to a larger deficit. Note that deficit financing of government expenditure can be viewed as a deferral of taxes, increasing current disposable income and reducing future disposable income. This rearrangement of the timing of taxes may leave expected permanent income basically unchanged compared to the case where taxes were levied at the same time as the government expenditure occurred. While the Keynesian consumption function predicts that consumption would increase with the increase in current disposable income, the permanent-income hypothesis (PIH), discussed in the appendix to Chapter 32, predicts that households' consumption is related to their lifetime or permanent income, not their current disposable income. If the PIH is an accurate description of behavior, deficit finance will have little effect on consumption behavior.

Thus it is possible to identify a set of conditions that would mean that government expenditure have the same effect on the economy whether it is financed by raising current taxes or by issuing government bonds. That imaginary world, first considered by David Ricardo in 1817 and recently revived by Professor Robert Barro, is populated by far-sighted individuals whose consumption decisions depend on their "permanent" income only. Thus changes in the time pattern of income receipts that leave their permanent income unchanged would have no effect on private-sector expenditure decisions.

In this world government bonds would not be net wealth because the financial value of a bond would be matched exactly by a corresponding liability for future tax payments needed to service the debt. Specifically, households would be indifferent between paying $1 of current taxes and paying a stream of future taxes that has a present value of $1 when discounted at the market interest rate. In this case the government deficit would not matter; bond rather than tax finance would merely represent a rearrangement in the timing of income receipts that the private sector could (and would) offset in capital markets. Issuing bonds now and raising taxes later would be viewed as equivalent to raising taxes now.

The theory underlying this analysis requires that households have an infinite planning horizon, as in the PIH discussed in the Appendix to Chapter 32. Otherwise taxes accruing after the household's lifetime would not offset interest payments received during the household's lifetime, and government bonds would be viewed as net wealth by the household. Hence deficits would increase households' perceived net wealth, households would increase their consumption, and deficit-financed government expenditure would be more expansionary than tax-financed expenditure.

Barro's contribution was to show that debt neutrality could arise even in the context of the life-cycle hypothesis if the household's concern for its heirs caused its planning horizon to extend beyond its own lifetime. Suppose that the typical household, when making its own lifetime consumption plans, also plans for a positive bequest that it intends to leave to its heirs. Now consider the effects of a government decision to sell bonds rather than increase taxes in order to finance previously announced government expenditure; this of course increases the government budget deficit. (Thus we are focusing on the effects of the method of financing the expenditure, not on the effects of the expenditure itself.) If the households wished, they could simply spend the increased disposable income that results from not having to pay current taxes to finance the government expenditure, thus leaving the next generation with a liability to pay the taxes that will have to be levied when the government redeems the bonds. If the recipients behave in this manner, the fiscal authority's decision to rely on deficit financing will have stimulated the economy by inducing an increase in spending.

However, this behavior would reduce the net value of the bequest that the typical household would be leaving to its heirs, since the heirs now face an increased tax liability. This violates the notion that the members of a typical household make a rational plan that includes targets for their own consumption and for the bequest that they wish to leave to their heirs, since the government action does not change the options open to current households. The current households could have achieved this redistribution away from future generations toward themselves without the government action simply by increasing their own consumption and reducing the value of the estate they leave to their heirs.

If they wish to preserve their initial plan, all that current households need to do is maintain their spending plans and increase saving by the full amount of the increase in their disposable income, that is, by the increase in the government budget deficit. The resulting increase in the value of the next generation's inheritance will exactly offset the increase in tax liabilities that they face. Thus a government deficit that issues bonds now and "promises" taxes in the future would have no effect even if the taxes were expected only after the current generation were dead.

Note that the level of government expenditure is still important in this model—only the method of financing is irrelevant. But there are a number of reasons to believe that future taxes that have a present value of $1 are not equivalent to present taxes of $1 and thus that this debt-neutral Ricardian model does not provide an accurate description of the working of a modern economy. (Ricardo himself rejected it.) Let us cite but three reasons.

The private sector borrows on different terms than the government sector. This is perhaps the most important reason why deficit financing is not neutral in practice. In many circumstances households, and to some extent firms, face constraints that prevent them from borrowing all that they would like to at the prevailing market interest rate. Alternatively, they may be able to borrow but at a much higher interest rate than that facing the government. Consequently, when the government substitutes future taxes for present taxes by running a deficit, these "constrained" private-sector agents will feel wealthier and, consequently, will spend more.

Myopic perception. If some households imperfectly perceive the future tax liabilities implied by the government deficit, they will not offset government dissaving with private saving.

Finite lifetimes. Another reason why households might view future taxes as not equivalent to current taxes is that future taxes may extend beyond the expected lifetime of the household. Thus the household may anticipate escaping taxes by dying! As Barro points out, this would make no difference if households "care about their heirs"; in this case living households would simply alter any bequests they had planned to leave to their heirs by an amount equal to the expected increase in future taxes borne by their heirs. However, if currently alive households do not care or are unable to alter their bequests (perhaps because such bequests cannot be reduced below their current zero level), living households will in fact react to a change in the deficit in a manner that does not completely offset it.

Conclusions

The basic feature of the economy that makes government deficits and the public debt matter is that to a significant extent, current private-sector expenditure is tied to current private-sector income. The government deficit influences the current income of the private sector, since for a given level of government expenditure a larger deficit means lower current taxes and hence larger current private disposable income. In the first instance this debt finance simply causes an intertemporal rearrangement of private-sector income. But for the reasons noted, the private sector is not indifferent to this rearrangement of its income receipts. In particular, current private-sector expenditure rises in response to the increase in current income. This influence of government deficits on private spending not only creates the potential for a stabilization role for deficits over the business cycle, but it also creates the mechanism by which persistent deficits become costly and undesirable in the longer run.

PART ELEVEN

International Macroeconomics

40

Exchange Rates and the Balance of Payments

The value of the Canadian dollar is of great concern to many people. It affects the decisions of a Japanese firm wanting to sell cars in Canada, a Canadian wanting to buy a German government bond, a French exporter selling kitchen appliances to Canada, a Canadian firm hoping to sell commuter airplanes to American feeder airlines, and exporters of Canadian wood and mineral products in markets where prices are quoted in U.S. dollars. It also matters to Canadian tourists cashing their traveler's cheques in London, Athens, or Bangkok.

In this chapter we are concerned with what it means to speak of the "price of the dollar" and what causes that price to change. The discussion will bring together material on three topics studied elsewhere in this book: the theory of supply and demand (Chapter 4), the nature of money (Chapter 33), and international trade (Chapter 20).

We shall examine the simple case of a **small open economy (SOE),** which is an economy that can exert no influence on the world prices of traded goods. The quantities it exports and imports are small in relation to the total volume of world trade in these commodities. Thus the country must accept prices that are established in world markets. For many countries such as Canada, and for many commodities such as wheat, forest products, and minerals, this is a reasonable assumption.

The small open economy faces terms of trade that are fixed by forces beyond its control.

The Nature of Foreign Exchange Transactions

We have seen that money, which consists of any accepted medium of exchange, is vital in any sophisticated economy that relies on specialization and exchange. Yet money as we know it is a *national* matter, one closely controlled by national governments. If you live in Sweden, you will earn kronor and spend kronor; if you run a business in Austria, you borrow schillings and meet your payroll with schillings. The currency of a country is acceptable within the bounds of that country, but it will not usually be accepted by households and firms in another country. The Stockholm bus company will accept kronor for a fare but not Austrian schillings. The Austrian worker will not take Swedish kronor for wages but will accept schillings.

The situation is similar in Canada except that our proximity to the United States leads many Canadian sellers to accept U.S. dollars over the counter. Because U.S. dollars are so well known and so common, Canadian merchants are willing to accept them and then do what the customer would otherwise have had to do: take the money to the bank and exchange it for Canadian money.

When Canadian producers sell their products, they require payment in Canadian dollars. They must meet their wage bills, pay for their raw materials, and reinvest or distribute their profits. There is no problem when they sell to Canadian purchasers. However, if they sell their goods to Indian importers, either the Indians must exchange their rupees to acquire dollars to pay for the goods, or the Canadian producers must accept rupees. They will accept rupees only if they know that they can exchange the rupees for the dollars that they require. The same holds true for producers in all countries: They must eventually receive payment for the goods that they sell in terms of the currency of their own country.

In general, trade between nations can occur only if it is possible to exchange the currency of one nation for that of another.

The exchange rate. International payments that require the exchange of one national currency for another can be made in a bewildering variety of ways, but in essence they involve the exchange of currencies between people who have one currency and require another. Suppose that a Canadian firm wishes to acquire £3,000 for some purpose (£ is the symbol for the British pound sterling). The firm can go to its bank or to some other seller of foreign currency and buy a check that will be accepted in the United Kingdom as £3,000. How many *dollars* the firm must pay to purchase this check will depend on the price of pounds in terms of dollars.

The exchange of one currency for another is part of the process of foreign exchange. The term **foreign exchange** refers to the actual foreign currency or various claims on it, such as bank deposits

or promises to pay, that are traded for each other. The **exchange rate** is the price at which purchases and sales of foreign currency or claims on it take place; it is the amount of home currency that must be paid in order to obtain one unit of the foreign currency. For example, if one must give up $2.00 to get £1.00, the exchange rate is 2.[1]

A rise in the price of foreign exchange (i.e., a rise in the exchange rate) is a **depreciation** of the home currency. *Foreign currencies have become more expensive; therefore, the relative value of the home currency has fallen.* A fall in the price of foreign exchange (i.e., a fall in the exchange rate) is an **appreciation** of the home currency. *Foreign currencies have become cheaper; therefore, the relative value of home currency has risen.* For example, when the dollar price of sterling rises from $2.00 to $2.50 (in other words, the sterling price of the dollar falls from £.50 to £.40), the dollar has *depreciated* and the pound has *appreciated*.

The mechanism of foreign exchange transactions. Let us see how foreign exchange transactions are carried out. Suppose that a Canadian firm wishes to purchase a British sports car to sell in Canada. The British firm that made the car requires payment in pounds sterling. If the car is priced at £15,000, the Canadian firm will go to its bank, purchase a cheque for £15,000, and send the cheque to the British seller. Let us suppose this requires that the firm pay $15,000.[2] (The exchange rate in this transaction is £1.00 = $1.67, or $1.00 = £.60.) The British firm deposits the cheque in its bank.

Now assume that in the same period of time a British wholesale firm purchases 25 Canadian refrigerators to sell in Britain. If the refrigerators are priced at $1,000 each, the Canadian seller will have to be paid $25,000. To make this payment the British importing firm goes to its bank, writes a cheque on its account for £15,000, and receives a cheque drawn on a Canadian bank for $25,000. The cheque is sent to

---

[1] This expresses the relative values of the two currencies in terms of the dollar price of one pound sterling. Alternatively, one could consider the pound sterling price of $1.00 which in this example is £.50.

[2] Banks charge a small commission for making currency exchanges, but we shall ignore this and assume that parties can exchange moneys back and forth at the going exchange rate.

Canada and deposited in a Canadian bank. The effects of these transactions are shown in Table 40-1.

The two transactions cancel each other out, and there is no net change in international liabilities. No money need pass between British and Canadian banks; each bank merely increases the deposit of one domestic customer and lowers the deposit of another. Indeed, as long as the flow of payments between the two countries is equal (Canadians pay as much to British residents as British residents pay to Canadians), all payments can be managed as in the example, and there will be no need for a net payment from British banks to Canadian banks.

All these calculations involve comparing magnitudes measured in different currencies. These comparisons are done using the exchange rate. We now turn to an analysis of how such exchange rates are determined.

Determination of Exchange Rates

As a first step we must look at the link between exchange rates and the prices of a country's imports and exports.

Exchange Rates and the Domestic Prices of Traded Goods

A small open economy faces prices of internationally traded goods that are fixed in foreign currency. The exchange rate translates these into domestic prices. If, for example, the price of wheat is £2 a bushel on international wheat markets, its dollar price in Canada depends on the exchange rate. When the rate is $2 to the pound, the Canadian domestic price of wheat is $4. This is because $4 must be earned from domestic sales in order to match in value the amount that could be earned by selling the wheat internationally for £2 a bushel and by selling the pounds for $2 each.

In Figures 4A-1 and 4A-2 (pages 78 and 79) we showed how imports and exports were determined in an economy facing given world prices for traded goods. We drew the domestic demand and supply curves plotted against domestic prices. We then used the world price, *stated in units of domestic currency,* to determine the quantity of imports and exports of a product. To do this we needed, although we did not say so at the time, an exchange rate so that we could convert world prices into local currency. Recall that we express the exchange rate, *e,* as the number of units of domestic currency needed to buy one unit of foreign currency. The *domestic* price of traded goods, p_d, is then the *world* price of traded goods expressed in foreign currency, p_f, multiplied by the exchange rate:

$$p_d = (e) \ (p_f)$$

For example, when the international price of wheat is £2 per bushel and the exchange rate is $2 to the pound, the Canadian dollar price of wheat is £2 per bushel times $2 per pound, which is $4 per bushel.

It is now a simple matter to see the effect of a change in the exchange rate on the domestic prices of traded goods. Say, for example, that the Canadian dollar appreciates so that it takes only $1.50 to buy £1.00. The domestic price of a bushel of wheat that costs £2.00 is now only $3.00, since $3.00 is now sufficient to buy £2.00. For a second example, say that the Canadian dollar depreciates so that it now takes $2.50 to buy £1.00. Now the dollar price of wheat rises to $5.00 since it takes $5.00 to buy £2.00. (The formula $p_d = (e) \ (p_f)$ gives the right answer, since $2.50 per pound times £2 per bushel equals $5 per bushel.)

An appreciation of the domestic currency lowers the domestic prices of traded goods, whereas a depreciation raises these prices.

To see the effects of changes in the exchange rate, let us return to the example of the Appendix to Chapter 4, a country that is exporting wheat and importing cloth. A 10 percent depreciation of the country's currency would mean that the domestic currency prices of the two goods must rise by 10 percent. First consider the export good, wheat. Since the sale of a unit of wheat abroad still yields the same amount of foreign exchange, it now yields 10 percent more in terms of domestic currency. Domestic purchasers too

TABLE 40-1   Changes in the Balance Sheets of Two Banks As a Result of International Payments

U.K. bank			Canadian bank		
Assets	Liabilities		Assets	Liabilities	
No change	(1) Deposits of car exporter	+£15,000	No change	(1) Deposits of car importer	−$25,000
	(2) Deposits of refrigerator importer	−£15,000		(2) Deposits of refrigerator exporter	+$25,000
	Net change	0		Net change	0

International transactions involve a transfer of deposit liabilities among banks. The table records two separate international transactions at an exchange rate of $1.00 = £.60: (1) a Canadian purchase of a British car for £15,000 (= $25,000) and (2) a British purchase of Canadian refrigerators for $25,000 (= £15,000). The Canadian's import of a car reduces deposit liabilities to Canadian residents and increases deposit liabilities to British residents. The Britisher's import of refrigerators does the opposite. When a series of transactions are equal in value, there is only a transfer of deposit liabilities among individuals within a country. The Canadian refrigerator manufacturer received (in effect) the dollars the Canadian car purchaser gave up to get a British-made car.

will have to pay 10 percent more, for if the domestic price did not rise, producers would sell only in the export market. Similarly, the purchase of cloth still requires the same amount of foreign currency, but 10 percent more of the domestic currency must be paid to obtain the required amount of foreign currency. Thus the domestic currency price of imported cloth also rises by 10 percent.

The effects of these price changes are illustrated in Figures 40-1 and 40-2. In the markets for wheat and cloth, the increase in the domestic price causes the quantity supplied domestically to rise and the quantity demanded domestically to fall. As a result, the quantity of wheat exported, which is equal to the excess of the quantity supplied domestically over the quantity demanded domestically, *rises* (see Figure 40-1). In the market for cloth, the domestic price rise also causes quantity supplied to increase and quantity demanded to fall. However, since the initial situation was one where domestic supply exceeded domestic demand, this response reduces that excess. As a result, the quantity of cloth imported *decreases* (see Figure 40-2).

For a small country, a depreciation of the domestic currency causes the domestic prices of traded goods to rise, thereby increasing the quantity supplied and reducing the quantity demanded domestically. Therefore, the volume of exports increases while the volume of imports falls.

As a result of these changes, actual net exports, $X - M$, rises. Since $X - M$ is a component of aggregate demand, the depreciation increases the country's aggregate demand. This in turn tends to increase equilibrium national income.

Similarly, an *appreciation* of the domestic currency *lowers* the domestic prices of traded goods. This leads to a reduction in the quantity supplied and an increase in the quantity demanded domestically for both; the quantity of cloth imports now rises while the quantity of wheat exports falls. This is also shown in Figures 40-1 and 40-2.

The Exchange Rate Between Two Currencies

For simplicity we shall consider an example involving trade between Canada and the United Kingdom and the determination of the exchange rate between their two currencies, dollars and sterling. The two-country example simplifies things, but the principles apply to all foreign transactions. Thus sterling stands for foreign exchange in general, and the dollar price of sterling stands for the foreign exchange rate in general.

We can relate our example to the demand and

FIGURE 40-1 Effects of an Increase in the Domestic Currency Price of an Exported Good (Wheat)

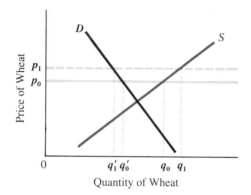

An increase in the domestic currency price of export goods leads to an increase in the volume of exports. Exports of wheat are determined by the domestic excess supply of the tradable good at the domestic price. (The domestic price is the world price adjusted by the exchange rate.) D and S are the domestic demand and supply schedules. If the world price expressed in domestic currency is p_0, quantity q_0 will be produced, of which q_0' will be consumed domestically and $q_0'q_0$ will be exported. A depreciation of the domestic currency or an increase in the world price causes the domestic currency price to rise to p_1. As a result, domestic consumption falls to q_1', quantity supplied rises to q_1, and exports rise to $q_1'q_1$.

FIGURE 40-2 Effects of an Increase in the Domestic Currency Price of an Imported Good (Cloth)

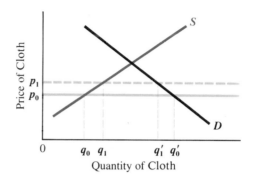

An increase in the domestic currency price of import goods leads to a decrease in the volume of imports. Imports of cloth are determined by the domestic excess demand for cloth at the domestic price. (The domestic price is the world price adjusted by the exchange rate.) D and S are the domestic demand and supply schedules. If the world price expressed in domestic currency is p_0, quantity q_0' will be consumed, of which q_0 will be produced domestically and $q_0'q_0$ will be imported. A depreciation of the domestic currency or an increase in the world price causes the domestic currency price to rise to p_1. As a result, quantity supplied rises to q_1, domestic consumption falls to q_1', and imports fall to $q_1'q_1$.

supply analysis of Chapter 4. To do so we need only to recognize that *in the market for pounds sterling,* the Canadian firm that wants pounds is a demander of pounds and the British firm that is selling pounds to buy dollars is a supplier of pounds. We can also look at the same transaction in the market for dollars: The Canadian firm is a supplier of dollars, and the British firm is a demander of dollars.

Because one currency is traded for another on the foreign exchange market, it follows that to demand dollars implies a willingness to supply foreign exchange, while to supply dollars implies a demand for foreign exchange.

When £1.00 equals $2.00, a British importer who offers to buy $6.00 with pounds must be offering to sell £3.00. Similarly, a Canadian importer who offers to sell $6.00 for pounds must be offering to buy £3.00. For this reason a theory of the exchange rate between dollars and pounds can deal either with the demand for and the supply of dollars or the demand for and the supply of pounds sterling; both need not be considered. We shall concentrate on the demand, supply, and price of pounds sterling (which may be taken to stand for all foreign exchange).

Figure 40-3 plots the exchange rate, the price of sterling measured in Canadian dollars, on the vertical axis, and the quantity of sterling on the horizontal axis. Moving down the vertical scale, the foreign currency (sterling) becomes *cheaper;* it is depreciating on the foreign market while the domestic currency

FIGURE 40-3   The Market for Foreign Exchange

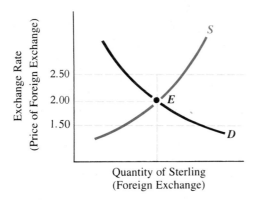

The equilibrium exchange rate equates the demand and supply of foreign exchange. The *S* curve is the supply of sterling to the foreign exchange market to be used to make purchases in Canada. The *D* curve is the demand for sterling in the foreign exchange market to be used to make purchases in the United Kingdom. The quantity of sterling demanded is equal to the quantity supplied at an exchange rate of $2.00 to the pound. If the price of sterling were low, say, $1.50, there would be an excess demand for sterling, which would bid its price up. If the price of sterling were high, say, $2.50, there would be an excess supply of sterling, which would bid its price down.

(the dollar) is appreciating. Moving up the scale, sterling becomes *more expensive;* it is appreciating while the dollar is depreciating.

In more general terms, Figure 40-3 represents the foreign exchange market. It plots the quantity of foreign exchange against the Canadian dollar price of foreign exchange, that is, the Canadian exchange rate. Although we continue to speak of sterling to make the argument easier to follow, everything said about sterling applies to any other foreign currency and to foreign exchange in general.

Supply of Sterling

The supply of sterling to the foreign exchange market arises to finance purchases by foreigners from Canadians. In addition to the purchase of exports studied before, there are purchases of assets previ-

ously owned or newly issued by Canadians (and Canadian governments). Such purchases are called **capital flows.** They play an important role in exchange markets, and we study them in detail later in this chapter; for the present, we continue to focus on international trade in goods and services.

Consider again a representative Canadian export good, wheat. What are the implications for the foreign exchange market of transactions in wheat? We saw in Figure 40-1 that a rise in the exchange rate (a depreciation of the dollar) led to an increase in the *quantity* of wheat exports. Since the pound sterling *price* of wheat is constant (being set on international wheat markets), the supply of pounds to the foreign exchange market must increase. People must be spending more pounds on Canadian wheat, and these pounds go to purchase the Canadian dollars needed to pay for this wheat.

What, then, is the shape of the supply curve of sterling? As we have just seen, if the exchange rate rises, the British will buy more Canadian wheat and will offer more sterling for this purpose. The quantity of pounds supplied will rise. In the opposite case, if the exchange rate falls, the British will buy less Canadian wheat and will thus spend fewer pounds sterling on it.

The supply curve of sterling on the foreign exchange market is upward-sloping when plotted against the dollar price of sterling—that is, against the exchange rate.

Demand for Sterling

In our two-country example, the demand for sterling on the foreign exchange market is merely the opposite side of the supply of dollars. Who wants to sell dollars for foreign exchange? In our example, Canadians seeking to purchase British cloth will require foreign exchange to make those transactions, and hence they will wish to supply dollars in exchange for pounds.[3]

---

[3] A demand for sterling may also result from capital flows if Canadians seek to buy pound sterling assets. As with the supply of sterling, we neglect this for now.

When the exchange rate rises (the Canadian dollar depreciates), the Canadian price of British cloth rises. As we saw in Figure 40-2, Canadians will import less of the now more expensive British cloth. Since the sterling price of cloth is unchanged, buying less cloth means needing less sterling to pay for it. Thus the Canadian demand for sterling falls.

When the exchange rate falls, British cloth exports to Canada become cheaper, and more will be sold. Since the sterling price of cloth is unchanged, buying more still means spending more sterling. Thus there is an increase in the amount of sterling demanded on the foreign exchange market. Together these two changes tell us the shape of the demand curve for sterling:

The demand curve for sterling on the foreign exchange market is downward-sloping when plotted against the dollar price of sterling—that is, against the exchange rate.

Equilibrium Exchange Rates in a Competitive Market

Consider a rate of exchange that is set on a freely competitive market. Like any competitive price, this rate fluctuates according to the conditions of demand and supply.

Assume that the current exchange rate is so low (say, $1.50 in Figure 40-3) that the quantity of sterling demanded exceeds the quantity supplied. Sterling will be in scarce supply; some people who require sterling to make payments to the U.K. will be unable to obtain it, and the price of sterling will be bid up. The dollar will depreciate against the pound, which is the same thing as the pound appreciating against the dollar.

As the dollar price of sterling rises, the dollar price of Canadian imports rise; hence the quantity of imports falls, as does the quantity of sterling demanded on the foreign exchange market to pay for these imports. This is a movement along the demand curve D in Figure 40-3. However, the depreciation of the dollar also leads to a rise in the dollar price of Canadian exports and a resulting increase in the quantity sold abroad. Thus the amount of sterling offered to buy more Canadian exports at an un-

changed sterling price must rise. This is a movement along the supply curve S in Figure 40-3.

Thus a rise in the dollar price of the sterling reduces the quantity of sterling demanded and increases the quantity of sterling supplied. Where the two curves intersect, quantity demanded equals quantity supplied, and the foreign exchange market is in equilibrium.

What happens if the price of foreign exchange is too high? The quantity of sterling demanded will be less than the quantity of sterling supplied. With sterling in excess supply, some people who wish to convert sterling into dollars will be unable to do so. The price of sterling will fall, less sterling will be supplied, more will be demanded, and an equilibrium will be re-established.

A foreign exchange market is like other competitive markets in that the forces of demand and supply tend to lead to an equilibrium price in which quantity demanded equals quantity supplied.

Changes in Exchange Rates

What causes exchange rates to vary? The simplest answer to this question is changes in demand or supply in the foreign exchange market. Anything that shifts the demand curve for sterling to the right or the supply curve for sterling to the left leads to a depreciation of the dollar. Anything that shifts the demand curve for sterling to the left or the supply curve for sterling to the right leads to an appreciation of the dollar. This is nothing more than a restatement of the laws of supply and demand, applied now to the market for foreign currencies.

But what causes the shifts in demand and supply that lead to changes in exchange rates? There are many causes, some of them transitory and some persistent; we shall mention several of the most important ones.

Foreign Inflation

First consider the case where the rest of the world inflates while the local country does not, so that its domestic costs and the prices of domestic (nontraded) goods remain unchanged. But the world price of all traded goods rises, so that at the initial exchange rate the prices of traded goods also rise in the domestic country.

We saw in Figures 40-1 and 40-2 that the rise in the prices of exported and imported goods leads our country to increase the quantity of its exports while decreasing the quantity of its imports. These changes will cause shifts in the demand and supply curves in the foreign exchange market. More Canadian exports sold at a higher world price mean more foreign exchange offered in return for Canadian dollars. The supply curve of foreign exchange shifts right, as shown in Figure 40-4. Fewer imports purchased at higher foreign prices means less spent on imports, as long as the percentage fall in the quantity demanded exceeds the percentage rise in the price.[4] The demand curve for foreign exchange shifts left, as shown in Figure 40-4.

Now at the original exchange rate there is an excess supply of foreign exchange, and the market exchange rate falls to its new equilibrium level. The exchange rate falls, which is the same thing as an appreciation of the Canadian dollar.

A foreign inflation, other things equal, will lead to an appreciation of the Canadian dollar.

Domestic Inflation

Suppose now that foreign prices are constant but there is an increase in domestic wages and other costs of production and in the price of local goods and services—things such as haircuts and restaurant meals that are not traded internationally. As a result of the rise in costs, the supply curves for imports and exports will shift upward. As a result of the rise in prices of nontraded goods, the demand curves for traded goods will shift upward. This is because at

---

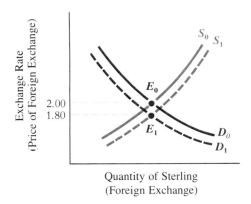

FIGURE 40-4   Foreign Inflation and the Exchange Rate

Foreign inflation will increase the supply of foreign exchange and decrease the demand, thus causing an appreciation of the dollar. The initial supply and demand curves are shown by the solid curves (labeled D_0 and S_0), and the initial equilibrium is at E_0. Now suppose that a foreign inflation occurs. This raises the foreign price of all tradable goods. At any given exchange rate, this will cause an increase in the dollar price of traded goods and, as we saw in Figures 40-1 and 40-2, the quantity of exports will increase and the quantity of imports will fall as a result. The increase in exports gives rise to an increase in the supply of sterling, as shown by the shift from S_0 to S_1. The decrease in imports gives rise to a fall in the demand for foreign exchange, as shown by the shift in the demand curve from D_0 to D_1. As a result, the dollar appreciates as the price of sterling falls from \$2.00 to \$1.80.

---

any given exchange rate, traded goods are now cheaper relative to domestic or nontraded goods, so more will be demanded and less will be supplied. As a result, the quantity of imports will rise and the quantity of exports will fall. This situation is shown in Figure 40-5.

At any given exchange rate, these changes in the quantities of imports and exports will cause the supply and demand of foreign exchange to change. The decrease in exports will cause the quantity of sterling supplied to the foreign exchange market to decrease—in terms of Figure 40-4, the supply curve of sterling shifts left from S_1 to S_0. The increase in

---

[4] This is true as long as the elasticity of demand for imports is greater than one—the fall in the volume of imports will then swamp the rise in price, and hence fewer dollars will be spent on them. This elasticity condition is related to a famous, long-standing issue in international economics. In what follows, we adopt the standard case of the condition's being met. In a more general form, it is called the *Marshall-Lerner condition* after two famous economists who first studied the problem.

imports will cause the quantity of sterling demanded in the foreign exchange market to increase—in terms of Figure 40-4, the demand curve shifts right from D_1 to D_0. As a result, the equilibrium moves from E_1 to E_0 and the exchange rate rises; that is, the dollar depreciates.

A local Canadian inflation will lead to a depreciation of the Canadian dollar (a rise in the exchange rate).

Inflation in Both Countries

Now consider a case where the domestic country suffers exactly the same rate of inflation as the rest of the world. Now the demand and supply curves for traded goods in Figure 40-5 shift upward as before, but so does the world price of imports and exports. (The rise in the world price is not shown in the figure.) The two shifts offset each other. The upward shifts in the curves tend to reduce exports and increase imports, while the upward shift in world prices tends to increase exports and reduce imports. With equal rates of inflation in Canada and the rest of the world, relative prices of Canadian and the other country's goods remain unchanged at the old exchange rate. There is no reason to expect any change in either country's demand for imports at the original exchange rate and hence in the demands for and supplies of foreign exchange. The inflations in the two countries leave the equilibrium exchange rate unchanged.

Offsetting inflation in two countries will leave the incentive to import and to export unchanged and thus will cause no change in the exchange rate.

Unequal Inflation

The foregoing analysis suggests that the *relative rates of inflation* between two trading countries is an important determinant of exchange rate changes. Differences in the inflation rates will cause changes in imports and exports and hence changes in quantities demanded and supplied on the foreign exchange market. Thus the exchange rate between the two

currencies will change. The general conclusion that follows from a simple extension of the cases just studied is this:

If the price level of one country is rising relative to that of another country, the equilibrium value of its currency will be falling relative to that of the second country.

Capital Movements

Major capital flows can exert strong influences on exchange rates. For example, an increased desire to invest in British assets will shift the demand curve for sterling to the right and cause the dollar to depreciate.

A movement of investment funds has the effect of appreciating the currency of the capital-importing country and depreciating the currency of the capital-exporting country.

This statement is true for all capital movements, short term or long term. Since the motives that lead to large capital movements are likely to be different in the short and long terms, however, it is worth considering each.

Short-term capital movements. A major motive for short-term capital flows is a change in interest rates. International traders hold transactions balances just as domestic traders do. These balances are often lent out on short-term loan rather than being left idle. Naturally, the holders of these balances will tend to lend them, other things being equal, in the markets where interest rates are highest. Thus if one major country's short-term rate of interest rises above the rates in most other countries, there will tend to be a large inflow of short-term capital into that country to take advantage of the high rate, and this will tend to appreciate the currency. If these short-term interest rates should fall, there will likely be a sudden shift away from that country as a source of transactions balances, and its currency will tend to depreciate.

A second motive for short-term capital movements is speculation about a country's exchange rate. If foreigners expect the dollar to appreciate, they will

FIGURE 40-5   Domestic Inflation and International Trade

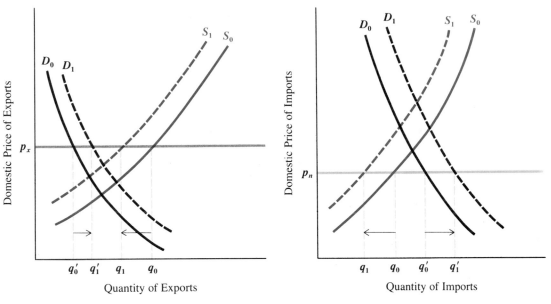

(i) The fall in exports

(ii) The rise in imports

Domestic inflation unmatched in the rest of the world increases the domestic demand for traded goods and reduces the domestic supply; as a result, the quantity of exports falls and the quantity of imports rises. The initial supply and demand curves are shown by the solid lines D_0 and S_0 in both parts of the figure. In each market the initial quantity supplied is given by q_0 and the initial quantity demanded by q_0'. Initial exports are given in part (i) by $q_0'q_0$ and initial imports in part (ii) by q_0q_0'.

A domestic inflation causes the demand curves for each traded good to shift rightward from D_0 to D_1 and the supply curve for each to shift leftward from S_0 to S_1. As a result, quantity demanded rises from q_0' to q_1' and quantity supplied falls from q_0 to q_1.

In the market for exports, where domestic supply initially exceeded demand, the inflation thus causes exports to fall, from $q_0'q_0$ to $q_1'q_1$. (In turn, this means that the demand for dollars in the foreign exchange market falls, as shown by a shift from D_1 to D_0 in Figure 40-4.)

In the market for imports, where domestic demand initially exceeded supply, the inflation thus causes imports to rise, from q_0q_0' to q_1q_1'. (In turn, this means that the supply of dollars to the foreign exchange market rises, as shown by a shift from S_1 to S_0 in Figure 40-4.)

rush to buy assets that pay off in dollars; if they expect the dollar to depreciate, they will be reluctant to buy or hold Canadian securities.

Long-term capital movements.   Long-term movements are largely influenced by long-term expectations about another country's profit opportunities

and the long-run value of its currency. A British firm would be more willing to purchase a Canadian factory if it expected that the dollar profits would buy more sterling in future years than the profits from investment in a British factory. This could happen if the Canadian firm earned greater profits than the British firm, with exchange rates unchanged. It could also happen if the profits were the same but the British firm expected the dollar to appreciate relative to the pound.

Structural Changes

An economy can undergo structural changes that alter the equilibrium exchange rate. *Structural change* is an omnibus term for a change in cost structures, the invention of new products, or anything else that affects the pattern of comparative advantage. For example, when a country's products do not improve as rapidly as those of some other country, consumer demand (at fixed prices) shifts slowly away from the first country's products and toward those of its foreign competitors. This causes a slow depreciation in the first country's currency because the demand for its currency is shifting slowly leftward.

The Balance of Payments

Balance-of-Payments Accounts

To know what is happening to the course of international trade, governments keep track of the transactions among countries. The record of such transactions is made in the **balance-of-payments accounts.** Each transaction, such as a shipment of exports or the arrival of imported goods, is classified according to the payments or receipts that would typically arise from it. Table 40-2 shows the major items in the Canadian balance-of-payments accounts for 1986.

Current Account

The **current account** records payments arising from trade in goods and services and from income in the form of interest, profits, and dividends arising from capital owned in one country and invested in another. The current account is divided into two main sections.

The first is variously called the **balance of trade,** the **trade account,** the **visible account,** and the **merchandise account.** It records payments and re-

TABLE 40-2 Canadian Balance of International Payments, 1986 *(billions of dollars)*

Current Account		
Merchandise exports	+	120.6
Merchandise imports	−	110.2
Balance of merchandise trade	+	10.4
Exports of services	+	17.7
Imports of services	−	20.9
Balance of trade	+	7.2
Net investment income	−	16.9
Transfers	+	1.5
Balance on current account	−	8.2
Capital Account		
New direct investment	+	1.6
Other long-term capital flows	+	15.9
Total long-term capital flows	+	17.5
Short-term capital flows	−	3.2
Balance on capital account	+	14.3
Current Plus Capital Account	+	6.1
Statistical discrepancy[a]	−	5.0
Use of official reserves (increase −, decrease +)	−	1.1
Overall balance of payments	(Always zero)[a]	

[a] In balance-of-payments accounts there is a "statistical discrepancy" item that results from the inability to measure some industrial items accurately. For example, many capital transactions are not recorded.

The overall balance of payments always balances, but the individual components do not have to. In 1986 Canada shows a positive (surplus) merchandise trade balance (exports exceed imports) and a negative (deficit) balance on current account. There is a positive (surplus) balance on capital account because capital exports exceeded capital imports. The capital *plus* current account balance is what is commonly referred to as the *balance of payments.* It is exactly matched by the balance in the official account, i.e., the use of official reserves.

ceipts arising from the import and export of tangible goods such as computers, cars, wheat, and shoes. Canadian imports require the use of foreign exchange and hence are entered as debit items on the visible account. Canadian exports earn foreign exchange and hence are recorded as credit items.

The second section of the current account is called the **invisible account** or the **service account.** It records payments arising out of trade in services and payments for the use of capital. Trade in such services as insurance, shipping, and tourism is entered in the invisible account, as are payments of interest, dividends, and profits made for capital used in one country but owned by residents of another country.

Items that use foreign exchange, such as purchases by Canadian residents of foreign insurance and shipping services, travel abroad by Canadians, and payments to foreign residents of interest earned in Canada, are entered as debit items. Items that earn foreign exchange, such as foreign purchases of Canadian insurance and shipping services, travel by foreigners in Canada, and payments to Canadian residents of interest earned abroad, are entered as credit items.

Given Canada's long history of being a net international borrower, the payment of interest and dividends on foreign loans and investments is a substantial item in the Canadian balance-of-payments accounts. When an American corporation owns a subsidiary in Canada, it receives dividend payments in Canadian dollars. If the American owners wish to spend these dividends at home, they will need to exchange Canadian for American dollars. Interest and dividends paid to foreigners thus use up foreign exchange and are entered as debit items on the balance of payments. Usually the debt-servicing entry is sufficiently large to cause the current account to be in deficit even when the trade account shows a substantial surplus. Some concerns about this tendency to run current account deficits are taken up in Box 40-1.

Capital Account

The second main division in the balance of payments is the **capital account,** which records transactions related to international movements of financial capital. The export of funds from Canada, called a *capital export,* uses foreign exchange and so is entered as a debit item in the Canadian payments accounts. The import of funds into Canada, called a *capital import,* earns foreign exchange and so is entered as a credit item in the payments statistics.

It may seem odd that a merchandise export is a credit item on current account but the export of capital is a debit item. To see that there is no con-

tradiction between the treatments of goods and capital, consider the export of Canadian funds for investment in a British bond. The capital transaction involves the purchase, and hence the *import,* of a British bond, and this has the same effect on the balance of payments as the purchase, and hence the import, of a British good. Both items involve payments to foreigners, and both use foreign exchange. Both are thus debit items in Canadian balance-of-payments accounts.

The capital account often distinguishes between movements of short-term and long-term capital. Short-term capital is money held in the form of highly liquid assets, such as bank accounts and short-term treasury bills. If a nonresident merchant buys dollars and places them in a deposit account in Toronto, this represents an inflow of short-term capital into Canada, and it will be recorded as a credit item on short-term capital account. Long-term capital represents funds coming into Canada (a credit item) or leaving Canada (a debit item) to be invested in less liquid assets such as long-term bonds or physical capital such as a new car assembly plant.

The two major subdivisions of the long-term part of the capital accounts are direct investment and portfolio investment. **Direct investment** relates to changes in nonresident ownership of domestic firms and resident ownership of foreign firms. Thus one form of direct investment in Canada is capital investment in a branch plant or subsidiary corporation in Canada in which the investor has voting control. Another form is a takeover in which a controlling interest in a firm previously controlled by residents is acquired by foreigners. **Portfolio investment,** by contrast, is investment in bonds or a minority holding of shares that does not involve legal control.

Use of Official Reserves

The final section in the balance-of-payments account represents transactions in the *official reserves* held by a country's central bank. These transactions reflect the financing of the balance on the remainder of the accounts. The central banks of most countries hold reserves of funds to use to buy and sell in the foreign exchange market. Some of these reserves are held in

BOX 40-1

Is Canada's Current Account a Cause for Alarm?

Some observers have expressed alarm at the long-term trend in Canada's balance of payments, which shows a large current account deficit matched by a large capital account surplus. Here we address two sources of this alarm.

Is Canada Headed for Financial Ruin?

Concern often arises from the belief that Canada is borrowing abroad to finance a current account deficit that reflects excessive spending. Tourist expenditures of Canadians traveling abroad and interest payments to service past debts are commonly singled out as "causes" of Canada's heavy foreign borrowing. Two contentions are involved: first, that the country is borrowing abroad to help cover a current account deficit, and second, that the policy of financing investment by foreign borrowing is in some way unsound.

The first contention mixes up cause and effect. The various items in the balance of payments represents unrelated decisions by many individuals, firms, and governments, each seeking the best possible economic position. The coordination and reconciliation of these independent actions is accomplished by the foreign exchange market. No one *decides* to borrow in the United States in order to finance an excess of current account payments over receipts. If Canada is to have capital imports, there must be a deficit on

current account. The currency will appreciate until the necessary deficit occurs.

If there had been less foreign borrowing during the period, the Canadian dollar would have depreciated, with the result that the foreign exchange required to finance Canadian travel abroad and the payment of interest and dividends to foreign investors would have been acquired in some other way. There would have been higher exports or lower imports or less travel abroad or more foreigners visiting Canada or some combination of these and other changes in individual balance-of-payments items.

The second contention is more easily dealt with. The relevant question to ask when assessing the economic implications of rapidly rising debt, whether foreign or domestic, is whether the funds raised are being used to finance new investment that will generate sufficient returns in the future to compensate for the burden of interest payments. If Canada's capacity to produce and export is being adequately enhanced by the investment, there is not reason to suppose the country is headed for financial ruin.

The current account deficit reflects the excess of current domestic spending over current income. If spending is high in part because investment is high, the deficit does not mean that Canada is "living beyond its means." If spending is high because current consumption expenditure is high, this may be justified

gold, some in foreign exchange, some as claims on various major foreign currencies, and some in an international currency called special drawing rights (which we study in Chapter 41).

The Bank of Canada, operating on behalf of the government, can intervene in the market for foreign exchange to influence the dollar's exchange rate. For example, to prevent the price of dollars from falling, the Bank must buy dollars. This means it must sell gold or foreign exchange. It can do so only if it holds reserves of these media. When the Bank wishes to stop the dollar from rising in value, it enters the

market and sells dollars. In this case, the Bank buys foreign exchange, which it then adds to its reserves.

The Meaning of Payments Balances and Imbalances

We have seen that the payments accounts show the total of receipts of foreign exchange (credit items) and payments of foreign exchange (debit items) on account of each category of payment. It is also common to calculate the *balance* on separate items or groups of items. The concept of the balance of pay-by the high expected *future* income arising from the current investment. When that income is being earned, the debts accruing due to current borrowing can be repaid, and there will be a current account surplus.

Only to the extent that the foreign borrowing is not accompanied by productive domestic investment is a current account deficit a cause for concern. Recent deterioration of the current account has been linked to the borrowing requirements due to the federal government deficit and has been cited as a potential problem in the future.

Structural Problems and the Balance of Trade

It is commonly alleged that the chronic current account deficit reflects serious structural problems in the Canadian economy. This means essentially that Canada produces the wrong combination of goods so that exports are too low and imports are too high.* In this view, one of the problems arising from the deficit is that the high propensity to import frustrates

---

* A related contention is that our exports are concentrated on raw materials rather than manufacturing goods. For 1986 the merchandise trade balance was a surplus of $10.4 billion, composed of a $16.9 billion surplus in raw materials and a $6.5 billion deficit in manufactured goods.

expansionary policy from having its desired impact on domestic output and employment. The implied policy remedies include the encouragement of domestic production of import substitutes through the use of tariffs and other forms of protection.

If it is true that Canada is not allocating resources properly to exploit its comparative advantage—and hence is producing the "wrong" mix of output—this will be reflected in a reduced value of total output produced. But this reduction in real income will carry with it a reduction in expenditure. A balance-of-trade deficit will arise only if the reduction in real income is greater than the reduction in domestic spending. To put it another way, correction of the structural problem will lead to higher real domestic income *and* therefore higher real domestic spending. The current account deficit will be improved only if income rises by more than spending. (See Box 31–2 on pages 650–651.)

Professor Neil Bruce of Queen's University has challenged the view that structural changes have led to the increased deficit. His research showed fairly constant long-term shares of raw materials and manufactures in Canada's trade. The facts of the Canadian case are that its raw materials base is so broad and varied that *at the aggregate level* there are only relatively moderate changes in the division of total output between the raw materials and manufacturing sectors.

ments is used in a number of ways. These can be confusing, so we must approach this issue in a series of steps.

The Balance of Payments Must Balance Overall

Notice two things about the payments accounts. First, they record *actual* payments, not *desired* payments. Second, they record *all* payments, whatever the reason for which they were made.

It is quite possible that at the existing exchange

rate between dollars and yen, holders of yen want to purchase more dollars than holders of dollars want to sell in exchange for yen. In this situation the quantity of dollars demanded exceeds the quantity supplied. But holders of yen cannot actually buy more dollars than holders of dollars actually sell; every yen that is bought must have been sold by someone, and every dollar that is sold must have been bought by someone.

It follows that if we add up all the receipts arising from (1) payments received by Canadian residents on account of Canadian exports of goods and ser-

BOX 40-2

Why the Balance of Payments Always Balances: An Illustration

Trade Between Two Countries

Suppose that the sole international transaction made this year by a small country called Myopia was an export to Canada of Myopian coconuts worth $1,000. Further suppose that the Myopian central bank issues a local currency, the stigma, but does not operate in the foreign exchange market, so there is no official financing. Finally, suppose that Myopia's self-sufficient inhabitants want no imports. Surely, then, you might think Myopia has an overall favorable balance of $1,000, which is a current account receipt (C_R) with no balancing item on the payments side.

To see why this is wrong, we must ask what the exporter of coconuts did with the dollars he received for his coconuts. If he deposited them in a Toronto bank, this transaction represents a capital export from Myopia. Myopians have accumulated claims on foreign exchange, which they hold in the form of a deposit with a foreign bank. Thus there are two entries in the Myopian accounts—one a credit item for the export of coconuts ($C_R = \$1,000$) and the other a debit item for the export of capital ($K_P = \$1,000$).

The fact that the same firm made both transactions is irrelevant. Although the current account shows a credit balance, the capital account exactly balances this with a debit item. Hence, looking at the *balance of payments* as a whole, the two sides of the account are equal. The balance of payments has balanced—as always it must.

Consider now a slightly more realistic case. If the coconut exporter wants to turn his $1,000 into Myopian stigmas so that he can pay his coconut pickers in local currency, he must find someone who wishes to buy his dollars in return for Myopian currency. But we have assumed that no one in Myopia wants to import, so no one wants to sell Myopian currency for current account reasons. Assume, however, that a wealthy Myopian landowner would like to invest $1,000 in Toronto by buying shares in a Canadian firm. To do so he needs $1,000. The coconut exporter can sell his $1,000 to the landowner in return for stigmas. Now he can pay his local bills. The landowner sells his stigmas to the exporter in return for dollars. Now he can buy the Canadian shares.

vices, (2) capital imports, and (3) purchase of foreign exchange or gold by the Bank of Canada, these must be exactly equal to all payments made by holders of dollars arising from (1) Canadian imports of goods and services, (2) exports of capital, and (3) sale of foreign exchange or gold by the Bank.

This relation is so important that it pays us to write it out in symbols. We let C, K, and F stand for current account, capital account, and use of official reserves, respectively, and use P for payments (debit items) and R for receipts (credit items). Now we can write

$$C_R + K_R + F_R = C_P + K_P + F_P \qquad [1]$$

All this tells us is that if we add up across all transactions, they must balance in total.

Although the relation given in the equation is necessarily true, it often worries students who feel that it need not be true. To help clarify the issue, some apparent exceptions are considered in Box 40-2.

Payments on Specific Parts of the Accounts Do Not Need to Balance

Although the overall total of payments must equal the overall total of receipts, the same zero balance does not have to hold on subsections of the overall accounts. We now look at the balances on parts of the accounts, balances that may be positive or negative. We do this first in relation to particular countries and then in relation to particular subsectors of the account.

Once again the Myopian balance of payments will show two entries, equal in size but opposite in sign. There is a credit item for the export of coconuts (the sale of coconuts earned foreign exchange) and a debit item for the export of capital (the purchase of the Canadian shares used foreign exchange).

Trade Involving Many Countries

In the example, Myopia had what is called a bilateral payments balance with Canada. The *bilateral balance of payments* between any two countries is the balance between the payments and receipts flowing between them. If there were only two countries in the world, their overall payments would have to be in bilateral balance; that is, one country's payments to the other would be equal to its receipts from the other. But this is not true when there are more than two countries.

Suppose that one year later Myopia again sells $1,000 worth of coconuts to Canada and that the landowner does not wish to invest further in Canada, but that the Myopian people wish to buy 200,000 yen's worth of parasols from Japan. (Assume also that on the foreign exchange market $1 trades for 200 yen.) Finally, assume that a Japanese importer wishes to buy $1,000 worth of skateboards from a Canadian company.

Now what in effect happens is that the Myopian coconut exporter sells his $1,000 to the Japanese skateboard importer for 200,000 yen, which the coconut dealer then sells to the Myopian parasol importer in return for Myopian stigmas. (In the real world the exchanges are all done through banks, but this is what happens in effect.) Now the Myopian payments statistics will show a $1,000 bilateral payments surplus with Canada—receipts of $1,000 from Canada on account of coconut exports and no payments to Canada—and a bilateral deficit with Japan of 200,000 yen (equal to $1,000)—$1,000 of payments to Japan on account of parasol imports and no receipts from Japan. But when both countries are considered, Myopia's multilateral payments are in balance.

Country balances. When all foreign countries are taken together, a country's balance of payments must balance, but a country can have bilateral surpluses or deficits with individual foreign countries or groups of countries. In general, the **multilateral balance of payments** refers to the balance between one country's payments to and receipts from the rest of the world. When all items are considered, every country must have a zero multilateral payments balance with the rest of the world, although it can have bilateral surpluses or deficits with individual countries. This important principle is illustrated in the second part of Box 40-2.

Subsection balances. The balance on visible account refers to the difference between the value of Canadian exports of goods and the value of imports of goods. A surplus occurs when exports of goods exceed imports of goods, while a deficit occurs when imports exceed exports. The balance on invisibles refers to the difference between the value of receipts on invisibles and the value of payments for invisibles. The **current account balance** is the sum of the balances on the visible and invisible accounts. It gives the balance between payments and receipts on all income-related items.

As a carryover from a long-discredited eighteenth century economic doctrine called mercantilism, a credit balance on current account (receipts exceed payments) is called a **favorable balance**, while a debit balance (payments exceed receipts) is called an **unfavorable balance**.

BOX 40-3

The Volume of Trade, the Balance of Trade, and the New Mercantilism

Media commentators, political figures, and much of the general public often judge the national balance of payments as they would the accounts of a single firm. Just as a firm is supposed to show a profit, the nation is supposed to secure a balance-of-payments surplus, with the benefits derived from international trade measured by the size of that surplus.

This view is related to the exploitation doctrine of international trade. Since one country's surplus is another country's deficit, one country's gain, judged by its surplus, must be another country's loss, judged by its deficit.

People who hold such views today are echoing an ancient economic doctrine called *mercantilism*. The mercantilists were a group of economists who preceded Adam Smith. They judged the success of trade by the size of the trade balance. In many cases this doctrine made sense in terms of their objective, which was to use international trade as a means of building up the political and military power of the state rather than raising the living standards of its citizens. A balance-of-payments surplus allowed the nation (then and now) to acquire foreign-exchange reserves. (In those days the reserves took the form of gold. Today they are a mixture of gold and claims on the currencies of other countries.) These reserves could then be used to pay armies, composed partly of foreign mercenaries; to purchase weapons from abroad; and generally to finance colonial adventures.

People who advocate this view in modern times are called *neo-mercantilists*. Insofar as their object is to increase the power of the state, they are choosing means that could achieve their ends. Insofar as they are drawing an analogy between what is a sensible objective for a business interested in its own material welfare and what is a sensible objective for a society interested in the material welfare of its citizens, their views are erroneous, for the analogy is false.

If we take the view that the object of economic activity is to promote the welfare and living standards of ordinary citizens, rather than the power of governments, the mercantilist focus on the balance of trade makes no sense. The law of comparative advantage shows that average living standards are maximized by having individuals, regions, and countries specialize in the things they can produce comparatively best and trading to obtain the things they can produce comparatively worst. The more specialization, the more trade.

In this view the gains from trade are to be judged by the volume of trade. A situation in which there is a *large volume* of trade but where each country has a *zero balance* of trade can thus be regarded as quite satisfactory. Furthermore, a change in commercial policy that results in a balanced increase in trade between two countries will bring gain, because it allows for specialization according to comparative advantage even though it causes no change in either country's trade balance.

To the business interested in private profit and to the government interested in the power of the state, it is the balance of trade that matters. To the person interested in the welfare of ordinary citizens, it is the volume of trade that matters.

Mercantilists, both ancient and modern, hold that the gains from trade arise from having a favorable balance of trade. This misses the whole point of the doctrine of comparative advantage, which states that countries can gain from a balanced increase in trade between themselves because of the opportunity it provides for each country to specialize according to its comparative advantage. The modern resurgence of mercantilist views is discussed in Box 40-3.

The balance on capital account gives the difference between receipts of foreign exchange and payments of foreign exchange arising out of capital movements. A surplus, or "favorable" balance, on capital account means that a country is a *net* importer of capital; while a deficit, or "unfavorable" balance, means that the country is a *net* exporter of capital.

Notice that a deficit on capital account, which is referred to as an unfavorable balance, merely indicates that a country is investing abroad. For a country to invest abroad and accumulate assets that will earn income in the future may be a desirable situation. So once again we observe that there is nothing necessarily unfavorable about having an "unfavorable" balance on any of the payments accounts.

A credit balance on official settlements account means that the Bank of Canada has bought more gold and foreign exchange than it has sold. This adds to its reserves of foreign exchange. A deficit balance means that the Bank has sold more gold and foreign exchange than it has bought. This reduces its foreign exchange reserves.

The Relation Between Various Balances

Two important points should be noted at this time. First, since overall payments must balance, the terms *balance-of-payments deficit* and *balance-of-payments surplus* refer to the balance on some part of the payments accounts. Second, because of the necessity for the balance of payments to balance overall, a deficit on any one part of the accounts implies an offsetting surplus on the rest of the accounts. We now consider two important applications of this second statement. The first concerns the balances on current and capital accounts, and the second concerns the use of official reserves and the balances on the remainder of the total accounts.

The current and capital account balances. To make the relation between current and capital balances clear, let us assume that the Bank of Canada does not engage in any foreign exchange transactions. This means that the use of official reserves is zero because both F_R and F_P in Equation 1 are zero.

Now any deficit or surplus on current account must be matched by an equal and opposite surplus or deficit on capital account. For example, if a country has a credit balance on current account, the foreign exchange earned must appear as a debit item in the capital account. The foreign exchange may be used to buy foreign assets or merely stashed away in

foreign bank accounts. In either case there is an outflow of capital from Canada. It is recorded as a debit item because it uses foreign exchange.

We can see this clearly if we return to Equation 1 and set F_R and F_P equal to zero to indicate no transactions by the Bank of Canada. This gives

$$C_R + K_R = C_P + K_P \qquad [2]$$

Now subtract C_P and K_R from both sides of the equation to get

$$C_R - C_P = K_P - K_R \qquad [3]$$

This expresses in equation form what we have just stated in words: A surplus on current account must be balanced by a deficit on capital account (i.e., an outflow of capital), and a deficit on current account must be matched by a surplus on capital account (i.e., an inflow of capital).

One important implication relates to capital transfers. A country that is importing capital has a surplus on capital account and so it *must* have a deficit on current account. This is the position that the United States was in during the mid 1980s. Because of the borrowing requirements of a massive government budget deficit and because the boom made the United States an attractive place in which to invest, there was a massive capital inflow into the United States. This inflow made a current account deficit inevitable. As long as the capital inflow persisted, no policy measure could remove the current account deficit. This issue is considered in more detail in Chapter 41.

Use of official reserves and the rest of the accounts. When people speak of a country as having an overall balance-of-payments deficit or surplus, they are usually referring to the *balance of all accounts excluding use of official reserves*. A balance-of-payments surplus means that the central bank is adding foreign exchange reserves to its holdings; a balance-of-payments deficit means that the central bank is reducing its reserves.

If the central bank does not operate in the foreign exchange market, there can be no overall balance-of-payments deficit or surplus on current plus capital account. Suppose that holders of dollars are trying to buy more foreign exchange than holders of foreign currencies wish to sell in return for dollars. There will be an excess supply of dollars and an excess demand for foreign exchange. The dollar will depreciate on the foreign exchange market until demand equals supply. At this point both desired and actual international payments are in balance.

If exchange rates are completely free to vary, balance-of-payments deficits and surpluses will be eliminated though exchange rate adjustments.

In today's world, though no country need have a balance-of-payments problem, many do have them. As long as governments intervene in foreign exchange markets, there will be balance-of-payments deficits and surpluses. Surpluses will occur whenever the currency is held below its equilibrium level. Persistent deficits will cause persistent losses of reserves; they are evidence that the government is trying to resist longer-term trends for changes in the exchange rate.

Summary

1. International trade can occur only when it is possible to exchange the currency of one country for that of another. The exchange rate between two currencies is the amount of one currency that must be paid to obtain one unit of another currency. Where more than two currencies are involved, there will be an exchange rate between each pair of currencies.

2. The determination of exchange rates in the free market is simply an application of the laws of supply and demand studied in Chapter 4; the item being bought and sold is a nation's money.

3. The supply of foreign exchange arises from Canadian exports of goods and services and from long-term and short-term capital flows into Canada. The demand for foreign exchange arises from Canadian imports of goods and services and from capital flows out of Canada.

4. A depreciation of the dollar (a rise in the exchange rate) raises the domestic price of traded goods. This increases the quantities of such goods supplied domestically and reduces the quantity demanded. As a result, the volume of exports rises and, with it, the supply of foreign exchange. But the volume of imports falls, and with it the demand for foreign exchange. Thus the supply curve for foreign exchange is upward-sloping and the demand curve for foreign exchange is downward-sloping when the quantities demanded and supplied are plotted against the price of foreign exchange measured in terms of Canadian dollars—that is, against the exchange rate.

5. A currency will tend to depreciate if there is a shift to the right of the demand curve for foreign exchange or a shift to the left of the supply curve. Shifts in the opposite directions will tend to appreciate the currency. Shifts are caused by such things as changes in the prices of imports and exports, the rates of inflation in different countries, capital movements, structural changes, expectations about future trends in earnings and exchange rates, and the level of confidence in the currency as a source of reserves.

6. Actual transactions among the firms, households, and governments

of various countries are kept track of and reported in the balance-of-payments accounts. In these accounts any transaction that uses foreign exchange is recorded as a debit item and any transaction that produces foreign exchange is recorded as a credit item. If all transactions are recorded, the sum of all credit items necessarily equals the sum of all debit items since the foreign exchange that is bought must also have been sold.

7. Major categories in the balance-of-payments account are the balance of trade (exports minus imports), current account, capital account, and official financing. The so-called balance of payments is the balance of the current plus capital accounts; that is, it excludes the transactions on official account. Ignoring official settlements, a balance on current account must be matched by a balance on capital account of equal magnitude but opposite sign.

8. There is nothing inherently good or bad about deficits or surpluses. Persistent deficits or surpluses cannot be sustained because the former will eventually exhaust a country's foreign exchange reserves and the latter will do the same to a trading partner's reserves.

Topics for Review

Foreign exchange and exchange rates
Appreciation and depreciation
Sources of the demand for and supply of foreign exchange
Effects on exchange rates of capital flows, inflation, interest rates, and expectations about exchange rates
Balance of trade and balance of payments
Current and capital account
Official financing items
Mercantilist views on the balance and volume of trade

Discussion Questions

1. What is the probable effect of each of the following on the exchange rate of a country, other things being equal?
   a. The quantity of oil imports is greatly increased, but the value of imported oil is lower due to price decreases.
   b. The country's inflation rate falls well below that of its trading partners.
   c. Rising labor costs of the country's manufacturers lead to a worsening ability to compete in world markets.
   d. The government greatly expands its gifts of food and machinery to underdeveloped countries.
   e. A major boom occurs with rising employment.
   f. The central bank raises interest rates sharply.
   g. More domestic oil is discovered and developed.
2. In the mid 1980s the United States became a major importer of capital, partly to finance the large internal budget deficit and partly because the American boom and the European slump made the

United States a highly attractive place in which to invest foreign funds. Predict the effects of this large capital inflow on the U.S. dollar exchange rate and on the balance of payments on current account. Would these developments have anything to do with the upsurge of protectionist sentiment in the Congress during the latter part of the 1980s?

3. In recent years money wages have risen substantially faster in Canada than in the United States. Many Canadians have expressed the fear that their rapidly rising costs will price them out of U.S. markets. Did this fear make sense when the Canadian exchange rate was fixed relative to the American dollar? Does it make sense today when exchange rates are free to vary on the open market?

4. Indicate whether each of the following transactions increases the demand for dollars, the supply of dollars, or neither on foreign exchange markets.

    a. IBM moves $10 million from bank accounts in Canada to banks in Paris to expand operations in France.

    b. The Canadian government extends a grant of $3 million to the government of Peru, which Peru uses to buy farm machinery from a Winnipeg firm.

    c. Canadian investors, responding to higher profits of American rather than Canadian corporations, buy stocks through the New York Stock Exchange.

    d. Several countries stop interest payments on their large debts to Canadian and American banks.

    e. Lower interest rates in Montreal than in London encourage British firms to borrow in the Montreal money market, converting the proceeds into pounds sterling for use at home.

5. "The necessity of the government to stabilize the balance of payments through the settlement account is a relic of the past. It was a by-product of the adherence to a policy of fixed exchange rates." Do you agree?

6. "If a country solves its balance-of-payments problems, it will have solved its foreign trade problems." Discuss.

7. Outline the reasoning behind the following summer 1983 newspaper headline: "U.S. dollar tumbles as American interest rates weaken."

41

Alternative Exchange Rate Systems

The nations of the world have tried many different international monetary systems. No system has been fully satisfactory, and periods of crisis have alternated with periods of stability.

The twentieth century began with a system of fixed exchange rates under the gold standard. This system suffered periodic crises in the post–World War I years but did not collapse until the onset of the Great Depression. The 1930s was a period of experimentation with flexible, market-determined exchange rates. This ended with World War II, when governments fixed exchange rates.

In 1944 the fixed exchange rate regime was formalized by international agreement at a conference in Bretton Woods, New Hampshire. The Bretton Woods system lasted for over a quarter of a century, but its shortcomings and the periods of crisis it induced finally prevailed over its advantages and the periods of stability it afforded. After several attempts to patch it up in the 1970s, the system finally broke down and was gradually abandoned as countries turned one by one to market-determined, flexible exchange rates.

Fixed and Flexible Exchange Rates

Among the principal international monetary systems two extremes can be distinguished. The first is a system in which exchange rates are fixed at announced par values. The gold standard was such a system, and so was Bretton Woods. (The operation and decline of both systems are discussed in the appendix to this chapter.)

The second is a system of freely fluctuating rates determined by market demand and supply in the absence of government intervention. Some countries have come close to this system, first in the 1930s and then since 1971.

Between these two "pure" systems are a variety of possible intermediate cases. The two that we will encounter are known as the *adjustable peg* and the *managed float*. In the adjustable peg system, governments set and attempt to maintain par values for their exchange rates, but they explicitly recognize that circumstances may arise in which they will change the par value. In a managed float, the central bank seeks to have some stabilizing influence on the exchange rate but does not try to fix it at some publicly announced par value.

The International Monetary Fund (also called the IMF and the Fund) was created as part of the Bretton Woods system. Under its original charter the Fund had several tasks. It tried to ensure that countries kept their exchange rates fixed in the short run. It was supposed to ensure that any exchange rate change was really needed to remove a persistent payments disequilibrium and that a single devaluation did not set off a self-canceling round of devaluations. It also made loans—out of funds subscribed by member nations—to governments to support their exchange rates in the face of temporary payments deficits.

The Bretton Woods system has been abandoned, but the Fund survives, although its tasks have changed. For example, the Jamaica Agreement of 1976 amended the IMF charter to ratify the adoption of floating exchange rates and deemphasize gold as a basis for the international payments system.

A Fixed Exchange Rate System

In a system of **fixed exchange rates,** each country's central bank intervenes in the foreign exchange market to prevent that country's exchange rate from going outside a narrow band on either side of its par value.

This system presents one immediate difficulty in that one country must take a passive role with respect to its exchange rate. This is because there is one less exchange rate to be determined than there are countries. In a two-country world containing only Japan and the United States, for example, if the Bank of Japan fixes the exchange rate at 150 yen to the dollar, the U.S. Federal Reserve cannot fix a different rate making the dollar worth, say, 200 yen. Under the Bretton Woods system, all foreign countries fixed their exchange rate against the U.S. dollar. The Fed adopted the passive role; it was the only central bank in the world that did not have to intervene to support a particular value of its currency.

Having picked a fixed exchange rate for its currency against, say, the U.S. dollar, each foreign central bank then had to manage matters so that the chosen rate could actually be maintained. The bank had to be prepared to offset imbalances in demand and supply by government sales or purchases of foreign exchange. In the face of short-term fluctuations in market demand and supply, each central bank could maintain its fixed exchange rate by entering the market and buying and selling as required.

To do this the central bank has to hold reserves

of acceptable foreign exchange. When there is an abnormally low demand for its country's currency on the market, the bank keeps the currency from depreciating by selling foreign exchange and buying up domestic currency. This depletes its reserves of foreign exchange. When there is an abnormally high demand for its country's currency on the foreign exchange market, the bank prevents the currency's appreciating by selling domestic currency in return for foreign exchange. This augments its stocks of foreign exchange.

As long as the central bank is trying to maintain an exchange rate that equates demand and supply for its currency on average, the policy can be successful. Sometimes the bank will be buying and other times selling, but its reserves will fluctuate around a constant average level.

If, however, there is a permanent shift in demand for or supply of a nation's currency on the foreign exchange market, the long-term equilibrium rate will move away from the **pegged rate,** that is, its par value. It will then be difficult to maintain the pegged rate. For example, if there is a major inflation in France while prices are stable in the United States, the equilibrium value of the franc will fall. In a free market the franc would depreciate and the U.S. dollar would appreciate. But a fixed exchange rate is not a free-market rate. If the Bank of France persists in trying to maintain the original exchange rate, it will have to meet the excess demand for U.S. dollars by selling from its reserves. This policy can persist only as long as the Bank has reserves that it is willing to spend to maintain an artificially high price of francs. But the Bank cannot do this indefinitely. Sooner or later the reserves that it has, and those that it can borrow, will be exhausted.

The management of a fixed rate is illustrated in Figure 41-1. The example used is the maintenance by the Bank of England of a fixed exchange rate between sterling and the U.S. dollar.

When the fixed rate is not near the free-market equilibrium rate, controls of various sorts may be introduced in an attempt to shift the demand curve for foreign exchange so that it intersects the supply curve at a rate close to the fixed rate. This is usually done by restricting imports of goods and services or by restricting the export of capital. If the central bank

FIGURE 41-1   A Fixed Exchange Rate

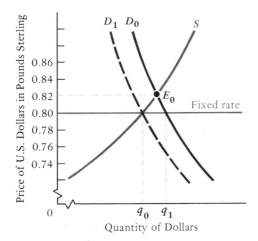

When an exchange rate is fixed at other than the equilibrium rate, either excess demand or excess supply will persist. Suppose demand and supply curves of dollars in the absence of government controls are D_0 and S; equilibrium is at E_0, with a price of £.82 per dollar. The equilibrium price of the pound is $1.22. Now the British authorities peg the price of the pound at $1.25; that is, they fix the price of the dollar at £.80. They have overvalued the pound and undervalued the dollar. As a result there is an excess of dollars demanded over dollars supplied of q_0q_1. To maintain the fixed rate it is necessary to shift either the demand curve or the supply curve (or both) so that the two intersect at the fixed rate. For example, demand might be shifted to D_1 by the British government's limiting imports. If the curves are not shifted, the fixed rate will have to be supported by the British government's supplying dollars in the amount of q_0q_1 per period out of its reserves.

cannot shift demand and supply in order to keep the equilibrium rate approximately as high as the fixed rate, it will have no alternative but to devalue its currency.

Problems with Fixed Exchange Rates

Three problems typically arise in a system of fixed exchange rates: (1) providing sufficient reserves, (2) adjusting to long-term trends, and (3) dealing with speculative crises.

Reserves. Reserves are needed to accommodate short-term balance-of-payments fluctuations arising from the current and the capital accounts. On current account, trade is subject to many short-term variations, some systematic and some random. This means that even if the value of imports does equal the value of exports on average over several years, there may be considerable imbalances over shorter periods.

With a market-determined exchange rate, fluctuations in current and capital account payments would cause the exchange rate to fluctuate. To prevent such fluctuations when rates are fixed, the monetary authorities buy and sell foreign exchange as required. These operations require the authorities to hold reserves of foreign exchange. If they run out of reserves, they cannot maintain the pegged rate.

As discussed in the appendix, the Bretton Woods system had difficulty providing sufficient reserves. This was because the ultimate reserve was gold, and there was not enough of it. As a result, the world's central banks held much of their reserves in U.S. dollars and British pounds sterling. Currencies that are widely held for this purpose are called **reserve currencies**.

This system worked well enough as long as these reserve currencies had a stable value. However, in the mid 1960s fear of an impending devaluation of sterling arose, and in the early 1970s a similar fear arose regarding the U.S. dollar. In both cases the fears were well founded: Sterling was devalued in late 1967, and the dollar was devalued in 1971 and again in 1973.

The devaluation of a reserve currency reduces the value of the reserves of that currency held by the world's central banks. Fear that a devaluation will occur reduces the acceptability of a currency as a means of holding reserves. This is discussed further in Box 41-1.

The problem of providing reserves, although serious, need not be insurmountable in any future system of fixed rates. After all, a balanced portfolio composed of some holdings of a number of currencies could be held as reserves. This would reduce the risks from holding reserves, since whenever one currency falls in value against a second currency, the second currency rises in value against the first.

BOX 41-1

Problems for Nations Whose Currency Is Held As a Reserve

Under the Bretton Woods system, the supply of gold was augmented by reserves of the key currencies, the U.S. dollar and the British pound sterling. While it is prestigious to have one's currency held as a reserve currency—and even advantageous as long as other countries are willing to increase their holdings of one's paper money without making claims on current output—there are both disadvantages and hazards for the country whose currency is involved.

Such a country is placed under great pressure not to devalue its currency. If it does devalue, all countries holding that currency will find the value of their reserves diminished. If it tries to avoid devaluation, the fear that it may be unable to do so will in any case impair the usefulness of the currency as a reserve because other countries will become reluctant to hold it. The result may well be that the domestic policy of the country whose currency is the reserve becomes unduly subservient to the overriding need to maintain its exchange rate.

The Loss of Confidence in the U.S. Dollar As a Reserve Currency

In the 1950s and 1960s America ran frequent deficits on its overall balance of payments. This resulted largely from American loans, investments, and contributions to other nations who were rebuilding their economies after World War II. As long as other nations were willing to accumulate dollar holdings, this caused no problem; indeed, the buildup of dollars provided the growth in foreign exchange reserves that was needed to finance the growing volume of world trade.

The effect of the dollar devaluations of the early 1970s.   Had everyone believed that the devaluations

of 1971 (7.9 percent) and 1973 (11 percent) were just isolated adjustments, they might well have licked their wounds and gone on as before. But no fundamental changes arose either in American policy or in international financial arrangements. Thus many believed that these devaluations were but preludes to inevitable future ones.

Fear of further devaluations not only made holders of U.S. dollars reluctant to increase their holdings but actually led many prudent holders to want to decrease reliance on such a shaky reserve. As people tried to get rid of U.S. dollars, the exchange rate began to slide. Between 1970 and 1973 the U.S. dollar declined 22 percent against the Japanese yen and 30 percent against the German mark. The lower value of the U.S. dollar reduced the adequacy of most countries' dollar reserves and threatened their financial stability.

Attempts to flee from the dollar.   While one country (or one bank) can readily reduce its holdings of U.S. dollars by buying gold or other currencies, for everyone to do so requires major changes in the value of the dollar and its alternatives. In the late 1970s the dollar fell sharply relative to the yen and the mark, and one cause of the startling rise in the price of gold in 1979–1980 from $250 to over $900 an ounce was the attempt of many holders of U.S. dollars to flee to gold.

The return to stable prices in the United States restored some faith in the dollar; indeed, in the period 1981–1984 most observers felt that the dollar was overvalued, so its sharp decline in 1984 was welcomed. While the use of SDRs and other currencies has increased, the dollar still remains the key currency, and the problems discussed in this box remain.

Long-term disequilibria.   With fixed exchange rates, long-term disequilibria can be expected to develop because of lasting shifts in the demands for and sup-

plies of foreign exchange. There are three important reasons for these shifts. First, different trading countries have different rates of inflation. Chapter 40 explained how these varying rates produce changes in the equilibrium rates of exchange; if the rate is fixed, these would produce excess supply or excess demand in each country's foreign exchange market. Second, changes in the demands for and supplies of imports and exports are associated with long-term economic growth. Because the economies of different countries grow at different rates, their demands for imports and their supplies of exports can be expected to shift at different rates. Third, structural changes, such as major new innovations or a change in the price of oil, cause major changes in imports and exports.

The associated shifts in demand and supply on the foreign exchange market imply that there is no reason to believe that the exchange rate consistent with equilibrium in the market for foreign exchange will be unchanged.

The exchange rate consistent with balance-of-payments equilibrium will change over time; over a decade the change can be substantial.

Government may react to long-term disequilibria in at least three ways.

1. The exchange rate can be changed whenever it is clear that a balance-of-payments deficit or surplus is the result of a long-term shift in demands and supplies in the foreign exchange market and not the result of some transient factor.

2. Domestic price levels can be allowed to change in an attempt to make the present fixed exchange rates become the equilibrium rate. To restore equilibrium, countries with overvalued currencies need to have deflations and countries with undervalued currencies need to have inflations. But changes in domestic price levels have all sorts of domestic repercussions. Deflations are difficult and costly to accomplish (e.g., reductions in aggregate demand intended to lower the price level are likely to raise unemployment), and often the explicit goal of government policy is to avoid inflation. One might expect governments to be more willing to change exchange rates than to try to change their price levels.

3. Restrictions can be imposed on trade and foreign payments. Imports and foreign spending by tourists and governments can be restricted, and the export of capital can be slowed or even stopped.

Surplus countries are often quick to criticize such restrictions on international trade and payments. But as long as exchange rates are fixed and price levels prove difficult to manipulate, deficit countries have little option but to restrict the quantity of foreign exchange their residents are permitted to obtain.

Since restrictions on trade and foreign payments are undesirable in a world economy characterized by large-scale international trade and foreign investment, and since deflations of the price level are difficult and costly to bring about, most countries will want to preserve the possibility of making occasional changes in their exchange rates even if fixed rates are the main rule of the day.

Under the Bretton Woods system, although most countries defended their exchange rates in the face of crises, there were still major rounds of exchange rate adjustments. Because exchange rates did have to be changed from time to time, the system of fixed rates under the Bretton Woods agreement was called an **adjustable peg system.**

Handling speculative crises. When enough people begin to doubt the government's ability to maintain the current exchange rate, speculative crises develop. The most important reason for such crises is that over time, equilibrium exchange rates get further and further away from any given set of fixed rates. When the disequilibrium becomes obvious to everyone, traders and speculators come to believe that a realignment of rates is due. There is a rush to buy currencies expected to be revalued and a rush to sell currencies expected to be devalued. Even if the authorities take drastic steps to remove the payments deficit, there may be doubt that these measures will work before the exchange reserves are exhausted. Speculative flows of funds can reach large proportions, and it may be impossible to avoid changing the exchange rate under such pressure.

Under an adjustable peg system, opportunities often arise for speculators to make large profits; this occurs when everyone knows the direction in which an exchange rate will be changed if it is to be changed at all.

As the equilibrium value of a country's currency changes, possibly under the impact of high inflation, it becomes obvious that the central bank is having more and more difficulty holding the pegged rate. So when a crisis arises, speculators sell the country's currency. If it is devalued, they can buy it back at a lower price and earn a profit. If it is not devalued, they can buy it back at the price at which they sold it and lose only the commission costs on the deal. This asymmetry, with speculators having a chance to make large profits by risking only a small loss, eventually destroyed the Bretton Woods system.

During the Bretton Woods period, governments tended to resist changing their exchange rates until they had no alternative. This made the situation so obvious that speculators could hardly lose, and their actions set off the final crises that forced exchange rate readjustments. If changes could be made more frequently and before they became inevitable, the number of speculative crises might diminish, and the system of fixed exchange rates might appear more viable. Such changes, however, would remove the day-to-day certainty that was one of the chief advantages of this system. Moreover, a surprise change might lead to suspicion that a devaluation was made to gain a competitive advantage for a country's exports rather than to remove a fundamental disequilibrium. After all, governments are not supposed to devalue under an adjustable peg system until it is *clear* that they are faced with a fundamental disequilibrium. If this is clear to them, it is also clear to ordinary traders and speculators.

Flexible Exchange Rates

Under a system of flexible exchange rates, demand and supply determine the rates without any government intervention. (This was illustrated in Figure 40-1 on page 878.) Such rates are called free, **flexible,** or **floating exchange rates**. Since the foreign exchange market always clears, the government can turn its attention to domestic problems of inflation and unemployment, leaving the balance of payments to take care of itself—at least so went the theory before flexible rates were introduced.

For reasons that we shall analyze later in this chapter, this optimistic picture did not materialize when the world went over to flexible exchange rates. Free-market fluctuations in rates were far greater, and

hence potentially more upsetting to the performance of national economies and to the flow of international trade, than many economists had anticipated. As a result, central banks have felt the need to intervene quite frequently and extensively to stabilize exchange rates.

Managed Floats

A major difference between the present system and Bretton Woods is that central banks no longer publicly announce values for exchange rates that they are committed in advance to defend even at heavy cost. Central banks are thus free to adjust their exchange rate targets as circumstances change. Sometimes they leave the rate completely free to fluctuate, and at other times they interfere actively to alter the exchange rate from its free-market value. Such a system is called a **managed float** or a **dirty float**.

Some countries have opted for what is called a *currency block* by pegging their exchange rates against each other and then indulging in a joint float against the outside world. The best-known currency block is the European **snake**. Under this arrangement the countries of the EEC, with the exception of the United Kingdom, maintain fixed rates among their own currencies but allow them to float as a block against the dollar.

What Determines the Exchange Rate in a Floating System?

One surprise to supporters of floating exchange rates has been the degree of exchange rate volatility. Why have rates been so volatile?

The average value of exchange rates over the long term depends on their **purchasing power parity (PPP)** values. The PPP exchange rate is the one that holds constant the relative price levels in two countries *when measured in a common currency*. For example, assume that the U.S. price level rises by 20 percent, while the German price level rises by only 5 percent over the same period. The PPP value of the German mark then appreciates by approximately 15 percent. This would mean that in Germany the prices of all goods (both German-produced and imported American goods) would rise by 5 percent measured in

German marks, while in the United States the prices of all goods (both American-produced and imported German goods) would rise by 20 percent measured in U.S. dollars.

The PPP exchange rate adjusts so that the relative price of the two nations' goods (measured in the same currency) is unchanged because the change in the relative values of two currencies compensates exactly for differences in national inflation rates.

If the actual exchange rate equals the PPP rate, the competitive positions of producers in the two countries will be unchanged. Firms located in countries with high inflation rates will still be able to sell their outputs on international markets, since the exchange rate adjusts to offset the effect of the higher domestic prices.

Figure 41-2 shows that the exchange rate between U.S. dollars and sterling has followed the PPP rate over the long run. But notice also the large fluctuations around the PPP rate.

During the Bretton Woods period of fixed exchange rates, the advocates of floating rates argued that speculators would stabilize the actual rates within a narrow band around the PPP rates. The argument was that since everyone knew the normal value was the PPP rate, speculators seeking a profit when the rate deviated from its PPP level would quickly force the rate back to that level. To illustrate, suppose the PPP rate is U.S. $1.25 = £1.00 and that the actual rate falls to U.S. $1.15 = £1.00. Speculators would rush to buy pounds at U.S. $1.15 each, expecting to sell them for U.S. $1.25 when the rate returns to its PPP level. This very action would raise the demand for sterling and help push its value back toward U.S. $1.25.

FIGURE 41-2   Actual and PPP Exchange Rate, U.S. Dollar and Pound Sterling, 1972–1987

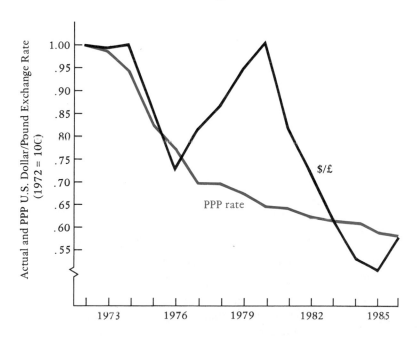

The actual exchange rate follows the trend value of the PPP exchange rate but fluctuates substantially around it. The black line shows the dollar/pound exchange rate; the colored line shows the ratio of the U.S. CPI to the British CPI. (Both series are set to 1.00 in 1972. The figures for 1987 are for the exchange rate at the end of April.)

The continual decline of the PPP exchange rate reflects the United Kingdom's higher inflation rate relative to that of the United States. Until 1976 the relative value of the pound fell in accordance with the PPP rate, but after 1976 the pound appreciated sharply through 1980. (Many observers associate this appreciation with the onset of production from large oil deposits in the North Sea and with high interest rates in 1979–1980.) In 1980 the relative value of the pound began to fall, bringing it back toward its PPP value. In 1983 the pound fell below its PPP value, and in 1985 it started to rise again toward its PPP value, and reached it by late 1986. *(Source: International Financial Statistics)*

Such speculative behavior would stabilize the exchange rate near its PPP value if speculators could be sure that the deviations would be small and short-lived. But in practice the swings around the PPP rate have been wide and have lasted for long periods. Thus if sterling fell to U.S. $1.15, speculators would know that it could go as low as U.S. $1.05 and stay there for quite a while before returning to U.S. $1.25. In that case it might be worth speculating on a price of U.S. $1.10 next week rather than a price of U.S. $1.25 in some indefinite future.

The wide swings in exchange rates that have occurred show that speculative buying and selling cannot be relied on to hold exchange rates close to their PPP values.

Why have these wide fluctuations occurred? One of the most important reasons is associated with international differences in interest rates.

Exchange Rate Overshooting

Suppose that American interest rates rise above those ruling in other major financial centers. A rush to lend money at the profitable rates found in the United States will lead to an appreciation of the U.S. dollar.

This process will stop only when the rise in value of the U.S. dollar on foreign exchange markets is large enough that investors expect the dollar subsequently to fall in value. This expected future depreciation then just offsets the interest premium from lending funds in U.S. dollars.

To illustrate, assume that interest rates are 4 percentage points higher in New York than in London due to a restrictive monetary policy in the United States. Investors believe the PPP rate is U.S. $1.60 = £1.00, but as they rush to buy dollars to take advantage of the higher U.S. interest rates, they drive the rate to, say, U.S. $1.40 = £1.00. (Since £1.00 now buys fewer U.S. dollars, sterling has depreciated, and since it takes fewer U.S. dollars to buy £1.00, the dollar has appreciated.) They do not believe this rate will be sustained and instead expect the U.S. dollar to lose value. If foreign investors expect it to depreciate at 4 percent per year, they will be indifferent between lending money in New York

and doing so in London. The extra 4 percent of interest they earn in New York per year is exactly offset by the 4 percent they expect to lose when they turn their money back into their own currency.

Any policy that raises domestic interest rates above world levels will cause the external value of the domestic currency to appreciate enough to create an expected future depreciation sufficient to offset the interest differential.

A central bank that is seeking to meet a monetary target may have to put up with large fluctuations in the exchange rate. If, in the example, the high U.S. interest rates were the result of a restrictive monetary policy, the overshooting of the U.S. dollar beyond its PPP rate may put export- and import-competing industries under temporary but severe pressure from foreign competition.

The other side of this coin is that the high value of the U.S. dollar creates inflationary pressure in other countries. U.S. goods become much more expensive abroad, thus putting upward pressure on foreign prices and wages. Authorities in those countries are faced with the uncomfortable choice of accepting this increased inflation or raising their own interest rates and thus maintaining their exchange rates in terms of the U.S. dollar. In the early 1980s many foreign central banks chose this latter option, and the tight U.S. monetary policies were quickly imitated in other countries. This combined monetary contraction contributed to the severity of the world recession, as discussed further in Box 41-2 (pages 904–905).

Current Problems[1]

The Lack of an Alternative to the Dollar As a Reserve Currency

Governments operating dirty floats need reserves, just like governments operating adjustable pegs. The search for an adequate supply of reserves has continued unabated since the demise of the Bretton Woods system.

[1] The rest of this chapter can be omitted without loss of continuity.

One major form in which reserves are held is U.S. dollars; another, one that is growing in size, is the **special drawing rights (SDRs)** held with the IMF. First introduced in 1969, SDRs were designed to provide a supplement to existing reserve assets. The Special Drawing Account of the IMF was set up and kept separate from all other operations of the Fund. Each member country was assigned an SDR quota that was guaranteed in terms of a fixed gold value. Each country could use its quota to acquire an equivalent amount of convertible currencies from other participants. SDRs could be used without prior consultation with the Fund, but only to cope with balance-of-payments difficulties. SDR allocations grew from about $10 billion in 1970 to over $50 billion in 1986.

The commitment to lower inflation initiated by the Reagan administration in 1981 has restored some confidence in the U.S. dollar as a reserve asset. But overall these developments have not been seen as long-term solutions to the reserve problem. Other national currencies could take over the reserve role played by the U.S. dollar, but this is not likely.

Why does the world not turn to an international paper reserve system based on SDRs or some similar creation? Such a solution has much support from academic economists, who see an appropriate international institution managing the supply of international currency to accommodate growth and to avoid inflation.

Critics of such a system—among them most of the world's central bankers—distrust the concept of an international paper currency, pointing out that few countries have managed their own money supplies effectively. However difficult the task of the U.S. Federal Reserve may be, the task of a World Reserve Bank would be more difficult. Further, private acceptance and use of the SDR has been virtually nonexistent, indicating the enormous difficulties inherent in creating a new currency.

Some who are skeptical of an international paper monetary standard have urged a return to the gold standard. This approach has critical disadvantages. In fact, the IMF and the U.S. government have at various times taken the lead in the attempt to "demonetarize" gold completely.

For the moment at least, the world cannot agree on an international monetary reserve. Until it does,

there will be crises whenever there is a desire to shift from one to another of the multiple sources of reserves: dollars, gold, SDRs, marks, francs, and yen. The speculative opportunities inherent in such a system remain large, as evidenced by the recent behavior of the price of gold shown in Figure 41-3 (see page 906).

The Impact of OPEC

One issue affecting the future payments system—and indeed the whole of international economic relations—is the variability of the price of oil.

Oil Price Increases

The OPEC cartel raised the price of oil dramatically in 1974 and again in 1979. In total these events led to a tenfold increase, which generated an unprecedented imbalance in the international economic system in the form of a massive payments surplus for the oil producers and a corresponding deficit for the oil-importing countries. The excess purchasing power in the hands of oil producers came to be called **petrodollars**. The cumulative stock of petrodollars may well have exceeded $500 billion. Petrodollars caused several different kinds of problems, some of them short term, others long term in nature.

Short-term problems of industrialized countries. Most petrodollars were eventually used for the purchase of consumption goods and services or investment goods from industrialized countries. But the oil-producing countries could not spend their oil revenues on goods and services as fast as they were earned in the late 1970s.[2] Nor could the industrialized oil-consuming countries produce the goods and services at the rate necessary for all the oil revenues to be spent without creating enormous inflationary pressures.

Thus in the short term the OPEC countries had excess dollars. They also had an understandable desire to earn a return on those funds. One way was

---

[2] There is a limit to the speed with which any country can absorb foreign goods, and many oil-producing countries were at that limit. Ships sometimes wait months to unload for want of dock capacity, unloaded goods sometimes sit in wharfside stockpiles for months, even years, for want of transportation capacity, and so on.

BOX 41-2

Beggar-My-Neighbor Policies, Past and Present

The Great Depression of the 1930s brought an end to the long-standing stability of the gold standard and ushered in a period of experimentation in exchange regimes. Experiments were tried with both fixed and fluctuating rates.

But the overriding feature of the decade was that considerations of massive unemployment came to dominate economic policies in almost every country, and all devices, including exchange rate manipulations, seemed fair game for dealing with them. Many of the policies adopted at this time were acts of desperation that would have made long-term sense only if other countries had not also been in crisis. Governments tended not to consider the long-term effects on trade or on their trading partners of the policies they adopted, hoping to gain short-term advantages before their policies provoked the inevitable reaction from others.

The use of devaluations to ease domestic unemployment rested on a simple and superficially plausible line of analysis: If a country has unemployed workers at home, why not substitute home production for imports and thus give jobs to one's citizens instead of to foreigners? One way to do this is to urge, say, Americans to "buy American." Another, probably more effective, way is to lower the prices of domestic goods relative to those of imports. The devaluation of one's currency does this by making foreign goods that much more expensive. (A 10 percent devaluation, means that it will take 10 percent more domestic

money to buy the same imports; this is equivalent to a 10 percent rise in the prices of all foreign goods.)

Of course, if this policy works, other countries will find *their* exports falling and unemployment rising as a consequence. Because such policies attempt to solve one country's problems by inflicting them on others, they are called **beggar-my-neighbor policies** and are described as attempts to "export one's unemployment."

In a situation of inadequate world demand, a beggar-my-neighbor policy on the part of one country can work only in the unlikely event that other countries do not try to protect themselves. A situation in which all countries devalue their currencies in an attempt to gain a competitive advantage over one another is called a situation of **competitive devaluations**.

This is what happened during the 1930s. One country would devalue its currency in an attempt to reduce its imports and stimulate exports. But because other countries were suffering from the same kinds of problems of unemployment, they did not sit idly by. Retaliation was swift, and devaluation followed devaluation. But the simultaneous attempt of all countries to cut imports without suffering a comparable cut in exports is bound to be self-defeating.

When unemployment is due to insufficient world aggregate demand, it cannot be cured by measures designed to redistribute among nations the fixed and inadequate total of demand.

---

to invest their surplus revenues in the advanced industrialized nations, thereby returning on capital account the purchasing power extracted from the current accounts of the oil-importing nations. This creates many serious problems.

One of the most important concerns the havoc brought to foreign exchange markets when surplus oil funds are invested in liquid assets and switched between currencies in response to changes in interest rates and expected capital gains arising from possible exchange rate alterations. Surplus petrodollars can also be used speculatively, and many observers believe that a good part of the wild rise and sudden fall

in gold prices in 1979–1980 was due to just such a use of petrodollars.

Short-term problems of underdeveloped countries. Consider an oil-importing country such as Kenya, for which the OPEC price increase turned a small trade surplus into a massive deficit overnight. The country was unable to generate revenues quickly enough to pay its oil bill, yet it could sharply decrease its use of oil only at the cost of a great slowdown in its domestic economy.

The IMF stepped in with loan arrangements to help countries most severely affected by the rising

These policies, along with other restrictive trade policies such as import duties, export subsidies, quotas, and prohibitions, led to a declining volume of world trade and brought no relief from the world-wide depression. Moreover, they contributed to a loss of faith in the economic system and in the ability of either economists or politicians to cope with economic crises.

To avoid a recurrence of the beggar-my-neighbor policies of the 1930s, trading nations designed some important institutions. The International Monetary Fund (IMF) was supposed to reduce the chances of competitive devaluations, and the General Agreement on Tariffs and Trade (GATT) was to reduce the chances of competitive increases in tariffs and other trade restrictions. These institutions worked well for over 30 years.

In 1980 the United States embarked on tight monetary policy, driving up U.S. interest rates and the external value of the U.S. dollar. Just as expansionary monetary policy in the face of world recession tends to "export unemployment" by leading to a depreciation of the home currency and reducing the demand for foreign goods, tight monetary policy in the face of the world inflation tends to "export inflation" by leading to an appreciation of the home currency and raising the demand for foreign goods.

Most other governments, notably Germany and Japan, were worried about the implications of this for their own inflation rates and reacted by also adopting tight monetary policies. This monetary tightness helped lead the world into the serious recession of 1981–1983.

Under the extreme pressures of this difficult economic situation, beggar-my-neighbor pressures surfaced, and many governments found them hard to resist politically. Throughout the 1980s American voters have shown strong support for advocates of increased tariffs. Many countries negotiated unofficial quotas restricting the importation of Japanese cars. European agricultural protectionism nearly wrecked the GATT negotiations in December 1982 and has been the focus of considerable debate in the United States for the past few years. Less-developed countries sought covert ways of protecting their own infant industries and complained, with some justice, that the developed nations paid lip service to, rather than really acting on, the slogan of "trade, not aid." It was clear that great pressure was being put on the whole postwar fabric designed to encourage trade and discourage beggar-my-neighbor policies. As the world recovered in the period from 1983 to 1986, some but not all of the pressures abated. But in the rest of the world in mid 1987 most observers were still worried about the threat of beggar-my-neighbor policies and the protectionist mood in the United States.

oil prices, the repayments of maturing loans were deferred, and the OPEC nations established a fund for short-term loans to such countries. Thus the purely short-term problems can be, and have been, solved through international cooperation and recognition of the need for accommodation on the part of creditor nations.

Oil Price Decreases

Many oil-exporting countries also borrowed heavily on the expectation of rising oil prices. In early 1983, however, OPEC had lost control of the market, and the price of oil started to fall. In early 1986 the price of crude oil fell sharply from over $30 a barrel to around $12.[3] Many international loans were threatened, including those made by large private banks to less-developed countries such as Mexico, which is heavily dependent on oil exports for repayment. The risk of a major default hangs over the system, and the IMF again finds itself facing the problem of rescheduling repayments of large international loans.

[3] Oil prices, like the prices of many other international commodities, are expressed in U.S. dollars.

FIGURE 41-3   Price of Gold, 1971–1987

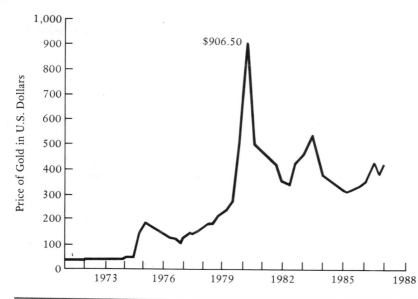

Gold soared in value and proved highly volatile after convertibility of the dollar was suspended in 1973. The two devaluations of the U.S. dollar in terms of gold that occurred under the adjustable peg system are barely visible. (These devaluations are discussed in the appendix to this chapter.) The effects of speculation on the price of gold is seen in subsequent experience. The price of gold more than quadrupled from 1977 to 1979, reaching a peak of over $900 per ounce. It subsequently fell to around $300 by 1981, then rose through 1984 before falling again.

Nevertheless, lower oil prices generally contributed to a reduction of interest rates and an increase in economic growth among the industrialized countries. Both of these contribute to the long-run health of the less-developed countries, whether oil exporting or not.

The U.S. Dollar and Protectionism

The dollar became overvalued during the period of tight monetary policy that began in 1980. If a temporary overshooting of the exchange rate was all that was involved in that overvaluation, the dollar would have come down shortly thereafter. Many economists expected it to do so, but in fact it remained high throughout 1981–1985.

Most observers believe that the dollar remained high because this period witnessed enormous capital inflows into the United States. These capital inflows were partly a result of the record U.S. government budget deficit. That deficit exceeded $200 billion in 1986 (over 5 percent of GNP); some of this was financed by domestic savings, but much also had to be financed by foreign borrowing, resulting in capital

inflows. The large capital inflows that occurred were also responding to the combination of low inflation and relative prosperity in the United States, which made the country a safe and profitable place in which to invest.

As we saw in Chapter 40, equilibrium in the foreign exchange market means that the capital inflow is *necessarily* matched by a current account deficit (see page 891). Only when these two are equal will the demand for dollars by foreign investors wishing to buy American capital assets be matched by the supply of dollars by those Americans wishing to import foreign goods and services. The large capital inflows thus meant that there also had to be a current account deficit; from this perspective the high value of the dollar was simply the mechanism by which the required current account deficit was brought about.

The high value of the dollar placed American firms that produce traded goods (i.e., goods for export and goods that face competition from imports) at a cost disadvantage relative to foreign producers. Falling production, rising unemployment, and many business failures resulted. These events, combined with the increase in the demand for imports resulting from the fall in their relative price, contributed to the growth of the current account deficit.

In spite of the vigorous expansion of the macro economy from 1984 through 1986, these traded goods sectors remained depressed; the recovery was focused in the nontraded sectors. Not surprisingly, the plight of the import-competing and export sectors led to a call for protection. The United States put pressure on Japan, Germany, and Canada to reduce their current account surpluses and itself took many steps to curb imports. Some steps were specific, such as the tariff imposed in May 1986 on Canadian cedar shakes and shingles. Further, in 1987 protectionist trade bills were being considered in both the Congress and the Senate.

While the motivation for these protectionist measures was easy enough to understand, most economists felt that the measures were seriously misguided. First, they threatened to upset the fabric of international trading relations and cooperation carefully built up through multilateral negotiation during the post–World War II period. The growing protectionist sentiment in Congress led to a serious split between that body and the administration; in late 1985 President Reagan, an avowed "free trader," warned of a "mindless stampede to protectionism."

Second, the measures were likely to be largely ineffective in terms of their goal of reducing the current account deficit. As we have seen, the current account deficit was a necessary counterpart to the capital inflows that the U.S. economy was experiencing. Unless the root causes of the capital inflows were dealt with, the current account deficit would persist with or without protectionist measures. If the government deficit remained large, and if the United States remained attractive to foreign investors, the current account would have to remain in deficit in order to match the capital inflows.

To see this very important point, assume that import tariffs, surcharges, and quotas succeeded in bringing the current account into balance but that people still wished to bring capital into the United States. With a balanced current account, there would not be anyone willing to supply the dollars to the would-be capital importers, and consequently the dollar would start to appreciate. This would lead to

a reduction in exports and an increase in imports until the original current account deficit was re-established.[4]

The Challenge for the Rest of the Century

The 1970s witnessed the replacement of a system of managed fixed exchange rates by a system of managed flexible exchange rates. The problems of the latter may have been revealed by the events of the last decade, but they cannot be said to have been solved. Officials understand the need to devise workable guidelines for managing flexible rates and to enhance cooperation more generally.

The Management of Exchange Rates

Managing floating rates poses several potential problems for the international monetary system. Let us discuss three key problems.

Inconsistent exchange rate policies. Different governments may try to fix their exchange rates at levels that are inconsistent with each other. For example, if the Fed's target is that the U.S. dollar should be worth 150 yen while the Bank of Japan's target is that the yen should be worth U.S. $0.005, both policies cannot succeed. If both banks persist in trying to meet such inconsistent targets, they can destabilize exchange markets.

Competitive devaluations. Countries may get involved in bouts of competitive devaluations similar to those that destabilized exchange markets in the 1920s and 1930s. For example, if one country devalues its currency in order to get a competitive advantage for its exports and other countries respond by devaluing their currencies, the rounds of successive devaluations will destabilize the exchange market without giving any country's exports a permanent advantage.

---

[4] Of course, to the extent that the tariffs create revenue and therefore reduce the government deficit, more domestic private saving would be available to finance domestic investment, and capital inflows and the current account both could be reduced correspondingly.

Destabilizing speculation.   Speculative behavior can destabilize exchange markets. Before the system of floating exchange rates was adopted, many economists felt that rates would stay fairly close to their equilibrium values. Economists expected that speculators would then stabilize rates even further by buying currencies that seemed temporarily low in price and selling those that seemed temporarily high. In that event, however, very large and persistent deviations of exchange rates from the long-run equilibrium values occurred. This left speculators less clear on which way a particular rate was likely to go in the near future. When a particular currency started to fall in value, speculators might conclude that a large and persistent fall was just beginning. In this case their rush to sell the currency before its expected further fall would bring the fall about.

To help avoid these problems, the IMF has issued guidelines for exchange rate management. The guidelines emphasize that exchange rate policy is a matter for international consultation and surveillance by the IMF and that intervention practices by individual central banks should be based on three principles: (1) Exchange authorities should prevent sudden and disproportionate short-term movements in exchange rates and ensure an orderly adjustment to longer-term pressures. (2) In consultation with the IMF, countries should establish a target zone for the medium-term values of their exchange rates and keep the actual rate within that target zone. (3) Countries should recognize that exchange rate management involves joint responsibilities and is not just the responsibility of the individual country in question.

The experiences of the last decade have underlined one of the most important unsolved problems of managed floating rates: coping with the massive volume of short-term funds that can be switched rapidly between financial centers. Short-term capital flows forced the abandonment of exchange rates that had been agreed on in 1971 and have often caused violent fluctuations in floating rates since then. Severe "currency misalignments" have arisen and persisted, rendering uncompetitive on world markets the export- and import-competing sectors in countries with overvalued currencies, while creating enormous profit opportunities in countries with undervalued currencies.

Capital flows often prevent the quick return of exchange rates to their PPP values. Various attempts have been made to limit such capital flows. Italy has adopted a two-tier foreign exchange market, with one price for foreign exchange to finance current account transactions and another price (and another set of controls) for foreign exchange to finance capital movements. Germany has used direct controls on overseas borrowing. There has also been a considerable extension of arrangements under which central banks in surplus countries lend the funds they are accumulating back to central banks in deficit countries. Through such arrangements, the ability of banks to maintain stable exchange rates in the face of short-term speculative flights of capital is enhanced.

The major problem in managing speculative flows is to identify them accurately. Experience suggests that exchange rate management can smooth out temporary fluctuations but cannot resist underlying trends in equilibrium rates caused by relative inflation rates, structural changes, and persistent nonspeculative capital flows. In day-to-day management it is not always easy to distinguish among them.

Nevertheless, the excessive variability and persistent misalignment of exchange rates that continued to plague the flexible exchange rate system led to a number of proposals for reform. These are discussed further in Box 41-3.

The Need for Cooperation

One of the most impressive aspects of the international payments history of the past 30 years has been the steady rise of effective international cooperation. When the gold standard collapsed and the Great Depression overwhelmed the countries of the world, "every nation for itself" was the rule of the day. Rising tariffs, competitive exchange rate devaluations, and all forms of beggar-my-neighbor policies abounded.

After World War II the countries of the world cooperated in bringing the Bretton Woods system and the IMF into being. The system itself was far from perfect, and it finally broke down as a result of its own internal contradictions. But the international cooperation that was necessary to set up the system

BOX 41-3

Proposals for International Monetary Reform

The high degree of variability and persistent misalignment of exchange rates that plagued the flexible exchange rate system for over the first decade of its operation led in the mid 1980s to a number of proposals for reform.

Fixed Exchange Rates

Some observers advocated a return to fixed exchange rates. In fact, some even wanted the new system to be based on gold or some other group of commodities. This proposal was apparently motivated by the belief that *ruling out* exchange rate changes would allow some of the problems noted in the text to be avoided.

This proposal has not received wide support among economists since most believe that the flaws that led to the demise of the Bretton Woods system were indeed fatal and that a system of fixed exchange rates would have performed worse, not better, than flexible exchange rates did in the face of the shocks that have disturbed the world economy since Bretton Woods was abandoned. Proponents of fixed exchange rates counter that many of those shocks were in fact the result of bad policies that were made possible only by the freedom for independent domestic policy that exists under flexible exchange rates. They argue that the discipline imposed by fixed exchange rates would have improved the performance of policy over the period.

Target Exchange Rate Zones

Another proposal was for establishing *target zones* for exchange rates. Some advocates proposed "hard" zones, that is, narrowly defined zones with automatic intervention required whenever exchange rates moved outside the defined limits. This amounts to a fixed exchange rate system, and, not surprisingly, debate on this type of proposal paralleled that on fixed exchange rates.

Alternatively, some advocates proposed "soft" zones, defined more loosely and departures from which simply served as a signal to authorities that some policy reaction might be appropriate. Although these soft zones were more acceptable to some observers, many expressed a good deal of skepticism about what such weak arrangements might accomplish.

Objective Indicators

Other participants in the debate promoted the idea that "objective indicators" be calculated to provide a signal to authorities when policies become mutually inconsistent. Such indicators, which might involve measures of performance such as real growth and inflation as well as policy measures such as money growth rates and fiscal deficits, are an extension of the soft zone for exchange rate targets in that they serve merely as an indicator and do not themselves trigger automatic policy responses.

Though many commentators were sympathetic to this idea, there was little consensus as to how to calculate such indicators and how exactly they might work to avoid the problems in the system. Indeed, proponents of all these reforms concede that the high variability and persistent misalignment of exchange rates are really just symptoms of the real problems in the international economy and that any real reform must address the root causes of such problems. Many of those root causes are beyond the control of policymakers, but some of the problems result from undesirable economic policies in the industrialized countries. Recognizing this, Western leaders attending the economic summit held in Tokyo in May 1986 reached an agreement to establish objective indicators in an effort to improve international cooperation in formulating economic policies.

survived. The joint cooperative actions of central banks allowed them to weather speculative crises in the 1970s that would have forced them to devalue their currencies in the 1950s.

Thus the collapse of Bretton Woods did not plunge the world into the same chaos that followed the breakdown of the gold standard. The world was also better able to cope with the terrible strains caused by the sharp rise in oil prices in the 1970s. Of course, enormous oil-related problems remain, and they are matters for continuing international dialogue. Further, it is not yet clear how well the world economy will weather the upsurge of American protectionism of the mid 1980s. Prior to this upsurge, the United States provided essential leadership in working for lower restrictions on international trade. It is a serious question, then, whether other nations will now follow the American lead to *increased* protectionism and thus join in a mutually destructive round of competitive tariff increases and other restrictions.

Whatever the problems of the future, the world has a better chance of solving them—or even just learning to live with them—when countries cooperate through the IMF and other international organizations than when each country seeks its own solution without concern for the interests of others.

Summary

1. Various systems of international monetary arrangements have been tried. All involve aspects of the two extremes of fixed exchange rates and flexible exchange rates.

2. Under fixed exchange rates the central bank intervenes in the foreign exchange market to maintain the exchange rate at or near an announced par value. To do this the central bank must hold sufficient stocks of foreign exchange reserves. Reserves have historically been held in the form of gold or reserve currencies, particularly the U.S. dollar. The SDR is a relatively new international paper money meant to provide additional international reserves linked neither to gold nor to the U.S. dollar.

3. Any fixed exchange rate system will face three major problems: (1) providing sufficient international reserves, (2) adjusting to long-term trends in receipts and payments, and (3) handling periodic speculative crises.

4. Under a system of flexible, or floating, exchange rates, the exchange rate is market-determined by supply and demand for the currency.

5. Since their adoption in the mid 1970s, flexible exchange rates have fluctuated substantially. As a result, central banks have often intervened to stabilize the fluctuations. Thus the present system is called a managed, or dirty, float.

6. Fluctuations in exchange rates can be understood as fluctuations around a trend value that is determined by the purchasing power parity (PPP) rate. The PPP rate adjusts in response to differences in national inflation rates.

7. Current problems include the need to find an adequate reserve not tied to a national currency, to accommodate both the short-term and the longer-term impact of OPEC, and to develop rules for managing flexible exchange rates. A continuing commitment to international cooperation will help the world cope with these problems.

Fixed and flexible exchange rates
Managed floats
Adjustable peg
Bretton Woods system
International Monetary Fund
Exchange rate overshooting
Petrodollars

Topics for Review

Discussion Questions

1. From mid 1985 through the end of 1986 the U.S. dollar fell sharply in terms of the Japanese yen and the major European currencies. However, the U.S. current account deficit did not fall. Can you think of any reasons why? What happened to the Canadian dollar over this period? What were the implications for Canada?
2. The U.S. dollar is no longer convertible into gold because of a change in U.S. policy. Does this lack of convertibility make the dollar any less useful as an international medium of exchange?
3. Are Americans benefited or hurt when the U.S. dollar is the standard form of international reserves?
4. "Under a flexible exchange rate system no country need suffer unemployment, for if its prices are low enough there will be more than enough demand to keep its factories and farms fully occupied." The evidence suggests that flexible rates have not generally eliminated unemployment. Can you explain why? Can changing exchange rates ever cure unemployment?
5. The OPEC oil price increases during the 1970s caused grave problems in international payments and increased the need for IMF loans. Why did market adjustment of exchange rates not solve the problem?
6. In November 1985 the five major industrialized countries met and agreed that a major realignment of the world's currencies was appropriate. Why? What did they do about it? What was the result?
7. What role in international payments does or did gold play under (a) the gold standard, (b) the adjustable peg Bretton Woods system, and (c) the present system?
8. Might a person who regards inflation as the number one economic danger favor a return to the pre-1914 gold standard? Would you predict non-inflationary results if in order to restore the gold standard, the price of gold had to be set at U.S. $1,600 per ounce, either all at once or gradually?

The Gold Standard and the Bretton Woods System

Two episodes with fixed exchange rates were experienced in the twentieth century. Each ultimately failed. The gold standard, whose origins are as old as currency itself, was used until the late 1920s and early 1930s. The Bretton Woods system, which was the only payments system ever to be designed and established by conscious action, was born out of World War II and collapsed a little less than 30 years later. Their histories are instructive, not least because many people continue to propose returning to one or the other of these systems.

The Gold Standard

The gold standard was not *designed;* it just happened. It arose out of the general acceptance of gold as the commodity to be used as money. In most countries paper currency was freely convertible into gold at a fixed rate. In 1914 the U.S. dollar was worth 0.053 standard ounces of gold, while the British pound sterling was worth 0.257 standard ounces. This meant that the pound was worth 4.86 times as much as the dollar in terms of gold, thus making £1 worth U.S. $4.86. (In practice the exchange rate fluctuated within narrow limits set by the cost of shipping gold.) As long as all countries were on the gold standard, a person in one country could be sure of being able to make payments to a person in another.

The Gold-Flow, Price-Level Mechanism

The gold standard was supposed to maintain a balance of international payments by causing adjustments in price levels within individual countries. Consider a country that had a balance-of-payments deficit because the value of its imports (i.e., purchases) from other countries exceeded the value of its exports (i.e., sales) to other countries. The demand for foreign exchange would exceed the supply on this country's foreign exchange market. Some people who wished to make foreign payments would need to convert their domestic currency into gold and ship the gold. Therefore, some people in a surplus country would receive gold in payment for exports. They would deposit this to their credit and accept claims on gold—in terms of convertible paper money or bank deposits—in return. Thus deficit countries would be losing gold, while surplus countries would be gaining it.

Under the gold standard, the whole money supply was linked to the supply of gold. The international movements of gold would therefore lead to a fall in the money supply in the deficit country and a rise in the surplus country.[1] If full employment prevails, changes in the domestic money supply will cause changes in domestic price levels. Deficit countries would thus have falling price levels, while surplus countries would have rising price levels. The exports of deficit countries would become relatively cheaper, while those of surplus countries would become relatively more expensive. The resulting changes in quantities bought and sold would move the balance of payments toward an equilibrium position.

Actual Experience of the Gold Standard

The half century before World War I was the heyday of the gold standard. During this relatively trouble-free period, the adjustment mechanism just described seemed to work well.

Subsequent research has suggested, however, that the gold standard succeeded during the period mainly because it was not called on to do much work. No major trading country found itself with a serious and

---

[1] When the person who received gold deposited it in a bank, the bank would be in the position of the bank in Table 33-4 on page 725, and a multiple expansion of deposit money would ensue.

persistent balance-of-payments deficit, so no major country was called on to restore equilibrium through a large change in its domestic price level. Short-run fluctuations were ironed out either by movements of short-run capital in response to changes in interest rates or by changes in national income and employment.

In the 1920s the gold standard was called on to do a major job. It failed utterly, and it was abandoned. How did this happen? During World War I most belligerent countries had suspended convertibility of currency (i.e., they went off the gold standard). Most countries suffered major inflations, but the degree of inflation differed from country to country. As we have seen, this will lead to changes in the equilibrium exchange rates.

After the war countries returned to the gold standard (i.e., they restored convertibility of their currencies into gold). For reasons of prestige, many insisted on returning at the prewar rates. This meant that some countries' goods were overpriced and other countries' goods were underpriced. Large deficits and surpluses in the balance of payments inevitably appeared, and the adjustment mechanism required that price levels should change in each of the countries in order to restore equilibrium. Exchange rates were not adjusted, and price levels changed very slowly. By the onset of the Great Depression, equilibrium price levels had not yet been attained. The financial chaos brought on by the depression destroyed the existing payments system.

Major Disabilities of a Gold Standard

One may ask whether an altered gold standard, based on more realistic exchange rates, might not have succeeded. Some modern economists, notably Robert Mundell of Columbia University, think it would; most others believe that the gold standard suffered from key weaknesses.

Like any other exchange rate system, it required a mechanism for orderly adjustment to changes in the supply and demand for a nation's currency. The price adjustment process worked too slowly and too imperfectly to cope with large and persistent disequilibrium.

Furthermore, gold as the basis for an international money supply suffered several special disadvantages.

These included a limited supply that could not be expanded as rapidly as increases in the volume of world trade required, an uneven distribution of existing and potential new gold supplies among the nations of the world, and a large and frequently volatile speculative demand for gold during periods of crisis. These factors could cause large, disruptive variations in the supply of gold available for international monetary purposes.

The Bretton Woods System

The one lesson that everyone thought had been learned from the 1930s was that a system of either freely fluctuating exchange rates or fixed rates with easily accomplished devaluations was a sure route to disaster. In order to achieve a system of orderly exchange rates that would facilitate the free flow of trade following World War II, representatives of most of the countries that had participated in the alliance against Germany, Italy, and Japan met at Bretton Woods, New Hampshire, in 1944. In the words of Charles Kindleberger of MIT, the Bretton Woods meeting was "the biggest constitution-writing exercise ever to occur in international monetary relations."

The Bretton Woods system had three objectives: (1) to create a set of rules that would maintain fixed exchange rates in the face of short-term fluctuations, (2) to guarantee that changes in exchange rates would occur only in the face of "fundamental" deficits or surpluses in the balance of payments, and (3) to ensure that when such changes did occur, they would not spark a series of competitive devaluations. The basic characteristic of the system was that U.S. dollars held by foreign monetary authorities were made directly convertible into gold at a price fixed by the U.S. government, while foreign governments fixed the prices at which their currencies were convertible into U.S. dollars. It was this characteristic that made the system a **gold exchange standard.** Gold was the ultimate reserve, but other currencies were held as reserves because directly or indirectly they could be exchanged for gold.

As we saw in the text, a system with a rate that is pegged against short-term fluctuations but can be adjusted from time to time is called an adjustable peg system. To maintain the convertibility of their currencies at fixed exchange rates, the monetary authorities of each country had to be ready to buy and sell their currency in foreign exchange markets to offset imbalances at the pegged rates.[2]

To be able to support the exchange market, the monetary authorities had to have reserves of acceptable foreign exchange. In the Bretton Woods system the authorities held reserves of gold and claims on key currencies, mainly the U.S. dollar and the British pound sterling. When a country's currency was in excess supply, its authorities would sell dollars, sterling, or gold. When a country's currency was in excess demand, its authorities would buy dollars or sterling. If they then wished to increase their gold reserves, they would use the dollars to purchase gold from the Fed, thus depleting the U.S. gold stock.

The problem for the United States was to have enough gold to maintain fixed-price convertibility of the dollar into gold as demanded by foreign monetary authorities. The problem for all other countries was to maintain convertibility (on either a restricted or unrestricted basis) between their currency and the U.S. dollar at a fixed rate of exchange.

Problems of the Adjustable Peg System

Here we see how the three problems of the Bretton Woods system discussed in the text actually worked out in the period after World War II.

Reserves to accommodate short-term fluctuations.
It is generally believed that the average size and frequency of the gaps between demand and supply on the foreign exchange market created when central banks peg their exchange rates will increase as the volume of international payments increases. Since there was a strong upward trend in the volume of overall international payments, there was also a strong upward trend in the demand for foreign exchange reserves.

The ultimate reserve in the Bretton Woods system was gold. The use of gold as a reserve caused two serious problems during the 1960s and early

1970s. First, the world's supply of monetary gold did not grow fast enough to provide adequate reserves for the expanding volume of trade. As a result of the fixed price of gold, rising costs of production, and rising commercial uses, the world's stock of monetary gold during the 1960s was rising at less than 2 percent per year, while trade was growing at nearly 10 percent per year. Gold, which had been 66 percent of the total monetary reserves in 1959, was only 40 percent in 1970, and had fallen to 30 percent by 1972. Over this period reserve holdings of dollars and sterling rose sharply. Clearly, the gold backing needed to maintain convertibility of these currencies was becoming increasingly inadequate.

Second, the country whose currency is convertible into gold must maintain sufficient reserves to ensure convertibility. During the 1960s the United States lost substantial gold reserves to other countries that had acquired dollar claims through their balance-of-payments surpluses with the United States. By the late 1960s the reduction in U.S. reserves had been sufficiently large to undermine confidence in America's continued ability to maintain dollar convertibility.

Adjusting to long-term disequilibria.
The second characteristic problem of a fixed-rate system is the adjustment to long-term disequilibria that develops because of secular shifts in the demands for and supplies of foreign exchange.

These disequilibria developed slowly. At first they led to a series of speculative crises as people expected a realignment of exchange rates to occur. Finally they led to a series of realignments that started in 1967. Each occurred amid quite spectacular flows of speculative funds that thoroughly disorganized normal trade and payments.

Speculative crises.
The adjustable peg system often leads to situations in which speculators are presented with one-way bets. In these disequilibria situations, there is an increasing chance of an exchange rate adjustment in one direction with little or no chance of a movement in the other direction. Speculators then have an opportunity to secure a large potential gain with no corresponding potential for loss. Speculative crises associated with the need to adjust to

[2] The exchange rates were not quite fixed; they were permitted to vary by 1 percent on either side of their par values. Later the bands of permitted fluctuation were widened to 2.25 percent on either side of par.

fundamental disequilibria were the downfall of the system.

Collapse of the Bretton Woods System

The Bretton Woods system worked reasonably well for nearly 20 years. Then it was beset by a series of crises of ever-increasing severity that reflected the system's underlying weaknesses.

Speculation against the British pound.   Throughout the 1950s and 1960s, the British economy was more inflation prone than the U.S. economy, and the British balance of payments was generally in deficit. Holders of sterling thus had reason to worry that the British government might not be able to keep sterling convertible into dollars at a fixed rate. When these fears grew strong, there would be speculative rushes to sell sterling before it was devalued.

The crises in the 1960s were of this kind. By the mid 1960s it was clear to everyone that the pound was seriously overvalued. Finally, in 1967 it was devalued in the midst of a serious speculative crisis. Many other countries with balance-of-payments deficits followed, bringing about the first major round of adjustments in the pegged rates since 1949.

Speculation against the American dollar.   The U.S. dollar was not devalued in 1967. The lower prices of the currencies that were devalued in 1967 plus the increasing Vietnam War expenditures combined to produce a growing deficit in the American balance of payments. This deficit led to the belief that the dollar itself was becoming seriously overvalued. People rushed to buy gold because a devaluation of the U.S. dollar would take the form of raising its gold price. (Under the Bretton Woods system, the dollar was devalued by raising the official price at which the Fed would convert dollars into gold.)

The first break in the Bretton Woods system came in 1968 when the major trading countries were forced to stop pegging the free-market price of gold. Speculative pressure to buy gold could not be resisted, and from that point there were two prices of gold: the official price at which monetary authorities could settle their debts with each other by transferring gold and the free-market price, determined by the forces of private demand and supply independent of any intervention by central banks. The free-market price quickly rose far above the official U.S. price of $35 an ounce (see Figure 41-3).

Once the free-market price of gold was allowed to be determined independently of the official price, speculation against the dollar shifted to those currencies that were clearly undervalued relative to the dollar.[3] The German mark and the Japanese yen were particularly popular targets, and during periods of crisis billions and billions of dollars flowed into speculative holdings of these currencies. The ability of central banks to maintain pegged exchange rates in the face of such vast flights of funds was in question; on several occasions all exchange markets had to be closed for periods of up to a week.

Devaluation of the dollar.   By 1971 the American authorities had concluded that the dollar would have to be devalued. This uncovered a problem, inherent in the Bretton Woods system, that had so far gone virtually unnoted. Because the system required each foreign country to fix its exchange rate against the dollar, the American authorities could not independently fix their exchange rate against other currencies.[4]

But when the U.S. economy began to inflate rapidly, it became necessary to devalue the U.S. dollar relative to most other currencies. Any other country in this situation would merely unilaterally devalue its currency. But the only way that the required U.S. devaluation could be brought about was for all other countries to agree to revalue their currencies relative to the dollar.

Prompted by continuing speculation against the

[3] When the free-market price of gold was held the same as the official price, a devaluation of the dollar entailed a rise in the free-market price—and hence profit for all holders of gold. Once the free-market price was left to be determined by the forces of private demand and supply independent of any central bank intervention, there was no reason to believe that a rise in the official price of gold would affect the (much higher) free-market price. Speculators against the dollar then had to hold other currencies whose price was sure to rise against the dollar in the event of the dollar's being devalued.

[4] If, for example, the British authorities pegged the pound sterling at $2.40, as they did in 1967, the dollar was pegged at £.417, and the Fed could not independently decide on another rate. Similar considerations applied to all other currencies.

dollar, President Nixon suspended gold convertibility of the dollar in August 1971. He also announced the intention of the United States to achieve a de facto devaluation of the dollar by persuading those nations whose balance of payments were in surplus to allow their rates to float upward against the dollar.

By ending the gold convertibility of the dollar, the U.S. government brought the gold exchange standard aspect of the Bretton Woods system officially to an end. The fixed-exchange-rate aspect of the system lasted a little longer.

The immediate response to the announced intention of devaluing the dollar was a speculative run against that currency. The crisis was so severe that for the second time that year foreign exchange markets were closed throughout Europe. When the markets reopened after a week, several countries allowed their rates to float. The Japanese, however, announced their intention of retaining their existing rate. Despite severe Japanese controls, $4 billion in speculative funds managed to find its way into yen in the last two weeks of August, and the Japanese were forced to abandon their fixed-rate policy by allowing the yen to float upward.

After some hard bargaining, an agreement among the major trading nations was signed at the Smithsonian Institution in Washington, D.C. in December 1971. The main element of the agreement was that all countries consented to a 7.9 percent devaluation of the dollar against their currencies.

De facto dollar standard.   Following the Smithsonian agreements, the world was on a de facto **dollar standard**. Foreign monetary authorities held their reserves in the form of dollars and settled their international debts with dollars. But the dollar was not convertible into gold or anything else. The ultimate value of the dollar was given not by gold but by the American goods, services, and assets that dollars could be used to purchase.

One major problem with such a system is that the kind of American inflation that upset the Bretton Woods system is no less upsetting to a dollar standard because the real purchasing-power value of the world's dollar reserves is eroded by such an inflation.

Final breakdown of fixed exchange rates.   The Smithsonian agreements did not lead to a new period of international payments stability. This doomed the hope that a de facto dollar standard could provide the basis for an international payments system free of crises and devaluations.

The U.S. inflation continued unchecked, and the U.S. balance of payments never returned to the relatively satisfactory position that had been maintained throughout the 1960s. Within a year of the agreements speculators began to believe that a further realignment of rates was necessary. In January 1973 speculative movements of capital once again occurred. In February the United States proposed a further 11 percent devaluation of the dollar. This was to be accomplished by raising the official price of gold to $42.22 an ounce and by not keeping other currencies tied to the dollar at the old rates. Intense speculative activity followed the announcement.

Five member countries of the European Economic Community then decided to stabilize their currencies against each other but to let them float together against the dollar. This joint float was called the *snake*. Norway and Sweden later joined the snake arrangement. The other EEC countries (Ireland, Italy, and the United Kingdom) and Japan announced their intention to allow their currencies to float in value. In June 1972 the Bank of England had abandoned the de facto dollar standard with the announcement that it had "temporarily" abandoned its commitment to support sterling at a fixed par value against the U.S. dollar. The events of 1973 led "temporarily" to become "indefinitely."

Fluctuations in exchange rates were severe. By early July 1973 the snake currencies had appreciated about 30 percent against the dollar, but by the end of the year they had nearly returned to their February values.

The dollar devaluation formally took effect in October. Most industrialized countries maintained the nominal values of their currencies in terms of gold and SDRs, thereby appreciating them in terms of the U.S. dollar by 11 percent. The devaluation quickly became redundant, for despite attempts to restore fixed rates, the drift to flexible rates had become irresistible by the end of 1973.

42

Macroeconomic Policy in an Open Economy

When we shift our attention to an *open* economy, we encounter a number of features that are of particular interest to the study of macroeconomic policy. New complications arise. These include the behavior of the terms of trade and their influence on net exports and national income, the nature and extent of foreign borrowing, and changes in foreign interest and inflation rates. The response of the economy to various policies is altered. For example, as we saw in Chapter 40, the size of the simple multiplier is smaller than that in a closed economy. Also, as we shall see in this chapter, since Canadian interest rates are closely tied to those prevailing in foreign markets, the mechanism by which macroeconomic policies influence the economy can differ sharply from the closed-economy mechanisms studied so far in this book.

Consideration of the openness of the economy also introduces some new policy targets that may be in conflict with policy targets arising solely from domestic considerations. In the next section we introduce the study of macroeconomic policy in an open economy by considering these possibly conflicting targets.

Internal and External Balance

In this chapter we summarize the domestic policy objectives in terms of a target level of real national income. Restricting our attention to one domestic policy target is done primarily for simplicity. However, it is perhaps more general than would first appear. For example, if one objective is to reduce the domestic rate of inflation, we know from our analysis in Chapter 36 that this can be accomplished by choosing a target level of real national income below the capacity level. When real national income is at its target level, we say the economy has achieved **internal balance.**

In this section we focus on the trade account as the external policy target. As we saw in Chapter 40, the trade account is related to the current and capital accounts. Hence such things as the level of interest payments that must be paid to foreigners, the need to accumulate or decumulate foreign exchange reserves, or the need for capital flows to finance new investment may influence the target level of the trade balance.[1] When the trade account is equal to its target level, we say the economy has achieved **external balance.**

In this section we also treat the exchange rate as fixed. Later in the chapter we study the complications that arise when the capital account and a flexible exchange rate are considered.

The conditions for internal and external balance are illustrated in Figure 42-1.

The Potential for Conflict Between Objectives

When policies used to move the economy closer to one objective move the economy further from the other objective, the objectives are said to be in conflict.

Policies to eliminate a recessionary gap will also influence the trade account by causing a movement along the net export function (which is negatively sloped). Whether there is a conflict between the objectives of internal and external balance depends on how the trade account and real national income compare to their target values.

For simplicity, we now make the assumption that the target level of real national income is the capacity level of output and that the target for the trade account is a zero balance.[2] Hence we can identify the initial situation relative to the targets simply in terms of the signs of the output gap and the trade account balance. There are four possible cases:

1. A trade account *deficit* combined with an *inflationary gap* poses no conflict, because the contraction of aggregate demand to eliminate the inflationary gap leads to a reduction in imports and hence reduces the trade deficit.

---

[1] For example, a nation with a large undeveloped natural resource base may have a low current national income yet anticipate a high future national income when the resource base is developed. High current investment to develop the resource base and high current consumption in anticipation of that high future income will together lead to high imports and a trade account deficit. Hence the *target* trade account in such a circumstance may well be a deficit. (See also the discussion in Box 40-1 on page 886–887.)

[2] We emphasize that this assumption is made only to simplify the discussion and that the actual targets may often differ from these. The same principles apply regardless of the actual values of the targets.

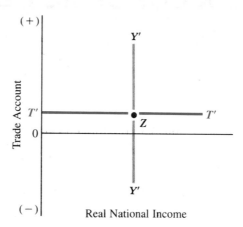

FIGURE 42-1   Internal and External Balance

Internal and external balance are simultaneously attained at point Z. Internal balance is defined in terms of a target level of real national income and is depicted by the vertical line $Y'Y'$. External balance is defined in terms of a target level of the trade account and is depicted by the horizontal line $T'T'$. Only at the intersection, point Z, are both internal and external balance attained.

2. A trade account *deficit* combined with a *recessionary gap* does pose a conflict, because the expansion of aggregate demand to eliminate the recessionary gap leads to an increase in imports and hence a worsening of the trade deficit.
3. A trade account *surplus* combined with a *recessionary gap* poses no conflict, because the expansion of aggregate demand to eliminate the recessionary gap increases imports and hence reduces the trade surplus.
4. A trade account *surplus* combined with an *inflationary gap* does pose a conflict, because the contraction of aggregate demand to eliminate the inflationary gap leads to a reduction in imports and hence an increase in the trade surplus.

The four cases are depicted in Figure 42-2.

Conflict Cases

In case 2 in our list the trade account deficit calls for a decrease in national income, but the recessionary gap calls for an increase. In case 4 the trade account

FIGURE 42-2 Conflicts Between Internal and External Balance

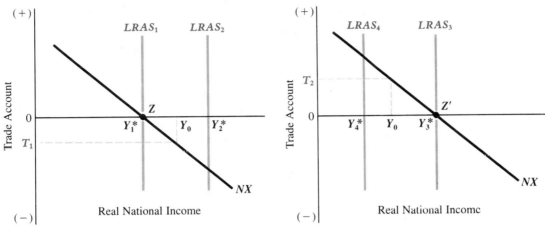

(i) A trade account deficit

(ii) A trade account surplus

Of the four different possible combinations of signs of the output gap and the trade account, only two pose conflicts. In both parts of the figure, the net export function, which relates the trade account to real national income, is shown by the black line labeled NX. The actual level of income is given by Y_0, so in part (i) there is a trade account deficit of T_1, while in part (ii) there is a trade account surplus of T_2.

In part (i), if potential output is given by Y_1^* so there is an inflationary gap (case 1), there is no conflict, since adjustment of actual real national income to achieve one target will also achieve the other target, at point Z. However, if potential output is given by Y_2^* so there is a recessionary gap (case 2), there is a conflict, since movement of actual real national income to achieve either target will cause a movement away from the other target.

In part (ii), if potential income is given by Y_3^* so there is a recessionary gap (case 3), there is no conflict, since adjustment of actual real national income to achieve one target will also achieve the other target, at point Z'. However, if potential output is given by Y_4^* so there is an inflationary gap (case 4), there is a conflict, since a change in actual real national income to achieve either target will cause a movement away from the other target.

---

surplus calls for an increase in national income, but the inflationary gap calls for a decrease.[3]

A conflict arises between the objectives of internal and external balance when the two call for opposite changes in the level of national income.

[3] Case 2 has traditionally attracted the most attention, perhaps because a trade deficit is generally viewed as being a more serious problem than a trade surplus, and—at least in the past—unemployment has been considered a more serious problem than inflation. Case 2 is often referred to as a situation in which there is a "balance-of-payments constraint" on domestic stabilization policy.

Basically, the conflicts arise from *movements along* the net export function; we now see that resolution of such conflict arises from *shifts in* the net export function.

Expenditure-changing and Expenditure-switching Policies

We start by repeating the basic equilibrium condition, that national income equal aggregate desired expenditure.

$$Y = C + I + G + (X - M)$$ 　　　**[1]**

The total $C + I + G$ is often referred to as domestic absorption, or simply absorption. This concept, which was discussed in Box 31-2 on pages 650–651, refers to total expenditure on goods for use in the economy. Denoting absorption by the letter A, we can rewrite the national income equilibrium condition as

$$Y = A + (X - M) \qquad [2]$$

This condition states that equilibrium national income is equal to aggregate desired expenditure, which in turn is equal to domestic absorption plus net exports.

Equation 2 is useful in distinguishing between two types of policies that might be used to maintain internal and external balance. Policies that maintain the level of aggregate desired expenditure but influence its composition between domestic absorption and net exports are called **expenditure-switching** policies. Policies that change aggregate desired expenditure are called **expenditure-changing** policies.

Expenditure-changing policies involve moving along a given net export function, so changes in the trade balance and national income must be *negatively* related. If the initial situation calls for them to move in the same direction, the use of expenditure-changing policies necessarily involves a conflict.

The conflicts between the objectives of internal and external balance arise from the use of expenditure-changing policies.

An expenditure-switching policy shifts the net export function. As we shall see, this can lead to *positively* related changes in the trade balance and national income. Devaluation or revaluation of the domestic currency, restrictions on international trade such as tariffs or quotas, and domestic inflation or deflation relative to foreign conditions are all expenditure-switching policies.[4]

---

[4] When restrictions on international trade, such as tariffs or quotas, are used in this manner, they are referred to as *commercial policy.* Commercial policy may in some circumstances be useful for macroeconomic purposes, but it is never the case that commercial policy *must* be used; other expenditure-switching policies will have the same macroeconomic effects.

A Trade Account Deficit

As we have seen, a trade account deficit means that national income is less than domestic absorption. Now consider policies to eliminate the trade account deficit; to be successful, the policies must raise national income *relative* to absorption.

Case 1: A deficit combined with an inflationary gap: No conflict. If the economy already has an inflationary gap, national income should not be increased further. The trade account deficit indicates that domestic absorption is above the current level of national income and hence, by virtue of the inflationary gap, above the full-employment level. To eliminate the deficit, absorption must be lowered. In other words, if net exports are to rise, resources must be released through a reduction in domestic usage. This calls for *expenditure-reducing* policies such as reductions in the money supply, cuts in government expenditure, and increases in taxes. No conflict for expenditure-changing policies arises in this case, because the expenditure reduction cuts the inflationary gap and improves the trade account by inducing a movement along the net export function.

Case 2: A deficit combined with a recessionary gap: Conflict. When national income is below its capacity level, income can be expanded. But an expansion in national income with a fixed net export function would worsen the trade account, so expenditure-increasing policies are not appropriate. A reduction in national income to reduce the trade deficit would worsen unemployment, so expenditure-reducing policies are not appropriate. What is needed is a switch in expenditure away from foreign goods (thus reducing the trade deficit) and toward domestic goods (thus reducing the recessionary gap).

Policies to induce a *switch* of some expenditure from foreign goods to domestic goods—thereby *shifting* the net export function rightward and raising national income—will alleviate the conflict posed by a recessionary gap combined with a trade deficit.

Such policies include devaluation of the currency and protective measures such as tariffs and quotas. This is illustrated in Figure 42-3.[5]

[5] From the discussion in Chapter 40, it would appear that there should be two shifts in the *NX* function. The first is due to the switch in expenditure; the second, which will be in the opposite direction to the first, is due to the induced change in the price of domestic goods as national income changes. The analysis in Figure 42-3, and in this chapter, incorporates this second effect in the response of *NX* national income by using the *SRAS* curve to capture the price effect. [54]

A Trade Account Surplus

Cases 3 and 4 in our list both involve a trade account surplus. An expansion of national income will therefore cause a move toward external balance by raising imports. Hence in case 3, where there is a recessionary gap, no conflict arises, and expenditure-raising policies will lead to movement toward both targets. In case 4, where there is an inflationary gap, a conflict does arise; external balance calls for expenditure in-

FIGURE 42-3   A Trade Deficit and a Recessionary Gap

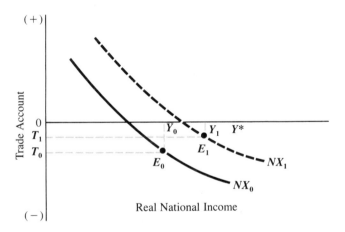

(i) Net export function

A policy to switch expenditure away from foreign goods and toward domestic goods can be used to resolve the conflict posed by a trade deficit combined with a recessionary gap. Initially, the net export function is given by NX_0 in part (i), and aggregate demand is given by AD_0 in part (ii). Equilibrium is at E_0 with real national income equal to Y_0. There is a recessionary gap of Y_0Y^* and a trade deficit of T_0.

An expenditure-switching policy raises net exports at each level of income, so the net export function shifts right to NX_1 in part (i). The policy also raises aggregate demand, so the AD curve shifts right to AD_1 in part (ii). The new equilibrium is at E_1, with real national income of Y_1 and a trade deficit of T_1. Hence both the recessionary gap and the trade deficit are reduced.

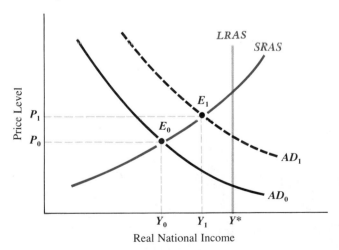

(ii) Determination of national income

creases, but internal balance calls for expenditure reduction. What is needed is a *switch* in expenditure away from domestic goods (thus reducing the inflationary gap) and toward foreign goods (thus reducing the trade account surplus).

Policies to induce a switch of expenditure from domestic goods to foreign goods—thereby *shifting* the net export function leftward and lowering national income—will alleviate the con- flict posed by an inflationary gap combined with a trade surplus.

This is illustrated in Figure 42-4.

A General Statement

We have now seen the difference in the effects of the two types of expenditure policies in an open economy.

FIGURE 42-4   A Trade Surplus and an Inflationary Gap

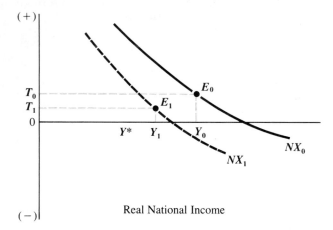

(i) Net export function

A policy to switch expenditure away from domestic goods and toward foreign goods can be used to solve the conflict posed by a trade surplus combined with an inflationary gap. Initially, the net export function is given by NX_0 in part (i), and aggregate demand is given by AD_0 in part (ii). Equilibrium is at E_0 with real national income equal to Y_0. This is an inflationary gap of Y^*Y_0 and a trade surplus of T_0.

An expenditure-switching policy lowers net exports at each level of income, so the net export function shifts left to NX_1 in part (ii). The policy also lowers aggregate demand, so the aggregate demand curve shifts left to AD_1 in part (ii). The equilibrium moves from E_0 to E_1, real national income falls to Y_1, and the trade surplus falls to T_1. Hence both the inflationary gap and the trade surplus are reduced.

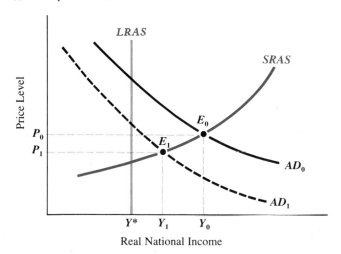

(ii) Determination of national income

To achieve internal and external balance, a combination of expenditure-changing and expenditure-switching policies is generally required.

In the conflict situations, expenditure-switching policies will result in movement *toward* both targets. But they alone cannot be expected exactly to achieve both internal and external balance. Hence both types of policies are generally required. Expenditure-switching policies are necessary to shift the net export function in order to make the two objectives consistent. [In terms of Figures 42-3(i) and 42-4(i) this means that expenditure-switching policies should be used to ensure that the *NX* curve cuts the horizontal axis at Y^*. There is no assurance, however, that the effects of such policies on the aggregate demand curve will give rise to actual real national income of Y^*.] Then expenditure-changing policies—which shift the aggregate demand curve but not the net export curve—can be used to attain both internal and external balance simultaneously.

Some long-run aspects of such policies are taken up in Box 42-1.

Macroeconomic Policy and the Capital Account

The capital account of the balance of payments records international movements of investment funds. When foreign investors buy securities issued by Canadian corporations or governments or invest in Canadian industry, this capital inflow is recorded as a receipt in the balance of payments, because it gives rise to an increase in the amount of foreign currency offered for Canadian dollars in the foreign exchange market. Conversely, the acquisition of foreign assets by Canadians represents a capital outflow and is recorded as a payment because foreign currency is used up by such transactions.

The primary means by which capital flows can be influenced by the policy authorities is through domestic interest rates. International traders hold transactions balances just like domestic traders. These balances are often lent out on a short-term basis rather than being left idle. Naturally enough, holders of these balances will tend to lend them,

other things being equal, in markets where interest rates are highest. If short-term interest rates are raised in Canada, this will induce an inflow of short-run capital to take advantage of the higher Canadian rates. A lowering of Canadian interest rates will have the opposite effect, as capital moves elsewhere to take advantage of the now relatively higher foreign rates.

Long-term capital flows are typically less sensitive to interest-rate differentials, but they are nevertheless likely to show some response. In particular, Canadian corporations and governments attempt to minimize the cost of long-term borrowing by selling bonds in foreign markets when the foreign interest rate is lower than the Canadian rate.

In discussing the trade account in the first part of this chapter, we did not distinguish between the effects of monetary and fiscal policy. However, capital flows respond to interest rates, and monetary and fiscal policies that have the same influence on income have opposite effects on interest rates. As we saw in Chapter 34, in a closed economy expansionary monetary policy exerts its influence on income by reducing interest rates. Fiscal policy influences aggregate demand directly, and fiscal-policy-induced increases in national income create an excess demand for money, which in a closed economy causes interest rates to rise. In discussing capital flows in an open economy it is therefore necessary to distinguish between the operation of monetary and fiscal policies.

Fiscal Policy and the Capital Account

The effects of fiscal policy on the capital account of an open economy are related to the interest-rate effects it would have in a closed economy. Expansionary fiscal policy, for example, leads to increased federal government borrowing in domestic capital markets. In a closed economy this forces interest rates up; in an open economy it forces other domestic borrowers to import their capital requirements from foreign financial centers. Many provincial governments finance their deficits by borrowing abroad themselves, thereby giving rise directly to a capital account surplus. In summary:

An expansionary fiscal policy will put upward pressure on interest rates and lead to an inflow

BOX 42-1

Expenditure-switching Policies in the Long Run

Use of expenditure-switching policies such as devaluation has often been very controversial. Supporters point to the increase in output and the reduction in the trade account deficit shown in Figure 42-3. Opponents focus on the inflationary impact indicated by the rise in the price level also shown in Figure 42-3. The controversy often hinges on disagreement about the relative size of these two effects. Some of the controversy can be defused by distinguishing between the long-run and short-run effects of such policies.

In the text we focused on the short-run effects of expenditure-switching policies, treating the *SRAS* curve as fixed and studying the shifts in the *NX* and *AD* curves. One alternative to using such policies is to do nothing, and let the monetary adjustment mechanism studied in Chapter 34 operate to eliminate the recessionary gap. (Similar automatic mechanism also exist that establish external balance in the long run.) Justification for using devaluation, for example, in the face of a recessionary gap and a trade deficit is that these automatic adjustment mechanisms are very slow to operate. Hence support for devaluation and other expenditure-switching policies focuses on their ability to influence output and the trade account *in the short run.*

Note, however, that such policies do not alter potential output (they do not shift the *LRAS* curve), and hence they have no effect on output in the long run. But by circumventing the monetary adjustment mechanism and stimulating aggregate demand, expenditure-switching policies ensure that when potential income is attained in the long run, the price level will be higher than it would have been in their absence. Opponents of such policies focus on this price-level effect, since that is the only long-run effect the policies have. Typically these opponents believe the automatic adjustment mechanisms are strong enough so that the long-run effect would be achieved fairly quickly without intervention or that devaluations set up expectations of price rises that quickly feed into wages and hence create very little real response of output and employment even in the short run.

The key policy implication of this debate is that devaluation and other expenditure-switching policies should be directed toward the external target, but they should be combined with expenditure-changing policies that focus on the internal target. In particular, a devaluation should be accompanied by expenditure-reducing policies to offset any inflationary gap caused by the devaluation in the short run and hence to avoid the price-level increase that would otherwise ensue in the long run.

of foreign capital, thereby moving the capital account toward a surplus. A contractionary fiscal policy will have the opposite effects.

Monetary Policy and the Capital Account

Since monetary policy influences interest rates in a closed economy, it will also influence the capital account in an open economy:

An expansionary monetary policy will put downward pressure on interest rates and lead to an outflow of capital, thereby moving the capital account toward a deficit. A contractionary monetary policy will have the opposite effects.

An Alternative Target for External Balance

So far in this chapter we have used *external balance* to mean achieving the target level of the trade account. Consideration of international capital flows suggests an expansion of this target to incorporate the capital account and interest payments on the foreign debt as well.

We now specify external balance in terms of a target level of the overall balance of payments.

For simplicity, we take external balance to mean a zero overall balance of payments so that any current account imbalance is exactly offset by capital account transactions.

Before turning to a discussion of how monetary and fiscal policy might be combined to achieve internal and external balance in this circumstance, it will be useful to examine the relationship between the money supply and the overall balance of payments.

The Balance of Payments and the Money Supply

Suppose that Canada is experiencing a balance-of-payments deficit and that the Bank of Canada intervenes in the foreign exchange market to maintain the value of the Canadian dollar. The Bank will be selling

TABLE 42-1   Balance Sheet Changes Caused by a Sale of Foreign Currency by the Central Bank

Nonbank private sector	
Assets	Liabilities
Foreign currency (equivalent value in Canadian dollars) +100	
Deposits −100	

Chartered banks	
Assets	Liabilities
Reserves (deposits with central bank) −100	Demand deposits −100

Central bank	
Assets	Liabilities
Foreign currency −100	Deposits of chartered banks −100

The money supply is reduced when the central bank sells foreign currency to maintain a fixed exchange rate when there is a balance-of-payments deficit. A deficit of 100 leads to an excess demand for foreign currency of 100, which is met by a reduction of official reserves by this amount. When the central bank receives payment in the form of a cheque drawn on a chartered bank, bank reserves fall by 100. There will then be a multiple contraction of deposit money through the process analyzed in Chapter 33.

foreign currency in exchange for Canadian dollars and thereby running down its stock of official reserves. Payment for the foreign currency acquired by private participants in the market will normally be made in the form of a Canadian dollar cheque drawn on one of the chartered banks. This cheque will be cleared by reducing the deposits of the chartered bank at the Bank of Canada. These transactions are summarized in Table 42-1.

If there are no offsetting transactions, a balance-of-payments deficit will lead to a decrease both in bank reserves and in bank deposits equal to the amount of foreign exchange sold by the central bank. A surplus will lead to an increase in bank reserves and deposits.

Thus a balance-of-payments deficit will lead to a contraction of the money supply. Of course, the central bank has the option of preventing this from happening by undertaking other offsetting transactions. For example, the decrease in bank reserves can be offset by an open-market purchase of bonds, which will have the effect of increasing bank reserves. This procedure of insulating the domestic money supply from the effects of balance-of-payments deficits or surpluses is known as **sterilization.**

Fixed Exchange Rates

Monetary Policy

To see the limitations of monetary policy under a fixed exchange rate, consider the following sequence of events. Suppose that interest rates in Canada are at levels similar to those in the rest of the world, and thus there is no inducement for large international movements of capital. Suppose now that the Bank of Canada, faced with a large recessionary gap, seeks to stimulate demand through an expansionary monetary policy. The Bank buys bonds in the open market, thereby increasing the money supply and reducing interest rates.

Lower interest rates stimulate an outflow of capital from Canada and thus a deficit on the capital account. To the extent that national income rises, movement along the net export function creates a deficit on the trade account. Thus the overall balance of payments moves into deficit. To maintain the fixed exchange rate, the Bank will have to intervene in the foreign exchange market and sell foreign currency. This will have the effect of *reducing* the money supply and thus *reversing* the increase brought about by the initial open-market operation.

If no other transactions are initiated by the Bank of Canada, national income and the money supply will fall and domestic interest rates will rise until they all return to their initial levels. Thus the deficit will be self-correcting, and the Bank's expansionary policy will be nullified.

Suppose now that the Bank of Canada attempts to sterilize the impact on the money supply of the balance-of-payments deficit. The difficulty with this strategy is that it can be continued only as long as the Bank has sufficient reserves of foreign exchange. If capital flows are highly sensitive to interest rates, as a great deal of evidence suggests is the case, these reserves will be run down at a rapid rate and the Bank will be forced to abandon its expansionary policy.

Under a fixed exchange rate, there is little scope for the use of monetary policy for domestic stabilization purposes because of the sensitivity of international capital flows to interest rates. The central bank will be forced to maintain domestic interest rates close to the levels existing in the rest of the world, and it will not be able to bring about substantial changes in the domestic money supply.

Fiscal Policy

Consider now the effectiveness of fiscal policy under fixed exchange rates. Suppose again that Canadian interest rates are in line with those of the rest of the world when an expansionary fiscal policy is introduced, aimed at reducing a large recessionary gap. The fiscal expansion raises the level of domestic interest rates and national income.

Higher interest rates stimulate a flow of capital into Canada, thereby leading to a surplus on the capital account. If the capital flows are large, as they

are likely to be in Canada because of the close integration of Canadian and American capital markets, the surplus on capital account will exceed the current account deficit arising from the increased national income. Hence there will be an overall balance-of-payments surplus.

To maintain the fixed exchange rate, the Bank of Canada will have to intervene in the foreign exchange market and buy foreign currency. This will have the effect of increasing the money supply, thus reinforcing the initial fiscal stimulus.

Under a fixed exchange rate, interest-sensitive international capital flows stabilize the domestic interest rate and enhance the effectiveness of fiscal policy.

Combining Monetary and Fiscal Policy

Consider an attempt to increase employment with expansionary monetary policy that reduces interest rates and thereby stimulates investment and other interest-sensitive expenditure. The decline in domestic interest rates makes it more attractive to invest short-term capital abroad rather than at home. The outflow of short-term capital to be invested at more attractive rates in foreign financial centers worsens the balance of payments on the short-term capital account. Of course, if the expansionary policy succeeds in raising income, there will be additional strain on the balance of payments on current account as a consequence of the increased expenditure on imports caused by the rise in income.

In principle, the conflict can be removed by an appropriate combination of monetary and fiscal policy. Consider the country with full employment and a balance-of-payments deficit. It could eliminate the deficit by following a tighter monetary policy to increase domestic interest rates and attract short-term capital. At the same time, the contractionary effect of tight money on domestic expenditure and employment could be offset by raising government expenditures or cutting taxes. Thus the two goals can both be achieved through a combination of tight monetary policy and expansionary fiscal policy.

This strategy is unlikely to be a satisfactory solution to a persistent current account deficit. The country will find it increasingly difficult to maintain its exchange rate by importing short-term capital. Short-term international capital flows are extremely volatile, and they are particularly sensitive to shifts in expectations concerning exchange rates. If investors lose confidence in a country's ability to maintain its existing exchange rate, capital outflows will build up, and ultimately a devaluation will be required to reduce the deficit and restore confidence.

Flexible Exchange Rates

A major advantage of a flexible exchange rate is that it removes any conflict between domestic stabilization objectives and the balance of payments, because deficits or surpluses are automatically eliminated through movements in the exchange rate. In addition, a flexible rate often cushions the domestic economy against cyclical variations in economic activity in other countries. If, for example, the U.S. economy goes into a recession, the decline in U.S. income will lead to a reduction in demand for goods exported from Canada. The fall in exports will reduce income in Canada through the multiplier effect. But if the value of the Canadian dollar is allowed to respond to market forces, there will also be a depreciation. This fall in the external value of our currency will stimulate demand for our exports and encourage the substitution of domestically produced goods for imports. Thus the depreciation will provide a stimulus to demand in Canada that will at least partially offset the depressing effect of the U.S. recession.

Box 42-2 discusses some further aspects of fluctuating exchange rates.

Fiscal Policy

Suppose the government seeks to remove a recessionary gap by expansionary fiscal policy. An increase in government expenditures and/or a reduction in taxes will increase income through the multiplier effect and reduce the size of the gap. This will also tend to cause a movement along the net export function, leading to a deterioration of the trade account. However, this is not the whole story, for there will also be repercussions on the capital account and the exchange rate.

Capital flows and the crowding-out effect. In a closed economy, fiscal policy causes domestic interest rates to rise. This causes interest-sensitive private expenditures to fall, thus partially offsetting the initial expansionary effect of the fiscal stimulus. As we saw in Chapter 32, this *crowding-out effect* plays an important role in the analysis of fiscal policy in a closed economy. In an open economy the crowding-out effect will operate differently, due to international capital flows.

Higher domestic interest rates will induce a capital inflow and cause the domestic currency to appreciate. If capital flows are highly interest-elastic, the external value of the currency is likely to rise substantially. This will depress demand by discouraging exports and encouraging the substitution of imports for domestically produced goods. The initial fiscal stimulus will be *offset* by the expenditure-switching effects of currency appreciation.

Under flexible exchange rates there will be a strong crowding out of net exports that will greatly reduce the effectiveness of fiscal policy.

However, it is possible to eliminate the crowding-out effect by supporting the fiscal policy with an accommodating monetary policy. Suppose that the central bank responds to the increase in the demand for money induced by the fiscal expansion by increasing the supply of money so as to maintain domestic interest rates at their initial level. There will then be no capital inflow and no tendency for the currency to appreciate. Income will expand by the usual multiplier process.

The effectiveness of fiscal policy under flexible exchange rates can be enhanced by an accommodating monetary policy.

Monetary Policy

We have seen that there is little scope under fixed exchange rates for the use of monetary policy for domestic stabilization purposes. Under flexible exchange rates the situation is reversed, and monetary policy becomes a very powerful tool.

Suppose the Bank of Canada seeks to stimulate

BOX 42-2

Understanding Exchange Rate Changes

Since reaching a peak of over $1.05 U.S. in early 1976, the Canadian dollar has depreciated steadily, briefly falling below 70 cents U.S. in 1986 before rising again to around 76 cents U.S. by mid 1987. This fall, shown by the black line in the figure, has prompted news reports of a national crisis of disaster proportions and a source of national shame. Several considerations, however, help us put this slide in some perspective.

Currencies can appreciate or depreciate for many reasons. To take pride in the external price on one's currency is to commit oneself in advance to be proud of a great ragbag of events, some of which will seem undesirable to all reasonable people. Until the public and the media see the folly in viewing the value of a country's currency the way shareholders of a corporation view the price of its stock, there is little hope of a rational discussion of exchange rate policy.

In fact, the fall in the value of the Canadian dollar reflects a number of very different events, some with very different implications.

The fall in the early part of the period reflected higher Canadian inflation and was necessary to restore the competitive position of Canadian industry. Inflation was the problem; depreciation was part of the "solution."

The underlying trend value of the Canadian dollar in terms of the U.S. dollar changes as the Canadian price level changes relative to the American price level.* During the 1960s American inflation exceeded Canadian inflation, and the Canadian dollar rose above the U.S. dollar. From 1971 to 1976 Canadian inflation exceeded U.S. inflation, and the trend PPP value of the Canadian dollar fell steadily, reaching the range 89 to 91 units by the end of 1972. For a while capital flows and other events kept the value of the Canadian dollar above its trend rate, but in 1976 it fell rapidly toward its trend value. The actual value had to fall sooner or later to its trend value, and it is a good thing—it helped restore the international competitiveness of Canadian industry.

From 1981 through 1984 the fall in the Canadian dollar reflected different pressures. In 1980 tight monetary policy in the United States drove up interest rates in that country. As we saw in Chapter 41 (see especially page 902), this presented the Bank of Canada with a policy dilemma: Either let Canadian interest rates rise or let the Canadian dollar fall. The Bank tried to take a middle stance between these two, and

* Recall the discussion of the purchasing power parity exchange rate in Chapter 41, especially pages 900–901.

demand through an expansionary monetary policy. The Bank buys bonds in the open market, thereby increasing bank reserves and the money supply and reducing interest rates. Lower interest rates will cause an outflow of capital from Canada and thus a deficit on the capital account.

Under a fixed rate we saw that the Bank may be forced to reverse its policy in order to stem the loss of foreign reserves. Under a flexible rate, however, the Canadian dollar can be allowed to depreciate. This will stimulate exports and discourage imports so that the deficit on the capital account will be offset by a surplus on the current account.

Domestic employment will be stimulated not only by the fall in interest rates but also by the increased demand for domestically produced goods brought about by a depreciation of the currency. The initial monetary stimulus will be *reinforced* by the expenditure-switching effects of currency depreciation.

Under flexible exchange rates, monetary policy is a powerful tool for stabilizing domestic income and employment. If capital flows are highly interest-elastic, the main channel by which an increase in the money supply stimulates demand for domestically produced goods is a depreciation of the currency.

as a result the value of the Canadian dollar in terms of the U.S. dollar fell gradually between 1980 and 1986.

Is the Canadian Dollar Weak?

A related point is that over the period 1981–1985 the apparent weakness of the Canadian dollar actually reflects the strength of the U.S. dollar. This is shown by the colored line in the figure, where we plot the average or trade-weighted Canadian dollar exchange rate in terms of all Canada's trading partners. The divergent path, with the Canadian dollar falling against the U.S. dollar but rising against the rest of Canada's trading partners, results from the fact that the U.S. dollar was rising even more against European currencies and the Japanese yen during this period. From this perspective the widespread perception of a weak Canadian dollar in the 1981–1985 period was just wrong.

As noted, in early 1986 strong speculative pressures drove the Canadian dollar to just under 70 cents U.S., but later in the year and especially in 1987 the Canadian currency strengthened considerably in terms of the American. This meant that the large depreciation that the U.S. dollar experienced in terms

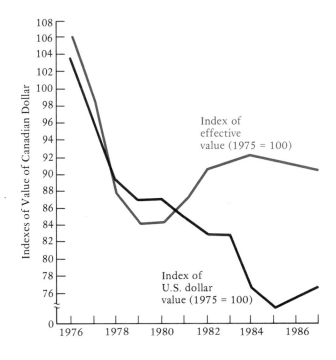

of the offshore currencies did not lead to as large a depreciation of the Canadian dollar in terms of those currencies.

Canadian Stabilization Policy and External Balance

The foregoing arguments suggest that the choice between a fixed rate and a flexible rate can influence the operation of stabilization policy. It is instructive to examine recent Canadian experience from this perspective.

1950–1961: Introduction of Flexible Exchange Rates

Canada operated under a flexible exchange rate from 1950 to 1961. The one major cyclical fluctuation of

the economy in this period began with the recovery from the mild recession of 1954.

The Canadian economy experienced large capital inflows during the period 1955 to 1961 in response to the attractive investment opportunities that existed in Canada. As shown in Figure 42-5, the price of one U.S. dollar remained below one dollar Canadian and at times fell to around 95 cents Canadian. By the end of 1957, however, the economy had turned down, and the unemployment rate rose sharply.

How did monetary policy respond to this serious recession? Although the money supply grew rapidly during 1958, the period 1959–1961 was characterized by a very restrictive monetary policy.

FIGURE 42-5   The Canadian–U.S. Dollar Exchange Rate, 1950–1986

The price of a U.S. dollar has fluctuated from about $0.92 Canadian to over $1.40 Canadian. The exchange rate was determined largely by market forces during the 1950s, when flexible exchange rates were in use. During that period, the price of a U.S. dollar fluctuated from $1.08 Canadian to about $0.92 Canadian. From 1962 to 1970 the exchange rate was pegged in a narrow band around $1.08 Canadian. Since 1970 the exchange rate has again been largely market-determined. After an initial appreciation in the early 1970s, the Canadian dollar fluctuated around or above parity until 1976. From 1976 through 1986, the Canadian dollar steadily depreciated in terms of the U.S. dollar, as indicated by the rise in the price of the U.S. dollar. In 1986 and early 1987 the Canadian dollar appreciated somewhat.

As the theory outlined before indicates, what was needed was an expansionary policy that would have reduced interest rates and discouraged capital inflows. This would have caused the Canadian dollar to depreciate and stimulated the economy. Unfortunately, the advantages of a flexible exchange rate were not used to deal with the serious unemployment problem, and the hoped-for expansion of the money supply and depreciation of the Canadian dollar did not occur until 1961. This episode is discussed further in Box 42-3.

1962–1970: Fixed Exchange Rate

The exchange rate was pegged at $1.08 Canadian to the U.S. dollar throughout the period 1962–1970—that is, the Canadian dollar was worth 92.5 cents U.S. This period witnessed the buildup of boom conditions in the United States, fueled by government expenditures related to the Vietnam War. As is to be expected under a fixed exchange rate, the resulting rise in inflation in the United States spilled over into Canada. In the late 1960s the Canadian

BOX 42-3

The Coyne Affair

The late 1950s witnessed a high level of unemployment and a current account deficit in Canada. Part of the problem was that the U.S. economy was in a mild recession. Several Canadian economists maintained that the Canadian recession, in particular Canadian unemployment, was in fact being aggravated by the restrictive monetary policy pursued by the Bank of Canada. They argued that if monetary policy were loosened, aggregate demand would increase and unemployment would be reduced. They also argued that the current account deficit was primarily due to unusually low levels of exports caused by the U.S. recession; when the American recession ended, they contended, the current account would improve.

The governor of the Bank of Canada, James Coyne, argued that the current account deficit indicated that the Canadian economy was living beyond its means, financed by unusually large capital inflows. He defended the Bank's tight monetary policy on the grounds that if the money supply grew and interest rates fell, capital inflows would *increase.* This would cause an appreciation of the dollar and a further worsening of unemployment. Moreover, the increased current account deficit could be financed only by even larger capital inflows. Thus, in Coyne's view, an expansionary monetary policy would only exacerbate

the problem, and contractionary policy was needed to restrain demand and eliminate the current account deficit.

After considerable controversy in academic and political arenas, the Bank of Canada's policies were repudiated. It was decided that expansionary policies were needed. Since he could not agree with these policies, Coyne was replaced as governor in July 1961, establishing the important precedent that in circumstances of fundamental disagreement, the governor of the Bank of Canada, an appointed official, must either agree to pursue the policies of the elected government as put forward by the minister of finance or resign.

The money supply began to expand. We saw in the text that expansionary monetary policy under flexible exchange rates will lead to a capital outflow, a currency depreciation, and effective expansion of aggregate demand. These predictions were all borne out by developments during this period. Unemployment began to fall almost immediately, and the recession was quickly ended. Downward pressure was put on the Canadian dollar, and in May 1962 the government pegged the Canadian dollar at 92.5 U.S. cents, lower than it had been throughout the previous 10 years.

---

government decided that control of inflation was its primary policy objective. Contractionary monetary policy was introduced, and the restriction in aggregate demand had the desired domestic result: By 1970 inflation had fallen to 3.3 percent. But unemployment had risen, reaching almost 6 percent.

As the analysis earlier in this chapter predicts, a tight monetary policy under fixed exchange rates led to a large balance-of-payments surplus. The Bank of Canada accumulated foreign exchange rapidly; it tried to sterilize the effects that its purchases of foreign exchange would otherwise have had on the domestic money supply, but it had only limited success. In the end, faced with the alternative of accepting a

rapid rate of domestic monetary expansion or dropping the fixed exchange rate, the Bank chose the latter. On May 31, 1970, the Bank announced that it would no longer maintain the Canadian dollar at a fixed par value. Canada had reverted to a flexible exchange rate.

The attempt to inflate at a slower rate than the United States was incompatible with fixed exchange rates; in the face of a high balance-of-payments surplus, either the economy had to be allowed to expand faster or the exchange rate had to be freed. The latter course was chosen.

BOX 42-4

Foreign Inflation: Imported or Insulated?

Two distinct circumstances can lead to an appreciation of the Canadian dollar. One is a change in the price at which the Bank of Canada intervenes in the foreign exchange market; the other is a change in the foreign prices of traded goods in the absence of Bank of Canada intervention. The two circumstances have very different implications for the "competitiveness" of domestic industry. Many critics of Bank of Canada policy in the 1970s argue that the Bank has failed to recognize the distinction between the two cases. Let us examine this contention.

At given foreign-currency prices of traded goods, an increase in the foreign exchange value of the Canadian dollar as maintained by the Bank of Canada will lead to a reduction in the domestic price of traded goods. Output in both the export- and import-competing sectors will fall. In this case appreciation of the Canadian dollar *is* harmful to the international competitive position of Canadian industry, because it lowers the prices of traded goods relative to domestic costs.

At a given value of the exchange rate, an increase in foreign-currency prices of traded goods leads to

an increase in exports and a reduction in imports. The first increases the supply of foreign exchange; the second reduces the demand for foreign exchange. As a result, the Canadian dollar appreciates.

This appreciation offsets the inflationary effects of the foreign-price rise on domestic prices and output. In this case appreciation of the Canadian dollar *is not* harmful to the international competitive position of Canadian industry; the appreciation is a response to foreign disturbances and is instrumental in the process that restores domestic costs and prices to their initial position relative to those of foreign industries.

Nevertheless, in the face of foreign inflation, increases in the value of the Canadian dollar are often opposed, and that opposition is sometimes strong enough to influence policy.

What happens when foreign prices increase and the Canadian dollar is not allowed to appreciate in the manner just outlined? The answer is simple: The Canadian price of traded goods must also rise. In the end, Canadian prices must equal foreign prices adjusted for the exchange rate. If the exchange rate does not change, Canadian prices must change. This is

1970–1975: Return to Floating

Once it was freed, the Canadian dollar rapidly rose in value almost to par with the U.S. dollar. The stage was now set for Canada to continue to pursue its policy of striving for a lower rate of inflation than that in the United States. If Canada were to achieve this goal, it would be necessary that the value of the Canadian dollar *continue to rise* at a rate approximately equal to the excess of the U.S. inflation rate over the Canadian inflation rate.[6]

However, the Bank of Canada, after adopting a flexible exchange rate in order to be able to pursue its anti-inflation policy, simultaneously adopted a more expansionary posture. In particular, it adopted a managed float, commonly referred to as a **dirty**

[6] The discussion of the PPP exchange rate on pages 900–901 could usefully be reviewed at this stage.

float. A dirty float prevails when a central bank operates to regulate closely the foreign exchange value of the domestic currency without undertaking an explicit commitment to maintain it at or near a publicly announced value.

There are two ways to manage a dirty float. One is to intervene directly in the foreign exchange market to stabilize the exchange rate. A balance-of-payments surplus such as Canada was experiencing at the time would mean that the Bank of Canada would have to buy foreign exchange to keep the Canadian dollar from appreciating. Of course, the purchase of foreign exchange by the Bank of Canada would have meant that the supply of Canadian dollars would be rising.

The second method of managing a dirty float is to set domestic monetary conditions (rates of interest and rates of monetary expansion) so that the ex-

known as *imported inflation.*

Many economists argue that precisely such imported inflation occurred in Canada in 1974–1975. At that time OPEC price increases caused enormous increases in inflation in our major trading partners, in particular the United States. Canada then was basically self-sufficient in oil and hence was not adversely affected by the oil shock. The decrease in the relative price of Canadian goods resulting from the American inflation led to an increase in exports and a decrease in imports, causing upward pressure on the Canadian dollar.

The Bank of Canada met this by selling Canadian dollars, thereby stabilizing the exchange rate. Although Canada was on a de jure floating exchange rate at that time, the exchange rate did not in fact perform its "insulation" function because it was not allowed to float de facto. By fixing the exchange rate, the Bank of Canada allowed the rapid takeoff into double-digit inflation in the rest of the world to result in a similar inflation in Canada.

This policy error is not unique to the Canadian experience; it is similar to what has happened in other high-inflation countries such as Israel and Sweden. Attempts to protect domestic industry from the supposed ravages of appreciation end in a situation of imported inflation. But the *real* position of the domestic export sector is ultimately unchanged. Either the exchange rate adjusts, allowing domestic money wages and prices to remain constant, or the exchange rate is held constant and domestic inflation occurs. In the latter event, the inflation bids up domestic wages, causing the domestic price of traded goods to rise. The competitiveness of domestic industry remains the same as under the flexible exchange rate option, because in both cases the foreign-currency prices of our goods rise.

Similar arguments were being made when the United States inflation rate took off to 16 and 17 percent in early 1979; there was pressure on the Bank of Canada to intervene to prevent the Canadian dollar from appreciating. Fortunately, the high American inflation did not last very long, and the problem disappeared. But what would have happened had the U.S. inflation persisted? Have we learned, or will we repeat past mistakes?

change market clears at the desired exchange rate without substantial government intervention in the foreign exchange market. Essentially, this means adopting the monetary policy that would be consistent with fixed rates (and hence might better be termed a "dirty fix").

The Bank of Canada chose the second method, and it led to a more rapid expansion of the money supply than would have been consistent with the goal of reducing inflation. Indeed, it led predictably to a rate of inflation roughly equal to that in the United States and higher than the target rate that led to the monetary contraction of the late 1960s and the adoption of a flexible exchange rate in 1970. Indirectly, by maintaining policies consistent with a stable exchange rate, inflation was imported from the United States.

One reason often put forward to explain this apparent policy mistake is discussed in Box 42-4. Canadian export industries had a significant competitive advantage during the period of the late 1960s, when Canada was maintaining a fixed exchange rate and inflating more slowly than the United States, and this competitive advantage was reflected in the current account surplus experienced over that period. The revaluation that followed the floating of the exchange rate in June 1970 eroded much of the competitive advantage because Canadian costs in terms of U.S. dollars also rose.

As a result, further appreciation of the Canadian dollar was opposed on the grounds that it would further harm the competitive position of the export sector. As Box 42-4 emphasizes, this is not the case when the appreciation arises from a low domestic inflation rate relative to the foreign rate. Stabilizing the exchange rate merely led to increased domestic inflation with no gain in competitive advantage for the domestic export sector. Costs in terms of U.S. dollars still rose, not as a result of a rise in the value of the Canadian dollar but rather as a result of increased domestic factor costs, especially wages.

An alternative explanation or justification for the dirty float was that by the middle of 1970 unemployment had become so high that the government had decided it had become the most important problem. Accordingly, from 1970 through 1973, fiscal policy and monetary policy became expansionary.

In any event, Canada appears to have missed an opportunity to avoid at least some of the inflation that plagued the world economy in the 1970s. The full benefits of a flexible rate were not realized because the Bank of Canada resisted the appreciation of the Canadian dollar and permitted high rates of growth of the money supply. The experience of this period illustrates dramatically the futility of trying to protect Canada's export industries by holding the value of the Canadian dollar below its equilibrium level. This could only be done by increasing the rate of growth of the money supply, which had the effect of raising the domestic rate of inflation.

Whatever was gained by Canada's export industries from a lower Canadian dollar was subsequently lost through a higher rate of inflation. The nation's competitive position in world markets depends on its costs of production relative to those of other countries measured in terms of the same currency. The cost of production in Canada, measured in terms of, say, U.S. dollars, will rise as a result of either an appreciation of the Canadian dollar or an increase in domestic wages and prices. In view of the other undesirable effects of inflation, it seems clear that an appreciation of the Canadian dollar would have been less harmful to the Canadian economy.

1975–1980: Monetary Targeting

In 1975 the Bank of Canada began to follow policies that made use of the monetary independence created by flexible exchange rates. The Bank started announcing target rates of growth for the money supply. While on the surface this policy appeared to meet some of the earlier objections to the use of monetary policy under flexible exchange rates, most econo-

mists believed nevertheless that the policy was still one of a "dirty float."

In 1978–1979 a large number of wage contracts, following the unwinding of wage and price controls, were coming up for renewal. At the same time, the Canadian dollar was under substantial pressure. The Bank of Canada, worried that an inflationary surge coming from a depreciation would trigger an unacceptable increase in wages, intervened to support the dollar. However, many economists were skeptical of the importance of the direct influence of the exchange rate on wages; they believed that the harmful disruptions to financial markets caused by the uncertainty arising from the Bank's departure from its independent monetary stance were likely to be larger than any possible gains on the wage front. This experience was discussed in detail in Chapters 35 and 36.

1980–1983: Imported Monetary Restraint

In the early 1980s a problem for Canadian monetary and exchange rate management arose from the high average level and volatile behavior of interest rates in the United States. A rise in foreign interest rates leads, other things being equal, to large outflows of short-term capital and a depreciation of the domestic currency. Hence a rise in foreign interest rates such as occurred in the United States in 1980 and again in 1981 must be matched by a rise in Canadian rates, a depreciation of the Canadian dollar, or some combination of the two.

In the 1980 episodes Canadian interest rates rose, but by less than those in the United States. The resulting interest differential attracted capital to the United States, and as a result the Canadian dollar fell from a peak of 87 U.S. cents in July to 82.5 U.S. cents in December. When the next round of U.S. interest rate increases occurred in 1981, Canadian interest rates rose virtually as high as their U.S. counterparts, and the dollar remained relatively stable at around 83 U.S. cents. Again the Bank of Canada was criticized for pursuing a "dirty float."

Although nominal interest rates in the United States fell in 1983, real interest rates remained high. The Bank of Canada walked a middle ground between high Canadian real interest rates and depreciation of the Canadian dollar. While the value of the Canadian dollar fell slowly but steadily from 1982 on, it is widely agreed that the Bank of Canada acted to "protect the exchange rate" and that monetary policy in Canada was tighter than it would have been in the absence of the very tight U.S. monetary policy. This had benefits in the form of a substantial fall in inflation in the 1982–1984 period. It also had costs in terms of the severity of the 1982 recession and the persistent high unemployment of the 1983–1984 recovery.

1984–1987: Recovery and Stable Inflation

During the period 1984–1987 the Bank of Canada was able to reap the benefits of the monetary tightness that it pursued in the first years of the decade. The economy experienced a sustained recovery, inflation remained stable in the 4 percent range, and interest rates fell dramatically. As a result, the central focus of monetary policy was the re-entry problem discussed in Chapter 35—it had to accommodate the growth in the demand for real balance while not rekindling inflation. The exchange rate did not play

a central role in the overall design or execution of monetary policy in this period, although exchange rate fluctuations were large and on occasion attracted the interest of the Bank and economic commentary.

The period was dominated by the dramatic fall in the value of the U.S. dollar in terms of the Japanese yen and the major European currencies. In late 1985 and early 1986 the Canadian dollar fell in terms of the U.S. dollar; during a brief period in January 1986 speculative pressures—apparently motivated by concern over Canada's large government budget deficit—drove the Canadian dollar below 70 cents U.S. The Canadian dollar thus experienced an even more dramatic depreciation in terms of the offshore currencies. The Bank of Canada took strong measures to counter the speculative attacks and kept to its medium-term goal of stabilizing the inflation rate. In late 1986 and early 1987 the market acknowledged its faith in these policies, and the Canadian dollar strengthened considerably in terms of the U.S. dollar, rising to around 74 cents U.S. This mitigated the depreciation experienced in terms of the overseas currencies, and the Canadian dollar stayed almost constant in terms of a trade-weighted average of all currencies.

Summary

1. Policymakers in an open economy are faced with policy targets or objectives relating to the foreign sector as well as to the domestic sector. Attainment of these targets is often called achieving external and internal balance, respectively. When policies to move the economy toward one target cause it to move away from the other, the targets are said to be in conflict.
2. Expenditure-changing policy used to control the level of national income will also influence the trade balance by altering imports. There will be a conflict of objectives if there is a trade account deficit and a recessionary gap or if there is a trade account surplus and an inflationary gap. Expenditure-switching policies that shift the net export function can be used to deal with conflict situations.
3. In general, both expenditure-switching and expenditure-changing policies are needed to attain internal and external balance.
4. The capital account is influenced by both fiscal and monetary policy because both influence domestic interest rates.
5. Under a fixed exchange rate, there is little scope for the use of monetary policy for domestic stabilization purposes. Because of the

sensitivity of international capital flows to interest rates, the central bank will be forced to maintain domestic interest rates close to the levels in the rest of the world, and it will not be able to bring about substantial changes in the domestic money supply.

6. Under a fixed exchange rate, capital flows will act to reinforce the effectiveness of fiscal policy.

7. Under a flexible exchange rate, fiscal policy actions will be offset by a crowding-out effect unless they are accompanied by an accommodating monetary policy that prevents changes in interest rates and the exchange rate.

8. Under a flexible exchange rate, monetary policy is a powerful tool. When capital flows are highly interest-elastic, the main channel by which an increase in the money supply increases demand for domestically produced goods is a depreciation of the exchange rate.

9. During the period 1950–1961 Canada was on a flexible exchange rate. The Bank of Canada failed to use monetary policy effectively to deal with a serious unemployment problem. In the late 1960s Canada was on a fixed exchange rate that prevented the authorities from avoiding the rising inflation rates experienced by other countries.

10. The floating of the Canadian dollar in 1970 did not remove the inflationary pressure coming from abroad because the Bank of Canada permitted excessively high rates of growth of the money supply during the period 1971–1975.

11. From 1975 to 1980 the Bank of Canada followed a policy of controlling the rate of growth of the money supply. Nevertheless, there were episodes in which a "dirty float" was maintained.

12. From 1980 to 1983 the Bank of Canada has tried to defend the value of the Canadian dollar. Nevertheless, high U.S. interest rates have led to both tight monetary policy in Canada and some depreciation of the Canadian dollar. Since 1984 monetary policy has been focused on maintaining economic recovery combined with stable inflation, with occasional focus on the exchange rate.

Topics for Review

Internal and external balance
Conflicts between objectives
Expenditure-changing and expenditure-switching policies
Monetary and fiscal policy under fixed exchange rates
Sterilization
Monetary and fiscal policy under flexible exchange rates
Dirty float

Discussion Questions

1. Explain how a country can influence the external value of its currency by (a) direct intervention in the foreign exchange market, (b) fiscal policy, (c) monetary policy.

2. One message of this chapter is that despite a formal commitment to flexible exchange rates, central banks often try to stabilize the exchange rate and to "mimic" policies of major countries' policies. Why might a central bank oppose both a depreciation and an appreciation of its currency? How has Canadian monetary policy performed in this respect in the past two or three years?

3. In a speech in December 1980, Bank of Canada governor Gerald Bouey stated that "the rapid run-up of U.S. short-term [interest] rates is bound to have a major impact on Canada through increases in interest rates here or through a fall in the foreign exchange value of the Canadian dollar, or some combination of the two." Why must one of these responses occur? What policies can the Bank of Canada follow in order to influence which of the possible responses occurs? Which is preferable?

4. In his annual report for 1977, Bank of Canada governor Gerald Bouey said: "If we in Canada continue our progress towards better control of our prices and costs we shall unquestionably benefit from higher levels of employment and output than would otherwise be possible. Better price performance will improve the competitive position of Canadian suppliers in foreign markets and in relation to foreign goods in Canadian markets." Why should Canada be concerned with its competitive position under a flexible exchange rate? In what other ways might a lowering of the rate of inflation lead to increased employment?

5. Which of the following pairs of policy goals can be reached simultaneously using an appropriate macroeconomic policy, and which involve conflicting objectives? Indicate the policies you would advocate in each case.
   a. Lower rate of inflation and a reduced trade deficit
   b. Elimination of an inflationary gap and a trade deficit
   c. Lower rate of unemployment and a reduced trade deficit
   d. Lower rate of unemployment and a reduced overall balance-of-payments deficit

6. Explain why the use of monetary policy for domestic stabilization is limited under a fixed exchange rate.

7. A country that maintains a fixed exchange rate will have to allow its inflation rate to adjust to the level occurring in the rest of the world. Is this inconsistent with the theories of demand-pull and expectational inflation discussed in Chapter 36?

Mathematical Notes

1. Since it is impermissible to divide by zero, the ratio $\Delta Y/\Delta X$ cannot be evaluated when $\Delta X = 0$. But the limit of the ratio as ΔX approaches zero can be evaluated, and it is infinity.

$$\lim_{\Delta X \to 0} \frac{\Delta Y}{\Delta X} = \infty$$

2. Many variables affect the quantity demanded. Using functional notation, the argument of the next several pages of the text can be anticipated. Let Q^D represent the quantity of a commodity demanded and

$$T, \overline{Y}, N, Y^*, p, p_j$$

represent, respectively, tastes, average household income, population, income distribution, its price, and the price of the jth other commodity.

The demand function is

$$Q^D = D(T, \overline{Y}, N, Y^*, p, p_j), \ j = 1, \ldots, n$$

The demand schedule or curve looks at

$$Q^D = q(p) \bigg|_{T, \overline{Y}, N, Y^*, p_j}$$

where the notation means that the variables to the right of the vertical line are held constant.

This function is correctly described as the demand function with respect to price, all other variables held constant. This function, often written concisely as $q = q(p)$, shifts in response to changes in other variables. Consider a change in average income. If, as is usually hypothesized, $\partial Q^D/\partial \overline{Y} > 0$, then increases in average income shift $q = q(p)$ rightward and decreases in average income shift $q = q(p)$ leftward. Changes in other variables likewise shift this function in the direction implied by the relationship of that variable to the quantity demanded.

3. Quantity demanded is a simple, straightforward, but frequently misunderstood concept in everyday use, but it has a clear mathematical meaning.

It refers to the dependent variable in the demand function from note 2:

$$Q^D = D(T, \overline{Y}, N, Y^*, p, p_j)$$

It takes on a specific value, therefore, whenever a specific value is assigned to each of the independent variables. A change in Q^D occurs whenever the specific value of any independent variable is changed. Q^D could change, for example, from 10,000 tons per month to 20,000 tons per month as a result of a *ceteris paribus* change in any one price, in average income, in the distribution of income, in tastes, or in population. It could also change as a result of the net effect of changes in all of the independent variables occurring at once. Thus a change in the price of a commodity is a sufficient reason for a change in Q^D but not a necessary reason.

Some textbooks reserve the term *change in quantity demanded* for a movement along a demand curve, that is, a change in Q^D as a result of a change in p. They then use other words for a change in Q^D caused by a change in the other variables in the demand function. This usage gives the single variable Q^D more than one name, and this is potentially confusing.

Our usage, which corresponds to that in all intermediate and advanced treatments, avoids this confusion. We call Q^D *quantity demanded* and refer to *any* change in Q^D as a *change in quantity demanded*. In this usage it is correct to say that a movement along a demand curve is a change in quantity demanded. But it is incorrect to say that a change in quantity demanded can occur only because of a movement along a demand curve (since Q^D can change for other reasons, for example, a *ceteris paribus* change in average household income).

4. Continuing the development of note 2, let Q^S represent the quantity of a commodity supplied and

$$G, X, p, w_i$$

represent, respectively, producers' goals, technology, the products' own price, and the price of the ith input.

The supply function is

$$Q^S = S(G,X,p,w_i), \ i = 1, 2, \ldots, m$$

The supply schedule or supply curve looks at

$$Q^S = s(p) \ \bigg|_{G,X,w_i}$$

This is the supply function with respect to price, all other variables held constant. This function, often written concisely $q = s(p)$, shifts in response to changes in other variables.

5. Continuing the development of notes 2 through 4, equilibrium occurs where $Q^D = Q^S$. *For specified values of all other variables,* this requires that

$$q(p) = s(p) \tag{1}$$

Equation 1 defines an equilibrium value of p; hence although p is an *independent* variable in each of the supply and demand functions, it is an *endogenous* variable in the economic model that imposes the equilibrium condition expressed in Equation 1. Price is endogenous because it is assumed to adjust to bring about equality between quantity demanded and quantity supplied. Equilibrium quantity, also an endogenous variable, is determined by substituting the equilibrium price into either $q(p)$ or $s(p)$.

Graphically, Equation 1 is satisfied only at the point where demand and supply curves intersect. Thus supply and demand curves are said to determine the equilibrium values of the endogenous variables, price and quantity. A shift in any of the independent variables held constant in the q and s functions will shift the demand or supply curves and lead to different equilibrium values for price and quantity.

6. The definition in the text uses finite changes and is called *arc elasticity.* The parallel definition using derivatives is

$$\eta = \frac{dq}{dp} \times \frac{p}{q}$$

and is called *point elasticity.* Further discussion appears in the Appendix to Chapter 5.

7. The propositions in the text are proven as follows. Letting TR stand for total revenue, we can write

$$TR = pq$$

$$\frac{dTR}{dp} = q + p\,\frac{dq}{dp} \tag{1}$$

But from the equation in note 6

$$q\eta = p\,\frac{dq}{dp} \tag{2}$$

which we can substitute in Equation 1 to obtain

$$\frac{dTR}{dp} = q + q\eta = q(1 + \eta) \tag{3}$$

Because η is a negative number, the sign of Equation 3 is negative if the absolute value of η exceeds unity (elastic demand) and positive if it is less than unity (inelastic demand).

8. The axis reversal arose in the following way. Marshall theorized in terms of "demand price" and "supply price," these being the prices that would lead to a given quantity being demanded or supplied. Thus

$$p^d = D(q) \tag{1}$$

$$p^s = S(q) \tag{2}$$

and the condition of equilibrium is

$$D(q) = S(q)$$

When graphing the behavioral relations expressed in Equations 1 and 2, Marshall naturally put the independent variable, q, on the horizontal axis.

Leon Walras, whose formulation of the working of a competitive market has become the accepted one, focused on quantity demanded and quantity supplied *at a given price.* Thus

$$q^d = q(p)$$

$$q^s = s(p)$$

and the condition of equilibrium is

$$q(p) = s(p)$$

Walras did not use graphical representation. Had he done so, he would surely have placed *p* (his independent variable) on the horizontal axis.

Marshall, among his other influences on later generations of economists, was the great popularizer of graphical analysis in economics. Today we use his graphs, even for Walras' analysis. The axis reversal is thus one of those historical accidents that seem odd to people who did not live through the "perfectly natural" sequence of steps that produced it.

9. The relationship of the slope of the budget line to relative prices can be seen as follows. In the two-commodity example, a change in expenditure (ΔE) is given by the equation

$$\Delta E = p_C \Delta C + p_F \Delta F \qquad [1]$$

Along a budget line, expenditure is constant, that is, $\Delta E = 0$. Thus, along such a line,

$$p_C \Delta C + p_F \Delta F = 0 \qquad [2]$$

whence

$$-\frac{\Delta C}{\Delta F} = \frac{p_F}{p_C} \qquad [3]$$

The ratio $-\Delta C / \Delta F$ is the slope of the budget line. It is negative because with a fixed budget, to consume more *F* one must consume less *C*. In other words, Equation 3 says that the negative of the slope of the budget line is the ratio of the absolute prices (i.e., the relative price). While prices do not show directly in Figure 7-3, they are implicit in the budget line: Its slope depends solely on the relative price, while its position, given a fixed money income, depends on the absolute prices of the two goods.

10. The distinction made between an incremental change and a marginal change is the distinction for the function $Y = Y(X)$ between $\Delta Y / \Delta X$ and the derivative $\frac{dY}{dX}$. The latter is the limit of the former as ΔX approaches zero. Precisely this sort of difference underlies the distinction between arc and point elasticity, and we shall meet it repeatedly—in this chapter in reference to mar-

ginal and incremental *utility* and in later chapters with respect to such concepts as marginal and incremental *product, cost,* and *revenue*. Where *Y* is a function of more than one variable—for example, $Y = f(X, Z)$—the marginal relationship between *Y* and *X* is the partial derivative $\frac{\partial Y}{\partial X}$ rather than the total derivative.

11. The hypothesis of diminishing marginal utility requires that we can measure utility of consumption by a function $U = U(X_1, X_2, \ldots, X_n)$ where $X_1, \ldots, X_n$ are quantities of the *n* goods consumed by a household. It really embodies two utility hypotheses. First, $\frac{\partial U}{\partial X_i} > 0$, which says that for some levels of consumption the consumer can get more utility by increasing consumption of the commodity. Second, $\frac{\partial^2 U}{\partial X_i^2} < 0$, which says that the marginal utility of additional consumption is declining.

12. Because the slope of the indifference curve is negative, it is the absolute value of the slope that declines as one moves downward to the right along the curve. The algebraic value, of course, increases. The phrase *diminishing marginal rate of substitution* thus refers to the absolute, not the algebraic, value of the slope.

13. Marginal product as defined in the text is really incremental product. More advanced treatments distinguish between this notion and its limit as ΔL approaches zero. Technically, *MP* measures the rate at which total product is changing as one factor is varied. The marginal product is the partial derivative of the total product with respect to the variable factor. In symbols,

$$MP = \frac{\partial TP}{\partial L}$$

14. We have referred specifically both to diminishing *marginal* product and to diminishing *average* product. In most cases, eventually diminishing marginal product implies eventually diminishing

average product. This is, however, not necessary, as the accompanying figure shows.

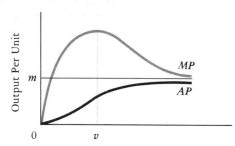

Units of the Variable Factor

In this case marginal product diminishes after v units of the variable factor are employed. Because marginal product falls toward, but never quite reaches, a value of m, average product rises continually toward, but never quite reaches, the same value.

15. Let q be the quantity of output and L the quantity of the variable factor. In the short run

$$TP = q = f(L) \qquad [1]$$

We now define

$$AP = \frac{q}{L} = \frac{f(L)}{L} \qquad [2]$$

$$MP = \frac{dq}{dL} \qquad [3]$$

We are concerned about the relation between these two. Whether average product is rising, at a maximum, or falling is determined by its derivative with respect to L.

$$\frac{d\frac{q}{L}}{dL} = \frac{L\frac{dq}{dL} - q}{L^2} \qquad [4]$$

This may be rewritten:

$$\frac{1}{L}\left(\frac{dq}{dL} - \frac{q}{L}\right) = \frac{1}{L}(MP - AP) \qquad [5]$$

Clearly, when MP is greater than AP, the expression in Equation 5 is positive and thus AP is rising. When MP is less than AP, AP is falling. When they are equal, AP is at a stationary value.

16. The mathematically correct definition of marginal costs is the rate of change of total cost, with respect to output, q. Thus $MC = dTC/dq$. From the definitions, $TC = TFC + TVC$. Fixed costs are not a function of output. Thus we may write $TC = K + f(q)$, where $f(q)$ is total variable costs and K is a constant. From this we see that $MC = df(q)/dq$. MC is thus independent of the size of the fixed costs.

17. This point is easily seen if a little algebra is used:

$$AVC = \frac{TVC}{q}$$

but

$$TVC = L \times w$$

and

$$q = AP \times L$$

where L is the quantity of the variable factor used and w is its cost per unit. Therefore

$$AVC = \frac{L \times w}{AP \times L} = \frac{w}{AP}$$

Since w is a constant, it follows that AVC and AP vary inversely with each other, and when AP is at its maximum value, AVC must be at its minimum value.

18. A little elementary calculus will prove the point.

$$MC = \frac{dTC}{dq} = \frac{dTVC}{dq}$$

$$= \frac{d(L \times w)}{dq}$$

If w does not vary with output,

$$MC = \frac{dL}{dq} \times w$$

But, referring to note 15, Equation 3,

$$\frac{dL}{dq} = \frac{1}{MP}$$

Thus

$$MC = \frac{w}{MP}$$

Since w is fixed, MC varies inversely with MP. When MP is at its maximum, MC must be at its minimum.

19. As we saw in note 18

$$MC = \frac{dTVC}{dq}$$

If we take the integral of the MC from zero to q_0 we get

$$\int_0^{q_0} MC\, dq = TVC_{q_0} + K$$

The first term gives the area under the marginal cost curve and hence the total variable cost of producing q_0 units; the second term, the constant of integration, is total fixed cost.

20. Strickly speaking, the marginal rate of substitution refers to the slope of the tangent to the isoquant at a particular point while the calculations in Table 11A-1 refer to the average rate of substitution between two distinct points on the isoquant. Assume a production function

$$Q = Q(K, L) \tag{1}$$

Isoquants are given by the function

$$K = I(L, \overline{Q}) \tag{2}$$

derived from Equation 1 by expressing K as an explicit function of L and Q. A single isoquant relates to a particular value $(\overline{Q})$ at which Q is held constant. Define Q_K and Q_L as an alternative, more compact notation for $\partial Q/\partial K$ and $\partial Q/\partial L$, the marginal products of capital and labor. Also, let Q_{KK} and Q_{LL} stand for $\partial^2 Q/\partial L^2$ and $\partial^2 Q/\partial K^2$, respectively. To obtain the slope of the isoquant, totally differentiate Equation 1 to obtain

$$dQ = Q_K dK + Q_L dL$$

Then, since we are moving along a single isoquant, set $dQ = 0$ to obtain

$$\frac{dK}{dL} = -\frac{Q_L}{Q_K} = MRS$$

Diminishing marginal productivity implies Q_{LL}, $Q_{KK} < 0$ and hence, as we move down the isoquant of Figure 11A-1, Q_K is rising and Q_L is falling, so the absolute value of MRS is diminishing. This is called the *hypothesis of a diminishing marginal rate of substitution.*

21. Formally, the problem is maximize $Q = Q(K, L)$ subject to the budget constraint

$$p_K K + p_L L = C$$

To do this, form the Lagrangean

$$Q(K, L) - \lambda(p_K K + p_L L - C)$$

The first-order conditions for finding the saddle point on this function are

$$Q_K - \lambda p_K = 0; \; Q_K = \lambda p_K \tag{1}$$

$$Q_L - \lambda p_L = 0; \; Q_L = \lambda p_L \tag{2}$$

$$-p_K K - p_L L + C = 0 \tag{3}$$

Dividing Equation 1 by Equation 2 yields

$$\frac{Q_K}{Q_L} = \frac{p_K}{p_L}$$

that is, the ratio of the marginal products, which is (-1) times the MRS, is equal to the ratio of the prices, which is (-1) times the slope of the isocost line.

22. For this note and the next two it is helpful first to define some terms. Let

$$\pi_n = TR_n - TC_n$$

where π_n is the profit when n units are sold.

If the firm is maximizing its profits by producing n units, it is necessary that the profits at output q_n are at least as large as the profits at output zero. If the firm is maximizing its profits at output n, then

$$\pi_n \geq \pi_0 \tag{1}$$

The condition says that profits from producing must be greater than profits from not producing. Condition 1 can be rewritten

$$TR_n - TVC_n - TFC_n \geq TR_0 - TVC_0 - TFC_0 \tag{2}$$

But note that by definition

$$TR_0 = 0 \quad [3]$$
$$TVC_0 = 0 \quad [4]$$
$$TFC_n = TFC_0 = K \quad [5]$$

where K is a constant. By substituting Equations 3, 4, and 5 into Condition 2, we get

$$TR_n - TVC_n \geq 0$$

from which we obtain

$$TR_n \geq TVC_n$$

This proves Rule 1.

On a per unit basis it becomes

$$\frac{TR_n}{q_n} \geq \frac{TVC_n}{q_n} \quad [6]$$

where q_n is the number of units.

Since $TR_n = q_n p_n$, where p_n is the price when n units are sold, Equation 6 may be rewritten

$$p_n \geq AVC_n$$

23. Using elementary calculus, Rule 2 may be proved.

$$\pi_n = TR_n - TC_n$$

each of which is a function of output q. To maximize π it is necessary that

$$\frac{d\pi}{dq} = 0 \quad [1]$$

and that

$$\frac{d^2\pi}{dq^2} < 0 \quad [2]$$

From the definitions

$$\frac{d\pi}{dq} = \frac{dTR}{dq} - \frac{dTC}{dq} = MR - MC \quad [3]$$

From Equations 1 and 3 a necessary condition of maximum π is $MR - MC = 0$, or $MR = MC$, as is required by Rule 2.

24. Not every point where $MR = MC$ is a point of profit maximization. Continuing the equations of math note 23,

$$\frac{d^2\pi}{dq^2} = \frac{dMR}{dq} - \frac{dMC}{dq} \quad [4]$$

From Equations 2 and 4 a necessary condition of maximum π is

$$\frac{dMR}{dq} - \frac{dMC}{dq} < 0$$

which says that the slope of MC must be greater than the slope of MR. Taken with the previous result, it implies that for q_n to maximize π, $MR_n = MC_n$ at a point where MC cuts MR from below.

25. Marginal revenue is mathematically the rate of change of total revenue with output, dTR/dq. Incremental revenue is $\Delta TR/\Delta q$. But the term *marginal revenue* is loosely used to refer to both concepts.

26. To prove that for a downward-sloping demand curve, marginal revenue is less than price, let $p = p(q)$. Then

$$TR = pq = p(q)q$$
$$MR = \frac{dTR}{dq} = q\frac{dp}{dq} + p$$

For a downward-sloping demand curve dp/dq is negative by definition, and thus MR is less than price for positive values of q.

27. The case of the linear demand curve is easily studied using calculus. Let $p = a - bq$, which is the general equation for a downward-sloping straight line ($b > 0$). Then

$$TR = pq = aq - bq^2$$

and

$$MR = \frac{dTR}{dq} = a - 2bq$$

More generally, the demand curve is $p = p(q)$ and total revenue is

$$TR = pq = p(q)q$$

So marginal revenue is

$$MR = qp'(q) + p(q)$$

and its slope is

$$p''(q) + p'(q)$$

We can infer nothing about the sign of this expression given only our knowledge that $p'(q) < 0$, given that the demand curve is negatively sloped.

28. A monopolist selling in two or more markets will set its marginal cost equal to marginal revenue in each market. Thus the condition $MC = MR_1 = MR_2$ is a profit-maximizing condition for a monopolist selling in two markets. In general, equal marginal revenues will mean unequal prices, for the ratio of price to marginal revenue is a function of elasticity of demand: The higher the elasticity, the lower the ratio. Thus equal marginal revenues imply a higher price in the market with the less elastic demand curve.

29. The marginal revenue produced by the factor involves two elements: first, the additional output that an extra unit of the factor makes possible and, second, the change in price of the product that the extra output causes. Let Q be output, R revenue, and L the number of units of labor hired. The contribution to revenue of additional labor is $\partial R/\partial L$. This in turn depends on the contribution of the extra labor to output $\partial Q/\partial L$ (the marginal product of the factor) and $\partial R/\partial Q$, the firm's marginal from the extra output. Thus

$$\frac{\partial R}{\partial L} = \frac{\partial Q}{\partial L} \cdot \frac{\partial R}{\partial Q}$$

We define the left-hand side as marginal revenue product, MRP. Thus

$$MRP = MP \cdot MR$$

30. The condition that for profit maximization MRP be downward sloping at the point where $w = MRP$ is just an application of the proposition (proved in math note 24) that for profit maximization MC must cut MR from below. Consider the output added by the last unit of the variable factor. Its marginal cost is w, and its marginal revenue is MRP. Thus w must cut MRP

from below. Since W is a horizontal line, MRP must be falling.

Putting the matter in standard mathematical terms,

$$w = MRP \qquad [1]$$

is a first-order condition of *either* maximizing or minimizing. The second-order condition for maximization is

$$\frac{dw}{dq} > \frac{dMRP}{dq} \qquad [2]$$

Since

$$\frac{dw}{dq} = 0 \qquad [3]$$

the slope of MRP must be negative to satisfy Equation 2; that is, it must be declining.

31. The proposition that the marginal labor cost is above the average labor cost when the average is rising is essentially the same proposition proved in math note 15. But let us do it again, using elementary calculus.

The quantity of labor depends on the wage rate: $L = f(w)$. The total labor cost is wL. The marginal cost of labor is $d(wL)/dL = w + L(dw/dL)$. This may be rewritten $MC = AC + L(dw/dL)$. As long as the supply curve slopes upward $dw/dL > 0$, therefore $MC > AC$.

32. Let t be the tax rate applied to the profits, π, of the firm. Thus the after-tax profits are $(1 - t)\pi$, where π is a function of output, q. To maximize profits after tax requires

$$\frac{d(1 - t)\pi}{dq} = 0$$

or

$$(1 - t)\frac{d\pi}{dq} = 0$$

Dividing through by $(1 - t)$ we can see that $d\pi/dq = 0$ depends on the level of q but is independent of the tax rate.

33. Calculating the ratio of the cost of purchasing a fixed bundle of commodities in two periods is the same thing as calculating the percentage change in each price and then averaging these by weighting each price by the proportion of total expenditure devoted to the commodity. The following expression illustrates the equivalence of these two procedures for the two-commodity case:

$$\frac{q^A p_1^A + q^B p_1^B}{q^A p_0^A + q^B p_0^B} =$$

$$\frac{p_1^A}{p_0^A}\left(\frac{q^A p_0^A}{q^A p_0^A + q^B p_0^B}\right) + \frac{p_1^B}{p_0^B}\left(\frac{q^B p_0^B}{q^A p_0^A + q^B p_0^B}\right)$$

Each q is a fixed quantity weight, and each p is a price. The superscripts A and B refer to two commodities; the subscripts 0 and 1 refer respectively to the base period and some subsequent time period. The expression on the left is the fixed bundle q^A and q^B valued at given year prices divided by its value in base year prices. The first term in the expression on the right gives the ratio of the price of good A in the given year and the base year multiplied by the proportion of total expenditure in the base year devoted to good A. The second term does the same for good B. Simple multiplication and division reduce the right-hand expression to the left-hand one.

34. In the text we define *MPC* as an incremental ratio. For mathematical treatments it is sometimes convenient to define all marginal concepts as derivatives: $MPC = dC/dY_d$, $MPS = dS/dY_d$, and so on.

35. The basic relation is

$$Y_d = C + S$$

Dividing through by Y_d yields

$$Y_d/Y_d = C/Y_d + S/Y_d \text{ or}$$

$$1 = APC + APS$$

Next take the first difference of the basic relation to yield

$$\Delta Y_d = \Delta C + \Delta S$$

Dividing through by ΔY_d gives

$$\Delta Y_d/\Delta Y_d = \Delta C/\Delta Y_d + \Delta S/\Delta Y_d \text{ or}$$

$$1 = MPC + MPS$$

36. This involves using functions of functions. We have $C = C(Y_d)$ and $Y_d = f(Y)$. So by substitution $C = C[f(Y)]$. In the linear expressions used in the text, $C = a + bY_d$, where b is the marginal propensity to consume. $Y_d = hY$, so $C = a + bhY$, where bh is thus the marginal response of C to a change in Y.

37. The elementary theory of national income can be described by the following set of equations (or model).

$$
\begin{array}{llr}
Y = AE & \text{(equilibrium condition)} & [1] \\
AE = C + I + G + (X - M) & & \\
 & \text{(definition of } AE) & [2] \\
C = a + hY & \text{(consumption function)} & [3] \\
M = mY & \text{(import function)} & [4] \\
Y_d = hY & \text{(disposable income)} & [5]
\end{array}
$$

where I, G, and X are all treated as constant. Substituting Equations 3, 4, and 5 and collecting terms in Y, we can obtain the aggregate expenditure function relating desired expenditure to income.

$$AE = (a + I + G + X) + (bh - m)Y$$

where the first term (in parentheses) is autonomous expenditure and the second term is induced expenditure. Using Equation 1, the equilibrium level of income can be derived by solving

$$Y = (a + I + G + X) + (bh - m)Y$$

to obtain

$$Y = \frac{1}{1 - bh + m}(a + I + G + X) \qquad [6]$$

The example in Table 28-6 has these values: $a = 100$, $I = 250$, $G = 170$, $X = 240$, $b = 0.80$, $h = 0.90$, and $m = 0.1$. Substituting into Equation 6 yields

$$Y = \frac{1}{1 - .72 + .10} (100 + 250 + 170 + 240)$$

$$= \frac{1}{.38} (760) = 2,000$$

38. The total expenditure over all rounds is the sum of an infinite series. Letting A stand for the initiating expenditure and z for the marginal propensity to spend, the change in expenditure is ΔA in the first round, $z\Delta A$ in the second, $z(z\Delta A) = z^2\Delta A$ in the third, and so on. This can be written

$$\Delta A(1 + z + z^2 + \cdots + z^n)$$

If z is less than 1, the series in parentheses converges to $1/(1 - z)$ as n approaches infinity. The change in total expenditure is thus $\Delta A/(1 - z)$. In the example in the box, $z = 0.80$; therefore, the change in total expenditure is five times ΔA.

39. As we saw in Box 28–2, the simple multiplier, K, is equal to the reciprocal of the marginal propensity not to spend, $1 - z$, also called the marginal propensity to withdraw, w.

$$K = \frac{1}{w}$$

In an open economy the marginal propensity to withdraw is equal to the sum of the marginal propensity to save, $1 - b$, plus the marginal propensity to import, m. Hence the multiplier in an open economy

$$K_o = \frac{1}{(1 - b) + m}$$

is less than that in a closed economy

$$K_c = \frac{1}{(1 - b)}$$

if the two economies had a common marginal propensity to consume, b. Note that the denominator of K_o can be written as $1 - (b - m)$ where $b - m$ is the marginal propensity to consume *home goods*.

40. Using the multiplier derived in math note 39, we see that an autonomous increase in exports leads to an increase in national income given by

$$\Delta Y = \frac{1}{(1 - b) + m} \Delta X$$

The resulting increase in imports is given by the marginal propensity to import times the change in national income.

$$\Delta M = m\Delta Y$$

Combining, we can calculate the change in the trade balance, $\Delta T = \Delta X - \Delta M$, as

$$\Delta T = \frac{1 - b}{(1 - b) + m} \Delta X = (1 - b) \Delta Y$$

which is positive since b is less than one.

41. The accelerator may be stated as a general macroeconomic theory. Define I_n as the volume of net investment this year and ΔY as the increase in national income from last year to this year. The accelerator theory is the relationship between I_n and ΔY.

Assume that the capital-output ratio is a constant

$$\frac{K}{Y} = \alpha, \text{ so } K = \alpha Y$$

If Y changes, K must be changed accordingly

$$\Delta K = \alpha\Delta Y$$

But the change in the capital stock (ΔK) is net investment, so

$$\Delta K = I_n = \alpha\Delta Y$$

42. This is easily proven. In equilibrium the banking system wants sufficient deposits (D) to establish the legal ratio (r) of deposits to reserves (R). This gives $R/D = r$. Any change in D of ΔD has to be accompanied by a change in R of ΔR of sufficient size to restore r. Thus $\Delta R/\Delta D = r$, so $\Delta D = \Delta R/r$, and $\Delta D/\Delta R = 1/r$.

43. Proof: Let r be the reserve ratio. Let $e = 1 - r$ be the excess reserves per dollar of new deposit. If X dollars are deposited in the system assumed in the text, the successive rounds of

new deposits will be X, eX, e^2X, e^3X. . . . The series

$$X + eX + e^2X + e^3X \cdots$$
$$= X(1 + e + e^2 + e^3 + \cdots)$$

has a limit

$$X\left(\frac{1}{1 - e}\right) = X\left[\frac{1}{1 - (1 - r)}\right] = \frac{X}{r}$$

44. Suppose that the public desires to hold a fraction, v, of deposits in cash. Now let the banking system receive an initial increase in its reserves of ΔR. It can expand deposits by an amount ΔD. As it does so, the banking system suffers a cash drain to the public of $v\Delta D$. The banking system can increase deposits only to the extent the required reserve ratio r makes possible. The maximum deposit expansion can be calculated from

$$r\Delta D = \Delta R - v\Delta D$$

which, collecting terms, can be written

$$(r + v)\,\Delta D = \Delta R$$

Hence

$$\Delta D = \frac{\Delta R}{r + v}$$

45. The argument is simply as follows, where prime marks stand for first derivatives:

$$M^D = F_1(T), \quad F'_1 > 0$$
$$T = F_2\,(Y), \quad F'_2 > 0$$

therefore,

$$M^D = F_1\,(F_2(Y))$$
$$= H\,(Y), \quad H' > 0$$

where H is the function of the function combining F_1 and F_2.

46. Let $L(Y, r)$ give the real demand for money measured in purchasing power units. Let M be the supply of money measured in nominal units and P an index of the price level so that M/P is the real supply of money. Now the equilibrium condition requiring equality between the demand

for money and the supply of money can be expressed in real terms as

$$L(Y, r) = M/P \qquad [1]$$

or by multiplying through by P in nominal terms as

$$PL(Y, r) = M \qquad [2]$$

In Equation 1 a rise in P disturbs equilibrium by lowering M/P, and in Equation 2 it disturbs equilibrium by raising $PL\,(Y, r)$.

47. This is expressed in functional notation as

$$DE = f(Y - Y^*)$$

where the restrictions are (a) that $f(0) = 0$ so when $Y = Y^*$ there is no demand effect; and (b) $f' > 0$ so that as Y rises, the demand effect rises. Together (a) and (b) imply that $DE > 0$ when $Y > Y^*$ and $DE < 0$ when $Y < Y^*$.

  Point 4 implies that $f'' > 0$; that is, that the Phillips curve gets steeper as Y rises.

48. The "rule of 72" is an approximation derived from the mathematics of compound interest. Any measure X_t will have the value $X_t = X_0 e^{rt}$ after t years at a continuous growth rate of r percent per year. Because $X_1/X_0 = 2$ requires $r \times t = 0.69$, a "rule of 69" would be correct for continuous growth. The "rule of 72" was developed in the context of compound interest, and if interest is compounded only once a year, the product of $r \times t$ for X to double is approximately 0.72.

49. The time taken to break even is a function of the *difference* in growth rates, not their level. Thus had 4 percent and 5 percent or 5 percent and 6 percent been used in the example, it still would have taken the same number of years. To see this quickly, recognize that we are interested in the ratio of two growth paths: $e^{r1t}/e^{r2t} = e^{(r1 - r2)t}$.

50. The equation for the *IS* curve is given by

$$y = c(y - T) + I(r) + G \qquad [1]$$

where $c'\,(y - T) > 0$ is the marginal propensity

to consume [$c'(y - T) = b$], $I_r < 0$ is the response of investment to a change in the interest rate, and T is taxes. Substituting $T = T_0 + ty$ into [1], and differentiating, we get

$$wdy = - b (dT_0 + ydt) + I_r dr + dG \qquad [2]$$

where w is equal to [$1 - b(1 - t)$], the marginal propensity not to spend. The *IS* curve is drawn for $dT_0 = dt = dG = 0$. Its slope is therefore

$$\frac{dr}{dy}\bigg|_{IS} = \frac{w}{I_r} < 0 \qquad [3]$$

The horizontal shift in the *IS* curve due to a change in any of the exogenous variables (T_0, t, or G) can be calculated from [2] by setting $dr = 0$. For example, a change in G shifts the *IS* curve by

$$\frac{dy}{dG}\bigg|_{dr = 0} = \frac{1}{w} > 0$$

while a change in tax rates causes a shift of

$$\frac{dy}{dt}\bigg|_{dr = 0} = \frac{-by}{w} < 0$$

51. The equation for the *LM* curve is given by

$$M = PL(y,r) \qquad [1]$$

where $L(y,r)$ represents the demand for real money balances which depends positively on income ($L_y > 0$) and negatively on the interest rate ($L_r < 0$). Differentiating Equation 1 we get

$$dM = L(y,r)dP + PL_y dy + PL_r dr \qquad [2]$$

The *LM* curve is drawn for $dM = dP = 0$. Its slope is therefore

$$\frac{dr}{dy}\bigg|_{LM} = -\frac{L_y}{L_r} > 0 \qquad [3]$$

The horizontal shift in the *LM* curve due to a change in the money supply can be calculated from Equation 2 by setting $dr = 0$.

$$\frac{dy}{dM}\bigg|_{dr = 0} = \frac{1}{LP_y} > 0 \qquad [4]$$

52. Equations 2 from each of the two previous math notes can be combined to give two relationships between dy and dr. Solving them simultaneously we can derive the following expressions for the effects of monetary and fiscal policy on national income and interest rates. Restricting our analysis of fiscal policy to the effects of government expenditure (so $dT = dt = 0$), and holding $dP = 0$, these are as follows:

$$\frac{dy}{dM} = \frac{- I_r}{D} > 0 \qquad \frac{dr}{dM} = \frac{- w}{D} < 0$$

$$\frac{dy}{dG} = \frac{- PL_r}{D} > 0 \qquad \frac{dr}{dG} = \frac{PL_y}{D} > 0$$

where $D = - (I_r PL_y + wPL_r) > 0$.

53. The aggregate demand curve can be written by solving Equations 1 from each of the math notes 50 and 51 to eliminate the interest rate, thus leaving a relationship between P and y. The relationship between *changes* in P and y can be written

$$Ddy = I_r L(y, P)dP - PL_r dG - I_r dM \qquad [1]$$

where D is as defined in note 52.

The *AD* curve is drawn from $dG = dM = 0$, so its slope is given by

$$\frac{dP}{dy}\bigg|_{AD} = \frac{I_r L(y, P)}{D} < 0 \qquad [2]$$

The horizontal shift in *AD* can be calculated from Equation 1 by setting $dP = 0$, so that the effects of monetary (dM) and fiscal (dG) policy with a constant price level can be written as follows:

$$\frac{dy}{dM}\bigg|_{dr = 0} = \frac{- I_r}{D} > 0$$

$$\frac{dy}{dG}\bigg|_{dr = 0} = \frac{- PL_r}{D} > 0$$

which, of course, are as in math note 52.

54. Net exports equals exports minus imports.

$$NX = X - M \qquad [1]$$

Exports depend on foreign income, Y^f, and on the terms of trade.

$$X = X_0 + m^f Y^f - b^f\left(\frac{P}{eP^f}\right) \qquad [2]$$

where X_0 is autonomous exports, m^f is the foreign marginal propensity to import, b^f is the response of exports to a change in relative prices, P is the domestic price level, e is the exchange rate, and P^f is foreign prices. Imports depend on domestic income and the terms of trade.

$$M = M_0 + mY + b\left(\frac{P}{eP^f}\right) \qquad [3]$$

Combining Equations 1, 2, and 3, we can write

$$NX = (X_0 - M_0) + m^f Y^f - mY - c\left(\frac{P}{eP^f}\right) \qquad [4]$$

where $c = b + b^f$. In Chapter 39 we considered this relationship in isolation and hence the slope of the NX curve when drawn against national income was taken to be $dNX/dY = -m$, where the other variables in Equation 4 were held constant. Now we have to take into account the fact that P changes as Y changes.

Writing the *SRAS* curve as

$$P = g(Y),\, g' > 0 \qquad [5]$$

and substituting Equation 5 into Equation 4, we eliminate P to yield

$$NX = (X_0 - M_0) + mY^f - mY - c\left(\frac{g(Y)}{eP^f}\right) \qquad [6]$$

The slope of the NX curve is now given by

$$dNX/dY = -(m + cg') < 0 \qquad [7]$$

Hence as Y rises, NX falls both because of the marginal propensity to import and because of substitution away from domestic goods as P rises.

Glossary

absolute advantage   The advantage one nation has over another in the production of a commodity when the same amount of resources will produce more of the commodity in that nation than in the other.

absolute price   The amount of money that must be spent to acquire a unit of a commodity. Also called *money price*.

acceleration hypothesis   The hypothesis that when national income is held above potential, the persistent inflationary gap will cause inflation to accelerate; and when national income is held below potential, the persistent recessionary gap will cause inflation to decelerate.

accelerator   The theory that relates the level of investment to the rate of change of national income.

actual GDP   The gross domestic product that the economy in fact produces.

adjustable peg system   A system in which exchange rates are fixed in the short term but are occasionally changed in response to persistent payments imbalances.

administered price   A price set by the conscious decision of the seller rather than by impersonal market forces.

ad valorem tariff   An import duty that is a percentage of the price of the imported product.

ad valorem tax   See *excise tax*.

adverse selection   Self-selection, within a single risk category, of persons of above average risk.

AE   See *aggregate expenditure*.

aggregate demand   Total desired purchases by all the buyers of an economy's output.

aggregate demand (AD) curve   A curve showing the combination of real national income and the price level that makes aggregate desired expenditure equal to national income and the demand for money equal to the supply of money; the curve thus relates the total amount of output that will be demanded to the price level of that output.

aggregate demand shock   A shift in the aggregate demand curve.

aggregate expenditure (AE)   Total expenditure on final output of the economy; $AE = C + I + G + (X - M)$, representing the four major components of aggregate desired expenditure.

aggregate supply   Total desired output of all the producers of an economy's output.

aggregate supply (AS) curve   A relation between the total amount of output that will be produced and the price level of that output.

aggregate supply shock   A shift in the aggregate supply curve.

allocation of resources   The distribution of the available factors of production among the various uses to which they might be put.

allocative efficiency   A situation in which no reorganization of production or consumption could make everyone better off (or, as it is sometimes stated, make at least one person better off while making no one worse off).

allocative inefficiency   The absence of allocative efficiency. A situation in which either production or consumption could be reorganized so as to make everyone better off (or, as it is sometimes stated, make at least one person better off while making no one worse off).

annuity   A given sum of money paid at stated intervals for a specific period of time or (in case of an *infinite annuity*) forever.

anticombine laws   Laws designed to prohibit the acquisition and exercise of monopoly power by business firms.

appreciation   A rise in the free-market value of domestic currency in terms of foreign currencies.

a priori   Literally, "at a prior time" or "in advance"; knowledge that is prior to actual experience.

arc elasticity   A measure of the average responsiveness of quantity to price over an interval of the demand curve. For analytical purposes it is usually defined by the formula

$$\eta = \frac{\Delta q/q}{\Delta p/p}$$

An alternative formula often used where computations are involved is

$$\eta = \frac{(q_2 - q_1)/(q_2 + q_1)}{(p_2 - p_1)/(p_2 + p_1)}$$

where p_1 and q_1 are the original price and quantity and p_2 and q_2 the new price and quantity.

With negatively sloped demand curves elasticity is a negative number. Sometimes the above expressions are therefore multiplied by -1 to make measured elasticity positive.

autonomous expenditure   In macroeconomics, elements of expenditure that do not vary systematically with other variables, such as national income and the interest rate, but that are determined by forces outside of the theory. Also called *exogenous expenditure*.

autonomous variable   See *exogenous variable*.

average cost (AC)   See *average total cost*.

average fixed cost (AFC)   Total fixed costs divided by the number of units of output.

average product (AP)   Total product divided by the number of units of the variable factor used in its production.

average propensity to consume (APC)   The proportion of income devoted to consumption; total consumption expenditure divided by disposable income ($APC = C/Y_d$).

average propensity to save (APS)   The proportion of income devoted to saving; total saving divided by disposable income ($APS = S/Y_d$).

average revenue (AR)   Total revenue divided by quantity sold.

average tax rate   The ratio of total tax paid to total income earned.

average total cost (ATC)   Total cost of producing a given output divided by the number of units of output; it can also be calculated as the sum of average fixed costs and average variable costs. Also called *cost per unit, unit cost, average cost*.

average variable cost (AVC)   Total variable costs divided by the number of units of output. Also called *direct unit cost, avoidable unit cost*.

balanced budget   A situation in which current revenue is exactly equal to current expenditures.

balanced budget multiplier   The change in income divided by the tax-financed change in government expenditure that brought it about.

balance-of-payments accounts   A summary record of a country's transactions that involve payments or receipts of foreign exchange.

balance of trade   The difference between the value of exports and the value of imports of visible items (goods).

balance sheet   A financial report showing a firm's assets and the claims against those assets at a moment in time.

bank notes   Paper money issued by commercial banks.

barter   A system in which goods and services are traded directly for other goods and services.

base control   The use of the monetary base as the instrument by which the central bank attempts to influence its target variables. See also *interest rate control*.

base period   A year or other point in time chosen for comparison purposes in order to express or compute index numbers or constant dollars. Also called *base year*.

beggar-my-neighbor policies   Policies designed to increase a country's prosperity (especially by reducing its unemployment) at the expense of reducing prosperity in other countries (especially by increasing their unemployment).

blacklist   An employer's list of workers who have been fired for union activity.

black market   A situation in which goods are sold illegally at prices above a legal price ceiling.

bond   An evidence of debt carrying a specified amount and schedule of interest payments and, usually, dates for redemption of the face value of the bond.

boom   A period in the business cycle characterized by high demand and increasing production at a level that exceeds potential GDP.

boycott   A concerted refusal to buy (buyers' boycott) or to sell (producers' or sellers' boycott) a commodity.

bread-and-butter unionism   A union movement whose major objectives are better wages and conditions of employment rather than political or social ends.

budget balance   The difference between total government revenue and total government expenditure.

budget deficit   The shortfall of current revenue below current expenditure.

budget line   Graphic representation of all combinations of commodities or factors that a household or firm may obtain if it spends a given amount of money at fixed prices of the commodities or factors. Also called *isocost line*.

budget surplus   The excess of current revenue over current expenditure.

built-in stabilizer   Anything that tends to adjust government revenues and expenditures automatically (i.e., without an explicit policy decision) so as to reduce inflationary and recessionary gaps whenever they develop.

business cycle   More or less regular, long-term patterns of fluctuations in the level of economic activity.

C   See *consumption expenditure*.

capacity   The level of output that corresponds to the minimum short-run average total cost. Also called *plant capacity*.

capital   A factor of production consisting of all manufactured aids to further production.

capital account   A part of the balance-of-payments accounts that records payments and receipts arising from the import and export of long-term and short-term financial capital.

capital consumption allowance   An estimate of the amount by which the capital stock is depleted through its contribution to current production. Also called *depreciation*.

capital deepening   Adding capital to the production process in such a way as to increase the ratio of capital to labor and other factors of production.

capitalized value   The value of an asset measured by the present value of the income stream it is expected to produce.

capital-labor ratio   The ratio of the amount of capital to the amount of labor used by a firm, an industry, or the whole economy.

capital-output ratio   The ratio of the value of capital to the annual value of output produced using it.

capital stock   The aggregate quantity of a society's capital goods or the total of a firm's capital goods.

capital widening   Adding capital to the production process in such a way as to leave factor proportions unchanged.

cartel   An organization of producers who agree to act as a single seller, thus limiting competition among themselves, in order to maximize joint profits.

ceiling price   See *price ceiling.*

central bank   A bank that acts as banker to the commercial banking system and often to the government as well. In the modern world, usually a government owned and operated institution that controls the banking system and is the sole money issuing authority.

certificate of deposit (CD)   A negotiable time deposit carrying a higher interest rate than that paid on ordinary time deposits.

ceteris paribus   Literally, "other things being equal"; usually used in economics to indicate that all variables except the ones specified are assumed not to change.

change in demand   An increase or decrease in the quantity demanded at each possible price of the commodity, represented by a shift in the whole demand curve.

change in quantity demanded   An increase or decrease in the specific quantity bought at a specified price, represented by a movement along a demand curve.

change in quantity supplied   An increase or decrease in the specific quantity supplied at a specified price, represented by a movement along a supply curve.

change in supply   An increase or decrease in the quantity supplied at each possible price of the commodity, represented by a shift in the whole supply curve.

chartered bank   Privately owned, profit-seeking institution that provides a variety of financial services, such as accepting deposits from customers, which it agrees to transfer when ordered by a cheque, and making loans and other investments.

classical unemployment   See *real wage unemployment.*

cleared market   A market in which buyers have been able to buy all they wish and sellers have been able to sell all they wish at the going price.

clearing house   An institution where interbank indebtedness arising from transfer of cheques between banks is computed, offset against each other, and net amounts owing are calculated.

closed shop   A place of employment in which a union has exclusive bargaining jurisdiction for all employees in a shop and only union members can be employed.

coefficient of determination (r^2 or R^2)   A measure of how closely a relationship between two variables holds. A coefficient showing the fraction of the total variance of the dependent variable that can be associated with the independent variables in the regression equation; r^2 is used for two variables and R^2 for three or more variables.

collective bargaining   The process by which unions and employers arrive at and enforce agreements.

collective consumption goods   Goods or services that if they provide benefits to anyone, necessarily provide benefits to a large group of people, possibly everyone in the country.

collusion   An agreement among sellers to act as though there were a single seller, for example, by setting a common price. Collusion may be overt or covert, explicit or tacit.

command economy   An economy in which the decisions of the government (as distinct from households and firms) exert the major influence over the allocation of resources.

commercial policy   Restrictions on the free flow of goods and services among nations.

commodities   Items produced to satisfy wants. Commodities may be either *goods,* which are tangible, or *services,* which are intangible.

common-property resource   A natural resource that is not privately owned and may be used by anyone.

common stock   A form of equity capital usually carrying voting rights and a residual claim to the assets and profits of the firm.

comparative advantage   The ability of one nation (region or individual) to produce a commodity at a lesser opportunity cost of other products foregone than another nation.

comparative statics   Short for comparative static equilibrium analysis; the derivation of predictions by analyzing the effect of a change in some exogenous variable on the equilibrium position.

competitive devaluations   A round of devaluations of exchange rates by a number of countries, each trying to gain a competitive advantage over the other and each failing to the extent that other countries also devalue.

complement   Two commodities are complements when they tend to be used jointly with each other; the degree of complementarity is measured by the size of the negative cross elasticity between the two goods.

comprehensive income taxation (CIT)   Use of a very broad tax base by defining taxable income to include income from most sources and thus eliminating most exemptions and deductions.

concentration ratio   The fraction of total market sales (or some other measure of market occupancy) controlled by a specified number of the industry's largest firms, four-firm and eight-firm concentration ratios being most frequently used.

conglomerate merger   See *merger.*

constant-cost industry   An industry in which costs of the most efficient size firm remain constant as the entire industry expands or contracts in the long run.

constant returns   A situation in which output increases proportionately with inputs as the scale of production is increased.

consumerism   A movement that asserts a conflict between the interests of firms and the public interest.

Consumer Price Index (CPI)   A measure of the average prices of commodities commonly bought by households; compiled monthly by *Statistics Canada*.

consumers' durables   See *durable good*.

consumers' surplus   The difference between the total value consumers place on all units consumed of a commodity and the payment they must make to purchase the same amount of the commodity.

consumption   The act of using commodities to satisfy wants.

consumption expenditure   In macroeconomics, household expenditure on all goods and services except housing. Represented by the symbol C as one of the four components of aggregate expenditure.

consumption function   The relationship between total desired consumption expenditure and all the factors that determine it; in a more specific sense, the relationship between desired consumption expenditure and disposable income.

corporation   A form of business organization in which the firm has a legal existence separate from that of the owners and ownership and financial responsibility are divided, limited, and shared among any number of individual and institutional shareholders.

cost (of output)   To a producing firm, the value of inputs used in producing output.

cost minimization   An implication of profit maximization that the firm will choose the method that produces specific output at the lowest attainable cost.

Cournot-Nash equilibrium   An equilibrium that results when each firm makes its decisions on the assumption that the behavior of all other firms will remain unchanged; also called the *non-cooperative equilibrium*.

CPI   See *Consumer Price Index*.

craft union   A union organized to include workers with a specified set of skills or occupations, regardless of where or in what industry they are employed.

cross elasticity of demand (η_x) A measure of the responsiveness of the quantity of a commodity demanded to changes in price of a related commodity, defined by the formula

$$\eta_x = \frac{\text{percentage change in quantity demanded of } X}{\text{percentage change in price of } Y}$$

cross-sectional data   Several different measurements or observations made at the same point in time.

crowding out effect   The offsetting reduction in private expenditure caused by the rise in interest rates that follows an expansionary fiscal policy.

current account   A part of the balance-of-payments accounts that records payments and receipts arising from trade in goods and services and from interest and dividends earned by capital owned in one country and invested in another.

cyclically adjusted deficit (CAD)   An estimate of the government budget deficit (expenditure minus tax revenue) not as it actually is but as it would be if national income were at its potential level.

day-to-day loan   Loan made by a chartered bank to an investment dealer. Such loans make up part of the *secondary reserves* of the chartered banks.

debt   Amounts owed to one's creditors, including banks and other financial institutions. That portion of a firm's money capital that has been borrowed from persons or institutions who are not owners of the firm.

decision lag   The period of time between perceiving some problem and reaching a decision on what to do about it.

decreasing returns   A situation in which output increases less than proportionately to inputs as the scale of production increases. A firm in this situation, with fixed factor prices, is an *increasing cost* firm.

demand   The entire relationship between the quantity of a commodity that buyers wish to purchase per period of time and the price of that commodity.

demand curve   The graphic representation of the relationship between the quantity of a commodity that buyers wish to purchase per period of time and the price of that commodity, other things equal.

demand deposit   A bank deposit that is withdrawable on demand (without notice of intention to withdraw) and transferable by means of a cheque.

demand for money   The total amount of money balances that the public wishes to hold for all purposes.

demand inflation   Inflation arising from excess aggregate demand, that is, when national income exceeds potential.

demand schedule   A table showing selected values of the quantity of a commodity that buyers wish to purchase per period of time and the corresponding price of that commodity, other things equal.

deposit money   Money held by the public in the form of demand deposits with commercial banks.

depreciation   (1) The loss in value of an asset over a period of time due to physical wear and tear and obsolescence. (2) The amount by which the capital stock is depleted through its contribution to current production. (3) A fall in the free-market value of domestic currency in terms of foreign currencies.

depression   A period of very low economic activity with very high unemployment and high excess capacity.

derived demand   The demand for a factor of production that results from the demand for products it is used to make.

differentiated product   A product sufficiently distinguishable from others within an industry that the producer of each has some power over its own price; the products of firms in monopolistically competitive industries.

diminishing marginal rate of substitution The hypothesis that the marginal rate of substitution changes systematically as the amounts of two commodities being consumed vary.

direct investment In balance-of-payments accounting, foreign investment in the form of a takeover or capital investment in a branch plant or subsidiary corporation in which the investor has voting control.

dirty float See *managed float*.

discount rate (1) In the United States, the rate at which the central bank is prepared to lend reserves to commercial banks. (2) More generally, the rate of interest used to discount a stream of future payments to arrive at their present value.

discouraged workers People who would like to work but have ceased looking for a job and hence have withdrawn from the labor force, because they believe that no suitable jobs are available.

discretionary fiscal policy Fiscal policy that is a conscious response (not according to any predetermined rule) to each particular state of the economy as it arises.

disembodied technical change Technical change that raises output without the necessity of building new capital to embody the new knowledge.

disequilibrium The absence of equilibrium. A market is in disequilibrium when there is either excess demand or excess supply.

disequilibrium price A price at which quantity demanded does not equal quantity supplied.

disposable income (Y_d) The income that households have available for spending and saving; GDP minus any part of it not actually paid to households minus personal income taxes paid by households.

distributed profits Profits paid out to owners of a firm. For incorporated firms the distributed profits are called *dividends*.

dividends That part of profits paid out to shareholders of a corporation.

division of labor The breaking up of a production process into a series of repetitive tasks, each done by a different worker.

dollar standard A system under which countries hold reserves in and settle debts with U.S. dollars, but the dollar is not backed by gold or any other physical source of monetary value.

domestic absorption (A) Total demand for goods for use by domestic residents; equal to the sum of $C + I + G$.

double counting In national income accounting, adding up the total outputs of all the sectors in the economy so that the value of intermediate goods is counted in the sector that produces them and every time they are purchased as an input by another sector.

dumping In international trade, the practice of selling a commodity at a lower price in the export market than in the domestic market for reasons not related to differences in costs of servicing the two markets.

duopoly An industry that contains only two firms.

durable good A good that yields its services over an extended period of time. Often divided into the subcategories *producers' durables* (e.g., machines, equipment) and *consumers' durables* (e.g., cars, appliances).

dynamic differential A difference in factor prices caused by disequilibrium that will tend to lead to corrective movements of resources and will be eliminated in equilibrium. Also called *disequilibrium differential*.

economic growth Increases in real, or constant dollar, potential GDP.

economic profits or losses The difference between the revenues received from the sale of output and the opportunity cost of the inputs used to make the output. Negative economic profits are economic losses. Also called simply *profits* or *losses*.

economic rent That part of the payment to a factor in excess of its transfer earnings.

economies of scale Reduction of costs per unit of output resulting from an expansion in output; a negatively sloped *LRAC* curve over a range of output.

economies of scope Economies achieved by a firm that is large enough to engage efficiently in multi-product production and associated large-scale distribution, advertising, and purchasing.

economy A set of interrelated production and consumption activities.

effective rate of tariff The tax charged on any imported commodity expressed as a percentage of the value added by the exporting industry.

effluent charge A fee, fine, or tax on a producer for polluting activity, usually on a per unit basis.

elastic demand The situation in which for a given percentage change in price there is a greater percentage change in quantity demanded; elasticity greater than unity.

elasticity of demand (η) A measure of the responsiveness of quantity of a commodity demanded to a change in market price, defined by the formula

$$\eta = \frac{\text{percentage change in quantity demanded}}{\text{percentage change in price}}$$

With negatively sloped demand curves, elasticity is a negative number. Sometimes the above expression is multiplied by -1 to make measured elasticity positive. Also called *demand elasticity, price elasticity*.

elasticity of supply (η_s) A measure of the responsiveness of the quantity of a commodity supplied to a change in the market price, defined by the formula

$$\eta_s = \frac{\text{percentage change in quantity supplied}}{\text{percentage change in price}}$$

embodied technical change   Technical change that can be utilized only when new capital, embodying the new techniques, is built.

employment   The number of adult workers (15 years of age and older) who hold jobs.

endogenous expenditure   See *induced expenditure.*

endogenous variable   A variable that is explained within a theory.

entry barrier   Legal or other artificial impediment to entry into an industry, such as patents, economies of scale, and established brand preferences.

envelope curve   Any curve that encloses, by being tangent to, a series of other curves. In particular, the *envelope cost curve* is the *LRAC* curve, which encloses the *SRAC* curves by being tangent to each without cutting any of them.

equalization payments   Transfers of tax revenues from the federal government to the low-income provinces to compensate them for their lower potential per capita tax yields.

equilibrium condition   A condition that must be fulfilled if some market or sector of the economy or the whole economy is to be in equilibrium.

equilibrium differential   A difference in factor prices that would persist in equilibrium, without any tendency for it to be removed.

equilibrium inflation   The rate of inflation that arises when there is no shock inflation, when output is held at potential so there is no demand inflation, and when there is monetary accommodation of expectational inflation.

equilibrium price   The price at which quantity demanded equals quantity supplied.

equity capital   Funds provided by the owners of a firm the return on which depends on the firm's profits.

error term   The difference between the measured value of a variable and the value as predicted by some theoretical or statistical relation.

excess capacity   The amount by which actual output falls short of capacity output (which is the output that corresponds to the minimum short-run average total cost).

excess capacity theorem   The proposition that equilibrium in a monopolistically competitive industry will occur where each firm has excess capacity.

excess demand   A situation in which, at the given price, quantity demanded exceeds quantity supplied. Also called a *shortage.*

excess reserves   Reserves held by a chartered bank in excess of the legally required minimum.

excess supply   A situation in which, at the given price, quantity supplied exceeds quantity demanded. Also called a *surplus.*

exchange rate   The price of one currency in terms of another.

excise tax   A tax on the sale of a particular commodity; may be a *specific tax* (fixed tax per unit of commodity) or an *ad valorem tax* (fixed percentage of the value of the commodity).

execution lag   The time it takes to put policies in place after the decision is made.

exogenous expenditure   See *autonomous expenditure.*

exogenous variable   A variable that influences other variables within a theory but is itself determined by factors outside the theory. Also called *autonomous variable.*

expectational inflation   Inflation that occurs because decision makers raise prices (so as to keep their relative prices constant) in the expectation that the price level is going to rise.

expectations augmented Phillips curve   The relationship between unemployment and the rate of increase of money wages or between national income and the rate of increase of money prices that arises when the demand and expectations components of inflation are combined.

expenditure-changing policies   Policies that change the level of aggregate desired expenditure.

expenditure-switching policies   Policies that maintain the level of aggregate desired expenditure but change the relative proportions of its components, domestic absorption, and net exports.

external balance   A situation where the balance of payments accounts, or some subset of them, are at their target levels.

externalities   Effects, either good or bad, on parties not directly involved in the production or use of a commodity. Also called *third-party effects.*

factor markets   Markets in which the services of factors of production are sold.

factor mobility   The ease with which factors can be transferred between uses.

factors of production   Resources used to produce goods and services; frequently divided into the basic categories of land, labor, and capital.

fair trade laws   Laws permitting duties to be applied to goods being traded "unfairly" because, for example, of subsidies or the practice of dumping.

falling-cost industry   An industry in which the lowest costs attainable by a firm fall as the scale of the industry expands.

favorable balance of payments   A credit balance on some part of the international payments account (receipts exceed payments); often refers to a favorable balance on current plus capital account (that is, everything except the official settlements account).

federation   In respect to labor unions, any loose organization of national unions.

fiat money   Paper money or coinage that is neither backed by nor convertible into anything else but is accepted as legal tender.

final output   Total output of goods and services excluding what is sold to other firms for use as a component in producing their output; sometimes called *final goods*.

financial capital   The funds used to finance a firm, including both equity capital and debt. Also called *money capital*.

fine tuning   The attempt to maintain national income at or near its full-employment level by means of frequent changes in fiscal or monetary policy.

firm   The unit that employs factors of production and produces goods and services to be sold to households, other firms, or the government.

fiscal drag   The tendency for an output gap to open up because tax revenues rise faster than government expenditure as full-employment income rises due to economic growth.

fiscal policy   The use of the government's revenue-raising and spending activities in an effort to influence the behavior of such macro variables as the GDP and total employment.

fixed cost   A cost that does not change with output. Also called *overhead cost, unavoidable cost*.

fixed exchange rate   An exchange rate that is maintained within a small range around its publicly stated par value by the intervention of a country's central bank in foreign market operations. Also called a *pegged rate*.

fixed factor   An input that cannot be increased in the short run.

fixed investment   Investment in plant and equipment.

flexible exchange rate   An exchange rate that is left free to be determined by the forces of demand and supply on the free market with no intervention by the monetary authorities. Also called *floating exchange rate*.

floating exchange rate   See *flexible exchange rate*.

floor price   A minimum permitted price.

foreign exchange   Actual foreign currency or various claims on it, such as bank balances or promises to pay, that are traded for each other.

45° line   In macroeconomics, the line that graphs the equilibrium condition that aggregate desired expenditure should equal national income ($AE = Y$).

fractional reserve system   A banking system in which chartered banks are required to keep only a fraction of their deposits in cash or on deposit with the central bank.

freedom of entry and exit   The absence of legal or other artificial barriers to entering into production or withdrawing assets from production.

free good   A commodity for which the quantity supplied exceeds the quantity demanded at a price of zero; therefore a good that does not command a positive price in a market economy.

free-market economy   An economy in which the decisions of individual households and firms (as distinct from the government) exert the major influence over the allocation of resources.

free trade   The absence of any form of government intervention in international trade, which implies that imports and exports must not be subject to special taxes or restrictions levied merely because of their status as "imports" or "exports."

frictional unemployment   Unemployment caused by the fact that it takes time for labor to move from one job to another.

fringe benefits   Compensation other than wages for the benefit of labor, such as company contributions to pension and welfare funds, sick leave, and paid holidays.

full-cost pricing   Setting price equal to average total cost at normal-capacity output plus a fixed markup.

full employment   Employment sufficient to produce the economy's potential output; all unemployment is frictional and structural.

function   Loosely, an expression of a relation between two or more variables. Precisely, Y is a function of the variables $X_1, \ldots, X_n$ if for every set of values of the variables $X_1, \ldots, X_n$, there is associated a unique value of the variable Y.

functional distribution of income   The distribution of income among major factors of production.

G   See *government expenditure*.

gains from trade   The increased national income that results from specialization and trade as opposed to self-sufficiency.

GDP deflator   See *implicit GDP deflator*.

Giffen good   An inferior good for which the negative income effect outweighs the substitution effect so that the demand curve is positively sloped.

gold exchange standard   A monetary system in which U.S. currency is directly convertible into gold and other countries' currencies are indirectly convertible by being convertible into the gold-backed U.S. dollar at a fixed rate.

goods   Tangible commodities, such as cars or shoes.

government   All public officials, agencies, and other organizations belonging to or under the control of state, local, or federal government.

government expenditure   Includes all government expenditure on currently produced goods and services and does not include government transfer payments. Represented by the symbol G as one of the four components of aggregate expenditure.

Gresham's law   The theory that "bad," or debased, money drives "good," or undebased, money out of circulation because people keep the good money for other purposes and use the bad money for transactions.

gross domestic product (GDP)   National income as measured by the output approach; equal to the sum of all values added in the economy or, what is the same thing, the values of all final goods produced in the economy.

gross investment   The total value of all investment

goods produced in the economy during a stated period of time.

gross national expenditure (GNE) National income as measured by the expenditure approach; equal to the sum of expenditures on consumption, investment, government production and net exports.

gross national product (GNP) National income as measured by the income approach; equal to the sum of all factor incomes earned plus depreciation plus (to get the valuation at market prices) indirect taxes minus subsidies.

gross return on capital The receipts from the sale of goods produced by a firm less the cost of purchased goods and materials, labor, land, manager's talents, and taxes.

homogeneous product In the eyes of purchasers every unit of the product is identical to every other unit.

horizontal equity Focuses on differences that may arise among individuals or families with the same income levels but different circumstances.

horizontal merger See *merger*.

household All the people who live under one roof and who make, or are subject to others making for them, joint financial decisions.

human capital The capitalized value of productive investments in persons; usually refers to value derived from expenditures on education, training, and health improvements.

hypothesis of diminishing returns The hypothesis that if increasing quantities of a variable factor are applied to a given quantity of fixed factors, the marginal product and average product of the variable factor will eventually decrease. Also called *law of diminishing returns, law of variable proportions*.

hypothesis of equal net advantage The hypothesis that owners of factors will choose the use of their factors that produces the greatest net advantage to themselves and therefore will move their factors among uses until net advantages are equalized.

I See *investment expenditure*.

implicit deflator An index number derived by dividing national income measured in current dollars by national income measured in constant dollars and multiplying by 100. In effect, a price index with current-year quantity weights measuring the average change in price of all the items in national income.

import quota A limit set by the government on the quantity of a foreign commodity that may be shipped into that country in a given period.

import substitution industry Domestic production for sale in the home market of goods previously imported; usually involves some form of protection or subsidy.

imputed costs The costs of using factors of production already owned by the firm, measured by the earnings they could have received in their best alternative employment.

income-consumption curve A curve drawn on an indifference curve diagram and connecting the points of tangency between a set of indifference curves and a set of parallel budget lines, showing how the consumption bundle changes as income changes, with relative prices held constant.

income effect The effect on quantity demanded of a change in real income.

income elasticity of demand A measure of the responsiveness of quantity demanded to a change in income, defined by the formula

$$\eta_Y = \frac{\text{percentage change in quantity demanded}}{\text{percentage change in income}}$$

incomes policy Any direct intervention by the government to influence wage and price formation.

income statement A financial report showing the revenues and costs that arise from the firm's use of inputs to produce outputs over a specified period of time.

increasing returns A situation in which output increases more than in proportion to inputs as the scale of a firm's production increases. A firm in this situation, with fixed factor prices, is a *decreasing cost* firm.

incremental cost See *marginal cost*.

incremental product See *marginal product*.

incremental revenue See *marginal revenue*.

indexing The automatic change in any money payment in proportion to the change in the price level.

index number An average that measures changes over time of variables such as the price level and industrial production; conventionally expressed as a percentage relative to a base period assigned the value 100.

indifference curve A curve showing all combinations of two commodities that give the household an equal amount of satisfaction and between which the household is thus indifferent.

indifference map A set of indifference curves based on a given set of household preferences.

induced expenditure In macroeconomics, elements of expenditure that are explained by variables within the theory. In the aggregate desired expenditure function it is any component of expenditure that is related to national income. Also called *endogenous expenditure*.

industrial union A union organized to include all workers in an industry, regardless of skills.

industry A group of firms producing similar products.

inelastic demand For a given percentage change in price there is a smaller percentage change in quantity demanded; elasticity less than unity.

infant industry argument for tariffs The argument that new domestic industries with potential economies of scale need to be protected from competition from established low-cost foreign producers so that they can grow large enough to achieve costs as low as those of foreign producers.

inferior good   A good for which income elasticity is negative.

inflation   A rise in the average level of all prices. Sometimes restricted to prolonged or sustained rises.

inflationary gap   A negative output gap, that is, a situation in which actual national income exceeds potential income.

inflation rate   Percentage change in some price index from one period to another.

infrastructure   The basic installations and facilities (especially transportation and communications systems) on which the commerce of a community depends.

injections   Income earned by domestic firms that does not arise out of the spending of domestic households and income earned by domestic households that does not arise out of the spending of domestic firms.

innovation   The introduction of an invention into methods of production.

inputs   Materials and factor services used in the process of production.

interest   The payment for the use of borrowed money.

interest rate   The price paid per dollar borrowed per year; expressed either as a fraction (e.g., 0.06) or as a percentage (e.g., 6 percent) See also *real interest rate.*

interest rate control   The use of the interest rate as the instrument by which the central bank attempts to influence its target variables. See also *base control.*

intermediate goods   All outputs that are used as inputs by other producers in a further stage of production.

intermediate targets   Variables that the government cannot control directly and does not seek to control ultimately, yet that have an important influence on policy variables.

internal balance   State of the economy when real national income is at its target level.

invention   The discovery of something new, such as a new production technique or a new product.

inventories   Stocks of raw materials, goods in process, and finished goods, held by firms to mitigate the effect of short-term fluctuations in production or sales.

investment expenditure   Expenditure on the production of goods not for present consumption.

investment goods   Goods produced not for present consumption, i.e., capital goods, inventories, and residential housing.

invisible account   A form of balance-of-payments account that records payments and receipts arising out of trade in services and the use of capital. Also called *service account.*

involuntary unemployment   Unemployment due to the inability of qualified persons who are seeking work to find jobs at the going wage rate.

isocost line   See *budget line.*

isoquant   A curve showing all technologically efficient factor combinations for producing a specified output.

isoquant map   A series of isoquants from the same production function, each isoquant relating to a specific level of output.

jurisdictional dispute   Dispute between unions over which has the right to organize a group of workers.

Keynesians   A label attached to economists who hold the view, derivative from the work of John Maynard Keynes, that active use of monetary and fiscal policy can be effective in stabilizing the economy. Often the term encompasses economists who advocate active policy intervention in general.

Keynesian short-run aggregate supply curve   A horizontal aggregate supply curve indicating that when national income is below potential, changes in national income can occur with little or no accompanying changes in prices.

***k* percent rule**   The proposition that the money supply should be increased at a constant percentage rate year in and year out, irrespective of cyclical changes in national income.

labor   A factor of production consisting of all physical and mental contributions provided by people.

labor boycott   An organized attempt to persuade customers to refrain from purchasing the products of a firm or industry whose employees are on strike.

labor force   The total number of people either employed or actively seeking work.

labor union   See *union.*

Laffer curve   A graph relating the revenue yield of a tax system to the marginal or average tax rate imposed.

laissez faire   Literally, "let do"; a policy advocating the absence of government intervention in a market economy.

land   A factor of production consisting of all gifts of nature, including raw materials and "land" as conventionally defined.

law of demand   The proposition that market price and quantity demanded in the market vary inversely with one another, that is, that demand curves slope downward.

law of diminishing returns   See *hypothesis of diminishing returns.*

law of variable proportions   See *hypothesis of diminishing returns.*

legal tender   Anything that by law must be accepted for the purchase of goods and services or in discharge of a debt.

less-developed countries (LDCs)   The lower-income countries of the world, most of which are in Asia, Africa, and South and Central America. Also called *underdeveloped countries, developing countries,* the *South.*

life-cycle hypothesis (LCH)   A hypothesis that relates the household's actual consumption to its expected lifetime income rather than (as in early Keynesian theory) to its current income.

lifetime income   See *permanent income.*

limited liability   The limitation of the financial responsibility of an owner (shareholder) of a corporation or a limited partner to the amount of money he or she has actually made available to the firm by purchasing its shares.

limited partnership   This is an ordinary partnership with the addition of one or more limited partners who do not participate in management while their personal liability for the debts of the firm is limited to the amount each has invested.

liquidity   The degree of ease and certainty with which an asset can be turned into the economy's medium of exchange.

liquidity preference (*LP*) function   The function that relates the demand for money to the rate of interest.

lockout   The closing of operations by an employer during a bargaining dispute; the employer's equivalent of a strike.

logarithmic scale   A scale in which equal proportional changes are shown as equal distances (for example, 1 inch may always represent doubling of a variable). Also called *log scale, ratio scale.*

long run   A period of time in which all inputs may be varied, but the basic technology of production cannot be changed.

long-run aggregate supply (*LRAS*) curve   The curve indicating total supply that is forthcoming when all wages and prices have adjusted; a vertical line at $Y = Y^*$.

long-run average cost (*LRAC*) curve   The curve showing the least-cost method of producing each level of output. Also called *long-run average total cost (LRATC) curve.*

long-run Phillips curve (*LRPC*)   The relation between national income and the price level when all goods and factor markets are in long-run equilibrium.

Lorenz curve   A graph showing the extent of departure from equality of income distribution.

lower turning point   The bottom point of the business cycle where a contraction turns into an expansion of economic activity.

Lucas aggregate supply curve   A curve expressing the hypothesis that national output varies positively with the ratio of the actual to the expected price level.

M   Imports; a country's total expenditure on imports.

M1   Currency plus demand deposits.

M1A   M1 plus chequable savings deposits plus nonpersonal notice deposits.

M2   M1A plus personal savings and fixed-term deposits.

M3   M2 plus nonpersonal fixed-term and foreign-currency deposits.

macroeconomics   The study of the determination of economic aggregates and averages, such as total output, total employment, the price level, and rate of economic growth.

managed float   Intervention in the foreign exchange market by a country's central bank to respond to particular circumstances in pursuit of an unofficial exchange rate target, but not to maintain an announced par value. Also called *dirty float.*

marginal cost (*MC*)   The increase in total cost resulting from raising the rate of production by one unit. Mathematically, the rate of change of cost with respect to output. Also called *incremental cost.*

marginal efficiency of capital (*MEC*)   The marginal rate of return on a nation's capital stock. The rate of return on one additional dollar of net investment, i.e., an addition of one dollar's worth of new capital to capital stock.

marginal efficiency of capital schedule   A schedule relating *MEC* to the size of the capital stock.

marginal efficiency of investment (*MEI*)   The function that relates the quantity of investment to the rate of interest.

marginal net private benefit (*MNPB*)   The difference between the contribution of a unit of production to a firm's revenue and its contribution to the firm's cost.

marginal net social benefit (*MNSB*)   The difference between marginal social benefit and marginal social cost.

marginal physical product (*MPP*)   See *marginal product.*

marginal product (*MP*)   The change in quantity of total output that results from using one unit more of a variable factor. Mathematically, the rate of change of output with respect to the quantity of the variable factor. Also called *incremental product* and *marginal physical product* (*MPP*).

marginal productivity theory of distribution   The theory that factors are paid the value of their marginal products so that the total earnings of each type of factor of production equal the value of the marginal product of that factor multiplied by the number of units of that factor that are employed.

marginal propensity not to spend   The fraction of any increment to national income that is not spent on domestic production (1 − the marginal propensity to spend; i.e., $1 - \Delta AE/\Delta Y$).

marginal propensity to consume (*MPC*)   The change in consumption divided by the change in disposable income that brought it about; mathematically, the rate of change of consumption with respect to disposable income ($MPC = \Delta C/\Delta Y_d$).

marginal propensity to save (*MPS*)   The change in

saving related to the change in disposable income that brought it about; the rate of change of saving divided by disposable income ($MPS = \Delta S/\Delta Y_d$).

marginal propensity to spend The fraction of any increment to national income that is spent on domestic production; it is measured by the change in aggregate expenditure divided by the change in income ($\Delta AE/\Delta Y$).

marginal rate of substitution (MRS) (1) In consumption, the slope of an indifference curve, showing how much more of one commodity must be provided to compensate for the giving up of one unit of another commodity if the level of satisfaction is to be held constant. (2) In production, the slope of an isoquant, showing how much more of one factor of production must be used to compensate for the use of one less unit of another factor of production if production is to be held constant.

marginal revenue (MR) The change in a firm's total revenue arising from a change in its rate of sales by one unit. Mathematically, the rate of change of revenue with respect to output. Also called *incremental revenue*.

marginal revenue product (MRP) The addition of revenue attributable to the last unit of a variable factor. $MRP = MP \times MR$. Mathematically, the rate of change of total revenue with respect to quantity of the variable factor.

marginal social benefit The contribution of a unit of production to social welfare.

marginal tax rate The amount of tax a taxpayer would pay on an additional dollar of income, i.e., the fraction of an additional dollar of income that is paid in taxes.

marginal utility The additional satisfaction obtained by a buyer from consuming one unit more of a good; mathematically, the rate of change of utility with respect to consumption; also called *marginal value*.

marginal value See *marginal utility*.

margin requirement The fraction of the price of a stock that must be paid in cash, while putting up the stock as security against a loan for the balance.

market A concept with many possible definitions. (1) An area over which buyers and sellers negotiate the exchange of a well-defined commodity. (2) From the point of view of a household, the firms from which it can buy a well-defined product. (3) From the point of view of a firm, the buyers to whom it can sell a well-defined product.

market-clearing price Price at which quantity demanded equals quantity supplied so that there are neither unsatisfied buyers nor unsatisfied sellers; that is, the equilibrium price.

market economy A society in which people specialize in productive activities and meet most of their material wants through exchanges voluntarily agreed upon by the contracting parties.

market failure Failure of the unregulated market system to achieve optimal allocative efficiency or social goals because of externalities, market impediments, or market imperfections.

market sector That portion of an economy in which commodities are bought and sold and in which producers must cover their costs from sales revenue.

market structure Characteristics of market organization that affect behavior and performance of firms, such as the number and size of sellers, the extent of knowledge about each other's actions, the degree of freedom of entry, and the degree of product differentiation.

markup The amount added to cost to determine price.

medium of exchange Anything that is generally acceptable in return for goods and services sold.

merchandise account See *visible account*.

merger The purchase of either the physical assets or the controlling share ownership of one company by another. In a *horizontal* merger both companies produce the same product; in a *vertical* merger one company is a supplier of the other; if the two are in unrelated industries, it is a *conglomerate* merger.

microeconomic policy Activities of governments designed to alter resource allocation and/or income distribution.

microeconomics The study of the allocation of resources and the distribution of income as they are affected by the workings of the price system and by government policies.

minimum efficient scale (MES) The level of output at which long-run average cost is at a minimum. The smallest size of firm required to achieve the economies of scale in production and/or distribution.

minimum wages Legally specified minimum rate of pay for labor in covered occupations.

mixed economy An economy in which some decisions about the allocation of resources are made by firms and households and some by the government.

monetarists A label attached to economists who stress monetary causes of cyclical fluctuations and inflations and who believe that an active stabilization policy is not normally required. Often the term encompasses conservative economists who oppose active policy intervention in general.

monetary base The sum of currency in circulation plus reserves of the chartered banks.

monetary equilibrium A situation in which the demand for money equals the supply of money.

monetary policy An attempt to influence the economy by operating on such monetary variables as the quantity of money and the rate of interest.

money Any generally accepted medium of exchange.

money capital See *financial capital*.

money income   Income measured in monetary units per period of time.

money rate of interest   See *interest rate.*

money substitute   Something that serves as a temporary medium of exchange but is not a store of value.

money supply   The total quantity of money in an economy at a point in time.

monopolistic competition   (1) A market structure of an industry in which there are many sellers and freedom of entry but in which each firm has a product somewhat differentiated from the others, giving it some control over its price. (2) More recently, any industry in which more than one firm sells differentiated products.

monopoly   A market situation in which the output of an industry is controlled by a single seller.

monopsony   A market situation in which there is a single buyer.

moral hazard   A situation in which an individual or firm takes advantage of special knowledge while engaging in socially uneconomic behavior.

multilateral balance of payments   The balance between one country's payments to and receipts from the rest of the world.

multiple regression analysis   See *regression analysis.*

multiplier   The ratio of the change in national income to the change in autonomous expenditure that brought it about.

Nash equilibrium   See *Cournot-Nash equilibrium.*

national debt   The current volume of outstanding federal government debt.

national income   In general, the value of total output and the value of the income generated by the production of that output.

national income accounting   The set of rules and techniques for measuring the total flow of output produced and incomes generated by this production.

natural monopoly   An industry characterized by economies of scale sufficiently large that one firm can most efficiently supply the entire market demand.

natural rate of unemployment   The rate of unemployment (due to frictional and structural causes) consistent with potential national income (Y^*). It is the rate of unemployment at which there is neither upward nor downward demand pressure on the price level.

natural scale   A scale in which equal absolute amounts are represented by equal distances.

near money   Liquid assets that are easily convertible into money without risk of significant loss of value and can be used as short-term stores of purchasing power, but are not themselves media of exchange.

negative income tax (NIT)   A tax system in which households with incomes below taxable levels receive payments from the government based on a percentage of the amount by which their income is below the minimum taxable level.

net domestic income (NDI) at factor cost   The sum of the four components of factor incomes (wages, rent, interest, and profits).

net exports   Total exports minus total imports. Represented by the expression $(X - M)$ as a component of aggregate expenditure, where X is total exports and M is total imports.

net investment   Gross investment minus replacement investment.

net national product (NNP) at market prices   Sum of wages, rent, interest, profits, and indirect taxes minus subsidies.

net private benefit (NPB)   The difference between private benefits and private costs.

net social benefit (NSB)   The difference between social benefits and social costs. Where private production produces externalities, it is net private benefit plus external benefits and minus external costs.

net unborrowed reserves   The total reserves of the commercial banking system minus required reserves minus the reserves that have been borrowed from the central bank.

neutrality of money   The doctrine that the money supply affects only the absolute level of prices and has no effect on relative prices and hence no effect on the allocation of resources or the distribution of income.

newly industrializing countries (NICs)   Formerly underdeveloped countries that have become major industrial exporters since World War II.

nominal GDP   See *nominal national income.*

nominal national income   Total output measured in dollars; the money value of national output. Also called *money national income* or *current dollar national income.*

nominal rate of interest   See *interest rate.*

nominal rate of tariff   The tax charged on any imported commodity.

nonmarket sector   That portion of an economy in which commodities are given away and producers must cover their costs from some source other than sales revenue.

nonprice competition   Competition by sellers for sales by means other than price cutting, such as advertising, product differentiation, trading stamps, and other promotional devices.

nontariff barriers to trade   Restrictions, other than tariffs, designed to reduce the flow of imported goods.

normal capacity output   The level of output that a firm hopes to maintain on average over the business cycle; typically, somewhat less than full capacity output.

normal good   A good for which income elasticity is positive.

normal profits   A term used by some economists for the imputed returns to capital and risk taking just necessary to keep the owners in the industry. They are included in what most economists, but not all businessmen, see as *total costs.*

normative statement   A statement about what ought to be, as opposed to what is, was, or will be true.

note   See *treasury bill*.

oligopoly   A market structure in which a small number of rival firms dominate the industry.

open market operations   The purchase and sale of securities on the open market by the central bank of securities (usually short-term government securities).

open shop   A place of employment in which a union represents its members but does not have bargaining jurisdiction for all workers in a shop and membership in the union is not a condition of getting or keeping a job.

operating regime   The combination of intermediate targets and policy instruments used to achieve those targets selected by a central bank in order to reach its policy goals.

opportunity cost   The cost of using resources for a certain purpose, measured by the benefit given up by not using them in their best alternative use.

organization theory   A set of hypotheses that predicts that the substance of the decisions of a firm is affected by its size and form of organization.

output gap   The difference between total output that could have been produced at the potential level and what is actually produced; that is, potential GDP minus actual GDP.

outputs   The goods and services that result from the process of production.

Pareto-efficiency   See *Pareto-optimality*.

Pareto-optimality   A situation in which it is impossible by reallocation of production or consumption activities to make all consumers better off without simultaneously making others worse off (or, as it is sometimes put, to make at least one person better off while making no one worse off). Also called *Pareto-efficiency*.

partnership   A form of business organization in which the firm has two or more joint owners, each of whom is personally responsible for all of the firm's actions and debts.

paternalism   Intervention in the free choices of individuals by others (including governments) to protect them against their own ignorance or folly.

pegged rate   See *fixed exchange rate*.

per capita GDP   GDP divided by total population.

perfect competition   A market structure in which all firms in an industry are price takers and in which there is freedom of entry into and exit from the industry.

permanent income   The maximum amount that a household can consume per year into the indefinite future without reducing its wealth. (A number of similar but not identical definitions are in common use.) Also called *lifetime income*.

permanent-income hypothesis (PIH)   A hypothesis that relates actual consumption to permanent income rather than (as in the original Keynesian theory) to current income.

personal income   Income earned by individuals before allowance for personal income taxes on that income.

petrodollars   Money earned by the oil-exporting countries and held by them in short-term, liquid investments.

Phillips curve   Originally, a relation between the percentage of the labor force unemployed and the rate of change of money wages. Now often drawn as a relation between the percentage of the labor force employed and the rate of price inflation or between actual national income and the rate of price inflation.

picket line   Striking workers parading at the entrances to a plant or firm on strike; a symbolic blockade of the entrance.

point elasticity   A measure of the responsiveness of quantity demanded to price at a particular point on the demand curve. The formula for point elasticity of demand is

$$\eta = \frac{\Delta q}{\Delta p} \times \frac{p}{q}$$

With negatively sloped demand curves elasticity is a negative number. Sometimes the above expression is multiplied by -1 to make elasticity positive.

point of diminishing average productivity   The level of output at which average product reaches a maximum.

point of diminishing marginal productivity   The level of output at which marginal product reaches a maximum.

policy instruments   The variables that the government can control directly to achieve its policy objectives.

policy variables   The variables that the government seeks to control, such as real national income and the rate of change of the price level.

political business cycle   Cyclical swings in the economy generated by fiscal and monetary policy for the purpose of winning elections.

portfolio investment   In balance-of-payments accounting, foreign investment in bonds or a minority holding of shares that does not involve legal control. See also *direct investment*.

positive statement   A statement about what is, was, or will be true, as opposed to what ought to be.

potential GDP (Y^*)   The real gross domestic product the economy could produce if its productive resources were fully employed at their normal intensity of use.

potential income   See *potential GDP*.

potential national income   See *potential GDP*.

poverty level   The official government estimate of the annual family income required to maintain a minimum adequate standard of living.

precautionary balances Money balances held for protection against the uncertainty of the timing of cash flows.

preferred stock A form of equity capital with a preference over common stock to receipt of dividends up to a stated maximum amount; may be voting or non-voting.

present value (*PV*) The value now of one or more payments to be received in the future; often referred to as the *discounted present value* of future payments.

price ceiling A maximum permissible price.

price-consumption line A line connecting the points of tangency between a set of indifference curves and a set of budget lines where one absolute price is fixed and the other varies, money income being held constant.

price control policy Any government policy that regulates the price at which a commodity can be bought and sold; often used to refer to the imposition of maximum prices on one or more commodities.

price discrimination The sale by a single firm of different units of a specific commodity at two or more different prices for reasons not associated with differences in cost.

price elasticity of demand See *elasticity of demand*.

price floor A minimum permissible price.

price index A number that shows the average percentage change that has occurred in some group of prices over some period of time; price indexes can be used to measure the price level at a given time relative to a base period.

price level The average level of a broad group of prices; it is usually measured by an index number.

price taker A firm that can alter its rate of production and sales without significantly affecting the market price of its product.

principle of substitution The implication of cost minimization that as the relative prices of the inputs vary, the proportions in which various inputs are used will vary so as to use relatively more of the cheaper inputs.

private cost The value of the best alternative use of resources used in production as valued by the producer.

private sector That portion of an economy in which the organizations that produce goods and services are owned and operated by private units such as households and firms.

producers' durables See *durable good*.

producers' surplus The difference between the total amount producers receive for all units sold of a commodity and the total variable cost of producing the commodity; it can be calculated by finding the difference between the marginal cost and marginal revenue associated with the production and sale of each unit of output and summing over all units of output.

product differentiation The existence of similar but not identical products sold by a single industry such as the breakfast food and the automobile industries.

production The act of making commodities.

production function A functional relation showing the maximum output that can be produced by each and every combination of inputs.

production possibility boundary A curve that shows which alternative combinations of commodities can just be attained if all available productive resources are used; it is thus the boundary between attainable and unattainable output combinations.

productive efficiency Production of any output at the lowest attainable cost for that level of output.

productivity Output produced per unit of resource input; frequently used to refer to *labor productivity,* measured by output per hour worked or per worker employed.

product markets Markets in which outputs of goods and services are sold.

profit (1) In ordinary usage, the difference between the value of outputs and the value of inputs. (2) In microeconomics, the difference between revenues received from the sale of goods and the value of inputs, which includes the opportunity cost of capital, so that profits are *economic profits*. (3) In macroeconomics, profits exclude interest on borrowed capital, but do not exclude the return to owner's capital.

progressive tax A tax that takes a larger percentage of income the higher the level of income.

progressivity of taxation The ratio of taxes to income as income increases. If the ratio decreases, the tax is *regressive;* if it remains constant, *proportional;* if it increases, *progressive.*

proportional tax A tax that takes a constant percentage of income at all levels of income and is thus neither progressive nor regressive.

protectionism Government intervention to provide partial or complete protection of domestic industries from foreign competition in domestic markets by use of tariff or nontariff barriers to trade.

proxy A document authorizing someone to exercise the voting rights of a stockholder in a corporation.

proxy fight A struggle between competing factions in a corporation to obtain the proxies for a majority of the outstanding shares.

public sector That portion of an economy in which production is owned and operated by the government or bodies appointed by it such as crown corporations.

public utility regulation Regulation of such things as prices and profit rates in industries that have been deemed to be natural monopolies.

purchase and resale agreement (PRA) An arrangement by which the Bank of Canada makes short-term advances as a lender of last resort to investment dealers. Government securities are sold to the Bank with an agreement to repurchase them.

purchasing power of money The amount of goods and services that can be purchased with a unit of money. Decreases in the purchasing power of money are measured by increases in a price index. Also called *value of money.*

purchasing power parity (PPP) exchange rate The exchange rate between two currencies that adjusts for relative inflation rates.

pure rate of interest The rate of interest that would rule in equilibrium in a riskless economy where all lending and borrowing are for investment in productive capital.

pure return on capital The amount capital can earn in a riskless investment; hence the transfer earnings of capital in a riskless investment.

quantity actually bought The amount of a commodity that households succeed in purchasing in some time period.

quantity actually sold The amount of a commodity that producers succeed in selling in some time period.

quantity demanded The amount of a commodity that households wish to purchase in some time period. An increase (decrease) in quantity demanded refers to a movement down (up) the demand curve in response to a fall (rise) in price.

quantity exchanged The identical amount of a commodity that households actually purchase and producers actually sell in some time period.

quantity supplied The amount of a commodity producers wish to sell in some time period. An increase (decrease) in quantity supplied refers to a movement up (down) the supply curve in response to a rise (fall) in price.

random sample A sample chosen from a group or population in such a way that every member of the group has an equal chance of being selected.

rate base The total allowable investment to which the rate of return allowed by a regulatory commission is applied.

rate of return The ratio of return to capital earned by a firm to total invested capital.

rate of return on capital Sometimes used synonymously with *rate of return.* Frequently used to refer to a specific capital good; the annual return to capital produced by a capital good, expressed as a percentage of the price of the good.

rational expectations The theory that people understand how the economy works and learn quickly from their mistakes, so that while random errors may be made, systematic and persistent errors are not made.

ratio scale See *logarithmic scale.*

real capital Physical assets of a firm, including plant, equipment, and inventories. Also called *physical capital.*

real income A household's or firm's income expressed in terms of the purchasing power of the income, that is, the quantity of goods and services that can be purchased with the income; it can be calculated as money income deflated by a price index.

real national income Total output measured in prices prevailing in some base year; changes in real national income reflect only changes in quantities produced. Also called *constant dollar national income.*

real product wage The proportion of each sales dollar accounted for by labor costs (including the pre-tax nominal wage rate, benefits, and payroll taxes).

real rate of interest The money rate of interest corrected for the change in the purchasing power of money by subtracting the inflation rate.

real wage unemployment Unemployment caused by too high a real product wage. Also called *classical unemployment.*

recession In general, a sustained downswing in the level of economic activity.

recessionary gap A positive output gap; that is, a situation in which actual national income is less than potential income.

regression analysis A quantitative measure of the relationship between two or more variables. *Simple regression* concerns the relation between Y and a single independent variable, X_1; *multiple regression* concerns the relation between Y and more than one independent variable, $X_1, \ldots, X_n$. Also called *correlation analysis.*

regression equation An equation describing the statistically determined best fit between variables, or best estimate of the average relationship between variables in regression analysis.

regressive tax A tax that takes a lower percentage of income the higher the level of income.

relative price The ratio of the money price of one commodity to the money price of another commodity; that is, a ratio of two absolute prices.

replacement investment The amount of investment that just maintains the existing capital stock intact.

required reserves The minimum amount of reserves a bank must, by law, keep either in currency or in deposits with the central bank.

reserve currencies Currencies (such as the U.S. dollar) commonly held by foreign central banks as international reserves.

reserve ratio The fraction of its deposits that a bank holds as reserves in the form of cash or deposits with a central bank.

resource allocation The allocation of an economy's scarce resources among alternative uses.

retained earnings See *undistributed profits.*

return to capital The total amount available for payments to owners of capital; the sum of pure returns to capital, risk premiums, and economic profits.

rising-cost industry An industry in which the minimum cost attainable by a firm rises as the scale of the industry expands.

rising supply price   A rising long-run supply curve, caused by increases in factor prices as output is increased or by diseconomies of scale.

risk premium   The return on capital necessary to compensate owners of capital for the risk of loss of their capital.

sample   A small number of items, chosen from a larger group or population, that is intended to be representative of the larger entity.

satisficing   A hypothesized objective of firms to achieve target levels of satisfactory performance rather than to *maximize* some objective.

saving   All disposable income that is not spent on consumption.

savings deposit   An interest-bearing deposit legally withdrawable only after a certain notice period. (Savings deposits were common prior to recent revisions in the Bank Act.)

scarce good   A commodity for which the quantity demanded exceeds the quantity supplied at a price of zero; and therefore a good that commands a positive price in a market economy.

scatter diagram   A graph of statistical observations of paired values of two variables, one measured on the horizontal and the other on the vertical axis. Each point on the coordinate grid represents the values of the variables for a particular unit of observation.

search unemployment   Unemployment caused by people continuing to search for a good job rather than accepting the first job they come across when unemployed.

secondary reserves   Interest-earning liquid assets held by banks. For purposes of the minimum ratio to deposits imposed by the Bank of Canada, secondary reserves are defined as holdings of *treasury bills, day-to-day loans,* and *excess cash reserves.*

sectors   Parts of an economy.

securities market   See *stock market.*

sellers' preferences   Allocation of commodities in excess demand by decisions of those who sell them.

service account   See *invisible account.*

services   Intangible commodities, such as haircuts or medical care.

short run   A period of time over which the quantity of some inputs cannot, as a practical matter, be varied.

short-run aggregate supply (SRAS) curve   A relation between the price level of final output and the quantity of output supplied on the assumption that all input prices (including wage rates) are held constant.

short-run equilibrium   Generally, equilibrium subject to fixed factors or other things that cannot change over the time period being considered. For a competitive firm, the output at which market price equals short-run marginal cost; for a competitive industry, the price and output at which industry demand equals short-run industry supply and all firms are in short-run equilibrium.

short-run Phillips curve (SRPC)   A relation between unemployment and the rate of wage inflation or between national income and the rate of price inflation, drawn for a given state of expectations about the future rate of inflation.

short-run supply curve   A curve showing the relation of quantity supplied to prices, when one or more factor is fixed; it is the horizontal sum of marginal cost curves (above the level of average variable costs) of all firms in an industry.

simple multiplier   The ratio of the change in equilibrium national income to the change in autonomous expenditure at a constant price level.

single proprietorship   A form of business organization in which the firm has one owner, who is personally responsible for all of the firm's actions and debts.

size distribution of income   The distribution of income among households by amount, without regard to source of income or social class of households.

slope   The ratio of the vertical change to the horizontal change between two points on a straight line.

Snake   An agreement among the countries of the European Community (except the U.K.) to fix exchange rates among their own currencies and then let their joint rate float against the dollar.

social cost   The value of the best alternative use of resources available to society as valued by society. Also called *social opportunity cost.*

special drawing rights (SDRs)   Financial liabilities of the IMF held in a special fund generated by contributions of member countries. Members can use SDRs to maintain supplies of convertible currencies when these are needed to support foreign exchanges.

specialization of labor   An organization of production in which individual workers specialize in the production of particular goods or services (and satisfy their wants by trading) rather than produce everything they consume (and satisfy their wants by being self-sufficient).

specific tariff   An import duty of a specific amount per unit of the product.

specific tax.   See *excise tax.*

speculative balances   Money balances held as a hedge against the uncertainty of the prices of other financial assets.

stabilization policy   Any policy designed to reduce the economy's cyclical fluctuations. Attempts by the government to remove inflationary and recessionary gaps when they appear.

stagflation   The coexistence of high rates of unemployment with high, and sometimes rising, rates of inflation.

sterilization   Operations undertaken by the central bank to offset the effects of the money supply of balance-of-payments surpluses or deficits.

stockholders   The owners of a corporation who have supplied money to the firm by purchasing its shares.

stock market   An organized market where stocks and bonds are bought and sold. Also called *securities market*.

strike   The concerted refusal of the members of a union to work.

strikebreakers   Nonunion workers brought in by management to operate the plant while a union is on strike (derisively called *scabs* by union members).

structural unemployment   Unemployment due to a mismatch between characteristics required by available jobs and characteristics possessed by the unemployed labor.

substitute   Two commodities are substitutes for each other when both satisfy similar needs or desires; the degree of substitutability is measured by the magnitude of the positive cross elasticity between the two.

substitution effect   A change in quantity of a good demanded resulting from a change in its relative price, eliminating the effect on real income of the change in price.

supply   The entire relationship between the quantity of some commodity that producers wish to make and sell per period of time and the price of that commodity, other things being equal.

supply curve   The graphic representation of the relation between the quantity of some commodity that producers wish to make and sell per period of time and the price of that commodity, other things being equal.

supply of effort   The total number of hours of work that the population is willing to supply. Also called *total supply of labor*.

supply of money   See *money supply*.

supply schedule   A table showing for selected values the relation between the quantity of some commodity that producers wish to make and sell per period of time and the price of that commodity, other things being equal.

tacit collusion   The adoption, without explicit agreement, of a common policy by sellers in an industry. Also called *conscious parallel action*. See also *collusion*.

takeover bid   See *tender offer*.

tariff   A tax applied on imports.

tax base   The aggregate amount of taxable income.

tax expenditures   Tax concessions, such as exemptions and deductions from taxable income and tax credits, designed to induce market responses considered to be desirable. They are called expenditures because they have the same effect as having no concessions and then spending money on subsidies and other transfers to the groups getting the concessions.

tax incidence   The location of the burden of a tax; that is, the identity of the ultimate bearer of the tax.

tax-related incomes policy (TIP)   Tax incentives for labor and management to encourage them to conform to wage and price guidelines.

tax-rental arrangements   An agreement by which the federal government makes a per capita payment to the provinces for the right to collect income taxes.

tender offer   An offer to buy directly some or all of the outstanding common stock of a corporation from its stockholders at a specified price per share, in an attempt to gain control of the corporation. Also called *takeover bid*.

term   See *term to maturity*.

term deposit   See *savings deposit*.

terms of trade   The ratio of the average price of a country's exports to the average price of its imports.

term to maturity   The period of time from the present to the redemption date of a bond. Also called simply the *term*.

third-party effects   See *externalities*.

time deposit   An interest-earning bank deposit, legally subject to notice before withdrawal (in practice the notice requirement is not normally enforced) and until recently transferable by cheque.

time-series data   A set of measurements or observations made on some variable at successive periods (or moments) of time. Contrasted with *cross-sectional data*.

total cost (*TC*)   The sum of the opportunity costs of the factors used to produce that output, it can be divided into total fixed costs and total variable costs of producing at a given level of output.

total fixed cost (*TFC*)   Total costs of producing that do not vary with level of output.

total product (*TP*)   Total amount produced during a given period of time by all the factors of production employed over that time period.

total revenue (*TR*)   Total receipts from the sale of a product; price times quantity.

total utility   The total satisfaction resulting from the consumption of a given commodity by a consumer in a period of time; also called *total value*.

total value   See *total utility*.

total variable cost (*TVC*)   Total costs of producing that vary directly with level of output.

trade account   See *visible account*.

trade union   See *union*.

transactions balances   Money balances held to finance payments because payments and receipts are not perfectly synchronized.

transactions costs   Costs incurred in effecting market transactions (such as negotiation costs, billing costs, and bad debts).

transfer earnings   That part of the payment to a factor in its present use that is just enough to keep it from transferring to another use.

transfer payment   A payment to a private person or institution that does not arise out of current productive activity; typically made by governments, as in welfare payments, but also made by businesses and private individuals in the form of charitable contributions.

transmission mechanism   The channels by which a change in the demand or supply of money leads to a shift of the aggregate demand curve.

treasury bill   The characteristic form of short-term government debt. A promise to pay a certain sum of money at a specified time in the future (usually 90 days to 1 year from date of issue). Although they carry no fixed interest payments, holders earn an interest return because they purchase them at a lower price than their redemption value. Also called *treasury note.*

undistributed profits   Earnings of a firm not distributed to shareholders as dividends, but retained by the firm. Also called *retained earnings.*

unemployment   The number of persons 15 years of age and older who are not employed and are actively searching for a job.

unemployment rate   Unemployment expressed as a percentage of the labor force.

unfavorable balance of payments   A debit balance on some part of the payments accounts (payments exceed receipts); often refers to the balance on current plus capital account (that is, everything except the official settlements account).

union   An association of workers authorized to represent them in bargaining with employers. Also called *trade union, labor union.*

union shop   A bargaining arrangement in which the employer may hire anyone at union wages, but every employee must join the union within a specified period of time (often 60 days).

unit costs   Costs per unit of output, equal to total cost divided by total output. Also called *average cost.*

upper turning point   The top point of the business cycle where an expansion turns into a contraction of economic activity.

utility   The satisfaction that results from the consumption of a commodity.

value added   The value of a firm's output minus the value of the inputs that it purchases from other firms.

value added tax (VAT)   A multi-stage tax collected on the value added to goods as they progress through the production and distribution systems.

value of money   See *purchasing power of money.*

variable   A magnitude (such as the price of a commodity) that can take on a specific value, but whose value will vary with time and place.

variable cost   A cost that varies directly with output. Also called *direct cost, avoidable cost.*

variable factor   An input that can be varied in the short run.

velocity of circulation   National income divided by quantity of money.

vertical equity   Focuses on comparisons among individuals or families with different levels of income.

very long run   A period of time in which the technological possibilities open to a firm are subject to change.

visible account   A form of balance-of-payments account that records payments and receipts arising from the import and export of tangible goods. Also called *trade account* and *merchandise account.*

voluntary export restriction (VER)   An agreement by an exporting country to limit the amount of a good exported to another country.

wage and price controls   Direct government intervention in wage and price formation with legal power to enforce the government's decisions on wages and prices.

wage-cost push inflation   An increase in the price level caused by increases in labor costs that are not themselves associated with excess aggregate demand for labor.

wealth   The sum of all the valuable assets owned minus liabilities.

windfall profit   A change in profits that arises out of an unanticipated change in market conditions such as a sudden increase in demand. Negative windfall profits are sometimes called *windfall losses.*

withdrawals   Income earned by households and not passed on to firms in return for goods and services purchased, and income earned by firms and not passed on to households in return for factor services purchased.

X   Exports; the value of all domestic production sold abroad.

X-inefficiency   The use of resources at a lower level of productivity than is possible, even if they are allocated efficiently, so that the economy is at a point inside its production possibility boundary.

X − M   See *net exports.*

Index

Common Abbreviations Used

Greek Letters

Δ	(delta)	change in
Σ	(sigma)	sum of
η	(eta)	elasticity
π	(pi)	profit

Abbreviations

AD	Aggregate Demand
AS	Aggregate Supply
AE	Aggregate Expenditure
ATC	Average Total Cost
AVC	Average Variable Cost
C	Consumption
CPI	Consumer Price Index
D	Demand
E	Equilibrium
G	Government Expenditure
GDP	Gross Domestic Product
GNE	Gross National Expenditure
GNP	Gross National Product
I	Investment Expenditure
i	rate of interest
LR	Long-run
M	Imports *or* Money Supply
M1, M1A, M2, etc.	Measures of Money Supply
MC	Marginal Cost
MEC	Marginal Efficiency of Capital
MES	Minimum Efficient Scale
MP	Marginal Product
MR	Marginal Revenue
MRP	Marginal Revenue Product
OPEC	Organization of Petroleum Exporting Countries
p	price
P	Price Level
q	quantity
r	rate of interest, rate of return
S	Supply *or* Saving
SR	Short-run
SRAS	Short-run Aggregate Supply
T	Taxes
TC	Total Cost
TR	Total Revenue
X	Exports
X-M	Net Exports
Y	National Income
Y*	Potential National Income
Y_d	Disposable Income

Federal Revenues, Expenditures, and Budget Balances, 1967–1986
(*percentage of GDP, national accounts basis*)

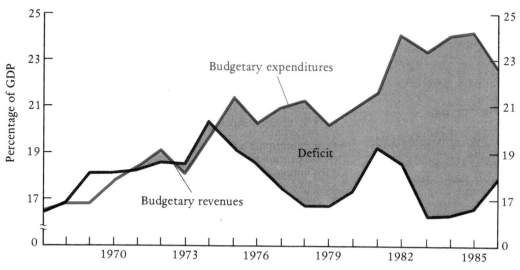

(i) Revenues and expenditures

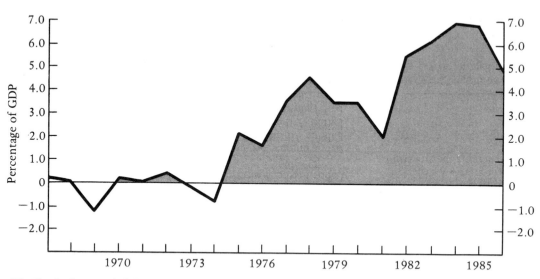

(ii) The budgetary deficit

Canadian Labor Force, Employment, and Unemployment, 1930–1986

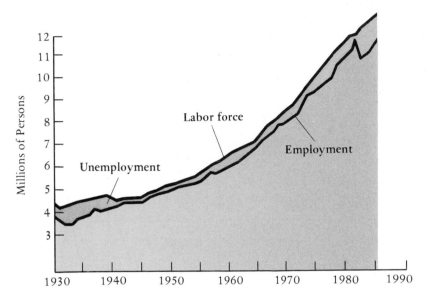

(i) Labor force, employment, and unemployment

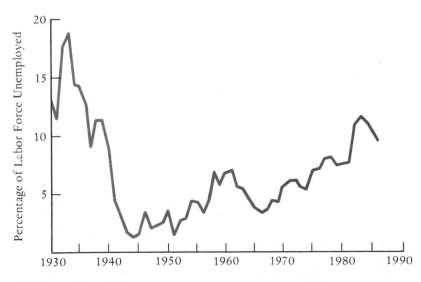

(ii) Unemployment rate

Selected Statistical Series for Canada, 1926–1986

Year	Nominal national income[a] in billions of current dollars	Implicit deflator (1981 = 100[b])	Real national income in billions of 1981 dollars	Population in millions	Real national income per capita in 1981 dollars
1926	5.1	15.0	34.0	9.5	3,579
1927	5.6	14.9	37.6	9.6	3,915
1928	6.1	14.8	41.2	9.8	4,206
1929	6.1	14.9	40.9	10.0	4,094
1930	5.7	14.6	39.2	10.2	3,846
1931	4.7	13.7	34.3	10.4	3,298
1932	3.8	12.4	30.9	10.5	2,939
1933	3.5	12.2	28.8	10.6	2,714
1934	4.0	12.3	32.4	10.7	3,027
1935	4.3	12.4	34.8	10.8	3,222
1936	4.7	12.8	36.4	11.0	3,305
1937	5.3	13.1	40.1	11.0	3,648
1938	5.3	13.1	40.3	11.2	3,597
1939	5.6	13.0	43.4	11.3	3,837
1940	6.7	13.6	49.6	11.4	4,349
1941	8.3	14.7	56.7	11.5	4,926
1942	10.3	15.3	67.5	11.7	5,769
1943	11.1	15.9	69.7	11.8	5,910
1944	11.9	16.4	72.3	11.9	6,072
1945	11.8	16.8	70.4	12.1	5,822
1946	11.9	17.3	68.5	12.3	5,569
1947	13.5	18.8	71.7	12.6	5,688
1948	15.5	21.2	73.2	12.8	5,715
1949	16.8	22.1	76.0	13.4	5,673
1950	18.5	22.5	82.2	13.7	5,999
1951	21.6	25.1	86.2	14.0	6,158
1952	24.6	26.2	93.8	14.5	6,472
1953	25.8	26.2	98.6	14.8	6,662
1954	25.9	26.6	97.4	15.3	6,368
1955	28.5	26.8	106.4	15.7	6,780
1956	32.1	27.8	115.3	16.1	7,163
1957	33.5	28.3	118.4	16.6	7,134
1958	34.8	28.8	120.8	17.1	7,062
1959	36.8	29.4	125.3	17.5	7,162
1960	38.4	29.7	129.2	17.9	7,215
1961	39.6	29.9	132.6	18.2	7,285
1962	42.9	30.2	142.1	18.6	7,642
1963	46.0	30.9	148.8	18.9	7,873
1964	50.3	31.7	158.6	19.3	8,218
1965	55.4	32.8	168.8	19.6	8,612
1966	61.8	34.4	179.7	20.0	8,987
1967	66.4	35.8	185.5	20.4	9,093
1968	72.6	37.1	195.6	20.7	9,452
1969	79.8	38.8	205.7	21.1	9,749
1970	85.7	40.6	211.0	21.4	9,862
1971	94.5	41.9	225.4	21.6	10,436
1972	105.2	44.2	238.1	21.8	10,921
1973	123.6	48.1	256.9	22.1	11,624
1974	147.5	55.1	267.7	22.4	11,953
1975	165.3	60.5	273.3	22.8	11,987
1976	191.9	65.8	291.6	23.0	12,677
1977	210.2	69.9	300.7	23.3	12,906
1978	232.2	74.1	313.4	23.5	13,335
1979	264.3	81.6	323.9	23.7	13,665
1980	297.6	90.2	329.9	23.9	13,803
1981	339.8	100.0	339.8	24.2	14,041
1982	358.3	108.7	329.6	24.5	13,454
1983	389.8	114.1	341.7	24.8	13,777
1984	420.9	117.9	357.0	25.1	14,222
1985	453.7	121.7	372.8	25.4	14,678
1986	488.4	125.3	389.8	25.6	15,226

Source: Department of Finance, *Quarterly Economic Review,* June 1987.

[a] Data for 1926 to 1947 based on GNP; post-1947 based on GDP.

[b] Figures for pre-1947 based on authors' calculations using series for 1971 = 100.